SO-AJC-782

Essential Papers on Masochism

Essential Papers in Psychoanalysis
General Editor: Leo Goldberger

Essential Papers on Borderline Disorders
Edited by Michael H. Stone, M.D.

Essential Papers on Object Relations
Edited by Peter Buckley, M.D.

Essential Papers on Narcissism
Edited by Andrew P. Morrison, M.D.

Essential Papers on Depression
Edited by James C. Coyne

Essential Papers on Psychosis
Edited by Peter Buckley, M.D.

Essential Papers on Countertransference
Edited by Benjamin Wolstein

Essential Papers on Character Neurosis and Treatment
Edited by Ruth F. Lax

Essential Papers on the Psychology of Women
Edited by Claudia Zanardi

Essential Papers on Transference
Edited by Aaron H. Esman, M.D.

Essential Papers on Dreams
Edited by Melvin R. Lansky, M.D.

Essential Papers on Literature and Psychoanalysis
Edited by Emanuel Berman

Essential Papers on Object Loss
Edited by Rita V. Frankiel

Essential Papers on Masochism
Edited by Margaret Ann Fitzpatrick Hanly

ESSENTIAL PAPERS ON MASOCHISM

Edited by
Margaret Ann Fitzpatrick Hanly

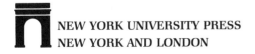

NEW YORK UNIVERSITY PRESS
NEW YORK AND LONDON

NEW YORK UNIVERSITY PRESS
New York and London

© 1995 by New York University Press

All rights reserved

Library of Congress Cataloging-in-Publication Data
Essential papers on masochism / edited by Margaret Ann Fitzpatrick
Hanly.
p. cm. —(Essential papers in psychoanalysis)
Includes bibliographical references and index.
ISBN 0-8147-3495-2. —ISBN 0-8147-3496-0 (pbk.)
1. Masochism. 2. Sadomasochism. I. Hanly, Margaret Ann
Fitzpatrick, 1948– . II. Series.
RC553.M36E87 1995
616.85′835—dc20   94-38513
                              CIP

New York University Press books are printed on acid-free paper,
and their binding materials are chosen for strength and durability.

Manufactured in the United States of America

10   9   8   7   6   5   4   3   2   1

ESSENTIAL PAPERS ON MASOCHISM

Edited by
Margaret Ann Fitzpatrick Hanly

NEW YORK UNIVERSITY PRESS
NEW YORK AND LONDON

NEW YORK UNIVERSITY PRESS
New York and London

© 1995 by New York University Press

All rights reserved

Library of Congress Cataloging-in-Publication Data
Essential papers on masochism / edited by Margaret Ann Fitzpatrick
Hanly.
p. cm.—(Essential papers in psychoanalysis)
Includes bibliographical references and index.
ISBN 0-8147-3495-2.—ISBN 0-8147-3496-0 (pbk.)
1. Masochism. 2. Sadomasochism. I. Hanly, Margaret Ann
Fitzpatrick, 1948– . II. Series.
RC553.M36E87   1995
616.85'835—dc20   94-38513
                          CIP

New York University Press books are printed on acid-free paper,
and their binding materials are chosen for strength and durability.

Manufactured in the United States of America

10   9   8   7   6   5   4   3   2   1

For Charles and Elizabeth

Contents

Introduction *Margaret Ann Fitzpatrick Hanly* 1

PART I: THREE INTRODUCTIONS TO THE PSYCHOANALYSIS OF MASOCHISM 13

  Introduction 15

1. *Le Masochisme*, Introduction *Sacha Nacht* 18

2. A Contribution to the Psychoanalytic Theory of Masochism *Rudolph M. Loewenstein* 35

3. The Masochistic Contract *Victor N. Smirnoff* 62

PART II: MASOCHISM, SEXUALITY, AND AGGRESSION 75

  Introduction 77

4. Three Essays on the Theory of Sexuality (An Excerpt) *Sigmund Freud* 84

5. Instincts and Their Vicissitudes (An Excerpt) *Sigmund Freud* 90

6. Aggressiveness and Sadomasochism ~~*Jacques*~~ Jean *Laplanche* 104

7. Pain, Aggression, Fantasy, and Concepts of Sadomasochism *William I. Grossman* 125

PART III: MASOCHISTIC PERVERSION: THE BEATING FANTASY 151

  Introduction 153

8. "A Child Is Being Beaten": A Contribution to the Study of the Origin of Sexual Perversions *Sigmund Freud* 159

9. Masochism in Paranoia *Robert C. Bak* 182

10. Psychodynamic Theory of Masochism *Bela Grunberger* 196

11. More about Rats and Rat People *Leonard Shengold* 215

12. The Essence of Masochism *Kerry Kelly Novick and Jack Novick* 237

PART IV: MORAL MASOCHISM: GUILT, FANTASY, AND THE OBJECT 265

Introduction 267

13. The Economic Problem of Masochism *Sigmund Freud* 274

14. Beating Fantasies and Daydreams *Anna Freud* 286

15. The Clinical Aspect of the Need for Punishment *Otto Fenichel* 300

16. The Characteristics of Masochism (An Excerpt) *Theodor Reik* 324

17. The Role of Object Relations in Moral Masochism *Bernhard Berliner* 344

18. The Masochistic Character: Genesis and Treatment *Charles Brenner* 360

19. The Excitement of Sadomasochism *Stanley J. Coen* 383

PART V: MASOCHISM AND FEMALE PSYCHOLOGY 403

Introduction 405

20. The Significance of Masochism in the Mental Life of Women *Helene Deutsch* 411

21. A Contribution to the Psychoanalysis of Extreme Submissiveness in Women *Annie Reich* 423

22. Some Biopsychical Aspects of Sado-Masochism *Marie Bonaparte* 432

23. Auto-Sadism, Eating Disorders, and Femininity: Reflections Based on Case Studies of Adult Women Who Experienced Eating Disorders as Adolescents *Janine Chasseguet-Smirgel* 453

PART VI: MASOCHISM AND THE NEGATIVE THERAPEUTIC REACTION   471

Introduction   473

24. A Contribution to the Analysis of the Negative Therapeutic Reaction   *Joan Riviere*   477

25. The Negative Therapeutic Reaction   *Stanley L. Olinick*   494

26. Addiction to Near-Death   *Betty Joseph*   511

Name Index   525

Subject Index   529

About the Editor   533

Introduction

Margaret Ann Fitzpatrick Hanly

Masochism is a psychoanalytic concept which has served as a vehicle to open up pathways of understanding into human lives where rituals of pain and sexual abusiveness prevail, and into unconscious fantasies constructed out of psychological pain, desperate need, and sexually excited, self-destruction. The term *masochism,* and that of *sadism,* come from literature, from the autobiographical writings and fiction of Sacher-Masoch and the Count de Sade. Possessing something of a literary imagination helps in understanding the paradox, reversal, repetition, and fantasy of sadomasochism. Much data about masochistic perversion remain in police files and known to prostitutes, not appearing in psychoanalytic offices.

Humiliation (Eidelberg 1959) and the desire to subjugate, with their diverse fantasy contents, lie at the heart of sadomasochism (Freud 1905; chapter 4 in this volume). Aggression, sexuality, and narcissistic pain all feed into the development of the masochist, driving double hooks into the vulnerable psyches of children. The humiliation of being a masochist, attached to a humiliating, sexualized way of pleading with the gods, and to a striving for passive, self-destructive victories, requires tact as it is opened up in the analytic dialogue.

The psychoanalytic literature on masochism and sadomasochism is as rich as any branch of our field. The contributions have sometimes been brilliant, and no analyst today works without the gains won through the capacity of earlier colleagues to imagine their way back into the experience of the vulnerable child, whose masochism or sadomasochism was the solution to the problem of finding some good out of evil, some position from which to long for revenge, and to hope for love and approval.

Essential papers may refer to those papers which best describe the histori-cal growth of a psychoanalytic concept, or to those which are the finest papers on isolated aspects of a topic, or to those which best describe the clinical phenomena. I have tried to select papers from all three of these categories, with an emphasis on historical development of ideas and their clinical relevance. Many wonderful papers on masochism, some of which represent landmarks in the field, are not republished in this volume. For various reasons, where papers on masochism have been gathered together in recent volumes, I have not reprinted them (Glick and Meyers 1988; Zanardi 1989; Shapiro 1991).

An introduction to "essential papers" can do no better than indicate why the papers were chosen and why the sections exist as they do. There is a pleasure in tracing complex ideas to their sources. And, as psychoanalysis is an intellectual discipline, we have the responsibility for maintaining the ethics of such a discipline, that is, for knowing where contributions were first made, and for maintaining our discourse at the level of complexity that has been achieved.

INTRODUCTIONS TO THE PSYCHOANALYSIS OF MASOCHISM

Masochism is too broad and many-faceted a concept to introduce adequately in a few pages. An introductory section of three papers—Nacht (1938, Loewenstein 1957), and Smirnoff (1969)—serves to open up the subject in chapters 1–3. Nacht's book is a window on the early psychoanalytic writers as well as a guide to many central clinical issues. Loewenstein's study is, perhaps, the leading paper in this field, very dense, each paragraph filled with ideas on how to think about and how to approach the masochistic patient. His bibliography, in itself, is a major contribution. Smirnoff introduces us to Sacher-Masoch and his writings, and elaborates on the meanings of the masochistic "scenario."

MASOCHISM, SEXUALITY, AND AGGRESSION

A recent convergence of attention on masochism in relation to the drives and early psychic functioning (Blum 1991) has led me to return to Freud's papers in these essential papers. The thinking of Shengold (1967, 1971, 1988) and Coen (1981, 1992) on overstimulation and sadomasochism, the recent approaches to sadomasochism in sexual excitement by Kernberg (1991), and to sadomasochism and the destruction of reality in the exigencies of the

Oedipus complex by Chasseguet-Smirgel (1991) and Blos (1991), lead us back to Freud's work (1905, 1915) on the childhood component instincts, on autoerotism, on the complex vicissitudes of infantile sexual excitations with their direct path into mature sex and adult perversion.

An excerpt from the "Three Essays on the Theory of Sexuality" (1905; chapter 4 in this volume) presents Freud's first consideration of sadism and masochism as component instincts rooted in the love and hate of the anaclitic bond. The specific language of these passages suggests that masochism was intrinsically an object relations theory for Freud.

In "Instincts and Their Vicissitudes" (1915; chapter 5 in this volume) we see sadomasochism in the contexts of Freud's exploration of sexual looking and exhibitionism, and of his exploration of infantile love and hate. Still the reference point for much psychoanalytic thinking on the dynamics of the paired opposites in the infantile psyche, this text is worth re-reading in any consideration of masochism. We can see, for instance, in the case presentations in Fenichel's work (1925) on the need for punishment, the interconnectedness and simultaneity of the three paired component instincts at the heart of the patient's fantasy and current symptoms.

Laplanche (1969; chapter 6 in this volume) revives the meanings of Freud's work on sadomasochism, carefully distinguishing the concepts of sadism from aggression which Freud did not do adequately, and looking for the moment when the self-destructive and sexual impulses are first united in fantasy. Laplanche (1969) illuminates the subtle continuities between Freud's paper on "Instincts" and that on the beating fantasy.

In "Pain, Aggression, Fantasy, and Concepts of Sadomasochism," Grossman (1991; chapter 7 in this volume) looks closely at the aggressive drive as it is stimulated by pain. His discussion draws on the study of post traumatic stress disorders and object relations factors, in understanding the "precocious development" of sadism which feeds the masochistic beating fantasy (Freud 1919; chapter 8 in this volume).

MASOCHISTIC PERVERSION:
THE BEATING FANTASY

In a recent article on sadomasochism, Chasseguet-Smirgel (1991) examines the basic sadomasochistic nature of the perversions. Her hypothesis is that even when the sadistic or masochistic nature of the contents is not obvious, the backdrop of perversions against which the various contents are enacted is *always* sadomasochistic.

Freud's paper, " 'A Child Is Being Beaten': A Contribution to the Study of the Origin of Sexual Perversions" (1919) places masochism in a special role in the formation, and resolution, of the Oedipus complex. As Laplanche (1969) suggests, the movements in the psyche depicted by Freud represent a symbolic action, a key moment in the constitution of human sexuality in its full nature as psychological and rooted in fantasy. When we think of Freud's saying that the neuroses are the negative of the perversion, we have some sense of the centrality of the masochistic fantasy.

Bak's (1946) work on masochism in the paranoia of male homosexuals (chapter 9 in this volume) articulates a very important aspect of male masochism. After reviewing some early literature, Bak explores the extreme intensification of the ambivalence in his patient, in the context of total rejection by the mother and a cold strictness in the father. Bak goes on to work out precise mechanisms, in four stages, which indicate that "paranoia is delusional masochism."

Grunberger (1956; chapter 10 in this volume) studies one key fantasy in the development of masochism, which corresponds somewhat to the first phase of the beating fantasy in Freud's (1919) conception. He sees the aggressive desire for the father's love (unconsciously represented as the wish to castrate, that is, to steal the phallic power, procreativity, and well-being of the father) as a central fantasy, developmentally. This fantasy attack on the phallus requires elaboration and working through, in both sexes, in order for the psyche to avoid a rebound into masochistic fantasies of humiliation or castration.

Shengold's (1971) depictions of overstimulation, and its consequent sadomasochistic rat fantasies and destructive impulses in his patients (chapter 11 in this volume), confront us with masochism in one of its most dangerous and narcissistic forms. His attention to trauma and to its effect on psychic structure and fantasy has been a significant adddition to clinical theory.

Novick and Novick (1987) reexamine the fixed beating fantasy as an outgrowth of infantile trauma (chapter 12 in this volume). Through the developmental stages, they trace the growth of the beating fantasy. They have found that the fantasy receives its final psychic structure only in the wake of the Oedipal incest fantasy, corroborating Freud's (1919) position.

MORAL MASOCHISM: GUILT, FANTASY, AND THE OBJECT

If Freud's paper "The Economic Problem of Masochism" (1924; chapter 13 in this volume) were divided, the larger portion of it belongs to the study of moral masochism. The clinical usefulness over the years of Freud's idea of the unconscious need for punishment has been immense. In a paper entitled "The Clinical Aspect of the Need for Punishment," Fenichel (1925) works out the details in two cases, of the connection between sexual instinct and the need for punishment. In his case of moral masochism, he shows us "the excessive sexualizing in it of all penalizing actions; the turning of the sadistic trends against the patient's self, and the change of the normal oedipus complex into the inverted form as a preliminary; further, the mechanism of guilt-borrowing at its most advantageous expression" (Fenichel 1925, 92).

Anna Freud's "Beating Fantasies and Daydreams" (1922; chapter 14 in this volume), which considers the role of beating fantasies in the imagination of a teenage girl, is both a link between masochistic perversion and neurosis and an important work in female psychology. She describes the moment when the beating fantasy ceased to yield the pleasure it had given before, a sexual masturbatory pleasure associated with "Father loves only me". The "nice stories" she then developed (her conscious narratives), which disguised the masochistic pleasure, were structured in a way that was identical with the unconscious beating fantasies.

Reik's (1940) paper (chapter 16 in this volume) is well known for its phrase "victory through defeat" which first captured the desperate unconscious search for control in the abused and sadomasochistic child. Reik's (1940) work on states of masochistic excitation is less well remembered but is confirmed in the work of Coen (1992) where it finds a contemporary articulation.

Berliner (1958; chapter 17 in this volume) emphasizes the object relations factors in the etiology of masochism, particularly the sadism of the parents and resulting trauma for children. This contribution of painful experience to the formation of masochism is also articulated by Fenichel: "Certain experiences may have so firmly established the conviction that sexual pleasure must be connected with pain that suffering has become the pre-requisite for sexual pleasure." (Fenichel 1945, 358).

Brenner's often-quoted paper (1959; chapter 18 in this volume) on masochistic character explores masochism as a normal component of the human personality, with the distinction between normal masochism and masochistic character understood as a matter of degree. He emphasizes that masochistic fantasies and character traits are always associated with sadistic ones, making the term sadomasochistic most appropriate. He shows masochistic character traits as having multiple functions and as being multiply determined, but determined always in part by infantile sexual conflicts. Like Loewenstein (1957) and Fenichel (1945), he finds that masochism is an important defense against the typical childhood anxieties. Moral masochism, seemingly the farthest removed from sexual perversion or erotogenic masochism, involves a symptomatology which is the opposite of sexual masochism: a severe restraint on sexual activity, an intense investment in Oedipal and pre-Oedipal prohibitions, and in pure ideals—ideals of sacrifice and self-abnegation for higher goals. The underlying sexual sadomasochistic fantasies in moral masochism are often difficult to uncover, having, as they do, a desperate shame attached to their hidden fantasy gratifications.

Coen's "Excitement of Sadomasochism" (1992; chapter 19 in this volume) brings together, in a contemporary way, the forces at work in the co-excitation of pleasure and pain, and trauma. He returns to, and revitalizes, the work of Freud (1905, 1915) and Reik (1940), demonstrating that attunement with a masochistic patient means staying with their sadistic and sexually excited impulses as we help to bring back and integrate memories of the sadomasochistic parent. Coen makes certain key distinctions between perversion and masochistic character, while understanding the similar underlying fantasy structures.

MASOCHISM AND FEMALE PSYCHOLOGY

Helene Deutsch's paper "The Significance of Masochism in the Mental Life of Women" (1930), which begins the section as chapter 20, strongly influenced Freud (1925, 1931, 1933) in his thinking on masochism and female psychology (Fliegel 1986). Because so few analysts are returning to read this historically significant paper, its extremes are not remembered. Much of the female psychology on which Deutsch's account of feminine masochism is based has been significantly revised (Horney 1935; Blum 1976). Despite Deutsch's emphasis on the "castrated" woman (Fliegel 1986), or through it, she gives us a vivid account of many still too familiar symptoms in submissive women and allows us to see some of the developmental cruxes out of which pathological submissiveness evolves. To understand where we are now in our thinking, it is worth recalling the original position.

Reich (1940; chapter 21 in this volume) vividly depicts the pre-Oedipal narcissistic trauma at the hands of the mother which lies behind the woman's overvaluation of the penis and her masochistic submission in love. Without entering the debate on female passivity and masochism explicitly, she sets the limits on normal "submissiveness."

Bonaparte's "Some Biopsychical Aspects of Sadomasochism" (1952; chapter 22 in this volume) focuses, in a dramatic way, on the connection between feminine genital anxieties, a subject which has been revived and newly elaborated in recent papers (Mayer 1985; Bernstein 1990; Richards 1992) and masochistic fantasies rooted in such anxieties. Her paper, which includes a critique of Freud's theory of primary masochism and the first excerpts from de Sade used in psychoanalytic literature, posits what might be called a biopsychical tendency to a particular masochism in women. While some aspects of Bonaparte's female psychology seem dated, her exploration of unconscious fantasies of penetration is of interest now, as we better understand female genital anxiety.

The final paper on sadomasochism and femininity, by Chasseguet-Smirgel (1993; chapter 23 in this volume), receives its first English publication here. Her consideration of eating disorders in women reviews important work on the childhood autoerotic experience. Chasseguet-Smirgel makes a distinction between healthy autoerotic developments and pathological types. With great rigor she traces the connection between infantile trauma and conflict (especially in the anal realm) and the teenage desperation to control the burgeoning body which feels like a domineering mother, in fantasy. She goes on to discuss the symptoms of adult women, including those of menopause, in connection with the same infantile fantasies. Chasseguet-Smirgel (1993) places eating disorders in the arena of the narcissistic disorders, which leaves us with the task of understanding theoretically how these narcissistic disorders encompass so many sadomasochistic desires and excitations.

NEGATIVE THERAPEUTIC REACTION: MASOCHISM
AND CLINICAL IMPASSE

The final section, on negative therapeutic reaction, attempts to delineate a clinical theory for unblocking massive resistance to the psychoanalytic process which involves a sadomasochistic transference and an important component of unconscious guilt. Modell (1965) worked with the factor of separation guilt in the reaction. Limentani (1981) and Pontalis (1988) thought through the positive meaning for the patient of the negative therapeutic reaction. Renik (1991) considered denial in a family system. Schafer (1988) revitalized the concept of "those wrecked by success." Valenstein (1973) explored attachment to painful feelings. The papers chosen for this volume review the literature and explore transference and countertransference in the negative therapeutic reaction.

Riviere's (1936; chapter 24 in this volume) work has been seminal in understanding the need to repair the bad and damaged internal object before the patient can allow the possibility of cure for her- or himself. Riviere explores the pressures on the analyst as the patient insists that the analysis is making them worse.

Olinick's paper (1964; chapter 25 in this volume), with its apt review of the literature and its attention to sadomasochistic fantasy, especially in the transference and countertransference, advances a well-conceived clinical strategy for treating the negative therapeutic reaction.

Joseph's paper, "Addiction to Near-Death" (1982; chapter 26 in this volume), brings us a close account of the analytic process in a sadomasochistic transference which threatened to "do down" the analysis unless the analyst was able to bring the patient to glimpse the sadomasochistic gratifications he or she experienced unconsciously, and to experience how they mobilized resistance to the analytic work.

My intention has been to present the problem of masochism in its different facets and to choose papers that articulate various aspects of the clinical and theoretical concept with sufficient complexity and clarity. Many papers have not been included which would have greatly increased the scope and detail of this work in a positive way. The topic of "masochism and narcissism" (Bergler 1949; Cooper 1988; Eidelberg 1959; Lampl-de-Groot 1937; Novick and Novick 1991; Rosenfeld 1988) is approached in many of the papers printed here, but no separate section was made. When the superego is the key factor in the turning back of aggressive love onto the self in the beating fantasy, moral masochism engages fully with issues of narcissism. When the masochist is most cut off from the object in autoerotic compulsive behaviors (Chasseguet-Smirgel 1993), the narcissist takes over (Kernberg 1988).

However, in this era of narcissism, the study of masochism offers a corrective to the view that everything in human nature can be seen as stemming from narcissism. The true masochist comes at life and its exigencies from another angle — one that strives for the object, with body and soul, one that results in bondage to the object, often in body and soul, with specific defensive and adaptive ways of using the object (Brenman 1952). The issues of sexual excitation, of the eroticization of hate and pain, of sexual humiliation, in short of sexuality in its infantile fixated component forms, is always close at hand in the case history of the masochist.

The workings of an omnipotent delusion in masochism (Novick and Novick 1991), the victory through defeat of Reik (1940), the workings of narcissistic wounds in the abject humiliation of a woman's sexual enthrallment to a man (Reich 1940), the self-destructive narcissism at the extreme edge of the spectrum of masochistic disorders (Rosenfeld 1988), where sexuality and object relations have retained little investment of any kind (Kernberg 1988) — these aspects of narcissism intertwined with masochism have been written about and interpreted throughout the century (Freud 1919). In achieving an even greater degree of precision in sorting out the relationship of narcissism to masochism, we have a chance of a more flexible interpretive strategy which handles the humiliation with tact, the sadism with empathy, the disturbing sexual fantasy with a sense of its bearing. The lessons learned in relation to the negative therapeutic reaction in its particular blend of narcissistic and masochistic issues have benefited all analytic work.

In terms of the overall historical currents and countercurrents in the psychoanalytic study of masochism, we can see that some of the fine early articulations have been neglected and then reinvented in contemporary terms. But there has been development too, in ideas which concern the handling of the sadomasochistic transference, in the distinctions between the various types of masochistic disorders, from the depressive through the perverse and narcissistic extremes (Kernberg 1988), in the understanding of the effects of trauma in the inevitably conflicted, sometimes humiliating world of the little child striving toward personal and sexual maturity.

BIBLIOGRAPHY

André, J. 1991. La sexualité féminine: Retour aux sources. In *Psychanalyste à l'Université*. Paris: Presses Universitaires de France.

Bak, R. 1946. Masochism in Paranoia. *Psychoanal. Quarterly* 15:285–301. (Chapter 9 in this volume.)

Bergler, E. 1949. *The Basic Neurosis: Oral Regression and Psychic Masochism.* New York: Grune & Stratton.

Berliner, B. 1958. The Role of Object Relations in Moral Masochism. *Psychoanal. Quarterly* 27:38–56. (Chapter 17 in this volume.)

Bernstein, D. 1990. Female Genital Anxieties, Conflicts and Typical Mastery Modes. *Int. J. Psycho-Anal.* 71:151–65.

Blos, P., Jr. 1991. Sadomasochism and the Defense against Recall of Painful Affect. *J. Amer. Psychoanal. Assn.* 39:417–30.

Blum, H. 1976. Masochism, the Ego Ideal, and the Psychology of Women. *J. Amer. Psychoanal. Assn.* 24:157–91.

———. 1991. Sadomasochism in the Psychoanalytic Process, Within and Beyond the Pleasure Principle. *J. Amer. Psychoanal. Assn.* 39:431–50.

Bonaparte, M. 1952. Some Biopsychical Aspects of Sado-Masochism. *Int. J. Psycho-Anal.* 33:373–84. (Chapter 22 in this volume.)

Brenman, M. 1952. On Teasing and Being Teased: And the Problem of Moral Masochism. *Psychoanal. Study Child* 7:264–85.

Brenner, C. 1959. The Masochistic Character: Genesis and Treatment. *J. Amer. Psychoanal. Assn.* 7:197–226. (Chapter 18 in this volume.)

Chasseguet-Smirgel, J. 1991. Sadomasochism in the Perversions: Some Thoughts on the Destruction of Reality. *J. Amer. Psychoanal. Assn.* 39:399–415.

———. 1993. Auto-Sadism, Eating Disorders, and Femininity. In French, in the *Canadian Journal of Psychoanalysis* 1, no. 1: 101–22. (In English, chapter 23 in this volume.)

Coen, S. 1981, Sexualization as a Predominant Mode of Defense. *J. Amer. Psychoanal. Assn.* 29:893–920.

———. 1992. The Excitement of Sadomasochism. In *The Misuse of Persons: Analyzing Pathological Dependency.* Hillsdale, N.J.: The Analytic Press, pp. 190–208. (Chapter 19 in this volume.)

Cooper, A. 1988. The Narcissistic-Masochistic Disorder. In *Masochism: Current Psychoanalytic Perspectives,* ed. R. Glick and D. Meyers. Hillsdale, N.J.: The Analytic Press, pp. 117–38.

Deutsch, H. 1930. The Significance of Masochism in the Mental Life of Women. *Int. J. Psycho-Anal.* 11:48–60. (Chapter 20 in this volume.)

Eidelberg, L. 1959. Humiliation and Masochism. *J. Amer. Psychoanal. Assn.* 7:274–83.

Fenichel, O. 1925. The Clinical Aspect of the Need for Punishment. In *The Collected Papers of Otto Fenichel: First Series.* New York: Norton, 1953, pp. 71–96. (Chapter 15 in this volume.)

———. 1945. *The Psychoanalytic Theory of Neurosis.* New York: Norton.

Fliegel, Z. 1986. Women's Development in Analytic Theory: Six Decades of Controversy. In *Psychoanalysis and Women,* ed. J. Alpert. Hillsdale, N.J.: The Analytic Press, pp. 3–31.

Freud, A. 1922. Beating Fantasies and Daydreams. *Int. J. Psycho-Anal.* 4:89–102. (Chapter 14 in this volume.)

Freud, S. 1905. Three Essays on the Theory of Sexuality (An Excerpt). In *S.E.* 7:135, 155–60. (Chapter 4 in this volume.)

———. 1915. Instincts and Their Vicissitudes (An Excerpt). In *S.E.* 14:125–40. (Chapter 5 in this volume.)

———. 1919. "A Child Is Being Beaten": A Contribution to the Study of the Origin of Sexual Perversions. In *S.E.* 17:179–204. (Chapter 8 in this volume.)

———. 1924. The Economic Problem of Masochism. In *S.E.* 19:159–70. (Chapter 13 in this volume.)

———. 1925. Some Psychical Consequences of the Anatomical Distinction between the Sexes. In *S.E.* 19:248–58.

————. 1931. Female Sexuality. In *S.E.* 21:225–43.

————. 1933. Femininity. In *S.E.* 22:112–35.

Glick, R., and Meyers, D., eds. 1988. *Masochism: Current Psychoanalytic Perspectives.* Hillsdale, N.J.: The Analytic Press.

Grossman, W. I. 1991. Pain, Aggression, Fantasy, and Concepts of Sadomasochism. *Psychoanal. Quarterly* 60:22–52. (Chapter 7 in this volume.)

Grunberger, B. 1956. Psychodynamic Theory of Masochism. In *Perversions, Psychodynamics and Therapy,* ed. S. Lorand and M. Balint. New York: Random House, 183–208. (Chapter 10 in this volume.)

Horney, K. 1935. The Problem of Feminine Masochism. *Psychoanal. Rev.* 22:241–57.

Joseph, B. 1982. Addiction to Near-Death. *Int. J. Psycho-Anal.* 63:449–456. (Chapter 26 in this volume.)

Kernberg, O. 1988. Clinical Dimensions of Masochism. In *Masochism: Current Psychoanalytic Perspectives,* ed. R. Glick and D. Meyers. Hillsdale, N.J.: The Analytic Press, pp. 61–79.

————. 1991. Sadomasochism, Sexual Excitement, and Perversion. *J. Amer. Psychoanal. Assn.* 39:333–62.

Lampl-de Groot, J. 1937. Masochism and Narcissism. In *The Development of the Mind.* New York: International Universities Press, 1965, 82–92.

Laplanche, J. 1969. Aggressiveness and Sadomasochism. In *Life and Death in Psychoanalysis.* Baltimore: Johns Hopkins University Press. (Chapter 6 in this volume.)

Limentani, Adam. 1981. On Some Positive Aspects of the Negative Therapeutic Reaction. *Int. J. Psycho-Anal.* 62:379–90.

Loewenstein, R. 1957. A Contribution to the Psychoanalytic Theory of Masochism. *J. Amer. Psychoanal. Assn.* 5:197–234. (Chapter 2 in this volume.)

Mayer, E. L., 1985. Everybody Must Be Just Like Me: Observations on Female Castration Anxiety. *Int. J. Psycho-Anal.* 66:331–48.

Modell, A. 1965. On Having the Right to Life: An Aspect of the Super-ego's Development. *Int. J. Psycho-Anal.* 46:323–31.

Nacht, S. 1938. Introduction. In *Le masochisme.* Paris: Payot, 1965. (Trans. M. A. Fitzpatrick Hanly, chapter 1 in this volume.)

Novick, K., and Novick, J. 1987. The Essence of Masochism. *Psychoanal. Study Child* 42:353–84. (Chapter 12 in this volume.)

————. 1991. Some Comments on Masochism and the Delusion of Omnipotence from a Developmental Perspective. *J. Amer. Psychoanal. Assn.* 39:307–31.

Olinick, S. L. 1964. The Negative Therapeutic Reaction. *Int. J. Psycho-Anal.* 45:540–48. (Chapter 25 in this volume.)

Pontalis, J.-B. 1988. Non, deux fois non. In *Perdre de vue.* Paris: Gallimard, pp. 73–101.

Reich, A. 1940. A Contribution to the Psycho-Analysis of Extreme Submissiveness in Women. *Psychoanal. Quarterly* 9:470–80. (Chapter 21 in this volume.)

Reik, T. 1940. The Characteristics of Masochism. *Am. Imago* 1:26–59. (In excerpt form, chapter 16 in this volume.)

Renik, Owen. 1991. One Kind of Negative Therapeutic Reaction. *J. Amer. Psychoanal. Assn.* 39:87–105.

Richards, A. 1992. The Influence of Sphincter Control and Genital Sensation on Body Image and Gender Identity in Women. *Psychoanal. Quarterly.* 61:331–51.

Riviere, J. 1936. A Contribution to the Analysis of the Negative Therapeutic Reaction. *Int. J. Psycho-Anal.* 17:304–20. (Chapter 24 in this volume.)

Rosenberg, B. 1988. *Masochisme mortifère et masochisme gardien de la vie.* Paris: Presses Universitaires de France.

Rosenfeld, H. 1988. On Masochism: A Theoretical and Clinical Approach. In *Masochism: Current Psychoanalytic Perspectives*. Hillsdale N.J.: Analytic Press.

Rothstein, A. 1991. Sadomasochism in the Neuroses Conceived of as a Pathological Compromise Formation. *J. Amer. Psychoanal. Assn.* 39:363–75.

Schafer, R. 1988. Those Wrecked by Success. In *Masochism: Current Psychoanalytic Perspectives,* ed. R. Glick and D. Meyers. Hillsdale, N.J.: The Analytic Press, pp. 81–91.

Shapiro, T., ed. 1991. *J. Amer. Psycho-Anal.* Madison, Conn.: International Universities Press, vol. 39.

Shengold, L. 1967. The Effects of Overstimulation: Rat People. *Int. J. Psycho-Anal.* 48:403–15.

———. 1971. More about Rats and Rat People. *Int. J. Psycho-Anal.* 52:277–88. (Chapter 11 in this volume.)

———. 1988. *Halo in the Sky*. New York: Guilford Press.

Smirnoff, V. 1969. The Masochistic Contract. *Int. J. Psycho-Anal.* 50:665–71. (Chapter 3 in this volume.)

Stoller, R. 1975. *Perversion*. New York: Pantheon.

Valenstein, A. 1973. On Attachment to Painful Feelings and the Negative Therapeutic Reaction. *Psychoanal. Study Child* 28:305–92.

Zanardi, C., ed. 1989. *Essential Papers on the Psychology of Women*. New York: New York University Press.

PART I

THREE INTRODUCTIONS TO THE PSYCHOANALYSIS OF MASOCHISM

Introduction

It is a sign of the many-faceted nature of masochism, and of its complex functions within the human psyche, that this volume begins with four introductions—a brief account concerning the selection of papers and three major works on masochism which carry the burden of introducing this topic.

In 1938, Nacht wrote a book on masochism which is still regularly cited in French papers on the subject. His introduction to this work (chapter 1 in this volume) serves as a set of basic reference points. He first reviews for us the history of the concept of masochism and its early development by Freud and his European followers. Nacht reminds us that the role of beating, or flagellation, in sexual excitation was pointed out by the most ancient observers, but only in the nineteenth century was masochism named and described as a sexual perversion. And only with Freud were the interrelated dynamics of the paired opposites—sadism and masochism—begun to be understood.

In the mid-1990s, when the sexual aspect of masochism is being disputed and repudiated even within psychoanalysis, Nacht's work reminds us of the connection of masochism to love—to sexual desire in its most human and binding forms, in the passive longing of the infant for the mother, in the ambivalent anaclitic love of the toddler, and in the strong possessive love of the Oedipal child. This rooting of the concept of masochism in sexual love rather than in destructivity, or the death instinct, places Nacht in what has been the mainstream North American view of masochism (see Berliner 1958; Brenner 1959), and it puts him, clearly, on one side of a still lively debate in France concerning the relationship of masochism to the death instinct (Laplanche 1992; Rosenberg 1988).

Because Loewenstein wrote papers on masochism both in French and in English, his work served as a bridge between Europe and North America. His reflexions on infantile passive longings and masochism are still pertinent today. Loewenstein (1957; chapter 2 in this volume) evokes the vulnerability of the passive infant to proto-masochistic defenses. He understood passivity as an infantile libidinal position and as a prerequisite for masochism. He notes however that "passivity is obviously not sufficient to explain the essential character of the masochistic perversion; namely that unpleasure is so intimately bound up with sexual gratification" (p. 37 in this volume). The author then reviews the various mechanisms that underlie masochistic perversions, which involve crucial problems with which human sexuality has to deal in its development: fear of the loss of the object and fear of the loss of its love, castration fear, and superego anxiety. Loewenstein reminds us of the tendency to passivity and helplessness, which may have the implicit aim of appealing to the mercy of the threatening and protective parental figure (Horney 1935). He describes the permitting of sexual gratification by apparently eliminating all responsibility for it, and the use of suffering as a prerequisite for sexual pleasure—as a price that must be paid to appease guilt feelings (Reich 1949). He recalls Rado's (1933) idea concerning the acceptance of suffering as a "lesser Evil." Loewenstein alludes to the turning against the self of active genital and aggressive impulses directed at incestuous objects. And he reminds us that the masochist uses mechanisms generally designed to deal with anxiety (Freud 1926), in trying to anticipate actively what might be feared to occur to one passively (Waelder 1933; Fenichel 1945). "By imagining or producing scenes of torturing or punishment which he himself devises, the masochist excludes the possibility of being tortured or punished in an unexpected and uncontrollable way (Eidelberg 1934). This is particularly evident in the cases that have been described as 'erotization of anxiety' (Laforgue 1930), and which lie somewhere between a neurosis and a perversion" (p. 37 in this volume). Loewenstein notes that these mechanisms explain the cases in which pain is a condition for pleasure but fail to account for the pleasure that is derived from suffering. His hypothesis is that masochistic perversions originate in traumatic events which involve "a mixture of prohibition, seduction and reassurance," such that "the masochistic perversions are modified repetitions of childhood situations and scenes in which sexual fantasies, erotic games, direct or indirect attempts at sexual rapprochement toward forbidden objects, particularly the mother, have met with disappointment or rebuff coupled with actual or imagined ridicule, threat, or punishment." Like Nacht, Loewenstein reminds us that the infant and child need and seek the love of the object and that masochism has many functions which are essentially object bound.

Smirnoff (1969; chapter 3 in this volume) develops the idea of a masochistic contract. He shows how Sacher-Masoch allayed anxiety about losing the impossible but desired object through the acting out of self-humiliation and self-punishment with the help of a phallic mother figure, and through the development of a scenario which repeats childhood trauma. He describes for us the way in which Sacher-Masoch, in his life and novels, brings alive this description of the infantile origins of sadomasochism. "Masochism is a defiance. It is expressed through the masochist's apparently passive behaviour, by his compliance with the inflicted pain and humiliation, by his claims of being enslaved and used. In fact, the masochist knows that his position is simply the result of his own power: the power of endowing the executioner with the obligation of playing the role of a master, when indeed he is only a slave, a creation of the masochist's desire" (p. 69 in this volume).

These three introductions to the psychoanalysis of masochism launch us into the complexities of a psychic process which taxes our analytic skills even more than our understanding.

BIBLIOGRAPHY

Berliner, B. 1958. The Role of Object Relations in Moral Masochism. *Psychoanal. Quarterly* 27:38–56. (Chapter 17 in this volume).

Brenner, C. 1959. The Masochistic Character: Genesis and Treatment. *J. Amer. Psychoanal. Assn.* 7:197–226. (Chapter 18 in this volume.)

Eidelberg, L. 1934. A Contribution to the Study of Masochism. In *Studies in Psychoanalysis*. New York: International Universities Press, 1952, pp. 31–40.

Fenichel, O. 1945. *The Psychoanalytic Theory of Neurosis*. New York: Norton.

Freud, S. 1926. Inhibitions, Symptoms, and Anxiety. *S.E.* 20:77–175.

Horney, K. 1935. The Problem of Feminine Masochism. *Psychoanal. Rev.* 22:241–57.

Laforgue, R. 1930. On the Eroticization of Anxiety. *Int. J. Psycho-Anal.* 11:312–26.

Laplanche, J. 1976. *Life and Death in Psychoanalysis*. Baltimore: Johns Hopkins University Press.

———. 1992. *La révolution copernicienne inachevée*. Paris: Aubier.

Loewenstein, R. 1957. A Contribution to the Psychoanalytic Theory of Masochism. *J. Amer. Psychoanal. Assn.* 5:197–234. (Chapter 2 in this volume.)

Nacht, S. 1938. Introduction. In *Le masochisme*. Paris: Payot, 1965, pp. 5–32. (Chapter 1 in this volume.)

Novick, K., and Novick, J. 1987. The Essence of Masochism. *Psychoanal. Study/Child.* 42:353–84. (Chapter 12 in this volume.)

Rado, S. 1933. Fear of Castration in Women. *Psychoanal. Quarterly.* 2:425–75.

Reich, W. 1949. The Masochistic Character. In *Character Analysis*. New York: Orgone Institute Press, 3d ed., pp. 208–47.

Rosenberg, B. 1988. *Masochisme mortifère et masochisme gardien de la Vie*. Paris: Presses Universitaires de France.

Smirnoff, V. 1969. The Masochistic Contract. *Int. J. Psycho-Anal.* 50:665–71. (Chapter 3 in this volume.)

Waelder, R. 1933. The Psychoanalytic Theory of Play. *Psychoanal. Quarterly.* 2:208–24.

1. *Le Masochisme,* Introduction

Sacha Nacht

Masochism is a neurotic state characterized by a search for suffering. The masochist feels a real need, an "appetite" for suffering.

The suffering is physical or moral, or both at the same time.

The masochistic person seeks suffering directly, knowingly, with the goal of an erotic genital satisfaction. This practice represents erotogenic masochism, or masochistic sexual perversion; this was the only manifestation of masochism known before psychoanalytic research.

This research discovered another much more widespread form of masochism—moral masochism.

Here, the suffering is indirectly and unconsciously sought, but the search is unavowed. Also, it goes beyond the realm of the genital to encompass the whole personality.

Moral masochism, alone, can develop into a real neurosis of behavior, usually designated in psychoanalytic literature under the name "masochistic character." Still more often, we see masochism in the form of masochistic tendencies, taking an essential part in the formation of most psychoneurotic states.

This wish for suffering, pushed to its extreme, reveals a veritable tendency in the order of a self-destructive drive. The biological universality of this tendency led Freud to consider it as an independent drive, called by him "the death instinct." We will have occasion more than once to come back to this concept which Freud took care, several times, to designate as purely speculative (metapsychological).

As for us, let us make it clear from the start that we are dedicated to the task of studying the question of masochism most particularly from the clinical and psychogenic point of view.

Reprinted by permission of Editions Payot & Rivages, from *Le Masochisme* by S. Nacht, 1965. Translated by Margaret Ann Fitzpatrick Hanly.

From this point of view, the concept of a primary masochism, expression of an instinctive self-destructive tendency, seems contradicted by the facts of clinical observation.

This tendency, in fact, would seem to have as a goal the realization of suffering for its own sake; whereas, clinically, masochism, whether it is erotogenic or moral, hardly ever appears as an end, but rather as a means.

We believe that we can show in this study that masoshism, an apparently paradoxical reaction, is a means of defense, pathological self-defense. As we will later demonstrate, things proceed as if the masochist, faced with the danger of losing everything (and the majority of psychoanalytic papers indicate—as we will see later—that this danger is conceived of, on the unconscious level, as castration), consents to a partial sacrifice to save the rest.

A mug's game, however, at least in the eyes of the beholder; for the sufferings and sacrifices which the masochist inflicts on himself are real, whereas the danger against which he struggles is only a fiction of the unconscious. However, the economy of the psychic apparatus succeeds in drawing out a certain gain from the situation.

Theodor Reik (1941), although finding my expression "a mug's game" a good one, objected that this is the point of view of the observer, but not of the subject. I never thought otherwise, for if the masochist had the same point of view he would not be a masochist.

All our psychoanalytic efforts are adapted precisely in order to lead the masochist toward this point of view, that of objective reality, which is distorted in him by subjective reality.

Most of the time, a combination of two mechanisms brings about this neurotic gain:

(a) the suffering is erotized;
(b) the suffering is used by the superego as a means of self-punishment meant to partially neutralize the guilt complex. So that libidinal needs, until then forbidden, can be authorized to find a certain satisfaction.

We will have more than one occasion to deepen our study of these mechanisms. An understanding of them facilitates the explanation, at least at the clinical level, of the most strange and harmful psychopathologies.

We will also see that if we want to call upon the concept of the death instinct, its role would be inconceivable except as a "second-degree mechanism" (Nacht 1963).

The clinical value in the concept is negligible, if not nonexistent, and, from a therapeutic point of view, the concept is sterile.

We are not on solid ground when we reflect on the origins of masochism, except in returning to Freud's first concept. This leads us to take up the history of the idea. But before doing so, it is worth making some remarks concerning psychoanalytic terminology.

Psychoanalysts know what great difficulties they encounter when they want to describe the facts of psychoanalytic observation. For the most part these difficulties stem from the lack of a terminology sufficiently adapted to the object of our studies. In the description of unconscious processes, we are constantly obliged to use terms which have a well enough defined psychological sense, but which do not apply with felicity to what we are trying to say. This gap can create a certain confusion and misunderstanding in the very framework of psychoanalytic research. It is certainly responsible for a great deal of the discomfort felt by those who take up our publications for the first time.

One example, among others, is provided by the complex called the *castration complex*. We designate by this term a group of infantile representations, translating the child's experience of a danger to his genital organs, representations which are certainly very different from the precise image evoked by the word *castration*.

Can we one day surmount the difficulties due to this particular terminology?

Following a similar train of thought, R. Loewenstein criticized my term *guilt complex*, used at the heart of this presentation, a term which he found inappropriate. But his arguments not having convinced us, and above all no other term having been proposed, we have kept the term, not believing it to be particularly good, but for want of a better.

Indeed, to use the term *Schuldgefühl* (feeling of guilt), generally employed by German-speaking analysts, would involve the same error as using the term *unconscious feeling of guilt,* which according to Freud himself is psychological non-sense. In the face of this difficulty, Freud advises that we speak only of the need for punishment, but as it is hardly possible to avoid referring to the notion of guilt attached to the need for punishment, this doesn't solve the problem.

Also, we felt we were closer to the truth in utilizing the term *guilt complex* each time it seemed necessary.

HISTORICAL

The strange relation between pain and sexual pleasure, between suffering and love, has been pointed out by the most ancient observers.

It is said that Solomon in old age had himself pricked by women to excite his failing virility. Flavius Josephe tells the story of his brother, Herod Pherosas, who had himself chained and beaten by women slaves, for the same reason.

Socrates, in his relations with his wife, Xantippe, presents an even more complete example of masochism.

The same is true for Aristotle and Phyllis. There are images of the philosopher on all fours, carrying his wife on his back, armed with a whip.

The fact that among the votive offerings of the ancient courtisans to Venus were found whips, bridles, and spurs, suggests clearly enough the erotic usage they could make of this apparatus.

In the *Satyricon,* Petronius has one of his characters beaten with nettles which stimulates his virility. Trenel (1902) has found masochistic scenes (equine masochism) on the bas-reliefs of the thirteenth century.

By the sixteenth century the role of flagellation in sexual excitation is described (Eulenburg 1902). In 1643, a monograph entitled *De usu flagorum in Re Venera* by Meibomius appeared.

Still, for a long time, authors saw these practices as a means of stimulation, as a sort of aphrodisiac. It was only in the nineteenth century that masochism came to be described as a sexual perversion.

In 1869, Krafft-Ebing (1906) describes in his *Psychopathia Sexualis* a perversion characterized by the seeking after a painful and humiliating submission which he baptized masochism, after Sacher-Masoch, a popular writer at the time, who perfectly illustrated by his work, as well as his life, the perversion which has since borne his name.

Krafft-Ebing's study remains the most comprehensive and complete document preceding psychoanalytic work.

Every clinical manifestation of masochism is mentioned: physical pain by pricks, blows, whipping, etc.; moral humiliation by attitudes of servile submission to women, accompanied by corporal punishments judged as indispensable. The role of masochistic fantasies did not escape the notice of Krafft-Ebing. Moreover, he indicates the link between masochism and its opposite sadism, and does not hesitate to consider the whole of masochism "as a pathological overlay of feminine psychic elements, as a morbid exaggeration of certain aspects of a woman's soul."

As for what concerns the origin of this perversion, he restricts himself to blaming constitutional tendencies.

Schrenck-Notzing (1892), Ferre (1899), Eulenburg (1902), and others studied masochism around 1900, most especially in their research on pain. In this work, they employed the terms *passive algolagnie* and *passive algophylie*.

For these authors, as for Binet (1888) and Gilbert Ballet (1903), the mechanism and origin of perversion remained obscure. They could only imagine the hypothesis of a perversion acquired through the infamous "mental degeneracy" to which, in that era, every human problem was attributed.

More recently, and in a more subtle way, Havelock Ellis devoted a long chapter to masochism, in his *Studies in the Psychology of Sex* (1897). As always with this author, we find here a very rich clinical documentation. Moreover, Ellis was inclined to attribute a biological instinctual origin to the function of the sexual stimulant which could take on pain. This pain would then represent a transformation of the anger and fear which characterize the "court" of the animals. Influenced by P. Janet, Ellis writes, "It is only under these neurasthenic or neuropathological conditions, that is, when an organism is weakened, irritable or fatigued by other causes, acquired or congenital—and ordinarily perhaps by both—that these manifestations can prosper so vigorously, so as to be in the foreground of sexual consciousness, and so as to attain such importance that they themselves take over the entire aim of sexual desire."

But it was Freud, and certain later psychoanalytic studies taken as a whole, which made masochism what it is today—one of the most important problems of psychopathology, at least in the domain of psychoanalytic research.

In the beginning, this research focused on gaining a better understanding of the origins and mechanisms of masochism; later, psychoanalysis, in discovering the true extent of moral masochism, could understand it as an essential and almost universal component in every psychopathological process. Freud's ideas on the structure of the psychic apparatus were, in their turn, influenced by the notions drawn from his more and more thorough knowledge of masochism.

Finally, in the years which followed, a great deal of psychoanalytic work was taken up by the study of the origin and interconnection of the instincts. It was masochism, again, which was the point of departure for this research.

Freud first expressed his ideas on masochism in the "Three Essays on the Theory of Sexuality" (1905).

Without yet formulating a full definition, he clearly indicated:

1. the participation of sadism and masochism as constitutive elements in sexual life, in general;
2. the passivity which characterized the masochist's attitude in relation to the sexual object;
3. the connection between sadism and masochism, one being the transformation of the other:

"We often note," he wrote, "that masochism is nothing other than a continuation of sadism, which takes the place of a sexual object."

Krafft-Ebing (1906) had already indicated the co-existence of sadism and masochism in the same person, but he had simply noted the fact as a coincidence.

Freud (1905) showed, for the first time, the link between the two apparently opposite tendencies. He wrote, "One could ask oneself whether masochism rather than being a primary phenomenon is not always a transformation of sadism." We will see how later Freud (1924) was led to renounce this idea, although clinical observation confirmed it and, at the same time, great therapeutic gains stemmed from it.

From then on he emphasized the probable role of the castration complex and the feeling of guilt in the fixation and exaggeration of the "original" passive sexual attitude (it would have been more precise to say "infantile" than "original").

The problem remained there for many years, the interest in psychoanalytic circles being directed to other fields. Then, Adler (1921), Steckel (1922), Sadger (1926), Federn (1914a and 1914b), and most recently T. Reik (1941) took up the study of sadomasochism again.

Federn (1914a and 1914b), came back to the opposition between active and passive. In a long article, he tried to show that masochism was only the reawakening of partial drives of infantile sexuality for which the passive character is inherent. Every satisfaction, for example resulting from tactile excitation, became a source of passive sexual satisfaction according to him. This was most notably the case with hollow organs: bladder, rectum, and later the vulva and vagina. From this would stem the dominant character of passivity in female sexuality and its special relationship to masochism.

On the other hand, all motor excitation can become the source of an erotic satisfaction, which has active, aggressive, and hence, virile character.

It was only in 1919 that Freud directly took up the question of masochism in his study of the beating fantasies, called "A Child Is Being Beaten" (Freud 1919).

Neurotic patients very often have more or less conscious fantasies, in which they create scenes which go something like this: Someone—usually a child—is beaten. Under analysis these fantasies appear as reflections of the Oedipal conflict. Freud reaffirmed that masochism resulted from the transformation of sadism. But he also clearly showed that the conditions for this transformation were special: "It is always the feeling of guilt which transforms sadism into masochism," he writes. This was the first time that we have, so clearly formulated, the hypothesis which has shown itself to be so fruitful in the psychoanalytic research which followed, concerning the role played by the guilt complex in the turning around of the sadistic-aggressive tendency into its opposite: the masochistic-passive tendency.

The beating fantasy, that is, the widespread neurotic fantasy of a child being beaten, shows a repressed desire in the patient to be beaten by the father. Here, the father is the object of the sexual Oedipal tendencies for the girl as well as for the boy. For the boy this creates what we call the negative Oedipus complex, which has great importance for many questions studied in this text.

Things proceed as if, through this fantasy, the desire to be beaten by the father is substituted for the repressed desire to be loved by him. The expression of this desire is translated into the form of a punishment, and, at the same time, the punishment can alleviate the sense of guilt implicated in the desire because of its Oedipal origins. From this stems the passive feminine, self-punishing aspect of these masochistic fantasies and of masochism in general.

From the "Three Essays on the Theory of Sexuality" on, Freud (1905) let it be understood that aggressivity alone could not explain masochism. In having the sense of guilt intervene, and above all showing that the masochistic attitude could represent one mode of the psyche's reaction to the Oedipus complex, Freud began to clarify the question.

If we maintain—and we will see in studying erotogenic masochism that this is in fact plausible—that in many cases the genesis of the masochistic fantasy is no different from the need for real punishment which the masochistic pervert undergoes, we will understand how and why, by a process of regression, he who has himself been beaten and humiliated can find therein a satisfaction.

We will understand also how a fixation on a specific mode of infantile sexual satisfaction does not imply from the beginning that this satisfaction existed before. Clinical amnesia shows that this is in fact quite rare.

Finally, we can conceive that the mere desire to receive punishment can suffice. Perhaps we can even say that the real punishment received has its true traumatic or fixating power, only insofar as conflicts move a child to seek the punishment.

But it was not only in the limited sphere of masochistic perversion that Freud's work brought precious new elements. The fact of having shown that masochism represented one of the ways of resolving the Oedipus complex led to new conceptions of the psychic apparatus, and also to new explanations of psychopathological phenomena. But we are now obliged to take a detour into the general history of psychoanalytic concepts before taking up masochism again.

During the first twenty years of its existence, psychoanalysis had studied, for the benefit of those with neurotic conflicts, unconscious tendencies wherein forces derived from the sexual instinct had undergone repression—in a word, repressed impulses.

Then, psychoanalysis took up the study of the forces of repression. Their study ended in a new psychology of the ego.

This displacement of interest from Freud's first work was of such importance that certain psychoanalysts spoke of a "new psychoanalysis." But in fact it was only a question of a development, magnificent in its continuity, of the same line of thought.

In reviewing the history of psychoanalytic ideas, I have often been struck to see that such and such a concept which was extremely important at a certain time—and justifiably so—can already be found as a hypothesis, or rudimentary idea, in the first works of Freud.

Jones made the same remark one day to the Psychoanalytic Society of Paris in relation to the subject which is now the focus of our attention: "Throughout the entire work of Freud, in the earliest as in the most recent writings, there exists the most rigorous continuity, even in regard to the superego; and the entire theory constitutes a whole organism, in the process of evolving and expanding" (Jones 1927).

Thus, from 1914, in his article on narcissism, Freud (1914) indicates the importance of the repressive forces which later became "personified" in the superego. This article marks a turning point in the evolution of ideas which concern the organization of libidinal instincts, which were at first observed as always and entirely oriented toward the outside, toward the objective world.

The study of dementia precox—and of all the neuroses called narcissistic—led Freud to admit, with Ferenczi, that libidinal drives could be turned back toward the subject, and directed toward the ego which would itself become an object of libido (secondary narcissism).

The existence of the possibility of this libidinal investment will be very useful later for understanding certain complex problems posed by masochism, notably its libidinal character.

Returning to the repressive forces, Freud showed in the same article how what he still called *conscience,* and what would later be called the *superego,* represented the introjection of the critical authority and prohibitions of the parents. He explained then how this introjection could take place under the influence of fear—especially fear of the loss of the parents' love or fear of sexual punishment (the castration complex). But we cannot succumb to the temptation to continue the analysis of these beautiful studies by Freud, which begin with the essay "On Naricissism" (1914) and move through "Mourning and Melancholia" (1915) to arrive at "Beyond the Pleasure Principle" (1920) and "The Ego and the Id" (1923), to the present conception of the psychic apparatus. We must be content to respect the framework of this presentation, and to draw out ideas concerning the superego—ideas which are indispensable for understanding a whole aspect of masochism.

The child, under the weight of the Oedipus complex and in order to avoid the fear of danger (loss of the parents' love, punishments, castration), a fear which is insurmountable and inherent in the conflict he is traversing, finds himself led into the subtle and helpful game of identifying, of introjecting and integrating, of making his own, all the criticisms and prohibitions— formulated or understood—coming principally from the parent of his own sex, in whom he senses the obstacle to the realization of his sexual needs.

But the fear and the love felt for the same being transform the rival into an ally: the child finds therein the strength to fight, that is, to repress his incestuous desires. This rival, become ally, doubles as a judge, if not an enemy, and represents, in the case of the boy, for instance, the father he loves, and in whom he respects the rights and authority (in which image he has an ally), but, at the same time, the father he fears, because jealousy makes the boy hate him (in which image he has an enemy). The "attributes" of the friend-enemy (ambivalence), interiorized by the work of identification and incorporated into the ego, will, in future, form an integral part of the child's psyche. This will be the superego, the heir of the Oedipus complex, as Freud has called it.

Indeed, the appearance of the superego marks the end of the Oedipus complex. The work of this new psychic agency which criticizes and forbids, on the father's behalf, the sexual impulses, ends, after repression, in desexualizing the link with the mother, in reducing also the fear of the father, that is, in putting down the conflict.

This peace is an "armed peace": the enemy is not exterminated, he is simply pushed back from the borders. The incestuous sexual impulses are repressed; they are not dissolved and they can reappear at any moment.

Thus the primitive external conflict, resulting from the conflict between the libidinal impulses shown by the child and the educational prohibitions of the parents, has become an internal conflict between the drives emerging from the "id" (or elementary unconscious) and the critical agency, the "superego." This psychic function manifests itself in two ways. One is conscious, it is the conscience, which, following the development of the whole being, stimulates and enriches moral aspirations, judged in importance, according to the scale of values employed. The other part of the superego, and the one which is the most important in pathology, remains unconscious; and it can become the implacable instrument of neurosis.

This is why we must pay the unconscious part the greatest attention. Indeed, this part of the superego remains infantile and does not follow the developmental process of the personality as a whole. Thus, it stays irrational.

The result is that one part of the personality takes an infantile and irrational attitude to the rest of the personality—especially to the sexual impulses. One part of the superego will have the tendency to treat the sexual drives of the adult in the same way parents and educators treated the same drives in the child: forbidding them, and punishing them. It is easy here to make certain links which bring us back to the very heart of the problem with which we are preoccupied, and from which we seemed to have drifted away. Doesn't the masochist show himself infantile precisely in his sexual life? Isn't every satisfaction forbidden to him? And doesn't punishment always follow satisfaction? The superego acts in just this way. The superego must therefore be present at the origin of the need to suffer, and to be punished, which the masochist experiences.

We have seen that what presides over the development of the superego is the fear of the father, in the boy, and the fear of the mother, in the girl.

And doesn't this fear come, above all, from the aggression felt against the feared adult? Once internalized, the same fear can later be felt by the ego when it faces the superego.

The excessive severity of the superego, whose punishments can be inflicted in the form of self-punishments, permit the ego to escape the internalized fear, which corresponds to the fear of castration. We can see, then, how the hostility and aggression primitively felt against the other, and then turned back by the person against himself, can persist under the form of a punishment administered against oneself, and isn't this one aspect of masochism?

We can now better understand the connection linking sadism to masochism, which has struck all observers.

We also know one of the means of transforming sadism into masochism. The superego appears to us as the path through which the aggressive drive finds a way of turning back against the subject in the form of a punishment.

But the same hatred experienced by the child before the refusal of satisfaction during the Oedipal conflict can be felt at other stages of the development of libido, during which he comes up against the impossibility of satisfying his libidinal tendencies.

It is very possible that part of this hatred follows the same path (although constrained, because repressed) in turning back against the subject himself and is situated at the origin of masochism. We can sum up what has been said in this way: every prohibition or refusal of libidinal satisfaction unleashes aggressive movements (the culminating point of which process is reached in the Oedipus complex). Normally the aggressivity cannot be acted out against the object (because the object is both feared and loved). The aggression returns then, after repression, against the subject himself in the form of masochism.

The person treats himself in the same way he would have treated his object, if he could have. The masochism appears, then, as a manifestation of aggression. Thus to seek the origin of masochism is to seek that also of sadism. For a long while, during which neither Freud, nor other analysts, deepened our understanding of the instincts, we considered sadism as a partial drive. But does it, like the other component instincts, really act as a sexual drive? Doesn't it faithfully accompany the sexual instinct in its evolution without ever being an integral part of it? At the time, this couldn't be said. While waiting we had to content ourselves with describing manifestations of the sadistic drive, within the framework of sexual development: oral, and above all sadistic-anal and genital.

Freud (1915) was later led to define sadism (made up of the whole gamut of the various states which it encompasses: hatred, animosity, cruelty, aggressiveness) as an instinct in itself, with an autonomous origin. A few years later, certain clinical facts obliged Freud (1924) to deepen the problem of the instincts in trying to define their origins and their interconnections.

These studies led to a veritable psychoanalytic theory of instincts, a theory which led Freud to change some of his previous concepts, especially those which concerned the origin of masochism.

Alexander (1927), Reik (1925), Nunberg (1926), Weiss (1930), etc. tried to apply these new concepts to their clinical work, risking changing the whole explanatory theory of the neuroses. Their attempt does not seem to have been fruitful. Perhaps what has emerged, despite some work of great interest, is more confusion than anything else.

To be schematic, one could have represented neurosis until then as the result of conflict: a conflict of the sexual drives with external reality (prohibitions). Neurotic symptoms thus represented a compromise allowing some of the hitherto refused libidinal satisfaction.

The introduction of a primary destructive drive changes this model, conflict no longer resulting from an opposition between libidinal drives and prohibitions coming from the external world (introjected in the form of the superego), but from the opposition of sexual drives and the self-destructive drive (the need for punishment); See, Alexander (1927 and Reik (1925).

In the French psychoanalytic literature of this period, masochism, as a process of self-punishment, received what was perhaps an excessive extension into all psychoneurotic manifestations; see Codet and Laforgue (1929) and Hesnard and Laforgue (1931).

As for Freud himself, despite the care he took to remind us more than once, that in this area of thought, he was in the realm of speculative hypothesis, he disconcerted a great many of those who were trying to follow him in all the breadth of his theory of the death instinct (1920). We must recall that, often, his thought had surprised and overwhelmed, before finally being understood.

Despite the difficulties that arose when we tried to accept the aggressive instinct, or death instinct, above all when we tried to test it against clinical observation, we could not forget that for Freud the point of departure was always to begin with clinical observation, and that from the discovery of the negative therapeutic reaction until *Civilization and Its Discontents* (1930) his work represents an admirable continuity.

However, as for masochism, while in "Instincts and Their Vicissitudes," which marks the beginning of the study of the instincts, Freud still considered it as a secondary phenomenon, derived from sadism, his new concepts led him to consider it as a primary phenomenon. It is no longer aggressiveness, turned back from the object and bent back onto the subject, which will become masochism, but the opposite. From the inmost depths of living matter emerges a primary "organic" tendency toward self-destruction. One part of this self-destructive tendency will be projected onto the external world, in the form of aggression; the other will continue to be a part of the human being, as the death instinct, and will constitute the root of primary masochism.

The phenomenon of the turning back of aggression onto the subject will continue to manifest itself, but will constitute a secondary masochism which will be added to primary masochism.

Clinically, doubtless, we can only confirm the secondary form of masochism. And if we "take off" from this point in the theory, nothing changes with respect to the mechanisms already studied which alone have a clinical and therapeutic interest. And so we will just take up the work of Freud (1924) again, with "The Economic Problem of Masochism."

To begin with, Freud pointed out the difficulty that he had in admitting the existence of the need to suffer in human beings, in the form of masochism, given the workings of the pleasure/unpleasure principle, which should oppose suffering, and act as the "guardian of life."

Only the bonds between the death instinct and the erotic vital (libidinal) instincts could explain this complicated problem if we admit that one part of the death instinct can undergo a transformation to become the pleasure principle. This transformation would result from the action of the vital libidinal instincts on the death instinct.

Thus, a part of this instinct would remain in the service of that tendency which seeks to take back the whole living being into a state of complete repose, of death (this is the principle called by Freud, after Barbara Low, "the nirvana principle").

Another part of the death instinct, under the influence of the life instincts, would become the pleasure principle, which would follow along with the death instinct even while apparently opposing it, for it too would have as its aim to bring the living organism peace, repose, eliminating the state of tension which characterizes unpleasure.

This fusion of the libidinal and destructive instincts would have the effect of a partial "supplying" of the death instinct with libidinal impulses. This destructive instinct is confronted by libido and the "libido has the task of making the destroying instinct innocuous" (Freud 1924, 163).

The means by which this result is obtained, Freud never indicates.

But what seems clear to him is that "this masochism (erotogenic-primary) would thus be evidence of, and a remainder from, the phase of development in which the coalescence, which is so important for life, between the death instinct and Eros took place" (Freud 1924, 164). He continues a little later:

> Erotogenic masochism accompanies the libido through all its developmental phases and derives from them its changing psychical coatings. . . .
> The fear of being eaten up by the totem animal (the father) originates from the primitive oral organization; the wish to be beaten by the father comes from the sadistic-anal phase which follows it; castration, although it is later disavowed, enters into the content of masochistic phantasies as a precipitate of the phallic stage or organization; and from the final genital organization there arise, of course, the situations of being copulated with and giving birth, which are characteristic of femaleness. (Freud 1924, 164–65)

This primary masochism appears then as a component of libido. How then does it become erotogenic masochism, "a mode of sexual excitation," or sexual perversion, that is, an abnormal component of libido? Freud does not explain.

The second form of masochism studied in this text, feminine masochism, is also based on "a primary erotogenic factor, the pleasure in suffering."

By feminine masochism, Freud understands a psychosexual behavior characteristic of "the nature of the woman" but adopted by certain neurotic men. The fantasies of these masochistic and impotent or nearly impotent men, approach the actual behavior of masochistic perverts; the fantasies represent a situation which is essentially infantile and feminine: to be bound, tied up, at the mercy of someone, beaten, mistreated, humiliated.

While indicating the fundamental role of the feeling of guilt in this form of masochism, Freud does not say why he considers it as primary nor why he differentiates it from the third form of masochism—moral masochism.

In moral masochism the man unconsciously seeks punishment on all levels, and seems, thus, to distance his masochism from the sexual arena. Freud conceives of this form of masochism as uniquely due to the need for punishment.

To be punished by the father signified regressively to be in a passive sexual situation with regard to him.

Thus, this form of masochism represents a reactivation of the negative Oedipus complex. A good part of the moral conscience, of the superego, of such a patient results in a regressive resexualization of morality.

With "The Economic Problem of Masochism," the work of Freud which is of interest to us here comes to an end.

His later work *Civilization and Its Discontents* (1930), or the *New Introductory Lectures* (1931) only contain restatements of these points of view, with no new bearing.

In passing, we made reference to the work of Reik, Alexander, and others, more particularly from the English Psychoanalytic school, witnessing an effort to apply the notion of the death instinct to the structure of the neuroses and psychoses.

We believe that this literature has already thrown a certain confusion into psychoanalytic thought. W. Reich (1932) has elsewhere vigorously spoken against it. He tried to show that masochism, far from representing a manifestation of the destructive instincts, represents instead a defensive reaction against castration anxiety. As for the origin of sadism, the reservoir of masochism, he sees it as the freeing up of the aggressive component of libido, each time that this is opposed by a refusal of satisfaction.

These concepts seem to us to come closer to clinical observation, and so it will appear in the second part of this work.

If, now, we wished to sort out the essence of this long foray into the history of masochism, we could say the following:

Masochism, while it is as old as the world, was only identified as a sexual anomaly in the nineteenth century by Krafft-Ebing, who gave it its name.

The relationship with its opposite, sadism, was intuited by this learned man, but not explained. Neither were the pathogenic mechanisms, nor the "moral" manifestations of behavior, formulated at this time.

Psychoanalytic studies have shown that masochism is derived from the aggressive forces by a turning round of these against the subject. This mechanism brings into play the guilt complex and its result: the need to be punished, that is, to suffer.

Then, seeking to get back to the origins of masochism, Freud was led to consider it as a primary instinct of self-destruction, a concept which, to our mind, has no aspect which can be used clinically or therapeutically. As to what there is to understand about the essential character of masochism—how what causes pain becomes sexual pleasure—no worthwhile explanation could be given.

Perhaps there is nothing surprising in this, for strictly speaking under the rubric of pain = pleasure, masochism really does not exist.

There is no true paradox here: This is the impression that emerges for us from the facts of observation, and which finally makes itself felt.

REFERENCES

Adler, A. 1921. *The Neurotic Constitution: Outlines of a Comparative Individualistic Psychology and Psychotherapy*. London: K. Paul.
Alexander, F. 1927. *Psychoanalyse der Gesamtpersönlichkeit*. Vienna: Internationaler psychoanalytischer Verlag.
Ballet, G. 1903. *Traité des pathologie mentale*. Paris: Doin.
Binet, 1888. Etudes de psychologie experimentale: Le fétichisme dans l'amour. Paris.
Codet, H., and Laforgue, R. 1929. Echecs sociaux et besoin inconscient d'auto-punition. *Revue Française de Psychanalyse* 3, no. 3: 448–63.
Ellis, H. 1897. *Studies in the Psychology of Sex*. London: Wilson and Macmillan.
Eulenburg, A. 1902. *Sadismus und Masochismus*. Wiesbaden: J. F. Bergmann.
Federn, P. 1914a. Beiträge zur Analyse des Sadismus und Masochismus: I. Die Quellen des männlichen Sadismus. *Internationale Zeitschrift für ärztliche Psychoanalyse* 1:29–49.
———. 1914b. The Infantile Roots of Masochism. *New York Medical Journal* C: 351–55.
Ferre, C. 1899. *L'instinct sexuel: Evolution et dissolution*. Paris: Alcan.
Freud, S. 1905. Three Essays on the Theory of Sexuality. In *S.E.* 7:123–245.
———. 1914. On Narcissism: An Introduction. In *S.E.* 14:67–107.
———. 1915. Mourning and Melancholia. In *S.E.* 14:237–60.
———. 1919. A Child Is Being Beaten: A Contribution to the Study of the Origin of Sexual Perversions. In *S.E.* 17:175–204.
———. 1920. Beyond the Pleasure Principle. In *S.E.* 18:1–64.
———. 1923. The Ego and the Id. In *S.E.* 19:1–66.
———. 1924. The Economic Problem of Masochism. In *S.E.* 19:157–70.
———. 1930. *Civilization and Its Discontents*. In *S.E.* 21:57–145.
———. 1931. *New Introductory Lectures on Psychoanalysis*. In *S.E.* 22:1–182.
Hesnard, A., and Laforgue, R. 1931. Les processus d'auto-punition. VIe Congrès des Psychanalystes de Langue Française, Paris.
Jones, E. 1927. La conception du sur-moi. *Revue Française de Psychanalyse* 1:324–36.
Krafft-Ebing, R. F. 1906. *Psychopathia Sexualis*. New York: Physicians and Surgeons Book Co., 1931.
Nacht, S. 1963. Instinct de mort ou instinct de vie. In *La Présence du psychanalyste*. Paris: Presses Universitaires de France, pp. 148–61.
Nunberg, H. 1926. Schuldgefühl und Strafbedürfnis. *Int. Zeitschrift f. Psychoanalyse* 12:348–59.

Reich, W. 1932. The Masochistic Character. *Int. Zeitschrift f. Psychoanalyse* B. 18:303–51.

Reik, T. 1925. *Geständnis, Zwang und Strafbedürfnis.* Leipzig: Internationaler psychoanalytischer Verlag.

————. 1941. *Masochism in Modern Man.* New York: Farrar, Straus.

Sadger, J. 1926. A Contribution to the Understanding of Sadomasochism. *Int. J. Pscho-Anal.* 7:484–91.

Schrenck-Notzing, A. von. 1892. *Die Suggestion-Thérapie bei krankhaften Erscheinungen des Geschlechtssinnes mit besonderer Berücksichtigung der conträran Sexualempfindung.* Stüttgart: F. Enke.

Steckel, W. 1922. Bisexual Love: The Homosexual Neurosis. Boston: Gorham Press.

Trenel. 1902. Le Masochisme dans l'art au Moyen-Age et le lai d'Aristote. *Revue Médicale Normande.*

Weiss, E. 1930. Todestrieb und Masochismus. *Imago* 21:393–411.

2. A Contribution to the Psychoanalytic Theory of Masochism[1]

Rudolph M. Loewenstein

I

When we speak of masochism we refer to a tendency to seek physical or mental suffering in order to achieve, be it consciously or not, sexual gratification in the widest sense. Quite apart from their clinical importance, these phenomena are so challenging because they seem to contradict a basic characteristic of the human mind: the trend to avoid pain and unpleasure, i.e., the pleasure principle. Indeed, to some masochists "physical or mental suffering at the hands of the sexual object is a condition" for sexual gratification (Freud, 32). Because of this paradox, one might expect that the study of masochism should also lead to interesting considerations dealing with the problems of the human mind when faced with some painful realities of the external and internal world.

In "The Economic Principle in Masochism" Freud (36) noted that masochism "comes under our observation in three shapes: as a condition under which sexual excitation may be roused; as an expression of feminine nature; and as a norm of behavior."

Theoretical considerations on masochism thus can deal with several types of problems. The first and the comparatively best known of these are the cases of masochistic perversion. They have been most widely studied clinically; they were well described already in pre-Freudian psychiatric literature, and psychoanalytic research has contributed substantially to their elucidation. Numerous authors, in addition to Freud, have examined these problems from various points of view.

Freud stressed the prevalence of pregenital features in the sexuality of masochists. He pointed out that in masochistic fantasies or actual gratifica-

Abridged by permission of International Universities Press, Inc., from JAPA 5 (1957):197–34.

tions men unconsciously identify themselves with a woman in her role in intercourse or childbirth, and that in these cases the pain or punishment which arouses them is a regressive expression of their passive genital desires; that, in these cases, the punishing or cruel woman possesses phallic attributes which thus indirectly indicate that a woman here stands for a man. However, it must be added that these phallic characteristics of the female sexual partner also point to another very essential feature of the masochist, namely, to his stress on denial of the absence of a penis in the woman, and thus on denial of the castration danger. We shall come back to this point later on.

Still another essential feature is the connection between passivity and masochism. Absence of activity is sometimes called passivity. In such cases it might be more precise to use the term inactivity. Another form of behavior referred to as passivity is the readiness to comply with the will of other people. In connection with drives and their derivatives, we understand passivity in a twofold way: (1) passivity as opposed to activity can be used in reference to opposite aims of the instinctual drive; (2) passively being loved can be distinguished from actively loving (Hartmann, Kris, Loewenstein, 52).

In both these latter meanings passivity is an essential feature of early infancy and childhood. The passive gratification of his vital and erotic needs is a prerequisite for the infant's survival. Even in the normal development of the phallic phase we can, I believe, distinguish two stages: an earlier one in which passive aims, e.g., being looked at, being touched or manipulated, are more prevalent than in the later one where wishes of active penetration appear. It is the transition toward this latter stage, of active phallic strivings and wishes, that most often meets with particularly strong inhibiting forces centering around the castration fear (Loewenstein, 66). A reversion to or fixation on passive phallic aims is one of the characteristics of masochism, but not of masochism alone; indeed, we can find it at the base of numerous perversions and neurotic potency disturbances. In all these cases it seems that the active penetration of the woman remains either taboo or, at least, less gratifying than passively experienced genital gratification (Loewenstein, 66). Thus we assume that passivity is not a result of masochism but, on the contrary, the prerequisite for it.

In certain female patients, in whom masochism is not even very pronounced, the erotic fantasies culminate in the wish to be a thing, a completely helpless infant taken care of by the beloved man. Indeed, it seems that the longing to revert to a stage of entire helplessness and of being completely taken care of by an all-powerful parent can frequently be observed both in men and in women, without necessarily entailing masochistic tendencies. We believe it is only when this wish is experienced as humiliating, and yet the latter feeling is being enjoyed too, that we are in the presence of real masochism. The distinction, it is true, is not always easy to make. Passivity is obviously not sufficient to explain the essential character of the masochistic perversion; namely, that unpleasure is so intimately bound up with sexual gratification.

Various mechanisms underlying masochistic perversions have been discovered and described in the psychoanalytic literature. They all center around the crucial problems with which human sexuality has to deal during its development; namely, fear of loss of the object and fear of loss of its love, castration fear and superego anxiety. Thus, for instance, the tendency to passivity and helplessness may have the implicit aim of appealing to the mercy of the threatening and protective parental figure (Horney, 53). By the same token, it permits sexual gratification by apparently eliminating all responsibility for it. Suffering may become a prerequisite for sexual pleasure, as a price that must be paid to appease guilt feelings (W. Reich, 79); or as a "lesser evil" (Rado, 77), a form of self-castration, to avoid actual castration. Or there may be a turning against the self of active genital and aggressive impulses directed at incestuous objects.

It has also been stressed that the masochist uses a mechanism generally designed to deal with anxiety (Freud, 38); namely, to anticipate actively what might be feared to occur to one passively (Waelder, 89; Fenichel, 28). By imagining or producing scenes of torture or punishment which he himself devises, the masochist excludes the possibility of being tortured or punished in an unexpected and uncontrollable way (Eidelberg, 20, 21, 22). This is particularly evident in the cases that have been described as "erotization of anxiety" (Laforgue, 59), and which lie somewhere between a neurosis and a perversion. Gruesome fairy tales, thrillers, mystery plays and horror films seem to be an institutionalized means of gratifying the same need (Freud, 32).

We have already referred to Freud's view that some masochistic fantasies cover up and represent a flight from a much more intense and dreaded desire; namely, from feminine wishes toward the father. In such cases the fear of castration is alleviated by the substitution of a female figure for the father, and of beatings and threats for the passive genital penetration.

These mechanisms may explain those cases of masochism where a man must first undergo a certain amount of suffering before he is able to behave in a sexually normal way. But this is not characteristic for those masochists who derive pleasure through suffering rather than after suffering (Fenichel, 28).

Freud insists on the role of pleasure in pain as being due to a regressive reinforcement of the erotogenic masochism. Indeed, fixation on pregenital and particularly on anal, muscular and cutaneous erotism plays an essential part in the genesis of masochism.

A very well-known clinical fact common to many cases of perversion has not been sufficiently taken into account in psychoanalytic writings; namely, that the patients themselves describe the origin of their perversion as being linked to a particular, specific scene in childhood. We have learned in analysis to take such a remark by the patient seriously and to look for an explanation. One might explain it by referring to the fact that all sexual development proceeds silently or unconsciously for a while, until it becomes conscious as a finished product. But while this unquestionably is so, it would not explain why these specific memories of sexual scenes should be so much more frequent among perverts than among neurotics. We know, moreover, that they most often are screen memories standing for more significant events. It must be assumed that these remembered scenes allude to traumatic events. Greenacre (43) has recently brought this to our attention by stressing the importance of traumatic overstimulation in certain cases of fetishism or severe neuroses. In masochism one must think, more specifically, of traumatic events which involve a mixture of prohibition, seduction and reassurance (Loewenstein, 67; Fenichel, 28; Bornstein, 11).

We come closer to a satisfactory understanding of the masochistic perversion by taking into account some of its peculiarities. Freud pointed out that the sufferings desired and instituted by masochists never go as far as those of sadists. He also mentioned that in masochism the genitals and eyes are never directly involved in the actual threat.[2]

Masochists seek only certain specific and individually variable forms of suffering and humiliation. As soon as these reach a greater intensity or take a different form, they are reacted to with the habitual fear and pain. We shall go into this problem again when discussing the relation of masochism with Freud's theory of the death instinct. In addition, what is characteristic for the masochist's enjoyment of suffering and humiliation is a tacit but essential prerequisite: namely, that the sexual partner participate in the sexual scene or in masturbatory fantasy. Thus, the partner's threats and punishments amount to something akin to play or make-believe (Loewenstein, 67; Fenichel, 28).[3]

We also know that the type of threat and suffering which the masochist strives for is invariably a more or less veiled threat of castration. The problem is how it comes about that the very threat of castration becomes the actual source of sexual gratification. One is led to the following conclusion:

The masochistic perversions are modified repetitions of childhood situations and scenes in which sexual fantasies, erotic games or direct or indirect attempts at sexual rapprochement toward forbidden objects, particularly the mother, have met with disapproval or rebuff coupled with actual or imaginary ridicule, threat or punishment. In perversion the object (i.e., parent) participates instead of rejecting; threat and punishment are only limited. The essential mechanism underlying the masochistic perversion is that, by inducing the sexual partner to enact a scene of castration threat or punishment, the masochist forces the prohibiting, threatening parent to annul and undo the rebuff and the castration threat through its simulated repetition while actually participating in the veiled incestuous gratification. The masochistic scene is thus a means of gratifying the forbidden, repressed incestuous fantasies, but with the castration threat undone (Loewenstein, 67).

II

A few clinical examples may illustrate this point.

A young male patient suffered from a neurotic depression after a disappointing love affair. The girl preferred a slightly younger and sexually more aggressive friend of his. The situation revived his old problems centering around rivalry with a younger, more aggressive and more precocious brother who had been preferred by the mother. Following his disappointment in love, my patient, who was a highly idealistic and even ascetically inclined young man and had never before had any sexual experience, started roaming through streets where he was certain of meeting prostitutes. Beset with guilt and doubts, he would resist temptation, even when accosted, until he happened to find a prostitute who intuitively knew the way to overcome his resistance: she ordered him peremptorily to follow her. He would do so and comply with her command to have intercourse with her. The meaning of this masochistic behavior became clear only when he described that at the very moment of orgasm he would freeze into anxious immobility. In analysis he remembered childhood scenes which he connected with this freezing-up during orgasm. There were memories of bed wetting in the morning, and of his mother leaving the preferred younger brother in order to come over to his bed and scold him for having wet the bed. He remembered the bed wetting as being similar to the orgasm with the prostitute; both willful and frightening, anticipating mother's threat and anger. These screen memories stood for much earlier fantasies of passive sexual rapprochement toward the mother.

Thus the scenes with the prostitute revive and at the same time undo both his recent disappointment and his childhood castration fear. He revenges himself on the unfaithful sweetheart and mother by going to a prostitute, thereby unconsciously debasing them in his mind. In childhood his bed wetting led the mother to proffer castration threats, but was also an unconscious appeal to her which, by the same token, forced her to take care of him. In the scene with the prostitute the lowered image of the mother aggressively induces him to seek sexual gratification with her, by being the strict and "angry" mother. But instead of forbidding sex, she incites him to it and participates in it.

In another case, where jealousy of a younger brother likewise played an essential role in the genesis of the patient's masochism, the masochistic desires would overwhelm the patient as soon as he began to imagine that his sexual partner preferred another man. He traced his masochistic wishes to a screen memory in which his mother took care of the preferred, one-year-old brother while he himself was lying very tightly swaddled in a crib, simultaneously enjoying this situation and suffering from it (screen memory for passive and masochistic fantasies).

The patient during his analysis was able to have an affair without any need for masochistic gratification, but this need reemerged violently when his girl friend decided to leave him. He begged her to beat and to tie him, as though hoping in this way to seduce her into the mother's sadistic role and thus to undo the desertion. He made use here of a mechanism, "seduction of the aggressor," which we shall discuss in some detail later. Incompleteness of the analysis in this instance did not permit a sufficient elucidation of the screen memory of being swaddled, but merely the guess that it alluded to the time when violent aggressive outbreaks against his mother for preferring the brother were squelched in him in order to regain the mother's love.

My third and last example refers to a case of beating fantasies in a female patient. The fantasies in this instance had the typical and well-known dual, sadomasochistic character.

It will be helpful, first, to recall the general kind of development which Freud discovered in this type of case. He described that the beating fantasies start out, at an early age, with a fantasy of a sibling being beaten. The motive for this fantasy is not yet clearly sexual; rather, it is the wish to make sure that the sibling is not loved by the parents. This phase then is followed by a second, usually unconscious one, in which the little boy's fantasies center around being beaten by the father. The shift, as Freud explained, occurs for two reasons. First, it is due to the guilt about the aggressive thoughts, which turns the aggression against the self. The second motive for this turning against the self are feminine-passive genital wishes toward the father, regressively expressed as being beaten. The actual beating fantasies as the patients remember them, which represent the third phase of this development, commonly occur at a later period, often in early latency. Their general content is that a child, usually a boy, is beaten by some unidentified man, frequently a teacher. At this stage the fantasy has a conscious, sexual character and continues with many variations for a more or less extended time. The unconscious motivation underlying the conscious beating fantasies of the latency period has to do with the repression of the oedipal wishes as well as with the conflict arising from penis envy and castration fear (Freud, 33).

In the case of my patient, the beating fantasies persisted into adult life and constituted the only condition under which she was able to experience any orgastic gratification. There were particular features in her childhood history which, on the one hand, made her beating fantasies more understandable and which, on the other hand, made them much more difficult to unravel. One was the fact that she was the only girl and between two brothers of whom the first, five years older than the patient, displayed a genuinely sadistic attitude toward her, whereas the younger one was born when she was five, shortly before the onset of her conscious beating fantasy. The main complications, however, were due to an actual, severe beating administered by the father when the patient was seven. This was a traumatic event of extraordinary intensity to which the patient consistently, and probably correctly, attributed the tenacity and power of her beating fantasies.

I do not intend here to describe the various types of beating fantasies which this patient had elaborated over the years, but will mention only one out of many fantasies of a type she had, on and off, all through her life. During most, though not all, of these fantasies she identified herself consciously with the powerful, cruel, sadistic figures in the imagined scenes. Unconsciously, however, the identification with a slave, who was being denied sexual gratification and aroused by this denial, had a particularly strong effect upon her.

The typical fantasy I want to describe dealt with two middleaged women conversing in the presence of two girls, daughters or servants, who were completely at their mercy. The high point of the scene was that these women would tell one or both of the girls that it would be good for them to refrain from any sexual activity for some time, and that the girls would humbly acquiesce in this, being at the same time aroused by it. The sexual arousal at that very moment extended also to the patient herself and implicitly, therefore, to the older women with whom she consciously identified herself. There was a particular note of hypocrisy, which seemed to pervade many of the patient's imagined scenes. In this instance it was that the pseudo-moralistic reasons advanced by the older woman for imposing abstinence on the younger were very transparently given in order to arouse herself as well as the victim. The cruel woman of the fantasy to a certain extent seems to represent the opposite of the patient's real mother, who never actually forbade her daughter any sexual gratification but bashfully avoided any mention of the girl's sexuality. Yet for the daughter she was the strongest deterrent to any gratifying love life. The patient, who was then in her forties, once said: "I'd rather kill myself than tell my mother that I might love a man or might want to get married." Indeed, she never did.

To return to the fantasy and its connection with the theory of masochism: we see here what Freud called a regressive resexualization of morality. Morality is upheld, but with a transparent and unmistakable hypocrisy which invariably is the hallmark of this sexualization and aggressivization of morality.[4] In the fantasies the prohibitive role of the mother is continually repeated in a disguise, and thus annulled; therefore this repetition amounts to an incestuous—in this case, homosexual—reunion with the mother. As a matter of fact, the patient in her fantasies frequently imagined two punishing figures; herself as a woman punishing girls, and a parallel figure of a man punishing boys. In other fantasies, where only a woman or only a man was the main punishing character, we must assume a condensation of both parental figures.

III

I believe that our explanation of the masochistic perversion contributes to its understanding. It does not, however, exhaust the problem of masochism, not even of the sexual manifestations of masochism, of the frequency of masochistic elements in the normal life of women, the frequency of masochistic traits in the sexual development of childhood and puberty and even of adult men who do not present any actual perversion.

Before continuing our discussion of masochism, let us for a moment recall what we know about the role of repetition of early events. Repetition exists in the transference, as an archaic form of remembrance due to a displacement onto the analyst of unconscious strivings. The repetition compulsion exists as a way of surmounting or mastering painful, past traumatic events (Freud, 34). A slightly modified form of repetition of formerly gratifying situations or fantasies exists, sometimes, as a form of self-punishment for wishes underlying them (Loewenstein, 69).

It happens that young men are initiated into normal sex life by women somewhat older than themselves and that such sexual affairs alone permit these men to overcome strong sexual inhibitions. It seems that in these real situations the conditions of some fairy tale come true. Punishment meted out by a bad witch can be undone only by another witch, a good fairy this time. We see here a parallel to what is going on in masochistic perversions.

Before going further, it might be useful to discuss the explanations of masochism proposed by some authors, and to compare them with the one suggested above. Eidelberg (23) pointed out that the masochist overcomes his anxiety by exercising control over the threats and sufferings he undergoes. Fenichel (28) makes reference to the presence in the masochistic behavior of mechanisms similar to those in the signal function of anxiety as described by Freud. Neither of these views is at variance with the ideas here presented; both deal with processes aiming at active mastery of a passively experienced danger. However, as we have seen, the mechanisms operative in masochism involve much more than defense mechanisms of the ego alone: they involve id changes and actions on outside objects that permit instinctual gratifications. I shall have occasion to discuss this further on in connection with some early precursors of masochism.

On the other hand, the theory which sees in masochism a kind of self-castration appears to be in striking contrast with the observable behavior of masochists. To be sure, their masturbatory fantasies and perverse devices abound in allusions to castration threats, and these patients wallow in them. But the physiological reactions to these threats reveal that castration is invoked here precisely in order to annul it (Fenichel, 28). Self-castration does not result in erection or orgasm, whereas the masochist's actual sexual gratification represents a triumph over the danger of castration (in the man) or an overcoming of it (in the woman).

Another point that has to be considered here is the role of bisexuality and of femininity in masochism. There is no doubt that bisexuality plays a very important role in the masochism of men. But bisexuality and identification with a woman is not specific for masochism. Indeed, it plays an even more important and even a specific role in certain forms of homosexuality. In masochistic men feminine wishes toward the father exist, but they manifest themselves in a form in which genital gratification is bound up with suffering. The latter point is decisive and specific for this perversion. Furthermore, femininity and female sexuality are not identical with masochism. Masochistically tinged sexuality is very much more frequent in women than in men, but there are also women whose sexuality is practically devoid of masochism. Moreover, there are women who present actual masochistic perversions. It does not seem adequate to consider the latter cases as typical representatives of female sexuality. Freud (40) advised against equating any particular psychological trait, even such opposites as activity and passivity, with either masculinity or femininity. To equate masochism with femininity would not solve the problems presented by masochism. For all these reasons it seems preferable not to follow the classification of masochism, as proposed by Freud (36) in 1924, which placed masochistic perversions under the heading of feminine masochism.

The time of appearance of the masochistic perversion, never before the oedipal period and frequently in early latency, also contributes to our understanding that they are, as Freud put it, "scars" formed by the passing of the oedipus complex. Although one can observe occasional masochistic activities and fantasies earlier in children, they do not yet possess all the characteristics of later perversions and, particularly, lack the involvement of genital excitation. Yet they all hinge on the existence of erotogenic masochism and on the ability of the human being to act occasionally counter to the pleasure principle, to deceive the "guardian of our life," to derive pleasure from bodily or mental unpleasure.

In developing his ideas, Freud elaborated three distinct theories to account for the masochistic component drive. He first pointed out that, like all human sensations, pain also could be giving rise to sexual excitation. Later on he expressed his opinion in the following manner, which can best be conveyed by quoting him: ". . . there seems to be a confirmation of the view that masochism is not the manifestation of a primary instinct, but originates from sadism which has been turned round and directed upon the self, that is to say, by means of regression from an object to the ego . . . The transformation of sadism into masochism appears to be due to the influence of the sense of guilt . . ." (Freud, 33).

We know that he later modified this view and conceived the masochism due to transformation of sadism as being a secondary one, derived from what he then termed primary masochism. "A section of this [death] instinct is placed directly in the service of the sexual function, where it has an important part to play: this is true sadism. Another part is not included in this displacement outwards; it remains within the organism and is 'bound' there libidinally with the help of the accompanying sexual excitation mentioned above: this we must recognize as the original erotogenic masochism" (Freud, 36).

This conception thus hinges entirely on whether the speculation on the existence of a death instinct is a valid one or not. We believe that this question may only be decided, some day, through biological research and not by psychoanalysts. However, we assume the existence of two independent instinctual drives: the sexual and the aggressive (Hartmann, Kris, Loewenstein, 52). . . .

IV

Psychoanalytic experience invariably confirms Freud's view that masochistic perversions in men, as well as the moral masochism, result from a turning of sadism against the self under the influence of guilt feelings. The latter seem less decisive in the masochistic component in the sexuality of women, although here, too, the yielding to superior power adds the relief from guilt feelings which is so important in sexual enjoyment. However, in a more general way the theory of masochism must take into account the vicissitudes of the aggressive drive in its relations to the libido as well as to the ego. Both from analytic work and from direct observation of young children one gains the impression that in childhood a seeking of pleasure in unpleasure exists, which is not based on this turning of aggression against the self; moreover, that the turning of aggression against the self has precursors in which guilt feelings do not yet play a role.

Let us turn, now, to the early manifestations pertinent to the development of what will in the course of time be recognizable as masochism. It might be advisable, in this respect, to distinguish between pleasurable reactions to two types of unpleasure: the physical and the mental. It seems that pleasure bound up with mental unpleasure appears at the end of the first year of life, very closely on the footsteps of the earliest forms of object relation. An example will describe what I mean.

Many years ago I witnessed a little girl of eleven months being jokingly scolded by her grandmother for putting her thumb in her mouth. The baby would, with visible fright, observe the stern face of her grandmother; but as soon as she saw the grandmother smile, she would start to laugh and put her thumb back into her mouth, with a naughty and provoking expression. And so the game would go on. When the prohibition became serious, however, i.e., when the grandmother's face remained serious, the child burst into tears. Needless to say that she would try to transform every prohibition into a game of this sort, to elicit the smile of the grownup, to create that affectionate complicity which undoes the prohibition and eliminates the danger of not being loved (Loewenstein, 67).

In other varieties of these playful activities between adults and children, both the threat and its pleasurable removal almost coincide in one and the same act, such as playfully attacking and frightening the child. It is well known how eagerly children ask for endless repetition of these games.

This type of behavior, this *seduction of the aggressor* which one can find in all children, already contains elements of future, actually masochistic behavior: the seeking for situations that entail danger, fear and unpleasure, and their attenuation through a loving, erotic complicity of the threatening person. It is true, the pleasure in these situations at first is not yet derived from the pain itself but from its removal, from cessation of the threat through a loving reunion with the parent. But one can observe that soon the two, i.e., the unpleasure of the threat and the pleasure of its removal, become intimately tied together. For instance, one can very well see how the child's unpleasure at being thrown into the air or being made to lose his equilibrium, or at being threatened with pain or really hurt slightly, becomes actually pleasurable in itself, provided the parents participate with a loving complicity. These games thus come even more closely to resemble the patterns we have described in masochistic perversion.

Although this normal behavior pattern in children obviously does not always lead to masochism, it contains the essential elements to serve as a prototype for an eventual masochistic perversion. The readiness with which some children pass from enjoying removal of the threat to enjoying the unpleasure itself may serve as a measure of their predisposition for future masochism. While such a predisposition may be constitutionally variable, there is no doubt that it can be reinforced or fixated through excessive stimulation, serving as actual seduction of the child, by a parent who overindulges in these games. But whenever one speaks of fixations which may become pathogenic, it might be wise to consider that they also may occur as a result of insufficient gratification of some libidinal needs in childhood.

This is not the place to attempt a comparative study of "seduction of the aggressor" with other behavior patterns representing defensive ego mechanisms. But it can be pointed out that the latter are mainly endopsychic mechanisms aimed to ward off undesirable instinctual demands or external danger, although they, too, may be much more than that. While the seduction of the aggressor likewise endeavors to ward off threats of loss of love, or of bodily injury, and while it unquestionably also uses an ego mechanism of the type known to us from anxiety formation, essentially it is very different from a defensive ego mechanism. Seduction of the aggressor consists of behavior which seeks and frequently achieves to change an unloving to a loving attitude in the parent. And while thus mobilizing libido in both, it wards off anxiety in the child and aggression in the parent. Although it occurs as a particular form of childhood play, it is different from other games inasmuch as it actually changes the behavior of another person and thus comes close to actions successfully adjusting reality to the needs of the child. However, eventually, it can also be modified and put to use by fantasy and play in ways similar to those described by Freud (34) and Waelder (89).[5]

Should one call this normal behavior of children masochistic, inasmuch as it reveals mechanisms which later on will underlie masochistic perversions? It is more appropriate to term it *proto- or premasochistic,* as long as any involvement of the genital apparatus is absent. If it is permissible to consider these prototypes of future masochistic behavior from a point of view of survival, one might say that their function is to prepare the child to deal with frustrations and dangers imposed by one human being on another. In these games the roles of the protagonists are always the same; the child is in the "protomasochistic," the parent in the aggressive role. In the complicity of the adult there looms the shadow of erotic response which gives it a sadistic tinge. For the child these games thus have the function, aside from mastering the threat (Freud, 34; Waelder, 89), to seduce the parent, to soften his potential aggressions that might be really threatening the child (Loewenstein, 67).

The gradual development of sexuality, of aggression and of the ego leads the child to deal with new types of gratification and new forms of danger.

The behavior of infants, as it was described above, does not stop there. Children evolve ways of enjoying imaginary danger in the form of fairy tales and later on, when they grow older, enjoy terrifying mystery stories. A source of gratification in these childhood activities is the same: the underlying reassurance that the parents love them in spite of punishments, that their threats should not be taken too seriously and would not really endanger the child.

Freud pointed out that all sensations and feelings, even painful ones, might give rise to pleasure when they reach a certain intensity. It is correct to assume that they are pleasurable merely within certain limits,[6] beyond which they are only painful. But it is difficult to determine where the threshold is in each case. There can be no doubt that this fundamental peculiarity underlies all masochistic phenomena. There certainly exist variations as to the extent to which individuals are predisposed to react in this way, and as to the nature of the painful sensations capable of eliciting pleasure in them.

It is well known that in sadomasochism the erogeneity both of musculature and skin plays a great role. Since we assume the existence of an aggressive drive concomitant to a sexual one, we must suppose that in all autoerotic as well as object-directed erotic activities both libido and aggression are being discharged (Hartmann, Kris, Loewenstein, 52; Kris, 57). The musculature and skin can thus give rise to aggressive as well as libidinal gratifications which may be both active and passive in form; moreover, these gratifications may be bound up in various ways with the object. Active double gratification (aggressive and libidinal) may be elicited from an attack on an outside object or on the self;[7] a passive double gratification can be produced by an action from an object as well as from oneself.

In all these mixed autoaggressive and autoerotic activities, pain might be bound up with pleasure. There are some phenomena in which the order is inverted; i.e., in which the pain is present first, and the reaction to it has an autoerotic and autoaggressive character. I refer to a painful sensation, such as itching or the sensations produced by swelling of the mucosae of the gums, eliciting reflex responses in the individual that are simultaneously pain-relieving, painful and pleasurable: scratching, clamping the jaws, teeth-grinding and biting.[8] These phenomena might serve as prototypes for some sadomasochistic reactions to actual or anticipated pain at the hands of the aggressor.

V

Guilt feeling as the motive for the turning of the aggression against the self, so essential in masochistic perversions and in moral masochism, appears later in childhood. We have dwelt in detail upon mechanisms of an earlier period, which may be made use of in the course of the later development of both the ego and the superego.[9]

Though we do not intend here to elaborate on the origin, development and function of guilt feelings, we can say that they may arise early in consequence of expectation of punishment; they may be the outcome of a conflict of love and hate for the same object; but mainly they are the result of the gradual development of superego functions. As important for the formation of guilt feeling and of masochism, however, must be stressed one point in the child's development; namely, when identification with the parents enables him to behave in various ways at the same time. He can be the threatening parent or the punished child; he can employ seduction of the aggressor and also be the (internalized) seduced aggressor. The child then is able to use this identification for the undoing of punishment as well as for self-punishment or for provocation of punishment. Later on the identification with the parents becomes involved in the oedipal conflicts and in superego formation. The superego eventually brings permanence and continuity to the turning of the aggressive drives against the self.

The oedipus complex adds new intensity and new dimensions to the conflicts between the aggressive and libidinal drives as well as between these drives and the ego and superego. In the normal development of men, the castration fear puts an end to the incestuous genital desires. In masochism this process does not succeed. Instead of a passing of the oedipal wishes, a regression occurs to earlier strivings, to pregenital stages of development where to suffer or to inflict suffering, to be humiliated or to humiliate, stands for feminine or masculine, for being castrated or possessing a penis (Freud, 33). In this regression the genital involvement stems from the oedipal phase, the form and condition of the genital excitation—inflicting or undergoing suffering—from the earlier stage whose various modes of interrelation between pleasure and unpleasure were described above.

We know that in boys the oedipal strivings may take a negative form, of a passive feminine attachment to the father. Most frequently and perhaps regularly this homosexual attachment to the dangerous rival-father has the function of giving up the incestuous wishes for the mother, in order to appease him and thus to avoid the danger of castration. The identification with the woman is a utilization, on the phallic level, of a pregenital mechanism existing irrespectively of sex differences since infancy: the seduction of the aggressor. Viewed from this angle, masochism represents one form, although not the only one, of this attempt at solving the conflicts of the oedipal phase.

As for masochism in women, it is essential to bear in mind that the early instinctual development of the female child, as opposed to that of the male, reflects the anatomical and developmental differences between them. In contrast to the boy, the normal girl enters the oedipal phase by giving up both the original love object (the mother) and the sexual organ (the clitoris). Her masculine, phallic attachment to her mother is being replaced by a feminine attachment to her father, in which the primacy of the clitoris yields to the pre-eminence of the vagina. For the girl, therefore, the entering into a feminine, heterosexual attachment presupposes an acceptance of "being castrated" (Freud, 37, 39, 40; Deutsch, 16; Lampl-de Groot, 60; Brunswick, 14). And this acceptance may become bound up with the pregenitally preformed pleasure in unpleasure.

The little girl seems to present a greater tendency to suppress aggressive strivings than does the boy, which might well be due to her congenital equipment as well as to social pressure (Freud, 40). The absence of an organ for sexual aggression may reinforce this tendency (Deutsch, 16) and may, moreover, favor the bending inward of her aggression (Lampl-de Groot, 62).

Indeed, the importance of a masochistic component in the sexuality of women was related by Deutsch (18) to women's greater passivity as well as to the fact that suffering is bound up with their sexual organs and functions. Marie Bonaparte (8) has pointed out that the conformation of their genitalia, their concavity, demands a penetration which their self-preservatory forces oppose. This danger to their bodily integrity evokes aggressive reactions against the male which are, furthermore, reinforced by their active phallic strivings. Thus it seems that a stronger erotic "concave" striving, combined with the bending inward of the woman's aggressive tendencies through superior aggression and with the mechanism of "seduction of the aggressor," leads her to enjoy the unconsciously dreaded sexual aggression of the male. Through this mechanism women disarm the dangerous man by seducing him, and are themselves seduced by this threatening situation.

VI

We must add to our discussion of masochism a few remarks about its relations to object choice. Masochism may be involved in particular ways in the choice of a love object. In the masochistically tinged sexuality of women pleasure in pain appears as a factor heightening sexual gratification, but may also be a stimulus for the choice of a love object. Deutsch (18) describes several cases of women slavishly attached to men who inflicted severe physical pain and humiliation on them.[10]

In the love life of both women and men, an exclusive attachment to a single object is frequently regarded as a most highly integrated form of emotional development. However, in some cases this exclusivity is the result of a particular and limited balance of forces; such, for instance, that some men or women can be sexually gratified only by a certain partner whose own sexuality presents peculiarities without which they are unable to be potent or to reach an orgasm. Among these various peculiarities are those which gratify some perverse "conditions" for sexual gratification. Masochistic persons, for example, who find in some partners a corresponding form of sadism, might become exclusively attached to those partners. One gains the impression that masochism may be the prerequisite or the consequence of some extreme cases of infatuation built on the model of early incestuous attachments. Thus a certain lack of exclusivity in the choice of love objects may represent a "lower" form of integration and yet on the whole a less vulnerable form of sexuality, less limited by some particular balance of "ingredients" in the partner's emotional make-up.

On the other hand, the sexuality of individuals for whom the value of the love object as a person is unimportant and the partner merely counts as a means of sexual gratification, without other emotional tie, might certainly be considered limited or arrested in its development. In the case of certain perverts, very often indeed the partner counts only in terms of gratifying the specific perversion. One would hardly refer as a love object to the special shape of shoe or foot all-important to a fetishist. The same may apply, more or less, to some masochists for whom the sexual object is not a person, or is so only by virtue of behaving in a particular way which satisfies their condition for sexual gratification.

This pattern must be especially pronounced in the cases we mentioned before as appearing probably in police records but not in the consultation room of the psychoanalyst. Those may very well be the kinds of perversion in which some have seen a special affinity to psychoses. In such cases one might assume the existence of a severe ego disturbance pertaining to object relations, a disturbance which on the one hand leads to psychosis, and on the other hand precludes any integration of the partial drives under the aegis of genitality related to a real and stable object. However, there exists an unquestionable correlation between masochistic characters and paranoic conditions (Freud, 33; Waelder, 90; Nacht, 75; Bak, 1; Brenman, 12). But in our opinion these cases do not justify the belief in a general affinity between "perversion" and "psychosis." Because of their considerable variations in terms of relationship to objects, perversions encompass a heterogeneous group of disorders which cannot easily be pigeonholed under a single heading like "The Perversion" whose only common denominator would be a negative one: "deviation" from normal sexual behavior.

VII

Whatever the mechanisms and the motives for turning the aggression against the self, clinically and theoretically masochism and its counterpart, sadism, are intimately bound together. In both of them suffering, pain, unpleasure are the conditions for sexual excitation, and this is the very point about which we do not know enough. To be sure, we know that in sadism and masochism libido and aggression exist in a certain state of fusion. But we know them also to be observable in a state of fusion outside of sadism and masochism. What, then, is the difference between these two kinds of fusion? If we assume, as we do, two different drives, the sexual and the aggressive, the gratification of each of which is accompanied by a specific form of pleasure (Hartmann, Kris, Loewenstein, 52), might the difference between the two types of fusion—or degrees of defusion—be found to reside in different types of mixtures of these specific, pleasurable experiences? Could it be that in sadomasochism the pleasure of aggressive gratification has retained a greater independence from the pleasures afforded by libidinal gratifications? We do not know it.

Whatever it may be, both sadism and masochism presuppose a rather evolved object relation (Hartmann, Kris, Loewenstein, 52). In both, the enjoyment of causing or suffering pain is clearly perceived in the sexual partner and is an essential part of the perversion. One of the functions of sadism and masochism is thus to maintain object relations, however precarious, in the face of aggressions which threaten the object world or the individual himself.

VIII

Of the various factors we have described as entering into the formation of masochism, not all seem to be of equal importance in its various forms.

Erotogenic masochism expresses mainly the fundamental property of the human mind, of experiencing as pleasurable some painful processes. The very early mechanisms of turning aggression against the self or passively bending it inward, with or without intervention of guilt feelings, and the mechanism of seduction of the aggressor make use of this property. In its individual development the aggressive drive is very closely bound up with the libidinal development. During this development, both active and passive forms of these fused drives manifest themselves. Thus the passive forms, i.e., the erotogenic masochism, according to the stage of libidinal development, take on the shape of the wish (or fear): to be devoured, to be beaten, to be castrated, to play the role of a woman in intercourse (Freud, 36).

The importance of the *masochistic component in the normal sex life of women* has the same basis, with particular importance of the mechanism of seduction of the aggressor due to the additional factor of passivity and to the psychological consequences resulting from the conformation and functions of the female genital apparatus. These factors undoubtedly are reinforced by turning of aggressions against the self, due to guilt feelings derived from the girl's castrative as well as from her incestuous fantasies. However, guilt feelings here do not seem to have the paramount role which they play in masochistic perversions and in moral masochism.

We must assume that in the *masochistic perversions* the inherent proclivity to experience some painful sensations as pleasurable is particularly pronounced. This may be due to some congenital equipment or to environmental influences, such as early traumatic stimulations or seductions. In these perversions, the role of guilt feelings in the turning of the aggression against the self seems to be superimposed upon the erotogenic masochism. Masochistic perversion, be it in men or in women, is the result of a process in which the reinforced erotogenic masochism has undergone a particular development by having been "brought in relation with the Oedipus complex" (Freud, 33). It represents "the legacy of that complex" (Freud), inasmuch as the masochist's sexual gratification never severs its connection with it. The fixation on the incestuous object choice, and the guilt and anxiety connected with it, pervade the masochist's sex life. Indeed, the sexual partner is expected to behave like a threatening, punishing parental figure. Masochists unconsciously use the early mechanism of seduction of the aggressor toward the heterosexual as well as the homosexual parental object. And the very function of the perversion, which allows the masochist to have an erection and an orgasm, resides in the undoing of both guilt feeling and castration threat, and in the unconscious incestuous gratification.

There are instances of masochism where one of the factors, i.e., the reinforced erotogenic masochism, has greater importance, and others in which the role of the "legacy of the Oedipus complex" predominates. The former would obtain when enjoyment of physical pain is the essential point, the latter when enjoyment of threats and humiliation is the condition for gratification. In cases where the "legacy of the Oedipus complex" is of little importance, masochism or other perversions might also be due to a severe disorder of the ego in the area of object relations.

We can distinguish three forms of *masochistic behavior:* the masochistic character, the behavior caused by what is called the "mentality of a slave," and the moral masochism. In all three the connection with sexuality is loosened, though in an unequal degree. The connection with aggression, however, is not lost in all of them to the same extent.

In cases of *masochistic character,* suffering as a means of aggression is very obvious (W. Reich, 79; Berliner, 5). Genetically it can be traced to early forms of "passive aggression." Since these disorders are those of character formation, we must assume that they are based not only on particular forms of instinctual development, but to a great extent also on that of the ego (Berliner, 5).

In childhood, shutting the mouth to food and closing the anal sphincter as a refusal to defecate may be prototypes of this behavior (Bergler, 3). Guilt feelings inhibit active manifestations of aggression and, by turning them against the self, reinforce the passive forms of aggression. Since he himself suffers, the masochist feels justified in having his suffering cause pain to others. In childhood a normal form of this behavior is well known: sulking is a powerful means of aggression against the mother and frequently an effective one in forcing her into manifestations of love.[11] Feeling sorry for oneself and the *"délectation morose"* or being a "comic teasee" (Brenman, 12) usually entail far less aggression against the outside world. In adult life the behavior of the masochistic character is usually more effective in causing the subject himself to suffer than in swaying other adults into a behavior resembling that of a loving mother. Occasionally adults may, by deliberately using similar mechanisms, achieve effects on the outside world which no other method might afford; I am alluding here to hunger strikes, for instance.

In masochistic character disorders the interplay between the drives and the ego is a complex one. On the one hand, the warded-off masochistic tendencies, persisting unconsciously, influence the development of the ego in such a way that its functions lend themselves to an unconscious gratification of related instinctual demands. On the other hand, faced with actual or imagined human aggression or loss of love, the ego uses mechanisms which reactivate masochistic tendencies in order to find pleasure in suffering and to attenuate aggression. (The ego may thus, for instance, indirectly reactivate the mechanism of seduction of the aggressor.) We may assume that both these processes are always at work in such character structures. Their results manifest themselves as character neuroses, as behavior patterns bound up with considerable sensitivity to actual or potential aggression from without. The presumed aggressor is made to feel guilty and therefore often actually becomes aggressive. The teasee displays an uncanny skill in provoking actual teasing (Brenman, 12). Thus in such cases the unconscious masochism is being gratified by actual aggression from the outside, which perpetuates these neurotic mechanisms.

The behavior caused by the *"mentality of a slave"* occurs in people subserviently submitting to a victor and identifying themselves with him on the level of the superego without neutralization of the aggression and with libidinization of self-destructive tendencies (Hartmann, Kris, Loewenstein, 52). Inmates of concentration camps were observed to take over the mannerisms of their S.S. tormentors and their sadistic behavior toward other captives as soon as they had the opportunity to do so (Bettelheim, 6). It is not unlikely that such behavior occurs when the submission to aggression initially elicited a masochistically tinged sexual attachment to the aggressor.

About the *moral masochism,* we know (Freud, 35, 36) that it exists in two forms: as sadism of the superego and as masochism of the ego. These two types of attitudes of the superego toward the ego reflect the two forms of gratification in aggressions against the self in early childhood. In the one, the discharge of libido and aggression is paramount, be it directed against an outside object or the self. In the other, unconscious libidinal gratification is effected by undergoing aggression, be it from outside or from oneself. The relationship of moral masochism to sexuality is quite remarkable and puzzling. The moral masochist does not derive any manifest sexual gratification from suffering, and there does not seem to exist any obvious correlation between masochistic perversion and its moral counterpart. In the perversion, both "crime and punishment" remain in the sexual sphere; not so, apparently, in moral masochism. Freud pointed out that even the condition that suffering be inflicted by a loved person seems to have disappeared. On the other hand, the relationship of superego and ego in moral masochism is more sexualized (Freud, 36) and aggressivized, i.e., less neutralized, than it is in people not afflicted by it. In its masochistic relationship toward the superego, the ego appears to have reactivated early passive homosexual wishes toward the father in their regressive form of suffering and punishment (Hartmann, Kris, Loewenstein, 52). Thus, we must say, moral masochism is not completely devoid of connection with a love object; even when the masochist seeks suffering "caused by impersonal forces or circumstances" (Freud, 36), he longs for parental love in this disguise. Does not the religious person accept God's punishment as proof of His love? Fate, as Freud pointed out, is unconsciously conceived of as personal, as a remote representative of the parents. Underlying the self-destructive tendencies involved in moral masochism, one can see at work in it the desperate attempt to seduce the aggressor, the harsh conscience, to appease the gods or fate by suffering; i.e., to revert to childhood, to the state when threats and dangers could actually be averted or minimized by using the method which was effective then.

The masochistic perversion as well as the behavioral masochism originate in the early processes of sexualization of mental and physical unpleasure. But they derive from them on different pathways and perform different functions. In the perversion, conscious pain is sought in order to reach conscious sexual gratification. In the masochistic behavior we observe an unconscious libidinization of suffering caused by aggressions from without and within.

In discussing masochistic behavior we have been led to consider not only problems of drive development but also those of survival. Viewed from this angle, masochism seems to be the weapon of the weak—i.e., of every child—faced with danger of human aggression. The masochistic perversion does not deal with the survival of the individual, but one can say that it permits a limited and precarious survival of genitality. Female masochism is linked to survival, however, inasmuch as it permits the woman to overcome dangers to her bodily integrity that are inherent in her sexual functions. The mechanism of "seduction of the aggressor," which we have found to be operative in masochism and its forerunners since childhood, appears at that early age to ensure the existence of parental love, at a time when parental love is as necessary for the development of sexuality as it is for survival. It continues to be operative in both, even when they have parted ways and at times even oppose one another.

BIBLIOGRAPHY

1. Bak, R. C. Masochism in paranoia. *Psychoanal. Quart., 15*:285–301, 1946.
2. Bak, R. C. Fetishism. *JAPA, 1*:285–298, 1953.
3. Bergler, E. *The Basic Neurosis.* New York: Grune & Stratton, 1949.
4. Berliner, B. Libido and reality in masochism. *Psychoanal. Quart., 9*:322–333, 1940.
5. Berliner, B. On some psychodynamics of masochism. *Psychoanal. Quart., 16*:459–471, 1947.
6. Bettelheim, B. Individual and mass behavior in extreme situations. *J. Abn. & Soc. Psychol., 38*:417–452, 1943.
7. Bonaparte, M. Des autocrotismes agressifs par la griffe et par la dent. *Rev. Franç. Psychanal., 6*:192–216, 1933.
8. Bonaparte, M. Passivité, masochisme et féminité. *Rev. Franç. Psychanal., 8*:208–216, 1935.
9. Bonaparte, M. *Female Sexuality.* New York: International Universities Press, 1953.
10. Borel, A. and Robin, G. *Les Bouderies morbides.* Paris: N. R. F., 1925.
11. Bornstein, B. The analysis of a phobic child. Some problems of theory and technique in child analysis. *The Psychoanalytic Study of the Child, 3/4*:181–226. New York: International Universities Press, 1949.
12. Brenman, M. On teasing and being teased: and the problem of "moral masochism." *The Psychoanalytic Study of the Child, 7*:264–285. New York: International Universities Press, 1952.
13. Bromberg, N. Maternal influences in the development of moral masochism. *Am. J. Orthopsychiat., 25*:802–812, 1955.
14. Brunswick, R. M. The preoedipal phase of the libido development. *Psychoanal. Quart., 9*:293–319, 1940.
15. Burlingham, D. T. Die Einfühlung des Kleinkindes in die Mutter. *Imago, 21*:429–444, 1935.
16. Deutsch, H. The psychology of women in relation to the functions of reproduction. *Int. J. Psychoanal., 6*:405–418, 1925.
17. Deutsch, H. The significance of masochism in the mental life of women. *Int. J. Psychoanal., 11*:48–60, 1930.
18. Deutsch, H. *The Psychology of Women, 1.* New York: Grune & Stratton, 1944.
19. Dooley, L. The relation of humor to masochism. *Psychoanal. Rev., 28*:37–46, 1941.
20. Eidelberg, L. Zur Metapsychologie des Masochismus. *Int. Ztsch. Psychoanal., 19*:615–616, 1933.
21. Eidelberg, L. Zur Theorie und Klinik der Perversion. *Int. Ztsch. Psychoanal., 19*:620–621, 1933.

22. Eidelberg, L. Beiträge zum Studium des Masochismus. *Int. Ztsch. Psychoanal.*, *20*:336–353, 1934.

23. Eidelberg, L. *A Comparative Pathology of the Neuroses*. New York: International Universities Press, 1954.

24. Eissler, K. R. A clinical note on moral masochism: Eckermann's relationship to Goethe. In: *Drives, Affects, Behavior*, ed. R. M. Loewenstein. New York: International Universities Press, 1953, pp. 285–326.

25. Feldman, S. S. Anxiety and orgasm. *Psychoanal. Quart.*, *20*:528–549, 1951.

26. Fenichel, O. The clinical aspect of the need for punishment. *Collected Papers*, *1*:71–92, New York: W. W. Norton, 1953.

27. Fenichel, O. A critique of the death instinct. *Collected Papers*, *1*:363–372. New York: W. W. Norton, 1953.

28. Fenichel, O. *The Psychoanalytic Theory of Neurosis*. New York: W. W. Norton, 1945.

29. Ferenczi, S. Stages in the development of the sense of reality. In: *Sex in Psychoanalysis*. New York: Basic Books, 1950, pp. 213–239.

30. Freud, A. Schlagephantasie und Tagtraum. *Imago*, *8*:317–332, 1922.

31. Freud, A. *The Ego and the Mechanisms of Defense*. New York: International Universities Press, 1946.

32. Freud, S. Three essays on the theory of sexuality (1905). *Standard Edition*, *7*:123–245. London: Hogarth Press, 1953.

33. Freud, S. A child is being beaten (1919). *Collected Papers*, *2*:172–201. London: Hogarth Press, 1924.

34. Freud, S. Beyond the pleasure principle (1920). *Standard Edition*, *18*:1–64, London: Hogarth Press, 1955.

35. Freud, S. Certain neurotic mechanisms in jealousy, paranoia and homosexuality (1922). *Standard Edition*, *18*:221–232. London: Hogarth Press, 1955.

36. Freud, S. The economic principle in masochism (1924). *Collected Papers*, *2*:255–268. London: Hogarth Press, 1924.

37. Freud, S. Some psychological consequences of the anatomical distinction between the sexes (1925). *Collected Papers*, *5*:186–197. London: Hogarth Press, 1950.

38. Freud, S. *The Problem of Anxiety* (1926). New York: W. W. Norton, 1936.

39. Freud, S. Female sexuality (1931). *Collected Papers*, *5*:252–272. London: Hogarth Press, 1950.

40. Freud, S. *New Introductory Lectures on Psychoanalysis* (1932). New York: W. W. Norton, 1933.

41. Freud, S. Analysis terminable and interminable (1937). *Collected Papers*, *5*:316–357. London: Hogarth Press, 1950.

42. Greenacre, P. *Trauma, Growth and Personality*. New York: W. W. Norton, 1952.

43. Greenacre, P. Certain relationships between fetishism and faulty development of the body image. *The Psychoanalytic Study of the Child*, *8*:79–98. New York: International Universities Press, 1953.

44. Greenacre, P. Contribution to the discussion on problems of infantile neurosis. *The Psychoanalytic Study of the Child*, *9*:18–24. New York: International Universities Press, 1954.

45. Greenacre, P. Further considerations regarding fetishism. *The Psychoanalytic Study of the Child*, *10*:187–194. New York: International Universities Press, 1955.

46. Greenson, R. R. On empathy and sublimation. Paper read at the Midwinter Meeting of the American Psychoanalytic Association, 1954.

47. Grunberger, S. Esquisse d'une théorie psychanalytique du masochisme. *Rev. Franç. Psychanal.*, *18*:193–214, 1954.

48. Hartmann, H. Ich-Psychologie und Anpassungsproblem. *Int. Ztsch. Psychoanal. & Imago.*, 24:62–135, 1939.
49. Hartmann, H. Comments on the psychoanalytic theory of the ego. *The Psychoanalytic Study of the Child*, 5:74–96. New York: International Universities Press, 1950.
50. Hartmann, H. The mutual influences in the development of ego and id. *The Psychoanalytic Study of the Child*, 7:9–30. New York: International Universities Press, 1952.
51. Hartmann, H. Notes on the theory of sublimation. *The Psychoanalytic Study of the Child*, 10:9–29. New York: International Universities Press, 1955.
52. Hartmann, H.; Kris, E.; Loewenstein, R. M. Notes on the theory of aggression. *The Psychoanalytic Study of the Child*, 3/4:9–36. New York: International Universities Press, 1949.
53. Horney, K. The problem of feminine masochism. *Psychoanal. Rev.*, 22:241–257, 1935.
54. Kaplan, L. *Psychoanalytische Probleme*. Vienna: Deuticke, 1916.
55. Keiser, S. The fear of sexual passivity in the masochist. *Int. J. Psychoanal.*, 30:162–171, 1949.
56. Kris, E. Notes on the development and on some current problems of psychoanalytic child psychology. *The Psychoanalytic Study of the Child*, 5:24–46. New York: International Universities Press, 1950.
57. Kris, E. Some comments and observations on early autoerotic activities. *The Psychoanalytic Study of the Child*, 6:95–116, 1951.
58. Kris, E. Neutralization and sublimation: observations on young children. *The Psychoanalytic Study of the Child*, 10:30–46. New York: International Universities Press, 1955.
59. Laforgue, R. On the erotization of anxiety. *Int. J. Psychoanal.*, 11:312–326, 1930.
60. Lampl-de Groot, J. The evolution of the oedipus complex in women. *Int. J. Psychoanal.*, 9:332–345, 1928.
61. Lampl-de Groot, J. Problems of femininity. *Psychoanal. Quart.*, 2:489–518, 1933.
62. Lampl-de Groot, J. Masochismus und Narzissmus. *Int. Ztsch. Psychoanal.*, 23:479–489, 1937.
63. Lampl-de Groot, J. Depression and aggression. In: *Drives, Affects, Behavior*, ed. R. M. Loewenstein. New York: International Universities Press, 1953, pp. 153–168.
64. Lewin, B. D. *The Psychoanalysis of Elation*. New York: W. W. Norton, 1950.
65. Loewenstein, R. M. D'un mécanisme auto-punitif. *Rev. Franç. Psychoanal.*, 5:141–151, 1932.
66. Loewenstein, R. M. Phallic passivity in men. *Int. J. Psychoanal.*, 16:334–340, 1935.
67. Loewenstein, R. M. L'origine du masochisme et la théorie des instincts. *Rev. Franç. Psychanal.*, 10:293–321, 1938.
68. Loewenstein, R. M. The vital and somatic instincts. *Int. J. Psychoanal.*, 21:377–400, 1940.
69. Loewenstein, R. M. A special form of self-punishment. *Psychoanal. Quart.*, 21:377–400, 1940.
70. Loewenstein, R. M. Contribution to the discussion on problems of infantile neurosis. *The Psychoanalytic Study of the Child*, 9:47–48. New York: International Universities Press, 1954.
71. Menaker, E. Masochism—a defense reaction of the ego. *Psychoanal. Quart.*, 22:205–220, 1953.
72. Menninger, K. A. *Man Against Himself*. New York: Harcourt, Brace. 1938.
73. Menninger, K. A. *Love Against Hate*. New York: Harcourt, Brace, 1942.
74. Monchy, R. de. Masochism as a pathological and as a normal phenomenon in the human mind. *Int. J. Psychoanal.*, 31:95–97, 1950.

75. Nacht, S. Le masochisme. *Rev. Franç. Psychanal., 10*:173–291, 1938.
76. Nunberg, H. *Principles of Psychoanalysis. Their Application to the Neuroses.* New York: International Universities Press, 1955.
77. Rado, S. Fear of castration in women. *Psychoanal. Quart., 2*:425–475, 1933.
78. Reich, A. The structure of the grotesque-comic sublimation. *Bull. Menninger Clin., 13*:160–171, 1949.
79. Reich, W. The masochistic character. In: *Character Analysis.* New York: Orgone Institute Press, 3rd ed., 1949, pp. 208–247.
80. Reik, T. Psycho-analysis of the unconscious sense of guilt. *Int. J. Psychoanal., 5*:439–450, 1924.
81. Reik, T. *Geständniszwang und Strafbedürfnis.* Vienna: Internationaler Psychoanalytischer Verlag, 1925.
82. Reik, T. The characteristics of masochism. *Am. Imago, 1*:26–59, 1940.
83. Reik, T. *Masochism in Modern Man.* New York: Farrar & Rhinehart, 1941.
84. Schilder, P. *The Image and Appearance of the Human Body.* New York: International Universities Press, 1950.
85. Spitz, R. A. Aggression: its role in the establishment of object relations. In: *Drives, Affects, Behavior,* ed. R. M. Loewenstein. New York: International Universities Press, 1953, pp. 126–138.
86. Spitz, R. A. The primal cavity. *The Psychoanalytic Study of the Child, 10*:215–240, New York: International Universities Press, 1955.
87. Spitz, R. A. and Wolf, K. M. Anaclitic depression. *The Psychoanalytic Study of the Child, 2*:313–342. New York: International Universities Press, 1946.
88. Spitz, R. A. and Wolf, K. M. Autoerotism. Some empirical findings and hypotheses on three of its manifestations in the first year of life. *The Psychoanalytic Study of the Child, 3/4*:85–120. New York: International Universities Press, 1949.
89. Waelder, R. The psychoanalytic theory of play. *Psychoanal. Quart., 2*:208–224, 1933.
90. Waelder, R. The principle of multiple function: observations on overdetermination. *Psychoanal. Quart., 5*:45–62, 1936.
91. Wittels, F. The mystery of masochism. *Psychoanal. Rev., 24*:139–149, 1937.
92. Zilboorg, G. Considerations on suicide, with particular reference to that of the young. *Am. J. Orthopsychiat., 7*:15–31, 1937.

NOTES

1. A brief version of this paper was presented at the Midwinter Meeting of the American Psychoanalytic Association, December 3, 1955.
2. This may not always be correct. We have seen cases of women as well as men in whom light and playful beatings of the genital organs produce a highly arousing effect.
3. "If we assume that a similar erotogenic effect attaches even to intensely painful feelings, especially when the pain is toned down or kept at a distance by some accompanying condition, we should here have one of the main roots of the masochistic-sadistic instinct, into whose numerous complexities we are very gradually gaining some insight" (Freud, 32).
4. More correctly one would say that either neutralization may never have been completely achieved or morality may have regressively deneutralized.
5. Seduction of the aggressor hinges on the infant's very early ability to "perceive" the emotions of the mother. The child acquires this essential function for every object relation and for survival in the social world very soon (Loewenstein, 70). This is made possible by

the fact that the infant, while nursing at the breast, looks at the mother's face, a phenomenon that has recently been stressed by Spitz (86) in another context. Whatever may be the mechanisms through which this perception of the mother's emotion can be achieved, an introjection of her feelings becomes possible at all only after they have been "perceived." As to the mechanism of projection, one may conjecture that it is used concomitantly with introjection so as to distinguish or compare the child's own emotions and those being perceived in her, as a kind of trial-and-error procedure in the gradual acquisition of this knowledge about the mother's emotions. From the example of the little girl "seducing the aggressor," we must conclude that children are able quite early to "perceive the meaning" of an adult's facial expression and to distinguish between the disapproving or angry and the loving expression, the erotic component in the adult's behavior (Kaplan, 54; Schilder, 84; Burlingham, 15; Greenson, 46). Thus it is not surprising that even when faced with severe bodily punishment by a sadistic mother (as in a case of E. Kris, discussed in connection with this paper), the child does maintain an object relation with her. The sadism of the mother is a form of loving which the child perceives in spite of the punishment.

6. Dr. Elisabeth R. Geleerd suggested this point of view.
7. We were accustomed to describe the transformation of the libidinal object relation into autoerotic activity as a narcissistic phenomenon, as a turning of the libido upon the ego. It is more correct to define it as a libidinal investment of the self (Loewenstein, 68; Hartmann, 49; Kris, 57).
8. Clamping of the jaws is an expression of anger; "one's hands itch" to hit someone.
9. These points will be discussed by Hartmann, Kris and myself in a paper devoted to the study of superego functions.
10. The greater role of object relation in the little girl, which is mentioned by Freud (40), thus may be an additional factor predisposing to future masochism.
11. For its role in psychopathology, see also Borel and Robin (10).

3. The Masochistic Contract

Victor N. Smirnoff

Clinical features of masochism have been discussed by Freud (1924), who made the distinction between moral, feminine and erotogenic masochism; Reik (1941), who described moral masochism at length; and Lagache (1961), who emphasized the importance of aggressivity. Most writers, however, insist on the problem of masochism as a character trait or as a sexual perversion, and many discussions have centred on the question of primary or secondary masochism (Reich, 1932) as well as on guilt feelings (Nacht, 1938). All of these studies have added considerably to our understanding of the metapsychology of masochism. Nevertheless, many questions still remain unsolved.

The first question is the very definition of masochism. The first clinical descriptions of algolagnia or sexual algophobia emphasized the element of pain or suffering as the specific element. This remains true of Freud's (1924) description, in which he distinguishes three forms of the masochistic syndrome. It is all too apparent that this 'longing for suffering' is present in most cases, if not in all. But is it really possible to consider this longing as the basic requirement of the masochistic fantasy?

Suffering, as Darcourt (1968) points out, is after all a subjective experience and there is some inner contradiction in saying that the masochist 'feels pleasure through pain', a contradiction that was mentioned by Freud. When Lagache (1961) remarks that one can speak of the passivity of the masochist by saying that

the passive, dependent, submissive child must experience some satisfactions at being submitted to the beneficent omnipotence of the other,

he makes an important point in replacing 'suffering' by 'state of well-being', a state of diminished tension which initiates pleasure. This, of course, applies

Reprinted by permission of the author and the *International Journal of Psycho-Analysis* 50 (1969):665–71. Copyright © Institute of Psycho-Analysis.

to what Lagache (1961) has called the 'narcissistic masochistic position', which does not cover all the varieties of masochistic behaviour, but is enough to prove that suffering *per se* is not a constant and indispensable symptom and that it cannot be used for an over-all definition of masochism. By going one step further, we can also underline the discrepancy between what the masochist himself has to say about his 'sufferings' and how we try to label his feelings 'objectively'. The satisfied masochist seems to enjoy a situation in which pain or humiliation would be the expected reaction. Lagache's (1961) definition of masochism as being a 'search for submission' seems to be of great importance, since it emphasizes a major point: that the essential phenomena of masochism may well be not in the suffering but in the position of the masochist in the masochistic relationship.

This masochistic position is one of the major interests of Sacher-Masoch's life and writing, which in his case are more intimately interrelated than usually appears in the work of artists. The confusion between the facts and fantasies in Sacher-Masoch's life and his written work is exemplified by comparing his best-known novel *Venus in Furs* (1870) and the history of his agitated marriage to Wanda. The basic and first confusion can be seen in the choice of his wife's name: her maiden name was Aurore Rumelin, but she signed her first letters with the name of Wanda von Dunajew, the heroine of *Venus in Furs*. She kept Wanda as her first name after marrying Sacher-Masoch (and again kept the full name Wanda von Sacher-Masoch, even after her divorce). In this strange and turbulent relationship it seems that the confusion between fact and fiction is present at the very beginning. But one more remark is necessary. *Venus im Pelz* was published in 1870, at least a year before the first meeting with Aurora-Wanda took place. *Venus,* although probably somewhat inspired by Sacher-Masoch's adventure with Fanny Pistor, is a work of fantasy, and it is important to keep in mind that it precedes Sacher-Masoch's marriage. But although *Venus* is a fictitious account, nothing in the whole novel is quite improbable. In fact, many of the situations depicted in it were actually to take place (under a somewhat different, but not essentially different form) during the following years. In spite of the fact that *Venus* is not an autobiographical novel, its main interest is that it can be used as an elaborate model of Sacher-Masoch's fantasy, a fantasy which he was to try to put into action.

One example of the extreme intricacy of Sacher-Masoch's life and work may be found in his promise to his wife Wanda. She reported to him that a literary critic had made some derogatory remarks about his work, saying how monotonous his recent novels had become, because most of the female characters were shaped after a single pattern. Wanda advised him to get rid of this type of woman, to erase this woman *from his life* and that by doing so she would not reappear in his books. Sacher-Masoch replied that such a woman was actually *missing* in his life and, for that very reason, present in his writings; that all of Wanda's furs were not enough to satisfy him and what he really needed was 'a whip', since to be mistreated by his own wife was his only real voluptuous pleasure. 'You shall have to mistreat me and I promise that all these cruel females will disappear for ever from my books.' Wanda accepted this 'deal'. She even got used to her role of flogging her husband, although she claims that she never enjoyed her part but was obeying through sheer necessity. One wonders whether Wanda had nothing on her mind but her husband's literary career, but it is quite true that none of the novels after this contained any flogging scenes, nor any true 'masochistic' machinery. It is also true that Sacher-Masoch's fame is not based on those novels, but this may not be entirely his fault.

This 'deal' was actually recorded: it is one of the many contracts which are to be found both in Sacher-Masoch's life, and signed by him and Fanny Pistor or Wanda von Sacher-Masoch, and in the contract between Severin Kusiemski and Wanda de Dunajew in *Venus in Furs*. It is remarkable how the contents and the wording of those contracts are identical in reality and in the work of fiction; it certainly shows the close interrelation of life and work, as demonstrated by the apparent ease with which the acting out of masochistic fantasies was able to replace the 'fantasy in writing'.

Those contracts have been quoted by many authors (Krafft-Ebing, 1893); their most important characteristic is that these contracts are in fact the arrangement of a certain immutable setting. Although Wanda in her autobiography (1906) points out that her husband abided by his decision, i.e. to give up using the masochistic scenes as a literary subject, she also complains that, having forced her to accept his conditions, he strained his ingenuity in order to make *her* part 'as painful as possible', forcing her to use even more elaborate contraptions, such as specially fabricated whips and a six-lashed knout fitted with sharp nails. But as to the remaining conditions mentioned, few improvisations altered the initial scheme.

But what does Wanda mean by saying that Sacher-Masoch tried to make her performance as painful as possible? Painful for whom? If one is to trust Wanda's claim, it would mean that Sacher-Masoch was making her task irksome and trying, as if to increase the discomfort of the executioner. It would also mean that the conditions imposed are an essential part of the masochistic position: the masochist is not looking for a consenting accomplice, eager to inflict pain or to torture the victim. There is an analogous demand on the sadist's part, who does not want his victim to submit too readily to the pleasure of being tortured or abused. As we shall see, there is no complementary agreement between the sadistic and the masochistic desire.

This is the real meaning of the masochistic contract, which tries to render the executioner's task more oppressive. The conditions imposed are clear enough: the tormentor's panoply only underlines his role, he must wear a uniform to remind him that he is merely an employee, a slave of the self-styled victim. The whole setting tends to harness the victim's delight, not to be simply defined as the agonizing pain of the masochist, but to define, and refine, the respective positions of the two parties. But we must not forget that it is the victim who lays down the rules.

Let us return to what we have called the 'masochistic position'. Moral suffering or physical pain matter less than the laws that regulate the partnership. This is reminiscent of what Khan (1965) describes in his article on intimacy in perversions, when he says that the

technique of intimacy is to establish a make-believe situation, involving in most cases the willing seduced cooperation of an external object.

We shall see later on whether this 'willingness' is an authentic one. It is of less importance to know whether the masochist enjoys his sufferings or experiences pleasure at being flogged, than to locate the exact position and define the functions of the masochist.

Neither the flogging nor the moral suffering is sufficient to define the specificity of the masochistic pleasure, which is mainly determined by the 'casting' of the play.

An example can be found in *Venus in Furs*. At the end of the novel, Wanda's lover, Alexis Papadopolis, alias the Greek, has to take over the flogging while Wanda leaves the scene for ever. Alexis takes his role seriously. Sacher-Masoch emphasizes his cruel disposition and bulging muscles, his strength and his callousness. But the flogging does not elicit any pleasure in Severin, merely disgust and dismay, an unpleasant humiliation, although theoretically Severin should feel elated: could he dream of a more truly satisfying 'masochistic' situation than that of being cruelly beaten by his triumphant rival?

This is a clear-cut example that pain is not enough, or even has little to do with pleasure even in masochism. Because Alexis Papadopolis is a real sadist, who fully and wholeheartedly enjoys his role as a tormentor and is not being coerced into this role, he cannot satisfy the masochist because he is not part of the contract; he has subscribed to nothing that puts him into the position of an employee. He is his own master and exerts his wilful cruelty, which is not at all what Severin wants.

The final chapter of *Venus in Furs* is purely a moral superstructure to exploit the reader's naivety. Severin pretends that he has been cured by excess of torture: an absurd claim coming from a masochist. He may be cured, not through punishment, but because he has been fooled in the process by Wanda's betrayal. What cures Severin is not the lashing, but Wanda's derisive laughter as she leaves the scene. She tells Severin that she too has betrayed him, by rejecting the treaty, which stipulated that the executioner must be his victim.

It is just as important to qualify the pleasure: in *Venus in Furs,* Sacher-Masoch uses the word *übersinnlich.* This can be translated by either 'over-sensory' or 'over-sensitive', as Deleuze (1967) points out in his excellent commentary. But we would rather render this as 'beyond sensuality', which connotes the fact that the masochistic 'pleasure' transgresses the borders of perception and sensibility: it is beyond the realm of vision, touch, pain or kinaesthesia. Even if this 'pleasure' incorporates all these various modalities, the multivalence is not, by itself, a sufficient criterion for defining it, since the masochistic pleasure takes on its full effect in the interplay between the victim and the executioner. In such a topology the masochistic position has often been defined as that of a consenting and demanding victim: *victima,* a person immolated in order to appease the gods. If such a direction is to be pursued, the concept of pain and pleasure must be complemented by that of sacrifice. *Übersinnlich,* beyond sensuality, also applies to the way in which this sacrifice is experienced by the victim. As the writings and the iconography concerning martyrdom so clearly show, there is always a basic component of ecstasy: the mystical trance, the tortured and languid body exposed to blows, the exquisite agonies, the often orgasmic quality of posture and facial expression. And those same elements are to be encountered in all erotic literature and pictorial representations of masochism. In 'beyond sensuality' we find the suspended gesture of sacrificial moment.

Such a gesture can be found in almost any mythical representation of

sacrifice. Whether in Abraham's suspended knife over the body of his beloved son, and echoed in a fourfold repetition by Kierkegaard in *Fear and
Trembling,* or the brandished knife above Iphigenia, who is sacrificed by her
father to appease the gods, the moment before Agamemnon's, Orestes' and
Aegisthus' fate is sealed forever. This last moment before the fate of things
to come is settled is the exact equivalent of what is described by Freud (1927)
as the decisive moment in the choice of a fetish:

It seems rather that when the fetish is instituted some process occurs which reminds
one of the stopping of memory in traumatic amnesia. As in this latter case, the
subject's interest comes to a halt half-way, as it were; it is as though the last
impression before the uncanny and traumatic one is retained as a fetish.

It is possible to recognize the nature of the fetish as a screen formation,
just as it is possible to identify the whipping scene as a screen memory. In
fact, such a scene had actually taken place in Sacher-Masoch's life and has
been reported by Schlichtegroll (1901), as well as by Sacher-Masoch himself:
the scene where Sacher-Masoch, as a young boy, is the involuntary witness
of his aunt's, Countess Xenobie von X's, adulterous sexual relations. The
scene is interrupted by the Countess' husband: she goes into a fury and
chases everybody out of her room. Leopold is discovered by his aunt and
severely chastised with a riding whip. He admits having felt some pleasure,
but it is important to note that, to say the least, this is a rather involved scene
and that many elements contribute to young Leopold's excitement.

It seems far too easy to relate Sacher-Masoch's perversion to this 'traumatic' event. But if we admit that this scene is really a screen memory—or
at least fulfils the function of a screen memory—the fetish, that is the whip
and his aunt's attire (the *Kazabaika,* a short, fur-lined jacket), becomes the
symbolic representation just before the feminine image is shattered to pieces,
the very point where the guilty sexual relations and the guilt of the scoptophilic pleasure (although Sacher-Masoch pretends that he closed his eyes and
covered his ears so as not to see or hear anything) come to be related to the
violence which gives him a unique and intense pleasure: Leopold crouching
under the suspended horsewhip of his adulterous aunt, and Leopold wincing
under the flogging are two distinct moments of the masochistic expectancy
and the masochistic ordeal.

This is where the intricate relationship between Sacher-Masoch's life and
writing starts and ends. The childhood scene—closely resembling the spanking of Jean-Jacques Rousseau by Mademoiselle Lambercier—merely ex-

plains the obvious: a first incident, well remembered and often told, but which only assumes its true significance because of the already included meaning. This so-called 'traumatic scene' can be nothing but a screen memory and, as such, reality can only assume its meaning through its already established symbolic network. This is why a genetic explanation can be only a preparatory exercise, a *Vorarbeit,* in order to release the underlying symbolic structure as it appears in fantasies or dreams.

The underlying fantasy can well be described as that of a sacrifice. As in the biblical story of Abraham and in the myth of Agamemnon, there is a covenant between the subject and God: neither Abraham nor Agamemnon performs sadistic deeds, but they are obliged, by virtue of an order, to sacrifice their child. They are bound by this obligation and have no possible choice of avoiding the imposed task. In the case of the masochistic scene, a similar contract binds the executioner and the victim, as we have already shown. But here again the victim is not being persecuted by a self-appointed sadistic executioner, since the latter is not pursuing his own private pleasure; also because a sadistic executioner would put the masochist into an absurd position.

The sadist cannot be satisfied in carrying out his activities on a willing victim, since the sadist's desire is to elicit pleasure in spite of the victim's initial refusal. The sadistic fantasy contains its own sequence: every detail must be commanded and performed according to the sadist's whim and will, in an almost improvised sequence of events. Everything is built up little by little, detail by detail, minutely arranged; as things go on, orders are issued, precise instructions given and a constant rearrangement of the procedure takes place while the performance proceeds. This sadistic happening can be compared with a rehearsal, where everything is being set in order to lead to a final and definitive version, but it never goes beyond these rehearsals: the final performance is delayed for ever.

Not so in the masochistic ceremony: there everything is settled from the very start; the general pattern of the execution is well arranged in advance and little can be changed once the scene is set. There can be no possible sadistic-masochistic meeting: the sadist only accepts to be the tormentor of an innocent and protesting victim; the masochist can only be the victim of a reluctant executioner *malgré lui.*

There are strict rules to this game. The masochistic 'victim' must bear witness to its own victimized status, and the evidence inscribed into his own flesh. Here again there is no simple opposition between the sadistic and the masochistic pursuit. The sadist aims at the ultimate destruction of the victim, and tries to mutilate and annihilate him. The masochist is not seeking to be killed or destroyed, but to be branded. Not by the absolute power of the other, but by the fictitious power that he himself has bestowed on the executioner: a power that the victim has, by way of contract, forced on the executioner, who can exercise it only at the victim's order.

Masochism is a defiance. It is expressed through the masochist's apparently passive behaviour, by his compliance with the inflicted pain and humiliation, by his claims of being enslaved and used. In fact, the masochist knows that his position is simply the result of his own power: the power of endowing the executioner with the obligation of playing the role of a master, when indeed he is only a slave, a creation of the masochist's desire.

A great deal of attention has been given in psychoanalytic literature to the love object of the masochist. We shall only try to emphasize one aspect of it: the dual feminine ideal of the masochist.

It might be interesting to compare what Wanda von Sacher-Masoch has to say about this in her *Confessions* (1906) and how Sacher-Masoch depicts it himself in *Venus*.

Wanda von Sacher-Masoch reports that her husband, speaking about his mother, said that she

represented the noblest and highest of all women, unattainable in her perfection and her pureness.

This reminds us of the Rousseauistic preconception of the primitive unspoilt human nature. Sacher-Masoch further states that social conventions spoil all women and make them 'bad':

The best of them are nothing but a caricature of what they could have been if one had not interfered with their natural development.

And this is even worse since 'they do not realize their own falseness and mental deformity'. Nothing is more repugnant for Sacher-Masoch, so he claims, than falsity and artificiality; and since this unobtainable goal is forgone for ever, nothing is left to him but to use the opposite image: the 'evil' woman. She at least admits to her brutality, her bad instincts and her egotism. His most passionate desire was to find a

noble and strong woman: not having found her, he had to turn to *another ideal.*

It would be quite justifiable to try to fit this statement into psychoanalytic theory: to identify Sacher-Masoch's experience as a phenomenon of disillusion (Winnicott, 1953), and to remark that the maternal image which is actually missing in Sacher-Masoch's life is the 'good-enough mother'; that his ego defences are mobilized by the lack of or the impossibility of establishing an inner object and that the 'idealized evil woman' marks the spot of the transitional area. The close relationship between fetishism and masochism has so far not been sufficiently explored, but it would appear that the 'idealized evil woman' is actually taking the place of a fetish. This would be rather confirmed by Sacher-Masoch's own fantasy, which seems to be closely related to the *deadness* of the internal object.

In Sacher-Masoch's own words, he prefers 'to be destroyed' by a beautiful demon rather than to be bound to a so-called 'virtuous woman'. He prefers 'an hour of vulgar sensual pleasure to a whole century of *emptiness*' (italics mine). This could also be described as the explicit image of female duplicity: on one hand, the burning image of an evil and rejecting woman; on the other, the cold and empty image of purity. As has been shown by Karl Abraham and Melanie Klein, but even better by Freud in his article on the 'Splitting of the Ego' (1940), the picture described by Sacher-Masoch is the projection of the split ego on the primary love object. But the characteristic aspect here refers to a bipartite object, and not two separate parts: an intricate figure, divided but not separated into two distinct parts. Two figures which can never be perceived simultaneously, but who coexist on two sides of the same coin. The passage from the good ideal object to the evil idealized one and vice versa is always possible, since they are both supported by a single figure. Such an object is described by Sacher-Masoch in *Venus* when Severin talks about his mistress. She is, in various disguises, both the harsh and evil woman, clad in velvet, in a dress clinging to her body, which appears as a marble statue, and the sweet and loving one, in her white and vaporous nightgown of lace and muslin.

The dual structure of the love object is clearly stated, since clothes, rather than the physical core, determine the status of the love object: and this dual structure must remain throughout the whole story. This is also one of the purposes of the masochistic contract, which stipulates when and how Wanda can play her successive roles. And it is essential that these two roles should be played *by the same woman,* the masochist's wife or mistress.

This is where the use of dresses, uniforms and accessories is of utmost importance. They are the indispensable means of maintaining these two images apart (from each other), lest their coalescence might nullify the ego defences and give place to delusion.

Such is the masochist's tragedy: he must love the cold, inhuman image in order to be loved by the other one.

Any work of art contains its own basic metaphor. *Venus in Furs* is no exception:

> A very young, very beautiful and very rich widow had come to spend some weeks at the boardinghouse where the narrator, Severin Kusiemski, is staying. But Severin is not interested in her: he has fallen in love with a marble statue of Venus. He is fascinated by her beauty, her coldness, her petrified smile. One night, while walking in the garden, he is seized by panic: he has seen the statue clad from head to foot in furs. He flees, then tries to come back, loses his way, and suddenly comes upon 'his' Venus, the beautiful stone figure, but she is sitting on a bench: she is alive, her flesh is warm and her heart is beating. The miracle has happened, but only to some extent: her white dress is glittering like the moonlight and her hair appears as if of stone. Such is the first appearance of Wanda de Dunajew, the novel's heroine, already cast in her dual role.

There is a paradigmatic value to this first encounter. It shows that the masochist's quest can be approached along two different lines: the dual aspect of the maternal imago, or the split in his own ego. Here again the fetishistic part of masochism is in full view.

There is still another point to be made. The issue of the masochistic position is further exemplified by the character who appears at the end of *Venus:* Wanda's lover, the cruel Alexis Papadopolis, alias the Greek. Through him we find one more confusion in Severin's relationship to his love object. At first Severin thinks that the Greek is a woman in disguise: 'it would have been easy to believe that this person was a transvestite', but he is soon informed that this person is a prince, famous for his cruelty, courage and 'racist' attitudes. Severin sums up his impression: 'A man indeed'. This 'hermaphrodite' takes over the crucial role at the end of the novel. We have already reported the final whipping, Wanda's derisive laughter, her leaving and Severin's 'cure'. But is Severin really cured of his masochistic needs?

We should keep in mind that Sacher-Masoch's life story would point to the contrary. In his case he has given up the writing of fantasy masochism, because he found his Wanda in real life. But then *Venus* had been written before this happened, and besides, *Venus* is his own fantasy.

We have already pointed out that Severin attributes his cure to the severe flogging: too much pain and too much humiliation. We have said that certainly the most important part in this 'cure' was the fact that Severin met a 'real' sadist and that the masochistic position became untenable for him. But there is still another reason. Through the Greek, the initial confusion of man-woman is finally resolved. A man, indeed! A man who puts an end to the phallic femininity of Wanda, nullifying Severin's efforts to maintain his fantasy of the phallic Venus. She, the Greek goddess, has found her complement in the Greek: the Alexis-Apollo who has skinned Marsyas and who now brands Severin with the sign of the masculine power; he is whipping Severin with unquestionable pleasure and not because he has signed any contract. Wanda leaves in her furs which, by now, are only a derisive disguise: there is no secret fantasy left. Wanda and Alexis have assumed their real roles: a woman and a man. Severin, the abandoned Pygmalion, is left behind. He might have animated the statue of Aphrodite, but he could not change her into a phallic woman. Severin is now confronted with the real nature of womanhood. He has to accept the uselessness of disavowal, the necessity of confronting the problem of castration in the open, and not behind the mask of the masochistic panoply.

To institute and enact the endless repetition of this denial, masochism can only be based on a contract that is also an alliance. By instituting such a ritual, with all the compulsive elements included, the executioner must be part of the masochistic position, not an outside figure. Sacher-Masoch does not use the vocabulary of a victim, but that of the director of this play. Thus the masochist does not appear as the victimized accomplice to a sadistic executioner, but as his educator—just as the sadist is the pedagogue of his reluctant victim. It is of the utmost importance to redefine masochism—in any of its clinical forms—not through the 'pleasure in pain' element, but as the actualization of a contract which must regulate the relationship in the masochistic performance.

The symbiotic relation, as found in masochism, makes use of suffering, pain and humiliation, not in order to obtain pleasure, but as a symbolic representative of both the unattainable fusion with the impossible separation from the primary sexual object.

REFERENCES

Anzieu, D. (1968). De la mythologie particulière à chaque type de masochisme. *Bull. Ass. Psychanal. France*, no. 4, 84–91.
Cain, J. (1968). Le masochisme chez Masoch. *Bull. Ass. Psychanal. France*, no. 4, 64–75.
Darcourt, G. (1968). Définition clinique du masochisme moral. *Bull. Ass. Psychanal. France*, no. 4, 3–34.

Deleuze, G. (1967). *Présentation de Sacher-Masoch*. Paris: Éditions de Minuit.

Fedida, P. (1968). Le corps et sa mise en scène dans le fantasme masochiste. *Bull. Ass. Psychanal. France,* no. 4, 92–102.

Freud, S. (1924). The economic problem of masochism. *S.E.* **19.**

Freud, S. (1927). Fetishism. *S.E.* **21.**

Freud, S. (1940). Splitting of the ego in the process of defence. *S.E.* **23.**

Khan, M. M. R. (1965). The function of intimacy and acting out in perversions. In R. Slovenko (ed.), *Sexual Behavior and the Law*. Springfield, Ill.: Thomas.

Krafft-Ebing, F. (1893). *Psychopathia Sexualis*.

Lagache, D. (1961). Situation de l'agressivité. *Bull. Psychol.* **14,** 99–112.

Laplanche, J. (1968). La position originaire du masochisme dans le champ de la pulsion sexuelle. *Bull. Ass. Psychanal. France,* no. 4, 35–53.

Laplanche, J. & Pontalis, J. B. (1968). *Vocabulaire de la Psychanalyse*. Paris: Presses Univ. de France, 2nd ed.

Nacht, S. (1938). *Le Masochisme*. Paris: Le François, 1948.

Reich, W. (1932). The masochistic character. In *Character Analysis*. New York: Orgone Institute Press, 1949.

Reik, T. (1941). *Masochism in Modern Man*. New York: Farrar, Straus, 1949.

Sacher-Masoch, L. von (1870). *Venus im Pelz*.

Sacher-Masoch, L. von (1880). *L'Esthétique de la Laideur*. Paris: Buchet-Castel, 1967.

Sacher-Masoch, W. von (1906). *Confessions de ma vie*. Paris: Tchou, 1967.

Schlichtegroll, C. F. von (1901). *Sacher-Masoch und Masochismus*. Dresden.

Smirnoff, V. N. (1967). Le souvenir-écran. *Bull. Ass. Psychanal. France,* no. 2, 27–60.

Winnicott, D. W. (1953). Transitional objects and transitional phenomena. In *Collected Papers*. London: Tavistock Publications, 1958.

PART II

MASOCHISM, SEXUALITY, AND AGGRESSION

Introduction

Freud (1905; chapter 4 in this volume) looked at masochism, explicitly, as a component instinct, a vicissitude of childhood libido, and, implicitly, as a position of ego, in humiliation and subjection to the loved and needed object:

The most common and the most significant of all the perversions—the desire to inflict pain on the sexual object, and its reverse—received from Krafft-Ebing the names "sadism" and "masochism" for its active and passive forms respectively. . . . the names chosen by Krafft-Ebing bring into prominence the pleasure in any form of humiliation or subjection. (p. 86 in this volume)

In exploring masochism and sadism in the context of "Instincts and Their Vicissitudes," Freud (1915; chapter 5 in this volume) developed his account of pre-Oedipal ambivalence, that is, of love and hate to the mother, describing the unconscious processes which bind the complementary tendencies of masochism and sadism together in relation to the love object. In the light of Freud's original contributions, masochism is, essentially, an object relations theory of an aggressive sexual love, in a regressed and fixated form. The simultaneity and volatility of the instinctual urges of early childhood are the stuff out of which both fairy tales and maternal fatigue are made. Dependent on the containment of love and hate, the small child is subject to the stimulus of the sexuality of parents through contact with their bodies (Laplanche 1992), and to the stimulus of the infantile sexuality arising from their own bodies and imaginations. In "Instincts and Their Vicissitudes," Freud (1915) opened up the inner world of the child who wishes to possess the mother, or father, "from every direction" (Freud 1905). To see and be seen with sensations of pleasure forms an inevitable part of the positive narcissism of children, rooted in the attraction in the parents' eyes. To feel the pain of overstimulation in the parents' too intrusive sexuality, or the pain of sadistic disregard, turns love to hate (Shengold 1971). And this sadomasochistic relation can overlay a still earlier oral destructiveness created in the baby's dawning recognition of the mother's separateness, which can be raised to acute levels of hatred when she has not appeased hunger or anxiety in time to prevent a sense of catastrophe (Green 1990). The development of the body ego and the sense of self integral to it involves sexual looking and being looked at, and the testing of the positions of masochistic submission and sadistic attack, which accompany the shifts from intense loving into hating— the hallmark of the small child's emotional life (Freud 1915). We are aided in our understanding of masochism if we recall all three "pairs of opposites" (Freud 1915) which, simultaneously, characterize the multifaceted early phases of psychic development in which masochism has its roots: "The hate, which has its real motives, is here reinforced by a regression of the love to the sadistic preliminary stage; so that the hate acquires an erotic character and the continuity of a love-relation is ensured" (p. 101 in this volume).

INFANTILE PASSIVITY AND HUMILIATION

One of Freud's (1905) implicit questions about masochism concerned how it is that the normal passive longing of the infant, to be held, to be caressed, and to be loved, becomes masochistic, turns into the wish for, or accepted condition of, suffering for the love object. As Freud uncovered the workings of guilt in the incest fantasy, and its exacerbation through a precociously developed sadism (1919; chapter 8 in this volume), he saw the full power of the unconscious beating fantasy as deriving not from aggression and guilt only, but from a degradation of the child's struggling, possessive love, one geared into survival as well as into the essential satisfactions of this stage of development (A. Freud 1922; chapter 14 in this volume).

Early papers by Bak (1946; chapter 9 in this volume) and by Reich (1940; chapter 21 in this volume) add to the sadomasochistic dynamics Freud discovered, a fuller picture of the disturbed object relations which exacerbate a potentially dangerous position of the human psyche, in a combined passivity and co-excitation of pleasure and pain. Masochism in this light appears as a hybrid phenomenon, a defense and adaptation of the ego, and a turned back, frustrated, or attacked instinctual need (Brenman 1952).

MASOCHISM AS A VICISSITUDE OF AGGRESSION TOWARD THE LOVE OBJECT

Throughout the discussion of sadism and masochism in these early papers, Freud (1905, 1915) mixes what later became more distinct theoretical entities: aggression and sadism. As Laplanche (1976; chapter 6 in this volume) demonstrates, Freud referred to ordinary childhood aggression, that is, to the attempt at mastery of the environment and the mother, as sadism, just barely differentiating this from what he called sadism "properly speaking," the taking of pleasure in the mother's pain. Laplanche corrects for this blurring of distinct concepts. The first true linking of destructiveness and sexual excitation takes place, according to Laplanche (1976), in the masochistic position, in the moment when the aggression to the love object bends back in a fantasy of self-abuse, which involves the co-excitation of sexual pleasure and pain. Grossman's (1991; chapter 7 in this volume) work on pain as a source of aggression, and on the psychic structure that develops to express and regulate aggression, also explores the impairment of fantasy by child abuse and trauma.

SADOMASOCHISM AND THE OEDIPUS COMPLEX

The unique blend of libido and aggression in the intensity of Oedipal love appears to be the context in which the final fantasy structure of sadomasochism is created (Freud 1919; Nacht 1938; Novick and Novick 1987; chapter 12 in this volume), even if the Oedipus complex is "scarcely effected" (Freud 1919). From his first words on masochism, Freud focused on humiliation before the mother and on the subjection of the love object: "The sexuality of most male human beings contains an element of *aggressiveness*—a desire to subjugate." (The gender specificity of this observation has undergone appropriate revision [Fliegel 1986; Lax 1992].) Freud will continue to see the Oedipal stage, involving new and more focused capacities for object love and object subjugation, as a pivotal stage for the development of fixed adult sadomasochistic fantasies. Anna Freud (1922) underlines that it is love and not predominantly aggression that fuels the beating fantasy: "the function of the beating fantasy is the disguised representation of a never-changing sensual love situation which it expresses in the language of the anal-sadistic organization as an act of beating" (p. 296 in this volume).

THE THEORY OF CO-EXCITATION

In the co-excitation of infantile masochism, painful excitations are experienced as sexually exciting. Many writers who have not found Freud's hypothesis of the death instinct either verifiable or clinically useful (Nacht 1938; Loewenstein 1938, Brenner 1959; chapter 18 in this volume), have considered his theory of co-excitation (1905, 1924; chapter 13 in this volume) as an adequate account of the primitive core in severe masochism

(Laplanche 1992). In her chapter on primary masochism and primary narcissism, Jacobson (1964) discussed the possibility of inner directed discharges in the infant's more or less undifferentiated psychobiological beginnings. Excitations coming from hunger and from the life energies of the central nervous system can be directed to the outside in cries and gestures, or to the inside in movements of the organs and inner investments of attention. When these inner investments reach a certain level of intensity they may become sexually pleasurable, that is, attached to an organ such as the skin or anus, and subject to a wish for repetition. The theory of "anaclisis" or "etayage" which Laplanche (1976) has developed out of Freud's (1905) theory of central nervous system excitations comes into play in the theory of co-excitation. The initial survival needs of the infant, which involve being fed orally and being touched in all the acts of infant care-taking, can turn a vital activity into an expected pleasure and, in states of excitation, to sexual pleasure which sets desire for repetition in place. Fenichel (1945) pointed out that in a poor environment, the expectation of considerable pain in contiguity with infantile pleasure leads to the sense that pain and pleasure are inseparable. Later, pain will be sought as the forerunner of basic satisfactions (Berliner 1958; chapter 17 in this volume). Shengold (1971) and Kucera (1959) have considered the spilling over of cutaneous pain into erotic sensation. They have considered an intermingling of sexual excitement and pain in teething: "the change to tension and unpleasure of a predominantly pleasure giving zone at a time when the ego is beginning to coalesce may be more significant than has been thought" (Shengold 1971, p. 226 in this volume). The theory of co-excitation has been used by psychoanalysts in their search for the infantile roots of the most serious forms of masochism to which some patients regress in severe sadomasochitic addictive states. The theory of co-excitation, as such, has not received a great deal of articulation in psychoanalytic literature, though in a recent paper Laplanche has returned to it, suggesting that this theory is sufficient to all the clinical and theoretical demands masochism places on psychoanalytic theory. Laplanche (1992) maintains that there is in fact no inherent paradox in masochism. Masochism only appears to contravene the pleasure principle if we define pleasure and pain in too simple a way, without making important distinctions between a sexual fore-pleasure which involves rising levels of tension excitation, and sexual pleasure in orgasm which involves the release of tension excitation. The tensions in the body do not in themselves define pleasure or pain; the fantasies and fantasy expectations, and the rhythm of tension and release they promise or deny are important differentiating factors, as Freud noted in reference to masturbation. Early on, Reik (1941) characterized one style of a masochist, who uses sexual tension states in a self-abusive way, drawing out the moment of tension till the possibility of release passes and no pleasure is achieved.

PRIMARY MASOCHISM AND THE DEATH INSTINCT

Freud's (1924) final explanation for the origins of masochism is linked to his theory of the death instinct and attempts to clarify extreme self-destructive behaviors. Jacobson (1964) writes that in Freud's death instinct theory the drives are aimed at discharge on the primal self. Through the means of early projection, the inner directed destructive impulses can be externalized and possibly contained by the mother (Freud 1924; Rosenberg 1988). The destructive drive which remains inside (for not all can be projected) must be bound by libido in order to be rendered less dangerous to survival. This instinctual binding or fusion (Freud 1924) is the primary masochism which is the guardian of life (Rosenberg 1988). It is a defensive solution in the primal psychobiological self threatened by the destructive impulse. Freud redescribes the theory of co-excitation, indicating that this is the mechanism whereby the binding of the destructive instinct takes place in the infant. Jacobson's (1964) difficulty with Freud's solution, which receives elaboration in contemporary French psychoanalytic literature (Rosenberg 1988; Gauthier 1994) is that while she understands that fusions between aggression and libido can render destructive impulses harmless, she believes that this capacity develops at a much later infantile period and is connected with the partial neutralization of the drives. Whether or not the death instinct exists, infantile destructive impulses in a self partially undifferentiated from the other will be experienced as directed, at least diffusely, against the self. The need for projection, binding, or containment is a point of agreement in all current articulations concerning early sadomasochistic tendencies.

In this context of converging explanatory views for the earliest protomasochisms (Loewenstein 1957; chapter 2 in this volume) and those that lead to the negative therapeutic reaction, the gap between the French or Kleinian considerations of primary masochism, and the theories derived from infant mother research in North America and Britain is narrowing. In the undifferentiated psychobiological beginnings of the infant (Jacobson 1964) inevitable bits of rage from frustration turn into destructive impulses at a time when self and other (mother) are partially merged, and safety is threatened (Grossman

1991). How certain excitations of comingled pain and pleasure are created and then sorted out in the infant's relatively undifferentiated psyche and how the infant manages the subsequent task of responding to pleasure and pain appropriately depends on both constitutional factors and on the physical and psychological handling by the mother. The mother's physical response to the baby carries a great deal from her unconscious into the infant's world. Her psychological responsiveness in interpreting and normalizing aggressivity or destructiveness carries the organization of her ego back to the primary process world of the infant, actually altering the effectiveness of the pleasure principle (Rosenberg 1988; Blum 1991).

The early psychobiological patterns for masochistic reactions are only the beginning of the story, and do not in themselves necessarily make the difference between pathological and normal masochism. The complex roots of masochism lie in both the instincts of libido and aggression and in the narcissistic resources and ego organizations that develop to receive and sort out stimuli of pleasure and pain.

BIBLIOGRAPHY

Bak, R. 1946. Masochism in Paranoia. *Psychoanal. Quarterly* 15:285–301. (Chapter 9 in this volume.)
———. 1974. Distortions of the Concept of Fetishism. *Psychoanal. Study Child* 29:191–214.
Berliner, B. 1958. The Role of Object Relations in Moral Masochism. *Psychoanal. Quarterly* 27:38–56. (Chapter 17 in this volume.)
Blum, H. 1991. Sasomasochism in the Psychoanalytic Process, Within and Beyond the Pleasure Principle: Discussion. *J. Amer. Psychoanal. Assn.* 39:431–50.
Brenman, M. 1952. On Teasing and Being Teased: And the Problem of Moral Masochism. *Psychoanal. Study Child* 7:264–85.
Brenner, C. 1959. The Masochistic Character: Genesis and Treatment. *J. Amer. Psychoanal. Assn.* 7:197–226. (Chapter 18 in this volume.)
Coen, S. 1992. The Excitement of Sadomasochism. In *The Misuse of Persons: Analyzing Pathological Dependency.* Hillsdale, N.J.: The Analytic Press, pp. 190–208. (Chapter 19 in this volume.)
Fenichel, O. 1945. *The Psychoanalytic Theory of Neurosis.* New York: Norton.
Fliegel, Z. 1986. Women's Development in Analytic Theory: Six Decades of Controversy. In *Psychoanalysis and Women,* ed. J. Alpert. Hillsdale, N.J.: The Analytic Press, pp. 3–31.
Freud, A. 1922. Beating Fantasies and Daydreams. *Int. J. Psycho-Anal.* 4:89–109. (Chapter 14 in this volume.)
Freud, S. 1905. Three Essays on the Theory of Sexuality. In *S.E.* 7:135–243. (In excerpt form, chapter 4 in this volume.)
———. 1915. Instincts and Their Vicissitudes. In *S.E.* 14:117–40. (In excerpt form, chapter 5 in this volume.)

————. 1919. "A Child Is Being Beaten:" A Contribution to the Study of the Origin of Sexual Perversions. In *S.E.* 17:179–204. (Chapter 8 in this volume.)

————. 1924. The Economic Problem of Masochism. In *S.E.* 19:159–70. (Chapter 13 in this volume.)

Gauthier, M. 1994. De l'objet secourable: Désaide et masochisme. In *Les Actes A.P.P.Q. du Collogue de l'Au 1994.* Quebec.

Green, A. 1990. Pourquoi le mal. In *La Folie privée.* Paris: Gallimard.

Grossman, W. I. 1991. Pain, Aggression, Fantasy, and Concepts of Sadomasochism. *Psychoanal. Quarterly* 60:22–52. (Chapter 7 in this volume.)

Jacobson, E. 1964. *The Self and the Object World.* New York: International Universities Press.

Kernberg, O. 1988. Clinical Dimensions of Masochism. *J. Amer. Psychoanal. Assn.* 36:1005–29.

Kucera, O. 1959. On Teething. *J. Amer. Psychoanal. Assn.* 7:284–91.

Laplanche, J. 1976. Aggressiveness and Sadomasochism. In *Life and Death in Psychoanalysis.* Baltimore: John Hopkins University Press. (Chapter 6 in this volume.)

————. 1992. *La révolution copernicienne inachevée.* Paris: Aubier.

Lax, R. 1992. A Variation on Freud's Theme in "A Child Is Being Beaten"—Mother's Role: Some Implications for Super-Ego Development in Women. *J. Amer. Psychoanal. Assn.* 40:455–73.

Loewenstein, R. 1938. L'origine du masochisme et la théorie des instincts. *Rev. Franc. Psychanal.,* 10:293–321.

————. 1957. A Contribution to the Psychoanalytic Theory of Masochism. *J. Amer. Psychoanal. Assn.* 5:197–234. (Chapter 2 in this volume.)

Modell, A. 1965. On Having the Right to Life: An Aspect of the Super-ego's Development. *Int. J. Psycho-Anal.* 46:323–31.

Nacht, S. 1938. *Le masochisme.* Paris: Payot. 1965.

Novick, K., and Novick, J. 1987. The Essence of Masochism. *Psychoanal. Study Child.* 42:353–84. (Chapter 12 in this volume.)

Reich, A. 1940. A Contribution to the Psycho-Analysis of Extreme Submissiveness in Women. *Psychoanal. Quarterly* 9:470–80. (Chapter 21 in this volume.)

Reik, T. 1941. *Masochism in Modern Man.* New York: Farrar and Rinehart.

Rosenberg, B. 1988. *Masochisme mortifère et masochisme gardien de la vie.* Paris: Presses Universitaires de France.

Shengold, L. 1971. More about Rats and Rat People. *Int. J. Psycho-Anal.* 52:277–88. (Chapter 11 in this volume.)

4. Three Essays on the Theory of Sexuality (An Excerpt)

Sigmund Freud

I. THE SEXUAL ABERRATIONS [1]

The fact of the existence of sexual needs in human beings and animals is expressed in biology by the assumption of a 'sexual instinct', on the analogy of the instinct of nutrition, that is of hunger. Everyday language possesses no counterpart to the word 'hunger', but science makes use of the word 'libido' for that purpose. [2]

Popular opinion has quite definite ideas about the nature and characteristics of this sexual instinct. It is generally understood to be absent in childhood, to set in at the time of puberty in connection with the process of coming to maturity and to be revealed in the manifestations of an irresistible attraction exercised by one sex upon the other; while its aim is presumed to be sexual union, or at all events actions leading in that direction. We have every reason to believe, however, that these views give a very false picture of the true situation. If we look into them more closely we shall find that they contain a number of errors, inaccuracies and hasty conclusions. . . .

Fixations of Preliminary Sexual Aims

Appearance of New Aims. Every external or internal factor that hinders or postpones the attainment of the normal sexual aim (such as impotence, the high price of the sexual object or the danger of the sexual act) will evidently lend support to the tendency to linger over the preparatory activities and to turn them into new sexual aims that can take the place of the normal one.

Reprinted by permission of Sigmund Freud Copyrights, The Institute of Psycho-Analysis, the Hogarth Press, and Basic Books, a division of HarperCollins Publishers, Inc., from *The Standard Edition of the Complete Psychological Works of Sigmund Freud,* translated and edited by James Strachey, vol. 7: (1960) 135, 155–60.

Attentive examination always shows that even what seem to be the strangest of these new aims are already hinted at in the normal sexual process.

Touching and Looking. A certain amount of touching is indispensable (at all events among human beings) before the normal sexual aim can be attained. And everyone knows what a source of pleasure on the one hand and what an influx of fresh excitation on the other is afforded by tactile sensations of the skin of the sexual object. So that lingering over the stage of touching can scarcely be counted a perversion, provided that in the long run the sexual act is carried further.

The same holds true of seeing—an activity that is ultimately derived from touching. Visual impressions remain the most frequent pathway along which libidinal excitation is aroused; indeed, natural selection counts upon the accessibility of this pathway—if such a teleological form of statement is permissible[3]—when it encourages the development of beauty in the sexual object. The progressive concealment of the body which goes along with civilization keeps sexual curiosity awake. This curiosity seeks to complete the sexual object by revealing its hidden parts. It can, however, be diverted ('sublimated') in the direction of art, if its interest can be shifted away from the genitals on to the shape of the body as a whole.[4] It is usual for most normal people to linger to some extent over the intermediate sexual aim of a looking that has a sexual tinge to it; indeed, this offers them a possibility of directing some proportion of their libido on to higher artistic aims. On the other hand, this pleasure in looking [scopophilia] becomes a perversion *(a)* if it is restricted exclusively to the genitals, or *(b)* if it is connected with the overriding of disgust (as in the case of *voyeurs* or people who look on at excretory functions), or *(c)* if, instead of being *preparatory* to the normal sexual aim, it supplants it. This last is markedly true of exhibitionists, who, if I may trust the findings of several analyses,[5] exhibit their own genitals in order to obtain a reciprocal view of the genitals of the other person.[6]

In the perversions which are directed towards looking and being looked at, we come across a very remarkable characteristic with which we shall be still more intensely concerned in the aberration that we shall consider next: in these perversions the sexual aim occurs in two forms, an *active* and a *passive* one.

The force which opposes scopophilia, but which may be overridden by it (in a manner parallel to what we have previously seen in the case of disgust), is *shame*.

Sadism and Masochism. The most common and the most significant of all the perversions—the desire to inflict pain upon the sexual object, and its reverse—received from Krafft-Ebing the names of 'sadism' and 'masochism' for its active and passive forms respectively. Other writers [e.g. Schrenck-Notzing "Literaturzusam-menstellung über die Psychologie und Psychopathologie der Vita sexualis" (1899)] have preferred the narrower term 'algolagnia'. This emphasizes the pleasure in *pain,* the cruelty; whereas the names chosen by Krafft-Ebing bring into prominence the pleasure in any form of humiliation or subjection.

As regards active algolagnia, sadism, the roots are easy to detect in the normal. The sexuality of most male human beings contains an element of *aggressiveness*—a desire to subjugate; the biological significance of it seems to lie in the need for overcoming the resistance of the sexual object by means other than the process of wooing. Thus sadism would correspond to an aggressive component of the sexual instinct which has become independent and exaggerated and, by displacement, has usurped the leading position.[7]

In ordinary speech the connotation of sadism oscillates between, on the one hand, cases merely characterized by an active or violent attitude to the sexual object, and, on the other hand, cases in which satisfaction is entirely conditional on the humiliation and maltreatment of the object. Strictly speaking, it is only this last extreme instance which deserves to be described as a perversion.

Similarly, the term masochism comprises any passive attitude towards sexual life and the sexual object, the extreme instance of which appears to be that in which satisfaction is conditional upon suffering physical or mental pain at the hands of the sexual object. Masochism, in the form of a perversion, seems to be further removed from the normal sexual aim than its counterpart; it may be doubted at first whether it can ever occur as a primary phenomenon or whether, on the contrary, it may not invariably arise from a transformation of sadism.[8] It can often be shown that masochism is nothing more than an extension of sadism turned round upon the subject's own self, which thus, to begin with, takes the place of the sexual object. Clinical analysis of extreme cases of masochistic perversion show that a great number of factors (such as the castration complex and the sense of guilt) have combined to exaggerate and fixate the original passive sexual attitude.

Pain, which is overridden in such cases, thus falls into line with disgust and shame as a force that stands in opposition and resistance to the libido.[9]

Sadism and masochism occupy a special position among the perversions, since the contrast between activity and passivity which lies behind them is among the universal characteristics of sexual life. The history of human civilization shows beyond any doubt that there is an intimate connection between cruelty and the sexual instinct; but nothing has been done towards explaining the connection, apart from laying emphasis on the aggressive factor in the libido. According to some authorities this aggressive element of the sexual instinct is in reality a relic of cannibalistic desires—that is, it is a contribution derived from the apparatus for obtaining mastery, which is concerned with the satisfaction of the other and, ontogenetically, the older of the great instinctual needs.[10] It has also been maintained that every pain contains in itself the possibility of a feeling of pleasure. All that need be said is that no satisfactory explanation of this perversion has been put forward and that it seems possible that a number of mental impulses are combined in it to produce a single resultant.[11]

But the most remarkable feature of this perversion is that its active and passive forms are habitually found to occur together in the same individual. A person who feels pleasure in producing pain in someone else in a sexual relationship is also capable of enjoying as pleasure any pain which he may himself derive from sexual relations. A sadist is always at the same time a masochist, although the active or the passive aspect of the perversion may be the more strongly developed in him and may represent his predominant sexual activity.[12]

We find, then, that certain among the impulses to perversion occur regularly as pairs of opposites; and this, taken in conjunction with material which will be brought forward later, has a high theoretical significance.[13] It is, moreover, a suggestive fact that the existence of the pair of opposites formed by sadism and masochism cannot be attributed merely to the element of aggressiveness. We should rather be inclined to connect the simultaneous presence of these opposites with the opposing masculinity and femininity which are combined in bisexuality—a contrast which often has to be replaced in psycho-analysis by that between activity and passivity.[14]

NOTES

1. The information contained in this first essay is derived from the well-known writings of Krafft-Ebing, Moll, Moebius, Havelock Ellis, Schrenck-Notzing, Löwenfeld, Eulenburg,

Bloch and Hirschfeld, and from the *Jahrbuch für sexuelle Zwischenstufen,* published under the direction of the last-named author. Since full bibliographies of the remaining literature of the subject will be found in the works of these writers, I have been able to spare myself the necessity for giving detailed references. [*Added* 1910:] The data obtained from the psycho-analytic investigation of inverts are based upon material supplied to me by I. Sadger and upon my own findings.

2. [*Footnote added* 1910:] The only appropriate word in the German language, *'Lust',* is unfortunately ambiguous, and is used to denote the experience both of a need and of a gratification. [Unlike the English 'lust' it can mean either 'desire' or 'pleasure'.]

3. [The words in this parenthesis were added in 1915.]

4. [This seems to be Freud's first published use of the term 'sublimate', though it occurs as early as May 2, 1897, in the Fliess correspondence (Freud, 1950, Letter 61). It also appears in the 'Dora' case history, 1905, actually published later than the present work though drafted in 1901.—*Footnote added* 1915:] There is to my mind no doubt that the concept of 'beautiful' has its roots in sexual excitation and that its original meaning was 'sexually stimulating'. [There is an allusion in the original to the fact that the German word *'Reiz'* is commonly used both as the technical term for 'stimulus' and, in ordinary language, as an equivalent to the English 'charm' or 'attraction'.] This is related to the fact that we never regard the genitals themselves, which produce the strongest sexual excitation, as really 'beautiful'.

5. [In the editions before 1924 this read 'of a single analysis'.]

6. [*Footnote added* 1920:] Under analysis, these perversions—and indeed most others— reveal a surprising variety of motives and determinants. The compulsion to exhibit, for instance, is also closely dependent on the castration complex: it is a means of constantly insisting upon the integrity of the subject's own (male) genitals and it reiterates his infantile satisfaction at the absence of a penis in those of women.

7. [In the editions of 1905 and 1910 the following two sentences appeared in the text at this point: 'One at least of the roots of masochism can be inferred with equal certainty. It arises from sexual overvaluation as a necessary psychical consequence of the choice of a sexual object.' From 1915 onwards these sentences were omitted and the next two paragraphs were inserted in their place.]

8. [*Footnote added* 1924:] My opinion of masochism has been to a large extent altered by later reflection, based upon certain hypotheses as to the structure of the apparatus of the mind and the classes of instincts operating in it. I have been led to distinguish a primary or *erotogenic* masochism, out of which two later forms, *feminine* and *moral* masochism, have developed. Sadism which cannot find employment in actual life is turned round upon the subject's own self and so produces a *secondary* masochism, which is superadded to the primary kind.

9. [This short paragraph was in the first edition (1905), but the last two, as well as the next one, were only added in 1915.]

10. [*Footnote added* 1915:] Cf. my remarks below on the pregenital phases of sexual development, which confirm this view.

11. [*Footnote added* 1924:] The enquiry mentioned above [note 8] has led me to assign a peculiar position, based upon the origin of the instincts, to the pair of opposites constituted by sadism and masochism, and to place them outside the class of the remaining 'perversions'.

12. Instead of multiplying the evidence for this statement, I will quote a passage from Havelock Ellis *[Studies in the Psychology of Sex,* vol. 6: *Sex in Relation to Society]* (1913, 119): 'The investigation of histories of sadism and masochism, even those given by Krafft-Ebing (as

indeed Colin Scott and Féré have already pointed out), constantly reveals traces of both groups of phenomena in the same individual.'

13. [*Footnote added* 1915:] Cf. my discussion of 'ambivalence'.]

14. [The last clause did not occur in the 1905 or 1910 editions. In 1915 the following clause was added: 'a contrast whose significance is reduced in psycho-analysis to that between activity and passivity.' This was replaced in 1924 by the words now appearing in the text.]

5. Instincts and Their Vicissitudes (An Excerpt)

Sigmund Freud

. . . .

Since a study of instinctual life from the direction of consciousness presents almost insuperable difficulties, the principal source of our knowledge
remains the psycho-analytic investigation of mental disturbances. Psycho-
analysis, however, in consequence of the course taken by its development,
has hitherto been able to give us information of a fairly satisfactory nature
only about the *sexual* instincts; for it is precisely that group which alone can
be observed in isolation, as it were, in the psychoneuroses. With the extension of psycho-analysis to the other neurotic affections, we shall no doubt
find a basis for our knowledge of the ego-instincts as well, though it would
be rash to expect equally favourable conditions for observation in this further
field of research.

This much can be said by way of a general characterization of the sexual
instincts. They are numerous, emanate from a great variety of organic
sources, act in the first instance independently of one another and only
achieve a more or less complete synthesis at a late stage. The aim which each
of them strives for is the attainment of 'organ-pleasure';[1] only when synthesis is achieved do they enter the service of the reproductive function and
thereupon become generally recognizable as sexual instincts. At their first
appearance they are attached to the instincts of self-preservation, from which
they only gradually become separated; in their choice of object, too, they
follow the paths that are indicated to them by the ego-instincts.[2] A portion of
them remains associated with the ego-instincts throughout life and furnishes

Reprinted by permission of Sigmund Freud Copyrights, The Institute of Psycho-Analysis, the
Hogarth Press, from *The Standard Edition of the Complete Psychological Words of Sigmund
Freud*, translated and edited by James Strachey, vol. 4: (1915) 125–40.

them with libidinal components, which in normal functioning easily escape notice and are revealed clearly only by the onset of illness.[3] They are distinguished by possessing the capacity to act vicariously for one another to a wide extent and by being able to change their objects readily. In consequence of the latter properties they are capable of functions which are far removed from their original purposive actions—capable, that is, of 'sublimation'.

Our inquiry into the various vicissitudes which instincts undergo in the process of development and in the course of life must be confined to the sexual instincts, which are the more familiar to us. Observation shows us that an instinct may undergo the following vicissitudes:—

Reversal into its opposite.

Turning round upon the subject's own self.

Repression.

Sublimation.

Since I do not intend to treat of sublimation here[4] and since repression requires a special chapter to itself, it only remains for us to describe and discuss the two first points. Bearing in mind that there are motive forces which work against an instinct's being carried through in an unmodified form, we may also regard these vicissitudes as modes of *defence* against the instincts.

Reversal of an instinct into its opposite resolves on closer examination into two different processes: a change from activity to passivity, and a reversal of its content. The two processes, being different in their nature, must be treated separately.

Examples of the first process are met with in the two pairs of opposites: sadism—masochism and scopophilia—exhibitionism. The reversal affects only the *aims* of the instincts. The active aim (to torture, to look at) is replaced by the passive aim (to be tortured, to be looked at). Reversal of *content* is found in the single instance of the transformation of love into hate.

The turning round of an instinct upon the subject's own self is made plausible by the reflection that masochism is actually sadism turned round upon the subject's own ego, and that exhibitionism includes looking at his own body. Analytic observation, indeed, leaves us in no doubt that the masochist shares in the enjoyment of the assault upon himself, and that the exhibitionist shares in the enjoyment of [the sight of] his exposure. The essence of the process is thus the change of the *object*, while the aim remains unchanged. We cannot fail to notice, however, that in these examples the turning round upon the subject's self and the transformation from activity to passivity converge or coincide.

To elucidate the situation, a more thorough investigation is essential.

In the case of the pair of opposites sadism—masochism, the process may be represented as follows:

(a) Sadism consists in the exercise of violence or power upon some other person as object.

(b) This object is given up and replaced by the subject's self. With the turning round upon the self the change from an active to a passive instinctual aim is also effected.

(c) An extraneous person is once more sought as object; this person, in consequence of the alteration which has taken place in the instinctual aim, has to take over the role of the subject.[5]

Case (c) is what is commonly termed masochism. Here, too, satisfaction follows along the path of the original sadism, the passive ego placing itself back in phantasy in its first role, which has now in fact been taken over by the extraneous subject.[6] Whether there is, besides this, a more direct masochistic satisfaction is highly doubtful. A primary masochism, not derived from sadism in the manner I have described, seems not to be met with.[7] That it is not superfluous to assume the existence of stage (b) is to be seen from the behaviour of the sadistic instinct in obsessional neurosis. There there is a turning round upon the subject's self *without* an attitude of passivity towards another person: the change has only got as far as stage (b). The desire to torture has turned into self-torture and self-punishment, not into masochism. The active voice is changed, not into the passive, but into the reflexive, middle voice.[8]

Our view of sadism is further prejudiced by the circumstance that this instinct, side by side with its general aim (or perhaps, rather, within it), seems to strive towards the accomplishment of a quite special aim—not only to humiliate and master, but, in addition, to inflict pains. Psycho-analysis would appear to show that the infliction of pain plays no part among the original purposive actions of the instinct. A sadistic child takes no account of whether or not he inflicts pains, nor does he intend to do so. But when once the transformation into masochism has taken place, the pains are very well fitted to provide a passive masochistic aim; for we have every reason to believe that sensations of pain, like other unpleasurable sensations, trench upon sexual excitation and produce a pleasurable condition, for the sake of which the subject will even willingly experience the unpleasure of pain.[9] When once feeling pains has become a masochistic aim, the sadistic aim of *causing* pains can arise also, retrogressively; for while these pains are being inflicted on other people, they are enjoyed masochistically by the subject through his identification of himself with the suffering object. In both cases, of course, it is not the pain itself which is enjoyed, but the accompanying sexual excitation—so that this can be done especially conveniently from the sadistic position. The enjoyment of pain would thus be an aim which was originally masochistic, but which can only become an instinctual aim in someone who was originally sadistic.

For the sake of completeness I may add that feelings of pity cannot be described as a result of a transformation of instinct occurring in sadism, but necessitate the notion of a *reaction-formation* against that instinct. (For the difference, see later.)[10]

Rather different and simpler findings are afforded by the investigation of another pair of opposites—the instincts whose respective aim is to look and to display oneself (scopophilia and exhibitionism, in the language of the perversions). Here again we may postulate the same stages as in the previous instance:—*(a)* Looking as an *activity* directed towards an extraneous object. *(b)* Giving up of the object and turning of the scopophilic instinct towards a part of the subject's own body; with this, transformation to passivity and setting up of a new aim—that of being looked at. *(c)* Introduction of a new subject[11] to whom one displays oneself in order to be looked at by him. Here, too, it can hardly be doubted that the active aim appears before the passive, that looking precedes being looked at. But there is an important divergence from what happens in the case of sadism, in that we can recognize in the case of the scopophilic instinct a yet earlier stage than that described as *(a)*. For the beginning of its activity the scopophilic instinct is auto-erotic: it has indeed an object, but that object is part of the subject's own body. It is only later that the instinct is led, by a process of comparison, to exchange this object for an analogous part of someone else's body—stage *(a)*. This preliminary stage is interesting because it is the source of *both* the situations represented in the resulting pair of opposites, the one or the other according to which element in the original situation is changed. The following might serve as a diagrammatic picture of the scopophilic instinct:—

(α) Oneself looking at a sexual = organ	A sexual organ being looked at by oneself
│	│
(β) Oneself looking at an extraneous object (active scopophilia)	(γ) An object which is oneself or part of oneself being looked at by an extraneous person (exhibitionism)

A preliminary stage of this kind is absent in sadism, which from the outset is directed upon an extraneous object, although it might not be altogether unreasonable to construct such a stage out of the child's efforts to gain control over his own limbs.[12]

With regard to both the instincts which we have just taken as examples, it should be remarked that their transformation by a reversal from activity to passivity and by a turning round upon the subject never in fact involves the whole quota of the instinctual impulse. The earlier active direction of the instinct persists to some degree side by side with its later passive direction, even when the process of its transformation has been very extensive. The only correct statement to make about the scopophilic instinct would be that all the stages of its development, its auto-erotic, preliminary stage as well as its final active or passive form, co-exist alongside one another; and the truth of this becomes obvious if we base our opinion, not on the actions to which the instinct leads, but on the mechanism of its satisfaction. Perhaps, however, it is permissible to look at the matter and represent it in yet another way. We can divide the life of each instinct into a series of separate successive waves, each of which is homogeneous during whatever period of time it may last, and whose relation to one another is comparable to that of successive eruptions of lava. We can then perhaps picture the first, original eruption of the instinct as proceeding in an unchanged form and undergoing no development at all. The next wave would be modified from the outset— being turned, for instance, from active to passive—and would then, with this new characteristic, be added to the earlier wave, and so on. If we were then to take a survey of the instinctual impulse from its beginning up to a given point, the succession of waves which we have described would inevitably present the picture of a definite development of the instinct.

The fact that, at this[13] later period of development of an instinctual impulse, its (passive) opposite may be observed alongside of it deserves to be marked by the very apt term introduced by Bleuler—'ambivalence'.[14]

This reference to the developmental history of instincts and the permanence of their intermediate stages should make the development of instincts fairly intelligible to us. Experience shows that the amount of demonstrable ambivalence varies greatly between individuals, groups and races. Marked instinctual ambivalence in a human being living at the present day may be regarded as an archaic inheritance, for we have reason to suppose that the part played in instinctual life by the active impulses in their unmodified form was greater in primaeval times than it is on an average to-day.[15]

We have become accustomed to call the early phase of the development of the ego, during which its sexual instincts find auto-erotic satisfaction, 'narcissism', without at once entering on any discussion of the relation between auto-erotism and narcissism. It follows that the preliminary stage of the scopophilic instinct, in which the subject's own body is the object of the scopophilia, must be classed under narcissism, and that we must describe it as a narcissistic formation. The active scopophilic instinct develops from this, by leaving narcissism behind. The passive scopophilic instinct, on the contrary, holds fast to the narcissistic object. Similarly, the transformation of sadism into masochism implies a return to the narcissistic object. And in both these cases [i.e. in passive scopophilia and masochism] the narcissistic *subject* is, through identification, replaced by another, extraneous ego. If we take into account our constructed preliminary narcissistic stage of sadism, we shall be approaching a more general realization—namely, that the instinctual vicissitudes which consist in the instinct's being turned round upon the subject's own ego and undergoing reversal from activity to passivity are dependent on the narcissistic organization of the ego and bear the stamp of that phase. They perhaps correspond to the attempts at defence which at higher stages of the development of the ego are effected by other means.

At this point we may call to mind that so far we have considered only two pairs of opposite instincts: sadism—masochism and scopophilia—exhibitionism. These are the best-known sexual instincts that appear in an ambivalent manner. The other components of the later sexual function are not yet sufficiently accessible to analysis for us to be able to discuss them in a similar way. In general we can assert of them that their activities are *auto-erotic;* that is to say, their object is negligible in comparison with the organ which is their source, and as a rule coincides with that organ. The object of the scopophilic instinct, however, though it too is in the first instance a part of the subject's own body, is not the eye itself; and in sadism the organic source, which is probably the muscular apparatus with its capacity for action, points unequivocally at an object other than itself, even though that object is part of the subject's own body. In the auto-erotic instincts, the part played by the organic source is so decisive that, according to a plausible suggestion of Federn ["Beiträge zur Analyse des Sadismus und Masochismus, I: Die Quellen des männlichen Sadismus"] (1913) and Jekels ["Einige Bemerkungen zur Trieblehre"] (1913), the form and function of the organ determine the activity or passivity of the instinctual aim.

The change of the *content* [cf. p. 91] of an instinct into its opposite is observed in a single instance only—the transformation of *love into hate*.[16] Since it is particularly common to find both these directed simultaneously towards the same object, their co-existence furnishes the most important example of ambivalence of feeling. [See note 14.]

The case of love and hate acquires a special interest from the circumstance that it refuses to be fitted into our scheme of the instincts. It is impossible to doubt that there is the most intimate relation between these two opposite feelings and sexual life, but we are naturally unwilling to think of love as being some kind of special component instinct of sexuality in the same way as the others we have been discussing. We should prefer to regard loving as the expression of the *whole* sexual current of feeling; but this idea does not clear up our difficulties, and we cannot see what meaning to attach to an opposite content of this current.

Loving admits not merely of one, but of three opposites. In addition to the antithesis 'loving—hating', there is the other one of 'loving—being loved'; and, in addition to these, loving and hating taken together are the opposite of the condition of unconcern or indifference. The second of these three antitheses, loving—being loved, corresponds exactly to the transformation from activity to passivity and may be traced to an underlying situation in the same way as in the case of the scopophilic instinct. This situation is that of *loving oneself*, which we regard as the characteristic feature of narcissism. Then, according as the object or the subject is replaced by an extraneous one, what results is the active aim of loving or the passive one of being loved—the latter remaining near to narcissism.

Perhaps we shall come to a better understanding of the several opposites of loving if we reflect that our mental life as a whole is governed by *three polarities,* the antitheses

Subject (ego)—Object (external world),

Pleasure—Unpleasure, and

Active—Passive.

The antithesis ego—non-ego (external), i.e. subject—object, is, as we have already said, thrust upon the individual organism at an early stage, by the experience that it can silence *external* stimuli by means of muscular action but is defenceless against *instinctual* stimuli. This antithesis remains, above all, sovereign in our intellectual activity and creates for research the basic situation which no efforts can alter. The polarity of pleasure—unpleasure is attached to a scale of feelings, whose paramount importance in determining our actions (our will) has already been emphasized. The antithesis active—passive must not be confused with the antithesis ego-subject—external world-object. The relation of the ego to the external world is passive in so far as it receives stimuli from it and active when it reacts to these. It is forced by its instincts into a quite special degree of activity towards the external world, so that we might bring out the essential point if we say that the ego-subject is passive in respect of external stimuli but active through its own instincts. The antithesis active—passive coalesces later with the antithesis masculine—feminine, which, until this has taken place, has no psychological meaning. The coupling of activity with masculinity and of passivity with femininity meets us, indeed, as a biological fact; but it is by no means so invariably complete and exclusive as we are inclined to assume.[17]

The three polarities of the mind are connected with one another in various highly significant ways. There is a primal psychical situation in which two of them coincide. Originally, at the very beginning of mental life, the ego is cathected with instincts and is to some extent capable of satisfying them on itself. We call this condition 'narcissism' and this way of obtaining satisfaction 'auto-erotic'.[18] At this time the external world is not cathected with interest (in a general sense) and is indifferent for purposes of satisfaction. During this period, therefore, the ego-subject coincides with what is pleasurable and the external world with what is indifferent (or possibly unpleasurable, as being a source of stimulation). If for the moment we define loving as the relation of the ego to its sources of pleasure, the situation in which the ego loves itself only and is indifferent to the external world illustrates the first of the opposites which we found to 'loving'.[19]

In so far as the ego is auto-erotic, it has no need of the external world, but, in consequence of experiences undergone by the instincts of self-preservation, it acquires objects from that world, and, in spite of everything, it cannot avoid feeling internal instinctual stimuli for a time as unpleasurable. Under the dominance of the pleasure principle a further development now takes place in the ego. In so far as the objects which are presented to it are sources of pleasure, it takes them into itself, 'introjects' them (to use Ferenczi's [1909] term [20]); and, on the other hand, it expels whatever within itself becomes a cause of unpleasure.

Thus the original 'reality-ego', which distinguished internal and external by means of a sound objective criterion,[21] changes into a purified 'pleasure-ego', which places the characteristic of pleasure above all others. For the pleasure-ego the external world is divided into a part that is pleasurable, which it has incorporated into itself, and a remainder that is extraneous to it. It has separated off a part of its own self, which it projects into the external world and feels as hostile. After this new arrangement, the two polarities coincide once more: the ego-subject coincides with pleasure, and the external world with unpleasure (with what was earlier indifference).

When, during the stage of primary narcissism, the object makes its appearance, the second opposite to loving, namely hating, also attains its development.

As we have seen, the object is brought to the ego from the external world in the first instance by the instincts of self-preservation; and it cannot be denied that hating, too, originally characterized the relation of the ego to the alien external world with the stimuli it introduces. Indifference falls into place as a special case of hate or dislike, after having first appeared as their forerunner. At the very beginning, it seems, the external world, objects, and what is hated are identical. If later on an object turns out to be a source of pleasure, it is loved, but it is also incorporated into the ego; so that for the purified pleasure-ego once again objects coincide with what is extraneous and hated.

Now, however, we may note that just as the pair of opposites love—indifference reflects the polarity ego—external world, so the second antithesis love—hate [22] reproduces the polarity pleasure—unpleasure, which is linked to the first polarity. When the purely narcissistic stage has given place to the object-stage, pleasure and unpleasure signify relations of the ego to the object. If the object becomes a source of pleasurable feelings, a motor urge is set up which seeks to bring the object closer to the ego and to incorporate it into the ego. We then speak of the 'attraction' exercised by the pleasure-giving object, and say that we 'love' that object. Conversely, if the object is a source of unpleasurable feelings, there is an urge which endeavours to increase the distance between the object and the ego and to repeat in relation to the object the original attempt at flight from the external world with its emission of stimuli. We feel the 'repulsion' of the object, and hate it; this hate can afterwards be intensified to the point of an aggressive inclination against the object—an intention to destroy it.

We might at a pinch say of an instinct that it 'loves' the objects towards which it strives for purposes of satisfaction; but to say that an instinct 'hates' an object strikes us as odd. Thus we become aware that the attitudes[23] of love and hate cannot be made use of for the relations of *instincts* to their objects, but are reserved for the relations of the *total ego* to objects. But if we consider linguistic usage, which is certainly not without significance, we shall see that there is a further limitation to the meaning of love and hate. We do not say of objects which serve the interests of self-preservation that we *love* them; we emphasize the fact that we *need* them, and perhaps express an additional, different kind of relation to them by using words that denote a much reduced degree of love—such as, for example, 'being fond of', 'liking' or 'finding agreeable'.

Thus the word 'to love' moves further and further into the sphere of the pure pleasure-relation of the ego to the object and finally becomes fixed to sexual objects in the narrower sense and to those which satisfy the needs of sublimated sexual instincts. The distinction between the ego-instincts and the sexual instincts which we have imposed upon our psychology is thus seen to be in conformity with the spirit of our language. The fact that we are not in the habit of saying of a single sexual instinct that it loves its object, but regard the relation of the ego to its sexual object as the most appropriate case in which to employ the word 'love'—this fact teaches us that the word can only begin to be applied in this relation after there has been a synthesis of all the component instincts of sexuality under the primacy of the genitals and in the service of the reproductive function.

It is noteworthy that in the use of the word 'hate' no such intimate connection with sexual pleasure and the sexual function appears. The relation of *unpleasure* seems to be the sole decisive one. The ego hates, abhors and pursues with intent to destroy all objects which are a source of unpleasurable feeling for it, without taking into account whether they mean a frustration of sexual satisfaction or of the satisfaction of self-preservative needs. Indeed, it may be asserted that the true prototypes of the relation of hate are derived not from sexual life, but from the ego's struggle to preserve and maintain itself.

So we see that love and hate, which present themselves to us as complete opposites in their content, do not after all stand in any simple relation to each other. They did not arise from the cleavage of any originally common entity, but sprang from different sources, and had each its own development before the influence of the pleasure—unpleasure relation made them into opposites.

It now remains for us to put together what we know of the genesis of love and hate. Love is derived from the capacity of the ego to satisfy some of its instinctual impulses auto-erotically by obtaining organ-pleasure. It is originally narcissistic, then passes over on to objects, which have been incorporated into the extended ego, and expresses the motor efforts of the ego towards these objects as sources of pleasure. It becomes intimately linked with the activity of the later sexual instincts and, when these have been completely synthesized, coincides with the sexual impulsion as a whole. Preliminary stages of love emerge as provisional sexual aims while the sexual instincts are passing through their complicated development. As the first of these aims we recognize the phase of incorporating or devouring—a type of love which is consistent with abolishing the object's separate existence and which may therefore be described as ambivalent.[24] At the higher stage of the pregenital sadistic-anal organization,[25] the striving for the object appears in the form of an urge for mastery, to which injury or annihilation of the object is a matter of indifference. Love in this form and at this preliminary stage is hardly to be distinguished from hate in its attitude towards the object. Not until the genital organization is established does love become the opposite of hate.

Hate, as a relation to objects, is older than love. It derives from the narcissistic ego's primordial repudiation of the external world with its outpouring of stimuli. As an expression of the reaction of unpleasure evoked by objects, it always remains in an intimate relation with the self-preservative instincts; so that sexual and ego-instincts can readily develop an antithesis which repeats that of love and hate. When the ego-instincts dominate the sexual function, as is the case at the stage of the sadistic-anal organization, they impart the qualities of hate to the instinctual aim as well.

The history of the origins and relations of love makes us understand how it is that love so frequently manifests itself as 'ambivalent'—i.e. as accompanied by impulses of hate against the same object.[26] The hate which is admixed with the love is in part derived from the preliminary stages of loving which have not been wholly surmounted; it is also in part based on reactions of repudiation by the ego-instincts, which, in view of the frequent conflicts between the interests of the ego and those of love, can find grounds in real and contemporary motives. In both cases, therefore, the admixed hate has as its source the self-preservative instincts. If a love-relation with a given object is broken off, hate not infrequently emerges in its place, so that we get the impression of a transformation of love into hate. This account of what happens leads on to the view that the hate, which has its real motives, is here reinforced by a regression of the love to the sadistic preliminary stage; so that the hate acquires an erotic character and the continuity of a love-relation is ensured.

The third antithesis of loving, the transformation of loving into being loved,[27] corresponds to the operation of the polarity of activity and passivity, and is to be judged in the same way as the cases of scopophilia and sadism.[28]

We may sum up by saying that the essential feature in the vicissitudes undergone by instincts lies in *the subjection of the instinctual impulses to the influences of the three great polarities that dominate mental life.* Of these three polarities we might describe that of activity—passivity as the *biological,* that of ego—external world as the *real,* and finally that of pleasure—unpleasure as the *economic* polarity.

The instinctual vicissitude of *repression* will form the subject of an inquiry which follows.

NOTES

1. ['Organ-pleasure' (i.e. pleasure attached to one particular bodily organ) seems to be used here for the first time by Freud. The term is discussed at greater length in the early part of Lecture XXI of the *Introductory Lectures* (1916–17). The underlying idea, of course, goes back much earlier. See, for instance, the opening passage of the third of the *Three Essays* (1905), *Standard Ed.,* 7, 207.]
2. [Cf. 'On Narcissism'.]
3. [Ibid.]
4. [Sublimation had already been touched upon in the paper on narcissism; but it seems possible that it formed the subject of one of the lost metapsychological papers.]
5. [Though the general sense of these passages is clear, there may be some confusion in the use of the word 'subject'. As a rule 'subject' and 'object' are used respectively for the person in whom an instinct (or other state of mind) originates, and the person or thing to which it is directed. Here, however, 'subject' seems to be used for the person who plays

the active part in the relationship—the agent. The word is more obviously used in this sense in the parallel passage on p. 97 and elsewhere.]

6. [See last footnote.]

7. [*Footnote added* 1924:] In later works (cf. 'The Economic Problem of Masochism', 1924) relating to problems of instinctual life I have expressed an opposite view.

8. [The allusion here is to the voices of the Greek verb.]

9. [See a passage near the end of the second of the *Three Essays* (1905), *Standard Ed.*, **7**, 203–4.]

10. [It is not clear to what passage this is intended to refer, unless, again, it was included in a missing paper on sublimation. There is in fact some discussion of the subject in 'Thoughts for the Times on War and Death' (1915). But this cannot have been what Freud had in mind, for it was originally published in a different volume. In a footnote added in 1915 (the year in which the present paper was written) to the *Three Essays* (1905), Freud insists that sublimation and reaction-formation are to be regarded as distinct processes (*Standard Ed.*, **7**, 178 *n.*).—The German word for 'pity' is *'Mitleid'*, literally "suffering with', 'compassion'. Another view of the origin of the feeling is expressed in the 'Wolf Man' analysis (1918), *Standard Ed.*, **17**, 88, which was actually written, in all probability, at the end of 1914, a few months earlier than the present paper.]

11. [I.e. agent; see note 5.]

12. [*Footnote added* 1924:] Cf. note 7.

13. ['*Jener*'. In the first edition only, '*jeder*', 'every'.]

14. [The term 'ambivalence', coined by Bleuler ("Vortrag über Ambivalenz" *Dementia Praecox,* oder Giuppe der Schizophrenien, 1910, and 1911, 43 and 305), seems not to have been used by him in this sense. He distinguished three kinds of ambivalence: (1) emotional, i.e. oscillation between love and hate, (2) voluntary, i.e. inability to decide on an action, and (3) intellectual, i.e. belief in contradictory propositions. Freud generally uses the term in the first of these senses. See, for instance, the first occasion on which he seems to have adopted it, near the end of his paper on 'The Dynamics of Transference' (1912), and later in the present paper (pp. 100–101). The passage in the text is one of the few in which he has applied the term to activity and passivity. For another instance of this exceptional use see a passage in Section III of the 'Wolf Man' case history (1918), *Standard Ed.,* **17,** 26.]

15. [See *Totem and Taboo* (1912–13), *Standard Ed.,* **13,** 66.]

16. [In the German editions previous to 1924 this reads 'the transformation of *love and hate*'.]

17. [This question is discussed at much greater length in a footnote added in 1915 (the year in which the present paper was written) to the third of Freud's *Three Essays* (1905), *Standard Ed.,* **7,** 219 f.]

18. Some of the sexual instincts are, as we know, capable of this auto-erotic satisfaction, and so are adapted to being the vehicle for the development under the dominance of the pleasure principle [from the original 'reality-ego' into the 'pleasure-ego'] which we are about to describe [in the next paragraphs of the text]. Those sexual instincts which from the outset require an object, and the needs of the ego-instincts, which are never capable of auto-erotic satisfaction, naturally disturb this state [of primal narcissism] and so pave the way for an advance from it. Indeed, the primal narcissistic state would not be able to follow the development [that is to be described] if it were not for the fact that every individual passes through a period during which he is helpless and has to be looked after and during which his pressing needs are satisfied by an external agency and are thus prevented from becoming greater.—[This very condensed footnote might have been easier to understand if it had been placed two or three paragraphs further on. It may perhaps be expanded as follows. In

his paper on the 'Two Principles of Mental Functioning' (1911) Freud had introduced the idea of the transformation of an early 'pleasure-ego' into a 'reality-ego'. In the passage which follows in the text above, he argues that there is in fact a still earlier *original* 'reality-ego'. This original 'reality-ego', instead of proceeding directly into the *final* 'reality-ego', is replaced, under the dominating influence of the pleasure principle, by a 'pleasure-ego'. The footnote enumerates those factors, on the one hand, which would favour this latter turn of events, and those factors, on the other hand, which would work against it. The existence of auto-erotic libidinal instincts would encourage the diversion to a 'pleasure-ego', while the *non*-auto-erotic libidinal instincts and the self-preservative instincts would be likely instead to bring about a direct transition to the final adult 'reality-ego'. This latter result would, he remarks, in fact come about, if it were not that parental care of the helpless infant satisfies this second set of instincts, artificially prolongs the primary state of narcissism, and so helps to make the establishment of the 'pleasure-ego' possible.]

19. [On p. 96 Freud enumerates the opposites of loving in the following order: (1) hating, (2) being loved and (3) indifference. In the present passage, and below on pp. 98 and 100, he adopts a different order: (1) indifference, (2) hating and (3) being loved. It seems probable that in this second arrangement he gives indifference the first place as being the first to appear in the course of development.]

20. [This seems to be the first occasion on which Freud himself used the term.]

21. [The 'reality-ego' and the 'pleasure-ego' had already been introduced in the paper on the two principles of mental functioning (1911).]

22. [See note 19.]

23. [German *'Beziehungen'*, literally 'relations'. In the first edition this word is printed *'Bezeichnungen'*, 'descriptions' or 'terms'—which seems to make better sense. The word 'relations' in the later part of the sentence stands for *'Relationen'* in the German text.]

24. [Freud's first published account of the oral stage was given in a paragraph added to the third (1915) edition of his *Three Essays, Standard Ed.*, **7**, 198. The preface to that edition is dated 'October 1914'—some months before the present paper was written.]

25. [See 'The Disposition to Obsessional Neurosis' (1913).]

26. [See note 14.]

27. [See note 19.]

28. [The relation between love and hate was further discussed by Freud, in the light of his hypothesis of a death-instinct, in Chapter IV of *The Ego and the Id* (1923).]

6. Aggressiveness and Sadomasochism

Jean
~~Jacques~~ Laplanche

. . . .

Within Freud's thought and, more generally, within psychoanalytic practice as it developed before 1920 or even before 1915, it would be easy to make a list of those numerous places or moments in which "aggressive manifestations" may be observed: the oedipal complex, always described with both negative and positive components; love-hate ambivalence (in particular, in obsessional neurosis); negative manifestations in therapy (negative transference, resistance, etc.); sadomasochistic perversion; sadistic aspects of pregenital stages; etc. When Freud, in his role as historian of Freudian theory, retrospectively minimizes his appreciation of such phenomena before 1920, he is able to invoke two principal arguments: the absence of any *theoretical* recognition of an aggressive *drive* and, in addition, the failure to perceive the primacy of self-aggression over heteroaggression. That retrospective view—which is partially falsified, as is invariably the case when Freud turns toward a history of his own thought—can serve as a point of departure for our considerations.

The first argument, in any event, should not be overestimated. To be sure, before 1920, not only does the aggressive drive not appear,[1] but the term *aggressiveness* itself is practically absent. But nonrecognition of an aggressive drive does not necessarily mean neglect of the theory of aggressiveness, sadomasochism, and hatred: a theory which is explicitly developed, particularly in "Instincts and Their Vicissitudes" (1915). Similarly, we are somewhat astonished to see Freud categorizing under the same heading of "affective" resistance to the recognition of aggressiveness both his own thought before 1920 and the theory of those advocates of a fundamentally "good

Reprinted by permission of Johns Hopkins University Press, from *Life and Death in Psychoanalysis* by J. Laplanche, 1976.

human nature."[2] Such would seem to betray, if not an ignorance, at least an underestimation of a vast pessimistic tendency reigning both in Western philosophical and political thought and in Freud's own inspiration from their very beginnings.

And yet, the essential dimension of the affirmation of a death drive lies neither in the discovery of aggressiveness, nor in its theorization, nor even in the fact of hypostatizing it as a biological tendency or a metaphysical universal. It is in the idea that the aggressiveness is first of all directed against the subject and, as it were, stagnant within him, before being deflected toward the outside—"subject" here being understood at every level: the most elementary biological being, a protist or cell, as well as the multicellular biological organism, and, of course, the human individual both in his biological individuality and his "psychical life." Such is the thesis of "primary masochism," and there appears to be massive evidence leading us to suppose that that thesis is profoundly new, that it emerges only with the positing, in 1920, of the mythical being called the death drive. Nevertheless, without wishing to minimize the novelty of Freud's last theory of drives, we shall attempt to show precisely the tenuous but solid link binding it to the thesis evolved in 1915 from both clinical and dialectical considerations concerning the genesis of sadomasochism. That theory—which is implicit, no doubt imperfectly elaborated by Freud himself, and, above all, quickly covered over—entails, we believe, a double armature: the use of the notion of "propping" or anaclisis in the theory of sadomasochism, and the priority of the masochistic moment in the genesis of the sadomasochistic drive insofar as the latter is a sexual drive (and consequently a drive in the true sense of the Freudian *Trieb*).

If it is true that these two propositions can be rediscovered interlaced in the fabric of Freud's argument, but also that they are frequently eclipsed or hidden in it, it becomes appropriate, in order to bring them to light, to make use of a kind of index that alone gives them their relief: the distinction between the "sexual" and the "nonsexual." That distinction is explicitly posited by Freud in every text in which he studies sadomasochism: *Three Essays on the Theory of Sexuality,* already in its first edition, and in every one of its revisions; "Instincts and their Vicissitudes"; "The Economic Problem in Masochism" (1924); the *New Introductory Lectures* (1936); etc. But that opposition is not normally stabilized into an absolute terminological distinction: "sadism" and "masochism" are occasionally used, at a few lines' distance, at times to designate nonsexual violence, at others for an activity associated more or less narrowly with a sexual pleasure. A comparable "confusion" tends to reappear, even when Freud seems to want to restrict the terms of sadism and masochism to the aspect of violence that is sexualized. In such cases, he is occasionally obliged to endow the terms with a determination distinguishing them: he speaks of "sadism properly speaking" or "masochism properly speaking." At such moments, we are faced with a "terminological" problem that engages the thing itself: in our view, the slippage that Freud allows to occur within conceptual oppositions that he is perfectly aware of and that even serve as the guiding line in his argument *is nothing else than the slippage effected, within the genesis of the sexual drive, by the movement of anaclisis or propping.* But once that interaction of Freud's text and the terms it uses with the dialectic of what it describes is posited, we are obliged, as readers of Freud, in order better to control and detect the cases of slippage in operation, to force the text in the direction of a certain terminological stability: we shall consequently reserve the terms *sadistic (sadism)* and *masochistic (masochism)* for tendencies, activities, fantasies, etc., that necessarily involve, either consciously or unconsciously, an element of *sexual* excitement or enjoyment. In so doing, we shall distinguish them from the notion of aggressiveness (self- or heteroaggression), which will be considered as essentially nonsexual. This preliminary distinction in no way prejudges the actual existence of a nonsexual aggressiveness, and inversely, it does not invalidate a priori the proposition that behavior commonly called "sadistic" may, in fact, spring from nonsexual instinctual components.[3]

If, as we believe, the Freudian theory of "propping" should be used as the guiding scheme in understanding the problem of sadomasochism, it is important to recall briefly two major aspects of that theory: the marginal genesis of sexuality and the genesis of sexuality in a moment of turning round upon the self. On the one hand, indeed, propping implies that sexuality—the drive—emerges from nonsexual, instinctual activities: organ pleasure from functional pleasure. Every activity, modification of the organism, or perturbation is capable of becoming the source of a marginal effect, which is precisely the sexual excitation at the point at which that perturbation is produced. Propping is thus that leaning of nascent sexuality on nonsexual activities, but the *actual* emergence of sexuality is not yet there. Sexuality appears as a drive that can be isolated and observed only at the moment at which the nonsexual activity, the vital function, becomes detached from its natural object or loses it. For sexuality, it is the reflexive *(selbst* or *auto-)*

moment that is constitutive: the moment of a turning back towards self, an "autoerotism" in which the object has been replaced by a fantasy, by an object *reflected* within the subject.

If the theory of propping came to be relegated increasingly to a secondary role and even repressed, this is understandably even more the case for its application to the problem of masochism. And yet two of Freud's major texts, "Instincts and Their Vicissitudes" and "The Economic Problem in Masochism," clearly bear its imprint. Those two texts are separated by the turning point of 1920, but despite that separation, a quite remarkable convergence, perhaps unperceived by Freud himself, may be discovered between them. "Instincts and Their Vicissitudes" examines, as is known, fundamental modifications that can be studied as forming their own dialectic, within the drive itself, regardless of the fact that these "vicissitudes" may give rise to defense mechanisms. Concerning sadism and masochism, there are two contiguous "vicissitudes" that come into play: "reversal into the opposite, for example, would be the change in a drive from active to passive, or vice versa, which leads to the conception of a kind of complementarity between the two positions, just as one can move grammatically from an active to a passive proposition through a simple, reversible "transformation." The "turning round upon the subject," on the other hand, concerns the "object" of the drive, an object that can be exchanged and—though formerly external—become an internal object: the ego itself. Freud notes at the outset, however, that in the transition, sadism to masochism, the two vicissitudes are intimately interconnected and can be distinguished only abstractly.

Freud's text, in its great density, progresses like a spiral, presenting a whole series of approximations and schemes that do not invalidate each other but gradually come to complete the image of a common "genetic" structure. In addition, the scheme presented for the "pair of opposites" voyeurism-exhibitionism would also have to be considered, as Freud suggests. Before entering into some detail concerning Freud's *schemata,* we shall indicate what is at stake in the question. Historians of Freud's thought, and Freud himself, admit that after 1920, what is considered as the initial stage is the reflexive, masochistic moment: to make oneself suffer or to destroy oneself. It is from this "primary masochism" that—through "turning round"—both perverse sadism and masochism would be derived: to find someone else capable of making one suffer. Before 1920, on the contrary, and particularly in "Instincts and Their Vicissitudes," it would be the activity directed towards an external object—sadism—that would be first (destroy the other, make him suffer, aggress him), whereas masochism would only be the turning round of this initial attitude, a turning round that is, moreover, easily understandable in terms of obstacles encountered in the external world and, above all, of the guilt caused by aggression.

Now this turning round upon the self is not unknown to us within the vicissitudes of *sexuality in general,* since it is just such a process that constitutes the transition to autoerotism. But we know that within that autoerotic turning round, there is a kind of hiatus, deception, or slippage, whose result is that the *activity which turns round upon the subject is not the same one that was directed toward the external world* but a "derivative" of it (according to a complex movement of metaphorico-metonymical derivation). Thus, sexual activity breaks loose while turning round from a nonsexual activity directed towards a vital object. If, then, we would show that Freud's theory of sadomasochism conforms to the scheme of propping, it will be by bringing into focus:

(a) that the first active phase, directed towards an external object, is designated by Freud as sadistic in a manner that can only be regarded as improper, or by extension—since what is in question is a stage that is nonsexual—and is thus, properly speaking, aggressive or destructive;

(b) that sexuality emerges only with the turning round upon the self, thus with masochism, so that, within *the field of sexuality,* masochism is already considered as primary.

We shall present successively three schemes of derivation, or, as Freud would put it, three *vicissitudes:* a double turning round, active form-reflexive form-active form; a turning round with reversal into its opposite, active form-reflexive form-passive form; finally, a double symmetrical derivation, which, starting with the reflexive form, can result in the active as well as the passive form.

1. The central passage of the entire text is one which shows destructive activity turning round into masochism, and the latter again becoming the point of departure for sadistic activity.[4] But the text can be used only if we interpolate into it our own commentary and, through that commentary, the distinction, at every juncture, between what is nonsexual activity and what is linked to sexual pleasure. By means of that distinction (which merely follows Freud's quite clear indications), the passage finds its only possible interpretation in terms of the theory of "propping":

Our view of sadism is further prejudiced by the circumstance that this drive, side by side with its general aim (or perhaps, rather, within it), seems to strive towards the accomplishment of a quite special aim—

[Thus at the outset the problem of the dual nature and the dual aim of sadistic activity is posited.]

not only to humiliate and master . . .

[the aims of aggressiveness]

but, in addition, to inflict pains . . .

[a properly sexual aim, and consequently sadistic "properly speaking"]

Psychoanalysis would appear to show that the infliction of pain plays no part among the original purposive actions of the drive . . .

[Thus what is primary is an aggressiveness that is directed outward but not sexual. That instinct is the one that Freud calls the "instinct to master," or the tendency to make oneself the master of one's fellow being in order to achieve one's ends, but without that action—which could be characterized as entirely instrumental—implying any sexual pleasure in itself.]

A sadistic child takes no account of whether or not he inflicts pains, nor does he intend to do so . . .

[Here, we are obliged to substitute, for the "sadistic child," the "aggressive child." For the child is alleged to destroy what he finds in his path, without that destruction in itself being what is intended, nor for that matter the subjectivity of the other (i.e., his pain), and even less the pleasure discovered in the other's pain. It is of little concern to us, moreover, whether this description of the child, as a simple force of nature, seeking to accomplish its aims and breaking everything in its way, is the description of an actual— however fleeting—stage, or the positing of an ideal moment: in any event, what is presented is an ideal genesis.]

But when once the transformation into masochism has taken place . . .

[Thus the turning round of the aggressiveness onto the self; but here "masochism" is taken in its literal sense, at once sexual and nonsexual.]

the pains are very well fitted to provide a passive masochistic aim; for we have every reason to believe that sensations of pain, like other unpleasurable sensations . . .

[It will be seen that Freud distinguishes clearly, within the general domain of unpleasure, the quite specific phenomenon of pain, and that it is *pain that is linked to the essence of masochism.*]

trench upon sexual excitation and produce a pleasurable condition, for the sake of which the subject will even willingly experience the unpleasure of pain . . .

[Thus pain is a perturbation like any other perturbation; like all those which Freud had already begun listing in the *Three Essays,* it can be an "indirect source of sexuality," in the same way as, for example, physical exercise or intellectual effort. The idea of "trenching" upon the domain of sexual excitation effectively evokes the "marginal" character of this production of pleasure.]

When once feeling pains has become a masochistic aim, the sadistic aim of *causing* pains can arise also, retrogressively . . .

[This time, we should read: "sadistic, properly speaking," in the sexual sense, since what is being considered is the emergence of a new aim that did not exist in the initial active phase of pure destructiveness.]

for while these pains are being inflicted on other people, they are enjoyed masochistically by the subject through his identification of himself with the suffering object . . .

[Thus, whether what is under discussion is fantasy or sexuality, in both cases the masochistic moment is first. The masochistic fantasy is fundamental, whereas the sadistic fantasy implies an identification with the suffering object; it is within the suffering position that the enjoyment lies.]

In both cases, of course, it is not the pain itself which is enjoyed, but the accompanying sexual excitation—so that this can be done especially conveniently from the sadistic position.

[Here Freud is attempting to elude the difficulty of "enjoying pain" by displacing the problem; but the formula "enjoying the excitation" leads to the same impasse, at least if it is considered from the "economic" point of view. We shall return to this question later.]

The enjoyment of pain . . .

["In both cases," thus one's own pain as well as the other's pain.]

would thus be an aim which was originally masochistic . . .

[And there we have the whole of "primary" masochism.]

but which can only become the aim of a drive . . .

[To become a drive in the proper sense of the term is to become sexuality.] in someone who was originally sadistic.

[Unless we are prepared to eliminate every possible interpretation of this passage, we shall have to resolve to redefine "sadistic" once again as "aggressive": the sadomasochistic sexual drive, the enjoyment of pain, has its origin in the masochistic phase, but on the basis of a turning round of a primary heteroaggressiveness.]

In the same spirit as Freud's in the text under discussion, we shall schematize below this first vicissitude with its double turning-around:

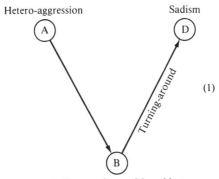

2. A second scheme is presented which, through various slight alterations, is interesting in its specification of the transition from sadism to masochism. The latter, on this occasion, is presented to us in two different aspects: "what is commonly termed masochism," which implies passivity towards an extraneous subject; and an intermediate stage in which "there is a turning round upon the subject's self *without* an attitude of passivity towards another person."[5] The three stages are thus:

(a) "The exercise of violence or power upon some other person as its object," an activity that Freud terms sadism, but in which, it is specified, sexuality does not enter into play.

(b) A turning around upon the self: "The active voice is changed, not into the passive, but into the reflexive, middle voice."[6] This is self-inflicted torment, which is not yet true masochism.

(c) Passive masochism, in which the active aim is transformed into a passive aim, which implies the search for another person as "object" (object of the drive, but subject of the action).

The first appearance of the sexual component, through propping, is linked to the turning round of the aggressiveness into self-aggression, so that it is always the reflexive "self-" phase to which the emergence of sexuality corresponds. We should note as well that during this reflexive phase the object is lost and is regained only in the fantasmatic doubling (in phase *b*) and then in the search in phase *c* in which the inversion of active and passive roles intervenes.[7]

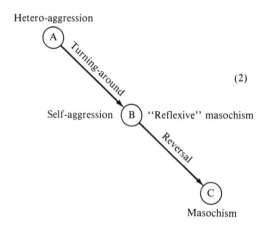

Hetero-aggression

Self-aggression ("Reflexive" masochism)

(2)

Masochism

3. Finally, a third and rather different model is presented concerning the vicissitudes of the "scopophilic drive." At stake is the genesis from the middle or reflexive position of the two active and passive positions. What one finds is not a reversal, but a kind of primary position, constituted by the "autoerotic" phase. The active position would result from the search in the external world for an extraneous object capable of being substituted for the original object, whereas the passive position would have an extraneous person substituted for the subject himself.

We reproduce this scheme below, first in its application to the scopophilic drive:

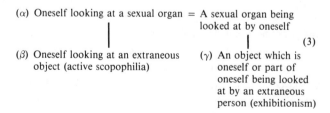

(α) Oneself looking at a sexual organ = A sexual organ being looked at by oneself

(3)

(β) Oneself looking at an extraneous object (active scopophilia)

(γ) An object which is oneself or part of oneself being looked at by an extraneous person (exhibitionism) and then transposed into more abstract terms:

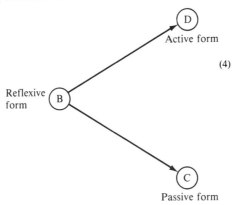

(4)

What should be observed is that Freud envisages the possibility of applying such a scheme to the case of sadomasochism, i.e., to derive from it the active and passive forms of a primally reflexive position. No doubt he explicitly dismisses this possibility, although conceding that "it might not be altogether unreasonable."[8] This scheme indeed *seems* to him to be in contradiction with the previously affirmed priority of heteroaggression. In the choice between a priority of the active relation to the object and a priority of the reflexive or "self-" phase, we rediscover a familiar debate that we have already evoked: is what is first a reflexive, objectless state closed in upon itself, as our last diagram seems to indicate, or, on the contrary, a would-be primary relation to the object? Now, our entire interpretation has tended to show that this is a false debate, and that the two statements are quite reconcilable, to the extent that they are not located on the same level: Diagrams 3 and 4, which derive everything from a primal reflexive phase, are located entirely on the level of sexuality: in the problem of the scopophilic drive, already in reflexive phase α, what is in question is "looking at a *sexual organ*" or "a *sexual organ's* being looked at." On the contrary, in the sequences moving from the active form to the reflexive form and from there either again to activity (Diagram 1) or to passivity (Diagram 2), we progressed from an initial stage which was, strictly speaking, nonsexual, since sexuality emerged only in the second stage. All of this might be expressed by saying that the transition from A to B is located in the *genesis* of sexuality, whereas the subsequent transformations, starting from B, represent the *vicissitudes* of sexuality.

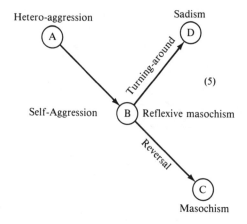

We have consequently taken the liberty of combining and even superimposing the various diagrams suggested by Freud's successive analyses, first by situating them on the same level, as in Diagram 5, then in a three-dimensional model intended to bring into relief the existence of two different surfaces—self-preservation and sexuality—and to bring into play the process of propping as the line at which the two surfaces intersect (see Diagram 6).

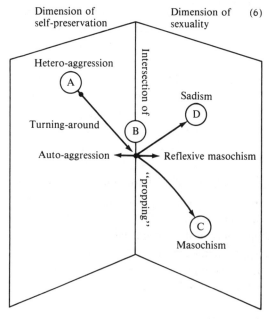

Such a diagram reveals clearly just how the problem of primary masochism is posed by Freud, and how the hesitations he proliferates—and eagerly bears witness to, for instance in the notes appended after 1920 to the text of "Instincts and Their Vicissitudes"—lag considerably behind what had already (and from the outset) been evolved in his thinking on sexuality, an idea that did not and will not vary, whatever form is taken by the notion of (nonsexual) aggressiveness.

The counter-proof of our interpretation might be found in a text of Freud's that takes up the same question: "The Economic Problem in Masochism."

We are in 1924. The great metabiological opposition of death drives and life drives constitutes from this point on the basis for any Freudian consideration concerning a problem of origins. At the beginning, the unsurpassable presence of two great opposing forces, at work from the start within, must be postulated. It is therefore all the more striking to note that this metaphysical postulation does not prevent Freud from beginning his consideration of *erotogenic masochism* by recalling the first thesis concerning the emergence of sexual excitation:

In my *Three Essays on the Theory of Sexuality,* in the section on the sources of infantile sexuality, I put forward the proposition that sexual excitation arises as an accessory effect of a large series of internal processes as soon as the intensity of these processes has exceeded certain quantitative limits; indeed that perhaps nothing very important takes place within the organism without contributing a component to the excitation of the sexual drive. According to this, an excitation of physical pain and feelings of distress would surely also have this effect.[9]

It is this "libidinal sympathetic excitation" that would provide the physiological foundation of erotogenic masochism.

The reader will recognize in the notion of *sympathetic excitation (Miterregung)* the exact counterpart of the "marginal action" or "marginal gain" by which Freud very early defined "organ pleasure" in relation to the functional pleasure in which it takes support. No doubt this explanation is considered "insufficient," and Freud will immediately refer to the great ontological struggle between destruction and libido. And yet, if it is true that "we never have to deal with pure life-drives and death-drives at all, but only with combinations of them in different degrees,"[10] it is indeed one of those alloys, "primary erotogenic masochism," that is first for us, and this erotogenic masochism emerges through the phenomenon of "sympathetic excitation": "Another part [of the death or destructive drive] is not included in this displacement outwards; it remains within the organism and *is 'bound' there libidinally with the help of the accompanying [sympathetic] sexual excitation mentioned above:* this we must recognize as the original erotogenic masochism."[11]

No doubt the fruitful notion of propping will gradually be replaced by the more abstract and mechanical notion of fusion and defusion *(Mischung/ Entmischung)* or by the all too convenient commonplace of "erotization." The crucial point, however, is that its place remains staked out at the same spot in the development of the drive: in the stage in which self-aggression is transformed, in place, into reflexive masochism.

We shall soon have to inquire into the thesis that such self-aggression, for its part, is an original datum and not the result of a turning round. But at present we are following a different line of thought that is closer to Freud's first intuitions concerning sexuality. Those intuitions posited autoerotism as a second stage, following a turning round or a brushing back of a self-preservative activity that was initially directed outwards. Now, if the genesis of reflexive masochism is to be understood as a turning round upon the self, that turning round must still be examined, for it is proposed to us in two different senses: first of all, self-aggression can be conceived of as an actual or even physiological process: domination or conquest of oneself. Freud proposes that general direction by evoking, in "Instincts and Their Vicissitudes," the virtual existence of a reflexive phase from which would emerge both sadism and passive masochism: "It might not be altogether unreasonable to construct such a [preliminary] stage out of the child's efforts to gain control over his own limbs."[12]

The other possible meaning of this turning round would be, to all appearances, quite different, since it would entail an internalization of the whole of the action on the psychical level, a process of an entirely different order from a real activity (e.g., of the muscles), since what would be implied would be a fantasmatization. And yet in the general description of autoerotism, these two types of internalization were already encountered: the withdrawal to an erogenous zone and brushing back into fantasy. These two modalities would seem not to be reducible to each other: one could be described in terms of sheer behavior or physiology; the other implies the dimension of "interiority." *Introjecting the suffering object, fantasizing the suffering object, making the object suffer inside oneself, making oneself suffer:* these are four rather different formulations, but our practice shows the subject constantly moving from one to the other. An author like Melanie Klein takes seriously (as well one should) the apparent absurdity of those equivalences and of that movement, entailing a mode of thought that would adhere with maximal fidelity to the experience of psychoanalysis—without introducing into it a logic of the excluded middle—and would posit the identity of the internalized object and the fantasy of the object.[13] But in that case, we are obliged to admit that a fantasy, the introjection of the object, is a perturbation and, in its essence (whether its "content" be pleasant or unpleasant), a generator of autoerotic excitation.[14] Similarly, as an effraction, the fantasy is the first psychical pain[15] and is thus intimately related, in its origin, to the emergence of the masochistic sexual drive.

In order to illustrate this process of a "turning back into fantasy," we should like to evoke the analysis undertaken by Freud, in "A Child Is Being Beaten" (1919), of the genesis of a sadomasochistic fantasy. It turns out to be a veritable clinical confirmation of "Instincts and Their Vicissitudes," since in it we follow the development of a drive through the dialectic binding the successive versions of the ideational representatives or fantasy to which the drive is attached. We encounter the vicissitudes of the drive, or perhaps even its genesis, if the distinction proposed earlier is accepted.

We shall recall the three phases of the evolution of the beating fantasy, as Freud describes them in women and more specifically in neurotic (mostly obsessional) women:

1. My father is beating the child whom I hate.
2. I am being beaten by my father.
3. A child is being beaten.

The third phase corresponds to a symptom that is confessed, not without difficulty, in the course of the analysis. For convenience of exposition it can itself be analyzed into the following two aspects: on the one hand, its accompaniment in "affect" and "discharge," and, on the other, its ideational content. The two manifestations regularly accompanying the evocation of the fantasy are an intense sexual excitation, almost always leading to masturbatory gratification, and a violent feeling of guilt, apparently related to the masturbation but, more profoundly, to the ideas evoked. As for the "fantasmatic representation" itself, it entails an imagined scene according to a relatively unchanging scenario, none of which prevents each of the three terms (beater/beaten/the action) from being relatively undetermined or variable, borrowed as each is from an undefined series of possible paradigms. As in the case of every fantasy, it should be emphasized, we are dealing with an imagined scene, particularly in its visual aspect. The sentence "A child is being beaten" is the way in which that scene is transposed by the subject in the discourse of therapy, and by Freud himself in his presentation. And yet that transcription into the language of words has the merit of bringing to light the grammar of the fantasy itself, and, in what follows, Freud's analysis will be based (just as in "Instincts and Their Vicissitudes") essentially on the successive modifications of the utterance of the fantasy.

"A child is being beaten": the intentional indeterminacy of the proposition manifests the neutrality that the patient would maintain in relation to the elements of the scene: "The figure of the child who is producing the beating-fantasy no longer itself appears in it. In reply to pressing inquiries patients only declare: 'I am probably looking on.' "[16] It may be noted, moreover, that the French translation, "On bat un enfant," inverts the position of the subject and object in relation to the German formula: "Ein Kind wird geschlagen." We note this, not in order to point out an imprecision in translation, but, on the contrary, to indicate that at this stage of the fantasy, there is an indeterminacy or in any event a reversibility between the active and passive formulations:

One beating child = child being beaten by one.

Inevitably, one thinks here of the equation proposed by Freud in order to translate what he called the reflexive stage of the scopophilic fantasy.[17]

The series of three formulations recalled here is presented by Freud as a chronological sequence. The first two phases, unlike the third, have to be rediscovered in the course of the work of analysis. But at this point a fundamental difference appears between phases 1 and 2: phase 1 may be remembered in the course of the analysis; phase 2, on the contrary, has to be reconstructed: "This second phase is the most important and the most momentous of all. But we may say of it in a certain sense that it has never had a real existence. It is never remembered, it has never succeeded in becoming conscious. It is a construction of analysis, but it is no less a necessity on that account."[18]

It is precisely on the difference in nature between phases 1 and 2 and on the transition between the two that we shall insist in order to reveal clearly in them the process of a turning back into autoerotism:

Phase 1 corresponds to one or several real scenes, in the course of which the child may have actually seen her father mistreat a little brother or sister: "One may hesitate to say whether the characteristics of a 'fantasy' can yet be ascribed to this first step towards the later beating-fantasy. It is perhaps rather a question of recollections of events which have been witnessed, or of desires which have arisen on various occasions."[19] As opposed to this, phase 2 is entirely fantasmatic; it is the first phase of the fantasy properly speaking, a point which Freud underlines by designating as the "original fantasy" *(ursprüngliche Phantasie)* the scenario "I am being beaten by my father."[20]

Phase 1 is consciously remembered, rediscovered through an investigative effort pursued in common by Freud and his patient. We may, in fact, doubt that it was ever truly repressed. As opposed to this, phase 2 is profoundly interred in the unconscious and generally inaccessible.

Finally, the first phase is barely sexual, or rather, to take up a term already used in the context of the "seduction theory," it is "sexual-presexual." If we accept a terminological distinction advanced above, its bearing is aggressive and not, properly speaking, sadistic:

Doubt remains, therefore, whether the fantasy ought to be described as purely "sexual," nor can one venture to call it "sadistic." . . . So perhaps we may say in terms recalling the prophecy made by the Three Witches to Banquo: "Not clearly sexual, not in itself sadistic, but yet the stuff from which both will later come." In any case, however, there is no ground for suspecting that in this first phase the fantasy is already at the service of an excitation which involves the genitals and finds its outlet in a masturbatory act.[21]

As opposed to this, the unconscious fantasy "I am being beaten by my father" is masochistic in the proper sense of the word: it expresses in "regressive" form the fantasy of sexual pleasure obtained from the father. The presence of sexual excitation already in phase 2 is attested to for Freud by the fact that certain patients "say that with them masturbation made its appearance before the third phase," which "inclines one to assume that the masturbation was at first under the dominance of unconscious fantasies and that conscious ones were substituted for them later."[22]

It may be seen that it is in the transition to phase 2 that *the fantasy, the unconscious,* and *sexuality* in the form of *masochistic excitation* together emerge in a single movement. In addition, in the fantasmatic *content,* the transition from phase 1 to phase 2, entailing a "turning round upon the subject," encourages us to recall the diagram of the *genesis* of the sadomasochistic drive:

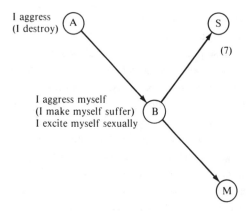

and then to inscribe in it the Freudian statements:

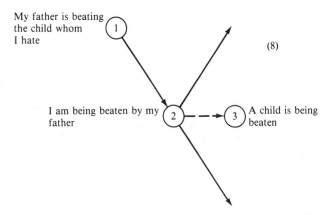

To be sure, the application of the general model to the case of the beating-fantasy cannot be purely mechanical. There remain discordances and discrepancies; but these, far from being totally irreducible, turn out to be fruitful for further considerations.

1. In phase A, characterized as heteroaggressive, it was *ego* (the individual in question) that was the subject of the action. In "A Child Is Being Beaten," in 1, it is "my father" who is doing the beating.

This difference does not seem essential to us. Ego wants to destroy the person in his way, the obstacle to his "self-preservation," and it matters little, at this precise level, whether he does it directly or through another person. Between father and ego, there is a kind of implicit transitivism, which should be distinguished scrupulously, moreover, from a fantasmatic introjection.

The important point is that the essential aspect of the action is situated on the level of vital or "egoistic" interests: "The fantasy [in its first phase] obviously gratifies the child's jealousy and is dependent upon the erotic side of his life, but is also powerfully reinforced by the child's egoistic interests."[23]

2. But we proceed only further into paradox by insisting on the aggressive, nonsexual aspect of the first phase; what is considered as presexual, linked to self-preservation and the "egoistic" tendencies is what Freud openly designates as the parental complex or the oedipus complex! In a purely chronological interpretation, we would arrive at the following absurdity: far from its being the case that the oedipal comes from sexuality, it would be sexuality which comes from the oedipal, which would itself allegedly take place on an initially presexual level, that of self-preservation or of "tenderness." The notion of a regression to the anal-sadistic stage, invoked in this text by Freud in order to account for sexualization, would only reinforce the absurdity if we limited ourselves to a purely linear chronology: the nonsexual oedipus complex would take on its sexual meaning through regression to an earlier stage of the libido.

An extended discussion of this question would necessitate a highly complex ordering of the different modes of temporality with which we deal in psychoanalysis, and would go beyond the limits of our inquiry. What is important for us, in the present paradox, is to emphasize that the so-called sequence of *propping* functions according to a temporality that it is impossible to superimpose on any other (that of sexual stages or that of the structuring of the object or Oedipus); newly formed sexuality seems able to take as its point of departure *absolute anything:* the vital functions, to be sure, but also, ultimately, the "oedipal" relation itself in its entirety, taken as a natural relation with a function of preservation and survival.

Moreover, what confirms this interpretation is that the oedipal complex is approached by Freud obliquely in this context, from a particular angle: from the point of view of drives, what is in the foreground is not the erotic relation, but the relation of "tenderness"; but above all, in the structure, the triangle under consideration is not the oedipal one: ego (little girl)-father-mother, but the triangle of rivalry, called in other circumstances the "fraternal complex": ego-parents-brother or sister.[24]

3. This clinical example afforded Freud the opportunity to examine the problem of repression from various points of view: the relation of repression to regression, the relation of repression to sexual role, masculine or feminine, and so on. We shall simply add a remark intended to render explicit the

identity of the *object* on which repression bears: it is essentially on the second phase, or on the fantasy at its emergence. It is, nevertheless, quite common to speak of repressed childhood memories, and not without clinical basis. In fact though, *what is repressed is not the memory but the fantasy derived from it or subtending it:* in this case, not the actual scene in which the father would have beaten another child, but the fantasy of being beaten by father. And yet it is clear that the repression of the fantasy can drag along with it into the unconscious the memory itself, a memory which after the event *[après-coup]* takes on a sexual meaning: "My father is beating another child—he loves me (sexually)." Just as the object to be refound is not the lost object, but its metonym, so the "scene" is not that of the memory, but that of the sexual fantasy derived from it.

4. Finally, we have situated, in the position of what we called reflexive masochism, or the middle voice, a fantasy which, however, has a properly masochistic content in the "passive" sense: I am being beaten by my father. But that is because, as we have emphasized, the process of turning-around is not to be thought of only at the level of the content of the fantasy, but *in the very movement of fantasmatization.* To shift to the reflexive is not only or even necessarily to give a reflexive content to the "sentence" of the fantasy; it is also and above all to reflect the action, internalize it, make it enter into oneself as fantasy. To fantasize aggression is to turn it around upon oneself, to aggress oneself: such is the moment of autoerotism, in which the indissoluble bond between fantasy as such, sexuality, and the unconscious is confirmed.

If we press that idea to its necessary conclusion, we are led to emphasize the privileged character of masochism in human sexuality. The analysis, in its very content, of an essential fantasy—the "primal scene"—would illustrate it as well: the child, impotent in his crib, is Ulysses tied to the mast or Tantalus, on whom is imposed the spectacle of parental intercourse. Corresponding to the perturbation of pain is the "sympathetic excitation" which can only be translated regressively through the emission of feces: the passive position of the child in relation to the adult is not simply a passivity in relation to adult activity, but passivity in relation to the adult fantasy intruding within him.[25]

NOTES

1. Except as an object of criticism when Adler proposes it.
2. *New Introductory Lectures on Psychoanalysis,* in *SE,* 22:104.
3. Our usage here differs from that of Melanie Klein, for whom "sadism" is purely and simply a synonym of aggressiveness or destructiveness. With her too there is a slippage of meaning, but the movement is from the sexual sense to the nonsexual sense, and in addition, there is no retention of that first meaning nor of the transition itself. There has simply been a change of meaning, a desexualization of sadism.
4. *SE,* 14:128.
5. "Instincts and Their Vicissitudes," p. 128.
6. Ibid.
7. The connection established by Freud between the instinctual—or better, drive—"vicissitudes" *(Triebschicksale),* on the one hand, and grammatical transformations, on the other, while remarkably innovative and intriguing is somewhat clouded by a certain confusion. Thus Freud confuses the "middle" and "reflexive" voices. And yet there is every reason to distinguish the middle from the reflexive form within the structure of fantasy, just as they are quite distinct grammatically and semantically, even if the *form of their expression* is occasionally identical. Thus the expression *se cogner* ("to knock [oneself]") corresponds both to the middle form (*En marchant dans l'obscurité, je me suis cogné à la table,* "Walking in the dark, I knocked [myself] into the table") and to the reflexive form (*Je me cogne la tête contre les murs,* "I knock [myself] my head against the walls"). The reflexive form distinguishes more clearly the subject and the object of the action, allowing the fantasied exchanges of position to take place. In the "middle" form, the terms of the fantasy remain in something of a state of coalescence.
8. "Instincts and Their Vicissitudes," p. 130.
9. "The Economic Problem of Masochism," in *SE,* 19:163.
10. Ibid., p. 164.
11. Ibid. Emphasis added.
12. "Instincts and Their Vicissitudes," p. 130.
13. There is an absolute realism of the thought process; thought is in the body, in the head, and is an internal object—which is to say that in a certain sense, there is no "scientific psychology" based on psychoanalysis.
14. "The dream *is* the fulfillment of a wish"; "the hallucination *is* a satisfaction"—these theses, which are central to psychoanalysis, defy every experimental observation. Freud, moreover, has a certain difficulty in fending off the objection that would admit that dreams express intentions and meanings, but would refuse the notions that those meanings are solely wishes or desires. For indeed, why not include as well hope, fear, resignation, regret, etc.? In order to justify Freud's a priori position (beyond any verification, which would always be suspect), we would have to admit that the fantasy *is in itself* a sexual perturbation.
15. We speak here of a "first pain" as Freud, in the *Project,* speaks of a "first hysterical lie or deceit." The two models are connected in an essential way.
16. "A Child Is Being Beaten," in *SE,* 17:186.
17. See p. 94.
18. *SE,* 12:185.
19. Ibid.

20. Ibid., p. 199.
21. Ibid., p. 187.
22. Ibid., p. 190.
23. Ibid., p. 187.
24. We are not, of course, suggesting that this triangle of rivalry is chronologically "prior" to the "sexual" triangle of the oedipus complex.
25. Where shall we situate the third stage of the fantasy "A child is being beaten"? Freud himself hesitated to qualify it as either sadistic or masochistic and finally concluded that "only the *form* of this fantasy is sadistic; the satisfaction which is derived from it is masochistic." *SE,* 17:191.

   The question strikes us as somewhat formalistic to the extent that we, along with Freud, would affirm "the regular and close connections of masochism with its counterpart in instinctual life, sadism." "The Economic Problem of Masochism," p. 163. That complementarity, authorizing us to retain the concept of "sadomasochism," has nothing to do, it should be emphasized, with an actual complementarity between the sadistic and masochistic *perversions,* nor with the possibility of an actual transition from one to the other (through a "turning-around," for example). Perversion always presupposes the fixation of *ego* at one of the poles of the fantasy. The diagram we have extracted from "Instincts and Their Vicissitudes" (Diagram 7) shows in its simplicity that there can be no direct transition from position S to position M, even though they both stem from a common "primal fantasy."

   But in that case, the conscious fantasy "a child is being beaten" should be considered neither sadistic nor masochistic *in the sense of a perversion.* As a sadomasochistic fantasy, it is part of "reflexive masochism," which can also be considered as "reflexive sadism." In "Instincts and Their Vicissitudes" Freud treats "reflexive" masochism as a characteristic of obsessional *neurosis,* and it is not by chance that the patients Freud refers to in "A Child Is Being Beaten" present symptoms which are predominantly obsessional. Thus "Ein Kind wird geschlagen = a child is being beaten" is a neutralized, neurotic, conscious derivative of the primal reflexive fantasy.

7. Pain, Aggression, Fantasy, and Concepts of Sadomasochism

William I. Grossman

Traumatized infants and children may exhibit syndromes of aggressive, pain-seeking, and self-destructive behavior resembling the so-called sadomasochism seen in adults. Three hypotheses are offered to account for the repetition of sadomasochistic phenomena in childhood and later character disorders: 1) pain and painful affects are sources of aggression; 2) the need to control aggression plays an important role in the development of psychic structure; 3) child abuse and trauma impair the ability to use fantasy for the mastery of impulses. Difficulty in expression and control of aggression are central issues in character disorders.

. . . children have become the main subject of psychoanalytic research and have thus replaced in importance the neurotics on whom its studies began. Analysis has shown how the child lives on, almost unchanged, in the sick man as well as in the dreamer and the artist; it has thrown light on the motive forces and trends which set its characteristic stamp upon the childish nature. . . .

—Freud (1925, p. 273)

INTRODUCTION

There is a growing consensus among psychoanalysts that there are many combinations of pleasure and pain, or unpleasure, in fantasy and behavior, which can be labeled "sadomasochism," and that there is a variety of developmental routes to these syndromes (Grossman, 1986b; Kernberg, 1988a;

Reprinted by permission of the author and *The Psychoanalytic Quarterly* 60 (1991):22–52.

Maleson, 1984; Novick and Novick, 1987; Panel, 1988). Only the obligatory combination of something pleasurable with something unpleasant, particularly the seeking of sexual excitement and satisfaction in pain or humiliation, characterizes all the traits, symptoms, and behavior referred to as sadism and masochism. This wide spectrum of phenomena includes self-injury in infancy, perversions and perverse fantasies, and unconsciously motivated behavior that leads to apparently accidental suffering and "bad luck." It has become clear that there is no single, well-defined entity, syndrome, disease, or pathogenic agent that lies at the core of all the neurotic, characterologic, psychotic, and perverse behavior that we call "sadomasochistic."

One sense in which the meaning of the term sadomasochism seems to be specific is the simple descriptive sense of a conscious or unconscious fantasy that is similar to sadistic or masochistic perversions, which are the behavioral enactment of fantasies (Grossman, 1986b). The deliberate pursuit of manifestly aggressive, destructive, and self-destructive behavior is also frequently called sadomasochism (regarding usage, see Maleson [1984]). This loosely descriptive, nontechnical usage of the term "sadomasochism" is followed in this paper, because the papers referred to here use the term with varying meanings.

It might be more correct to speak of "the sadomasochisms" in the same way that we speak of the depressions and Bleuler spoke of the schizophrenias. These terms imply some common surface characteristics, possibly with some interrelated etiological features. The idea of different interruptions of some common pathways to behavioral expression might also come to mind — the idea of sadomasochistic fantasies as a "final common path." However, sadomasochistic fantasies vary greatly in their content; the differences have been linked to different kinds of integration of ego and object relations (Kernberg, 1988a, 1988b).

Are there factors underlying sadomasochism(s) that might be thought to provide a foundation for the linkage of pleasure and pain throughout life? Freud's (1924) idea of "erotogenic masochism" suggests this possibility, as do formulations involving underlying physiological functions that join sexual pleasure and pain. There is evidence supporting the view that mechanisms leading to the association of pleasure with painful experience are present in everyone (Solomon, 1980), although organized and expressed differently in different people. In addition, the rapidly growing literature on the early and late sequelae of trauma and child abuse documents the accompanying disturbance of physiological, affective, cognitive, and memory functions relevant to an understanding of sadomasochism.

From our clinical, psychoanalytic perspective, an examination of the development of the drives, ego, and object relations provides a view of the way diverse kinds of experiences, affects, appetites, and satisfactions can be joined as a result of conflict resolution and patterned experiences with important figures in a person's life. The search for the sources and precursors of "sadomasochism" has brought to light important phenomena of infancy and childhood associated with childhood illness and child abuse. To be comprehensive, formulations of the origins of sadomasochism would have to account in some measure for the sadomasochistic phenomena occurring in the wake of trauma both in childhood and in adult life.

As data have accumulated from many sources, it has become clear that there is no satisfactory conceptualization that is general enough to unify the entire range of observations while retaining a psychodynamic orientation. At one extreme, there are data from child observations of the apparently preconflictual automatic repetitions of destructive and self-injurious behavior in infancy. Analogues of these phenomena occur in some of the symptoms of the post-traumatic disorders of adults. On the other hand, there are the clinical formulations concerning the self-destructiveness associated with unconscious guilt (Freud, 1924) and "entrenched suffering" (Schafer, 1984) in adults.

The purpose of this paper is to consider the range of so-called sadomasochistic phenomena, and to sketch a model that takes into account diverse observations from clinical psychoanalysis, infant observation, the study of abused children, and traumatic experiences of adults. Such an integrative formulation—to be something other than a reconstruction of early infantile fantasies—would have to begin to bridge the conceptual divide between the mental life of early childhood and the complex mental structures of neurotic adults and adults with perversions and severe character disorders. In addition, it would have to find a place for new discoveries about the physiological effects of trauma and their role in the mechanisms of repetition. However, as has always been the case in psychoanalysis, the aim is to find a psychological conceptualization that will lead to an understanding of the role of mental conflict in these problems. I shall offer formulations from the viewpoint of pain, aggression, the capacity for fantasy, and object relations.

THREE HYPOTHESES ON FANTASY, AGGRESSION, AND PAIN IN SADOMASOCHISM

For the beginning of a psychoanalytic framework for the exploration of what is loosely called sadomasochism, I suggest three basic hypotheses.

The first hypothesis is that mental organization (or structure) acquires some of its most important characteristics as the child learns to express and regulate aggression. As this occurs, the development of (unconscious) defenses against aggression contributes to both ego and superego formation. A corollary is that disturbances in the resolution of conflicts related to aggression may lead to distortions of ego and superego development and to stereotyped repetition of aggressive behavior.

The second hypothesis is that pain and painful affects are "sources" of aggression. This idea involves a number of complex theoretical questions, not the least of which are the reasons for employing the idea of an aggressive drive and the relationship of drives and affects. Consideration of these issues would lead in other directions than those to be explored here. The essential point for this discussion is that bodily experiences are a "source" for an aggressive drive in the same way that libido has a "source" in bodily experiences. The word "source" in these instances refers to the somatic locus to which personal experience assigns the sensations associated with sexual and aggressive arousal. From this viewpoint, the aggressive and sexual drives are more similar than they are usually considered to be.

The third hypothesis is that the psychological effects of trauma, whether in infancy or adult life, are best understood in connection with the development and functioning of the capacity to fantasize. Fantasy formation is an important and complex function that both contributes to and is dependent on ego integration. I suggest that to the extent that fantasy formation is possible, some transformation and mastery of traumatic experience is possible. Severe trauma impairs the capacity for fantasy (Fish-Murray et al., 1987), leading to a failure to transform the traumatic experience through mental activity. Instead, repetitive behavior and intrusive imagery that repeat or attempt to undo the traumatic experience are possible consequences. In addition, or alternatively, inhibitions, avoidances, and withdrawal may be attempts to avoid painful, repeated occurrences of a traumatic state. Repetitions in fantasy may contribute to the mastery of trauma, a function ascribed by Freud (1920) to the traumatic dream.[1]

These formulations diminish our interest in questions about the "nature," "essence," and "origins" of sadomasochism. The problems of sadomasochism are more usefully conceptualized as the problems of the development and management of aggression in relation to psychosexual attachments and the development of psychic structure. If this is so, we need to consider, in terms that are also relevant to the formulation of later intrapsychic processes, the ways in which traumatic experiences contribute to the development of aggressive impulses and their transformations.

The development, expression, and regulation of affects are factors whose importance for understanding trauma and its effects have long been recognized by analysts (see Krystal, 1978). Because of this, I shall mention them only in passing. My purpose is not to minimize or neglect these important issues, but rather to contribute to a psychological conceptualization of the way such factors are expressed in the mental life as we study it clinically in psychoanalysis.

TWO SCHEMAS OF OBJECT RELATIONS AND SADOMASOCHISM IN INFANCY

The considerations outlined above were first presented in response to observations reported at meetings of the American Psychoanalytic Association in a Workshop on the Vulnerable Child in 1983 and in a Panel on Sadomasochism in Children (Panel, 1985; Grossman, 1986a).[2] Reports that contributed to these ideas included observations on premature infants who had been subjected to procedures that, although they were lifesaving, were also painful; observations of family interactions between children and parents in which abusive parental behavior could be seen; observations of play by children whose histories were known to have involved abuse, sometimes of a sexual kind; therapy with children and families in which child abuse had occurred (Galenson, 1983, 1986, 1988; Glenn, 1978, 1984; Herzog, 1983, and in Panel, 1985; Panel, 1985; Ruttenberg, in Workshop, 1983). Some psychoanalytic data from child and adolescent analyses were reported as well.

In all of these cases, the traumatized children had also become, in some fashion, provokers of attacks on themselves and attackers of others. Some longitudinal studies correlating trauma in childhood with aggressive behavior were also presented. The cases were dramatic and at times startling in their documentation of the fact that from early infancy on, there is a capacity to respond to traumatic treatment with destructive and self-destructive behavior.

The phase-specific conflicts occurring in connection with feeding, toileting, birth of siblings, and sexual activities have long been known as possible origins of common traumatic experiences. In addition, an overview of data on children severely traumatized in other ways suggests two broad developmental constellations, each having a different significance for the development of sadomasochistic syndromes. In one type, events external to the child's relations with its caretaker require management of a painful or traumatic situation by the caretaker, and psychological mastery of the experience by the child. In these cases, the pain or trauma organizes the object relations.

The second constellation consists of situations in which the object relations were the source of the pain, whether mental or somatic. While in the first constellation, the relations between parent and child are shaped by outside forces, in the second group, something in the relationship between the participants is the source of pain or painful affects—fear, disappointment, dejection, and so on—for the child.

The most dramatic example of the first constellation is the "neonatal pain syndrome" described by Herzog (1983), who has written extensively on the subject of abuse and trauma in infancy and childhood. The neonatal pain syndrome occurs in some premature infants who are subjected to painful procedures during the first months of life. A small number of these infants develop self-injurious behavior and provoke others to hurt them. Herzog describes two such infants. One child, Marta, was eight weeks premature. She was placed on a respirator, intravenously fed, had catheters in place, and was tied down. Later, she was noted to be hyper-responsive to stimulation. At six weeks of age, she seemed irritable and appeared to be angry and to glare at the nurse and her mother. At follow-up over a period of months, she was reported to attack other children. She also tried to provoke others, including her parents, to hurt her, and when she could speak, she was explicit in her requests. Herzog explores the disturbed relationship between Marta's father and her depressed mother, from the time of the pregnancy until they separated when she was twenty-two months old. Reviewing the literature on the factors that may be assumed to bias neurophysiological development, Herzog discusses the possible interplay between these factors and the disturbed family interaction. Marta was still preoccupied with pain and with causing pain in her fantasies at twenty-eight months of age. However, her mother, who had formed a new relationship with a supportive man, did not comply with her requests to be hurt. In contrast, Herzog describes a similar child and her single mother whose relationship was organized around hurting one another.

Illness, medical treatment, and painful experiences of other kinds in infants and older children may make demands on the mother and other caretakers for some modification of the painful ordeal. The effects of these traumatic incidents can be greatly modified by sensitive care, even in the intensive care nursery (Gorski, 1983). The object relations are organized by the need to respond to these situations. It is of considerable interest that a relatively small proportion of children develop the markedly disturbed responses to the care in the premature nursery.

The various studies of children in this constellation show that the way the painful experience is elaborated in the mental life of the child and the way it functions in the child's relationships depends a great deal on the parental response. Parental guilt and depression, or angry responses to the child's provocative reactions to pain and discomfort, can stabilize self-destructive and provocative behavior in the child. For this reason, the relationship between early trauma and later psychological development is not a simple one.

Subsequent object relations and their attendant conflicts reflect the fantasies that evolve in the effort to deal with painful experience and the role of significant objects in it. This could be seen in the analysis, described by Glenn (1978), of a child with an anal fissure at the age of two years who later produced pain by withholding her stools.

In a general way, these childhood experiences organized around pain fit the classic model of trauma. The organizing situation, and presumably the experience, is one of being overwhelmed and helpless while being subjected to pain. In the traditional model, the response is an effort at mastery followed by the elaboration of fantasies serving libidinal gratification. The activities may involve direct sexual satisfaction and may be elaborated, in any case, as sexual fantasies.

The second constellation, in which the relationship with the parent or some other person is the source of pain is exemplified by the common forms of child abuse. For example, Herzog (Panel, 1985) described an extreme example of an infant boy whose mother forced him into painful sexual activities with her, activities which he tried to initiate later with both children and adults. Fraiberg (1982) has also described some dramatic instances of this type. She suggested that such behavior is the outcome of primitive modes of defensive adaptation. Defensive reactions, such as selective avoidance of the mother, may appear as early as three months of age. Before a year old, children may laugh giddily and kick in response to mother's aggression, as well as throw their toys provocatively. Fraiberg also discusses a "defense" she calls "transformation of affect." This is seen in the description of a mother feeding her nine-month-old son. As the baby sucks, the mother takes the bottle out of his mouth and holds it up, allowing the milk to fall into her own mouth. To the astonishment of the observers, the child laughs and kicks his feet excitedly. The author remarks: "This game is repeated six times in the course of the feeding. It is intolerable to watch" (p. 628). Other children showing a "defense" called "reversal" bump, fall, and bang their heads without apparent experience of pain. One child with this defense not only destroyed her toys but also tore her toenails until they bled. Her mother had been schizophrenic. At three, the child played with dolls, speaking in the voices of persecutors and persecuted.

Children whose usual relationship with some other person is the source of pain (physical or mental) are also familiar to us in the common pathogenic experiences of later childhood that we often hear about in analysis. For them, sadomasochistic fantasies are both the vehicle and the product of the resolution of conflicts generated in the object relations.

Describing these two constellations emphasizes only the initial organizing conditions, and certainly oversimplifies matters. However, this approach has the advantage of highlighting the range of parent-infant interactions, and the possible roles of parents as helpers or instigators in traumatic events of infancy. The trauma of painful experience in childhood includes some experience of the parent or caretaker. When the mother is the cause, or experienced as the cause, the hatred of the mother, a fantasy (or other representative of the experience), and aggression toward the mother are traumatic components of the painful experience. Isaacs (1929) emphasized the role of privation leading to frustration in the evocation of aggressive wishes and fantasies toward the mother, which in turn became projected and led to perceiving the mother as being sadistic.

These more dramatic examples may serve as models for thinking about the effects of less traumatic and more varied interactions. Complex variations occur in which some defect in the child—congenital or birth-related—may initially cause little discomfort to the child. For the mother, on the other hand, the damage to the child's appearance or function may be a severe narcissistic injury and may lead to depression or rejection of the child (Lax, 1972). The extent to which such reactions occur or are manageable may depend to a significant degree on the father's attitudes toward both mother and child. Therefore, we can see that relationships between infants and their parents may be organized initially around factors beyond the ordinary, but that the significance of such events for later development depends on the evolving meanings of these factors to parents and child. These interactions are elaborated in the mental life of the child along "final common paths" of fantasy structures and behavior.

ON THE ORIGINS OF SADOMASOCHISM

The observations mentioned above involve infants and children who have been subjected to painful and aggressive treatment and who go on to provoke the repetition of similar experiences, as well as inflicting them on others. These children behave in ways that resemble some adult behavior that is called sadomasochistic. Are the phenomena of infancy and those of adult life simply analogous, or are they manifestations of some similar processes occurring at different stages of development? Is the source of the sadomasochism that is studied on the couch in psychoanalysis by and since Freud (1919, 1924) to be found in these florid cases of abuse in infancy, or do we need to look elsewhere to account for psychoanalytic clinical findings?

According to one line of thought, we may find the "origins" of later, so-called sadomasochism in infancy. For example, some of the infants described by Fraiberg and Herzog showed the evolution of sadomasochistic behavior after the period of trauma. It is also possible that the abuse of infants is responsible for severe and intractable forms of sadistic and masochistic behavior in later life.

Loewenstein (1938, 1957) described a far more benign version of an infant's teasing game which he named the "seduction of the aggressor." He had observed an eleven-month-old girl "being jokingly scolded by her grandmother for putting her thumb in her mouth. The baby would, with visible fright, observe the stern face of her grandmother; but as soon as she saw the grandmother smile, she would start to laugh and put her thumb back into her mouth, with a naughty and provoking expression. . . . When the prohibition became serious, however, i.e., when the grandmother's face remained serious, the child burst into tears" (Loewenstein, 1957, p. 214). Loewenstein used the term "protomasochism," since he believed this playful teasing between children and adults contained the "essential elements" of later masochism and served as its prototype.

Adopting Loewenstein's term, Galenson (1988) suggested that there is indeed a "protomasochism," and the idea of a developmental line has been considered by others. Such ideas suggest a unitary disposition or even an origin of some kind occurring early in life and undergoing a sort of evolution. A related, though more fundamental, conception is Brenner's (1982a, 1982b) suggestion that masochism of some degree is universal as an accompaniment to superego formation. Some disposition of this kind might be an explanation for the commonplace transient and later unconscious masochistic fantasies found in a wide variety of patients.

Considerable evidence suggests, however, that there are many sources of sadomasochistic phenomena, that they can develop at any age, and that they are derived from many factors in development (see also, Blum, 1978). Moreover, it is evident that many different kinds of phenomena are considered "sadomasochism" so that the term has only the most general sort of significance.

An earlier review (Grossman, 1986b) concluded that the term "masochism" lacks specificity except when used to refer to a scenario combining some kind of sexual gratification with something (generally thought to be painful or) unpleasurable, and presented in conscious or unconscious fantasy, or in manifest perversions that are the enactment of such fantasies. Although one might use the term masochism to refer to the behavior that is a disguised expression, that is, a derivative, of such fantasies, this usage becomes confusing since the behavior usually has other, perhaps more significant, meanings and value as well. The same considerations apply to "sadomasochism."

From a purely descriptive point of view, there are many similarities in the activities that are self-destructive or harmful to others throughout childhood and adult life. The same kinds of behavior can disclose a wide variety of meanings in different people and in the same person at different times.

Since terms like masochism and sadomasochism cannot be used precisely, it is not surprising that the search for the origins of sadomasochism reveals a lack of specific precursors for this final outcome which itself lacks specificity. This is the reason why most commentators agree that there are many precursors, many pathways, and many outcomes on the road to the sadomasochistic spectrum.

Consequently, over the years, psychoanalysts offered many motives to explain why children and adults displaying masochistic phenomena of neurotic, perverse, or characterological types might want to seek out experiences of pain or unpleasure. The following is a partial list: the sensation of pain was a source of pleasure "in itself"; it created excitement; it brought relief of tension; it gave a sense of reality; it avoided a fantasied other pain; it prevented punishment; it paid for another pleasure, such as sexual gratification; it avoided true pain and passivity; it served to manipulate a more powerful person; it was a means of inflicting suffering on others; it maintained magical control; it protected loved objects from destruction; suffering for a valued goal, or at the hands of an admired, feared or loved person, may be a source of great narcissistic satisfaction.

This list shows that the unpleasure might in some cases be required as a condition for pleasure, or that obtaining pleasure might be a way of making unpleasure acceptable in object relations of different kinds. It is also evident that what is considered pain or unpleasure is sometimes in the eye of the beholder.

The essential points are the following.

(1) What appears unpleasurable to an observer may be pleasurable to the patient. Even what is unpleasurable for a person in one respect may be pleasurable in another.

(2) There are motives for self-injury that serve to control aggression and to win over or control the love object, rather than to bring pleasure (Loewenstein, 1938, 1957, 1972).

(3) Such apparently painful activities may also become sources of pleasure and serve sexuality.

(4) The decisive issue seems to be whether aggression is turned against the self because of love, fear of object loss, or threat from a feared, powerful person or, instead, because these dangers have been internalized. That is, the formation of the inner control against aggression involves the internalization of representations of the relationship, an identification with the threatening adult directing its aggression toward the self. This is the model of superego formation.

(5) Behavior patterns and styles of object relatedness may appear to be stable from childhood onward, although their meaning changes in the context of advancing development. Therefore, the multiple meanings noted evolve because experiences that are painful at one time in development may become the subject of fantasies, perhaps even providing pleasure, at a later time.

(6) Physical pain has a meaning, a fact that has a great deal to do with pain tolerance. Imagined "pain" in fantasies may represent a particular relationship, among other possibilities, and may reflect the effects of fantasy formation under the impact of superego formation. Therefore,

fantasies of pain may bring conscious pleasure, while serving an unconscious need for punishment. However, the enactment of those fantasies may be avoided because the real pain associated with the enactment is unacceptable.

Although the considerations outlined here argue against the idea of a common source of sadomasochistic phenomena in childhood, these studies do have relevance to clinical work with adults. By providing indications of the forms the primitive mental life may take, the observation of infants and children can show how sexual and aggressive conflicts develop in relation to one another at various ages. In an overview from a developmental viewpoint, Glenn (1985) outlined issues at different stages of child development that may lead to sexualized self-directed aggression. His outline of the developmental sources of so-called sadomasochistic phenomena might be correlated with the different motives for combining painful and sexual experiences that one can discern with clinical observation.

Glenn's observations do not support the idea of a true "developmental line" for "sadomasochism." In other words, traumatic experiences both in early infancy and at later ages may be the basis for eventual aggressive and self-destructive behavior. On the other hand, children with similar painful and traumatic experiences in infancy fare differently because of their varied object relations and conflict resolutions in later childhood and beyond.

Supplementing the data derived from infant studies, clinical study of older children by Novick and Novick (1987) demonstrates the variety of conflict and object relations leading to sadomasochistic behavior at different ages. Roiphe (1991) describes the relationship between a tormentor and his victim in a nursery drama, illustrating erotized aggression in teasing before the age of two.

PAIN AND AGGRESSION

The stereotyped, automatic, and urgently repetitive character of the destructive and self-destructive behavior developing out of the painful situations of childhood and child abuse often seems to be unresponsive to interpretation. Concepts like the "repetition compulsion" and the "economic point of view" address the possibility that the explanation for these behaviors is not to be found solely in the person's mental activity and conflict (A. Freud, 1967). These concepts draw our attention to factors that form the foundation on which psychological organization and conflict are developing and will develop and function. A related view suggests that very early mental development builds ego structures and a cohesive self, while later mental development involves conflict among structures and its resolution. According to the formulations to be developed here, an essential feature of the pre-ego/post-ego distinction is the extent to which the capacity for fantasizing mediates the generation of behavior, rather than behavior being a re-enactment of what has been experienced passively.

The same observations that lead to concepts of preconflictual or nonconflictual factors point to the possibility of some physiological effects, either in the form of "imprinting" or "neurophysiological biasing" (Herzog, 1983). Although such terms lack specificity and we have no clear idea of what we might mean here by organicity, there is still much to encourage attention to organic factors. There is a growing literature demonstrating the lasting effects of severe trauma in both infants and adults. The evidence shows that severe psychological trauma produces longlasting or permanent physiological and psychological change (Fish-Murray et al., 1987; Herzog, 1983; Kolb, 1987; van der Kolk and Greenberg, 1987). It is important to remember, in any case, that these considerations bring us to a point where it becomes difficult to differentiate the physiological and psychological determinants of mental function. After all, learning and training, too, have an organic side to them. On the other hand, interpersonal and psychological factors play an important role in physiological function. After all, learning and training, too, have an organic side to them. On the other hand, interpersonal and psychological factors play an important role in physiological function. In addition, what makes a trauma a trauma is, to a significant extent, determined by psychological factors, by what the situation means to the person involved. In effect, when we come to a consideration of the consequences of trauma, especially in infancy, we cannot assume that the physiological basis for psychic function is operating as it does in the average healthy adult. Although we can say little about organic and physiological factors from our clinical point of view, it is helpful to be alert to the points in our psychological explanations at which such factors may become relevant. We are at such a point when we discuss the interactions of trauma, drives, and ego organization.

The meaning and the effect of traumatic situations depend on such factors as ego and self-development and the capacity for self-regulation. The character of the fantasies and the nature of the fears and wishes all play a role. Superego development and the allocation of authority, too, will determine not only what is traumatic, but how traumatic it is and what resources are available for the management of these experiences and their psychological components. Implicit in these considerations is the idea that when we say economic factors are important, we recognize that ego functioning depends on conditions like the state of arousal, need, and drive intensity. In childhood, the availability of caretakers to help regulate these conditions is especially significant. However, in both children and adults, maximal developmental attainments of functional capacity are not necessarily maintained under stress or even under most ordinary circumstances. Therefore, it is imaginable that some state of affective arousal could be so great that ordinary levels of ego function cannot be maintained.

The interrelationships of fantasy, pain, and aggression provide a psychological focus in this vast psychosomatic subject of how traumatic experiences operate and produce such tenacious effects. I shall discuss, first, a relationship between pain and aggression and, second, the way fantasy helps to master trauma or is stunted by it.

A consideration of the way pain becomes a focal point, as either something to be suffered, something to inflict on others, or a source or vehicle for pleasure, leads to the problem of the relationship between pain and the drives, specifically, aggression. I suggest that one of the ways that pain becomes a *goal* in the object relations of sadomasochistic syndromes is through its relation to aggression. It is true that various ways that pain and pleasure are connected are important and give some support to the idea of "erotogenic masochism" (Freud, 1924; see also, Solomon, 1980).[3] However, clinical data suggest that the process of mastering the hostile aggression associated with pain and painful affects organizes the psychological mechanisms required to cement the object relations in sadomasochistic character pathology and related syndromes. Observations of development and pathology (Galenson, Glenn, Herzog, and Ruttenberg in Panel, 1985; Galenson, 1986, 1988; McDevitt, 1983; Roiphe, 1991) are consistent with this formulation and indicate that it may be of value in understanding "normal" development.

The hypothesis I suggest is as follows: pain and painful affect (anxiety, shame, guilt, humiliation, fear) are ordinarily occurring sources of the aggressive drive, though perhaps not the only ones (Grossman, 1986a, 1986b). Accordingly, any somatic pain might be thought of as a somatic source of the aggressive drive, much as stimulation of the erotogenic zones can be regarded as sources of libido. The erotogenic zones are not the *cause* of sexual stimulation or the sexual impulses in the sense of being literally generators of those impulses. They are, however, the places that are normally sources of pleasurable sensations when stimulated and are normally stimulated during child care. In addition, erotogenic zones normally figure in sexual fantasies as sites of pleasurable activities and sensations. Pain and painful affect figure similarly in aggressive fantasies and experience. Whatever the associated physiological mechanisms may be that contribute to the tenacity of the attachment to pain, psychological development organizes the formation of fantasy structures to regulate the responses to pain and the attendant aggression. The affectionate and sexual relationships with other people are the matrix for this process.

Both pain and unpleasurable affect are obviously commonplaces throughout life. In childhood, pain arises from external and internal sources in the ordinary course of care. We have, therefore, an arousable and inevitably stimulated source of the aggressive drive which can be either mitigated or intensified by maternal care throughout the course of development. Although no special circumstances are required for its arousal, special circumstances lead to special necessities in relation to the management of pain, anger, and aggression by the child and by the caretaker.

Pain and painful affect evoke aggression toward those people who are perceived as the perpetrators. To preserve the relationship, the expression of aggressive impulses directed against other people who are more powerful, gratifying or dangerous, threatening, and in control must be modified in some way. In some cases, sexual activity is utilized, as are other pleasurable experiences. Sometimes, the sexual activity itself may be a part of an enforced relationship, and its pleasurable quality may be ambiguous. In childhood, as well as in the traumatic situations of later life, pleasure-unpleasure fantasies become another vehicle for the management and channeling of aggression, leading to some familiar forms of sadomasochistic fantasies.

At any age, the need to control aggressive impulses evokes the development of defenses against aggression. Whatever else this may entail in the earliest stages of development, the capacity to experience pleasure in connection with unpleasure is a universal disposition from infancy onward, although with "changing psychical coatings" as Freud (1924) said. This is probably one reason why we see traumatic situations provoking sadomasochistic phenomena at any period of life (see Blum, 1978).

An added complication arises from the fact that insofar as the child's angry and aggressive responses to pain may be upsetting to the caretaker, it is possible that the latter may respond with anger or aggressive actions in turn. This is a powerful process by which painful and aggressive interactions become entrenched and repetitive. Consequently, the person is repeatedly involved with others in sexual and aggressive struggles of dominance and possession that are reflections of impaired self-object differentiation. The caretaker has the double task of relieving the sources of distress and helping with the benign management of aggression.

Patients whose behavior expresses conscious or unconscious fantasies that are organized around aggressive conflicts may try to force anyone who is supposed to be a helper or an authority, to collude in some fashion in forcing, controlling, or hurting them. Although the motives for seeking or inflicting pain may vary, as noted earlier, the partner is often required to do things that he or she might ordinarily regard as reprehensible. The fact that the partner has to struggle against being turned into an attacker may become an essential factor in any of the person's relationships—assistance, management, treatment, child care, and marriage. For a variety of motives that increase in complexity during the course of development, the patients become increasingly skilled in understanding the sensibilities of their parents, helpers, and partners. Successful provocation cements the relationship and sustains sadomasochism. To paraphrase Theodor Reik, defeat is its own reward, or rather, self-determined defeat and victory may be identical. This is one more instance of the way diverse kinds of experiences, affects, appetites, and satisfactions can be joined as a result of conflict resolutions patterned on experiences with important figures in one's life.

Such relationships have a remarkable stability. The cycles of aggressive excitement and relief, added to other associated satisfactions, help to preserve the object tie. Similarly, patients with significant sadomasochistic fantasies display "negative therapeutic reactions." They attempt to enact their fantasies in the transference, soliciting anger and abuse. This poses a serious threat to the analyst's neutrality, and may lead to a stalemate in an "interminable" treatment.

Defensive control of aggressive impulses supports the structure of the relationship and the formation of mental structures. Processes of identification and the concomitant internalization of both roles of the relationship are associated with the generation of unpleasurable affect, such as guilt, in relation to internal conflict, leading in turn to other kinds of defenses.

Patients whose transferences take the form of sadomasochistic fantasy enactments may, by their insistent invitation to attack, induce similar conflicts in the therapist. Sometimes in subtle ways, sometimes overtly, the therapist may be placed in a position requiring submission or some aggressive behavior. Many of the difficulties in the management of such patients arise when they arouse aggression in the therapist who must struggle against it. The capacity to provoke the anger of the therapist who threatens or punishes, or must find satisfactory defenses, keeps the self-destructiveness as a source of a number of satisfactions. Even in the best of treatments of such patients, the therapist will at some time gratify and thus reinforce the patient's self-destructive method of obtaining satisfaction. At times, the therapist's hurtfulness is unconscious or rationalized as realistic, neutral, or in the best interests of the patient. In the childhood recollections of such patients, as well as in their accounts of prior treatment, we often hear of help and treatment, realistically necessary, whose administration appears to have been accomplished with a certain sadistic satisfaction.

This model of the role of aggression in mental development and treatment is familiar, since it is based on Freud's (1923, 1930) formulations concerning superego formation and the way the aggressiveness of the child increases the severity of the superego. In particular, superego functions are based in part on the internalization of the authority for control of aggression as personified by the parents. However, if we include the superego precursors of turning passivity into activity and the identification with the aggressor, the model seems to fit throughout development as a model of mental structure formation, from the most primitive to the most complex.

The various disruptions of ego functioning associated with trauma, as noted earlier, coupled with the aggressive conflicts outlined here, contribute to impaired superego development. With the elaboration of fantasy and conflict, the occasions for pain and unpleasure, for painful and unpleasurable affects, change throughout development, just as do the danger situations (Freud, 1926) and the calamities (Brenner, 1979).

Ever since "The Economic Problem of Masochism" (Freud, 1924), psychoanalytic discussions of masochism have had more to do with the superego issues associated with the concepts of moral masochism and the negative therapeutic reaction than with perversion. Derivatives of unconscious sadomasochistic fantasies, such as humor (Dooley, 1941) and teasing (Brenman, 1952), are thought to depend on processes of superego formation for their development. Therefore, in addressing what we think are the central issues of the management of aggressive impulses, we are not surprised to find differences depending on the degree to which the control of the drive depends on the differentiation of the self and object, and on the degree of integration of superego precursors (Grossman, 1986b; Kernberg, 1984). In other words, it is a question of the ways in which the authority for the control of aggression has been internalized. These differences in superego development appear to account for important differences between the so-called sadomasochistic phenomena of children and those of adults.

FANTASY AND THE MASTERY OF PAIN AND TRAUMA

The capacity to combine unpleasurable and pleasurable, especially sexual, aims in fantasy and action appears to be present all through life. Freud (1920) discussed children's fantasies as expressed in their play as a means of taking over the active role of the object who imposes pain or frustration. To this he added that the "artistic play and artistic imitation carried out by adults . . . do not spare the spectators (for instance, in tragedy) the most painful experiences and can yet be felt by them as highly enjoyable. This is convincing proof that, even under the dominance of the pleasure principle, there are ways and means enough of making what is in itself unpleasurable into a subject to be recollected and worked over in the mind" (p. 17).

In describing children with sadomasochistic behavior, I have tried to show that the ways pleasure and unpleasure, pain and aggression, are combined in their behavior resemble adult sadomasochistic fantasies and behavior. We can see that in some cases the behavior is first instigated by adults by means of sadomasochistic games. Even where nothing so consciously structured as a game is involved, parental activities expressing conscious or unconscious fantasies, for instance, in regard to feeding, bowel training, and masturbation, have a similar shaping influence. In effect, parental fantasy structures the relationship with the infant by playing out unconscious games. In other cases, the meaning and origin of specific behavior is less clear.

The specific forms of fantasy and behavior that issue from traumatic events depend on the point or points in development of drives, ego, and object relations at which the core conflicts develop and are reshaped. An important factor is the way in which these traumatic events support or limit developing ego functions and expand or restrict further developmental possibilities. Such "alterations of the ego" (Freud, 1937) may be conceptualized as lying on a continuum from organic impairments of nervous system function as a result of trauma, to the development of impulsive or inhibitory patterns of behavior and learning, to neurotic compromise formations leading to character traits and symptoms.

The role of parental fantasy in structuring the relationship with the infant has already been mentioned in connection with infant syndromes. The children I described earlier were subjected to situations in which the child's experience was narrowly channeled by a totally controlling environment with repeated experiences of helplessness and disregard of his/her feelings. In some of the cases involving frank abuse, there was a monotonous repetition of situations of torment, helplessness, enforced compliance, and a limitation of experience. These elements suggest that whatever neurophysiological factors are involved are given a form and a developmental path that, at least for a time, is organized by the caretaker and derives its reinforcement from pain and fear.

The most extreme forms of abuse are reminiscent of the model offered by Ferenczi's "Taming of a Wild Horse" (1913).[4] These are the infants who are overpowered and painfully controlled by the people who also tend them and provide them with whatever satisfactions they have. They are forced into patterns of interaction either by circumstances of medical care, physical or mental defects, or by disturbed parents and caretakers in whose fantasies the children are forced to take a prescribed part, in spite of and counter to their own needs. The patterns of their early ego development, object relations, and responses are shaped by these experiences that are so overwhelming that they may preclude all mental activity other than the effort to respond in some way to these experiences. With their limited ego development, young children may be able only to repeat these experiences in imagery and action, i.e., according to the sensorimotor organization described by Piaget.

The mode of mastery is restricted by a limited capacity for mental elaboration and representation.[5] Thus, while normal adult mastery of experience relies on mental working over of experience and elaboration of plans and fantasies, this avenue will be less available the younger the child. Developing capacity for mental representation offers more possibility for the utilization of this method of mastery, as well as for the greater range of interpretation of the situation to be mastered. Greater symbolic capacity opens up the possibility of other adaptive responses. In the most immature cases, the patterns forced on the child will eventually achieve some mental representation and elaboration, unless the continuation of the traumatizing relationship interferes even further with ego development. (Herzog [Panel, 1985] has provided longitudinal data on children demonstrating both conditions.) At this end of the spectrum, the developmental problem, from the point of view of the ego, is to surmount the traumatic events from which helplessness prevents escape and to develop a capacity for mental representation and fantasy along with adaptive behavior.

There are analogues in the situations of complete helplessness suffered by adults in wartime and captivity, hostage situations, and concentration camps. The effects of this kind of treatment in adults are said to be lasting, too, which is one of the observations that suggest physiological change. In traumatic neuroses, the representations of the traumatic situations in dreams and fantasy undergo changes and are eventually repeated with distortions and elaborations, showing that they have become assimilated to the representational life. Similarly, adult patients who have been severely traumatized in childhood often behave in ways that seem to repeat the early patterns of object relations, and induce others, often unknowingly and helplessly, to repeat these patterns with them. At the same time, the fantasies embodying self- and object representations show that those patterns have found mental elaboration.

Whatever the organic substrate, the requirement for massive self-control and compliance with the powerful person in control is bound to instill methods of activity in response to impulses and to objects that are limiting to the satisfaction of libidinal and aggressive needs. To the extent that this way of looking at the problem is correct, it is not only that pain creates a change in the nervous system, but that the associated relations shape the "alterations of the ego" and the later forms of defense.

In addition to pain and helplessness, the traumatic situations of infancy involve poverty of opportunity for the explorations and gradual acquisition of the control of self-satisfaction that develops into creation of fantasies from the elements of experience. These are extreme instances of "soul murder" that Shengold (1974, 1979, 1989) has discussed. If the victims of trauma, whether adults or children, cannot turn enforced behavior patterns into mental activity that can in some way serve to overcome the painful experiences, compulsive repetitive action and ideation are evident. In the more brutally treated individuals, there may be little transformation of the traumatic experiences that are later re-enacted with monotonous repetition, with the subject in the role of victim or aggressor, perhaps alternately. Dissociative states are another means of walling off the memory of experiences that cannot be transformed through fantasy.[6]

We may see various versions of these phenomena in analytic work with older children and adults in whom mental elaboration of traumatic experiences involves representation of both the conflict with the other person and the inner effort of control. The fantasy elaboration of the childhood experiences takes many forms, including literary transformations like those of Sacher-Masoch and de Sade (see also, Shengold, 1989). Sadomasochistic perversions enact such transformations in fantasy and turn the frightening or punitive adult of childhood into a sexual accomplice (Loewenstein, 1938; Stoller, 1975). In these enactments, as in their characterological equivalents and derivatives, identification with the pleasure of the partner is an important factor. Havelock Ellis (1936) quoted a letter from a woman who wrote:

"I believe that, when a person takes pleasure in inflicting pain, he or she imagines himself or herself in the victim's place. This would account for the transmutability of the two sets of feelings." To which she added: "I cannot understand how (as in the case mentioned by Krafft-Ebing) a man could find any pleasure in binding a girl's hands except by imagining what he supposed were her feelings, though he would probably be unconscious that he had put himself in her place" (pp. 160–161).

With the sort of model I have outlined in mind, we can see why it is, in fact, possible for attentive and thoughtful caretakers to modify the impact of traumatic illness, injury, and medical intervention. Similarly, we may understand both the mitigating effects and the limitations of later corrective developmental experiences. Where there is some opportunity for mitigation, the elements of experience of object relations and bodily sensations can be synthesized into fantasy. The fantasy becomes the mediator and the generator of behavior, our usual concept of the role of fantasy in development and daily experience.

This, then, is an outline of the role of fantasy in the mastery of traumatic experience, and the role of the child's relation to the abusing adult in the impairment of the functions of fantasy which include development of representational capacities and achievement of a sense of reality and reality testing. Insofar as fantasy is a crucial ego function, or rather a set of ego functions, we have here an important aspect of the role of the ego in the mastery of trauma, the impact of traumatic experience on ego function, and the alteration of the ego in the process.

SUMMARY

The term "sadomasochism" is currently used to designate a heterogeneous group of fantasies and behaviors that are characterized by pleasure obtained through hostile aggression and destructiveness. A more specifically psychoanalytic point of view uses the term for fantasies which are the expression of the obligatory combination of sexual satisfaction and its derivatives with aggression. In such fantasies, the person may be the one who acts aggressively or is the target of the aggression that leads to pleasure.

The three hypotheses outlined here place clinical and developmental issues of sadomasochism (loosely defined) in the framework of drives and structure. The hypothesis that pain and painful affects are "sources" of the aggressive drive provides links among psychoanalytic clinical observation, child development observation, and clinical, psychological, and physiological studies of affects. The hypothesis that stresses the role of aggressive conflict and defenses against aggression in mental structure formation and stereotypic repetition, compulsive and impulsive, contributes to understanding some of the phenomena associated with trauma and child abuse. The hypothesis that fantasy formation is a factor in the overcoming of trauma, but may be impaired by trauma, places psychoanalytic observations in a framework related to psychological studies of cognition and memory organization. In effect, these formulations on "sadomasochism" form a bridge between psychoanalytic clinical observation, child development observation, and physiological and psychological studies of the effects of trauma of various kinds.

At various points in the discussion, physiological factors have been mentioned because it appears that information from both psychological and physiological research is relevant to understanding particular problems. For instance, severe trauma in both infants and adults produces long-lasting or permanent changes in psychological functioning that appear to have an organic basis. However, when we come to the interplay of physiological, psychological, and interpersonal factors in learning, memory, the attachment to pain, and the experience of trauma, the relationships are not easily sorted into primary and secondary. The issues of psychological organization and physiological functions come together, at some point, in considering both drive and ego activities. In traditional formulations, both the concept of the "repetition compulsion" and of the "economic point of view" address the possibility that some explanations of behavior require consideration of mental activity (conflict and object relations) and factors that form the foundation on which psychological organization and conflict develop and function.

It may be that hypotheses such as those offered here will be helpful in exploring the interface between psychoanalytic, psychological, and physiological studies of "sadomasochism" and trauma.

NOTES

1. These ideas on fantasy and its role in the mastery of trauma have been developed on the basis of psychoanalytic considerations. However, an excellent recent review by van der Kolk and van der Hart (1989) shows that the psychoanalytic viewpoint, based on Freud's and Piaget's ideas, owes a great deal to Janet's conceptualization of trauma, dissociation, and automatism.
2. This paper is a considerably modified version of Grossman (1986a).
3. Solomon (1980) presents evidence showing that painful and unpleasurable stimuli, in both humans and animals, produce unpleasant sensations first, and are then followed by pleasurable sensations. The same reversal takes place for pleasure. In this way, secondary motives can develop in which the unpleasurable experience is sought for its pleasurable after-effects, a mechanism that Loewenstein has described. The extent to which these processes can be shown to operate is truly impressive and provides a well-studied behavioral psychology basis with some probable physiological mechanisms associated with it. The nature of this process can be shown to account for some features of addiction as well as many other kinds of activities. So to this extent, the capacity for experiencing pleasure in unpleasure is, no doubt, truly universal. Similarly, the discoveries involving the release of endorphins in both sexual highs and painful experiences point in this direction.
4. In a brief note, Ferenczi (1913) described how a noted trainer tamed a restrained wild horse by alternately striking him on the nose with some metal rings, and then speaking softly to him while feeding him sugar.
5. The issues under discussion concern the broader issues of developmental theory in psychoanalysis today—the relationships between developmental deficit and conflict. This touches on the interesting question of whether we can conceptualize some kind of inner conflict, other than that proposed by Melanie Klein, in the early stages of development. I believe we should attempt to do this (see also Spitz, 1966). In the early cases, the issue seems to be self-control out of fear in conflict with the caretaker, but we know nothing about its mental elaboration. Presumably there is greater representation in fantasy of this self-control the more symbolic capacity there is. This early self-control generated out of fear and pain may perhaps be considered to be the precursor of inner conflict occurring at a presymbolic, sensorimotor level of development. It may not be conflict at the level of tripartite structure, but it may be conflict. The resolution of the conflict between impulse, the effort of control, and the interaction with the other person must have some kind of representation in memory, however primitive. It may be, however, that the representation is to be found only in the behavioral organization underlying character.
6. See van der Kolk and van der Hart (1989) for an interesting discussion of Janet's ideas on these issues.

REFERENCES

Blum, H. P. (1978). Psychoanalytic study of an unusual perversion. Discussion. *J. Amer. Psychoanal. Assn.*, 26:785–792.

Brenman, M. (1952). On teasing and being teased: and the problem of "moral masochism." *Psychoanal. Study Child*, 7:264–285.

Brenner, C. (1979). The components of psychic conflict and its consequences in mental life. *Psychoanal. Q.*, 48:547–567.

——— (1982a). The concept of the superego: a reformulation. *Psychoanal. Q.*, 51:501–525.

——— (1982b). *The Mind in Conflict*. New York: Int. Univ. Press.

Dooley, L. (1941). The relation of humor to masochism. *Psychoanal. Rev.*, 28:37–46.

Ellis, H. (1936). *Studies in the Psychology of Sex, Vol. 1*. New York: Random House.

Ferenczi, S. (1913). Taming of a wild horse. In *Final Contributions to the Problems and Methods of Psychoanalysis*. New York: Basic Books, 1955, pp. 336–340.

Fish-Murray, C. C., Koby, E. V. & Van Der Kolk, B. A. (1987). Evolving ideas: the effect of abuse on children's thought. In *Psychological Trauma*, ed. B. A. van der Kolk. Washington, D.C.: American Psychiatric Press, pp. 89–110.

Fraiberg, S. (1982). Pathological defenses in infancy. *Psychoanal. Q.*, 51:612–635.

Freud, A. (1967). Comments on psychic trauma. In *The Writings of Anna Freud, Vol. 5. Research at the Hampstead Child-Therapy Clinic and Other Papers, 1956–1965*. New York: Int. Univ. Press, pp. 221–241.

Freud, S. (1919). 'A child is being beaten': a contribution to the study of the origin of sexual perversions. *S.E.*, 17.

——— (1920). Beyond the pleasure principle. *S.E.*, 18.

——— (1923). The ego and the id. *S.E.*, 19.

——— (1924). The economic problem of masochism. *S.E.*, 19.

——— (1925). Preface to Aichhorn's *Wayward Youth*. *S.E.*, 19.

——— (1926). Inhibitions, symptoms and anxiety. *S.E.*, 20.

——— (1930). Civilization and its discontents. *S.E.*, 21.

——— (1937). Analysis terminable and interminable. *S.E.*, 23.

Galenson, E. (1983). A Pain-Pleasure Behavioral Complex in Mothers and Infants. Presented at the meeting of the American Psychoanalytic Association, December 15.

——— (1986). Some thoughts about infant psychopathology and aggressive development. *Int. Rev. Psychoanal.*, 13:349–354.

——— (1988). The precursors of masochism. In *Fantasy, Myth, and Realty: Essays in Honor of Jacob A. Arlow*, ed. H. P. Blum, et al. Madison, CT: Int. Univ. Press, pp. 371–379.

Glenn, J., Editor. (1978). *Child Analysis and Therapy*. New York/London: Aronson.

——— (1984). A note on loss, pain, and masochism in children. *J. Amer. Psychoanal. Assn.*, 32:63–73.

——— (1985). A Developmental Approach to Masochism. New York University Post-Doctoral Seminar, June 1.

Gorski, P. A. (1983). Premature infant behavioral and physiological responses to caregiving interventions in the intensive care nursery. In *Frontiers of Infant Psychiatry*, ed. J. D. Call, et al. New York: Basic Books, pp. 256–263.

Grossman, W. I. (1986a). Dolore, aggressività e fantasia all'origine del sadomasochismo. *Rivista di Psicoanalisi*, 32:557–571.

———— (1986b). Notes on masochism: a discussion of the history and development of a psychoanalytic concept. *Psychoanal. Q.*, 55:379–413.

Herzog, J. M. (1983). A neonatal intensive care syndrome: a pain complex involving neuroplasticity and psychic trauma. In *Frontiers of Infant Psychiatry*, ed. J. D. Call, et al. New York: Basic Books, pp. 291–300.

Isaacs, S. (1929). Privation and guilt. *Int. J. Psychoanal.*, 10:335–347.

Kernberg, O. F. (1984). *Severe Personality Disorders: Psychotherapeutic Strategies*. New Haven/London: Yale Univ. Press.

———— (1988a). Clinical dimensions of masochism. *J. Amer. Psychoanal. Assn.*, 36:1005–1029.

———— (1988b). Sadomasochism, sexual excitement, and perversion. Presented at the meeting of the American Psychoanalytic Association, December 17.

Kolb, L. C. (1987). A neuropsychological hypothesis explaining posttraumatic stress disorders. *Amer. J. Psychiat.*, 144:989–995.

Krystal, H. (1978). Trauma and affects. *Psychoanal. Study Child*, 33:81–116.

Lax, R. F. (1972). Some aspects of the interaction between mother and impaired child: mother's narcissistic trauma. *Int. J. Psychoanal.*, 53:339–344.

Loewenstein, R. M. (1938). L'origine du masochisme et la théorie des pulsions. *Rev. Française Psychanalyse*, 10:293–321.

———— (1957). A contribution to the psychoanalytic theory of masochism. *J. Amer. Psychoanal. Assn.*, 5:197–234.

———— (1972). Ego autonomy and psychoanalytic technique. *Psychoanal. Q.*, 41:1–22.

Maleson, F. G. (1984). The multiple meanings of masochism in psychoanalytic discourse. *J. Amer. Psychoanal. Assn.*, 32:325–356.

McDevitt, J. B. (1983). The emergence of hostile aggression and its defensive and adaptive modifications during the separation-individuation process. *J. Amer. Psychoanal. Assn.*, Suppl., 31:273–300.

Novick, K. K. & Novick, J. (1987). The essence of masochism. *Psychoanal. Study Child*, 42:353–384.

Panel (1985). Sadomasochism in Children. Meeting of the American Psychoanalytic Association, December 22.

———— (1988). Four sequential panels on Sadism and Masochism in the Psychoanalytic Process at the meeting of the American Psychoanalytic Association, December 14–18.

Roiphe, H. (1991). The Tormentor and the Victim in the Nursery. In press.

Schafer, R. (1984). The pursuit of failure and the idealization of unhappiness. *Amer. Psychologist*, 39:398–405.

Shengold, L. (1974). Soul murder: a review. *Int. J. Psychoanal. Psychother.*, 3:366–373.

———— (1979). Child abuse and deprivation: soul murder. *J. Amer. Psychoanal. Assn.*, 27:533–559.

———— (1989). *Soul Murder: The Effects of Childhood Abuse and Deprivation*. New Haven/London: Yale University Press.

Solomon, R. L. (1980). The opponent-process theory of acquired motivation: the costs of pleasure and the benefits of pain. *Amer. Psychologist*, 35:691–712.

Spitz, R. A. (1966). Metapsychology and direct infant observation. In *Psychoanalysis—A General Psychology. Essays in Honor of Heinz Hartmann*, ed. R. M. Loewenstein, et al. New York: Int. Univ. Press, pp. 123–151.

Stoller, R. J. (1975). *Perversion: The Erotic Form of Hatred*. New York: Pantheon.

Van Der Kolk, B. A. & Greenberg, M. S. (1987). The psychobiology of the trauma response: hyperarousal, constriction, and addiction to traumatic reexposure. In *Psychological*

Trauma, ed. B. A. van der Kolk. Washington, D.C.: American Psychiatric Press, pp. 63–88.

——— & Van Der Hart, O. (1989). Pierre Janet and the breakdown of adaptation in psychological trauma. *Amer. J. Psychiat.,* 146:1530–1540.

Workshop (1983). The Vulnerable Child. Meetings of the American Psychoanalytic Association, December 15.

PART III

MASOCHISTIC PERVERSION: THE BEATING FANTASY

Introduction

Fenichel (1945) writes, "perversions are something universally human . . . practiced in all ages and among all races" (p. 325). A measure of sadomasochism is an ingredient in the psychosexual development of all human beings (Brenner 1959, chapter 18 in this volume; Kernberg 1991); the perversion is created with the fixation of infantile positions. In the masochistic "mise-en-scène" (Grunberger, 1956; chapter 10 in this volume) or "masochistic contract" (Smirnoff 1969; chapter 3 in this volume), masochism is inextricably bound to fantasy. Masochistic fantasies are caused when aggressive libidinal demands on the object, bend back on the self and form a fantasy of sexually excited humiliation or self-harm.

In " 'A Child Is Being Beaten': A Contribution to the Study of the Origin of Sexual Perversions," Freud (1919; chapter 8 in this volume) maintained that the structure of the beating fantasy is bound to the structure of the Oedipus complex. In the cases he refers to, there was a premature repression of the negative Oedipal feelings in the boys, and a repression and regression of the passive incestuous Oedipal desires in the girls. Freud located the forces and fantasies involved in the origin of masochistic perversion during the period between the ages of two and five, when a precociously developed sadism becomes fused with repressed incest wishes. One of the fascinating aspects of this work is his attempt to look at the transformations of a fantasy over time.

The place of object relations in the intensification of sadism is important in Freud's paper (though contained in brief vignettes). Freud (1919) paints a vivid picture of paternal seductiveness and exacerbated sibling rivalry: "The affections of the little girl are fixed on her father, who has probably done all he could to win her love, and in this way has sown the seeds of an attitude of hatred and rivalry towards her mother" (pp. 165–66 in this volume). "There are other children in the nursery, only a few years older or younger, who are disliked . . . chiefly because the parents' love has to be shared with them, and for this reason they are repelled with all the wild energy characteristic of the emotional life of those years" (p. 166 in this volume). Freud notes that the child who is being beaten feels deprived of love and humiliated, and feels cast down from an imaginary omnipotence. The instigators of the trauma are the seductiveness of the father, the wild childhood energy which is hostile to new babies, and the experience of loss of love (anxiety) and humiliation (narcissistic injury). The first fantasy "my father is beating a child" has the reassuring meaning, "my father does not love this other child, he loves only me." And thus, Freud describes the narcissistic stability, as well as libidinal gratification, gained through the fantasy. "The phantasy . . . is also powerfully reinforced by the child's egoistic interests. Doubt remains, therefore, whether the phantasy ought to be described as purely 'sexual', nor can one venture to call it 'sadistic' " (p. 166 in this volume). The first phase of the fantasy, aims at the repair of a narcissistic injury by the assurance of the object's truest love. The second phase of the fantasy involves the essence of masochism: "No, he does not love you, for he is beating you" (p. 167 in this volume). Guilt for the incest fantasy or the sibling rivalry, generated by fear of reprisals (Nacht 1938; chapter 1 in this volume), turns the aggression, or aggressive sexual love, back on the self (Laplanche 1976; chapter 6 in this volume). Yet, Freud reiterates that the necessary condition for what the Novicks have called the "fixed" beating fantasy is the precociously developed sadistic component and a "scarcely effected" Oedipus complex which is met by repression.

Reich (1940; chapter 21 in this volume), Bak (1946; chapter 9 in this volume), Berliner (1958; chapter 17 in this volume), Shengold (1967) and (1971; chapter 11 in this volume), Novick and Novick (1987; chapter 12 in this volume), and Coen (1992; chapter 19 in this volume) present cases which clearly demonstrate that rage and erotic excitement, caused by the neglect and seductiveness of sadomasochistic parents, precociously intensify and fixate sadomasochism in the child. Freud's example of what leads to sadomasochism chiefly concerns sibling rivalry, the hatred (as well as attachment) that comes when a child's ability to get enough satisfaction from his or her parents is threatened. This precocious sadism does not in itself create the fixed beating fantasy which leads to perversion; the disturbed incest fantasy of the "scarcely effected" Oedipus adds an essential component (Freud 1919; Nacht 1938; Bak 1946; Novick and Novick 1987).

Along with the question of the place of instinctual forces and object relations in perverse masochism is the question of whether there is a radical distinction to be made between the worst cases of perversion which may involve psychosis and the more isolated perversion in neurotic characters. And there is a question whether at the more severe end of the spectrum, narcissistic aims become dominant. Coen (1992) makes a distinction between the higher level sadomasochistic pervert who uses the perverse behavior to "permit sexual functioning and orgasm" and to defend "against castration anxiety and oedipal guilt," and a lower level which involves "sexualization in the service of narcissism, closeness, need satisfaction, defense repair, adaptation, and the preservation of psychic equilibrium and structure" (p. 398 in this volume). Kernberg (1988) draws a distinction between perversion at the neurotic level and perversion with severely self-destructive or other regressive features. Close in thinking to Smirnoff (1969; chapter 3 in this volume), he describes the sexual masochism at the neurotic level as "a 'scenario' enacted in the context of an object relation that is experienced as safe . . . centering on . . . the need to deny castration anxiety and to assuage a cruel super-ego in order to obtain sexual gratification that has incestuous meanings" (Kernberg 1988, 70). In patients with borderline personality organization, the sexual perversion "breaks out of the 'as if' or play-acting frame, and may bring about an authentic threat to the patient's survival" (p. 72).

The relation of the perversions to childhood sexuality and the object relations available to children, makes the observations of child analysts more and more pertinent to theorizing on masochistic perversion. Novick and Novick (1972, 1987) have taken a large sampling of children in analysis and explored the beating fantasy. They found that there are two types of beating fantasy, a normal transitory one and a "fixed fantasy." They see the epigenesis of masochism as an adaptation to a disturbed environment, a defense against aggression, and a mode of instinctual gratification. Their findings agree with Freud, in that the organized beating fantasies were formed only post-Oedipally, while the determinants could be traced to earlier phases; "the beating wish, sadistic intercourse theory, and phallic beating games could be seen in some form in all the young children" (p. 238 in this volume). Novick and Novick (1987) believe that what masochistic perversions and moral masochism have in common is the underlying fantasy structure.

Several analysts (Loewenstein 1957, chapter 2 in this volume; Brenner 1959) have asked if there are always factors of contingency or conditionality, which mean that sexual pleasure is not sought directly through the medium of pain? De M'Uzan's (1973) paper is unique in its account of the way in which pain increases the sexual pleasure. His case of perverse masochism includes an appalling cutting and tormenting of the genitals and whole body causing gross scarring. He questions whether this violent discharge of sexual libido is an end in itself? He answers "yes" and "no," believing that the pain does contribute to the sexual pleasure, but that the pain is exquisitely suited to the setting of ego boundaries. Shapiro (1981) emphasizes the fact that the masochistic pervert experiences himself as seeking pleasure through the pain. He observes that Freud and numerous others have postulated a biological basis (apart from the death instinct) for the relation of pain and sexual excitement, to which the pervert can regress. Certain kinds of pain, especially cutaneous pain, are closely akin to erotic sensation and easily spill over into it. Shengold (1967, 1971), like Kucera (1959), considers the idea of a masochism through co-excitation, related to early infantile intermingling of sexual excitement and pain, in teething: "The change to tension and unpleasure of a hitherto predominantly pleasure giving erogeneous zone at a time when the ego is beginning to coalesce may be more significant than has been thought" (p. 226 in this volume). Co-excitation, the capacity of the organism to experience any intense stimulation, including painful stimulation, as sexually exciting (Brenner 1959), which we have considered in relation to the drives, has considerable explanatory power in masochistic perversion. Shengold (1967, 1971) elaborates a particular beating fantasy, the rat fantasy, derived from infantile co-excitation in the context of overstimulation and neglect.

The sadomasochistic scenarios, such as those described by Smirnoff (1969) and earlier by Reik (1940), involve a kind of tension that is both painful and sexual, but not to be identified with the release of sexual tension in end-pleasure. In the worst cases of masochism, according to de M'Uzan (1973), orgasm seems only to plunge the pervert back into the necessity to repeat the painful state of sexual tension. Laplanche (1992) believes that the so-called paradox of masochism, the simultaneity of sexual pleasure in pain, is not a paradox in nature but a problem in terminology. A differentiation between sexual excitation and orgastic pleasure shows that that it is only the tension of sexual excitation which is intermingled with, or facilitated by pain, and not the sexual pleasure of release in orgasm.

There have always been many theories of masochism which have looked at pain as a condition for pleasure and as a defense, rather than as an instinctual paradox (Freud 1919; Nacht 1938; Fenichel 1945; Brenner 1959). The theory that masochistic perversion is a defense against anxieties which are still more painful is explicit in Freud's (1919) paper on the beating fantasy. Anxiety over a loss of love and protection from the father and a closely connected castration anxiety are essential features in the development of the beating fantasy (Bak 1946; Fenichel 1945; Loewenstein 1957; Brenner

1959; Smirnoff 1969; Coen 1992). But how does masochism, which courts humiliation, avoid castration anxiety, or separation anxiety? "It seems a paradox," writes Fenichel (1945), in elaborating the relationship of perversion to castration anxiety, "that a feared pain might be avoided or denied by actually suffering pain" (p. 358). Grunberger (1956; chapter 10 in this volume) focuses on "masochism as the negation of anxiety," anxiety created by the aim to castrate the father (the fountain of narcissistic well-being) and, hence, to introject the paternal penis in an anal-sadistic manner.

Reik's (1940; in excerpt form, chapter 16 in this volume) thesis of the masochist attaining a victory through defeat, through painful humiliation, suggests that control of the object can be attained by submitting in a repetitive, ritualized way to the punishing object. Once the punishment is undergone, and is less than castration, relief ensues. Bak (1946), too, presents cases in which the longing for the father's love becomes debased and turned back into a beating fantasy, which helps to control the passive fears of castration anxiety. Smirnoff (1969) believes that the "idealized evil woman" who whips the masochist is taking the place of a fetish, in the struggle against castration anxiety (see also Bak 1953 and Coen 1992). Taking castration anxiety back to its roots in infantile separation anxiety, Smirnoff comments, the masochistic scene can be the "symbolic representative of both the unattainable fusion with, and the impossible separation from the primary sexual object" (1969; p. 72 in this volume). Here, the defensive function of masochism joins with the problem of pain in masochistic perversion.

BIBLIOGRAPHY

Bak, R. 1946. Masochism in Paranoia. *Psychoanal. Quarterly* 15:285–301. (Chapter 9 in this volume.)

———. 1953. Fetishism. *J. Amer. Psychoanal. Assn.* 1:285–98.

Berliner, B. 1958. The Role of Object Relations in Moral Masochism. *Psychoanal. Quarterly* 27:38–56. (Chapter 17 in this volume.)

Brenner, C. 1959. The Masochistic Character: Genesis and Treatment. *J. Amer. Psychoanal. Assn.* 5:197–234. (Chapter 18 in this volume.)

Chasseguet-Smirgel, J. 1991. Sadomasochism in the Perversions: Some thoughts on the Destruction of Reality. *J. Amer. Psychoanal. Assn.* 39:399–415.

Coen, S. 1992. The Excitement of Sadomasochism. In *The Misuse of Persons: Analyzing Pathological Dependency.* Hillsdale, N.J.: The Analytic Press, pp. 197–226. (Chapter 19 in this volume.)

de M'Uzan, M. 1973. A Case of Masochistic Perversion and an Outline of a Theory. *Int. J. Psycho-Anal.* 54:455–67.

Fenichel, O. 1945. *The Psychoanalytic Theory of Neurosis.* New York: Norton.

Freud, S. 1905. Three Essays on the Theory of Sexuality. In *S.E.* 14:135–243. (In excerpt form, chapter 4 in this volume.)

———. 1919. "A Child Is Being Beaten": A Contribution to the Study of the Origin of Sexual Perversions. In *S.E.* 17:179–204. (Chapter 8 in this volume.)

Grunberger, B. 1956. Psychodynamic Theory of Masochism. In *Perversions, Psychodynamics, and Therapy,* ed. S. Lorand and M. Balint. New York: Random House, pp. 183–208. (Chapter 10 in this volume.)

Kernberg, O. 1988. Clinical Dimensions of Masochism. In *Masochism: Current Psychoanalytic Perspectives,* ed. R. Glick and D. Meyers. Hillsdale, N.J.: The Analytic Press, pp. 61–79.

———. 1991. Sadomasochism, Sexual Excitement, and Perversion. *J. Amer. Psychoanal. Assn.* 39:333–62.

Kucera, O. 1959. On Teething. *J. Amer. Psychoanal. Assn.* 7:284–91.

Laplanche, J. 1976. Aggressiveness and Sadomasochism. In *Life and Death in Psychoanalysis.* Baltimore: John Hopkins University Press. (Chapter 6 in this volume.)

———. 1992. *La révolution copernicienne inachevée,* Paris: Aubier.

Loewenstein, R. 1957. A Contribution to the Psychoanalytic Theory of Masochism. *J. Amer. Psychoanal. Assn.* 5:197–234. (Chapter 2 in this volume.)

Nacht, S. 1938. Introduction. In *Le masochisme.* Paris: Payot, 1965. (Chapter 1 in this volume.)

Novick, K., and Novick, J. 1972. Beating Fantasies in Children. *Int. J. Psycho-Anal.* 53:237–42.

———. 1987. The Essence of Masochism. *Psychoanal. Study Child* 42:353–84. (Chapter 12 in this volume.)

Reich, A. 1940. A Contribution to the Psycho-Analysis of Extreme Submissiveness in Women. *Psychoanal. Quarterly* 9:470–80. (Chapter 21 in this volume.)

Reik, T. 1940. The Characteristics of Masochism. *Am. Imago* 1:29–59. (In excerpt form, chapter 16 in this volume.)

Shapiro, D. 1981. *Autonomy and Rigid Character.* New York: Basic Books.

Shengold, L. 1967. The Effects of Overstimulation: Rat People. *Int. J. Psycho-Anal.* 48:403–15.

———. 1971. More about Rats and Rat People. *Int. J. Psycho-Anal.* 52:277–88. (Chapter 11 in this volume.)

Smirnoff, V. 1969. The Masochistic Contract. *Int. J. Psycho-Anal.* 50:665–71. (Chapter 3 in this volume.)

8. "A Child Is Being Beaten": A Contribution to the Study of the Origin of Sexual Perversions

Sigmund Freud

I

It is surprising how often people who seek analytic treatment for hysteria or an obsessional neurosis confess to having indulged in the phantasy: 'A child is being beaten.' Very probably there are still more frequent instances of it among the far greater number of people who have not been obliged to come to analysis by manifest illness.

The phantasy has feelings of pleasure attached to it, and on their account the patient has reproduced it on innumerable occasions in the past or may even still be doing so. At the climax of the imaginary situation there is almost invariably a masturbatory satisfaction—carried out, that is to say, on the genitals. At first this takes place voluntarily, but later on it does so in spite of the patient's efforts, and with the characteristics of an obsession.

It is only with hesitation that this phantasy is confessed to. Its first appearance is recollected with uncertainty. The analytic treatment of the topic is met by unmistakable resistance. Shame and a sense of guilt are perhaps more strongly excited in this connection than when similar accounts are given of memories of the beginning of sexual life.

Eventually it becomes possible to establish that the first phantasies of the kind were entertained very early in life: certainly before school age, and not later than in the fifth or sixth year. When the child was at school and saw other children being beaten by the teacher, then, if the phantasies had become dormant, this experience called them up again, or, if they were still present,

Reprinted by permission of Sigmund Freud Copyrights, The Institute of Psycho-Analysis, the Hogarth Press, from *The Standard Edition of the Complete Psychological Works of Sigmund Freud*, translated and edited by James Strachey, vol. 17: (1919) 179–204.

it reinforced them and noticeably modified their content. From that time forward it was 'an indefinite number' of children that were being beaten. The influence of the school was so clear that the patients concerned were at first tempted to trace back their beating-phantasies exclusively to these impressions of school life, which dated from later than their sixth year. But it was never possible for them to maintain that position; the phantasies had already been in existence before.

Though in the higher forms at school the children were no longer beaten, the influence of such occasions was replaced and more than replaced by the effects of reading, of which the importance was soon to be felt. In my patients' *milieu* it was almost always the same books whose contents gave a new stimulus to the beating-phantasies: those accessible to young people, such as what was known as the *'Bibliothèque rose'* [1], *Uncle Tom's Cabin*, etc. The child began to compete with these works of fiction by producing his own phantasies and by constructing a wealth of situations and institutions, in which children were beaten, or were punished and disciplined in some other way, because of their naughtiness and bad behaviour.

This phantasy—'a child is being beaten'—was invariably cathected with a high degree of pleasure and had its issue in an act of pleasurable auto-erotic satisfaction. It might therefore be expected that the sight of another child being beaten at school would also be a source of similar enjoyment. But as a matter of fact this was never so. The experience of real scenes of beating at school produced in the child who witnessed them a peculiarly excited feeling which was probably of a mixed character and in which repugnance had a large share. In a few cases the real experience of the scenes of beating was felt to be intolerable. Moreover, it was always a condition of the more sophisticated phantasies of later years that the punishment should do the children no serious injury.

The question was bound to arise of what relation there might be between the importance of the beating-phantasies and the part that real corporal punishment might have played in the child's bringing up at home. It was impossible, on account of the one-sidedness of the material, to confirm the first suspicion that the relation was an inverse one. The individuals from whom the data for these analyses were derived had very seldom been beaten in their childhood, or were at all events not brought up by the help of the rod. Naturally, however, each of these children was bound to have become aware at one time or another of the superior physical strength of its parents or educators; the fact that in every nursery the children themselves at times come to blows requires no special emphasis.

As regards the early and simple phantasies which could not be obviously traced to the influence of school impressions or of scenes taken from books, further information would have been welcome. Who was the child that was being beaten? The one who was himself producing the phantasy or another? Was it always the same child or as often as not a different one? Who was it that was beating the child? A grown-up person? And if so, who? Or did the child imagine that he himself was beating another one? Nothing could be ascertained that threw any light upon all these questions—only the hesitant reply: 'I know nothing more about it: a child is being beaten.'

Enquiries as to the sex of the child that was being beaten met with more success, but none the less brought no enlightenment. Sometimes the answer was: 'Always boys', or 'Only girls'; more often it was: 'I don't know', or 'It doesn't matter which'. But the point to which the questions were directed, the discovery of some constant relation between the sex of the child producing the phantasy and that of the child that was being beaten, was never established. Now and again another characteristic detail of the content of the phantasy came to light: 'A small child is being beaten on its naked bottom.'

In these circumstances it was impossible at first even to decide whether the pleasure attaching to the beating-phantasy was to be described as sadistic or masochistic.

II

A phantasy of this kind, arising, perhaps from accidental causes, in early childhood and retained for the purpose of auto-erotic satisfaction, can, in the light of our present knowledge, only be regarded as a primary trait of perversion. One of the components of the sexual function has, it seems, developed in advance of the rest, has made itself prematurely independent, has undergone fixation and in consequence been withdrawn from the later processes of development, and has in this way given evidence of a peculiar and abnormal constitution in the individual. We know that an infantile perversion of this sort need not persist for a whole lifetime; later on it can be subjected to repression, be replaced by a reaction-formation, or be transformed by sublimation. (It is possible that sublimation arises out of some special process[2] which would be held back by repression.) But if these processes do not take place, then the perversion persists to maturity; and whenever we find a sexual aberration in adults—perversion, fetishism, inversion—we are justified in expecting that anamnestic investigation will reveal an event such as I have suggested, leading to a fixation in childhood. Indeed, long before the days of psycho-analysis, observers like Binet were able to trace the strange sexual aberrations of maturity back to similar impressions and to precisely the same period of childhood, namely, the fifth or sixth year.[3] But at this point the enquiry was confronted with the limitations of our knowledge; for the impressions that brought about the fixation were without any traumatic force. They were for the most part commonplace and unexciting to other people. It was impossible to say why the sexual impulse had undergone fixation particularly upon them. It was possible, however, to look for their significance in the fact that they offered an occasion for fixation (even though it was an accidental one) to precisely that component which was prematurely developed and ready to press forward. We had in any case to be prepared to come to a provisional end somewhere or other in tracing back the train of causal connection; and the congenital constitution seemed exactly to correspond with what was required for a stopping-place of that kind.

If the sexual component which has broken loose prematurely is the sadistic one, then we may expect, on the basis of knowledge derived from other sources, that its subsequent repression will result in a disposition to an obsessional neurosis.[4] This expectation cannot be said to be contradicted by the results of enquiry. The present short paper is based on the exhaustive study of six cases (four female and two male). Of these, two were cases of obsessional neurosis; one extremely severe and incapacitating, the other of moderate severity and quite well accessible to influence. There was also a third case which at all events exhibited clearly marked individual traits of obsessional neurosis. The fourth case, it must be admitted, was one of straightforward hysteria, with pains and inhibitions; and the fifth patient, who had come to be analysed merely on account of indecisiveness in life, would not have been classified at all by coarse clinical diagnosis, or would have been dismissed as 'psychasthenic'.[5] There is no need for feeling disappointed over these statistics. In the first place, we know that not every disposition is necessarily developed into a disorder; in the second place, we ought to be content to explain the facts before us, and ought as a rule to avoid the additional task of making it clear why something has *not* taken place.

The present state of our knowledge would allow us to make our way so far and no further towards the comprehension of beating-phantasies. In the mind of the analytic physician, it is true, there remains an uneasy suspicion that this is not a final solution of the problem. He is obliged to admit to himself that to a great extent these phantasies subsist apart from the rest of the content of a neurosis, and find no proper place in its structure. But impressions of this kind, as I know from my own experience, are only too willingly put on one side.

III

Strictly considered—and why should this question not be considered with all possible strictness?—analytic work deserves to be recognized as genuine psycho-analysis only when it has succeeded in removing the amnesia which conceals from the adult his knowledge of his childhood from its beginning (that is, from about the second to the fifth year). This cannot be said among analysts too emphatically or repeated too often. The motives for disregarding this reminder are, indeed, intelligible. It would be desirable to obtain practical results in a shorter period and with less trouble. But at the present time theoretical knowledge is still far more important to all of us than therapeutic success, and anyone who neglects childhood analysis is bound to fall into the most disastrous errors. The emphasis which is laid here upon the importance of the earliest experiences does not imply any underestimation of the influence of later ones. But the later impressions of life speak loudly enough through the mouth of the patient, while it is the physician who has to raise his voice on behalf of the claims of childhood.

It is in the years of childhood between the ages of two and four or five that the congenital libidinal factors are first awakened by actual experiences and become attached to certain complexes. The beating-phantasies which are now under discussion show themselves only towards the end of this period or after its termination. So it may quite well be that they have an earlier history, that they go through a process of development, that they represent an end-product and not an initial manifestation.

This suspicion is confirmed by analysis. A systematic application of it shows that beating-phantasies have a historical development which is by no means simple, and in the course of which they are changed in most respects more than once—as regards their relation to the author of the phantasy, and as regards their object, their content and their significance.

In order to make it easier to follow these transformations in beating-phantasies I shall now venture to confine my descriptions to the female cases, which, since they are four as against two, in any case constitute the greater part of my material. Moreover, beating-phantasies in men are connected with another subject, which I shall leave on one side in this paper.[6] In my description I shall be careful to avoid being more schematic than is inevitable for the presentation of an average case. If then on further observation a greater complexity of circumstances should come to light, I shall nevertheless be sure of having before us a typical occurrence, and one, moreover, that is not of an uncommon kind.

The first phase of beating-phantasies among girls, then, must belong to a very early period of childhood. Some features remain curiously indefinite, as though they were a matter of indifference. The scanty information given by the patients in their first statement, 'a child is being beaten', seems to be justified in respect to this phase. But another of their features can be established with certainty, and to the same effect in every case. The child being beaten is never the one producing the phantasy, but is invariably another child, most often a brother or a sister if there is any. Since this other child may be a boy or a girl, there is no constant relation between the sex of the child producing the phantasy and that of the child being beaten. The phantasy, then, is certainly not masochistic. It would be tempting to call it sadistic, but one cannot neglect the fact that the child producing the phantasy is never doing the beating herself. The actual identity of the person who does the beating remains obscure at first. Only this much can be established: it is not a child but an adult. Later on this indeterminate grown-up person becomes recognizable clearly and unambiguously as the (girl's) *father*.

This first phase of the beating-phantasy is therefore completely represented by the phrase: '*My father is beating the child.*' I am betraying a great deal of what is to be brought forward later when instead of this I say: 'My father is beating the child *whom I hate.*' Moreover, one may hesitate to say whether the characteristics of a 'phantasy' can yet be ascribed to this first step towards the later beating-phantasy. It is perhaps rather a question of recollections of events which have been witnessed, or of desires which have arisen on various occasions. But these doubts are of no importance.

Profound transformations have taken place between this first phase and the next. It is true that the person beating remains the same (that is, the father); but the child who is beaten has been changed into another one and is now invariably the child producing the phantasy. The phantasy is accompanied by a high degree of pleasure, and has now acquired a significant content, with the origin of which we shall be concerned later. Now, therefore, the wording runs: *'I am being beaten by my father.'* It is of an unmistakably masochistic character.

This second phase is the most important and the most momentous of all. But we may say of it in a certain sense that it has never had a real existence. It is never remembered, it has never succeeded in becoming conscious. It is a construction of analysis, but it is no less a necessity on that account.

The third phase once more resembles the first. It has the wording which is familiar to us from the patient's statement. The person beating is never the father, but is either left undetermined just as in the first phase, or turns in a characteristic way into a representative of the father, such as a teacher. The figure of the child who is producing the beating-phantasy no longer itself appears in it. In reply to pressing enquiries the patients only declare: 'I am probably looking on.' Instead of the one child that is being beaten, there are now a number of children present as a rule. Most frequently it is boys who are being beaten (in girls' phantasies), but none of them is personally known to the subject. The situation of being beaten, which was originally simple and monotonous, may go through the most complicated alterations and elaborations; and punishments and humiliations of another kind may be substituted for the beating itself. But the essential characteristic which distinguishes even the simplest phantasies of this phase from those of the first, and which establishes the connection with the intermediate phase, is this: the phantasy now has strong and unambiguous sexual excitement attached to it, and so provides a means for masturbatory satisfaction. But this is precisely what is puzzling. By what path has the phantasy of strange and unknown boys being beaten (a phantasy which has by this time become sadistic) found its way into the permanent possession of the little girl's libidinal trends?

Nor can we conceal from ourselves that the interrelations and sequence of the three phases of the beating-phantasy, as well as all its other peculiarities, have so far remained quite unintelligible.

IV

If the analysis is carried through the early period to which the beating-phantasies are referred and from which they are recollected, it shows us the child involved in the agitations of its parental complex.

The affections of the little girl are fixed on her father, who has probably done all he could to win her love, and in this way has sown the seeds of an attitude of hatred and rivalry towards her mother. This attitude exists side by side with a current of affectionate dependence on her, and as years go on it may be destined to come into consciousness more and more clearly and forcibly, or else to give an impetus to an excessive reaction of devotion to her. But it is not with the girl's relation to her mother that the beating-phantasy is connected. There are other children in the nursery, only a few years older or younger, who are disliked on all sorts of other grounds, but chiefly because the parents' love has to be shared with them, and for this reason they are repelled with all the wild energy characteristic of the emotional life of those years. If the child in question is a younger brother or sister (as in three of my four cases) it is despised as well as hated; yet it attracts to itself the share of affection which the blinded parents are always ready to give the youngest child, and this is a spectacle the sight of which cannot be avoided. One soon learns that being beaten, even if it does not hurt very much, signifies a deprivation of love and a humiliation. And many children who believed themselves securely enthroned in the unshakable affection of their parents have by a single blow been cast down from all the heavens of their imaginary omnipotence. The idea of the father beating this hateful child is therefore an agreeable one, quite apart from whether he has actually been seen doing so. It means: 'My father does not love this other child, *he loves only me.*'

This then is the content and meaning of the beating-phantasy in its first phase. The phantasy obviously gratifies the child's jealousy and is dependent upon the erotic side of its life, but is also powerfully reinforced by the child's egoistic interests. Doubt remains, therefore, whether the phantasy ought to be described as purely 'sexual', nor can one venture to call it 'sadistic'.

As is well known, all the signs on which we are accustomed to base our distinctions tend to lose their clarity as we come nearer to the source. So perhaps we may say in terms recalling the prophecy made by the Three Witches to Banquo: 'Not clearly sexual, not in itself sadistic, but yet the stuff from which both will later come.' In any case, however, there is no ground for suspecting that in this first phase the phantasy is already at the service of an excitation which involves the genitals and finds its outlet in a masturbatory act.

It is clear that the child's sexual life has reached the stage of genital organization, now that its incestuous love has achieved this premature choice of an object. This can be demonstrated more easily in the case of boys, but is also indisputable in the case of girls. Something like a premonition of what are later to be the final and normal sexual aims governs the child's libidinal trends. We may justly wonder why this should be so, but we may regard it as a proof of the fact that the genitals have already begun playing their part in the process of excitation. With boys the wish to beget a child from their mother is never absent, with girls the wish to have a child by their father is equally constant; and this in spite of their being completely incapable of forming any clear idea of the means for fulfilling these wishes. The child seems to be convinced that the genitals have something to do with the matter, even though in its constant brooding it may look for the essence of the presumed intimacy between its parents in relations of another sort, such as in their sleeping together, micturating in each other's presence, etc.; and material of the latter kind can be more easily apprehended in verbal images than the mystery that is connected with the genitals.

But the time comes when this early blossoming is nipped by the frost. None of these incestuous loves can avoid the fate of repression. They may succumb to it on the occasion of some discoverable external event which leads to disillusionment—such as unexpected slights, the unwelcome birth of a new brother or sister (which is felt as faithlessness), etc.; or the same thing may happen owing to internal conditions apart from any such events, perhaps simply because their yearning remains unsatisfied too long. It is unquestionably true that such events are not the *effective* causes, but that these love-affairs are bound to come to grief sooner or later, though we cannot say on what particular stumbling block. Most probably they pass away because their time is over, because the children have entered upon a new phase of development in which they are compelled to recapitulate from the history of mankind the repression of an incestuous object-choice, just as at an earlier stage they were obliged to effect an object-choice of that very sort.[7] In the new phase no mental product of the incestuous love-impulses that is present unconsciously is taken over by consciousness; and anything that has already come into consciousness is expelled from it. At the same time as this process of repression takes place, a sense of guilt appears. This is also of unknown origin, but there is no doubt whatever that it is connected with the incestuous wishes, and that it is justified by the persistence of those wishes in the unconscious.[8]

The phantasy of the period of incestuous love had said: 'He (my father) loves only me, and not the other child, for he is beating it.' The sense of guilt can discover no punishment more severe than the reversal of this triumph: 'No, he does not love you, for he is beating you.' In this way the phantasy of the second phase, that of being beaten by her father, is a direct expression of the girl's sense of guilt, to which her love for her father has now succumbed. The phantasy, therefore, has become masochistic. So far as I know, this is always so; a sense of guilt is invariably the factor that transforms sadism into masochism. But this is certainly not the whole content of masochism. The sense of guilt cannot have won the field alone; a share must also fall to the love-impulse. We must remember that we are dealing with children in whom the sadistic component was able for constitutional reasons to develop prematurely and in isolation. We need not abandon this point of view. It is precisely such children who find it particularly easy to hark back to the pregenital, sadistic-anal organization of their sexual life. If the genital organization, when it has scarcely been effected, is met by repression, the result is not only that every psychical representation of the incestuous love becomes unconscious, or remains so, but there is another result as well: a regressive debasement of the genital organization itself to a lower level. 'My father loves me' was meant in a genital sense; owing to the regression it is turned into 'My father is beating me (I am being beaten by my father)'. This being beaten is now a convergence of the sense of guilt and sexual love. *It is not only the punishment for the forbidden genital relation, but also the regressive substitute for that relation,* and from this latter source it derives the libidinal excitation which is from this time forward attached to it, and which finds its outlet in masturbatory acts. Here for the first time we have the essence of masochism.

This second phase—the child's phantasy of being itself beaten by its father—remains unconscious as a rule, probably in consequence of the intensity of the repression. I cannot explain why nevertheless in one of my six cases, that of a male, it was consciously remembered. This man, now grown up, had preserved the fact clearly in his memory that he used to employ the idea of being beaten by his mother for the purpose of masturbation, though to be sure he soon substituted for his own mother the mothers of his school-fellows or other women who in some way resembled her. It must not be forgotten that when a boy's incestuous phantasy is transformed into the corresponding masochistic one, one more reversal has to take place than in the case of a girl, namely the substitution of passivity for activity; and this additional degree of distortion may save the phantasy from having to remain unconscious as a result of repression. In this way the sense of guilt would be satisfied by regression instead of by repression. In the female cases the sense of guilt, in itself perhaps more exacting, could be appeased only by a combination of the two.

In two of my four female cases an elaborate superstructure of day-dreams, which was of great significance for the life of the person concerned, had grown up over the masochistic beating-phantasy. The function of this superstructure was to make possible a feeling of satisfied excitation, even though the masturbatory act was abstained from. In one of these cases the content— being beaten by the father—was allowed to venture again into consciousness, so long as the subject's own ego was made unrecognizable by a thin disguise. The hero of these stories was invariably beaten (or later only punished, humiliated, etc.) by his father.

I repeat, however, that as a rule the phantasy remains unconscious, and can only be reconstructed in the course of the analysis. This fact perhaps vindicates patients who say they remember that with them masturbation made its appearance before the third phase of the beating-phantasy (shortly to be discussed), and that this phase was only a later addition, made perhaps under the impression of scenes at school. Every time I have given credit to these statements I have felt inclined to assume that the masturbation was at first under the dominance of unconscious phantasies and that conscious ones were substituted for them later.

I look upon the beating-phantasy in its familiar third phase, which is its final form, as a substitute of this sort. Here the child who produces the phantasy appears almost as a spectator, while the father persists in the shape of a teacher or some other person in authority. The phantasy, which now resembles that of the first phase, seems to have become sadistic once more. It appears as though in the phrase, 'My father is beating the child, he loves only me', the stress has been shifted back on to the first part after the second part has undergone repression. But only the *form* of this phantasy is sadistic; the satisfaction which is derived from it is masochistic. Its significance lies in the fact that it has taken over the libidinal cathexis of the repressed portion and at the same time the sense of guilt which is attached to the content of that portion. All of the many unspecified children who are being beaten by the teacher are, after all, nothing more than substitutes for the child itself.

We find here for the first time, too, something like a constancy of sex in the persons who play a part in the phantasy. The children who are being beaten are almost invariably boys, in the phantasies of boys just as much as in those of girls. This characteristic is naturally not to be explained by any rivalry between the sexes, as otherwise of course in the phantasies of boys it would be girls who would be being beaten; and it has nothing to do with the sex of the child who was hated in the first phase. But it points to a complication in the case of girls. When they turn away from their incestuous love for their father, with its genital significance, they easily abandon their feminine role. They spur their 'masculinity complex' (Van Ophuijsen, 1917) into activity, and from that time forward only want to be boys. For that reason the whipping-boys who represent them are boys too. In both the cases of day-dreaming—one of which almost rose to the level of a work of art—the heroes were always young men; indeed women used not to come into these creations at all, and only made their first appearance after many years, and then in minor parts.

V

I hope I have brought forward my analytic observations in sufficient detail, and I should only like to add that the six cases I have mentioned so often do not exhaust my material. Like other analysts, I have at my disposal a far larger number of cases which have been investigated less thoroughly. These observations can be made use of along various lines: for elucidating the genesis of the perversions in general and of masochism in particular, and for estimating the part played by difference of sex in the dynamics of neurosis.

The most obvious result of such a discussion is its application to the origin of the perversions. The view which brought into the foreground in this connection the constitutional reinforcement or premature growth of a single sexual component is not shaken, indeed; but it is seen not to comprise the whole truth. The perversion is no longer an isolated fact in the child's sexual life, but falls into its place among the typical, not to say normal, processes of development which are familiar to us. It is brought into relation with the child's incestuous love-object, with its Oedipus complex. It first comes into prominence in the sphere of this complex, and after the complex has broken down it remains over, often quite by itself, the inheritor of the charge of libido from that complex and weighed down by the sense of guilt that was attached to it. The abnormal sexual constitution, finally, has shown its strength by forcing the Oedipus complex into a particular direction, and by compelling it to leave an unusual residue behind.

A perversion in childhood, as is well known, may become the basis for the construction of a perversion having a similar sense and persisting throughout life, one which consumes the subject's whole sexual life. On the other hand the perversion may be broken off and remain in the background of a normal sexual development, from which, however, it continues to withdraw a certain amount of energy. The first of these alternatives was already known before the days of analysis. Analytic investigation, however, of such fully-developed cases almost bridges the gulf between the two. For we find often enough with these perverts that they too made an attempt at developing normal sexual activity, usually at the age of puberty; but their attempt had not enough force in it and was abandoned in the face of the first obstacles which inevitably arise, whereupon they fell back upon their infantile fixation once and for all.

It would naturally be important to know whether the origin of infantile perversions from the Oedipus complex can be asserted as a general principle. While this cannot be decided without further investigation, it does not seem impossible. When we recall the anamneses which have been obtained in adult cases of perversion we cannot fail to notice that the decisive impression, the 'first experience', of all these perverts, fetishists, etc., is scarcely ever referred back to a time earlier than the sixth year. At this time, however, the dominance of the Oedipus complex is already over; the experience which is recalled, and which has been effective in such a puzzling way, may very well have represented the legacy of that complex. The connections between the experience and the complex which is by this time repressed are bound to remain obscure so long as analysis has not thrown any light on the time before the first 'pathogenic' impression. So it may be imagined how little value is to be attached, for instance, to an assertion that a case of homosexuality is congenital, when the ground given for this belief is that ever since his eighth or sixth year the person in question has felt inclinations only towards his own sex.

If, however, the derivation of perversions from the Oedipus complex can be generally established, our estimate of its importance will have gained added strength. For in our opinion the Oedipus complex is the actual nucleus of neuroses, and the infantile sexuality which culminates in this complex is the true determinant of neuroses. What remains of the complex in the unconscious represents the disposition to the later development of neuroses in the adult. In this way the beating-phantasy and other analogous perverse fixations would also only be precipitates of the Oedipus complex, scars, so to say, left behind after the process has ended, just as the notorious 'sense of inferiority' corresponds to a narcissistic scar of the same sort. In taking this view of the matter I must express my unreserved agreement with Marcinowski (1918), who has recently put it forward most happily. As is well known, this neurotic delusion of inferiority is only a partial one, and is completely compatible with the existence of a self-overvaluation derived from other sources. The origin of the Oedipus complex itself, and the destiny which compels man, probably alone among all animals, to begin his sexual life twice over, first like all other creatures in his early childhood, and then after a long interruption once more at the age of puberty—all the problems that are connected with man's 'archaic heritage'—have been discussed by me elsewhere, and I have no intention of going into them in this place.[9]

Little light is thrown upon the genesis of masochism by our discussion of the beating-phantasy. To begin with, there seems to be a confirmation of the view that masochism is not the manifestation of a primary instinct, but originates from sadism which has been turned round upon the self—that is to say, by means of regression from an object to the ego.[10] Instincts with a passive aim must be taken for granted as existing, especially among women. But passivity is not the whole of masochism. The characteristic of unpleasure belongs to it as well,—a bewildering accompaniment to the satisfaction of an instinct. The transformation of sadism into masochism appears to be due to the influence of the sense of guilt which takes part in the act of repression. Thus repression is operative here in three ways: it renders the consequences of the genital organization unconscious, it compels that organization itself to regress to the earlier sadistic-anal stage, and it transforms the sadism of this stage into masochism, which is passive and again in a certain sense narcissistic. The second of these three effects is made possible by the weakness of the genital organization, which must be presupposed in these cases. The third becomes necessary because the sense of guilt takes as much objection to sadism as to incestuous object-choice genitally conceived. Again, the analyses do not tell us the origin of the sense of guilt itself. It seems to be brought along by the new phase upon which the child is entering, and, if it afterwards persists, it seems to correspond to a scar-like formation which is similar to the sense of inferiority. According to our present orientation in the structure of the ego, which is as yet uncertain, we should assign it to the agency in the mind which sets itself up as a critical conscience over against the rest of the ego, which produces Silberer's functional phenomenon in dreams, and which cuts itself loose from the ego in delusions of being watched.[11]

We may note too in passing that the analysis of the infantile perversion dealt with here is also of help in solving an old riddle—one which, it is true, has always troubled those who have not accepted psycho-analysis more than analysts themselves. Yet quite recently even Bleuler regarded it as a remarkable and inexplicable fact that neurotics make masturbation the central point of their sense of guilt. We have long assumed that this sense of guilt relates to the masturbation of early childhood and not to that of puberty, and that in the main it is to be connected not with the act of masturbation but with the phantasy which, although unconscious, lies at its root—that is to say, with the Oedipus complex.[12]

As regards the third and apparently sadistic phase of the beating-phantasy, I have already [p. 165] discussed the significance that it gains as the vehicle of the excitation impelling towards masturbation; and I have shown how it arouses activities of the imagination which on the one hand continue the phantasy along the same line, and on the other hand neutralize it through compensation. Nevertheless the second phase, the unconscious and masochistic one, in which the child itself is being beaten by its father, is incomparably the more important. This is not only because it continues to operate through the agency of the phase that takes its place; we can also detect effects upon the character, which are directly derived from its unconscious form. People who harbour phantasies of this kind develop a special sensitiveness and irritability towards anyone whom they can include in the class of fathers. They are easily offended by a person of this kind, and in that way (to their own sorrow and cost) bring about the realization of the imagined situation of being beaten by their father. I should not be surprised if it were one day possible to prove that the same phantasy is the basis of the delusional litigiousness of paranoia.

VI

It would have been quite impossible to give a clear survey of infantile beating-phantasies if I had not limited it, except in one or two connections, to the state of things in females. I will briefly recapitulate my conclusions. The little girl's beating-phantasy passes through three phases, of which the first and third are consciously remembered, the middle one remaining unconscious. The two conscious phases appear to be sadistic, whereas the middle and unconscious one is undoubtedly of a masochistic nature; its content consists in the child's being beaten by her father, and it carries with it the libidinal charge and the sense of guilt. In the first and third phantasies the child who is being beaten is always someone other than the subject; in the middle phase it is always the child herself; in the third phase it is almost invariably only boys who are being beaten. The person who does the beating is from the first her father, replaced later on by a substitute taken from the class of fathers. The unconscious phantasy of the middle phase had primarily a genital significance and developed by means of repression and regression out of an incestuous wish to be loved by the father. Another fact, though its connection with the rest does not appear to be close, is that between the second and third phases the girls change their sex, for in the phantasies of the latter phase they turn into boys.

I have not been able to get so far in my knowledge of beating-phantasies in boys, perhaps because my material was unfavourable. I naturally expected to find a complete analogy between the state of things in the case of boys and in that of girls, the mother taking the father's place in the phantasy. This expectation seemed to be fulfilled; for the content of the boy's phantasy which was taken to be the corresponding one was actually his being beaten by his mother (or later on by a substitute for her). But this phantasy, in which the boy's own self was retained as the person who was being beaten, differed from the second phase in girls in that it was able to become conscious. If on this account, however, we attempt to draw a parallel between it and the *third* phase of the girl's phantasy, a new difference is found, for the figure of the boy himself is not replaced by a number of unknown, and unspecified children, least of all by a number of girls. Therefore the expectation of there being a complete parallel was mistaken.

My male cases with an infantile beating-phantasy comprised only a few who did not exhibit some other gross injury to their sexual activities; again they included a fairly large number of persons who would have to be described as true masochists in the sense of being sexual perverts. They were either people who obtained their sexual satisfaction exclusively from masturbation accompanied by masochistic phantasies; or they were people who had succeeded in combining masochism with their genital activity in such a way that, along with masochistic performances and under similar conditions, they were able to bring about erection and emission or to carry out normal intercourse. In addition to this there was the rarer case in which a masochist is interfered with in his perverse activities by the appearance of obsessional ideas of unbearable intensity. Now perverts who can obtain satisfaction do not often have occasion to come for analysis. But as regards the three classes of masochists that have been mentioned there may be strong motives to induce them to go to an analyst. The masochist masturbator finds that he is absolutely impotent if after all he does attempt intercourse with a woman; and the man who has hitherto effected intercourse with the help of a masochistic idea or performance may suddenly make the discovery that the alliance which was so convenient for him has broken down, his genital organs no longer reacting to the masochistic stimulus. We are accustomed confidently to promise recovery to psychically impotent patients who come to us for treatment; but we ought to be more guarded in making this prognosis so long as the dynamics of the disturbance are unknown to us. It comes as a disagreeable surprise if the analysis reveals the cause of the 'merely psychical' impotence to be a typically masochistic attitude, perhaps deeply embedded since infancy.

As regards these masochistic men, however, a discovery is made at this point which warns us not to pursue the analogy between their case and that of women any further at present, but to judge each independently. For the fact emerges that in their masochistic phantasies, as well as in the performances they go through for their realization, they invariably transfer themselves into the part of a woman; that is to say, their masochistic attitude coincides with a *feminine* one. This can easily be demonstrated from details of the phantasies; but many patients are even aware of it themselves, and give expression to it as a subjective conviction. It makes no difference if in a fanciful embellishment of the masochistic scene they keep up the fiction that a mischievous boy, or page, or apprentice is going to be punished. On the other hand the persons who administer chastisement are always women, both in the phantasies and the performances. This is confusing enough; and the further question must be asked whether this feminine attitude already forms the basis of the masochistic element in the *infantile* beating-phantasy.[13]

Let us therefore leave aside consideration of the state of things in cases of adult masochism, which it is so hard to clear up, and turn to the infantile beating-phantasy in the male sex. Analysis of the earliest years of childhood once more allows us to make a surprising discovery in this field. The phantasy which has as its content being beaten by the mother, and which is conscious or can become so, is not a primary one. It possesses a preceding stage which is invariably unconscious and has as its content: *'I am being beaten by my father.'* This preliminary stage, then, really corresponds to the second phase of the phantasy in the girl. The familiar and conscious phantasy: 'I am being beaten by my mother', takes the place of the third phase in the girl, in which, as has been mentioned already, unknown boys are the objects that are being beaten. I have not been able to demonstrate among boys a preliminary stage of a sadistic nature that could be set beside the first phase of the phantasy in girls, but I will not now express any final disbelief in its existence, for I can readily see the possibility of meeting with more complicated types.

In the male phantasy—as I shall call it briefly, and, I hope, without any risk of being misunderstood—the being beaten also stands for being loved (in a genital sense), though this has been debased to a lower level owing to regression. So the original form of the unconscious male phantasy was not the provisional one that we have hitherto given: 'I am being beaten by my father', but rather: *'I am loved by my father'*. The phantasy has been transformed by the processes with which we are familiar into the conscious phantasy: *'I am being beaten by my mother*. The boy's beating-phantasy is therefore passive from the very beginning, and is derived from a feminine attitude towards his father. It corresponds with the Oedipus complex just as the female one (that of the girl) does; only the parallel relation which we expected to find between the two must be given up in favour of a common character of another kind. *In both cases the beating-phantasy has its origin in an incestuous attachment to the father.*[14]

It will help to make matters clearer if at this point I enumerate the other similarities and differences between beating-phantasies in the two sexes. In the case of the girl the unconscious masochistic phantasy starts from the normal Oedipus attitude; in that of the boy it starts from the inverted attitude, in which the father is taken as the object of love. In the case of the girl the phantasy has a preliminary stage (the first phase), in which the beating bears no special significance and is performed upon a person who is viewed with jealous hatred. Both of these features are absent in the case of the boy, but this particular difference is one which might be removed by more fortunate observation. In her transition to the conscious phantasy [the third phase] which takes the place of the unconscious one, the girl retains the figure of her father, and in that way keeps unchanged the sex of the person beating; but she changes the figure and sex of the person being beaten, so that eventually a man is beating male children. The boy, on the contrary, changes the figure and sex of the person beating, by putting his mother in the place of his father; but he retains his own figure, with the result that the person beating and the person being beaten are of opposite sexes. In the case of the girl what was originally a masochistic (passive) situation is transformed into a sadistic one by means of repression, and its sexual quality is almost effaced. In the case of the boy the situation remains masochistic, and shows a greater resemblance to the original phantasy with its genital significance, since there is a difference of sex between the person beating and the person being beaten. The boy evades his homosexuality by repressing and remodelling his unconscious phantasy: and the remarkable thing about his later conscious phantasy is that it has for its content a feminine attitude without a homosexual object-choice. By the same process, on the other hand, the girl escapes from the demands of the erotic side of her life altogether. She turns herself in phantasy into a man, without herself becoming active in a masculine way, and is no longer anything but a spectator of the event which takes the place of a sexual act.

We are justified in assuming that no great change is effected by the *repression* of the original unconscious phantasy. Whatever is repressed from consciousness or replaced in it by something else remains intact and potentially operative in the unconscious. The effect of *regression* to an earlier stage of the sexual organization is quite another matter. As regards this we are led to believe that the state of things changes in the unconscious as well. Thus in both sexes the masochistic phantasy of being beaten by the father, though not the passive phantasy of being loved by him, lives on in the unconscious after repression has taken place. There are, besides, plenty of indications that the repression has only very incompletely attained its object. The boy, who has tried to escape from a homosexual object-choice, and who has not changed his sex, nevertheless feels like a woman in his conscious phantasies, and endows the women who are beating him with masculine attributes and characteristics. The girl, who has even renounced her sex, and who has on the whole accomplished a more thoroughgoing work of repression, nevertheless does not become freed from her father; she does not venture to do the beating herself; and since she has herself become a boy, it is principally boys whom she causes to be beaten.

I am aware that the differences that I have here described between the two sexes in regard to the nature of the beating-phantasy have not been cleared up sufficiently. But I shall not attempt to unravel these complications by tracing out their dependence on other factors, as I do not consider that the material for observation is exhaustive. So far as it goes, however, I should like to make use of it as a test for two theories. These theories stand in opposition to each other, though both of them deal with the relation between

repression and sexual character, and each, according to its own view, represents the relation as a very intimate one. I may say at once that I have always
regarded both theories as incorrect and misleading.

The first of these theories is anonymous. It was brought to my notice
many years ago by a colleague with whom I was at that time on friendly
terms.[15] The theory is so attractive on account of its bold simplicity that the
only wonder is that it should not have found its way into the literature of the
subject except in a few scattered allusions. It is based on the fact of the
bisexual constitution of human beings, and asserts that the motive force of
repression in each individual is a struggle between the two sexual characters.
The dominant sex of the person, that which is the more strongly developed,
has repressed the mental representation of the subordinated sex into the
unconscious. Therefore the nucleus of the unconscious (that is to say, the
repressed) is in each human being that side of him which belongs to the
opposite sex. Such a theory as this can only have an intelligible meaning if
we assume that a person's sex is to be determined by the formation of his
genitals; for otherwise it would not be certain which is a person's stronger
sex and we should run the risk of reaching from the results of our enquiry the
very fact which has to serve as its point of departure. To put the theory
briefly: with men, what is unconscious and repressed can be brought down to
feminine instinctual impulses; and conversely with women.

The second theory is of more recent origin.[16] It is in agreement with the
first one in so far as it too represents the struggle between the two sexes as
being the decisive cause of repression. In other respects it comes into conflict
with the former theory; moreover, it looks for support to sociological rather
than biological sources. According to this theory of the 'masculine protest',
formulated by Alfred Adler, every individual makes efforts not to remain
on the inferior 'feminine line [of development]' and struggles towards the
'masculine line', from which satisfaction can alone be derived. Adler makes
the masculine protest responsible for the whole formation both of character
and of neuroses. Unfortunately he makes so little distinction between the two
processes, which certainly have to be kept separate, and sets altogether so
little store in general by the fact of repression, that to attempt to apply the
doctrine of the masculine protest to repression brings with it the risk of
misunderstanding. In my opinion such an attempt could only lead us to infer
that the masculine protest, the desire to break away from the feminine line,
was in every case the motive force of repression. The repressing agency,
therefore, would always be a masculine instinctual impulse, and the re-

pressed would be a feminine one. But symptoms would also be the result of a feminine impulse, for we cannot discard the characteristic feature of symptoms—that they are substitutes for the repressed, substitutes that have made their way out in spite of repression.

Now let us take these two theories, which may be said to have in common a sexualization of the process of repression, and test them by applying them to the example of the beating-phantasies which we have been studying. The original phantasy, 'I am being beaten by my father', corresponds, in the case of the boy, to a feminine attitude, and is therefore an expression of that part of his disposition which belongs to the opposite sex. If this part of him undergoes repression, the first theory seems shown to be correct; for this theory set it up as a rule that what belongs to the opposite sex is identical with the repressed. It scarcely answers to our expectations, it is true, when we find that the conscious phantasy, which arises after repression has been accomplished, nevertheless exhibits the feminine attitude once more, though this time directed towards the mother. But we will not go into such doubtful points, when the whole question can be so quickly decided. There can be no doubt that the original phantasy in the case of the girl, 'I am being beaten (i.e. I am loved) by my father', represents a feminine attitude, and corresponds to her dominant and manifest sex; according to the theory, therefore, it ought to escape repression, and there would be no need for its becoming unconscious. But as a matter of fact it does become unconscious, and is replaced by a conscious phantasy which disavows the girl's manifest sexual character. The theory is therefore useless as an explanation of beating-phantasies, and is contradicted by the facts. It might be objected that it is precisely in unmanly boys and unwomanly girls that these beating-phantasies appeared and went through these vicissitudes; or that it was a trait of femininity in the boy and of masculinity in the girl which must be made responsible for the production of a passive phantasy in the boy, and its repression in the girl. We should be inclined to agree with this view, but it would not be any the less impossible to defend the supposed relation between manifest sexual character and the choice of what is destined for repression. In the last resort we can only see that both in male and female individuals masculine as well as feminine instinctual impulses are found, and that each can equally well undergo repression and so become unconscious.

The theory of the masculine protest seems to maintain its ground very much better on being tested in regard to the beating-phantasies. In the case of both boys and girls the beating-phantasy corresponds with a feminine attitude—one, that is, in which the individual is lingering on the 'feminine line'—and both sexes hasten to get free from this attitude by repressing the phantasy. Nevertheless, it seems to be only with the girl that the masculine protest is attended with complete success, and in that instance, indeed, an ideal example is to be found of the operation of the masculine protest. With the boy the result is not entirely satisfactory; the feminine line is not given up, and the boy is certainly not 'on top' in his conscious masochistic phantasy. It would therefore agree with the expectations derived from the theory if we were to recognize that this phantasy was a symptom which had come into existence through the failure of the masculine protest. It is a disturbing fact, to be sure, that the girl's phantasy, which owes its origin to the forces of repression, also has the value and meaning of a symptom. In this instance, where the masculine protest has completely achieved its object, surely the determining condition for the formation of a symptom must be absent.

Before we are led by this difficulty to a suspicion that the whole conception of the masculine protest is inadequate to meet the problem of neuroses and perversions, and that its application to them is unfruitful, we will for a moment leave the passive beating-phantasies and turn our attention to other instinctual manifestations of infantile sexual life—manifestations which have equally undergone repression. No one can doubt that there are also wishes and phantasies which keep to the masculine line from their very nature, and which are the expression of masculine instinctual impulses—sadistic tendencies, for instance, or a boy's lustful feelings towards his mother arising out of the normal Oedipus complex. It is no less certain that these impulses, too, are overtaken by repression. If the masculine protest is to be taken as having satisfactorily explained the repression of passive phantasies (which later become masochistic), then it becomes for that very reason totally inapplicable to the opposite case of active phantasies. That is to say, the doctrine of the masculine protest is altogether incompatible with the fact of repression. Unless we are prepared to throw away all that has been acquired in psychology since Breuer's first cathartic treatment and through its agency, we cannot expect that the principle of the masculine protest will acquire any significance in the elucidation of the neuroses and perversions.

The theory of psycho-analysis (a theory based on observation) holds firmly to the view that the motive forces of repression must not be sexualized. Man's archaic heritage forms the nucleus of the unconscious mind; and whatever part of that heritage has to be left behind in the advance to later phases of development, because it is unserviceable or incompatible with what is new and harmful to it, falls a victim to the process of repression. This selection is made more successfully with one group of instincts than with the other. In virtue of special circumstances which have often been pointed out already,[17] the latter group, that of the sexual instincts, are able to defeat the intentions of repression, and to enforce their representation by substitutive formations of a disturbing kind. For this reason infantile sexuality, which is held under repression, acts as the chief motive force in the formation of symptoms; and the essential part of its content, the Oedipus complex, is the nuclear complex of neuroses. I hope that in this paper I have raised an expectation that the sexual aberrations of childhood, as well as those of mature life, are ramifications of the same complex.

NOTES

1. [A well-known series of books by Mme. de Ségur, of which *Les Malheurs de Sophie* was perhaps the most popular.]
2. [This may be related to the theory of sublimation touched upon in Chapter III of *The Ego and the Id* (1923).]
3. [This observation of Binet's (1888) was mentioned by Freud in his *Three Essays* (1905) and commented upon in a footnote added to that work in 1920 (*Standard Ed., 7,* 154).]
4. [See 'The Predisposition to Obsessional Neurosis' (1913).]
5. [Nothing is said here of the sixth case.]
6. [Freud does in fact discuss beating-phantasies in men below (p. 174 ff.). Their specifically feminine basis is what he probably has in mind in speaking of 'another subject'.]
7. Compare the part played by Fate in the myth of Oedipus.
8. [*Footnote added* 1924:] See the continuation of this line of thought in 'The Dissolution of the Oedipus Complex' (1924).
9. [Freud had discussed these questions at length, not long before, in his *Introductory Lectures* (1916–17), especially in Lectures XXI and XXIII.]
10. Cf. 'Instincts and their Vicissitudes' (1915).—[In *Beyond the Pleasure Principle* (1920), *Standard Ed., 18,* 54–5, Freud suggested that there might after all be a primary masochism.]
11. [See Part III of Freud's paper on narcissism (1914). This agency was, of course, later described as the 'super-ego'. Cf. Chapter III of *The Ego and the Id* (1923).]
12. [See for example a discussion in the 'Rat Man' case history (1909), *Standard Ed., 10,* 202 ff.]
13. [*Footnote added* 1924:] Further remarks on this subject will be found in 'The Economic Problem of Masochism' (1924).
14. [A beating-phantasy plays some little part in the analysis of the 'Wolf Man' (1918).]
15. [Near the end of Freud's 'Analysis Terminable and Interminable' (1937), where he refers back to the present passage, he attributes this theory to Wilhelm Fliess.]
16. [Adler's theory of repression was discussed briefly in the case history of the 'Wolf Man' (1918).]

9. Masochism in Paranoia

Robert C. Bak

Until the works of Ferenczi *(1)* and Freud gave us essential insight into paranoia, Kraepelin's point of view dominated. Kraepelin gave the classic description, delineating the symptom complex, and the bulk of the ensuing research attempted to isolate paranoia as a disease entity. With the separation of the paraphrenias from dementia præcox, the sole two remaining clinical forms of sensitive paranoia were the paranoia of jealousy and litigious paranoia. Most investigators held that the psychosis was characterogenic, originating in a specific paranoid constitution, which manifested itself in certain personality traits. The psychosis was supposed to develop under the influence of certain experiences as an exaggeration of the underlying constitution. Among the precipitating experiences were particularly emphasized injuries to the ego, such as slights, frustrated ambitions, injustices.

Freud *(2)* emerged with his brilliant genetic theory of paranoia, demonstrated by means of Schreber's autobiography. Essentially this theory states that in paranoia the ego sets up defenses against homosexuality, from which there results a regression from sublimated homosexuality to narcissism. The libido is withdrawn from the loved person, the homosexual trend ('I love him') is denied and turned into its opposite ('I hate him'), and the hatred is then projected ('because he persecutes me'). Projection undoes the withdrawal. The subsequent formation of delusions is a work of reconstruction, which carries the libido back to the object, but with a negative prefix. This ingenious theory seemed applicable to the various clinical forms of paranoia.

Clinical psychiatry took over elements of Freud's theory but in an attenuated form. Schulte *(3)* developed the 'we' theory of paranoia, translating the idea of reconstruction into Gestalt terminology. He stated that the paranoiac regains contact with the group in his delusional relations, thus 'closing the

Read before the New York Psychoanalytic Society on June 19, 1945.
Reprinted by permission of *The Psychoanalytic Quarterly* 15 (1946):285–301.

wound' of isolation. Cameron *(4)* recently, and similarly, attributed paranoid delusions to a defective development of role-taking and a relative inadequacy in social perspectives. In place of projection and reconstruction he introduced the concept of 'pseudo-community', organized by the paranoiac's reaction to his own preoccupations out of fragments of the social behavior of others. Mayer-Gross *(5)*, paraphrasing the idea of libido withdrawal, derived persecutory delusions from the 'cooling of sympathetic emotions', which are then projected on the outside world. Kretschmer *(6)* in his study of the *'sensitive Beziehungswahn'* stressed the sexual ethical conflict as the main factor, and derived the paranoid reaction from the interplay of character and environment: a weak sexual endowment is manifested in an 'uncertainty of instinctual drives', while psychical trauma and exhaustion serve as precipitating factors.

In psychoanalytic circles at the time of Freud's paper on Schreber, interest was mainly focused on libidinal trends and the defense against them; hence, the discovery of the role of homosexuality was of enormous significance for an understanding of paranoia. To this emphasis, perhaps, may be due the inadequate answer to the main and specific question, namely, why the beloved person should be transformed into a persecutor.

Stärcke *(7)* and van Ophuijsen *(8)* attempted to explain this particular vicissitude of the homosexual trend. In their valuable contributions, still dominated by the reigning interest in phases of libido development, they upheld the view that the original persecutor is the scybalum, and that the delusions of persecution are derived mainly by elaboration and symbolizations of anal sensations. But this addition to the homosexual aspect did not provide sufficient clarification.

Another factor had to be considered. The enormous role played by aggression in paranoia could not elude Freud very long *(9)*. In the Ego and the Id, discussing the duality of instincts, he stated that the paranoiac does not directly transform the personal relationship from love into hate. From the start there is present an ambivalence; the transformation takes place by a reactive shifting of cathexis. The quantity of energy withdrawn from erotic trends is added to the hostile impulses.

This new important point clarified the second defensive step of the ego in paranoia. The first step is the withdrawal of love as a defense against the sexual wish. Reënforcement of hostility by the liberated energy constitutes the second step, and this second step accounts for the hatred felt for the previously loved person. The way in which this hatred is rationalized and nourished by interpretations of other persons' unconscious wishes was illuminated earlier by Freud in the article, Certain Neurotic Mechanisms in Jealousy, Paranoia and Homosexuality *(10)*. But hatred and hostility are not by any means paranoia. Therefore it seemed that somewhere in the third step of Freud's scheme, that of the projection of the aggression, lay the secret of persecutory delusional formation.

Klein *(11)*, who refers also to Róheim's *(12)* findings, believes that the fixation point of paranoia lies in the period of maximal sadism, during which the mother's body is attacked by means of dangerous and poisonous excreta. The delusions of persecution are supposed to arise from the anxiety attached to these attacks.

Nunberg *(13)* in his much quoted paper, Homosexuality, Magic and Aggression, gives us a profound hint in a somewhat different direction. He describes a particular type of homosexual, in whom the sexual act satisfies simultaneously both aggressive and libidinal impulses. In this type the ego ideal is projected onto the love object, which then receives sadistic treatment in the sexual act. In paranoia the sadism is turned largely into its opposite, into masochism. This paper, following a somewhat similar line of thought, will corroborate Nunberg's view.

The patient, a man of thirty-seven, began his analysis after an acute anxiety state with depression, for which he had spent four weeks in a hospital. He improved considerably but felt the need of further help to get at the cause of his acute breakdown. A few weeks prior to his hospitalization, he had become apprehensive about his relations with his fiancée. As the wedding day approached, although he was intensely desirous of being married, his anxiety mounted. He started to examine his penis and to worry about his ordinarily well-functioning potency. With increasing panic he observed a slackening of his mental faculties. He felt as if a catastrophe impended, as if he were sitting on a volcano whose eruption would sweep him away. At this point he asked for psychiatric help and was hospitalized.

In the hospital he was preoccupied mainly with three topics. In the first place he thought that he had lost his mind, which seemed proved to him by his own difficulty in thinking and by his suicidal impulses. Second, he thought he was incapable of getting married; this it was which made him think of suicide as the only way of avoiding the prospect of remaining a bachelor and leading 'a lonely, horrid, hideous existence'. Third, he feared his nervous breakdown would be interpreted by people to be the result of some sexual aberration, and that they might spread gossip about him in this connection. This was his first definitely paranoid idea, which later turned out to be related to childhood experiences of 'being buggered' (anal intercourse). Early in his treatment it became evident that the patient's main difficulty lay in his relation to men. Among women he was successful, especially in sexual relations, yet he had not developed any emotional tie up to the time of his engagement. His life was void of male friendships. His contacts were mainly restricted to the professional field, but even these relations proved to be very fragile. Previous to and during treatment, he got into states of anxiety which ran according to a more or less similar pattern. In most instances, he felt slighted by either of his older superiors, or by one of his rivals with whom he had had pleasant relations prior to the conflict; or he felt as though some injustice was inflicted upon him. A variation of these feelings occurred when he tried to get out of a situation in which he felt some obligation. The feeling that something was expected of him was experienced as something forced upon him. He was afraid he might be taken advantage of, 'used' and 'reduced to a mere tool'.

During a short absence from treatment he went through a typical episode which he communicated to me in a letter that gives insight into the structure and course of such a conflict.

'I am writing you regarding the recurrence of my troubles. Their cause is concerned with some of my personal relationships which are in reality getting out of hand. I realize that I am abnormally conscious of and concerned with these matters. But, this consciousness and concern is part of the cycle of wanting good personal relations, of being conscious of their status, of anxiety about them and of deterioration in them, partly because of the concern.

'A month ago, I moved to another building. The people were unfriendly and made no welcome and while I made some efforts to cultivate several members, I was not very successful. As a result of a strained feeling I refused to attend two of their private parties and that seems to have facilitated their resentment (which I feel, whether it exists or not). And during the course of a drinking bout indulged in by one of them, some quite serious indignities were inflicted on all members including me.

'The indignities as such are a minor problem. However, other reactions are much more disturbing and are making me seriously consider drastic measures. The main reactions are: sleeplessness, marked tension and much the same feeling of "sitting on a volcano" which I have described to you. In addition, I feel ill at ease with people, noncommunicative, and the anxiety, which is apparently detectable, spoils relationships with people with whom I had previously made a considerable favorable contact.

'The fear that I feel has been tremendous too, and is probably greater than I've experienced for eighteen months. As far as I can analyze it, the fear comes from the idea that I'll eventually have *to batter and beat one or more people—or be battered and beaten.*[1] Some of it is from the feeling that I'll get into a physical combat and will be disgraced and "talked about" by other members of the community—disgraced because of "starting a fight" (if I win), or because of getting a licking (if I lose). Some of these aspects have tortured me day and night for a week and that means that it has been more distressing than any situation since before I stopped seeing you regularly. If one feature is most disturbing, it is the fear which may be noticeable to others and thus tends (because of that) to cause more panic.

'At times like last night, I become almost panic-stricken when my mind "runs away" with all sorts of paranoid ideas. It would not be possible to name all of these, but most of them have to do with suspicion of conspiracies against me. I am moderately sure (during saner moments) that there are no conspiracies other than perhaps some small talk between the two people whom I dislike and distrust the most. I seriously suspect them of it, however, whether or not it is true.'

The scene of 'indignities' referred to in the letter was truly remarkable. The patient remained seated, motionless while a drunken, boisterous person spilled beer around the room, challenging him to fight, spilling beer on him, making him soaking wet. He could neither protest nor leave. He sat there in a kind of paralyzed fascination, waiting for the assault. Only later was he overwhelmed by a desire to 'split that man's head, and ruining the reputation of the whole place in case he was not rehabilitated'.

The conflict with one individual tended to include the group of which the individual was a member (Jews, Catholics, or various nationalities). When precipitated by the transference, as a 'transitive transference' reaction *(14)* only the conflict with the group became conscious. Thus, at one time the patient felt particularly slighted by taxi drivers. They were impolite, they cut in front of him, bumped into his car, pushed him out of their way; further-more, sailors spat in front of him, salesmen 'threw the change' in his face. He was fairly convinced in these phases that these were not chance happen-ings, but that they were directed against him. The reaction to these experi-ences was impulses of violence 'against the inferior mob or race', anxiety about them, and the desire to flee. He was on the way to developing the paranoiac pattern of the 'haunted man' whose fate is fleeing from one city to another.

Further clinical details which confirm the diagnosis of paranoia are omit-ted: systematization, excessive vulnerability, traces of megalomania, marked tendency to projection, ideas of reference and persecution, and litigious fan-tasies.

There is in the patient's history an organic factor that shaped his entire future. He was born with hypospadias. This seems to have remained unnoticed until the age of five, when he entered school. He became conspicuous through his urination: 'He can piss through a nut-hole', the boys teased him. His first name was distorted into a nickname similar to one of the vulgar expressions for the penis. They also changed his name into that of a woman. The vague notion that something was wrong became certainty when his mother said to him from an adjoining room, 'You are not quite like other boys', but avoided further explanation. The fact that she did not tell him made her appear guilty. At about the same age he agreed with his younger brother to mutual fellatio, which he performed. When the brother's turn came, he refused. This, he reasoned, occurred because his penis was unattractive. His enuresis was ridiculed by his brother and his parents. The ardent desire to be 'one of the boys', and his ostracism from the group became early realities. His envy of other boys and his hostility against them were vividly remembered. Later he heard that he was taken by his mother to several doctors, and that they might have operated on him.

He frequently examined his penis, found some scars on it, and thought they might have been caused by circumcision or by some other kind of operation. Up to an adult age, he could not decide whether the missing part of his foreskin was congenital or surgical.

A remarkable fantasy at the age of nine relates to this problem. It is probably a retrograde projection. In the fantasy he is not a child of his parents but the product of an experiment, the result of some chemical concoction. He thought he would have to go through further experiments and ordeals and probably come to a terrible end.

During puberty he became concerned with the relative enlargement of the glans penis and thought this might cause difficulty in withdrawing his penis from the vagina. From his first sexual intercourse with a prostitute he contracted gonorrhœa requiring long and painful treatments. The idea of injury done by women to the penis was thus confirmed. The evil role of women was represented in the dream:

'I was incarcerated in a sort of prison. A great many people were making efforts to get me out. I finally got out. You were standing in the background.'

Before the dream he had been pondering whether he should give up his affair with his current girl, a divorcee. The associations led through the links *carnis,* flesh, vulva to a memory which he was hesitant about confiding. 'It's too base and cruel', he said. As a boy of four or five he was playing with another child when they saw two dogs stuck together in coitus. They did not know quite what it was, and they chased the dogs with sticks toward a barbed-wire fence. The dogs became entangled in the barbed wire and hung suspended on the fence, their skins torn by the wire. He then got the vague idea that the dog's penis was cut off and that the bitch ran away with the male's penis inside of her.

Why he should discontinue his friendship with the divorcee became clear only later. Separation in time from her husband was not sufficient. He could not escape the feeling that the penis of the former husband was left in the wife's vagina. He had been told by his mother as a youngster that only a first marriage counts in heaven. He then visualized the second husband, roaming alone, lonely, having no place anywhere.

The notion persisted in the unconscious that woman inflicts injury on the man's penis, can tear it off and harbor it in the vagina. In the act of marriage not only his name but the man's penis is bestowed. The mother possesses the father's penis, and has power to destroy it.

The mother's treatment of the boy was total rejection. He felt he had been reared without any love at all. He could not recall any token of affection from his mother, no memory of caressing or tenderness. By contrast, the remembrance of a maid clasping him to her bosom, and the attendant feeling of her softness and warmth stood out in relief in his memory. The mother was no protection for him from his father; they presented a common front and participated in punishing the child. 'Wait until father comes home' was her repetitive admonition. Being the eldest, he saw the arrival of six children, one every second year.

Whatever the 'constitutional predisposition', the hypospadias more than paved the way to a preponderantly negative œdipus. The feminine component of his bisexuality was supplemented by his mother's harsh treatment, and by his fantasy of her threatening image. The convergence of these factors resulted in an identification with the castrating parent, the aggressive, phallic mother.

He turned to his father to be loved and appreciated by him. The father was a withdrawn, cold, strict, hard-working farmer. It was impossible to get in his good graces. The patient remembered often, with tears, how unapprecia-tive his father was of him. As a child of six, he was helping his father gather hay. He worked diligently the whole day, and driving home from the fields he asked his father if his work that day was worth fifty cents, and if so whether he could have it. The father ignored him completely. He pleaded, and finally in desperation asked if his work was worth at least a nickel. His father brushed him off as before. The emotional cathexis of these memories was tremendous. Not being loved, and particularly not having had any physical contact as a token of love, caused him a great deal of suffering. He felt very much moved when a neighbor's son put his arms around him. He felt a strong desire to go hand in hand with his father and for many years resented that the father did not play with him and did not teach him to fight. 'Together with father' he would have been strong, powerful, and a member of the male group. But instead of the close relationship and gentle physical contact he was beaten by the father for the slightest mischief. If he got into a fight with his brothers, which they started, he was nevertheless beaten by his father, being told he was older and should know better. Sometimes he waited for hours in a cold sweat for the threatened beating. The beatings, with a stick, were ruthlessly sadistic. He was always found to be in the wrong and was never exonerated. He fantasied though, with great clarity, picking up a shovel, or getting hold of the stick and attacking his father. After one beating he vowed that when he grew up he would beat up his father.

Such powerful aggression in this helpless boy, who craved for love and physical affection, intensified his ambivalence. One part of the aggression remained in fantasy, and developed into manifold sadistic reveries. He day-dreamed, for instance, that women were stationed in stalls like racing horses. Every woman was set and alert, bent forward on her toes in the stall. The patient, the boss, was beating them using his penis as a rod. He remembered a beating in the fields, his father starting back for the house, his being left behind overwhelmed by rage and sorrow, the idea flashing through his mind, 'Now he is going back to the house to screw mother'. The patient advanced the theory that his father 'was taking something out on him' at that time. There must have been a 'lack of sexual synchronization between my parents'. He recalled vaguely that his father had some sort of 'nervous breakdown' about that time. We have noted that 'nervous breakdown' was linked in the patient's mind to sexual (anal) aberration. It becomes obvious that in the unconscious the experience of being beaten by the father became libidinized into being sexually abused by him. The yearning for affection was regressively debased into masochistic degradation. In the masochistic act, part of the sadism took a circuitous path to gratification. During prostatic treatment the patient dreamed:

'I am going to the doctor for treatment. He looks like a debonair Frenchman, with a goatee. He could be a psychiatrist. The doctor starts to finger my anus, then it seems to change to intercourse. Finally I find myself dancing around in the room like a witch with a broomstick in my arse.'

To get hold of the father's stick, to castrate him, is achieved when anally he incorporates the father's penis, playing the part of the castrating woman, ultimately the role of the phallic mother. The patient's pugnacity and his lifelong preoccupation with preparing himself for physical fights by 'jiu-jitsu' lessons and 'commando training' also become understandable.

The constellation in which the paranoid reaction originates, as we know from Freud, is homosexuality. One of the prominent strivings in our patient had been the ambition to be recognized, appreciated and loved by important, outstanding men. The infantile desire to gain the father's recognition was never abandoned. Before the acute phase of his illness he dreamed that he went home, resolved the differences with his father, and at the final reconciliation they both wept. In his daydreams he became the favorite son as a reward for his successes and achievements. Fulfilment of the ego ideal, and being loved according to this ideal, is a sublimation which binds large quantities of homosexual and narcissistic libido. We know, however, that relationships on this basis prove to be very fragile, undermined as they are by strong ambivalence.

In such an unstable psychological structure economic changes in the ego or in the id result in a threat to the ego, and put the ego's defenses in action. An increase in homosexual libido may be due to biological or to situational factors (seduction, frustration); however, a greater role seems to be played in the further development by injuries inflicted directly upon the ego. Slights, frustrations, and disappointments reverse sublimations and liberate homosexual libido *(15):* 'You are not a man. You should be treated as a woman.' The failure of sublimation and the direct threat of castration lead to a retreat from phallic activity and induce a masochistic regression (homosexuality) where, according to the phallic and anal-sadistic organization, the desires to be castrated, beaten, and anally abused are reactivated.

A dream illustrates this point:

'Hitler, Mussolini, and Hirohito are about to be executed, but Hirohito cannot be found. I offer to replace him. The execution looks like a decapitation. I put my head on the scaffold; they separate the scalp from my skull, and push a knife into the back of my head.'

Through masochistic identification he could become the father, the powerful and loved enemy. The price he had to pay was castration (circumcision and anal intercourse).

This regression from sublimated homosexuality to masochism is an essential feature of the paranoid reaction, and constitutes the *first* defensive action of the ego. The withdrawal of love that follows is the *second* step in the defense through which the ego protects itself from the masochistic threat coming from the id. Alienation, feelings of estrangement, detachment from the previously beloved person, and free floating anxiety are the clinical corollaries of this stage. The *third* step is an increase of hostility, hatred of the love object, and the appearance of sadistic fantasies. In making the transition from love to hate the ego makes use of the displaceable energies contained in the originally ambivalent attitude. Sadism then fulfils several functions: the ego succeeds in turning passivity into activity and exploiting it as a countercathexis against masochism; furthermore, it reënforces the ego feelings (male attitude), and represents a recathexis of phallic activity. At this point mastery of the increased sadism is the primary task of the ego. That it fails is due to the interplay of several factors: weakness of the ego, masochistic fixation, and castration anxiety. The ego has to get rid of the increased tension and of the feelings of isolation, and this it manages by projecting a part of the sadism. The projection of sadism then would be the *fourth* step of defense. It is 'the paranoid mechanism proper', and it is a restitution. Projection is possible partly through the unconscious hostility of the actual and past participants and runs according to this preordained path. *In the projection of the sadism the masochism is bound to return.* The patient's preoccupation with precipitating a 'physical showdown' (being assaulted) and its ramified delusional elaborations, as being mistreated, injured, and persecuted, gratify the original masochistic desires of castration, beating, and abuse by the father. The delusion is a return of the repressed, and *paranoia is delusional masochism.*

The ego aligns itself on the side of sadism. Masochism (id) serves to reëstablish object cathexis and to hinder further 'defusion'. The antagonistic hypercathexis of the two psychic agencies is an attempt to achieve equilibrium. Depending on economic factors, the outcome may be flight, murder, suicide, or subsiding of the tension and cessation of the attack. Megalomania seems to be a later development when quantities of masochistic cathexis are further withdrawn.

Omitting the individual persecutory mechanism, let us examine briefly another characteristic feature of paranoia, that of an expanding, generalized persecution by a group. The answer may be found in the family constellation, perhaps more specifically in a vicissitude of sibling rivalry. The infantile prototype of this cohesive, hostile group may be traced in the fused image of the parents, their 'common front', representing the image of the phallic mother. This concept is later widened and includes the group of siblings. In the course of development these concepts in the ego ideal are further extended but seem to preserve their fused character and highly ambivalent cathexis. By regression they undergo a masochistic transformation to which can be applied Freud's *(16)* formulation in a modified version: 'My father loves me, I am the favorite, and he beats my brothers'. The libidinal and sadistic impulse after having undergone masochistic transformation is: 'My father beats me; I am hated; they all want to beat me', and this masochistic turn seems to correspond to reality. The love object, the father, was the original persecutor. The family was aligned against the patient in a 'common front'. His schoolmates ridiculed him. He was not accepted in fraternities, and his religious group was looked down on. Here we meet some of the real elements in delusion to which Freud referred in one of his last papers, Constructions in Analysis. True, to a large extent, the patient brought it on himself; but the paranoiac is not infrequently a person who has been persecuted in his past.

The sociological significance of this type of personality is well known. Our patient also turns violently against underprivileged minority groups. But once, when he witnessed a scene in which a fragile, small, Jewish-looking man was threatened with beating, he suddenly felt as if he himself were Jewish. He identifies himself with the persecuted minority on the basis of his history and on the basis of his masochistic propensity. In releasing his sadism against these groups, he not only defends himself against his own masochism, but realizes the beating fantasy through dramatization.

To what extent have these observations general validity in relation to paranoia? This case history is selected from a vast number of clinical experiences in the study of paranoid psychoses and from the analyses of paranoid personalities. We are indebted for the subtle and thorough analysis of a case of paranoia to Ruth Mack Brunswick *(17)*. In addition to this we are in possession of the full infantile history of this patient described in Freud's *(18)* inimitable way in the 'Wolf-man', in The History of an Infantile Neurosis, and this patient's later paranoid condition, observed by Brunswick.

The paranoia that started about twelve years after the analysis with Freud centered around a hypochondriac idea. The patient felt that his nose was swollen and disfigured by a scar due to operations that were performed on it by a dermatologist (who was a substitute for Freud). He felt crippled, and ruined for life, and claimed that 'he could not go on living that way', thereby repeating his mother's words which were related to her abdominal illness. The injury to the nose was originally self-inflicted and only later treated by the dermatologist. Brunswick stated:

'The patient's failure to be satisfied by his self-castration reveals a motive beyond the usual masochistic one of guilt, which, regardless of the perpetrator, would be satisfied by the act itself. The further motive is, of course, the libidinal one, the desire for castration at the hands of the father as an expression in anal-sadistic language of that father's love.' In discussing the patient's change of character, Brunswick relates it to the 'irritable and aggressive' period of childhood. 'Behind his tempers lay the masochistic desire for punishment at the hands of the father; but the outward form of his character was at that time sadistic. . . . In the present character change, the same regression to the anal-sadistic or masochistic level was present, but the role of the patient was passive. He was tormented and abused, instead of being the tormentor.' About the hypochondriac idea Brunswick wrote: 'The [childhood] fantasy of being beaten on the penis was reflected in the delusion of being injured on the nose by X [the dermatologist]'. There are many more masochistic elements in the case history, but still in the final analysis they are deprived of their due role. Brunswick derives the loss of psychic equilibrium in the patient from the flaring up of his love for the fatally ill Freud (father). This love represents a danger of castration, the love then is repressed and turned into hostility and has to be projected. It is true that the sight of the fatally ill Freud stirred up in the patient his old compassion for his father. In his childhood the sight of his sick father in a sanitarium became the prototype for his compassion for cripples, beggars, poor, and consumptive people, in whose presence he had to breathe noisily so as not to become like them. It was one of his defenses against identification with the castrated father.

We must add only some emphasis to Brunswick's analysis. Love for the ill Freud (father), which had the unconscious implication of the patient's being a 'woman', underwent regressive change into being castrated and beaten. *The homosexual object choice regressed into masochistic identification. We think that this form of regression constitutes the prerequisite of a paranoid development,* and the subsequent course in this patient also supports this assumption. In his hypochondria he consistently manœuvred to bring about his castration and at the same time defended himself against it by aggressive and litigious fantasies. This was the repetition of the sado-masochistic phase of his childhood, to which he had been thrown back partly because of a threat of castration. At that time he had been a tormentor of animals and men, but, at the same time, he indulged in fantasies of boys being beaten, and especially of being beaten on the penis. In a variation of these fantasies, 'the Czarevitch . . . is shut up in a room (the wardrobe) and beaten'. The Czarevitch was evidently himself. As we know, in hypochondriac and persecutory delusions, these fantasies find renewed expression.

A vast number of questions remains unanswered. The primary aim of this presentation has been to demonstrate the crucial role that masochism plays in the paranoid mechanism. In his paper, 'A Child Is Being Beaten', referring to the masochistic beating fantasies, Freud wrote:

'People who harbor fantasies of this kind develop a special sensitiveness and irritability towards anyone whom they can put among the class of fathers. They allow themselves to be easily offended by a person of this kind, and in that way (to their own sorrow and cost) bring about the realization of the imagined situation of being beaten by their father. I should not be surprised if it were one day possible to prove that the same fantasy is the basis of the delusional litigiousness of paranoia.'

NOTES

1. Italics mine.

REFERENCES

1. Ferenczi, Sándor: On the Part Played by Homosexuality in the Pathogenesis of Paranoia. In *Contributions to Psychoanalysis*. Boston: Richard C. Badger, 1916.
2. Freud: Psychoanalytic Notes Upon an Autobiographical Account of a Case of Paranoia (Dementia Paranoides), 1911. *Coll. Papers*, III, pp. 390–470.
3. Schulte, H.: *Versuch einer Theorie der paranoischen Eigenbeziehung und Wahnbildung*. Psychologische Forschung, V, 1924, pp. 1–23.
4. Cameron, N.: *The Development of Paranoic Thinking*. Psychol. Rev., L, 1943, pp. 219–233.
5. Mayer-Gross, W.: *Handbuch der Geisteskrankheiten*. Spez. T. Bd. V. pp. 303, ff. Editor: Bumke. Berlin: Springer, 1932.
6. Kretschmer, E.: *Die sensitive Beziehungswahn*. Berlin: Springer, 1924.

7. Stärcke, A.: *Die Rolle der analen und oralen Quantitäten im Verfolgungswahn und in analogen Systemgedanken*. Int. Ztschr. f. Psa., XXI, 1935, pp. 5–22.

8. Van Ophuijsen, J. H. W.: *On the Origin of the Feeling of Persecution*. Int. J. Psa., I, 1920, pp. 235–239.

9. Freud: *The Ego and the Id*. London: Hogarth Press, 1927.

10. ———: Certain Neurotic Mechanisms in Jealousy, Paranoia and Homosexuality, 1922. *Coll. Papers,* II, pp. 232–243.

11. Klein, Melanie: *The Psychoanalysis of Children*. London: Hogarth Press, 1937.

12. Róheim, Géza: *Nach dem Tode des Urvaters*. Imago, IX, 1923, pp. 83–121.

13. Nunberg, Hermann: *Homosexualität, Magie und Aggression*. Int. Ztschr. f. Psa., XXII, 1936, pp. 5–18.

14. Herman, Imre: *Die Psychoanalyse als Methode*. Vienna: Int. Psa. Verlag, 1936.

15. Freud: On Narcissism: an Introduction, 1914. *Coll. Papers,* IV, pp. 30–59.

16. ———: 'A Child Is Being Beaten'. A Contribution to the Study of the Origin of Sexual Perversions, 1919. *Coll. Papers,* II, pp. 172–201.

17. Brunswick, Ruth Mack: *A Supplement to Freud's 'History of an Infantile Neurosis'*. Int. J. Psa., IX, 1928, pp. 439–476.

18. Freud: From the History of an Infantile Neurosis, 1918. *Coll. Papers,* III, pp. 471–519.

10. Psychodynamic Theory of Masochism

Bela Grunberger

Deux instincts sont en moi,
Vertige et déraison,
J'ai l'effroi du bonheur,
Et la soif du poison.
AMIEL [1]

[I]

I once had occasion to quote the above lines during a discussion of this subject with a friend and colleague. "Masochism!" he exclaimed. "Be careful. Amiel was a great obsessional."

Amiel was indeed an obsessional. Sacher-Masoch, the worthy godfather of masochism, was a hysteric. Nacht, in his important work on the subject,[26] demonstrates the part played by masochism in practically all psychopathology. Much importance is also attached to the role of masochism in the new field of psychosomatic medicine. Thus one comes across it everywhere. It transcends established clinical concepts, principally in two dimensions. In the first place, in the horizontal respect, we find it transcending the hysterical pattern, whether the latter is obsessional or not, and lying at the back of everything else; and in a way the same is true in a vertical respect, since masochism transcends and seems to be consubstantial with human nature itself. (This observation might even be extended to three dimensions; in the course of treatment masochism often outlasts other symptoms, thus being transcendental in time also.) Certain writers, such as Reik[31] and Berliner,[5]

Reprinted from *Perversions, Psychodynamics and Therapy,* edited by S. Lorand and M. Balint, 1956.

have made investigations in this direction. Freud [14,18] refers on a number of occasions to non-neurotic masochists and to immanent masochism. That offers a very tempting prospect and opens up large horizons but, in my opinion, it is inappropriate from the point of view of psychoanalytic research, the specific goal of which must be better knowledge of the neuroses and psychoses. Whether masochism appears in the guise of a neurotic tendency or morbid behavior, whether it be instinct or symptom, code of conduct or system of ethics or philosophy, we must seek to individualize it as rigorously as possible within the nosological framework and, for this purpose, we must circumscribe the phenomenon rather than expand it to infinity. Disengaging the "masochistic mechanism" with the precision desired will not only help us to a better knowledge of the masochism which dominates all human psychopathology but will also yield us information about the neuroses in general.

[II]

Those who concern themselves with "the famous and terrible problem of masochism" (Odier [28]) run the risk of being immediately attracted and fascinated by the paradoxical combination of pain and pleasure. Confronted with the strange phenomenon of the search for pain, the inquirer is tempted to concentrate on it, and this often leads him into reflections which are more speculative than clinical. Moreover, in this he will meet with eager cooperation on the part of his patients, who will obligingly supply him with material capable of being used for the setting up of hypotheses based, for example, on narcissistic gratification (Eidelberg [7]; Lampl-de Groot [21]). These, however, are rationalizations and, even if light can be thrown on certain aspects of masochism by these methods, the clarifications thus obtained cannot be considered satisfactory. We shall therefore renounce pain as the point of departure for our investigations and concentrate our attention on the pleasure element instead.

We know that, apart from searching out pain, the masochist is characterized by total inhibition in the face of pleasure, pleasure of every kind. This is a point to which we shall return. In his chapter on the masochistic character, Nacht [26] draws attention to the inability to enjoy pleasures of life as a typical masochistic character trait. He mentions this last of all. To my way of thinking, however, it seems the most important feature. (Without wishing to insist on the point here, it seems to me that the masochist's incapacity to enjoy pleasure extends to all the phases of instinctual gratification, both genital and pregenital. Beneath this incapacity, however, there exists a strong wish to achieve pleasure all the same. It is this that causes the patient to accept analysis, and, in some measure, it is the presence of a masochistic element in every neurosis which causes the patient to submit to analysis and continue with it to a successful conclusion.) The masochist pursues pleasure, which he, like everyone else, desires. He even desires it—as is, indeed, only natural—more than other people do, as is proved by his conscious and unconscious life in its most diverse manifestations. It is at the moment of achieving pleasure, at the moment of taking a decisive, even if indirect, step toward it, that he recoils. He recoils from the anxiety which invariably arises in the presence of the pleasure-object, no matter in what form the latter appears, and returns to his former position, which is not one of renunciation pure and simple but of the opposite of pleasure, namely unpleasure. Without entering more deeply into details, we can conclude that what has been achieved by this is the disappearance of anxiety.

Various authors—Reik,[31] for instance—have drawn attention to the avoidance of anxiety in masochism. But, to my way of thinking, Reik's theory does not take the mechanism of masochistic pleasure sufficiently into account. Lewinsky[23] writes of masochism as the negation of anxiety but puts forward no solution for the problem as a whole.

The masochist Waldemar led a dangerous life, full of difficulties and privations, which he bore perfectly well. His mental and physical health left little to be desired. The masochist mechanism worked smoothly and without friction until the day when, by a fortunate and extraordinary combination of circumstances, he found himself face to face with a business opportunity which called for no effort on his part but would bring a fortune his way involving a complete change in his material circumstances. No sooner did he realize this than he was seized with anxiety, which grew until it became intolerable, reaching a point at which he felt an imperious need to do something immediately to rid himself of the opportunity, which he accordingly declined. That done, he breathed freely again, returned to his former situation, and resumed his old life. What a relief! He had had a narrow shave, had escaped by the skin of his teeth.

Can we say that Waldemar was searching for pain and finding pleasure in it? It does not seem so. He simply turned his back on pleasure in order to seek shelter from anxiety. If we insist on the pleasure element, it is because Waldemar's privations were not absolute. He had a sexual life and was able to enjoy mediocre, more or less "de-hedonized" gratifications. But, at the slightest attempt to cross the threshold which separated him from rich and genuine instinctual gratifications, anxiety made its implacable appearance. Generally, he unconsciously managed his life in such a way that this dangerous threshold was never reached, and all the dangerous drives in that direction were kept well repressed. Only analysis could release them and the anxiety associated with them. But, in everyday life, the anxiety remained more or less latent. In the neurosis of failure only the failure is evident and, in mental masochism, only the pain.

[III]

With anxiety, we touch on the core of the masochistic problem and the much debated question of the fear of castration as a motivation of masochistic behavior. (Nacht[26] says: "Everything happens as if the masochist, faced with the danger of losing everything, consents to the sacrifice of a part to save the rest.") However, I think it useless to resume this discussion again in detail though I do not propose to ignore it entirely. Actually, it throws a certain light on the solution of the problem of masochism as I foresee it.

Let me explain. Observation of a patient shows us that, during a certain phase of the analysis, there occur two parallel developments which sometimes, however, take place independently of each other. On the one hand, the patient abreacts his anxiety. We shall not examine the development of this abreaction here, for it would take us far from our subject. We shall say, however, that in general it all takes place in silence, the anxiety being by definition experienced as being non-objectual. On the other hand, the patient periodically shows us his castration complex, and does so with a certain ostentation, to state it no more strongly than that. These manifestations can be dramatic but often remain on a superficial level and obviously serve the purpose of display. During this period, there is not the slightest trace of real anxiety. On the contrary, the patient may adopt an amused tone which may extend to outright hilarity. This is not a defense but the whole complex functioning as a (temporarily successful) defense against anxiety. Here is a lapidary statement made by one of my patients, a masochistic obsessional:

"I have only to wish for some part of my body to be cut off, and then I have no more anxiety."

A young woman who made her husband beat her during sexual intercourse complained of frigidity and, in particular, of extremely severe attacks of anxiety. After three months' analysis, her anxiety ceased. A dream coinciding with the improvement, and accompanied by transference material having similar significance, shows us the same device, with the active participation of the superego:

"I was in a sanatorium, talking to another young woman and trying to convince her that I had a cavity. In fact I knew that I had no cavity, but maintained the opposite. She said that my condition was not serious, and that irritated me."

Associations: "I was among the least seriously ill in the sanatorium, but nobody was as tired as I was. I should have liked to tell everyone: 'You see, I am ill,' etc."

The masochistic pervert's *mise-en-scène* and all the self-castration material appearing in the masochist's dreams, phantasies and real life present the same picture. Freud[17] says that "the tortures of the masochist rarely appear as serious as the cruelties of the sadist." Feldman describes sado-masochistic regression as hypocritical.[8] Loewenstein[24] rejects this term and prefers to talk of "play" and "make-believe." We are confronted with a defense system *en bloc,* and Reik[31] understood as much when he said that the fear of castration, as it appears in masochism, is itself masochism, and that one should not set out to explain a phenomenon by the phenomenon itself. In any case, there is nothing specific about the fear of castration, as is pointed out by Berliner.[5] On the contrary, interpreting what has gone before, I believe the specific feature of masochism to be the utilization for defensive purposes, in a factitious and ostentatory manner, of a way of behavior that is genuine in itself, e.g., the fear of castration.

[IV]

I have glanced at the relationship between masochism and the fear of castration (on the genital level) in order to show that, as the explanation of masochism, it has led us into an *impasse.* If we turn to the pregenital phase, we notice immediately that much recourse has been had to orality to explain the genesis of masochism. It would be tedious to mention all the authors who have referred to oral conflict in this connection. However, we cannot omit mention of Bergler,[3] for whom there exists only one neurosis, the "basic neurosis," the sole manifestation of which is moral masochism. He regards this as deriving from oral conflict, the other neuroses being only "rescue stations" in which relief may be had from it. Rado[29] has attempted to build a whole theory of neurosis on masochism, starting out from the oral stage. Nacht[26,27] arrives at the conception of a "biological masochism" originating in the earliest pregenital phase, the pre-objectual phase during which the infant does not distinguish between its own body and its mother's breast. For the adherents of the theory of orality, masochism is a kind of recrudescence of oral frustration, and Bergler[3] even speaks of the desire to be frustrated. This frustration in itself would be a source of pleasure. Finally, in the view of Berliner,[5] the child identifies itself with the frustrating object, fixation on the wicked mother being the only way in which the child can be loved, there being historical reasons for this which can be verified in analysis.

Without entering into a detailed examination of these theories, the following criticisms may be made:

1. Those who support theories which derive masochism from oral conflict and frustration seem to take no account of the fact that masochism is, by definition, related above all to the anal-sadistic phase. Freud[9,12,16,10] always considered masochism to be the counterpart of sadism and firmly expressed his conviction that a solution of the problem of masochism could be attained only by way of sadism, the two being inseparable. Nacht's important contribution[26] to the study of masochism tends in the same direction. His taking the factor of aggression into account appears to me to be an important and decisive step toward the solution of this thorny problem.

2. Certain clinical objections can be made to the hypothesis of a purely oral genesis of masochism as envisaged, for instance, by W. Reich[30]: "The masochist always pursues pleasure, but invariably runs into frustration."

Freud himself was surprised to note[15] that the children who produced this phantasy ("a child is being beaten") had, so to speak, never been physically maltreated. Masochists are, in fact, mostly recruited from the ranks of spoiled children, a fact which is so obvious that Esther Menaker[25] used it as a point of departure for a theory of masochism. According to her, masochists were children who, because of lack of repeated oral frustrations, were unable sufficiently to reinforce their ego, this weakness of the ego constituting the frustration. Karen Horney[19] has argued that the masochist, in order to avoid anxiety, partly abandons his ego, keeping it weak, this being felt by him to be his only safeguard. Reik[31] once drew attention to the readiness with which women psychoanalysts in particular tended to consider female masochism as almost biological.

This observation leads me to repeat in connection with oral conflict what I have said in connection with the castration complex. The masochist uses it in the same way, and probably for the same purpose. The clinical material shows indeed that the patient gladly produces stories of oral frustration taken from his past life, just as in his present life and in his analysis he insists on playing the role of victim. One should therefore be extremely cautious before asserting the importance of oral frustration as a primary element in the history of the masochistic individual, as Keiser[20] does. ("In my observations, masochists have invariably had castrating mothers.") I recall a woman masochist whose whole analysis unfolded under the sign of a castrating mother and a weak and disappointing father. This situation was abundantly described and illustrated until the day came when we realized that this picture had been exaggerated for the purpose of reducing the patient's guilt, in accordance with the formula: "It was not I who castrated my father but my mother, who castrated me as well."

A young man, who was being analyzed, produced clinical material from which it emerged indisputably that in infancy he had been the victim of severe alimentary frustration. The patient produced a series of dreams and phantasies all converging toward a definite point which, in the end, it was possible to interpret as the "memory" of having been poisoned by his mother's milk. The fact that his mother had, in reality, had an abscess of the breast seemed to be a confirmation of this. But further investigation brought to light the fact that the abscess had occurred when his mother was nursing his brother, his junior by three years, and that his own nursing period had apparently passed off without trouble.

Apart from those patients who "come out with" their maternal conflict after a period generally devoted to their Oedipus conflict, there are some who produce it very quickly and even come to analysis with an open, violent and often actual maternal conflict. They insist on it at great length and with much freedom and evident satisfaction, and would like nothing better than to go on talking about it throughout the analysis. It is sometimes difficult to distinguish between the real, historical oral conflict and that deliberately put forward by the patient in order to mask something else.

Sometimes the process that takes place at the beginning or during the course of an analysis takes on an even clearer aspect toward the end or, rather, what should be the end of the analysis. At this stage, the patient makes a desperate effort to prevent the analyst from bringing the analysis to a successful conclusion. This appears in the form of a particularly tough resistance, manifesting itself in a sudden and violent reawakening of the oral conflict which one believed had been liquidated. This development is well adapted to make analysts despair, for it conjures up the "interminable analysis" bogy—all the more because the patient reacts to every new step taken by the analyst to bring the analysis to an end as a new oral frustration and responds to it all the more violently because that frustration serves as an excuse. Thus we find ourselves in a vicious circle which it is necessary to break.

[V]

The castration complex and the oral conflict exhaust the phenomenology of masochism. In life, as in analysis, all the specific aspects of masochistic behavior come within the framework of these two factors. The masochist, above all, arranges his life in such a way as to be castrated, that is to say, in such a way as to be incapable of pleasure in any field whatever; he is inhibited, poor, suffering, sick, diminished, "offended and humiliated." All these symptoms are negations of gratifications. Thus a young woman whom I treated for frigidity said to me that she considered her inability to have an orgasm as a shame to be concealed and a humiliation and, in her dreams, this humiliation took the form of castration. It may also be observed that the masochist frequently revives his oral conflict, with a grudge against his mother or mother-substitutes, these terms being understood in their functional sense, of course. His manifest complaints, to which he gives expression in a vindictive tone, show him in the light of a victim: no one likes him, he is treated badly, he has no luck, he is a victim of injustice. Whether he says so or not, the specifically masochistic part of his behavior is a never-ending demonstration of this state of affairs, a double demonstration with but a single purpose. Certainly this behavior appears equivocal and even paradoxical at times, as, in the very process of complaining (e.g., in analysis), he manages to exasperate his interlocutor, with the obvious purpose of provoking his rejection by the latter. His behavior becomes intelligible, however, if one considers that he is addressing himself to two figures at once, the mother and the father. The provocative attitude is intended to induce ill-treatment by the former, while the demonstration of what is taking place is directed at the latter. In the last resort, it is the frustrating mother who is the source of all the rejections, privations and ill-treatment of which the patient feels himself to be the victim, whether the ill-treatment is handed out by his love-partner or by his employer, by society or by God, by the stars or by the universe as a whole; and all the sufferings which she inflicts on the masochist are displayed for the benefit of the father. The masochist's ever-present interlocutor, whether real or imaginary, is a condensation of the mother and father figures. In analysis, there are three *dramatis personae,* two of whom are represented by the analyst, and the formula is not so much "Look what you are doing to me" as "Look how badly *she* treats me." We are confronted with a pre-Oedipal conflict, the object of which is not erotic rivalry with the parent of the same sex. The enemy is always the frustrating mother; the father plays a different role, to which we shall return. In studying the phantasies and *mise-en-scènes* of masochistic beating, one realizes that it is always the mother who does the beating, either overtly (in the case of men) or in disguise (in the case of women). In the latter's the man's role is often a humiliating attitude of indifference or neglect—a dramatized form of frustration imposed by the mother. The blows express coercion in the sense: "You will not do what you want to do unless forced to by me; that shows that you cannot attain your gratification of your own free will—you are castrated." There is, however, one striking detail in beating phantasies (a detailed analysis of which cannot be given here) which is, moreover, in accordance with Freud's observation that the phase in which the child is beaten by the father is very frequently repressed and can be brought to light only by analytic investigation. (In the exceptional cases in which the beating is done overtly by the father, we are probably confronted with less inhibited subjects who are content with a single defense: "It is he who is the castrator, and not I.") The woman who beats the masochistic pervert has male elements in her special attire (which is always the same, and is adapted to the affective position at an archaic level). Thus it is a condensed object which does the beating. But its masculine opponent nearly always has to remain unconscious. In this connection, Reik[31] reports a very characteristic case: during a masochist *mise-en-scène,* a patient discovered in his partner's attire something which reminded him of his father's beard. The erotic character of the scene vanished entirely and orgasm became impossible. How shall we interpret this incident?

We have seen that the content of the masochist's attitude is, on the one hand, being castrated and, on the other, being frustrated by the mother, his aim being the permanent demonstration of this state of affairs. Everything leads us to believe that the masochist cannot renounce this behavior which protects him from something that seems to him intolerable and, at the same time, blocks his path toward the gratification of his instinctual drives. Before trying to arrive at a general view of the situation, let us return to the phantasy of being beaten. Why must the paternal imago so often remain repressed and why is its unexpected emergence fatal in these cases to the success of the masochistic *mise-en-scène?* Purely and simply because the sole purpose of the whole masochistic structure is to maintain the repression. Freud[17] says that observation of the masochistic beating phantasy creates the impression that its subject has done something reprehensible (the nature of which is entirely vague) for which he must be punished. Our clinical material enables us to assert that, in all cases of masochism of every kind, we are confronted with castration of the father as an indispensable condition of gratification of the instinctual drive, and this in both sexes. The masochistic mechanism consists of a defense against this drive which, nevertheless, permits it to pursue and achieve its aim in a changed and disguised fashion which we shall describe later; and this aim is the castration of the father. In the course of analysis, one always discovers, behind the masochistic defense, the more or less disguised desire for and achievement of this castration or, rather, the introjection of the paternal penis in an anal-sadistic manner.

One of my patients, whose history will be told later, developed in the transference some reactions very characteristic of the masochistic mechanism revolving round the question of payment of fees. One day he handed me a check which, by mistake, he had made out for an excessive amount (simulated self-castration). Moreover, his bank balance was insufficient to meet the check. For days afterwards, he tormented himself on the subject. "Whenever I think of that check," he said, "I feel as if you were turning a knife in my heart. You have a weapon against me in your pocket." (In the meantime, I had returned to him the excess amount he had paid me and was waiting before presenting the check.) But he was forced to admit that, every time he planned to go to the bank to put the matter in order, he was prevented from doing so. When I drew his attention to the castration that he was inflicting on me, he was astonished but also said that, since his mistake, he had never been so potent sexually.

This distinction between the Oedipal murder of the father and the pregenital castration is very important. Actually, it seems that this introjection has to precede the transition to the Oedipal level which takes another phenomenological course. The victory over the father, his elimination as a rival on the Oedipal plane, cannot be superimposed on his sadistic castration which, moreover, is directed at a part-object's becoming a total object only by extension. In certain analyses, one observes that the reliving of the Oedipal combat and its interpretation awaken no opposition in the patient while, if he is shown the sadistic destruction of the paternal penis, he puts up the fiercest resistance. Killing of the father is acceptable, but not his castration; possession of his penis, but not its destruction. These *nuances* are important. Another proof that we are on the pregenital plane is the fact that the sadistic introjection in question is obligatory in both sexes and rouses greater guilt in women than in men. Behind the masochistic defense picture, the castration of the father in this sense is always present, though sometimes very much disguised.

Vincent dreamed that he saw, at a hotel window, a seductive young woman dressed in a gossamer nightgown. He went to look for her but lost his way in a succession of rooms. The search was very harrowing and painful. Vincent was assisted in his search by a number of male hotel employees. These were very helpful, were dressed in green (an allusion to my name), and were short in stature. Their help was vain, however, and they looked at Vincent with pity.

The situation was clear. Vincent was demonstrating to his superego—the analyst—that he considered himself castrated (unable to achieve pleasure) and that it was the woman (the inaccessible mother) who frustrated him. His friendly relations with the hotel men (the analyst) ill concealed the castration which he inflicted on them. The analyst is a hotel employee, short in stature and incapable of finding the way to the mother. (At a deeper level, the woman also represents the paternal penis.)

Otto came to analysis in an aggressive mood, complaining that he got nothing from me and that his analysis was getting nowhere (i.e., he remained castrated). He also said: "It's cold here [lack of maternal warmth]." Later he told me that he had seen a man's hairy arm in a café and had felt a desire to kiss it. "So, you see, you're not curing me." I showed him that he was castrating me and he replied immediately: "That's true. I've often thought that kissing is biting, cutting." Then he went on, without any transition, "I'm a little boy. My mother is beating me."

Véronique, aged forty, came to analysis because of various psychosomatic disorders; the picture, however, was rather of a failure neurosis. The first few months of analysis were devoted to an *exposé* at great length of a sharp and permanent conflict between her and her mother. She accepted the Oedipal interpretations without resistance, and even with obvious pleasure. But things changed on the day the positive transference produced anxiety as well as a new symptom, dysmenorrhoea. Her periods became painful and of abnormal duration. She complained bitterly of this and of the social injustice which made women "eternal victims." At one session, she delivered an onslaught on male prerogatives and produced a dream in which she saw herself during analysis bathing in her own blood and soiling the couch. Associations led her to talk about a film of Menotti's, *The Medium,* and she insisted on the tragic fate of the "victim," i.e., the principal woman character. Now, in the film, this woman kills a young boy, a fact which the patient completely obscured from herself; she was dumfounded when I reminded her of the fact. Shaken by this flash of insight, she produced material from which it emerged that she attributed a phallic significance to the real victim in the film, a black, semi-nude deaf-mute who was the playmate of the heroine's daughter. She further realized the anal-aggressive significance of her dream and, also, why her dysmenorrhoea regularly coincided with monthly complications about paying me my fee when it was due, the meaning of which was my castration. All this was followed by a massive emergence of memories relating to her impulses to castrate her father in an anal-sadistic fashion, as well as a number of similar phantasies.

Juliette, a journalist, aged twenty-eight, suffered from a complicated and atypical neurosis for which she had already been treated by another analyst. Analysis brought about a slow but definite improvement but she produced many acts of self-castration and had a great deal of difficulty in "coming out with" her positive transference. Actually, she seemed to be making a "transference dichotomy," reserving the positive side of the latter for her previous analyst whom, however, she persistently accused of having abandoned her. Being in possession of material which I cannot report here, I told her point-blank that her complaints about the other analyst, who represented her mother, enabled her more easily to castrate her father, that is to say, me. The effect of this intervention was dramatic. "I see your eyes, they are the eyes of my father, the eyes of an old man who is going to die," she said. "I am independent, and my father is old and helpless." Then, sobbing, she went on: "As he goes down, I go up. How could I love you, as I think only of your death?"

When she came next day she said: "You have entered into my analysis. I dreamed about you personally." The dream is too long to be reproduced here. She was mistaken in her comment, however, because she had had similar dreams before but had forgotten them immediately. But she identified herself with this dream and her transference attitude turned out to have been profoundly modified by this incident.

The typical masochistic elements appeal in all this material:

1. Self-castration
2. Frustration by the bad mother and identification with her.
3. Both concealing castration of the father.

[VI]

We have seen that masochism is a defense mechanism which enables the ego to mystify the superego. The object is to mask the wish to possess the paternal penis, in other words, to incorporate it in a sadistic manner. The defense mechanism expresses two things:

1. "I do not wish to castrate my father and, in any case, I could not, as I am castrated myself (I am castrated by my mother)."
2. "If I am in conflict, it is with my mother (and not with my father); the conflict is an oral conflict."

The structure of the defense may be different. One of my patients tried to prove:

1. That it was the analyst who was castrating her.
2. That it was the analyst (and not she) who was castrating her husband.
3. That it was the analyst's wife (and not she) who was castrating the analyst.

Since the masochist's behavior is an attempt to relieve himself from guilt, we can understand the role played in his life by pain, the architect of this relief from guilt. For the moral masochist, suffering is not a sacrifice accepted for the sake of achieving pleasure; he never achieves it. For the same reason, it is even less self-punishment. Nevertheless, the masochist considers suffering as having value, and sometimes it is the only value that he admits. (In this overevaluation of suffering, there is evidently a revival of the pleasure which it is supposed to repress; there is thus, to some extent, a return of the repressed under the mantle of the repressing forces.) It can be said that pain takes the place of pleasure; deep analysis reveals that it stands for the introjected penis—exactly like the whip of the masochistic pervert. It is only the level of introjection that is different; it is this which changes the character of the pleasure achieved.

Suffering ennobles and purifies. He who suffers is entitled to veneration for he is virtuous. Pleasure, indeed, being assimilated to castration of the father, it follows that suffering—i.e., being the castrated instead of the castrator—is a proof of innocence and a shelter against the accusations of the superego while, at the same time, permitting introjection at a deeper level. (I once overheard two women exchanging courtesies; one said to the other, with the air of granting her a diploma: "Of course I suffer, but what is my suffering compared with yours?" The diploma is the possession of the paternal penis. Those who suffer are proud of it and we know that the inmates of sanatoria look down on the healthy. A "fakir" once said: "When I suffer, I'm afraid of nobody.") This suffering is utilized, measured out, varied or stabilized, its intensity corresponding exactly to the amount of the fear to be neutralized by this technique. In analysis, we often observe patients who display their castration to the last, though they have been surreptitiously getting better all the time. They suffer and act castration just like the beggar who, sitting all day behind a placard with the word "blind" on it, goes home and reads the newspaper. I remember a young man who castrated himself from morning to night. I explained to him how, behind the mask of this behavior, he was managing to castrate me. No apparent change took place in him. But imagine my astonishment when I learned that this inhibited, impotent young man, who had led a completely parasitical existence, after breaking off the analysis ostensibly for financial reasons had started working successfully and now had a wife and child.

This also enables us to understand one of the most important aspects of masochism, namely, projection. For we observe that the masochist has constantly to provoke the object in order to project his own aggression on to him. He constantly puts himself in the position of a victim, according to the formula: "It is you who are castrating me" (i.e., "It is not I who am aggressive, but you."). Thus in the case of the masochist, we are confronted not, as Nacht[26] says, with a turning in of aggression against the self but with a projection of aggression on to the object. This projection is typical of the masochist. Freud[15] mentioned that, one day, it might be possible to classify masochism under the heading of paranoia. What is it the masochist projects, and on to whom? We have seen that the drive to be projected is that toward the anal castration of the father. The recipient of the projection is the mother, for reasons to which we shall return. Thus it is the bad mother who castrates the father and retains his penis. (Kleinian conception of the pregenital interpretation of sexual relations, as set forth by Lebovici and Diatkine.[22]) To obtain this penis, the masochist would have to introject the bad mother, therefore identifying himself with her. Berliner[5] thinks that the masochist seeks to carry out this identification in order to be loved and indicates that the type of masochist he was studying was the moral masochist. But the characteristic of the moral masochist is that he is unable to make this identification, for, if he were, he would not be a masochist but a sadist. The whole conduct of the moral masochist is characterized by a desperate and constant effort to prove to his superego that he is incapable of this identification and takes good care never to attempt it. All pleasure being subject to this condition, the masochist's reaction to it is always the same, namely, projection of the aggressive-sadistic component which endangers the paternal penis and consequently himself. This component has to be disposed of because of the unbearable anxiety it would provoke. It is as if the masochist, when brought face to face with pleasure—the good object—releases a trigger-mechanism, as it were, in order to find himself instead confronted with displeasure—the bad mother. But, as his instinctual drives demand satisfaction and are always present, he has continually to go through the same motion, day and night—as is proved by his dreams—in order to be able to live sheltered from anxiety. It is the need to pursue this projection continuously which forces him to live in suffering. It is not a simple inhibition but a display ("Look how she treats me!") and pleasure has automatically to become unpleasure. In the analyses and dreams of masochists, we invariably discover, behind the suffering, wishes of which it is the negation, the process being a strictly symmetrical one. The display is carried out in a logical manner, and the negative of success can only be failure, of happiness unhappiness, of health illness, of activity passivity, of triumph humiliation, and of the wish to castrate self-castration. One of my patients coined a phrase which summed it up. "I suffer from an opposite complex," he said.

In connection with the fear of identification with the bad mother we can quote Bergler.[4] He describes a masochistic husband who was completely put out and reduced to a state of terrible bewilderment and anxiety when, in response to his masochistic provocation—which Bergler considers "pseudo-aggressive"—his wife showed herself to be greatly hurt. Bergler's observation, which coincides with my own but is differently interpreted by him, seems to show the correctness of my point of view. The husband faced with this situation realizes that, though he has done all he can to demonstrate the opposite, his identification with the wicked mother has come about in spite of himself, so to speak. The result is that he founders in a sea of anxiety.

Here is a rather complicated case which is significant in this respect. It concerns a masochist who was deceived and badly treated by his wife (wicked mother). "My wife deceives and abuses me but that reassures me," he said. ("She is the wicked mother, not I.") He went on: "I ask her when she was last with her lover. 'At five-fifteen this afternoon,' she says. I become very excited, have an erection, and a very satisfactory coitus. I have the impression that, in telling me this, my wife is delivering the man up to me." (Castration of the father by identification with the mother in the guise of self-castration—he is the deceived husband.) "I have a feeling of superiority to the man, and am free from anxiety. But if my wife is difficult and argues and denies and I have to squabble with her, force her to confess [identification with the bad mother], I have heartbeats, feel anxiety and my erection subsides."

This apparently homosexual position (thanks to a large amount of transference material which lack of space prevents me from presenting) was analyzed as a defense against the desire to castrate the father in an anal-sadistic manner, and made possible transition to a most manifest Oedipal level. This shows that the homosexual attitudes of masochists are also projections on to the mother of the wish to castrate the father.

[VII]

What emerges from all this material is that the masochist can obtain pleasure when the introjection of the paternal penis has succeeded. This takes us back to the beginning of this discussion when we said that the masochist pursued his goal, reaching it or not according to circumstances. The goal is the castration of the father and, as the masochist has to carry out a preliminary identification with the bad mother to achieve this on the anal-sadistic level, the masochistic mechanism functions like a screen to conceal this identification. That is how the superego is deceived.

There are thus two kinds of masochists (with the whole range of mixed types in between):

1. Those who continue the diversionary maneuver as a defense against anxiety without ever achieving pleasure. These are the moral masochists.

2. Those who achieve their goal and obtain pleasure, orgasm, behind the protection of the masochistic mechanism. These are the masochistic perverts; and, provisionally, we must put in this category all those who seem to buy pleasure by what is generally and erroneously considered to be self-punishment.

Its fraudulent nature is demonstrated by the fact that, in extreme cases, a purely symbolic act is sufficient. I knew a woman masochist who had an orgasm every time she knelt. The ways in which masochists behave to attain their desired aim are very various, and the extent of the scale, which stretches from real pain on the one hand to a symbolic gesture on the other, is a function of the variations in strength and weakness of the ego in relation to the strength or weakness of the superego.

As for the moral masochist, he follows his path with less good fortune, but with all the more determination for that reason. Nothing will divert him from his goal, which is pleasure too. He is convinced that, one day, he will achieve it and the more he suffers, the sweeter will be his reward. Time does not exist for the unconscious and neither does death.

In analysis, the masochist behaves in the same fashion, with the difference that he learns to integrate his aggression and to overcome the obstacle which lies in its way. For this, it seems necessary for him to realize the identification with the wicked mother under the protection of its projection on to the analyst. That done, the introjection of the paternal penis—thanks to his released and normalized aggression—takes place on a level untainted with sadism. This, to use Bouvet's term,[6] is a "preservative introjection," the dynamic contribution which makes possible a transition to the Oedipal situation and its resolution.

Thus, at the root of masochism, we find dynamic disturbances which, though they originated, as always, in the oral period, did not really become pathogenic until the anal period because of the obstacles preventing the integration of the aggression which is so violently sought after at that stage. (If the spark is struck on the oral ground floor, the specific inflammable material is on the floor above.)

If it were a question of an oral conflict in the true sense of the term, we should find ourselves faced with specifically oral disorders, such as melancholia, depressive neuroses and psychoses, toxicomania, hysteria, etc. This point requires some clarification but I do not think I can embark on it here. Thanks to the clinical material, it seems to me sufficiently established:

1. That the introjection of the paternal penis is indispensable before Oedipal development can begin; this applies to both sexes.

2. That the disorder known as masochism indicates a disturbance of this process. The masochist is at grips with a dynamic problem and, to find a solution of his problem, we must abandon the libidinal framework and resolutely enter a dynamic framework, while keeping the role of the historic factor to a strict minimum. That is what I have attempted to do, being convinced that a distinct orientation in that direction represents assured progress.

CONCLUSION

I have omitted a number of the aspects in which masochism is so rich and which have in any case, been partially studied elsewhere; instead, I have made an attempt to establish the mechanism invariably to be found in masochism which, to my mind, can be regarded as specific of this disorder. This mechanism is as follows:

1. It is an ego defense aimed at persuading the superego that instinctual gratification has been renounced. This instinctual gratification is bound up with castration of the father and is denied by proof of its opposite in accordance with the formula:

(a) It is I who am castrated, not my father.

(b) My conflict brings me into conflict with my mother and not with my father.

2. This defense position is reinforced by constant projection on to the bad mother of the wish to castrate the father. The masochist simultaneously makes a display of wishing to maintain this projection, thus demonstrating his refusal to identify himself with the bad mother.

3. Behind the cover of these defense mechanisms, the moral masochist pursues his goal—which is castration of the father by anal-sadistic introjection—but consistently demonstrates his failure.

The masochistic pervert, thanks to the masochistic disguise, succeeds in deceiving his superego in the most complete and glaring manner and thus achieves genital pleasure.

REFERENCES

1. Amiel, H. F. *Fragments d'un journal intime.* Paris, 1922.
2. Bak, R. "Masochism in Paranoia." *Psychoanalytic Quarterly,* Vol. XV, 1946.
3. Bergler, E. *The Basic Neurosis.* New York, 1949.
4. ———. "Neurotic Helplessness in 'the Masochistic Situation in Reverse.' " *Psychiatric Quarterly,* Vol. XXI, 1947.
5. Berliner, B. "On Some Psychodynamics of Masochism." *Psychoanalytic Quarterly,* Vol. XVI, 1947.
6. Bouvet, M. "Le moi dans la névrose obsessionelle." *Revue Française de Psychanalyse,* 1953.
7. Eidelberg, L. "Zur Metapsychologie des Masochismus." *Internationale Zeitschrift für Psychoanalyse,* Vol. XIX, 1933.
8. Feldman, S. "Anxiety and Orgasm." *Psychoanalytic Quarterly,* Vol. XX, 1951.
9. Freud, Sigmund. *Three Essays on the Theory of Sexuality.* London, 1949.
10. ———. "Instincts and their Vicissitudes." *Coll. Papers,* Vol. IV. London, 1924.
11. ———. "Some Character Types Met with in Psychoanalytic Work." *Coll. Papers,* Vol. IV. London, 1924.
12. ———. *Introductory Lectures on Psychoanalysis.* New York, 1920.
13. ———. *New Introductory Lectures on Psychoanalysis.* New York, 1933.
14. ———. "From the History of an Infantile Neurosis." *Coll. Papers,* Vol. III. London, 1924.
15. ———. "A Child Is Being Beaten." *Coll. Papers,* Vol. II. London, 1924.
16. ———. *Beyond the Pleasure Principle.* London, 1922.
17. ———. "The Economic Problem in Masochism." *Coll. Papers,* Vol. II. London, 1924.
18. ———. "Dostoievsky and Parricide." *Coll. Papers,* Vol. V. London, 1950.
19. Horney, K. "The Problem of Feminine Masochism." *Psychoanalytic Review,* Vol. XVIII, 1935.
20. Keiser, S. "The Fear of Sexual Passivity in the Masochist." *International Journal of Psychoanalysis,* Vol. XXX, 1949.
21. Lampl-de Groot, J. "Masochismus und Narcissmus." *Internationale Zeitschrift für Psychoanalyse,* Vol. XXII, 1936.
22. Lebovici, S. and Diatkine, G. "Étude des fantasmes chez l'enfant." *Revue Française de Psychanalyse,* 1954.

23. Lewinsky, H. "On Some Aspects of Masochism." *International Journal of Psychoanalysis,* Vol. XXV, 1944.
24. Loewenstein, R. "L'origine du masochisme et la théorie des pulsions." *Revue Française de Psychanalyse,* 1938.
25. Menaker, E. "Masochism—A Defense Reaction of the Ego." *Psychoanalytic Quarterly,* Vol. XXII, 1953.
26. Nacht, S. "Le masochisme." *Revue Française de Psychanalyse,* 1938.
27. ———. "Essai sur la peur." *Ibid.,* 1952.
28. Odier, C. *L'homme esclave de son infériorité.* Paris.
29. Rado, S. "Fear of Castration in Women." *Psychoanalytic Quarterly,* Vol. II, 1933.
30. Reich, W. "Der masochistische Charakter." *Internationale Zeitschrift für Psychoanalyse,* Vol. XVIII, 1932.
31. Reik, T. *Le masochisme.* Paris.

11. More about Rats and Rat People

Leonard Shengold

In a previous paper (Shengold, 1967) I dealt with cannibalistic manifestations in adults who had undergone traumatic experiences as children—experiences that had resulted in ego regression and distortion, and in fixation on and regression to oral sadism and masochism. These manifestations include fears and wishes of being devoured associated with a particular vulnerability of the anal area; a characteristic 'cannibalistic' rage associated with the overstimulated state; the tendency to seek repetition of overstimulating experiences— and the massive defensive efforts needed to deal with all these: pervasive and intense isolation (isolation that is associated with vertical ego splits); autohypnotic states; denial and lying; and the turning of impulses alternately upon others and upon the self. These people have a split superego serving the opposing needs to repeat and to be punished for the cannibalistic experiences. I call these patients 'rat people' because, like Freud's Rat Man patient, they use the imago of rodents to carry connotations of overstimulation and cannibalism. I intend in this paper to explore rat symbolism, and to say something more about ego distortions in the 'rat people'.

RATS, CANNIBALISM AND OVERSTIMULATION

I begin with a literary quotation which connects rats, oral sadism and overstimulation. It comes from *Torture Garden* by Octave Mirbeau, which I believe to be the source of the story that obsessed Freud's famous patient, the Rat Man (Freud, 1909). This story was told the Rat Man by a sadistic army captain, who

'had *read* [my italics] of a specially horrible punishment used in the East . . . the criminal was tied up . . . a pot was turned upside down on his buttocks . . . some

Reprinted by permission of the author and the *International Journal of Psycho-Analysis* 52 (1971):277–88. Copyright © Institute of Psycho-Analysis.

rats were put into it . . . [the Rat Man is speaking and these hesitations are his] . . . and they . . .'—he got up again and was showing every sign of horror and resistance—'*bored their way in* . . .'—Into his anus, I [Freud] helped him out.[1]

Torture Garden was published in Paris in 1899, seven years before the Rat Man's encounter with the captain. During those years the book was widely read in Europe, having acquired a pornographic notoriety; it is, however, the work of a serious artist (Wilson, 1950). The book has a climactic episode about a rat torture; the garden is in China, the torturer Chinese; and the heroine, Clara, obsessed by torture, asks him (note the hesitations that are so similar to the Rat Man's):[2]

'What is this torture of the rat? . . . Can you describe it to us?' The Torturer answers, 'You take a condemned man, charming lady . . . or anybody else . . . you take a man, as young and strong as possible, whose muscles are quite resistant; in virtue of this principle: the more strength, the more struggle—and the more struggle, the more pain! Good! I don't know if I'm making myself understood? Then in a big pot, whose bottom is pierced with a little hole . . . a flowerpot, milady . . . you place a very fat rat,[3] whom it's wise to have deprived of nourishment for a couple of days, to excite its ferocity. And this pot, inhabited by this rat, you apply hermetically, like an enormous cupping-glass, to the back of the condemned by means of stout thongs attached to a leather girdle about the loins. Ah ha! Now the plot thickens!' He looked maliciously at [her] out of corners of his lowered lids, to judge the effect his words were producing. 'And then?' said Clara simply. 'Then milady, you introduce into the little hole in the pot . . . guess what?' The good fellow rubbed his hands, smiled horribly, and then continued: 'You introduce an iron rod, heated red hot at the fire of a forge . . . and when the iron rod is introduced, what happens? Ha Ha! Imagine what must happen, milady.' 'Oh, come on, you old gossip!' . . . 'A little patience, milady . . . Well, you introduce into the pot's hole, an iron rod, heated red hot . . . the rat tries to escape the burning of the rod and its dazzling light. It goes mad, cuts capers, leaps and bounds, crawls and gallops over the man's flesh, which it first tickles and then tears with its nails, and bites with its sharp teeth, seeking an exit through the torn and bleeding skin. But there is no exit. During the first frenzied moments, the rat can find none. And the iron rod, handled cleverly and slowly, still draws near the rat,, threatens it, scorches its fur. Its great merit lies in the fact that you must know how to prolong this initial operation as much as possible, for the laws of physiology teach us that there is nothing more horrible to the human flesh than the combination of tickling and biting. It may even happen that the victim goes mad from it. He howls and struggles; his body . . . heaves and contorts, shaken by agonizing shudders. But his limbs are firmly held by the chains, and the pot, by the thongs. And the movements of the condemned man only augment the rat's fury, to which the intoxication of blood is often added. It's sublime, milady. Finally, for I see you're anxious to know the climax of this wonderful and jolly story; finally—threatened by the glowing rod and thanks to the excitation of a few well chosen burns, the rat ends by finding an exit, milady. Ah ha ha! . . . you see, I'm proud of the interest you take in my torture. But wait! The rat penetrates the man's body, widening with claws and teeth the opening he madly digs, as in the earth. And he croaks, stifled, at the same time as the victim, who, after a half-hour of ineffable, incomparable torture, ends succumbing to a haemorrhage—when it isn't from too much suffering or even the congestion caused by a frightful insanity. In all cases, milady, and whatever the final cause of this death—you can be sure it's extremely beautiful!'

The anal erotism and the oral sadistic libido that are associated with the obsessions of the Rat Man are set forth here:[4] also the connotations of overstimulation and cannibalism. First, the rat is overstimulated with the red-hot iron rod (the danger throughout is that of a penetrative invasion by a phallus equipped with flesh-eating power); the rat 'goes mad' and tears and *bites* at the man's flesh, finally making a cannibalistic anal penetration after unbearably overstimulating the victim with the 'prolonged' and 'horrible . . . combination of tickling and biting.' Both rat and victim are overstimulated and die. Both are helpless in the face of increasing torment. The basic story of the victim's being eaten and anally penetrated by the rat is also present in displacement in relation to the glowing rod and the rat (here as victim); symbolically, it is presented through the heated iron rod and the flowerpot with the hole in its bottom; in attenuation the theme is repeated by way of the Torturer's teasing method of telling his story to the enthralled, over-excited Clara.

THE RAT AS CARRIER OF THE TOOTH

The words *rat* and *rodent* originate in tooth-connoting concepts. They are derived from the Latin *rodere:* to gnaw, consume. Related roots are *radere* (Latin): to scratch, and *radona* (Sanskrit): tooth (*Webster's Unabridged,* 1960).

The rat imago appears as a leading motif in the study of oral sadistic and masochistic phenomena (*tooth* phenomena).[5] The rat is a 'tooth-carrier' endowed with the power to creep back and forth from level to level of libidinal development, from one erogenous zone to another, biting and being bitten. The rat is one of the most common of many imagos that are first of all cannibalistic: carriers of the destructive tooth. These include the natural wolf, snake, spider; and the monstrous sphinx, vampire, werewolf. These are biting, sucking, crunching, devouring creatures.[6]

The rat is a very ancient animal. Remains of rats and men have been found together in fossils of the glacial period (Zinnser, 1935). There are no references to rats as such in classical or biblical literature; the term for *mouse* was used to indicate both kinds of animal.[7] The special designation for the rat was adopted in European languages only after the great invasions from Asia by the black rat in the 12th and 13th centuries. The black rat probably exterminated the prevailing indigenous rats and brought with it the devastating medieval plagues (*Encyclopaedia Britannica*, 1961, vol. 18). The brown rat, *Mus norvegicus*, swept over Europe in the early 18th century and has in its turn killed off the black rat in most parts of the world.

The resemblance between men and rats has often been pointed out, usually in relation to a tribute to their similar intraspecific destructive competitiveness. Lorenz (1966) indicates in rats 'the collective aggression of one community against another' as a model of what now threatens mankind. Both species demonstrate intraspecific *murderous* aggression: 'the gradual, relentless progressive extermination of the black rat by the brown has no parallel in nature so close as that of the similar extermination of one race of man by another' (Zinnser, 1935). There are other similarities:

The difficulties of combating the most successful biological opponent to man, the brown rat, lies chiefly in the fact that the rat operates basically with the same methods as those of man, by transmission of experience and its dissemination within the close community. (Lorenz, 1966)

The rat is usually described in literature as evil, and is detested. It persecutes and is persecuted, and evokes intense destructiveness. 'Rats are, indeed', wrote Charles Lamb, 'the most despised and contemptible parts of God's earth. I killed a rat the other day by punching him to pieces and I feel a weight of blood on me to this hour.' With a number of quotations, I want to illustrate how the rat is connected with overstimulation and cannibalism.

The rat is destructive and voracious: 'Ratborne diseases have resulted in the deaths of more people during the last 5000 years than the combined casualties of the wars taking place over those years' (Barker, 1951). 'Most rats kill birds or animals for their flesh and blood; others simply have a lust for killing' (Mills, 1959). 'Their diet is omnivorous; they eat anything, including human flesh . . . when driven by hunger they are so ravenous that neglected babies have been killed and eaten by them . . . [There are] a few cases of able-bodied men who have suffered a like fate when attacked by hordes of rats' (*Encyclopedia Americana*, 1957, vol. 23).

The rat is fecund so that if left unchecked it can overwhelm other species:

'They bear, four or five times in the year, four to 10 young, which can in turn breed in six months' (*Encyclopaedia Britannica*, 1961, vol. 18). 'The terrible rate at which the rat increases explains the slow process of extermination, despite the vast sums expended. It has been calculated that two rats, if left unchecked, would in the course of three to four years multiply into 20 millions' (Protheroe, 1940).

The rat is especially ferocious towards its own kind:

They change into horrible brutes as soon as they encounter members of any other society of their own species . . . What rats do when a member of a strange rat-clan enters their territory . . . is one of the most horrible and repulsive things which can be observed in animals . . . with their eyes bulging from their sockets, their hair standing on end, the rats set out on the rat hunt. They are so angry that if two of them meet they bite each other . . . [The strange rat] is slowly torn to pieces by its fellows. Only rarely does one see an animal in such desperation and panic, so conscious of the inevitability of a terrible death, as a rat which is about to be slain by rats. It ceases to defend itself. (Lorenz, 1966)

(In this description of the 'rat hunt' are found both the sadistic fury and the terrified masochistic submission that can be evoked by the rat.)

The rat, like all rodents, has amazing teeth: '[They] have a set of fierce looking gnawing teeth . . . [these] incisors sharpen themselves to chisel-like points as they are used. The owner rapidly grinds down these teeth with incessant gnawing, but they never wear out. A rodent's incisors continue to grow as the fingernails of people do' (Hegner, 1942). 'The rat's incisors grow at the rate of five inches a year' (Mills, 1959).

The rat must use his teeth or they can cause his death:

Should a member of this group have the misfortune to break a chisel tooth, he is often doomed to death. The broken tooth fails to meet the tooth opposite; both teeth grow unhindered. Since they are no longer ground off against each other, they grow wildly, sometimes circling the victim's face, locking his jaws, and causing starvation (Hegner, 1942).

The rat is continuously teething: 'The incisors grow, calcify and erupt continuously throughout the life of the animal' (Schour & Masser, 1949).

The rat is a fit object on which to project cannibalism. It is particularly linked with anal erogeneity because of its association with dirt and disease. Man has had continually to deal with the rat because of its omnipresence, its destructiveness and its great fecundity that makes extermination necessary but ineffectual. So the rat is both persecuting and persecuted. The problem of the continual increase in the number of rats, emphasized by the historical invasions of rats on a grand scale with accompanying cataclysmic deadly plagues, makes the rat particularly suited to represent, by allusion, overstimulation (too-muchness). And cannibalism is invoked. The linkage of rats, teeth and biting is evidenced by folklore from all parts of the world. And in relation to the rat's remarkable teeth, it may be said, paraphrasing Freud's dictum, that they must bite others or they will literally bite themselves.

MEANINGS OF THE RAT TO THE RAT MAN

The Rat Man came to Freud complaining about an obsession and compulsive actions that had begun when he was on military manoeuvres, after the sadistic army Captain N. (who, in my opinion, had read Mirbeau's *Torture Garden*) told him about the rat punishment and had also said something about paying back money that was owed to a third person. The violent symptomatic reaction that followed was analysed by Freud:

in the short interval between the captain's story and his request . . . to pay back the money, rats had acquired a series of symbolic meanings, to which, during the period that followed, fresh ones were continually being added

Rats, Freud says, are associated with anal eroticism. They are connected with dirt (faeces, money), infection (venereal disease) and with cruelty and sadism. Rats mean teeth and biting (the Rat Man felt that a rat was feeding off his father's corpse) and cannibalism. There is a condensation of meanings from the oral-sadistic and anal-sadistic libidinal stages. Most 'rat phenomena' of the Rat Man (and of 'rat people', for that matter) can be stratified in terms used by Fliess (1956): the erogeneity involved is anal, but the libido is oral-sadistic. This instinctual aim is destructive and ultimately cannibalistic; if turned against the self, the aim is to be destroyed and eaten.

The rat was equated with the penis by the Rat Man, especially in relation to anal intercourse (and sadistic intercourse). Here phallic power is equated with cannibalistic penetration—the penis has teeth and can bite (e.g. rat = syphilis that eats into the body). The rat as a phallic symbol is not only destructive (as are such symbols as knife, spear, club, gun) in contrast to more benign phallic symbols (stick, necktie, umbrella, balloon), but is specifically cannibalistic.

Rats can (like the penis: the 'little one') represent children, but these are dirty, biting, raging children. As vermin, rats can symbolize unwanted siblings or unwanted children[8] who evoke rage.

The law of talion applies to rats—if they bite, they can be bitten: 'But rats cannot be sharp-toothed, greedy and dirty with impunity; they are cruelly persecuted and mercilessly put to death by men' (Freud, 1909). If rat = penis, destructivity towards the rat involves castration. If rat = child, destructivity towards the rat involves murder.

I would like to stress the ubiquitous oral sadism and masochism in all these meanings that Freud and his patient found for rats: rats bite into the anus; the rat-penis has teeth; ratchildren bite and are bitten. The basic fantasy of castration here is that involving the *biting off* of the penis; intercourse is a *biting into* the cloaca.

The rat can stand for subject or object, part-subject or part-object. The Rat Man, 'a nasty little wretch who was apt to bite people when he was in a rage', was also subject to the rat: 'He remembered being castigated by his father at age 3–4 because he had bitten someone' and this had been taken as a castration threat. The father, here the rat-persecutor, is—in the fantasies of the adult Rat Man—himself eaten by a rat. Father, mother,[9] analyst could all be rats who could bite and be bitten.

Implicit in the clinical material and explicit in the rat torture is the association of overstimulation and rage with rats.

EGO REGRESSIONS IN THE RAT MAN
AND IN 'RAT PEOPLE'

Some of the regressive ego manifestations I have described in 'rat people' (Shengold, 1967; see also Shuren, 1967) are demonstrated in Freud's Rat Man. Freud (1909) outlines the symptoms and defences of obsessive-compulsive neurosis and their dynamic antecedents. I have written of the *intensity* and *massiveness* of the isolation needed by people who were seduced and beaten as children to split off and contain the impulses involved in, and the memories of, their traumatic overstimulating experiences. In the Rat Man paper, Freud describes two kinds of isolation. There is disconnexion between thought and affect, which is one of the mechanisms involved in disconnexion between idea and idea. Freud says:

repression is effected not by means of amnesia but by a severance of causal connexions brought about by a withdrawal of affect. These repressed connexions appear to persist *in some kind of shadowy form* . . . and they are thus transferred, in a process of projection, into the external world, where they bear witness to what has been effaced from consciousness [my italics].

The disconnexion between thoughts can also be accomplished by 'inserting a time interval' between them (Freud, 1909). Where such isolation is massive and intense, as with 'rat people', vertical splits occur in the mental apparatus, making possible such phenomena as the Orwellian 'double-think'[10] that is conditioned—again by rat torture—on to the victim-hero of *Nineteen Eighty-Four*. Freud tells of the Rat Man:

> He then went on to say that he would like to speak of a criminal act, whose author he did not recognize as himself, though he quite clearly recollected committing it. He quoted a saying of Nietzsche's: ' "I did this," says my Memory. "I cannot have done this," says my Pride and remains inexorable. In the end—Memory yields.' (Freud, 1909)

However, the 'yielding' for the Rat Man still leaves the memory in the 'shadowy' form described by Freud above and he goes on to tell it to Freud. These 'shadowy' memories make for two kinds of knowing: 'for he knows [things] in that he has not forgotten them, but he does not know them in that he is unaware of their significance'. Economic considerations in relation to these splits are conveyed by:

> He could not help believing in the premonitory power of dreams, for he [the Rat Man] had several remarkable experiences to prove it. Consciously he does not really believe in it. (The two views exist side by side, *but the critical one is sterile*.) [My italics.]

Freud gives another example in his early work, 'Studies on Hysteria' (1894), quoting the following dialogue between himself and his patient, Miss Lucy R. Freud had asked about her relationship with her employer (he knew, though she did not, that an incestuous attachment was involved):

> Freud: 'But if you knew you loved your employer, why didn't you tell me?'
> Lucy R.: 'I didn't know—or rather I didn't want to know. I wanted to drive it out of my mind and not think of it again, and latterly I believed I had succeeded.'

In a footnote written apparently somewhat later, Freud adds,

> I have never managed to give a better description than this of the strange state of mind in which one knows and does not know of a thing at the same time. It is clearly impossible to understand it unless one has been in such a state oneself. (Freud, 1894)

Freud goes on to tell about the 'very remarkable experience of this sort' he once had, and ends with a memorable turn of phrase appropriate to Oedipus, the discoverer of the oedipus complex, and to everyone:

I was afflicted by that *blindness of the seeing eye* which is so astonishing in the attitude of mothers to their daughters, husbands to their wives and rulers to their favourites. [My italics]

For Freud this was an occasional, an exceptional, experience but for *rat people* it represents a kind of thinking that (as in Orwell's *Nineteen Eighty-Four*) can dominate their mind and their world. Orwell shows how 'double-think' is aimed at the abolition of memories of the past.

By means of isolation and with the use of autohypnotic states involving alterations of consciousness (Breuer's 'hypnoid states': see Fliess, 1953; Dickes, 1965; Shengold, 1967), vertical splits in the ego take place—one major one is the split between the cognitive and the experiencing ego (see Shuren, 1967, whose formulations are based on clinical material similar to mine). A functioning of the ego necessary for the subjective feeling of identity—the ability to feel what is there to be felt[11]—is disrupted by this split; the personality is compartmentalized, not completely but in the 'shadowy' fashion Freud mentions so that there are provisional and alternating personae that can take over with slight alterations of consciousness. Freud describes the compartmentalization in the Rat Man twice. In the published case history he states his

impression that he [the Rat Man] had, as it were, disintegrated into three personalities: into one unconscious personality, that is to say, and into two preconscious ones between which his consciousness could oscillate. His unconscious comprised those of his impulses which had been suppressed at an early age and which might be described as passionate and evil impulses. In his normal state he was kind, cheerful, and sensible—an enlightened and superior kind of person—while in his third psychological organization he paid homage to superstition and asceticism. Thus he was able to have two different creeds and two different outlooks upon life.

This is more succinctly put, without the topographical (here really descriptively used) explanation, in the case record not meant for publication: 'He is made up of three personalities—one humorous and normal, another ascetic and religious and a third immoral and perverse.' In my patients these 'psychological organizations' (between which the patient can shift, thereby disrupting the ordinarily taken for granted consummation of feeling what is there—preconsciously—to be felt) are kept separated by 'hypnoid states'—alterations of consciousness. For example, a patient says: 'I know that I hate you and I want to bite off your penis but that part of me is wrapped in cellophane.' When fully 'awake' (the hypnotic wrapping dissolved), these feelings can be acknowledged—the patient can 'know' she hates in the experiential sense of the word. When analysis works for these people, the autohypnotic (largely defensively used) symptomatology is given up and the synthetic function of a 'knowing' ego is free to blend the disparate 'personalities' and the contradictory trends.

A SHAKESPEAREAN REVENGE FANTASY OF CANNIBALISTIC CASTRATION

A passage from *Macbeth* illustrates the universality of the rat meanings found in the Rat Man case.

The witches in *Macbeth* represent the bad primal parent (see Shengold, 1963): mendacious, destructive and terrifying—a phylogenetic figure whose counterpart in present-day reality can be a psychotic or psychopathic parent who attacks his children. The witches are ambiguously sexed, though primarily feminine (like the Sphinx; see Shengold, 1963). Banquo says to them, 'You should be women, and yet your beards forbid me to interpret that you are so.' These 'weird sisters' are to lead Macbeth to his destruction as well as to his murderous career. Like the bad primal parent they are liars, luring Macbeth on with seemingly sure guarantees of his invincibility. Just before they meet Macbeth and Banquo at the beginning of the play, the first witch and her sisters come on stage. The first witch is in a rage of oral frustration:

> A sailor's wife had chestnuts in her lap
> And mounched and mounched and mounched.
> 'Give me', quoth I.
> 'Aroint thee witch!', the rump-fed runyon cries.

'Rump-fed' shows that the witch's hunger is for flesh, not just for chestnuts, and that anal erogeneity is involved. The witch wants to use her teeth and 'mounch' on the chestnuts in the lap (genital area) of the orally satisfied object. The witch goes on to her plan of revenge which involves a transformation into a cannibalistic castrative rat:

> Her husband's to Aleppo gone, master o' the *Tiger*
> But in a sieve I'll thither sail,
> And like a rat without a tail
> I'll do, and I'll do, and I'll do.

The thrice iterated 'do' echoes the thrice iterated 'mounched'. The witch-as-rat will now castrate (the rat is castrated) with her teeth—first her vampire intent:

I'll drain him dry as hay . . .
Weary sev' night, nine times nine,
Shall he dwindle, peak, and pine . . .

Finally the castration:

                Look what I have.
2nd Witch: Show me!
1st Witch: Here I have a pilot's thumb,
                Wracked as homeward he did come.
                  (I: iii: 3–29)

TEETH AND TEETHING

To investigate further the rat as tooth-carrier, I want to deal with some of the phenomena connected with teeth and teething. There is much folklore linking rats, mice and teeth—especially in relation to the losing of teeth. This will be presented below. I mention it here to underline the impact of the amazing teeth of the rodent on human psychology where these teeth figure as an element in the external world that is used to express what is going on in the body.

Abraham (1924), in describing the second oral stage of libido development, pointed out that the development of the teeth coincides with the influx of sadism that occurs during that stage.

Undoubtedly the teeth are the first instruments with which the child can do damage to the outer world. For they are already effective at a time when the hands can at most only assist their activity by seizing and keeping hold of the object . . . the teeth are the only organs [small children] possess that are sufficiently hard to be able to injure objects around them. One has only to look at children to see how intense the impulse to bite is. This is the stage in which the cannibalistic impulses predominate.

Abraham quotes a comment of van Ophuijsen's, who believes 'that certain neurotic phenomena are due to a regression to the age when teeth were being formed'.

Subsequently, despite much that has been written on biting and oral sadism, the phenomenon of teething has been strangely neglected in psychoanalytic literature. Kucera's article (1959) is an exception. He points out that pleasure sucking is interfered with by teething, and that this intensifies the sadistic effect of the coming in of the teeth on the infant. He goes on to say that the 'experience which is regularly provoked during teeth eruption can be looked upon as the key situation for the origin of primary masochism, as its physiological organic foundation'. Without going into the moot questions of the existence and the origin of primary masochism, I want to deal with the *experience* of teething.

With the teeth painfully forcing their way through the mucosa of the gum, the infant can be said to bite himself (and experience being bitten) before he can bite anything else. Both during, and of course after, the eruption of the tooth, the infant bites himself. Tooth eruption produces the experience of being simultaneously the subject and the object of the biting for the owner of both the tooth and the surrounding mucosa. Of course, one cannot empathize with the child here since the ego at the time of teething is in a rudimentary state with incomplete differentiation of subject and object, of inside and outside. This differentiation is taking place during the oral sadistic phase of libido development.[12] During this phase the infant has to deal with an instinctual access of aggression which must be fused with libido. To deal with the frustration of need satisfaction and with overstimulation, a loving mother is needed to counteract the danger of a breakthrough of the stimulus barrier at the time of access of the aggressive instinct (see Hoffer, 1950; Mahler, 1952). Active discharge of the aggressive drive takes place by way of the teeth and the body musculature. Passive oral masochism is also experienced in the body (registering therefore in the forming body ego fundamental to the ego) in part by way of the teeth and their adjacent mucosa. It is probable that the phylogenetic significance of the tooth and of the teething experience is much greater than the ontogenetic. A look at animal life with evolution in mind, or at what Tennyson calls 'Nature red in tooth and claw', tends to suggest this. The continuously teething rat also epitomizes a primal common ancestor for man. I do not know that child observers have sufficiently 'looked at' teething. The change to tension and unpleasure of a hitherto predominantly pleasure-giving erogenous zone at a time when the ego is beginning to coalesce may be more significant than has been thought.

CANNIBALISTIC WISHES, INFANTILE EXPERIENCES AND TEETHING

Teething might furnish an 'ontogenetic root for the subjective reality of the cannibalistic act', the existence of which is questioned by Fliess (1956) who states that the second oral phase is the only phase of libido development where direct instinctual gratification is denied. Although the child does not discharge his oral impulses by eating the flesh from the breast, he does bite himself when he is teething, and the breast when he has teeth, at a time when 'I am the breast—the breast is part of me' (Freud, 1941). Lewin (1950) points out that the infant's wish to be devoured is not based on direct infant observation, but is 'a heuristic fiction . . . a construction based on inference'. Klein (1933) asserts that the fear of being eaten is *experienced* during the first year of life and that it is due to the projection of active oral-sadistic wishes on to the parent. Simmel (1944) speaks of cannibalistic fears and wishes as associated with the infant's identification with food. The food that is incorporated becomes a part of the baby's ego, becomes a part of the baby, and the baby 'might be considered as eating himself'. Autocannibalism, then, stems from the time that the mother's breast is still regarded as part of the body ego of the child. About the baby at the breast during this period, alternately chewing at his fingers and toes, Lewin (1950) states: 'one may say, with licence, that it indulges thereby in an act of autocannibalism'. I would ask the same licence for my formulation of teething as involving autocannibalism which supplements rather than supplants the other constructions.

TEETHING AS A PHYSIOLOGICAL PROTOTYPE OF PROJECTION

Teething also provides an experience of *discharge* of painful tension in the infant's first year (with an experiencing ego present):

> Fell sorrow's tooth doth never rankle more
> Than when it bites but lanceth not the sore
> *(Richard II,* I, iii, 301–2)

says Shakespeare. But when the tooth actually breaks through the mucosa of the gum, tension is discharged and the 'sore' is 'lanced'.[13] Perhaps this conditions some of the fantasies of explosive cannibalistic penetration, passive and active, that one gets from patients who have undergone experiences of overstimulation and, compulsively and repetitively, crave for a discharge of tension as if they were addicts—any kind of destructive penetration is sought out as a means of getting rid of the overstimulation.

At any rate, the infant can—*after* tooth eruption—bite others as well as bite himself. Aggression can be turned outwards, and also projected on to the environment so that a tension felt 'within' becomes 'without'; the eruption of the tooth acts like a material projection on to the environment. The tooth cannot only be used against others, but others can be endowed with it. Freud (1920) says about internal stimuli (like the drive representatives of oral masochism),

there is a tendency to treat them as though they were acting, not from the inside, but from the outside, so that it may be possible to bring the shield against stimuli into operation as a means of defence against them. This is the origin of projection . . .

The eruption of teeth can be seen as an experience that helps bring this about.

TEETH AND CASTRATION ANXIETY

There is much in the psychoanalytic literature about teeth and the phallic phase of libido development (e.g. tooth dreams referring to masturbation). These 'teeth phenomena' usually involve the falling out of the teeth rather than their eruption, and they invoke castration anxiety. I believe that it is because teeth can also connote the terror of passive masochistic annihilation that they can evoke the 'surprising, strong resistance' pointed out by Freud (1900). The resistance is in part ascribable to castration anxiety, but in addition the resistance relates to the intrapsychic phenomena connected with the 'tooth experience' earlier than the falling out of teeth: the biting and being bitten associated with the eruption of teeth. The two can coalesce; e.g. Fliess (1956) wonders 'whether castration is not in the last analysis conceived of as effected through biting?'

The phenomena related to teething have also been surrounded by a 'surprising, strong resistance', and not only by psychoanalysts whose very few contributions I have already mentioned. The fact of physiologically painful teething, familiar to any parent, has been minimized and even denied by generations of dentists and pediatricians (cf. Kucera, 1959).

THE OBJECT ENDOWED WITH A TOOTH

Fliess (1956) has pointed out how oral sadistic libido is regularly discharged in subsequent stages of libido development in situations both normal and pathological, so that any erogenic zone can be infused with cannibalistic libido. Any combination of sudden access of defused aggression and an ego regression, involving an impending loss of control of the instinctual access, means, if it goes far enough, a return to traumatic passive cannibalistic terror. In relation to the anal stage, for example, the Rat Man's terror concerns the rat *biting* its way into his body through his anus. The rat's many meanings for the Rat Man have been reviewed; it is above all the carrier of the tooth and thereby gains its full terrifying power. In dealing with another symbol that can be endowed with a tooth, the spider, Abraham (1922) (without stating that he does so) stratifies the meanings of a spider—with each added statement bringing in more terrifying connotations. The spider symbolizes the destructive phallic mother. It also symbolizes her destructive phallus, which can castrate. Abraham then quotes Nunberg, who states that the spider sucks blood, and finally quotes Freud, who adds that the female spider devours her mate—eats cannibalistically and thereby castrates by biting. The symbol for the phallic mother becomes terrifying when the phallus is endowed with teeth that can castrate and devour.

The tooth equips, accompanies and is the prototype for penetrative, devouring objects at any stage of libidinal development, involving any erogeneity that discharges oral sadistic libido. Differentiated objects that can be tooth-carriers are: the penetrative, castrating phallus of the parent (father or phallic mother); the faecal mass of the second anal stage that is clearly 'not-me'. The faecal stick that is 'me: not-me'; and the breast-mouth are the earlier subject and/or object that can be charged with cannibalistic libido. So both subject and object are equippable with teeth. This involves erogenous zones, partial object and subject: fantasies of the breast with teeth, vagina dentata, rectum dentata, urethra dentata (Keiser, 1954), phallus equipped with a mouth (Fliess, 1956). Fliess (1956) states: 'the mouth of this stage [second oral stage] is transferable on to all subsequent dominant erogenic zones'. Subject, object and erogenous zone can all be represented by cannibalist creatures like the rat which will appear, in analysis, in the associations of patients who have had traumatic overstimulating experiences.

MATERIAL FROM MYTHS AND FOLKLORE ILLUSTRATING THE ENDOWMENT OF OBJECTS WITH A TOOTH

The following myths about mice and rats demonstrate the connexion between the projection of cannibalistic aggression and the teeth. I quote from Frazer (1890) on 'contagious magic':

Thus in many parts of the world it is customary to put extracted teeth in some place where they will be found by *a mouse or a rat,* in the hope that through the sympathy which continues to exist between them and their former owner, his other teeth may acquire the same firmness and excellence as the teeth of these rodents. In Germany it is said to be almost a universal maxim that when you have a tooth taken out, you should insert it in a *mouse's hole*. To do so with a child's milk tooth . . . will prevent the child from having toothache. [My italics]

Lewis (1958) quotes folklore about the loss of teeth and mice and rats from Russia, Germany, Costa Rica, Oceania and from Polish Jews. Frazer has examples from Jews, Germans, Singhalese and Americans.

In this folklore the tooth is projected upon the rodent (literally), as in earlier development aggression is projected upon the mother to form the bad mother and the bad 'not-me'. To put it genetically, the breast is endowed with teeth: this is the basic meaning of the rat (into whose hole the lost tooth is to be put). The bad toothed breast is a projected part of the self at first, invested with narcissistic libido—part self, part object. After the establishment of object relations and a sense of self, the fear of being eaten and the sources of overstimulation are felt clearly as coming from the outside. This is eventually evidenced by the castration fear of the oedipal period which is, in regressive terms, so involved in these myths about losing teeth. The parent will not castrate the child if he loses, or has knocked out (as in puberty initiation rites), the penetrative tooth that symbolizes the penis. At a more regressive level, these myths are about not biting so as not to be bitten: The rat, not me, has the tooth.

CLINICAL ILLUSTRATIONS

The rat imago is used by patients who have been and continue to be overstimulated: besides themselves with rage; longing for a discharge to escape the traumatic state of too-muchness. I have described the concomitant ego and superego regressions. I want to add to previously published descriptions (Shengold, 1967) one literary and two short clinical examples.

A reading of Dostoyevski's *Notes from Underground* is to the point. The Underground Man characterizes himself repeatedly as a 'mouse' (he is predominantly masochistic), who lives in a rat hole-cloaca 'underground'. He gnashes his teeth, longs to bite; he suffers from toothache and finally enjoys it. He vents and courts spite: 'There in its nasty, stinking underground home our insulted, crushed and ridiculed mouse promptly becomes absorbed in cold, malignant and, above all, everlasting spite.' We see the vertical ego splits at work and at war in the Underground Man:

When petitioners would come to me . . . I used to grind my teeth at them, and felt intense enjoyment when I succeeded in making anybody unhappy. [He then says that he is conscious of not really being a spiteful man and that he wants to be loved.] 'I was lying when I said just now that I was a spiteful official. I was lying from spite. I was simply amusing myself with the petitioners . . . and in reality I never would become spiteful. I was conscious every moment in myself of many, very many elements absolutely opposite to that. I felt them positively swarming in myself, these opposite elements. . . .

The concomitant lack of identity and inability to love (like all 'rat people') are set forth:

Even in my underground dreams I did not imagine love except as a struggle. I began it always with hatred and ended it with moral subjugation, and afterwards I never knew what to do with the subjugated object.

The poor Underground Man is himself predominantly the Mouse, 'the subjugated object', although he confesses how he tormented and rejected the mousy young girl Liza after getting her to love him.

Patient 1

A young woman came to analysis complaining of pervasive feelings of worthlessness based on her reaction to what she called her 'bad' sexual impulses which were sadomasochistic and accompanied by great anger. These sexual impulses were ruthlessly suppressed in action, but at times the excitement was overwhelming and she felt compelled to masturbate. Her rage was rarely experienced although she was almost always aware it was there (the knowing and not knowing of the Rat Man). The rage would usually get discharged (and could be felt) against herself; she could act the role of a martyr and provoked people to treat her as one. Although her cruel impulses were conscious and were manifestly sexual in her masturbatory fantasies, they had no real significance for her. They were divided off from her 'official' personality; she was generally regarded, and with good reason, as a gentle and kind person (cf. the Rat Man). But when subject to rage and sexual excitement, she would go into an autohypnotic state and often would provoke something to happen. Sometimes she took a masochistic role, as when she 'found herself' inviting a strange and suspicious looking man into her apartment simply because he had rung the bell. Sometimes she would do something sadistic, but it was almost always disguised. In the analysis she was continually inviting and expecting rage and sexual attack but this was blocked off from her responsible awareness by her hypnoid states; what happened when she was 'wrapped in cotton wool', as she put it, did not count. It became clear that she wanted to be raped in her altered state of consciousness. This meant wishing a repetition of experiences from childhood with her sadistic and seductive father. The alterations of consciousness effectively deprived her of identity when she was the subject of her repeated overstimulated states. As the analysis proceeded and began to clarify this, she talked of herself as two personalities (as with the Rat Man these were in addition to her usual personality), which she called The Rat and The Mouse. To be The Mouse meant to be the little girl victim of her cruel father. As the Mouse she craved to have something violent and sexual done to her to end the traumatic overexcitement and provide a discharge. Her Rat personality was especially disowned; as the Rat she was aware of the wish to bite and to revenge herself—specifically she wanted to castrate by biting: to bite off the penis of the person who was overstimulating her. One day she talked of her excitement on reading Marlowe's *Edward II*, a play about a homosexual king who is killed by having a red-hot poker shoved up his anus. She wanted this done to herself, she wanted to do it to the analyst. In the Edward II story are some of the elements of the rat torture of *Torture Garden:* the red-hot poker, the anal penetration that kills. The rat was present in the patient's identification of herself as The Rat—the possessor of the cannibalistic penetrative 'toothed' penis that is seen as having the power to discharge the overstimulated condition. As a child she had many times sat on her father's lap and felt his erection. She was compelled to repeat this—to crave both to be the victim (the Mouse) and also to reverse roles—to become 'The Rat' and do it to 'the king'.

In subsequent analytic work the patient was able to feel fully, to remember fully and then to integrate the Mouse and Rat personae and thus undo their power.

Patient 2

A young Jewish man tells his analyst that when he was in the waiting room, he had walked to the window. Another patient, a woman, was then behind him; he had wanted to stare at her but had refrained. (It had been established many times that women in the waiting room were incestuous objects, belonging to the analyst.) As he looked out of the window far down at the street below, the patient had had the fantasy that the woman behind him would say,

'Don't jump—fall!' As he reported this, he felt that it was a kind of joke, but not a funny joke. Actually he had had a momentary impulse to jump. He then went into a resistant autohypnotic state, almost falling asleep. He 'woke up' with the following: 'I suddenly think of a story I read. It was about one of Freud's patients he called the Rat Man. Hungarians or Ukrainians put some rats upside down on his buttocks . . . God . . . how cruel. But . . . but the story . . . excited me [he reproduces the pauses of the Rat Man]. I felt that maybe if I could get away with it, I would do it.' At this point in the analysis the patient had not acknowledged his own predominantly passive anal cravings. Although the ambiguity of 'I would do it' allows for an expression of his being the rat-victim, he consciously meant that he would like to give the rat-treatment to someone else. But it had been the woman *behind* him in the waiting room that he had fantasied wanting him to fall (= to become a woman), and it was the arousal of anal excitement with the fantasy of a destructive penetration that had brought on his hypnosis.

The patient had distorted the 'Oriental torture' mentioned in the Rat Man case and connected it to Eastern Europe—to the Hungarians and Ukrainians who were his own ancestors. He associated to Hungarians and Ukrainians as being anti-Semitic; they would do things to Jews like him. But he himself had a Hungarian name, and was a Jewish anti-Semite. The hated analyst (who is 'behind him') is also Jewish. The anal erogeneity is associated with active and passive sadistic wishes. The patient went on to talk of his childhood traumatic experiences as the recipient of his mother's enemas.

His being at once a Jew and an anti-Semite was typical of the splits in this man's personality. He, like patient 1, was generally regarded (and thought of himself) as a kind and good-natured fellow. He too was subject to altered states of consciousness which defended him against the acknowledgement of his wishes and body feelings, while allowing for the repetitions of the past experiences on which these were based. He too performed and suffered cruelties that he refused to recognize.

One day, a high point in the analysis, he had felt great anger towards me and this was accompanied by fully acknowledged anal excitement. The next day he came in disturbed and hypnotic; with no mention of the previous session he went on to talk of his anger towards the whole world. His hypnoid state deepened and he actually went to sleep and had a dream on the couch: he dreamt that his mother-in-law was standing beside him: He woke, told me the dream and became very upset at the continuing hypnosis and 'sleepiness'. Then he said: 'Now I remember yesterday's session, but it's so vague. The man who had those feelings in his anus is someone else.' Later in the session, following long silences, I asked him about his dream: 'What comes to mind to your mother-in-law?' 'What dream? What mother-in-law?' he asked in consternation. He had completely suppressed the dream of ten minutes before. As he remembered it he said poignantly, 'My God! how bizarre! I'm not a person. I live in pieces.'

SUMMARY

I have reviewed some of the meanings of the rat imago for patients who have been seduced and traumatized as children. The rat is used as a hallmark for active and passive cannibalistic impulses, chiefly associated with anal erogeneity. I have stressed the importance of the tooth as the primal aggressive tool and speculated about the significance of teething. Some of the ego pathology of 'rat people' was described and exemplified, especially their extensive use of alterations of consciousness that makes possible vertical ego splits consisting of unacknowledged but powerful 'personalities' that appear and disappear. These people operate under the sway of the compulsion to repeat past traumata whose central content appears to be overstimulation.

NOTES

1. This remark of Freud's is cited by Kanzer (1952) as evidence of Freud's countertransference. The difficulty of saying 'into his anus' is demonstrated by its not being specifically stated in the Mirbeau story either. I think this evasion marks the special resistance evoked by the cannibalistic 'vulnerability' of the anal zone; it appears to be the principal site for the overwhelming stimulation (experienced as a being eaten into and a being eaten up) that can go on to ego dissolution.
2. These interstices are simultaneously attempts at isolation and a supplying of holes to be penetrated, i.e. 'peristaltic language'.
3. In the Rat Man's version (see below and Freud, 1909), the one rat becomes 'some rats'. We do not know if this is his distortion or the sadistic captain's. What does this multiplication mean? There are many possibilities: defensive (e.g. obfuscation) and revelatory (e.g. two as a female symbol), etc. One defensive meaning involves the keeping away from the *one* rat as the biting phallus. The Rat Man talks of both 'the rat punishment' and the 'punishment of the rats' but when the rat becomes singular it is clearly phallic: 'when he was wishing Constanze the rats he felt *a rat* gnawing at his own anus and had a visual image of it' (Freud, 1909).
4. The Rat Man told Freud of a dream of his involving oriental torture which he had dreamt in 1906—before the meeting with Captain N.
5. Lewin (1950), referring to the regression seen in pharmacothymic stupors, writes: 'The wish to be eaten sometimes makes its appearance starkly in the delirious hallucination of

menacing animals, large and small'. Rats are especially common in the hallucinations of DTs.

6. 'We get to look upon the child's fear of being devoured, or cut up, or torn to pieces . . . as a regular component of its mental life. And we know that the man-eating wolf . . . and all the evil monsters out of myths and fairy stories flourish and exert their unconscious influence in the phantasy of each individual child' (Klein, 1933).

REFERENCES

Abraham, K. (1922). The spider as a dream symbol. *Selected Papers*. London: Hogarth Press, 1949.

Abraham, K. (1924). The development of the libido. *Ibid.*

Barker, W. (1951). *Familiar Animals of America*. New York: Harper.

Dickes, R. (1965). The defensive function of an altered state of consciousness: a hypnoid state. *J. Am. psychoanal. Ass.* **13**, 365–403.

Fliess, R. (1953). The hypnotic evasion. *Psychoanal. Q.* **22**, 497–511.

Fliess, R. (1956). *Erogeneity and Libido*. New York: Int. Univ. Press.

Frazer, J. G. (1890). *The New Golden Bough,* ed. Gaster. New York: Criterion, 1959.

Freud, S. (1894). Studies on hysteria. *S.E.* **2**.

Freud, S. (1900). The interpretation of dreams. *S.E.* **4–5**.

Freud, S. (1909). Notes upon a case of obsessional neurosis. *S.E.* **10**.

Freud, S. (1920). Beyond the pleasure principle. *S.E.* **18**.

Freud, S. (1941). Schriften aus dem Nachlass. *G.W.* **17**.

Hegner, R. (1942). *A Parade of Familiar Animals*. New York: Macmillan.

Hoffer, W. (1950). Oral aggressiveness and ego development. *Int. J. Psycho-Anal.* **31**, 156–160.

Kanzer, M. (1952). The transference neurosis of the Rat Man. *Psychoanal. Q.* **21**, 181–189.

Keiser, S. (1954). Orality displaced to the urethra. *J. Am. psychoanal. Ass.* **2**, 263–279.

Klein, M. (1932). *The Psychoanalysis of Children*. London: Hogarth Press, 1949.

Klein, M. (1933). Early development of conscience in the child. *Contributions to Psycho-Analysis*. London: Hogarth Press, 1948.

Kucera, O. (1959). On teething. *J. Am. psychoanal. Ass.* **7**, 284–291.

Lamb, C. (1799). *Selected Letters,* ed. Matthews. New York: Farrar, Straus, 1956.

Lewin, B. D. (1950). *The Psychoanalysis of Elation*. New York: Norton.

Lewis, H. A. (1958). The effect of shedding the first deciduous tooth upon the passing of the oedipus complex of the male. *J. Am. psychoanal. Ass.* **6**, 5–37.

Lorenz, K. (1966). *On Aggression*. New York: Harcourt Brace.

Mahler, M. S. (1952). On child psychosis and schizophrenia. *Psychoanal. Study Child* **7**.

Mills, E. (1959). Rats, let's get rid of them. (U.S. Dept. of Interior circular, no. 22.)

Mirbeau, O. (1899). *Torture Garden*. New York: Citadel Press, 1948.

Protheroe, E. (1940). *New Illustrated Natural History of the World*. New York: Garden City Press.

Schour, I. & Masser, M. (1949). The teeth. In E. J. Farris & J. Q. Griffith (eds.), *The Rat in Laboratory Investigation*. Philadelphia: Lippincott.

Shengold, L. (1963). The parent as sphinx. *J. Am. psychoanal. Ass.* **11**, 725–751.

Shengold, L. (1967). The effects of overstimulation: rat people. *Int. J. Psycho-Anal.* **48**, 403–415.

Shuren, I. (1967). A contribution to the metapsychology of the preanalytic patient. *Psychoanal. Study Child* **22.**

Simmel, E. (1944). Self-preservation and the death instinct. *Psychoanal. Q.* **13,** 160–185.

Spock, B. (1957). *Baby and Child Care.* New York: Duell, Sloan.

Wilson, E. (1950). In memory of Octave Mirbeau. *Classics and Commercials.* New York: Farrar, Straus.

Zinnser, H. (1935). *Rats, Lice and History.* New York: Little, Brown.

12. The Essence of Masochism

Kerry Kelly Novick and Jack Novick

Despite putative shifts in the types of pathology presented to the modern psychoanalyst, our caseloads are in fact very similar to Freud's, since he too grappled with masochistic phenomena of varying intensity and pervasiveness in his daily work. The male cases cited in his paper on beating fantasies (1919) "included a fairly large number of persons who would have to be described as true masochists" (p. 196) and there are references to suicide in all of Freud's published cases except Little Hans (Litman, 1970; Novick, 1984). The difficulties in conceptualization and technical handling of masochism led Freud to repeated revisions of his formulations and ultimately to fundamental changes in psychoanalytic metapsychology.

Since Freud a vast literature has accumulated around the theoretical and clinical problems of masochism. Good summaries of the classical view are provided by Fenichel (1945), Loewenstein (1957), Bieber (1966), and Ferber (1975). Maleson (1984) says that masochism has acquired a "confusing array of meanings," with "little consistency or precision in its current usage" (p. 325). For Freud, all masochism was ultimately based on erotogenic masochism. The linkage of erotogenic and moral masochism takes place via the beating fantasy; morality for the masochist represents an unconscious, resexualized wish to be beaten by the father. In this way "the Oedipus complex is

Kerry Kelly Novick is on the faculty of the Michigan Psychoanalytic Institute; Jack Novick is a child and adolescent supervising analyst on the faculty of the Michigan's Psychoanalytic Institute, and an adjunct associate professor at Wayne State University Medical School.

Earlier versions of this paper were presented at the Arbor Clinic in May 1984, to the Michigan Association for Psychoanalysis in October 1984, and to a scientific meeting of the Michigan Psychoanalytic Society in May 1986.

Our thanks to Paul Brinich, Laurie Levinson, Steven Marans, Irene Marcus, Ava Bry Penman, and Katharine Rees for their helpful testing of our theoretical formulations against clinical data. Special thanks to Paul Brinich for his detailed review of the text.

Reprinted by permission of Yale University Press, from *The Psychoanalytic Study of the Child* 42 (1987):353–84.

revived and the way is opened for a regression from morality to the Oedipus complex" (1924, p. 169). Thus Freud reemphasized his earlier tenet that the beating fantasy is the "essence of masochism" (1919, p. 189).

If Freud's statement is valid, a detailed study of beating fantasies should help us to understand more fully the complex phenomena of masochism. In "The Economic Problem of Masochism" (1924) Freud sketched the genetic point of view; Loewenstein (1957) used a developmental perspective; and we too will apply this perspective to a study of beating fantasies to elucidate a developmental line of masochism.

A major finding of our 1972 study of beating fantasies in children was that there were two types of beating fantasies, a normal transitory one and a "fixed fantasy." The transitory fantasy was more often found in girls, was usually spontaneously modified, or easily gave way to interpretation, whereas the fixed fantasy became the permanent focus of the child's psychosexual life and was often impervious to years of interpretive work. In this paper we use the development of the fixed beating fantasy as a model to explicate aspects of the developmental line of masochism.

We use previously unpublished data from the cases of 11 children with beating fantasies as a framework. Further material from infant and toddler observation and from the psychoanalyses of children, adolescents, and adults is included. We delineate the epigenesis of masochism as an *adaptation* to a disturbed environment, a *defense* against aggression, and a *mode of instinctual gratification*. Further, we show that masochism is not only overdetermined but serves other ego functions.

INFANCY

The literature on masochism includes many controversies; one major issue devolves on the genesis of masochism in the preoedipal or oedipal stages. In our 1972 study we described material from child analyses and observations which showed that organized beating fantasies were formed only postoedipally, while the determinants could be traced to earlier phases. In the sample of 111 indexed cases at the Anna Freud Centre we found that "the beating wish, sadistic intercourse theory, and phallic beating games could be seen in some form in all the young children" (p. 239). The transitory beating fantasy seen in some girls arose postoedipally and represented, as Freud had described, both regressed oedipal strivings and punishment for them. In each instance, the dynamics followed the classical formulation of oedipal conflicts leading to regression to anal-phase fixations around aggression and the beating wish.

In contrast, the preoedipal determinants of masochistic behavior in those children with fixed beating fantasies derived from disturbances in the earliest months of their lives. Mark, who entered analysis at 8½ years of age, was later found to have a fixed beating fantasy. He was the second of two children. His mother described her "obsessive concern" during pregnancy with the older child's potential jealousy. Her concern intensified after Mark's birth to the point where she felt compelled to interrupt any ministrations to Mark, including feeding, whenever she thought of her first child. She described Mark's first year as extremely unhappy, the feeding as totally unsatisfactory, and Mark as a fussy, crying baby. Like other mothers in the sample, she described herself as depressed and preoccupied, unable to take any pleasure in her baby. Such descriptions of a mutual lack of pleasure on the part of both mother and baby were universal in the fixed beating fantasy sample and have recurred in all our subsequent cases of masochistic pathology where social history data have been available.

This finding contrasts strikingly with the histories of the children who were found to have a transitory beating fantasy. In that group, despite reports of various pathological interactions early in the child's life, there were nevertheless sources of available pleasure for both partners in the mother-child dyad. Emma's mother, for instance, said that she started her 3-week-old infant on solids and she continued a pattern of premature demands throughout infancy; Emma's precocious positive responses, however, provided intense gratification for her mother, which was returned to the child as loving praise and pleasure. Derivatives of this mutually pleasurable interaction may have formed a component in the transference relationship of pleasant working together which Emma was able to enjoy in her analysis at age 4.

While we should be extremely cautious in attributing later manifestations directly to experiences of early infancy, it is important to note the unanimous report of the therapists of the children with fixed beating fantasies that the treatments were arduous, joyless, and ungratifying for a long time.

Disturbances in the pleasure economy between mother and infant appeared in the histories of all the children with fixed beating fantasies, and were recreated in more specific forms in the transference relationship during analysis. Clinical material from child analyses suggests the links forged in very early life between the experience of lack of pleasure or unpleasure and the age-appropriate developmental needs of the infant. But in the transference relationships of adult patients the multitude of transformations which take place in the course of development to adulthood make discernment of the deviations of early infancy very complicated.

Mrs. S., a tall, attractive divorcee, sought analysis to deal with issues of unresolved mourning for her father. Although outwardly very successful, she was finding it increasingly difficult to reconcile the demands of her profession with the needs of her three children and her own social life. Early in the analysis, Mrs. S. described a beating fantasy which she used in order to achieve orgasm. In the fantasy she imagined her father telling her that she was bad, putting her across his knee, and spanking her. She only became conscious of the fantasy just before orgasm, and then habitually forgot it again. The fantasy surfaced in treatment in the context of sexualized pleasure in the joint analytic work, which was accompanied by pains in her lower back. After the interpretation that the pains seemed to be the condition under which she could experience pleasure, Mrs. S. remembered her beating fantasy and realized that she had "always" had it.

Subsequent material centered on her overstimulating relationship with her father and her unresolved oedipal conflicts and neurotic compromises. After these were worked through in the transference, successful mourning could be accomplished. After two years of work, her presenting symptoms had abated, she was functioning apparently well in all areas, and Mrs. S. wanted to finish her treatment. Despite the many positive changes, the analyst disagreed, because the beating fantasy was still central to Mrs. S.'s sexual life. She had strenuously resisted all attempts to relate any analytic material to her relationship with her mother, particularly in the transference.

During the course of her analysis, Mrs. S. had visibly gained weight and the analyst interpreted this as self-feeding to defend against her wishes and fears over reexperiencing the maternal relationship in the transference. Mrs. S. responded with stories about her childhood hitherto unreported because she considered them "irrelevant." She had been told by her mother that she had been a "poor feeder" from birth, had difficulty sucking, and had not gained weight for the first four months of her life. This history of her own failure-to-thrive had later been repeated when Mrs. S. became a mother and found the relationship with her own infant daughter unsatisfying and tense, with the outcome that Mrs. S.'s daughter was diagnosed failure-to-thrive at four months. Work on this previously omitted material revitalized the analysis, and the vicissitudes of her early painful relationship to her mother emerged in the transference to be understood as the first layer in the formation of masochistic relationships.

Reconstruction of the early mother-child relationship from analytic data can always benefit from corroborative evidence, so we will examine here some material from infant observation which pertains to pleasure and pain in infancy. From very early in life, the infant can differentiate among others via a wide range of perceptual modalities. Included in these capacities is the ability to differentiate between self and nonself at the body boundary of the skin. This takes place at the point where the skins of mother and child touch and are felt as separate, contiguous entities. Under normal circumstances, stimulation of infants occurs through multiple channels; but in a disturbed mother-child relationship, a reduction in possible channels occurs. One that may remain is skin contact, since this is not dependent on psychological or emotional synchrony, as are, for instance, eye contact, talking, or smiling.

We have been following the development of two infants who became hair-pullers. It appears that the development of this pain-seeking symptom represents an adaptation to a disturbed mother-child relationship. Both children were born to single adolescent mothers; both children were diagnosed failure-to-thrive at 4 months, when the mothers each went through a period of depression and withdrawal from the babies. While the etiology of failure-to-thrive is complicated and varied, some clear factors emerge from detailed observations, films, and interviews.[1] In films of feeding before 4 months, Nicole attempted to engage her mother in social interactions between bites. After each bite, Nicole's mother literally scraped the smile off Nicole's face with the spoon, until the sixth bite was followed by a frown. This is a good example of what Tronick and Gianino (1986) have called the failure to repair a mismatch between mother and baby. In our observations we could see the next step, in which the mother externalized her feelings of failure onto the baby: the mother then made clear that she found Nicole an unpleasant girl. Soon thereafter the mother's depression coincided with Nicole's failure-to-thrive.

Through the intervention of staff at the institution where they lived, useful feeding was reestablished and Nicole gained weight. But the effect of the sustained experience of dissynchrony persisted. Tronick and Gianino have found that infants of depressed mothers decrease their engagement with people and things and deploy more coping behaviors aimed at maintaining self-regulation. The child moves away from signaling the mother to self-comfort, such as rocking, withdrawal, or aversion. Nicole began to pull her hair, tweaking and twiddling it until it broke, just at the back top quarter of her head, the spot where her head rested in the crook of mother's arm, the one remaining point of contact with mother. For many months the spot was nearly bald; at 2½ years Nicole's hair was noticeably shorter and ragged at the same place. Despite excellent progress in both mother and child, this symptom persisted, appearing at moments when, for example, the nursery teacher failed to answer Nicole's question.

The hair-pulling in Nicole and the other infant is an example of pain-seeking as an adaptation to a pathological situation. Pain-seeking behavior represents an attempt to substitute for the withdrawal of cathexis by the mother. In Nicole the need for the object overrides the need for pleasure. For the children with beating fantasies or for the hair-pullers, safety resides in an object that induces pain rather than pleasure. These are mothers who, for a variety of reasons, cannot pay attention to their children's needs.

In our sample of children with beating fantasies we found a preponderance of mothers who were unable to absorb (Orgel, 1974) or contain the infant's helplessness, neediness, and rage, but blamed the child and externalized their own infantile affective states. Tronick and Gianino make the point that successful joint repair of mismatches by mother and child is experienced by the child as "effectance," and this may be what Winnicott (1960) and others have called the child's normal phase of omnipotence. Winnicott suggested that a child needs a long-enough stage of normal omnipotence before it can be relinquished. It is possible that extended periods of discomfort and dissatisfaction experienced in infancy by all the children with beating fantasies may have disrupted their normal stage of omnipotence prematurely. These children may have become aware too soon of their dependence on their mothers and felt deeply their inability to exert any control over the social realm. They turn to pathological solutions as an adaptation to this dilemma, as did the 11-month-old described by Loewenstein (1957) to illustrate his "protomasochistic" maneuver of "seduction of the aggressor."

The type of intervention with both mothers and infants described by Brinich (1984) and by Peter Blos, Jr. (1985) in his discussion of intergenerational pathology could correct this pattern; however, in our sample, it appeared that the mothers themselves experienced such difficulty in relation to activity, dependency needs, and feelings of helplessness that they attempted to resolve them by externalization of these hated, devalued parts of themselves onto their children. Abel's mother was cold and irritable, withdrawn emotionally from her crying baby whom she saw as a pathetically helpless child. Eric's mother denied her own feelings of castration and passivity by externalizing these aspects of her self representation onto all her male objects: thus her husband and her infant Eric were seen as damaged, hopeless, useless people.

Rather than a relationship based on the sensitive mutual repair of inevitable moments of mismatch, the infants who later developed masochistic pathology grew up in a milieu of painful externalizations. We could speculate that externalization of blame, failure, and devalued aspects of the self onto the child served as a major and early mode of relationship and may have become the "primary fault" (Balint, 1968) leading to the evolution of masochistic structures. We suggest that the first layer of masochism must be sought in early infancy, in the child's adaptation to a situation where safety resides only in a painful relationship with the mother. Glenn (1984) too found the roots of his patient's masochism in the relationship to a "parent associated with pain" (p. 72). Valenstein's description of "individuals whose attachment to pain signifies an original attachment to painfully perceived objects" (1973, p. 389) applies also to the patients in the 1972 sample and to those we have seen subsequently. Their beating fantasies encapsulated and perpetuated the painful relationship to the object, not only historically, but also in their clinging to unhappiness through all stages of treatment.

Mark, whose early history was referred to above, was typical of the group of children with fixed beating fantasies in our 1972 sample. His beating fantasy appeared against a background of severe pathology. He was referred for frequent tantrums, periods of overwhelming anxiety, multiple fears, and being bullied at school. Once he overcame his initial anxiety, he presented a picture of chaotic drive development with little or no phase dominance. Impulses from all libidinal levels coexisted: his anxieties were often oral in form, with fears of being poisoned or eaten; he said, "in intercourse the lady eats the man." Anal sexuality was manifest in excited preoccupation with feces, bottoms, and nose-picking. Mark, like the other children in the sample, was of superior intelligence and functioned adequately in school. In treatment, however, it soon became clear that his reality perception was distorted in relation to self and object representations. Mark, a slender boy in treatment with a plump woman, complained of being fat. His feelings about himself fluctuated between grandiose delusions of omnipotence and a sense of abject worthlessness.

As with the other children in the 1972 sample, the first two years of

Mark's treatment were marked by immediate discharge of wishes into action. His analyst said, "His behavior was wild and uncontrolled and there were long periods when I could make no contact with him. He would, for example, charge into the room with a pellet gun, shout, 'Alright, I'm going to kill you!' and fire the pellets at me. One moment he would be lying on the table, licking his snot, telling me he has no friends and the next moment he would shout at me, 'You fat pig, you'll die for this!' " As words could increasingly be linked to feelings and the range of affects broadened to include pleasure, Mark said, "When I'm feeling good, I feel all alone; when I'm feeling bad, I'm with my mother."

The need for pain seems to be at the core of the personalities of these patients; it arises early in life, whether from environmental causes or constitutional factors, as some have proposed (Olinick, 1964), persists throughout development, and can be seen to be at work even in the end phase of analysis. Mary was referred for analysis following a serious suicide attempt in adolescence. In her sixth year of treatment, she had graduated from university with highest honors and had a full scholarship for graduate studies where she was doing outstanding work. At the end of her first year of analysis the analyst described her as totally dependent on her mother, spending weekends and every evening in her room, sitting silently at meals and, other than studying, her only activity was rearranging furniture in her room, or spending hours trying to decide which side of the desk to put her pencils on. She was physically inhibited and looked like a prepubertal boy. At the time, the major concern was that she would become psychotic or kill herself.

After 6 years of analysis, she looked very feminine and attractive, had many friends, and had a long-standing relationship with a very suitable young man. They had arranged to share an apartment and were planning marriage. She had confronted her parents numerous times and had forced a change in the relationship which they enjoyed. Things were going well on all fronts, the end of analysis was in sight, and only one problem remained. The overt manifestation of the problem was Mary's continued difficulty in maintaining pleasurable feelings, especially with the analyst. As the suicide risk had receded, it had become apparent that Mary's primary pathology was not depression but an underlying severe masochistic disorder which subsumed both her depression and suicidal behavior. It became clear that her suicide attempt was an enactment of a fixed beating fantasy. As the determinants of Mary's underlying masochism were worked through, she could experience and maintain pleasure for longer periods of time outside of her therapy. She could feel pride and joy in her skills and competence, and take pleasure in her attractiveness and sexual activities. The conflicts around pleasure became centered almost entirely in the analysis. She would feel happy, proud of some achievement, until she walked in the door and then would feel gloomy and bad. Mary explained her need to feel unhappy with the analyst as follows:

When I'm happy, I feel I'm not with you.
To be unhappy is to be like you, to be with you, to sit quietly and depressed with the whole world right here in this room.
I tell you about something funny that happened in class and then I think, oh, you should have been there, and I realize you weren't there and I feel sad and lonely.
I sometimes think of my suicide as the best time. Everyone was with me, and loved me and felt sorry for me.

Throughout this paper, we will be examining the transformations through development of the child's involvement with pain, but what we are describing at the earliest level is a learned association. The clinical material of our masochistic patients supports Stern's (1985) view, based on infant observation, that "it is the actual shape of interpersonal reality, specified by the interpersonal invariants that really exist, that helps determine the developmental course. Coping operations occur as reality-based adaptations" (p. 255). As Mary said, "Feeling bad is something I know, it's safe, it's the smell of home."

Tronick and Gianino demonstrated the stability of the child's early coping styles, and Escalona (1968) has shown that it is *maladaptive* infant behavior which tends to persist. Thus the association of mother and unpleasure leads to the early adoption of an autoplastic, rather than alloplastic, mode of dealing with internal and external stimuli, which sets a pattern of discharge via the self which will affect all later developmental phases.

TODDLERHOOD

From the perspective of masochistic pathology, the toddler stage is crucial in determining the quality of aggressive impulses and in fixing the pattern of dealing with them. The normal developmental tasks, activities, and wishes of toddlerhood provide an opportunity to establish constructive defenses; a sound sense of self accompanied by feelings of effectance, joy, and safety; a loving relationship to constant objects; and an exponential expansion of ego control of motility and cognition. All of these are dependent on adequate drive fusion. In discussions of masochism, the concepts of fusion, libidiniza- tion, and binding are often used interchangeably, even by Freud. We feel it is important to differentiate them, as fusion denotes transformation of both drives by a mixture in which aggression is neutralized to some degree by libido, with resultant energy available for other purposes, such as defense formation or sublimation. Libidinization occurs in the formation of masochis- tic pathology, when aggressive impulses or painful experiences become sexualized; no transformation of either drive occurs. Binding is the structural inhibition of direct discharge. A striking feature of all the children with fixed beating fantasies was the extent of primitive aggressive behavior, apparently unfused by libido. In the first year of his analysis, Mark threw the toys all over the room, down the stairs, or out of the window. He would write on the wall, try to force open the files and lockers, and generally try to destroy the room. His uncontrolled behavior provoked the therapist to restrain him, which led to bitter accusations of attack. His mental world seemed dominated by fantasies of attack and counterattack, as he filled his sessions with com- plaints of being picked on by teachers, peers, his brother, and his parents.

Mary presented with alternating states of blank silence and overwhelming experiences of omnipotent rage. Her fantasies were characterized by primary process organization and her dreams were dominated by images of uncon- trolled, explosive destruction. For example, the central image in one dream was of stabbing a man over and over until he was reduced to a mound of indistinguishable flesh and blood. In a later dream, a room full of babies was shotgunned to the point of indiscriminate mess. Later in her analysis, when Mary became able to associate to these dreams, a repeated latent theme was anal explosiveness which would destroy her mother, who in reality had spent an inordinate amount of time scrubbing the bathrooms.

As Furman (1985) emphasized, the mother as auxiliary ego protects the child from excessive libidinal and aggressive stimulation. Our data confirm the findings of others (Rubinfine, 1965; Orgel, 1974; Brinich, 1984) that mothers of masochists seem less than normally able to contain their chil- dren's aggression and thus promote fusion. The result for the children is unfused, primitive, omnipotent aggression. Rather than containing and modi- fying the children's impulses and anxieties with the help of their own libidi- nal investment, each mother in the beating fantasy sample intensified the child's aggression by bodily intrusiveness, constraint of normal moves to- ward independence and autonomy, and interference with pleasure in messing and exploration.

Further, the mothers' own conflicts over instinctual impulses were dealt with by externalization onto the children. With Mary's mother this was a lifelong process, which continued even throughout Mary's treatment. For instance, Mary's mother insisted that family members and guests always enter through the back door and remove their shoes to protect the pale carpeting from any dirt they might bring in. She cleaned constantly, reproaching others for their dirtiness and mess. Once Mary "forgot" to remove her shoes and was overwhelmed with feelings of shame which were linked via associations to having soiled her pants as a young child. During the intake interview following Mary's suicide attempt, her mother's sole complaint was that Mary had accompanied a group of girls four years earlier as they threw eggs at an abandoned house. Despite the passage of time and the intervening near-death of her child, Mary's "vandalism," as she termed it, was the focus of her attention. In analysis, Mary recounted her continuing feeling of badness over the incident and her persistent fear that the police would still come after her.

Mrs. S.'s mother had a history of flamboyant sexual relationships with men who were unacceptable to her own family. Mrs. S. reported that, as a child, she masturbated openly. Though she had no recollection of her mother's reaction at the time, she described her mother's current practice of laughing accounts to friends of Mrs. S.'s "extreme uncontrollable childhood sexuality." From early adolescence, Mrs. S. was promiscuous, imperiling herself with sexual exploits which she recounted to her mother. In analysis, it became clear that Mrs. S.'s sexual behavior in childhood and adulthood represented an internalization of her mother's lack of control of impulses; the result was that Mrs. S. hated herself and contemplated suicide. Mary and Mrs. S., like the children with fixed beating fantasies, already had a proclivity developed in infancy toward autoplastic solutions to stress. It is in the toddler phase that the earlier use of the self to restore homeostasis joins with the mother's externalizations to create the mechanism of turning aggression against the self.

We found that all of the children in our sample dealt with their aggression by denying any sign of hostility between themselves and their mothers and struggled to maintain an idealized image of mother as loving and perfect. This included denial of the mother's castration, which Bak (1968) considered an important factor in perversions. Refusal to face imperfections in the mother was linked to omnipotence of thought, as mother's failings were attributed to the boy's own aggression. Mark felt that his penis was not his own; if his mother did not have one, it must be because he had stolen it from her. He felt his own defecation was a dangerous aggressive act (a result of his own wishes and his mother's attitude), and insisted that his mother could not do anything so terrible as defecate—he must be the only one in the world, and the worst person of all, to do so.

We see the defensive aspect of the underlying masochism expressed in the beating fantasy as following upon and reinforcing the child's prior submission to a threatening environment. What was initially an acceptance of the mother's externalizations (messy, dependent, aggressive) in the service of retaining the object becomes an active internalization used by the child to maintain the image of a loving, protective, perfect mother, safe from the destructive rage of his anal sadism. From the point of view of defense, the masochism can be seen as an attempt to defend against destructive wishes from each level of development, directed against the mother, utilizing the mechanisms of denial, displacement, internalization, and, via the internalization, turning of aggression against the body.

The operation of all these defenses can be seen in the form of the later beating fantasy. All the beating fantasies contained, implicitly in that they involved punishment or explicitly, the statement, "I am a naughty boy." Mark imagined that his strict paternal aunt entered the room; he took off his clothes, said, "I am a naughty boy," and then she spanked him. Despite the evidence from the boys' material which demonstrated that their mothers were experienced as threatening objects and the fact that the mothers were often the punishers in real life, the beater in the fantasies was usually the father or a father representative. Here we see a displacement of aggression from the more frightening, but more important, primary object to the father.

In reporting the beating fantasy the children usually stopped at the point where they had been beaten as if that were the end. Further work, especially by means of the transference relationship, revealed that there was more to the fantasy, and this remainder contained the main preoedipal libidinal and narcissistic goals of the fantasy—hence the reluctance of the children to disclose it. In this extension, someone important, often a woman, felt very sorry for the beaten child and comforted him; in many versions the child was then regarded as a very important and special person. One child fantasied that the beating would be followed by both parents apologizing and the mother putting soothing lotion on his bottom. In another child's fantasy, after he had been cruelly beaten by schoolboys, the headmaster told the assembled students, "He is the outstanding boy who has been treated badly. We have never had any other boy who has gone through so much." Analyses of adolescents who have attempted suicide show that this fantasied response by the object is crucial to the goals of the suicide (Novick, 1984). Mary imagined that, after her suicide, she would hover around to see how sorry everyone was, how they would feel guilty, and turn their full attention to her to gratify all her wishes. The defensive efforts to rid the mother-child relationship of omnipotent aggression by means of displacement and turning aggression against the self are the child's contribution to the joint attempt to create a "purified pleasure dyad" (Novick, 1980).

The mothers of children with beating fantasies were psychologically intrusive, via their externalizations. Through hypercathexis of their children's bodies well into prepuberty or adolescence, for active gratification of their own needs, they were also physically intrusive. Anna Freud (1960) commented on the increased impact of parental disturbance when the pathology is not contained in thought but moves into the realm of activity. For example, one mother constantly checked the child's anus and feces for signs of worms. Mark's mother wiped his bottom until he was 11 years old; she stopped only after three years of analytic work with Mark enabled him to resist her intrusion into the bathroom. In her analysis, Mary occasionally displayed a cognitive uncertainty which contrasted markedly with her high intelligence. Work on these states allowed for recovery of a memory of a voice asking, "Are you sure?" This phrase became a pointer to her symptomatic uncertainty at many levels, but specific associations led to the reconstruction of her mother's handling of her toilet training. Mary experienced a confirming shock of recognition when she saw her mother constantly asking her toddler grandchild if she had to go to the bathroom. When the child said "No," Mary's mother said, "Are you sure?" and then peeked into the grandchild's diaper while remarking to Mary, "You have to make sure."

In normal development, the self representation emerges out of and contains the body representation. This integration starts with the experience of pleasure in one's body at the hands of a loving object. The children with beating fantasies were unable to achieve integration of body and self. They experienced their bodies as owned and controlled by their mothers, and so preoedipal omnipotent aggression toward mother was defended against and expressed by attacks on the body. Mrs. S. was always ashamed of her breasts and had such antipathy to this part of her body that she was unable to breastfeed her children. When this was explored in analysis, there seemed no reality basis for her negative feelings, as her breast development was normal in all respects. Later in analysis, it emerged through dreams and associations that Mrs. S. did not feel that her breasts belonged to her. Her lack of pride in her own body and her inability to feed her own children were her way of expressing her rage and disappointment at her own mother's inability to breast-feed her. Autoaggressive behavior in infants as reported by Cain (1961) and the study of suicide cases confirm this finding (Novick, 1984).

A further effect of the intrusive pattern of interaction is the hypercathexis in the child of the receptive mode. This touches upon a major conceptual puzzle—the relation of masochism and passivity. Maleson (1984) notes that many analysts continue to equate the two, as Freud did originally. It might be helpful to distinguish between passivity and receptivity. We see passivity as an ego quality linked in its pathological extreme manifestations to the experience of an inattentive caretaker. An adolescent boy who had suffered from infancy from parental inability to sustain attention to his needs and feelings showed no signs of masochistic pathology, yet demonstrated extreme passivity in all areas of his life. Masochists are highly receptive and are ready to take in any stimuli from the outside world, ranging from subtle shifts in mother's moods to what one homosexual patient described as his wish for a "fist-fuck." Masochists are very active in their pursuit of pain and failure, in part to maintain the receptive relationship with an intrusive object. For example, Mary at 19 years endured taunts because she wore her hair cut so short that she looked like a schoolboy; she revealed after years of analysis that she went to her mother for her haircuts.

We have discussed the ways in which the toddler's aggression is intensified by failure in the mother-child relationship to promote fusion and integration. Further, the normal impulses toward separation and independent functioning which arise in the anal phase are experienced as aggression by both mother and child. The struggle for autonomy first takes place in the realm of bodily activity; the mothers of the children in our group opposed independence and reacted to normal assertion as attack. These children lost the battle for autonomy and felt that their mothers needed them only as helpless anal objects. Mother and child had become locked in an intense relationship which was experienced by the child as one in which each partner needed the other for survival and gratification. The child not only feared loss of the mother, but his guilt resided mainly in his normal wishes to separate from her and function independently. As Mark said, "Whenever I do something good without my mother, I think she is going to die." The beating in the fantasy formed later could then also be seen as a punishment for wishes to separate from the mother. In the fantasy the naughtiness for which they were beaten was usually left vague, but we have often found that the fantasy followed age-appropriate behavior, independent wishes, or achievements. Mark, at 14, was about to leave on a school trip and worried that his mother would be sad and upset, which she became. He hoped that he would be able to flirt with the girls, and at first he managed to talk to a girl he liked. Before the trip was actually under way, however, Mark created a fantasy that the school superintendent would cane him for flirting, and he spent the rest of the time preoccupied with this fantasy to the detriment of any of the social activities. Although this appears very similar to punishment for an oedipal wish, the subsequent material clearly indicated that Mark's flirting represented a breaking of the object tie to his mother, and it was for this disloyalty that he was being punished.

Similarly, other age-appropriate activities throughout development were experienced as aggressive attacks on the mother and could be performed only under conditions which counteracted any normal moves toward independence and separate functioning. For example, in adolescence several of the boys, including Mark, could not masturbate with their hands but rubbed their genitals against the sheets leaving the mess for their mothers to see and clean up. Instead of gratification in a private act which excluded mother, genital impulses were discharged in a form re-creating an anal mode of relating to their mothers. The dependent receptivity which is central to masochism and the beating fantasy can then be seen as a defense against the aggression attributed to activity, separation, and independent functioning.

Thus the child's pain-seeking adaptation to a pathological early relationship continues in the anal phase as the prime mode of attracting and retaining the object. The aggressive impulses of the anal phase are dealt with by the defense of turning the aggression against the self, which prevents destruction of the object and allows for discharge of aggression toward the internalized hated mother. In our view, the adaptive and defensive motives for the masochism which underlies the beating fantasy are preoedipal; the masochistic behavior of the child is not yet a sexual pleasure in itself but a means by which he attempts to survive and gratify other passive libidinal wishes. The clinical presentation of all the children in the 1972 sample was preoedipal. They entered treatment displaying a persistence of anal-phase ways of functioning, with excited preoccupation with seeing, smelling, and wiping bottoms, thoughts of defecating on people and smearing. One boy of 9 years still played with and hid feces, and several of them masturbated anally. The egos of these children had little ability to control discharge of the anal drive impulses; the defense systems were severely impaired, with predominant, often exclusive use of primitive defenses, such as denial and the variety of externalizations, including drive projection. Battling relationships were the norm at home, school, and in treatment. It is evident that these children carry into the phallic-oedipal phase the preexisting pathology; for this reason they will experience it very differently from the normal child. The phallic-oedipal period is crucial for the sexualization of masochism.

PHALLIC-OEDIPAL STAGE

The nature of the child's theory concerning parental intercourse has a profound effect on the development of masochism and the later beating fantasy. Sadistic intercourse theories are universal, but in normal children they coexist with other theories, whereas for the children we are discussing the notion that in intercourse the parents beat or hurt each other is the safest theory available to them. Just as being beaten represents the safest form of relating to the object in the beating fantasy, so the sadistic intercourse theory is preferred to more frightening ideas, such as chaotic, uncontrollable happenings (Niederland, 1958), mutual mutilation, castration, etc. This view is in line with Niederland's suggestion that the sadistic intercourse theory and the beating fantasy serve to structure unorganized, terrifying primal scene experiences and ideas. For these patients the primal scene is not a reconstructed hypothesis or a metaphor for the universal exclusion from parental activities but an ongoing reality, as parents of patients with masochistic pathology seem unable to protect them from repeated exposure to overwhelming experiences. Indeed, they often seem to inflict them on the patients. On the eve of a 13-year-old's entry into analysis, the parents happened to leave the bedroom door open; the boy walked in to see his parents in the act of intercourse, mother on top of father; the following day, preceding his first session, the patient broke his arm playing ball. Analysis revealed that this was but the latest in a series of events in which his mother had exposed him to traumatic situations which were invariably followed by self-injurious behavior. Furman (1984) has noted the role of parental pathology in the exposure to traumatic situations of suicidal patients.

The phallic excitement of this phase and the wish to participate in sadistic parental intercourse turn what had been a means to an end into an end in itself. To submit, to suffer, to be beaten, to be humiliated now come to represent the feminine receptive position in parental intercourse. The wish to be in this position becomes the instinctual motive for the masochism, the spur and the accompaniment to phallic masturbation. A crucial transformation occurs during this phase, when the painful experiences in the preoedipal parent-child interaction become libidinized and represent for the child participation in parental intercourse.

To the powerful motives for masochism of the earlier phases is added the circumvention of the normal oedipal exclusion, humiliation, and rage. Often the parents collude at each level in the development of the pathological relationship. Their involvement in the lack of resolution of the oedipus complex contributes to the maintenance of what we have called the "delusion of omnipotence." This ego defect is an important factor in the characteristically high level of anxiety in masochistic patients.

In the children with beating fantasies, drive material from all levels of libidinal development was available in consciousness. The children were convinced that these impulses could not be controlled either by themselves or by anyone else. They felt sure that their drive aims could and would be gratified; reality contradiction did not seem to affect this conviction. Mark, at 13, was convinced that his mother wanted to have intercourse with him. One of the sources of this attitude was the absence of an adequate system of defenses, which meant that internal controls were insufficient; none of these children had reached the stage of developing a structured superego. External controls were also missing, in that the fathers of these children were all particularly unsuitable to serve as strong, protective objects for identification. Two fathers had died, two fathers had psychotic breakdowns, and two were absent in the army during their children's early years. The others seemed to play no positive role in the family, showing undue dependence on the mothers. Conversely, the mothers were all described as powerful, domineering women, who ruled their families more or less overtly.

There was also a high degree of parental collusion in the gratification of inappropriate wishes. Several of the children in this group were allowed into the parental bed until ages of 11 and 12; others were helped with toileting up to 7 or 8 years; most ruled the house with their tantrums and rages, and in two cases there was danger of the child causing serious harm to a sibling. Mark regularly ousted his father from the parental bed, to which father's response was a depressive withdrawal. When Mark began displaying an interest in girls in adolescence, his father became acutely anxious and then announced that he was homosexual, although this apparently resulted in no action. Throughout her childhood, as far back as she could remember, Mrs. S. spent long evenings lying on her parents' bed watching television while her father stroked her body. She reported her childhood notion that mother had relinquished father to her while keeping the other children for herself. Rubinfine (1965) has suggested that such parents are unable to limit and contain the child's aggression, a point amply confirmed by our material. When it was suggested to Albert's mother that firmness might help control his wild behavior, she refused on the grounds that she did not want to risk upsetting the boy; in his teens, when his father became annoyed at Albert's resentment of his claims on his wife, one solution proposed by the family was that Albert and his mother should move into a flat together, leaving the rest of the family behind.

Both the delusion of omnipotence and the libidinization of painful experience persist in the pathology of adult patients. For example, a neurotic professional woman who lived out her beating fantasy in numerous unsuitable relationships reported a dream of marrying her father. In her associations, she revealed that she still thought that she really could marry her father and that no one could stop her from fulfilling her wishes. A male graduate student with beating fantasies had undergone frequent enemas as a child. For many years in analysis he recalled the enemas with enjoyment and remembered his older sister looking on with what he imagined to be jealousy. He said he felt special because he was the only one in the family to enjoy this exclusive relationship with his mother. His wish for an enema from the analyst figured as a central transference theme; only after many years of work could he begin to acknowledge and experience the rage he felt at his mother's gross bodily intrusion. In his early adolescence his mother bought him some bright purple shorts, which he described as the token of their exclusive relationship. Only after working through his libidinization of the enemas could he also recall that he was teased by the other boys for wearing the "faggy" shorts.

TRANSITION TO LATENCY

Fantasies and anxieties about pain and suffering are universal, as is the beating wish (Novick and Novick, 1972). With some resolution of the oedipus complex and the formation of the superego, children move into the latency period. Only at this point did a transitory beating fantasy emerge in some of the girls in our sample. When it occurred, it clearly represented both oedipal strivings in regressed form and punishment for them, as Freud described. Gradually sexual excitement and masturbation were divorced from the fantasy and the wishes appeared in increasingly distanced forms. In our study we concluded that this transitory beating fantasy was a normal transitional component of postoedipal development in girls and may be more common than is generally supposed. Female patients who present a beating fantasy may have regressed in or out of treatment to this postoedipal moment in development. As described above in the case of Mrs. S., it is only with clinical criteria of persistence and centrality of the fantasy, as well as the quality of the transference relationship, that the differentiation between a transitory and a fixed fantasy can be made.

In contrast, the children who later developed a fixed beating fantasy had no latency period to consolidate ego development and spent those years either in the enactment of preoedipal and oedipal sadomasochistic impulses or under the restriction of crippling inhibitions and severe obsessional symptomatology. For example, a potentially intelligent and creative woman with a fixed beating fantasy who sought analysis originally because of repeated work failure reported that she stopped learning in her school years and spent her time preoccupied with fantasies of imminent destruction which she contained by ritualistic repetitions of magical phrases.

PUBERTY AND ADOLESCENCE

The emergence of the fixed fantasy in the group of disturbed boys coincided with the onset of puberty, in all cases following the first emission. At 13 Mark reported a masturbation fantasy in which he first thought of undressing a girl in his class; the girl changed to an older woman and then, as his excitement mounted, the image changed to that of his mother. As he reached a climax the content shifted to his father walking in, holding him down and beating him on the buttocks. Mark, who was then as tall as his father, felt that he was "a Hitler" capable of killing his father. He not only wished to replace his father, but thought that his mother wanted him to do so. Pubertal changes in general give the stamp of reality to fantasies of gratifying infantile impulses. It was only because of the structural development fostered by years of analysis that the children in our sample could develop a fantasy outlet as an alternative to action. The capacity to contain impulses in fantasy represents an achievement. Less fortunate adolescents act out their impulses in self-injurious behavior or suicide.

Our children and adults used the *fixed* beating fantasy for important ego and superego functions which should have developed in latency, if these patients had been able to achieve a latency phase. These functions were control of anxiety, stabilization of the "representational world" (Sandler and Rosenblatt, 1962), and defense against direct drive discharge. The *transitory* beating fantasy found only in girls became progressively distanced from frightening oedipal wishes. The *fixed* beating fantasy, on the other hand, represented the most innocuous form of the wish; variations on the theme often involved more ominous fantasies of suicide, self-mutilation, and death. Abel had fantasies of being beaten by older boys, pop singers, and football players, but also masturbated with fantasies of having his penis and testicles burned or otherwise damaged. Further masturbation fantasies involved death and suicide; indeed, in late adolescence, some years after the termination of analysis, Abel attempted suicide. In the cases of Abel and the other boys with a fixed fantasy, we could see a diminution of anxiety when the beating fantasy was employed, whereas fantasies of death or mutilation soon became anxious preoccupations and led to feelings of overwhelming terror. One might say that in place of a fear of being destroyed or damaged, they created a pleasurable fantasy of being beaten, i.e., anxiety had become libidinized.

In the early phases of treatment of these children, it was often unclear who was standing for whom in the constant flux of externalizations, internalizations, and confusions with the object. In a brief sequence a child could become both the powerful attacking object and the victim of the attack. In the beating fantasy, however, there was a clear differentiation maintained between self and object. The subject was always the victim and the beater was invariably a person who figured in the child's real life, often the father or someone drawn from the class of father representatives. These characteristics may be seen in one boy's fantasy of being held down by two older boys from school and beaten on the buttocks. For the next two years, the fantasy remained basically unchanged, unlike the constantly elaborated imaginative productions of children with transitory beating fantasies, in which the characters were drawn from anywhere but real life. We would suggest that formation of the fixed fantasy not only required a modicum of stability of representations, but also seemed of itself to contribute to maintaining stability in the usual chaos of the representational world of these children.

Despite positive changes in these cases the "delusion of omnipotence" seemed unaltered. After 6 years of treatment Mark remained convinced that his death wishes would destroy the object. The work of Lamb (1976), Abelin

(1975, 1980), and others has underscored the importance of the father in the preoedipal development of the child. Through each stage in the development of the children in the fixed beating fantasy sample, the fathers failed to perform their necessary functions. As R. Furman (1986) so clearly describes, the father's initial role is to protect and support the primacy of the mother-child relationship. Mark's father reacted to his wife's pregnancy with intense jealousy, confirming the mother's pathological fantasies about the effect of the new baby on the other family members. Mary's father retreated into a busy professional life during the pregnancy and her first year, emerging periodically only to criticize mother's handling of the baby. During the toddler phase, Furman describes the importance of the father as a source of additional love for the child and support for the adult ego of the mother. Mark's father was as messy and uncontrolled as his toddler son; rather than taking pride in and fostering Mark's emerging autonomy, he joined with his wife in externalizations of the devalued anal aspects of his personality.

By the time Mark reached puberty and his analysis had helped him to approach the possibility of oedipal level impulses, he had no loving, consistent parental relationship to draw on as an internal resource in his struggle to control his incestuous wishes. After each achievement, which he experienced as an aggressive attack on the object, he immediately had to find out whether the analyst was still alive. It is in relation to this "delusion of omnipotence," the continuing lack of internal and external controls, that one of the important functions of the beating fantasy could be seen. From the material of these children, the timing of the emergence of the fantasy, and the content of the fantasy, it was evident that the beater in the fantasy represented a wished-for, ideal father, a strong male who would limit and control the fulfillment of omnipotent, libidinal and destructive wishes. The fathers of all these patients were particularly unsuitable to serve as strong, protective objects for identification. In the fantasy the beater was a father or father representative who was always a powerful, assertive figure punishing the child, often to stop him from gratifying a forbidden wish. Mark's fantasy was of attempting to go to bed with a middle-aged woman visitor; but before he could do so, his father stopped him, held him down, and beat him. In reality his father was a passive, ineffectual man who did not stop him from entering his mother's bed whenever he wanted to. Thus instead of internalizing a representation of a strong father, to build a superego, and defend against unacceptable impulses by means of age-adequate mechanisms such as repression, reaction formation, displacement, and especially sublimation, these children used the beating fantasy to control and limit drive discharge and gratification of omnipotent wishes. The fixed beating fantasy functioned in place of a super-ego, which would normally be formed in latency.

We have seen a similar outcome, arrived at by a different path, in the females with fixed beating fantasies. The fathers of the girls continued and intensified their denigration of the mothers and actively involved themselves in overstimulating relationships with their daughters from the oedipal phase on, with the result that a component in the masochistic pathology of the females was intense bisexual conflict and severe penis envy. The girls, like the boys, were unable to internalize an autonomous superego. In addition, the denigrated mother was not used as a feminine ego ideal. Mary entered treatment looking like a boy and declared her three vows—not to have a boyfriend, not to marry, and not to have children.

TECHNICAL IMPLICATIONS

Freud wrote to Jung in 1909, "In my practice, I am chiefly concerned with the problem of repressed sadism in my patients; I regard it as the most frequent cause of the failure of therapy. Revenge against the doctor combined with self-punishment. In general, sadism is becoming more and more important to me" (cited in Bergmann and Hartman, 1976, p. 33). In his last work, Freud still comments that we are "specially inadequate" (1940, p. 180) in dealing with masochistic patients. We may note that the Wolf-Man had a fixed beating fantasy and would have qualified for inclusion in our sample (Blum, 1974).

All of the children with fixed beating fantasies had many years of analysis. The change in the overt behavior and functioning of some was quite remarkable. Obvious manifestations of sadomasochistic relationships with peers or adults disappeared; they seemed to be coping well and even functioning quite independently. Frequently it was near termination that the child would first hint at and then disclose the existence of a beating fantasy. Analysis had fostered the development of certain ego functions, especially those necessary for the use of fantasy as a discharge channel, and had addressed some of the preoedipal determinants of the masochism. The formation of a beating fantasy at puberty was achieved on the basis of these gains. However, on follow-up, we found that some of these boys suffered psychotic breakdown in later adolescence, some attempted suicide, and others remained tied in a submissive, dependent relationship with an overpowering mother. Our findings on the various determinants of the fixed beating fantasy and the multiple ego functions it served suggest certain technical approaches which may improve the outcome of these cases.

For example, the fact that the beating fantasy served in lieu of important ego functions suggests that interpretation of the drive determinants will not be effective until concomitant work has been done on the ego pathology. Specifically, focus on the "delusion of omnipotence" would be important; if the patient could internalize and experience a capacity for controlling drive discharge, the necessity for a masochistic fantasy might diminish. Work could then turn to the determinants of the underlying masochism with special attention directed at the three aspects emphasized in this paper, i.e., the adaptive, defensive, and instinctual motives. The patient's masochistic behavior and fantasies would then be seen as a threefold attempt to (1) maintain a preoedipal object tie to his mother; (2) defend the object against his destructive wishes; and (3) participate in a sadomasochistic sexual relationship.

As noted earlier, Mark's mother reacted with increasing distress and ultimately depression to his adolescent moves toward separation. Extensive analysis of his omnipotent aggressive fantasies was not sufficient to help Mark separate from his mother without work on his denial of the reality of her preexisting problems around being left. When he saw her intense reaction to his brother's departure for college, he could not avoid recognizing her own hostile need to control those around her. The work could then return to his wishes to invite her control, thereby maintaining the narcissistically gratifying illusion that his mother clung to him out of love.

During the first two years of Mary's analysis, when she was 18 to 20 years old, she was completely dependent on her mother, who did her laundry, bought her clothes, cut her hair, and cooked for her. During this time much of the work focused on Mary's hurt and rage and her many ways of defending against the experience or expression of anger at her mother. The subsequent shift in her defense system, especially the infantile dependence, enabled her to become more active and self-sufficient. After an extended period of work, Mary managed to confront her mother over her intrusive behavior. Mother reacted by crying, and running away for several hours. Mary eventually moved to her own apartment and, when she first returned home for a weekend visit, her mother retreated to the attic and refused to come down to greet Mary. The accumulation of such incidents breached Mary's denial and she began to talk more in sessions about mother's "weirdness." When she turned to her father for reality confirmation, he did not validate her perceptions and support her healthy ego growth, but rather told her they must be involved in "some mother-daughter game." At that point she realized that the whole family had colluded for years to cover up mother's pathology. Mary moved then into a period of pleasure in her independent activity; she talked of "building a wall" between her and her mother, so that she could assign feelings to the appropriate person. She had earlier described her terror during electrical storms, but during this phase of treatment Mary realized that it was not she, but her mother who was so terrified. Mary herself actually enjoyed watching the lightning. Once this distinction had been made, it was much easier to work on Mary's contribution to the persisting infantile tie.

The ongoing preoedipal tie is the greatest stumbling block to progress. In order to break the tie the patient will have to become aware not only of his internal conflicts but also of his mother's pathology, especially her hostile opposition to progressive development. He will not only have to face his own destructive wishes but also relinquish his denial of his mother's hostility toward independence. Unless the preoedipal tie between mother and child can be broken, little change in the patient's underlying disturbance can be expected.

Work on the underlying motives must be accompanied by work on ego pathology, such as the persistence of omnipotent thinking and the inability to fuse drive impulses. For some time during the fourth year of Mary's analysis, material emerged which demonstrated the many ways she worked to maintain the delusion of the power of her wishes. If something she had wished for did not occur, she convinced herself that she had not wished her hardest. Habitually, on reaching the corner of the street, she looked at the stoplight, willing it to change color; when of course it did, she experienced a feeling of exultation in her power. This work prepared the way for material to emerge regarding another determinant of her experienced omnipotence. This was the lack of fusion of her aggressive impulses, which left them free to rage unchecked. Thus, any angry feeling in thought, fantasy, or dream instantaneously led to total bloody annihilation. For many years her dreams were filled with images of mutilation, horrible death, and destruction. After her love for her younger brother was acknowledged, she dreamed about a baby, which led to a fantasy of saying to her angry baby, "It's all right, I still love you."

In hindsight, looking at the timing of the emergence of the beating fantasy in the child sample and the follow-up data, it becomes apparent that some of the cases in the original group were terminated prematurely. The very achievements which contributed to the capacity for fantasy formation obscured the continued operation of masochistic pathology encapsulated in the beating fantasy. This attempt at a solution to needs from all levels of development could not stand up to the internal and external demands of life. Thus, indications for termination should be carefully scrutinized in these patients.

CONCLUSIONS

In elucidating a developmental line of masochism we have been working toward a definition of the term. Valenstein (Panel, 1981) noted that a discussion of masochism can easily "be obscured in a sea of words" (p. 674). Grossman (1986) surveyed the history of the concept and concluded that the term has only a restricted application. Maleson (1984) presents a broad definitional possibility which accepts existing usage and refers to all behavior, thoughts, fantasies, and symptoms or syndromes characterized by subjectively experienced pain or suffering which seems unnecessary, excessive, or self-induced. Unfortunately, this definition demands a judgment as to what is unnecessary or excessive pain. It also leads to the view that the choice of any experience or activity which may include pain, such as childbirth or self-sacrifice, is necessarily masochistic. We do not find any necessary relationship between feminine functions and masochism.

In addition to being too inclusive, this definition ignores the significant difference between a normal and a masochistic relationship to pain. For adaptive growth, a child must learn to tolerate pain within a certain range. Paradoxically, masochists who actively seek painful and humiliating experiences find ordinary levels of real pain intolerable.

But Maleson also suggests a narrow definition which would confine the label to states of physical or mental suffering in which a clear linkage to sexual, genital excitement is demonstrable. The experience of pain or suffering does not in itself warrant a conclusion that the behavior is masochistic, nor does the existence of genital excitement. We think it is possible, based on the work we have described in this paper, to come to a more satisfactory definition. Masochism is the active pursuit of psychic or physical pain, suffering, or humiliation in the service of adaptation, defense, and instinctual gratification at oral, anal, and phallic levels.

Masochism is a clinical concept, and the definition requires some concrete observational referents to be of any value. We are suggesting that the data base of the definition is the transference and counterreaction of the analytic situation. The patient's persistent search for pain or humiliation will be figured forth in the transference, often in subtle responses to interpretations. The counterreaction of the therapist may provide the first clue of an underlying masochistic fantasy in the patient. The therapist may feel the impulse to be sarcastic, impatient, or teasing. Less subtle reactions may take the form of being late, forgetting appointments, falling asleep, forced termination, etc. The epigenetic layering of masochism and its multiple functions emerge within the transference relationship, and must be dealt with in that context.

There has long been controversy over whether the determinants of masochism are preoedipal or oedipal, and whether the underlying conflicts primarily concern drive gratification or relate to maladaptive modes of coping with traumatic objects. These were questions posed in the 1984 Panel on masochism and depression. By examining the development of beating fantasies in particular, we have tried to throw light on the determinants of masochism in general. In our view, not only are derivatives of each phase discernible in masochism, but the painseeking behavior which starts in infancy alters and is altered by each subsequent phase, including the oedipal and postoedipal. Postoedipally, masochistic impulses are organized as conscious or unconscious fantasies which are fixed, resistant to modification by experience or analysis, serve multiple ego functions, and take the form, although not necessarily the content, of the beating fantasy. In the fantasies the subject is an innocent victim, who achieves through suffering reunion with the object, defense against aggressive destruction and loss of the object, avoidance of narcissistic pain, and instinctual gratification by fantasy participation in the oedipal situation. Suicidal pathology, masochistic perversions, certain forms of hypochondriasis and psychosomatic illness, and moral masochism have in common an *underlying fantasy structure*. In our view, this fantasy structure is the "essence of masochism" (Freud, 1919, p. 189).

NOTES

1. These cases are selected from an ongoing study of adolescent mothers and their babies. We are grateful to the other members of the study group, Drs. Kay and Linn Campbell, Connie Silver, A.M.L.S., and Don Silver, M.D.; the views presented here are our own and do not necessarily represent those of the group.

REFERENCES

Abelin, E. C. (1975). Some further observations and comments on the earliest role of the father. *Int. J. Psychoanal.*, 56:293–302.

――― (1980). Triangulation, the role of the father and the origins of core gender identity during the rapprochement subphase. In *Rapprochement*, ed., R. F. Lux, S. Bach, & J. A. Burland. New York: Jason Aronson, pp. 151–169.

Bak, R. C. (1968). The phallic woman. *Psychoanal. Study Child*, 23:37–46.

Balint, M. (1968). *The Basic Fault*. London: Tavistock Publications.

Bergmann, M. & Hartman, F. R. (1976). *The Evolution of Psychoanalytic Technique*. New York: Basic Books.

Bieber, I. (1966). Sadism and masochism. In *American Handbook of Psychiatry*, ed. S. Arieti. New York: Basic Books, pp. 256–270.

Blos, P., Jr. (1985). Intergenerational separation-individuation. *Psychoanal. Study Child*, 40:41–56.

Blum, H. P. (1974). The borderline childhood of the Wolf-Man. *J. Amer. Psychoanal. Assn.*, 22:721–742.

Brinich, P. M. (1984). Aggression in early childhood. *Psychoanal. Study Child*, 39:493–508.

Cain, A. C. (1961). The presuperego "turning inward of aggression." *Psychoanal. Q.*, 30:171–208.

Escalona, S. K. (1968). *The Roots of Individuality*. London: Tavistock Publications.

Fenichel, O. (1945). *The Psychoanalytic Theory of Neurosis*. New York: Norton.

Ferber, L. (1975). Beating fantasies. In *Masturbation from Infancy to Senescence*, ed. I. M. Marcus & J. J. Francis. New York: Int. Univ. Press, pp. 205–222.

Freud, A. (1960). The child guidance clinic as a center of prophylaxis and enlightenment. *W.*, 5:281–300.

Freud, S. (1905). Three essays on the theory of sexuality. *S.E.*, 7:125–243.

――― (1915). Instincts and their vicissitudes. *S.E.*, 14:109–140.

――― (1918). From the history of an infantile neurosis. *S.E.*, 17:3–123.

――― (1919). 'A child is being beaten.' *S.E.*, 17:175–204.

――― (1923). The ego and the id. *S.E.*, 19:3–66.

――― (1924). The economic problem of masochism. *S.E.*, 19:157–170.

――― (1940). An outline of psycho-analysis. *S.E.*, 23:141–207.

Furman, E. (1984). Some difficulties in assessing depression and suicide in childhood. In *Suicide in the Young*, ed. H. S. Sudak, A. B. Ford, & N. B. Rushforth. Boston: John Wright, pp. 245–258.

――― (1985). On fusion, integration, and feeling good. *Psychoanal. Study Child*, 40:81–110.

Furman, R. (1986). The father-child relationship. In *What Nursery School Teachers Ask Us About*, ed. E. Furman. New York: Int. Univ. Press, pp. 21–34.

Glenn, J. (1984). A note on loss, pain and masochism in children. *J. Amer. Psychoanal. Assn.*, 32:63–73.

Grossman, W. I. (1986). Notes on masochism. *Psychoanal. Q.*, 55:379–413.

Lamb, M. E. (1976). The role of the father. In *The Role of the Father in Child Development*, ed. M. E. Lamb. New York: John Wiley, pp. 1–63.

Lichtenberg, J. (1984). Continuities and transformations between infancy and adolescence. In *Late Adolescence*, ed. D. D. Brockman. New York: Int. Univ. Press, pp. 7–27.

Litman, R. E. (1970). Sigmund Freud on suicide. In *The Psychology of Suicide*. New York: Jason Aronson, pp. 555–586.

Loewenstein, R. M. (1957). A contribution to the psychoanalytic theory of masochism. *J. Amer. Psychoanal. Assn.*, 5:197–234.

Maleson, F. G. (1984). The multiple meanings of masochism in psychoanalytic discourse. *J. Amer. Psychoanal. Assn.*, 32:325–356.

Niederland, W. G. (1958). Early auditory experiences, beating fantasies, and primal scene. *Psychoanal. Study Child*, 13:471–504.

Novick, J. (1980). Negative therapeutic motivation and negative therapeutic alliance. *Psychoanal. Study Child*, 35:299–320.

——— (1984). Attempted suicide in adolescence. In *Suicide in the Young*, ed. H. S. Sudak, A. B. Ford, & N. B. Rushforth. Boston: John Wright, pp. 115–137.

——— & Novick, K. K. (1972). Beating fantasies in children. *Int. J. Psychoanal.*, 53:237–242.

Olinick, S. L. (1964). The negative therapeutic reaction. *Int. J. Psychoanal.*, 45:540–545.

Orgel, S. (1974). Fusion with the victim and suicide. *Int. J. Psychoanal.*, 55:532–538.

Panel (1981). Masochism: current concepts. N. Fischer, reporter. *J. Amer. Psychoanal. Assn.*, 29:673–688.

——— (1984). The relation between masochism and depression. J. Caston, reporter. *J. Amer. Psychoanal. Assn.*, 32:603–614.

Rubinfine, D. L. (1965). On beating fantasies. *Int. J. Psychoanal.*, 46:315–322.

Sandler, J. & Rosenblatt, B. (1962). The concept of the representational world. *Psychoanal. Study Child*, 17:128–145.

Stern, D. W. (1985). *The Interpersonal World of the Infant*. New York: Basic Books.

Tronick, E. Z. & Gianino, A. (1986). Interactive mismatch and repair. *Zero to Three*, 6:1–6.

Valenstein, A. (1973). On attachment to painful feelings and the negative therapeutic reaction. *Psychoanal. Study Child* 28:365–394.

Winnicott, D. W. (1960). The theory of the parent-infant relationship. In *The Maturational Processes and the Facilitating Environment*. New York: Int. Univ. Press, 1965, pp. 37–55.

PART IV

MORAL MASOCHISM: GUILT, FANTASY, AND THE OBJECT

Introduction

What is the relation between the sexual perversion and the character disorder that goes by the same name? Moral masochism can be distinguished from masochistic perversion in two main ways: at first glance, moral masochism does not seem to have any connection with the sexual functions; the seeking of pain as punishment for forbidden fantasy pleasure is not a conscious phenomenon. The moral masochist does not know he is masochistic; he is unaware of his part in creating his suffering; and unaware that these sufferings could constitute the very means of satisfying the needs of a fettered libido (Nacht 1938). The seeking of pain for sexual pleasure is conscious in perversion. Perversion can be rigorously defined as an adult psychopathological formation, consolidated through adolescent development, which is obligatory for adult sexual functioning (Coen 1992, chapter 19 in this volume; Bak 1974). This definition referring to the perverse act and its conscious purpose with respect to orgasm separates masochistic perversion from moral masochism, with its unconscious purpose.

Having suggested the important differences in the functioning of moral masochism and masochistic perversion, we can note that many authors find no major distinction in the underlying fantasy structure. Freud (1919, chapter 8 in this volume; 1924, chapter 13 in this volume) makes little distinction between the fantasy structure in perversion and in moral masochism. Reik (1940; in excerpt form, chapter 16 in this volume) carries on this tradition in showing the movements between fantasy in moral masochism and the scenarios set in perversion.

Anna Freud (1922; chapter 14 in this volume) describes the repression of the beating fantasy in the course of development of moral masochism. The paper is an important example of the fantasy structure of an adolescent girl. Freud describes the period in which the beating fantasy and the masturbatory pleasure that accompanied it were given up with self-reproaches and pangs of conscience, in which the "perverse" infantile component instinct moved toward the structure of moral masochism. The "nice stories" which came to preoccupy the patient were found to be analogous in construction to the beating fantasies, and parallel in content.

In the early days of Freud's (1924) discovery of unconscious guilt and its relation to the instincts and to symptom formation, a freshness is felt in the successful interpretive strategies described in such papers as Fenichel's "Clinical Aspect of the Need for Punishment" 1925; chapter 15 in this volume). Fenichel describes the sense of guilt as "a unique, primitive, ruthless thing." He writes up a case in which he sees "the genesis and constitution of moral masochism; the excessive sexualizing in it of all penalizing actions; the turning of the sadistic trends against the patient's self" (pp. 321–22 in this volume). Whatever more we have learned, this understanding of moral masochism has been fundamental to clinical psychoanalysis.

Reik (1940) begins his treatment of masochism stating that the "differences as to sex will be as little considered as the question of whether it concerns a masochistic phantasy or an actual scene of perversion" (p. 324 in this volume). He describes psychological phenomena which apply both to the perversion and to moral masochism, that is, to the underlying anxieties and to the leading defenses. The characteristics of masochism which Reik considers central are the special use of fantasy, the use of tension states, and a demonstrative (as opposed to exhibitionistic) tendency, a display of suffering or badness which leads to a negative victory. His idea that severe moral masochism is closer to perversion than to neurosis is articulated in some contemporary papers (Chasseguet-Smirgel 1991).

The difficulty in any attempt at precision in defining moral masochism is that the diagnostic category of masochism is never an exclusive one (Brenner 1959; chapter 18 in this volume). Nacht (1938) has sections on masochism in male homosexuality, masochism in obsessional neurosis, and masochism in melancholia. Bak (1946; chapter 9 in this volume) describes the masochistic aspects of paranoia; Fenichel (1945) outlines the masochism in obsessional neurosis; Grunberger (1956; chapter 10 in this volume) looks at the masochism as a vicissitude of phallic aggression which is particularly prone to pathological repression and turning round on the self. But despite the many-faceted nature of the subject, much concensus on the nature of moral masochism exists. The unconscious seeking after pain as a condition for pleasure (Brenner 1959) is the most consistent definition of moral masochism, where the pleasure, or reduction in unpleasure, may consist in the lessening of superego anxiety or the closer link to a bad but essential love object.

The transition from moral masochism to masochistic character involves the intensification of the masochistic trends into an organized and fixed set of attitudes to self and to others usually involving a relationship which allows for a permanent sense of injustice, or constant complaints concerning the object's failure to give enough, or endless sufferings experienced at the hands of the object in some other way (Nacht 1938).

A debate on the etiology of the masochistic character took place in the 1950s concerning the role of object relations in masochism. Some writers (Berliner 1947; 1958, chapter 17 in this volume; Menaker 1953) felt that the entire causation of moral masochism was to be found in the sadism of the parent or parents. Other analysts concentrated on a causation which varied and which involved many factors, among them, the exacerbation of ordinary aggressivity, intense incest wishes causing guilt, and attachment to regressed libidinal satisfaction (A. Freud 1922; Brenman 1952; Grunberger 1956; Brenner 1959): in other words, a complex interconnected blend of intrinsic human strivings and object relation factors.

Views of etiology influence approaches to therapy. The essays on masochism and object relations by Berliner (1947, 1958) and Menaker (1953) suggest that the main "analytic" task is to empathize with the patient insofar as he or she has been subject to the sadism of one or both parents, and has denied the parental sadism. Yet, when Berliner (1947) writes of the almost entirely unconscious aggression in the masochist and the difficulty of interpreting it to the patient, he is very close to Brenman (1952). One difference is that she sees the mechanism involved in rendering the aggression unconscious as a projection of the aggression (Brenman 1952). Berliner emphasizes the projection of love into the hating or ambivalent parent, and the denial of the parent's hatred, as the key defenses. Brenman (1952) describes a complex etiology for her severely masochistic patient. She recognizes a hating mother, but also, a libidinal satisfaction and self-punishment in the child's self-debasing humor, and, ultimately, a projection of hostile aggressivity onto the parent/therapist, which has the effect of a provocation. Her account of the multiple functions of, and multiple defenses involved in, the masochistic character suggests that we must be ready to see a unique variant of masochism in each patient. Brenner's (1959) case material suggests a similar flexibility of formulation. Grunberger (1956), in an attempt to see a fundamental psychodynamic in moral masochism, looks closely at a key unconscious fantasy. He finds clinical evidence to suggest that the fantasied wish to castrate the father (a critical point in the vicissitudes of normal aggression and narcissism) becomes, when not integrated, the basis for the formation of masochistic character. In his view, the unconscious fantasy of being castrated by father (so often cited as leading to masochism) is, in itself, a masochistic fantasy, both flooded with sexual exitations and having the castration wish bent back against the self. How can severe castration anxiety be both an explanation for, and a manifestation of masochistic trends (Grunberger 1956)? What emerges is a debate about analytic attitudes toward the patient's aggression and masochistic satisfactions. One group of analysts deplored any attitude of fault finding, what Freud so long ago warned against as the search for the criminality in a patient. Berliner (1958), therefore, emphasized the basic helplessness of the child in the anaclitic bond, and the child's need for love and protection of the parent however sadistic that parent might be. His analytic goal was to help the patient undo denials concerning the parent's sadistic behaviors. Another group of analysts see the patient as trapped by the unconscious nature of his or her aggression and libido which is silently turned back on the self. For them, helping a patient to integrate memories of frightening, but understandable, sadistic impulses, is a key analytic goal. It seems that some analysts have misread the "classical" attention to the unconscious aggression and sadomasochistic dynamics as a failure to see trauma or as an attack on the patient. But no major writer has indeed oversimplified the field of observation, or the clinical task, in this way.

The debate concerning masochism continues in the 1990s. The questions, for the most part, no longer need to be posed in terms of an either-or. Freud's sense that masochism is shaped by a skewed and "scarcely effected" Oedipus is seen to go hand in hand with the pre-Oedipal trauma and fixation of sadism which he saw as distorting the Oedipal situation (Freud 1919). The hatred and sadism parents act out toward their children is described along with the way in which the child's psychic structures are altered by their reactions to and defenses against that hatred, or neglect and seductiveness. Both parent and then, tragically, child, take up the sadomasochisic positions, simultaneously and in turn (Shengold 1967; 1971, chapter 11 in this volume; Coen 1992; Novick and Novick 1987, chapter 12 in this volume).

Implicit in the debate in the fifties is a question concerning the relative roles of sexual libido and aggression in the formation of masochistic character. While Berliner (1958) and Menaker (1953) underplay the child's ordinary aggression and sexuality and focus on the hatred and sadism of the parent, they do emphasize the child's need for the love object, which brings them round to the child's vulnerability to excitations and addictive attachments to sadistic objects. What finds a clearer focus in other papers is that a masochistic excitation grows up to complicate the need for love and a sadism complicates the frustration. In the nineties there is no longer debate about whether some trauma lies behind serious cases of masochistic character; instead there is a certain emphasis now on sadomasochism as purely a vicissitude of aggression (Blum 1991). And so the emphases shift over the years.

When masochism is seen as purely a vicissitude of aggression, we are led to ask what the difference is between masochism and depression. For superego guilt turning back aggression on the self and pre-Oedipal aggression turned back out of fear of loss of the object or fear of reprisals seems to define both depression and masochism. While there is some overlap in the psychic mechanisms, the particular need to manipulate the object into being sadistic, and the simultaneity of denial, projection, and introjection (Brenman 1952) which are characteristic of the masochistic character in a struggle with the love object, create a varied but identifiable set of clinical phenomena, appropriately called masochistic, or sadomasochistic. These are distinguishable from depression, which cuts off the object tie at certain points and becomes more isolated (Kernberg 1988). An object-bound struggle and excitations, covert or hidden, provoked by that struggle with the love object, are at the heart of masochism.

The question as to whether pre-Oedipal trauma is the sine qua non of masochistic character is still under discussion. The important distinction between primary and secondary guilt that Modell (1965) draws offers a way of understanding the unconscious need for punishment in the negative therapeutic reaction, without indicating much influence from the Oedipal stage. Modell (1965), quoting Freud, notes the fact that unconscious guilt precedes the formation of the superego. Primary guilt associated with aggression and accompanied by confusions of identity, can be diffuse, pervasive, and, at worst, can interfere with all personality functioning. This diffuse pre-Oedipal guilt, which distorts the Oedipus complex, then becomes fixed into the personality in specific masochistic fantasies through unconscious incest guilt (Novick and Novick 1987).

The aspect of masochistic character which has been called extreme submissiveness (Reich 1940; chapter 21 in this volume) or sexual enthrallment (Kernberg 1988) shows how sexual attachment to a humiliating object can be used to maintain narcissitic balance. The narcissitic function of masochism (Stolorow 1975) has led some analysts to consider a classification of narcissistic/masochistic character (Cooper 1988). And yet, careful distinctions have been made over time which separate masochism from narcissism (Reik 1941; Grunberger 1956; Kernberg 1988).

Moral masochism, then, is part of human psychic life, developed as an important function of the superego. The intensification of moral masochism into masochistic character, or its pathological role in homosexuality, obsessional neurosis, or paranoia have made it a central subject of psychoanalytic inquiry.

BIBLIOGRAPHY

Bak, R. 1946. Masochism in Paranoia. *Psychoanal. Quarterly* 15:285–301.(Chapter 9 in this volume.)

——— 1974. Distortions of the Concept of Fetishism. *Psychoanal. Study Child.* 29:191–214.

Berliner, B. 1947. On Some Psychodynamics of Masochism. *Psychoanal. Quarterly* 16:459–71.

——— 1958. The Role of Object Relations in Moral Masochism. *Psychoanal. Quarterly.* 27:38–56. (Chapter 17 in this volume.)

Blum, H. 1991. Sadomasochism in the Psychoanalytic Process, Within and Beyond the Pleasure Principle: Discussion. *J. Amer. Psychoanal. Assn.:* 39:431–50.

Brenman, M. 1952. On Teasing and Being Teased and the Problem of Moral Masochism. *Psychoanal. Study Child.* 8:264–85.

Brenner, C. 1959. The Masochistic Character: Genesis and Treatment. *J. Amer. Psychoanal. Assn.* 7:197–226. (Chapter 18 in this volume.)

Chasseguet-Smirgel, J. 1991. Sadomasochism in the Perversions: Some Thoughts on the Destruction of Reality. *J. Amer. Psychoanal. Assn.* 39:399–415.

Coen, S. 1992. The Excitement of Sadomasochism. In *The Misuse of Persons: Analyzing Pathological Dependency.* Hillsdale, N.J.: The Analytic Press, pp. 190–208. (Chapter 19 in this volume.)

Cooper, S. 1988. The Narcissistic-Masochistic Disorder. In *Masochism: Current Psychoanalytic Perspectives,* ed. R. Glick and D. Meyers. Hillsdale, N.J.: The Analytic Press, pp. 117–38.

Fenichel, O. 1925. The Clinical Aspect of the Need for Punishment. In *The Collected Papers of Otto Fenichel: First Series.* New York: Norton, 1953, pp. 71–96. (Chapter 15 in this volume.)

———. 1945. *The Psychoanalytic Theory of Neurosis.* New York: Norton.

Freud, A. 1922. Beating Fantasies and Daydreams. *Int. J. Psycho-Anal.:* 4:89–102. (Chapter 14 in this volume.)

Freud, S. 1919. A Child Is Being Beaten: A Contribution to the Study of the Origin of Sexual Perversions. In *S.E.* 17: 179–204. (Chapter 8 in this volume.)

———. 1924. The Economic Problem of Masochism. In *S. E.* 19:159–70. (Chapter 13 in this volume.)

Grossman, W. I. 1986. Notes on Masochism: A Discussion of the History and Development of a Psychoanalytic Concept. *Psychoanal. Quarterly.* 55:379–413.

———. 1991. Pain, Aggression, Fantasy and Concepts of Sadomasochism. *Psychoanal. Quarterly* 60:22–52. (Chapter 7 in this volume.)

Grunberger, B. 1956. Psychodynamic Theory of Masochism. In *Perversions, Psychodynamics and Therapy*, ed. S. Lorand and M. Balint. New York: Random House, pp. 183–208. (Chapter 10 in this volume.)

Kernberg, O. 1988. Clinical Dimensions of Masochism. In *Masochism: Current Analytic Perspectives*. Ed. R. Glick and D. Meyers. Hillsdale, N.J.: The Analytic Press, pp. 61–79.

Loewenstein, R. 1957. A Contribution to the Psychoanalytic Theory of Masochism. *J. Amer. Psychoanal. Assn.* 5:197–234. (Chapter 2 in this volume.)

Menaker, E. 1953. Masochism—A Defense Reaction of the Ego. *Psychoanal. Quarterly* 22:205–25.

Modell, A. 1965. On Having the Right to Life: An Aspect of the Super-ego's Development. *Int. J. Psycho-Anal.* 46:323–31.

Nacht, S. 1938. *Le masochisme*. Paris: Payot, 1965.

Novick, K., and Novick, J. 1987. The Essence of Masochism. *Psychoanal. Study Child* 42:353–84. (Chapter 12 in this volume.)

Reich, A. 1940. A Contribution to the Psycho-Analysis of Extreme Submissiveness in Women. *Psychoanal. Quarterly* 9:470–80. (Chapter 21 in this volume.)

Reik, T. 1940. The Characteristics of Masochism. *American Image* 1 (1940):26–59. (In excerpt form, chapter 16 in this volume.)

———. 1941. *Masochism and Modern Man*. New York: Farrar and Rinehart.

Shengold, L. 1967. The Effects of Overstimulation: Rat People. *Int. J. Psycho-Anal.* 48:403–15.

———. 1971. More About Rats and Rat People. *Int. J. Psycho-Anal.* 52:277–88. (Chapter 11 in this volume.)

Stolorow, R. D. 1975. The Narcissistic Function of Masochism. *Int. J. Psycho-Anal.* 56:441–48.

Valenstein, A. 1973. On Attachment to Painful Feelings and the Negative Therapeutic Reaction. *Psychoanal. Study Child* 28:305–92.

13. The Economic Problem of Masochism

Sigmund Freud

The existence of a masochistic trend in the instinctual life of human beings may justly be described as mysterious from the economic point of view. For if mental processes are governed by the pleasure principle in such a way that their first aim is the avoidance of unpleasure and the obtaining of pleasure, masochism is incomprehensible. If pain and unpleasure can be not simply warnings but actually aims, the pleasure principle is paralysed—it is as though the watchman over our mental life were put out of action by a drug.

Thus masochism appears to us in the light of a great danger, which is in no way true of its counterpart, sadism. We are tempted to call the pleasure principle the watchman over our life rather than merely over our mental life. But in that case we are faced with the task of investigating the relationship of the pleasure principle to the two classes of instincts which we have distinguished—the death instincts and the erotic (libidinal) life instincts; and we cannot proceed further in our consideration of the problem of masochism till we have accomplished that task.

It will be remembered that we have taken the view that the principle which governs all mental processes is a special case of Fechner's 'tendency towards stability',[1] and have accordingly attributed to the mental apparatus the purpose of reducing to nothing, or at least of keeping as low as possible, the sums of excitation which flow in upon it. Barbara Low [1920, 73] has suggested the name of 'Nirvana principle' for this supposed tendency, and we have accepted the term.[2] But we have unhesitatingly identified the pleasure-

Reprinted by permission of Sigmund Freud Copyrights, The Institute of Psycho-Analysis, the Hogarth Press, from *The Standard Edition of the Complete Psychological Works of Sigmund Freud*, translated and edited by James Strachey, vol. 19: (1961) 159–70.

unpleasure principle with this Nirvana principle. Every unpleasure ought thus to coincide with a heightening, and every pleasure with a lowering, of mental tension due to stimulus; the Nirvana principle (and the pleasure principle which is supposedly identical with it) would be entirely in the service of the death instincts, whose aim is to conduct the restlessness of life into the stability of the inorganic state, and it would have the function of giving warnings against the demands of the life instincts—the libido—which try to disturb the intended course of life. But such a view cannot be correct. It seems that in the series of feelings of tension we have a direct sense of the increase and decrease of amounts of stimulus, and it cannot be doubted that there are pleasurable tensions and unpleasurable relaxations of tension. The state of sexual excitation is the most striking example of a pleasurable increase of stimulus of this sort, but it is certainly not the only one.

Pleasure and unpleasure, therefore, cannot be referred to as increase or decrease of a quantity (which we describe as 'tension due to stimulus'), although they obviously have a great deal to do with that factor. It appears that they depend, not on this quantitative factor, but on some characteristic of it which we can only describe as a qualitative one. If we were able to say what this qualitative characteristic is, we should be much further advanced in psychology. Perhaps it is the rhythm, the temporal sequence of changes, rises and falls in the quantity of stimulus.[3] We do not know.

However this may be, we must perceive that the Nirvana principle, belonging as it does to the death instinct, has undergone a modification in living organisms through which it has become the pleasure principle; and we shall henceforward avoid regarding the two principles as one. It is not difficult, if we care to follow up this line of thought, to guess what power was the source of the modification. It can only be the life instinct, the libido, which has thus, alongside of the death instinct, seized upon a share in the regulation of the processes of life. In this way we obtain a small but interesting set of connections. The *Nirvana* principle expresses the trend of the death instinct; the *pleasure* principle represents the demands of the libido; and the modification of the latter principle, the *reality* principle,[4] represents the influence of the external world.

None of these three principles is actually put out of action by another. As a rule they are able to tolerate one another, although conflicts are bound to arise occasionally from the fact of the differing aims that are set for each— in one case a quantitative reduction of the load of the stimulus, in another a qualitative characteristic of the stimulus, and, lastly [in the third case], a postponement of the discharge of the stimulus and a temporary acquiescence in the unpleasure due to tension.

The conclusion to be drawn from these considerations is that the description of the pleasure principle as the watchman over our life cannot be rejected.[5]

To return to masochism. Masochism comes under our observation in three forms: as a condition imposed on sexual excitation, as an expression of the feminine nature, and as a norm of behaviour.[6] We may, accordingly, distinguish an *erotogenic*, a *feminine* and a *moral* masochism. The first, the erotogenic, masochism—pleasure in pain—lies at the bottom of the other two forms as well. Its basis must be sought along biological and constitutional lines and it remains incomprehensible unless one decides to make certain assumptions about matters that are extremely obscure. The third, and in some respects the most important, form assumed by masochism has only recently been recognized by psycho-analysis as a sense of guilt which is mostly unconscious; but it can already be completely explained and fitted into the rest of our knowledge. Feminine masochism, on the other hand, is the one that is most accessible to our observation and least problematical, and it can be surveyed in all its relations. We will begin our discussion with it.

We have sufficient acquaintance with this kind of masochism in men (to whom, owing to the material at my command, I shall restrict my remarks), derived from masochistic—and therefore often impotent—subjects whose phantasies either terminate in an act of masturbation or represent a sexual satisfaction in themselves.[7] The real-life performances of masochistic perverts tally completely with these phantasies, whether the performances are carried out as an end in themselves or serve to induce potency and to lead to the sexual act. In both cases—for the performances are, after all, only a carrying-out of the phantasies in play—the manifest content is of being gagged, bound, painfully beaten, whipped, in some way maltreated, forced into unconditional obedience, dirtied and debased. It is far more rare for mutilations to be included in the content, and then only subject to strict limitations. The obvious interpretation, and one easily arrived at, is that the masochist wants to be treated like a small and helpless child, but, particularly, like a naughty child. It is unnecessary to quote cases to illustrate this;

for the material is very uniform and is accessible to any observer, even to non-analysts. But if one has an opportunity of studying cases in which the masochistic phantasies have been especially richly elaborated, one quickly discovers that they place the subject in a characteristically female situation; they signify, that is, being castrated, or copulated with, or giving birth to a baby. For this reason I have called this form of masochism, *a potiori* as it were [i.e. on the basis of its extreme examples], the feminine form, although so many of its features point to infantile life. This superimposed stratification of the infantile and the feminine will find a simple explanation later on. Being castrated—or being blinded, which stands for it—often leaves a negative trace of itself in phantasies, in the condition that no injury is to occur precisely to the genitals or the eyes. (Masochistic tortures, incidentally, rarely make such a serious impression as the cruelties of sadism, whether imagined or performed.) A sense of guilt, too, finds expression in the manifest content of masochistic phantasies; the subject assumes that he has committed some crime (the nature of which is left indefinite) which is to be expiated by all these painful and tormenting procedures. This looks like a superficial rationalization of the masochistic subject-matter, but behind it there lies a connection with infantile masturbation. On the other hand, this factor of guilt provides a transition to the third, moral, form of masochism.

This feminine masochism which we have been describing is entirely based on the primary, erotogenic masochism, on pleasure in pain. This cannot be explained without taking our discussion very far back.

In my *Three Essays on the Theory of Sexuality,* in the section on the sources of infantile sexuality, I put forward the proposition that 'in the case of a great number of internal processes sexual excitation arises as a concomitant effect, as soon as the intensity of those processes passes beyond certain quantitative limits'. Indeed, 'it may well be that nothing of considerable importance can occur in the organism without contributing some component to the excitation of the sexual instinct'.[8] In accordance with this, the excitation of pain and unpleasure would be bound to have the same result, too.[9] The occurrence of such a libidinal sympathetic excitation when there is tension due to pain and unpleasure would be an infantile physiological mechanism which ceases to operate later on. It would attain a varying degree of development in different sexual constitutions; but in any case it would provide the physiological foundation on which the psychical structure of erotogenic masochism would afterwards be erected.

The inadequacy of this explanation is seen, however, in the fact that it throws no light on the regular and close connections of masochism with its counterpart in instinctual life, sadism. If we go back a little further, to our hypothesis of the two classes of instincts which we regard as operative in the living organism, we arrive at another derivation of masochism, which, however, is not in contradiction with the former one. In (multicellular) organisms the libido meets the instinct of death, or destruction, which is dominant in them and which seeks to disintegrate the cellular organism and to conduct each separate unicellular organism [composing it] into a state of inorganic stability (relative though this may be). The libido has the task of making the destroying instinct innocuous, and it fulfils the task by diverting that instinct to a great extent outwards—soon with the help of a special organic system, the muscular apparatus—towards objects in the external world. The instinct is then called the destructive instinct, the instinct for mastery, or the will to power. A portion of the instinct is placed directly in the service of the sexual function, where it has an important part to play. This is sadism proper. Another portion does not share in this transposition outwards; it remains inside the organism and, with the help of the accompanying sexual excitation described above, becomes libidinally bound there. It is in this portion that we have to recognize the original, erotogenic masochism.[10]

We are without any physiological understanding of the ways and means by which this taming;[11] of the death-instinct by the libido may be effected. So far as the psycho-analytic field of ideas is concerned, we can only assume that a very extensive fusion and amalgamation, in varying proportions, of the two classes of instincts takes place, so that we never have to deal with pure life instincts or pure death instincts but only with mixtures of them in different amounts. Corresponding to a fusion of instincts of this kind, there may, as a result of certain influences, be a defusion of them. How large the portions of the death instincts are which refuse to be tamed in this way by being bound to admixtures of libido we cannot at present guess.

If one is prepared to overlook a little inexactitude, it may be said that the death instinct which is operative in the organism—primal sadism—is identical with masochism. After the main portion of it has been transposed outwards on to objects, there remains inside, as a residuum of it, the erotogenic masochism proper, which on the one hand has become a component of the libido and, on the other, still has the self as its object. This masochism would thus be evidence of, and a remainder from, the phase of development in which the coalescence, which is so important for life, between the death instinct and Eros took place. We shall not be surprised to hear that in certain circumstances the sadism, or instinct of destruction, which has been directed outwards, projected, can be once more introjected, turned inwards, and in this way regress to its earlier situation. If this happens, a secondary masochism is produced, which is added to the original masochism.

Erotogenic masochism accompanies the libido through all its developmental phases and derives from them its changing psychical coatings.[12] The fear of being eaten up by the totem animal (the father) originates from the primitive oral organization; the wish to be beaten by the father comes from the sadistic-anal phase which follows it; castration, although it is later disavowed, enters into the content of masochistic phantasies as a precipitate of the phallic stage or organization;[13] and from the final genital organization there arise, of course, the situations of being copulated with and of giving birth, which are characteristic of femaleness. The part played in masochism by the nates, too, is easily understandable,[14] apart from its obvious basis in reality. The nates are the part of the body which is given erotogenic preference in the sadistic-anal phase, like the breast in the oral phase and the penis in the genital phase.

The third form of masochism, moral masochism,[15] is chiefly remarkable for having loosened its connection with what we recognize as sexuality. All other masochistic sufferings carry with them the condition that they shall emanate from the loved person and shall be endured at his command. This restriction has been dropped in moral masochism. The suffering itself is what matters; whether it is decreed by someone who is loved or by someone who is indifferent is of no importance. It may even be caused by impersonal powers or by circumstances; the true masochist always turns his cheek whenever he has a chance of receiving a blow. It is very tempting, in explaining this attitude, to leave the libido out of account and to confine oneself to assuming that in this case the destructive instinct has been turned inwards again and is now raging against the self; yet there must be some meaning in the fact that linguistic usage has not given up the connection between this norm of behaviour and erotism and calls these self-injurers masochists too.

Let us keep to a habit of our technique and consider first the extreme and unmistakably pathological form of this masochism. I have described elsewhere[16] how in analytic treatment we come across patients to whom, owing to their behaviour towards its therapeutic influence, we are obliged to ascribe an 'unconscious' sense of guilt. I pointed out the sign by which such people can be recognized (a 'negative therapeutic reaction') and I did not conceal the fact that the strength of such an impulse constitutes one of the most serious resistances and the greatest danger to the success of our medical or educative aims. The satisfaction of this unconscious sense of guilt is perhaps the most powerful bastion in the subject's (usually composite) gain from illness—in the sum of forces which struggle against his recovery and refuse to surrender his state of illness. The suffering entailed by neuroses is precisely the factor that makes them valuable to the masochistic trend. It is instructive, too, to find, contrary to all theory and expectation, that a neurosis which has defied every therapeutic effort may vanish if the subject becomes involved in the misery of an unhappy marriage, or loses all his money, or develops a dangerous organic disease. In such instances one form of suffering has been replaced by another; and we see that all that mattered was that it should be possible to maintain a certain amount of suffering.

Patients do not easily believe us when we tell them about the unconscious sense of guilt. They know only too well by what torments—the pangs of conscience—a conscious sense of guilt, a consciousness of guilt, expresses itself, and they therefore cannot admit that they could harbour exactly analogous impulses in themselves without being in the least aware of them. We may, I think, to some extent meet their objection if we give up the term 'unconscious sense of guilt', which is in any case psychologically incorrect,[17] and speak instead of a 'need for punishment', which covers the observed state of affairs just as aptly. We cannot, however, restrain ourselves from judging and localizing this unconscious sense of guilt in the same way as we do the conscious kind.

We have attributed the function of conscience to the super-ego and we have recognized the consciousness of guilt as an expression of a tension between the ego and the super-ego.[18] The ego reacts with feelings of anxiety (conscience anxiety)[19] to the perception that it has not come up to the demands made by its ideal, the super-ego. What we want to know is how the super-ego has come to play this demanding role and why the ego, in the case of a difference with its ideal, should have to be afraid.

We have said that the function of the ego is to unite and to reconcile the claims of the three agencies which it serves; and we may add that in doing so it also possesses in the super-ego a model which it can strive to follow. For this super-ego is as much a representative of the id as of the external world.[20]

It came into being through the introjection into the ego of the first objects of the id's libidinal impulses—namely, the two parents. In this process the relation to those objects was desexualized; it was diverted from its direct sexual aims. Only in this way was it possible for the Oedipus complex to be surmounted. The super-ego retained essential features of the introjected persons—their strength, their severity, their inclination to supervise and to punish. As I have said elsewhere,[21] it is easily conceivable that, thanks to the defusion of instinct which occurs along with this introduction into the ego, the severity was increased. The super-ego—the conscience at work in the ego—may then become harsh, cruel and inexorable against the ego which is in its charge. Kant's Categorical Imperative is thus the direct heir of the Oedipus complex.[22]

But the same figures who continue to operate in the super-ego as the agency we know as conscience after they have ceased to be objects of the libidinal impulses of the id—these same figures also belong to the real external world. It is from there that they were drawn; their power, behind which lie hidden all the influences of the past and of tradition, was one of the most strongly-felt manifestations of reality. In virtue of this concurrence, the super-ego, the substitute for the Oedipus complex, becomes a representative of the real external world as well and thus also becomes a model for the endeavours of the ego.

In this way the Oedipus complex proves to be—as has already been conjectured in a historical sense[23]—the source of our individual ethical sense, our morality. The course of childhood development leads to an ever-increasing detachment from parents, and their personal significance for the super-ego recedes into the background. To the imagos[24] they leave behind there are then linked the influences of teachers and authorities, self-chosen models and publicly recognized heroes, whose figures need no longer be introjected by an ego which has become more resistant. The last figure in the series that began with the parents is the dark power of Destiny which only the fewest of us are able to look upon as impersonal. There is little to be said against the Dutch writer Multatuli[25] when he replaces the Μοῖρα [Destiny] of the Greeks by the divine pair 'Λόγος καί 'Ανάγκη, [Reason and Necessity]';[26] but all who transfer the guidance of the world to Providence, to God, or to God and Nature, arouse a suspicion that they still look upon these ultimate and remotest powers as a parental couple, in a mythological sense, and believe themselves linked to them by libidinal ties. In *The Ego and the*

Id [p. 58] I made an attempt to derive mankind's realistic fear of death, too, from the same parental view of fate. It seems very hard to free oneself from it.

After these preliminaries we can return to our consideration of moral masochism. We have said[27] that, by their behaviour during treatment and in life, the individuals in question give an impression of being morally inhibited to an excessive degree, of being under the domination of an especially sensitive conscience, although they are not conscious of any of this ultramorality. On closer inspection, we can see the difference there is between an unconscious extension of morality of this kind and moral masochism. In the former, the accent falls on the heightened sadism of the super-ego to which the ego submits; in the latter, it falls on the ego's own masochism which seeks punishment, whether from the super-ego or from the parental powers outside. We may be forgiven for having confused the two to begin with; for in both cases it is a question of a relationship between the ego and the super-ego (or powers that are equivalent to it), and in both cases what is involved is a need which is satisfied by punishment and suffering. It can hardly be an insignificant detail, then, that the sadism of the super-ego becomes for the most part glaringly conscious, whereas the masochistic trend of the ego remains as a rule concealed from the subject and has to be inferred from his behaviour.

The fact that moral masochism is unconscious leads us to an obvious clue. We were able to translate the expression 'unconscious sense of guilt' as meaning a need for punishment at the hands of a parental power. We now know that the wish, which so frequently appears in phantasies, to be beaten by the father stands very close to the other wish, to have a passive (feminine) sexual relation to him and is only a regressive distortion of it. If we insert this explanation into the content of moral masochism, its hidden meaning becomes clear to us. Conscience and morality have arisen through the over-coming, the desexualization, of the Oedipus complex; but through moral masochism morality becomes sexualized once more, the Oedipus complex is revived and the way is opened for a regression from morality to the Oedipus complex. This is to the advantage neither of morality nor of the person concerned. An individual may, it is true, have preserved the whole or some measure of ethical sense alongside of his masochism; but, alternatively, a large part of his conscience may have vanished into his masochism. Again, masochism creates a temptation to perform 'sinful' actions, which must then be expiated by the reproaches of the sadistic conscience (as is exemplified in so many Russian character-types) or by chastisement from the great parental power of Destiny. In order to provoke punishment from this last representative of the parents, the masochist must do what is inexpedient, must act against his own interests, must ruin the prospects which open out to him in the real world and must, perhaps, destroy his own real existence.

The turning back of sadism against the self regularly occurs where a *cultural suppression of the instincts* holds back a large part of the subject's destructive instinctual components from being exercised in life. We may suppose that this portion of the destructive instinct which has retreated appears in the ego as an intensification of masochism. The phenomena of conscience, however, lead us to infer that the destructiveness which returns from the external world is also taken up by the super-ego, without any such transformation, and increases its sadism against the ego. The sadism of the super-ego and the masochism of the ego supplement each other and unite to produce the same effects. It is only in this way, I think, that we can understand how the suppression of an instinct can—frequently or quite generally—result in a sense of guilt and how a person's conscience becomes more severe and more sensitive the more he refrains from aggression against others.[28] One might expect that if a man knows that he is in the habit of avoiding the commission of acts of aggression that are undesirable from a cultural standpoint he will for that reason have a good conscience and will watch over his ego less suspiciously. The situation is usually presented as though ethical requirements were the primary thing and the renunciation of instinct followed from them. This leaves the origin of the ethical sense unexplained. Actually, it seems to be the other way about. The first instinctual renunciation is enforced by external powers, and it is only this which creates the ethical sense, which expresses itself in conscience and demands a further renunciation of instinct.[29]

Thus moral masochism becomes a classical piece of evidence for the existence of fusion of instinct. Its danger lies in the fact that it originates from the death instinct and corresponds to the part of that instinct which has escaped being turned outwards as an instinct of destruction. But since, on the other hand, it has the significance of an erotic component, even the subject's destruction of himself cannot take place without libidinal satisfaction.[30]

NOTES

1. *Beyond the Pleasure Principle* (1920) [*Standard Ed.*, **18**, 9].
2. [*Beyond the Pleasure Principle*, ibid., 56. Freud had previously given this same principle the name of 'the principle of constancy'. A full discussion of the history of Freud's use of these concepts and of their relation to the pleasure principle will be found in an Editor's footnote to 'Instincts and their Vicissitudes' (1915), *Standard Ed.*, **14**, 121.]
3. [This possibility had already been raised in *Beyond the Pleasure Principle*, *Standard Ed.*, **18**, 8 and 63.]
4. [Cf. 'Formulations on the Two Principles of Mental Functioning' (1911), *Standard Ed.*, **12**, 219.]
5. [Freud took up this discussion again in Chapter VIII of his *Outline* (1940 [1938]).]
6. [This last word is added in English in the original.]
7. [See Section VI of ' "A Child Is Being Beaten" ' (1919), *Standard Ed.*, **17**, 196ff.]
8. [*Three Essays* (1905), *Standard Ed.*, **7**, 204–5.]
9. [Ibid., 204.]
10. [For all of this see Chapter IV of *The Ego and the Id*. Cf. also another account in Chapter VI of *Beyond the Pleasure Principle*, *Standard Ed.*, **18**, 50.]
11. ['*Bändigung.*' Freud takes up the word again in the third section of his late paper on 'Analysis Terminable and Interminable' (1937). He had much earlier applied the idea to the 'taming' of memories in Section 3 of Part III of his 'Project' of 1895.]
12. ['*Psychische Umkleidungen.*' The image is an old one of Freud's. It occurs several times, for instance, in the 'Dora' case history (1905), *Standard Ed.*, **7**, 83, 84, and 99 *n*. 2.]
13. See 'The Infantile Genital Organization' (1923).
14. [Cf. a reference to this at the end of Section 4 of the second of the *Three Essays* (1905), *Standard Ed.*, **7**, 193.]
15. [In a paragraph added in 1909 to *The Interpretation of Dreams* (1900), Freud had proposed the term 'mental masochism' for people 'who find their pleasure, not in having *physical* pain inflicted on them, but in humiliation and mental torture'. (*Standard Ed.*, **4**, 159.)]
16. *The Ego and the Id* (1923).
17. [Feelings cannot properly be described as 'unconscious'. See Chapter II of *The Ego and the Id*.
18. [Ibid., Chapter III.]
19. ['*Gewissensangst.*' An Editor's footnote discussing this term will be found in Chapter VII of *Inhibitions, Symptoms and Anxiety* (1926), *Standard Ed.*, **20**, 128.]
20. [Cf. 'Neurosis and Psychosis' (1924).]
21. *The Ego and the Id.*
22. [Cf. ibid.]
23. In Essay IV of *Totem and Taboo* (1912–13).
24. [The term 'imago' was not often used by Freud, especially in his later writings. Its first appearance seems to be in his technical paper on 'The Dynamics of Transference' (1912), *Standard Ed.*, **12**, 100, where he attributes it to Jung. In this latter passage Jung tells us that he partly chose the word from the title of a novel of the same name by the Swiss writer, Carl Spitteler; and we learn from Hanns Sachs (1945, 63) that the psycho-analytic periodical *Imago*, started by him and Rank in 1912, also owed its title to the same source.]
25. E. D. Dekker (1820–87). ['Multatuli' had long been a favourite of Freud's. He heads the list of 'ten good books' which he drew up in 1907, *Standard Ed.*, **9**, 246.]
26. ['Aνάγχη had been named by Freud at least as early as in the Leonardo paper (1910),

Standard Ed., **11**, 125. Λόγοσ, on the other hand, seems to appear for the first time here. Both are discussed, and more especially Λόγοσ, in the closing passage of *The Future of an Illusion* (1927).]

27. [*The Ego and the Id.*]
28. [Cf. *The Ego and the Id.*]
29. [The subjects discussed in this paragraph were enlarged upon by Freud in Chapter VII of *Civilization and Its Discontents* (1930).]
30. [Freud discussed masochism in relation to psycho-analytic treatment once more in section VI of his paper on 'Analysis Terminable and Interminable' (1937).]

REFERENCES

Low, Barbara. 1920. *Psycho-Analysis,* London and New York.
Sachs, Hanns. 1945. *Freud, Master and Friend,* Cambridge, Mass., and London.

14. Beating Fantasies and Daydreams

Anna Freud

In his paper "A Child Is Being Beaten" Freud (1919) deals with a fantasy which, according to him, is met with in a surprising number of persons who seek analytic treatment on account of a hysteria or an obsessional neurosis. He thinks it very probable that it occurs even more often in other persons who have not been forced by a manifest illness to come to this decision. This "beating fantasy" is invariably invested with a high degree of pleasure and is discharged in an act of pleasurable autoerotic gratification. I shall take for granted that you are familiar with the content of Freud's paper—the description of the fantasy, the reconstruction of the phases which preceded it, and its derivation from the oedipus complex. In the course of my paper I shall frequently return to it.

In this paper Freud says: "In two of my four female cases an elaborate superstructure of day-dreams, which was of great significance for the life of the person concerned, had grown up over the masochistic beating fantasy. The function of this superstructure was to make possible a feeling of satisfied excitation, even though the masturbatory act was abstained from" (p. 190). I have been able to find one daydream, among a large variety of them, which seemed especially well suited to illustrate this brief remark. This daydream was formed by a girl of about fifteen, whose fantasy life, in spite of its abundance, had never come into conflict with reality. The origin, evolution, and termination of this daydream could be established with certainty, and its

This paper was written following several discussions with Lou Andreas-Salomé. It was first presented to the Vienna Psychoanalytic Society on May 31, 1922. It was published as "Schlagephantasie und Tagtraum" in *Imago*, 8:317–332, 1922. The English translation appeared in the *International Journal of Psycho-Analysis*, 4:89–102, 1923. A Spanish translation entitled "Relacion entre fantasias de flagelacion y sueño diurno" appeared in *Revista de Psicoanálisis*, 4:258–271, 1946. The version presented here has been revised.
Reprinted by permission of International Universities Press, Inc., from *The Writings of Anna Freud*, vol. 1, 1922–35, pp. 137–57.

derivation from and dependence on a beating fantasy of long standing were proved in a rather thoroughgoing analysis.

I

I shall now trace the development of the fantasy life of this daydreamer. In her fifth or sixth year—the exact date could not be established, but it was certainly before she entered school—this girl formed a beating fantasy of the type described by Freud. In the beginning its content was quite monotonous: "A boy is being beaten by a grownup." Somewhat later is changed to: "Many boys are being beaten by many grownups." The identity of the boys as well as that of the grownups, however, remained unknown, as did in almost all instances the misdeed for which the castigation was administered. We can assume that the various scenes were quite vivid in the child's imagination, but her references to them during the analysis were quite scanty and vague. Each one of the scenes she fantasied, frequently only very briefly, was accompanied by strong sexual excitement and terminated in a masturbatory act.

The sense of guilt which in the case of this girl, too, immediately became attached to this fantasy is explained by Freud in the following way. He says that this version of the beating fantasy is not the original one, but is the substitute in consciousness for an earlier unconscious phase in which the persons who have now become unrecognizable and indifferent were very well known and important: the boy who is being beaten is the child who produced the fantasy; the adult who beats, the child's own father. Yet even this phase is, according to Freud, not the primary one; it was preceded by an earlier phase which belongs to the period of the greatest activity of the oedipus complex and which by means of regression and repression was transformed into the version appearing in the second phase. In the first phase the person who beats also was the father; however, the child who was being beaten was not the fantasying child but other children, brothers or sisters, i.e., rivals for the father's love. In this first phase, therefore, the child claimed all the love for himself and left all the punishment and castigation to the others. With the repression of the oedipal strivings and the dawning sense of guilt, the punishment is subsequently turned back on the child himself. At the same time, however, as a consequence of regression from the genital to the pregenital anal-sadistic organization, the beating situation could still be used as an expression of a love situation. This is the reason for the formation of a second version which because of its all-too-significant content must remain unconscious and be replaced in consciousness by a third version that is more appropriate to the requirements of repression. This is how the third version or phase becomes the carrier of excitement and guilt; for the hidden meaning of this strange fantasy can still be expressed with the words: "Father loves only me."

In the case of our daydreamer the sense of guilt that arose in the wake of her repressed strivings for her father was at first attached less to the content of the fantasy itself—though the latter too was disapproved of from the beginning—than to the autoerotic gratification which regularly occurred at its termination. For a number of years, therefore, the little girl made ever-renewed but ever-failing attempts to separate the one from the other, i.e., to retain the fantasy as a source of pleasure and, at the same time, to give up the sexual gratification which could not be reconciled with the demands of her ego. During this period the fantasy itself was subjected to a great variety of alterations and elaborations. In the attempt to enjoy the permissible pleasure as long as possible and to put off the forbidden conclusion indefinitely, she added all sorts of accessory details that in themselves were quite indifferent but copiously described. The child invented complicated organizations and complete institutions, schools, and reformatories in which the beating scenes were to take place, and established definite rules and regulations which determined the conditions of gaining pleasure. At that time the persons administering the beatings were invariably teachers; only later and in exceptional cases the fathers of the boys were added—as spectators mostly. But even in these detailed elaborations of the fantasy, the acting figures remained schematic, all determining characteristics such as names, individual faces, and personal history being denied to them.

I certainly do not want to imply that such a postponement of the pleasurable scene, the prolongation and continuation of the entire fantasy, is always the expression of guilt feelings, a result of the attempt to separate the fantasy from the masturbatory activity. The same mechanism is used in fantasies which are not shaped by feelings of guilt. In such fantasies this mechanism simply serves the function of heightening the tension and thereby also the anticipated end pleasure.

Let us look at the further vicissitudes of the little girl's beating fantasy. With increasing age there occurred a strengthening of all the tendencies subserving the ego, in which the moral demands of the environment were now incorporated. As a result it became increasingly difficult for the fantasy in which the child's entire sexual life was concentrated to assert itself. She gave up her invariably unsuccessful attempts to separate the beating fantasy from the autoerotic gratification; the prohibition spread and now extended also to the content of the fantasy. Each breakthrough which now could occur only after a prolonged struggle in which strong forces opposed the temptation was followed by violent self-reproaches, pangs of conscience, and temporary depressed moods. The pleasure derived from the fantasy was more and more confined to a single pleasurable moment which seemed to be embedded in unpleasure that occurred before and after it. As the beating fantasy no longer served its function of providing pleasure, it occurred less and less frequently in the course of time.

II

At about the same time—probably between her eighth and tenth year (the exact age again could not be ascertained)—the girl initiated a new kind of fantasy activity which she herself called "nice stories" in contrast to the ugly beating fantasy. These "nice stories" seemed at first sight at least to depict nothing but pleasant, cheery scenes that all exemplify instances of kind, considerate, and affectionate behavior. All the figures in these nice stories had names, individual faces, external appearances that were detailed with great exactness, and personal histories which frequently reached far back into their fantasied past. The family circumstances of these figures, their friendships and acquaintances, and their relationship to each other were precisely specified and all incidents in their daily life were fashioned as true to reality as possible. The setting of the story readily changed with every change in the life of the daydreamer, just as she frequently incorporated bits and pieces of events she had read about. The conclusion of each rounded out episode was regularly accompanied by a strong feeling of happiness unclouded by any trace of guilt; certainly, there no longer was any autoerotic activity connected with it. This type of fantasy activity could therefore take over an ever-increasing part of the child's life. Here we encounter what Freud stressed in his paper: the artistic superstructure of daydreams which are of great significance for the person who forms them. In what follows I shall attempt to demonstrate the extent to which we are justified in regarding these daydreams as a superstructure built on a masochistic beating fantasy.

The daydreamer herself was quite unaware of any connection between the nice stories and the beating fantasy, and at that time would most certainly and without any hesitation have denied it. To her the beating fantasy represented everything that was ugly, reprehensible, and forbidden, while the nice stories were the expression of everything that brought beauty and happiness. A connection between the two simply could not exist; in fact, it was inconceivable that a figure playing a part in a nice story could even appear in the beating scene.

The two were kept apart so carefully that each occurrence of the beating fantasy—which on occasion did break through—had to be punished by a temporary renunciation of the nice stories.

I mentioned earlier that during the analysis the girl gave only the most cursory account of the beating fantasy—usually made with every indication of shame and resistance and in the form of brief, obscure allusions on the basis of which the analyst laboriously had to reconstruct the true picture. In contrast to this reticence, she was only too eager, once the initial difficulties had been overcome, to talk vividly and at length about the various fantasied episodes of her nice stories. In fact, one gained the impression that she never tired of talking and that in doing so she experienced a similar or even greater pleasure than in the daydreaming. In those circumstances it was not difficult to obtain a very clear picture of all the figures and the range of situation. It turned out that the girl had formed not one but a whole series of stories which deserve to be called "continued stories" in view of the constancy of the acting figures and the entire general setting. Among these continued stories one stood out as the most important: it contained the largest number of figures, persisted through the longest period of years, and underwent various transformations. Moreover, from it other stories branched off, which—as in legends and mythology—were elaborated into innumerable almost independent tales. Alongside the main story there existed various minor, more or less important stories which were used in turn but all of which were fashioned according to the same pattern. To gain insight into the structure of such a daydream I have selected as an example the briefest of the nice stories which because of its clarity and completeness is best suited to the purposes of this communication.

In her fourteenth or fifteenth year, after having formed a number of continued daydreams which she maintained side by side, the girl accidentally came upon a boy's storybook; it contained among others a short story set in the Middle Ages. She read through it once or twice with lively interest; when she had finished, she returned the book to its owner and did not see it again. Her imagination, however, was immediately captured by the various figures and their external circumstances which were described in the book. Taking possession of them, she further spun out the tale, just as if it had been her own spontaneous fantasy product, and henceforth accorded this daydream a not insignificant place in the series of her nice stories.

In spite of several attempts that were made during the analysis, it was not possible to establish even approximately the content of the story she had read. The original story had been so cut up into separate pieces, drained of their content, and overlaid by new fantasy material that it was impossible to distinguish between the borrowed and the spontaneously produced elements. All we can do therefore—and that was also what the analyst had to do—is to drop this distinction, which in any event has no practical significance, and deal with the entire content of the fantasied episodes regardless of their sources.

The material she used in this story was as follows: A medieval knight has been engaged in a long feud with a number of nobles who are in league against him. In the course of a battle a fifteen-year-old noble youth (i.e., the age of the daydreamer) is captured by the knight's henchmen. He is taken to the knight's castle where he is held prisoner for a long time. Finally, he is released.

Instead of spinning out and continuing the tale (as in a novel published in installments), the girl made use of the plot as a sort of outer frame for her daydream. Into this frame she inserted a variety of minor and major episodes, each a completed tale that was entirely independent of the others, and formed exactly like a real novel, containing an introduction, the development of a plot which leads to heightened tension and ultimately to a climax. In this she did not feel bound to work out a logical sequence of events. Depending on her mood she could revert to an earlier or later-occurring phase of the tale, or interpose a new situation between two already completed and contemporaneous scenes—until finally the frame of her stories was in danger of being shattered by the abundance of scenes and situations accommodated within it.

In this daydream, which was the simplest of them all, there were only two figures that were really important; all the others can be disregarded as incidental and subordinate by-players. One of these main figures is the noble youth whom the daydreamer has endowed with all possible good and attractive characteristics; the other one is the knight of the castle who is depicted as sinister and violent. The opposition between the two is further intensified by the addition of several incidents from their past family histories—so that the whole setting is one of apparently irreconcilable antagonism between one who is strong and mighty and another who is weak and in the power of the former.

A great introductory scene describes their first meeting during which the knight threatens to put the prisoner on the rack to force him to betray his secrets. The youth's conviction of his helplessness is thereby confirmed and his dread of the knight awakened. These two elements are the basis of all subsequent situations. For example, the knight in fact threatens the youth and makes ready to torture him, but at the last moment the knight desists. He nearly kills the youth through the long imprisonment, but just before it is too late the knight has him nursed back to health. As soon as the prisoner has recovered the knight threatens him again, but faced by the youth's fortitude the knight spares him again. And every time the knight is just about to inflict great harm, he grants the youth one favor after another.

Or let us take another example from a later phase of the story. The prisoner has strayed beyond the limits of his confine and meets the knight, but the latter does not as expected punish the youth with renewed imprisonment. Another time the knight surprises the youth in the very act of transgressing a specific prohibition, but he himself spares the youth the public humiliation which was to be the punishment for this crime. The knight imposes all sorts of deprivations and the prisoner then doubly savors the delights of what is granted again.

All this takes place in vividly animated and dramatically moving scenes. In each the daydreamer experiences the full excitement of the threatened youth's anxiety and fortitude. At the moment when the wrath and rage of the torturer are transformed into pity and benevolence—that is to say, at the climax of each scene—the excitement resolves itself into a feeling of happiness.

The enactment of these scenes in her imagination and the formation of ever new, but very similar scenes usually required a few days, at most some two weeks. The systematic elaboration and development of the single daydream elements usually succeed best at the beginning of each such phase of fantasying. At that time she already made extensive use of the possibility of disregarding the implications and consequences of each situation. As was previously mentioned, she could completely ignore what had happened before or after an incident. As a consequence she was each time fully convinced of the dangers threatening the prisoner and truly believed in the eventual unhappy ending of the scene. We thus see that the events leading to the climax—the preparation for it—were given ample scope. But if the fantasying persisted over a prolonged period of time, memory fragments of happy endings apparently were dragged along from scene to scene, contrary to the daydreamer's intentions. Then the anxiety and concern for the prisoner were described without real conviction, and the forgiving-loving mood of the climax, instead of being confined to a single brief moment of pleasure, began to spread until it finally also took over all that had previously served the purposes of introduction and development of the plot. But when this happened, the story no longer served its function and had now to be replaced (at least for several weeks) by another which after some time met with the same fate. The only exception was the main great daydream which by far outlasted all the minor insignificant stories. This was probably due to the great wealth of characters appearing in it as well as to its manifold ramifications. Nor is it unlikely that its broad design was carried through for the very purpose of ensuring it a longer life every time it emerged.

If we look at the various separate knight-youth daydreams as a continuous and connected series, we are surprised by their monotony, though the daydreamer herself never noticed it either in the course of fantasying or in talking about them in the analysis. Yet she was otherwise by no means an unintelligent girl and was in fact quite critical and exacting in the choice of her reading material. But the various scenes of the knight tale, divested of their accessory details which at first glance seemed to give them a vivid and individualized appearance, are in each case constructed on the same scaffold: antagonism between a strong and a weak person; a misdeed—mostly unintentional—on the part of the weak one which puts him at the other's mercy; the latter's menacing attitude which justifies the gravest apprehensions; a slowly mounting anxiety, often depicted by exquisitely appropriate means, until the tension becomes almost unendurable; and finally, as the pleasurable climax, the solution of the conflict, the pardoning of the sinner, reconciliation, and, for a moment, complete harmony between the former antagonists. Every one of the individual scenes of the other so-called "nice stories" had, with only a few variations, the same structure.

But this structure also contains the important analogy between the nice stories and the beating fantasy which our daydreamer did not suspect. In the beating fantasy, too, the protagonists are strong and weak persons who in their clearest delineation oppose each other as adults and children. There, too, it is regularly a matter of a misdeed, even though the latter is left as indefinite as the acting figures. There, too, we find a period of mounting fear and tension. The decisive difference between the two rests in their solution, which in the fantasy is brought about by beating, and in the daydream by forgiveness and reconciliation.

When in the analysis the girl's attention was drawn to these surprising similarities in structure, she could no longer reject the dawning awareness of a connection between these two, externally so different fantasy products. Once she had accepted the probability of their relatedness she immediately was struck by a series of other connections between them.

But despite the acknowledgment of their similar structure, the content of the beating fantasy seemed to have nothing in common with the nice stories. The assertion that their content differed, however, could not really be maintained. Closer observation showed that at various places the nice stories contained more or less clear traces of the old beating theme attempting to break through. The best example of this can be found in the knight daydream with which we already are familiar: the torture that is threatened, though not carried out, constitutes the background of a great number of scenes lending them a distinct coloring of anxiety. This threatened torture, however, is reminiscent of the old beating scene, the execution of which remains forbidden in the nice stories. Other forms of beating breaking through into the daydream can be found, not in this particular tale of the knight, but in other daydreams of this girl.

The following example is taken from the great main story, as far as it was revealed in the analysis. In many scenes the role of the passive, weak person (the youth in the tale of the knight) is enacted by two figures. Though both have the same antecedents, one is punished and the other pardoned. In this instance the punishment scene was neither pleasurably nor unpleasurably accentuated; it simply formed a backdrop to the love scene, their contrast serving to heighten the pleasure.

In another variation of the daydream, the passive person is made to recall all the past punishments he suffered while he is actually being treated affectionately. Here, too, the contrast serves to heighten the pleasurable accent.

In a third version, the active, strong person recalls, just as he is overcome by the conciliatory mood associated with the climax, a past act of punishment or beating which he, having committed the same crime, endured.

The four versions just described illustrate ways in which the beating theme can encroach upon the main theme of a daydream. But it also may be worked out in such a way that it constitutes the most essential theme of a daydream.

One of the prerequisites for this is the omission of an element that is indispensable in the beating fantasy, namely, the humiliation in being beaten. Thus the great main story of this girl contained several particularly impressive scenes which culminated in the descriptions of an act of beating or punishment, the former being described as unintentional, the latter as self-punishment.

Each of these examples of the beating theme erupting into the nice stories was furnished by the daydreamer herself, and each could be used as a further proof for the assertion that the two were related. But the most convincing evidence for their relatedness came later in the analysis in the form of a confession. The girl admitted that on some rare occasions a direct reversal of the nice stories into the beating fantasy had taken place. During difficult periods, i.e., at times of increased external demands or diminished internal capabilities, the nice stories no longer succeeded in fulfilling their task. And then it had frequently happened that at the conclusion and climax of a fantasied beautiful scene the pleasurable and pleasing love scene was suddenly replaced by the old beating situation together with the sexual gratification associated with it, which then led to a full discharge of the accumulated excitement. But such incidents were quickly forgotten, excluded from memory, and consequently treated as though they had never happened.

Our investigation of the relationship between beating fantasy and nice stories has so far established three important links: (1) a striking similarity in the construction of the individual stories; (2) a certain parallelism in their content; and (3) the possibility of a direct reversal of one into the other. The essential difference between the two lies in the fact that the nice stories admit the occurrence of unexpected affectionate scenes precisely at the point where the beating fantasy depicts the act of chastisement.

With these points in mind, I return to Freud's reconstruction of the history of the beating fantasy. As already mentioned, Freud says that the form in which we know the beating fantasy is not the original one, but is a substitute for an incestuous love scene that distorted by repression and regression to the anal-sadistic phase finds expression as a beating scene. This point of view suggests an explanation of the difference between beating fantasy and daydream: what appears to be an advance from beating fantasy to nice story is nothing but a return to an earlier phase. Being manifestly removed from the beating scene, the nice stories regain the latent meaning of the beating fantasy: the love situation hidden in it.

But this assertion still lacks an important link. We have learned that the climax of the beating fantasy is inseparably associated with the urge to obtain sexual gratification and the subsequently appearing feelings of guilt. In contrast, the climax of the nice stories is free of both. At first glance this seems to be inexplicable since we know that both sexual gratification and sense of guilt derive from the repressed love fantasy which is disguised in the beating fantasy but represented in the nice stories.

The problem resolves itself when we take into consideration that the nice stories also do not give expression to the repressed love fantasy without changing it. In this incestuous wish fantasy stemming from early childhood all the sexual drives were concentrated on a first love object, the father. The repression of the oedipus complex forced the child to renounce most of his infantile sexual aims. The early "sensual" aims were relegated to the unconscious. That they reemerge in the beating fantasy indicates a partial failure of the attempted repression.

While the beating fantasy thus represents a return of the repressed, the nice stories on the other hand represent its sublimation. In the beating fantasy the direct sexual drives are satisfied, whereas in the nice stories the aim-inhibited drives, as Freud calls them, find gratification. Just as in the development of a child's relations to his parents, the originally undivided current of love becomes separated into repressed sensual strivings (here expressed in the beating fantasy) and into a sublimated affectionate tie (represented by the nice stories).

The two fantasy products can now be compared in terms of the following scheme: the function of the beating fantasy is the disguised representation of a never-changing sensual love situation which it expresses in the language of the anal-sadistic organization as an act of beating. The function of the nice stories, on the other hand, is the representation of the various tender and affectionate stirrings. Its theme, however, is as monotonous as that of the beating fantasy. It consists in bringing about a friendship between a strong and a weak person, an adult and a boy, or, as many daydreams express it, between a superior and an inferior being.

The sublimation of sensual love into tender friendship is of course greatly facilitated by the fact that already in the early stages of the beating fantasy the girl abandoned the difference of the sexes and is invariably represented as a boy.

III

It was the object of this paper to examine the nature of the relationship between beating fantasies and daydreams which coexisted side by side. As far as possible their mutual dependence could be established. In what follows I shall use the opportunity provided by this case to follow the further development and fate of one of these continued daydreams.

Several years after the story of the knight first emerged, the girl put it in writing. She produced an absorbing short story which covers the period of the youth's imprisonment. It began with the prisoner's torture and ended with his refusal to escape. One suspects that his voluntary choice to remain at the castle is motivated by positive feelings for the knight. All events are depicted as having occurred in the past, the story being presented in the frame of a conversation between the knight and the prisoner's father.

While the written story thus retained the theme of the daydream, the method of its elaboration was changed. In the daydream the friendship between the strong and the weak characters had to be established over and over again in every single scene, while in the written story its development extends over the entire period of the action. In the course of this transformation the individual scenes of the daydream were lost; while some of the situational material that they contained returned in the written story, the individual climaxes were not replaced by a single great climax at the end of the written tale. Its aim—harmonious union between the former antagonists—is only anticipated but not really described. As a result, the interest, which in the daydream was concentrated on specific highpoints, is in the written version divided equally among all situations and protagonists.

This change of structure corresponds to a change in the mechanism of obtaining pleasure. In the daydream each new addition or repetition of a separate scene afforded a new opportunity for pleasurable instinctual gratification. In the written story, however, the direct pleasure gain is abandoned. While the actual writing was done in a state of happy excitement, similar to the state of daydreaming, the finished story itself does not elicit any such excitement. A reading of it does not lend itself to obtaining daydreamlike pleasures. In this respect it had no more effect on its author than the reading of any comparable story written by another person would have had.

These findings suggest a close connection between the two important differences between the daydream and the written story—the abandonment of the individual scenes and the renunciation of the daydreamlike pleasure gain at specific climaxes. The written story must have been motivated by different factors and serve other functions than the daydream. Otherwise the story of the knight would simply have become something unusable in its transformation from fantasy to written story.

When the girl was asked what had induced her to write down the story, she herself could give only one reason of which she was aware. She believed that she had turned to writing at a time when the daydream of the knight was especially obtrusive—that is to say, as a defense against excessive preoccupation with it. She had sought to create a kind of independent existence for the protagonists that had become all too vivid, in the hope that they then would no longer dominate her fantasy life. The daydream of the knight was in fact finished, as far as she was concerned, after it had been written down.

But this account of her motivation still leaves many things unexplained: the very situations that owing to their overvividness are supposed to have impelled her to write down the story are not included in it, whereas others that were not part of the daydream (e.g., the actual torturing) are dwelt on extensively. The same is true with regard to the protagonists: the written story omits several figures whose individual characterization was fully executed in the daydream and instead introduces entirely new ones, such as the prisoner's father.

A second motivation for writing the story can be derived from Bernfeld's observations (1924) of the creative attempts of adolescents. He remarks that the motive of writing down daydreams is not to be found in the daydream itself, but is extrinsic to it. He maintains that such creative endeavors are prompted by certain ambitious tendencies originating in the ego; for example, the adolescent's wish to influence others by poetry, or to gain the respect and love of others by these means. If we apply this theory to the girl's story of the knight, the development from the daydream to the written story may have been as follows:

In the service of such ambitious strivings as have just been mentioned, the private fantasy is turned into a communication addressed to others. In the course of this transformation regard for the personal needs of the daydreamer is replaced by regard for the prospective reader. The pleasure derived directly from the content of the story can be dispensed with, because the process of writing by satisfying the ambitious strivings indirectly produces pleasure in the author. This renunciation of the direct pleasure gain, however, also obviates the need to accord special treatment to certain parts of the story—the climax of the daydreams—which were especially suited to the purpose of obtaining pleasure. Likewise, the written story (as the inclusion of the torture scene demonstrates) can discard the restrictions imposed on the daydream in which the realization of situations stemming from the beating fantasy had been proscribed.

The written story treats all parts of the content of the daydream as equally objective material, the selection being guided solely by regard for their suitability for representation. For the better she succeeds in the presentation of her material, the greater will be the effect on others and therefore also her own indirect pleasure gain. By renouncing her private pleasure in favor of making an impression on others, the author has accomplished an important developmental step: the transformation of an autistic into a social activity. We could say: she has found the road that leads from her fantasy life back to reality.

REFERENCES

Bernfeld, R. 1924. *Von dichterischen Schaffen der Jugend.* Vienna and Leipzig: Internationaler psychoanalyitischer Verlag.

Freud, S. 1919. A Child Is Being Beaten: A Contribution to the Study of the Origin of Sexual Perversions. In *S.E.* 17:179–204.

15. The Clinical Aspect of the Need for Punishment

Otto Fenichel

I

Since Freud's work *The Ego and the Id* made profounder investigation of the psychology of the ego possible, this question has become the center of analytical interest. In particular the psychology of the sense of guilt has claimed special consideration, on account of its outstanding clinical and theoretical importance. Recognition of the importance of the sense of guilt is by no means confined to recent times. Apart from the part played by the conscious sense of guilt in manifestly neurotic forms of disease, Freud's doctrine of repression virtually implied that a sort of guilt feeling acted as a criterion for the decisions of the repressing faculty; in his description of the reaction formations of the obsessional neurotic, in his conception that every symptom complies with the repressing force as well, as with the claims of the repressed instinct, the idea of self-punishment was already contained. What is novel is simply our insight into the importance of the *unconscious* elements of feelings of guilt, and of the resultant penalties. We know that this insight formed the starting point of those of Freud's investigations which revealed the differentiation of the superego from the ego, the creation of the former by introjection of the objects of the oedipus complex, and the genesis of the sense of guilt from the discrepancy between the superego and the ego. According to Freud's latest doctrine of instincts, the conscious and unconscious feelings of guilt owe their distinctive position to the circumstance that they are representatives of the destructive instincts; and these have

First published in *Int. Z. Psa.*, Vol. II, 1925, pp. 469–487.
Reprinted by permission of W. W. Norton & Company, Inc., from *The Collected Papers of Otto Fenichel: First Series*, 1925. Collected and edited by Dr. Hanna Fenichel and Dr. David Rapaport, copyright 1953 by W. W. Norton & Company, Inc. Copyright renewed 1981 by Peter E. Lippet, executor of the Estate of Hanna Fenichel.

lost some of their neutralizing, libidinal components as a result of the instinctual defusion that goes on *pari passu* with introjection.

Once more it is only in extreme cases that the clinical significance of this fact becomes evident. Freud has at various times drawn attention to such cases; long before his latest works he described in "Those Wrecked by Success" and in "Criminality from a Sense of Guilt"[1] two neurotic types of person who become so enraged against themselves that they are driven either to self-destruction or, in order to avoid that, to the destruction of their surroundings. Even if the term "need for punishment" was first used only in his paper "The Economic Problem in Masochism,"[2] we know that Freud stated long before this that the most powerful resistances arise from a sense of guilt which finds discharge in the sufferings of a neurosis. He has, however, drawn attention to a special case in which the most obstinate resistances of this nature can be successfully dealt with. A footnote in *The Ego and the Id* deals with a "borrowed" sense of guilt, and runs as follows: "One has a special opportunity for influencing it when this Ucs. sense of guilt is a 'borrowed' one, i.e. when it is the product of an identification with some other person who was once the object of an erotic cathexis. When the sense of guilt has been adopted in this way it is often the sole remaining trace of the abandoned love relation, and not at all easy to recognize as such. (The likeness between this process and what happens in melancholia is unmistakable.) If one can unmask this former object cathexis behind the Ucs. sense of guilt, the therapeutic success is often brilliant, otherwise the outcome of one's efforts is by no means certain."[3]

Accordingly it is the libidinal element in the sense of guilt with which our therapeutics can deal successfully.[4]

Now in his paper on masochism Freud has contrasted the conscious "sadism of the superego" and unconscious "moral masochism," and has shown its close kinship with "erotogenic" and "feminine" masochism. Here, therefore, our therapeutic condition is fulfilled. We need only recall what he says about the "regression from morality to the oedipus complex," in order to understand the effect of this instinctual fusion. Its clinical application is immediately apparent. The masochism of the ego and the sadism of the superego certainly form a complemental series; but in practice it is important to discover which of the two trends predominates. Following Freud, in two cases, which it is instructive to compare with one another, I was able to observe in their origin the relationships (resulting from such instinctual fusions) between instinct and the need for punishment, and between the superego and the id (as well as the attitude taken up by the ego in regard to both). In part they exemplify clinically what has hitherto been only a matter of theory; i.e., they bring to completion our clinical observations,[5] and in part they fill in certain lacunae that have existed hitherto in our knowledge of this subject.

II

In the case history of a young patient the manifestations of his acutely conscious sense of guilt played a conspicuous part. When he indulged in the slightest luxury or pleasure he immediately experienced an inner command to be wretched, exhausted, and thoroughly ill. He was unable to do any work; his illness had cost him several years that should have been devoted to study. Among other things that happened to him, a short time before the beginning of the analysis he had been run over by a motorcar and severely injured; after this, while still in the hospital, he felt quite well and was able to write reproachful letters to his parents, against whom he was otherwise never able to utter a single word.

The patient's father is a clergyman in a small town. He belongs to a religious sect that professes a strict moral code, and is narrow and bigoted in his beliefs, although in other respects he is peaceable and easy to get on with. So far as authority is concerned, he is quite subordinate to his wife. She belongs to the same religious body, is a hysteric, and fanatical and temperamental. Her prohibitions to her children concerned not only all that related to sex, but everything that was at all worldly. She beat her children without restraint for trivial misdemeanors, and then forthwith overwhelmed them with excessive demonstrations of affection. There were three other members of the family, all younger than he. He told me of two "attacks" of "nervous cardiac trouble" which he had had in his twelfth and sixteenth years. In a *pavor nocturnus* which was characterized by hallucinations and fantasies of the end of the world, he cried out for his mother to come to his bedside (his father was unable to quiet him); he was unwilling to allow her to leave him, but was suddenly overtaken by the anxious fear that she knew everything, that he was betrayed, that she was laughing at him, and that he would have to confess all his sins to her, although he knew that she was already aware of them. On one occasion he even wrote out a list of his sins— like a confessional certificate. The second attack of this kind ended in an illness of several years' duration, in the course of which he was either unable to move at all, or at other times was only able to walk with the aid of crutches, and was for months under medical treatment at a hospital. Both he and his parents, contrary to medical opinion, thought that death was approaching. The occasions of these attacks were easily discoverable. The first took place on the day when his father had confirmed one of his boy friends; previous to that the patient had eagerly read some books which his mother had prohibited. The second attack occurred when a youth joined his class at school against whom his mother had warned him on account of his conduct with girls, but with whom he had consequently fallen violently in love. As a result of his illness he ceased attendance at school. He felt bound to confess his fondness for this youth to his mother, but believed, nevertheless, that she knew about it without being told. This belief in the omniscience of his parents was transferred afterward to physicians. Whenever his pulse was being felt it rose to 200, because he was convinced that the physician knew everything and that he was doomed.

We see therefore, this his attacks were the expression of a sense of guilt that had reference to his sexual curiosity and to infantile sexual practices. There was no reason to question the patient's idea that his curiosity had been aroused by observations of his parents' sexual intercourse made by him in his childhood, and that these observations were not only punished, but even reproduced, in his attacks. A series of dreams disclosed the effects of such scenes; as, for example: *During a tremendous catastrophe a monstrous dog thrust a knife into the earth.—A catastrophic outburst of fire altered the whole face of the world; his mother then built a very tiny house out of straw.—A monster destroyed the house of his father's superintendent.—*In a similar dream, *he runs away after the catastrophe with two heads, one with hair on it, the other shaved.*

It turned out that the attacks represented, in particular, attempts to defend himself against the identification with his mother that had been acquired in this way, i.e. they were a defense against homosexual tendencies. We are reminded here of a sentence of Freud's: "In the history of homosexuals one often hears that the change in them took place after the mother had praised another boy and set him up as a model."[6]

This statement has to undergo a characteristic modification for the case with which we are concerned. The first attack took place after the *father* had *praised* (confirmed) another boy; while the manifest (though aim-inhibited) homosexuality succeeded in breaking out only after the *mother* had *found fault with* another boy; the repression and, along with it, the second attack only occurred when the boy with whom he had fallen in love entered the same class at school, and came into very close proximity to him. The patient's compulsion to confess his homosexual love to his mother corresponded to a convulsive attempt to defend himself against this inclination and to find a heterosexual object once more in his mother. We see now why his father was unable to quiet him.

Let us now return to our investigation of the sense of guilt. Even when he was shouting furiously in unconcealed resistance to his conscientious compulsions, "Why should I always torment myself, why must I thrash myself, why, why?" yet he had first of all to beat himself in the most violent fashion with clenched fist on forehead and breast. He even thought of killing himself in order to deliver himself from his pangs of conscience, i.e. going to the furthest limit of acquiescence in his conflict with his superego. He was himself aware that the palpitation he felt during the attack was an inner self-scourging, indeed, an attempted suicide. The attack which was based on the earlier reaction of the childish observer to overhearing sexual intercourse between his parents thus included, in addition to an aggressive impulse against his parents (hindrance of their *current* intercourse), an aggressive element against his own ego. The connection between deed and punishment turned out, however, to be very much more close and complicated still.

The patient developed the fantasy of being at home and pretending to be insane, either by storming and smashing everything up—then he would not need to be ill any longer; or by lying quietly, not replying to anything and getting taken to an asylum—in this way, too, he would evade his illness. These fantasied outbreaks of insanity, as he saw himself, were the equivalents of his attacks, and, in particular, of the "compulsion to confess" which accompanied them. He said quite definitely: "If I had smashed up everything, I shouldn't have had to confess anything." The compulsion to confess, the imagined simulation of insanity, and the real illness are thus psychological equivalents. Accordingly, we are able to agree with Reik in regarding a confession as a weakened action which at the same time has to give satisfaction to the claims of the repressing forces, i.e. which has to be a punishment.[7] The original repressed instinctual trends could also break through relatively undisguised into consciousness, if only provision had been made for a preceding self-punishment. If his mother were to rebuke him again, he intended to hurl her to the ground, violate her, and then shout to her, "You see now what your crazy upbringing has led to!" He invented a whole series of complicated schemes by which he might at the same time injure both his mother and himself—e.g., he broke a large mirror belonging to his mother and cut himself with it. He failed at the school inspection in order to cast blame both on himself and on his teacher.

The patient's conduct in regard to onanism showed a remarkable condensation of sin and punishment. He had been conscious of (heterosexual) onanism in his early childhood. At puberty a peculiar form of inhibition of masturbation had set in, conditioned by the accompanying homosexual fantasies. At the date of the analysis he had in the main substituted for masturbation gymnastic and athletic activities which, although they were entirely ego-syntonic, were still affected by the full strength of the prohibition against masturbation. Contrary to his conscious will, he felt that he ought not to do gymnastics; they would make him healthy, whereas he ought to be ill. When he experienced the need for punishment after gymnastics, he had to masturbate without enjoyment until he felt quite ill. In this way what had been forbidden was reproduced afresh in the punishment in a far less disguised form than it had assumed in the act that merited punishment.[8] The special vehemence of this compulsive masturbation confirms Reik's idea that *forced* instinctual satisfactions arise from the need for punishment.[9]

Frequently, however, the patient broke off masturbation before ejaculation. He did this consciously to exacerbate his punishment; the analysis showed that this stood for a latent safeguard against punishment, since the ejaculation was regarded by his unconscious as castration. If on occasion he carried the masturbation as far as ejaculation, he afterwards swallowed his own emission. This was, in the first place, a simultaneous satisfaction of his bisexual trends, which sprang from his twofold identification with the parents whom he had overheard in the sexual act; he had actually dreamed that he ran away from the "catastrophe" with two heads, one with hair, i.e. feminine, and the other shaven, i.e. masculine. But it was further an avoidance of castration, since he took back the lost emission into his body, although at the same time it was a repetition of the castration: the swallowing of the emission corresponded to the incorporation of his own penis (oral mother-identification).

The castration idea, which here, as so often, meant both a punishment and a feminine instinctual aim, was able at times in spite of deep repression to penetrate into consciousness in a gross and undisguised form; its penal significance was then intended to mask the wish fulfillment. Thus for some time during his illness he walked on crutches. Occasionally he tied up his testicles with the intention of cutting them off: "Then I shall at least be freed from these instincts." The whole significance of the inferiority felt by seven-month children, recently described by Hollós,[10] appeared as a rationalization of the inferiority due to the castration complex when he once exclaimed: "I wish I had been a seven-month child! I am certainly utterly worthless, *but in that case I should at least have known the reason for it!*" In the same way he occasionally recognizes quite consciously the character of his neurosis as a simultaneous satisfaction of instinct and need for punishment; he scourges himself in order to suffer: "That will deliver me from my illness more quickly than the analysis will!" Just as naïvely he revealed the mechanism of criminality from a sense of guilt: "I will murder them all, and then at least I shall be put in prison, and shall not need a neurosis any longer."[11]

The conception that punishment also entails a license for the acts that follow it found confirmation in the relatively violent instinctual outbreaks that succeeded his self-chastisements without either a sense of guilt or a recognition of his morbidity. Reik has drawn attention to the fact that such outrageous and apparently guilt-free misdeeds, opposed to the patient's whole character but nevertheless permitted by the ego, are "crimes due to the sense of guilt."[12] Thus the patient seriously made up his mind to violate his sister or mother (in doing so he was, it is true, also aiming at a denial of deeply repressed homosexual incest wishes); he perpetrated exhibitionistic actions without having the least notion that his conduct represented an instinctual gratification, just as he was entirely ignorant of the sexual nature of his self-scourging. He tortured animals and dolls horribly, had nihilistic fantasies, wanted to kill the whole of humanity and destroy the whole world. These sadistic fantasies of his had, however, never been realized on other human beings. They lead us to a very clear comprehension of the manifold relations between his conduct and his self-punishment. His instinct-ridden outbursts were (a) the cause of his self-punishment (the act that gave rise to his need for punishment), (b) its result (criminality from a sense of guilt), (c) its equivalent (repetition of the act in the punishment), and (d) an attempt to free himself from it (they did not involve a sense of guilt or recognition of being ill).

The prototype of the patient's sadistic fantasies was his mother, who was so furious when he or any of the other children got into any mischief. The adoption of his mother into the patient's superego thus developed its effects in both directions: the mother's corrections were continued on his own person by his self-chastisements, while his sadistic fantasies were evidence of his longing to imitate his mother in his external relationships. At the same time his mother was the object of his aggressive impulses; he wished to conduct himself with regard to her exactly as she, on her part, had acted toward him. He dreamed that his mother was lying in his lap like a child. This reversal of situations had in its time resulted in a narcissistic, homosexual object choice. When he reached maturity he assumed a friendly, condescending attitude toward his mother, but exhibited from time to time irrational outbreaks of wrath; he recalled from his childhood days a similar alternation of conduct on her part.

In the analysis he spoke insultingly of his mother for hours together with terrible vehemence and monotony, described with the utmost indignation her behavior, her bigotry, her preposterous educational maxims, and had fantasies of either killing or violating her out of revenge. There is no doubt that this overdetermined hate against his mother served the purpose of concealing the normal oedipus attitude of hate against the weak father, as Boehm has shown with regard to homosexuals who hate their mothers.[13] Nevertheless, it was also very evident that the aggressions against his mother were the equivalents of aggressions against himself. He carried out in actual fact against himself the injury that he then said he wished to do to his mother. The mother whom he hated, who, he believed, demanded from him punishment, illness, death, proved to be a projection of his superego. In beating himself mercilessly, while reviling his conscience all the time, he was demonstrating in his own body how he would thrust a knife with delight into his mother's body. It was a kind of projection of his superego *backward* to the place in the external world from which it had come—a regressive projection. We recall the fact that Freud has already described[14] this decomposition of the function of conscience and its regressive projection into the external world in the case of paranoiac delusions of observation. The significance of such a projection is of an exquisitely *economic* character. This is immediately intelligible when we remember how Freud explains projection: "Towards the outer world there is a barrier against stimuli, and the mass of excitations coming up against it will take effect only on a reduced scale; towards what is within no protection against stimuli is possible. . . . There will be a tendency to treat them (such inner excitations as bring with them an overplus of pain) as though they were acting not from within but from without, in order for it to be possible to apply against them the defensive measures of the barrier against stimuli."[15]

The economic alleviation which projection affords was seen especially clearly in the occasional outcry of the patient, after he had been complaining about his rigorous conscious and had "resolved" never to punish himself again: "If anyone comes again to demand punishment from me, I will murder him in cold blood!" In his paranoid condition the transference, since it lay in a homosexual situation, furnished him with quite a special opportunity for projection. He had, for example, a "paranoid transference dream" of a kind similar to the one Freud once communicated.[16] The analyst had put on a beard like his father in order to force a father-transference on him; occasionally he believed that the analyst had sexual intentions with regard to him.

He also employed purely paranoidal projections for the purpose of self-punishment in his complicated schemes for provoking quarrels with his father and with the analyst: e.g., indirectly through him his father received a document which contained numerous implicit accusations against him; then he exaggerated a really trifling piece of fault-finding on his father's part, stormed at his father's lack of understanding, and railed against him for hours at a time. He maneuvered everything in such a way that his father would have to blame him and thus furnish a reason for his insulting him. In this way, by a rationalized projection, he would liberate himself from the compulsion to revile himself. Should the provocation prove ineffectual, should his father not scold him sufficiently, he would thereupon alter reality in the manner of a delusion of persecution. His "conscience thus encounters him in regressive form as an external, hostile influence."[17]

In the analysis, when the analyst casually remarked that he ought not to spend twenty minutes in excusing himself for being five minutes late, he declared that the analyst had apparently unconsciously felt that his being late was an aggression directed against him; the analyst was afraid of it, and in order to divert him from the subject, he had given him so severe a rebuke, and treated him so badly. Thus not only is the aggression which he feels himself transformed into one which the analyst feels, but he suspects, once more delusionally, an aggression on the part of the analyst simply in order to be attacked *from without*. By his persistent lateness and his hour-long, monotonous talk about it, he was fighting, as the analysis proved, not only against his homosexual transference love, but also against the constant pressure of his own conscience. The sexual element in this paranoid mechanism is evident; what relates to punishment in it falls into the following scheme: (a) a predominant sense of guilt, (b) a provocation of punishment (criminality from the sense of guilt), (c) when punishment does not take place, a perception of punishment of the nature of a delusion of persecution, (d) abuse externally directed, representing a projection of the ego as the object of the superego's aggression. Freud has characterized the delusion of persecution in the following way: "I do not love him—indeed, I hate him—he hates (persecutes) me";[18] in the case of our patient "I hate him" was intended to shout down not only "I love him" but "I hate myself." According to Reich those parts of the superego that have remained isolated from the ego—i.e., those parts of the superego that have not effected any ego alteration—are particularly well suited for this regressive projection.[19]

The projection of the patient's conscience went with an excessively aggressive attitude to the casual agents his conscience employed. He wanted, for instance, to have the chauffeur by whom he had let himself be run down arrested, or else to give him a merciless thrashing.

These extensive processes of condensation were facilitated by the actual sadistic behavior of his mother. Behind his sadistic fantasies in which he imitated his mother, he concealed his passive libidinal wishes and his need for punishment. For several nights during a transitory phase of the transference, he ran the streets looking for a girl. He never managed to get one. It happened every time that some old gentleman, whom he roundly abused, would snatch the girls away from him just when he was on the point of accosting them. In this way he repeated his infantile disillusionment, not only in the sense that his mother preferred his father to him, but also that his father preferred his mother to him. It was this passive homosexual attitude that evoked the sense of guilt and afterward, in a regressive form, took its place. On seeing an old man urinating he felt that he heard the command: "Now you must die!"

The sexualizing of his self-chastisements certainly gave the impression of being secondary in character. The sadism of his superego seemed to outweigh the masochism of the ego, just as he had also been conscious of his self-reproaches. Undoubtedly he felt that *death* was the punishment that was really awaiting him; it was only by chance that the accident with the motorcar passed off so lightly. He had forbidden himself gymnastics because, according to his idea, they were calculated to restore him to health. In a narcissistic game he set a picture of the Apoxyomenos alongside his own reflection, in order to compare himself with it; there, bodily confronted with one another, stood his actual ego and his ego-ideal, the conflict between which consisted in his illness. He said to himself he did not dare to be as healthy as that; when this prohibition came to him from without, he felt it only as an alleviation. On that account he could not believe even that the analyst wanted to cure him; just when he wished to study a symptom it disappeared—what a villain he must be!

We append the following summary: The first thing to be taken into account in the clinical picture was the bisexual predisposition aroused by the primal scene (dream of the two heads). The introjection of his mother had a pathogenic result. This was followed: (a) in the ego, by its becoming the representative of homosexuality, warded off in paranoid fashion; (b) in the superego, by his accepting all his mother's prohibitions, and ratifying them by his self-chastisement. On the other hand, his mother appeared to him in his sadistic fantasies as his ideal. He wished to imitate his mother (stand in the same relation as she to his father).

These conditions are complicated by the fact that we have also to assume analogous processes going on in connection with the father-identification. Not only do the object trends compete with the identifications, but the different identifications compete with one another. The sexualizing of punishment appeared to be secondary; it had more essentially the character of an unrelenting aggression of the superego than that of an instinctual gratification of the id. A "borrowed" guilt from the mother was certainly in some degree probable, but it was not corroborated by the analysis.

III

The second case furnishes a more distinct picture of "moral masochism." The patient's pangs of conscience were, as such, unconscious, and were manifested in the analysis as passive homosexual gratification. He came under analysis for impotence, but proved to be one of those patients about whom Freud has said: "We are usually able to make a confident promise of recovery to the psychically impotent, but, as long as we are ignorant of the dynamics of the disturbance, we ought to be more cautious in making this prognosis. An unpleasant surprise awaits us if the analysis discloses the cause of the 'purely psychical' impotence to be a typically masochistic attitude, perhaps embedded since infancy." [20]

At the root of the trouble there lay aggressive tendencies against the father, corresponding to the normal oedipus complex. These had led by reaction to a vast general inhibition of aggression, which had then been utilized for the satisfaction of a passive feminine attitude. The adoption of the mother into the ego which thus ensued was—in contrast to the earlier case—opposed by a *paternal* superego, to the influence of which one may ascribe the circumstance that the masochism originating in this way took a *moral* form. The identification with the father had miscarried in characteristic fashion, so that the borrowing of the sense of guilt from the father was quite impressive.

It was the trauma of an infantile observation of the maternal genitals that, as Freud has described,[21] activated the boy's castration anxiety and brought about a great mental revolution. In it he regressed from father- to mother-identification, and simultaneously from the phallic to the sadistic-anal stage. His neurosis could be recognized as a repetition of these early infantile libidinal vicissitudes, since his recent experience contained an exactly similar incident: he had been for the first time having sexual relations with a woman (she had seduced him, and was twice his age); but the necessity for amputation of a finger had then demonstrated the reality of the danger of castration (just as once before the glimpse of the feminine genitalia had done) and his neurosis broke out with impotence and so-called "states of depression." The latter became recognizable afterward as self-punishments—suffering caused by an overpowering sense of guilt.

From the beginning of the analysis there came clearly into view both the complete oedipus complex and the castration complex. At a deeper level the castration which he feared was desired: since it combined both punishment and the passive feminine attitude, I shall add a few observations regarding it.

The obscurity surrounding the sadistic conception of the sexual act in the patient's mind had led to a condensation of the threatener and the threatened, of the castrator and the castrated. Thus it came about that circumcised Jews, who were despised in the *milieu* in which the patient lived, became dangerously sexual castrators, and women and their genitals became a power which menaced the penis. According to an infantile theory, he imagined that the penis crumbled away in the sexual act and that bits of it remained in the vagina. There could plainly be discerned in the patient's unconscious mind two opposing types of castration: the one masculine, consisting in cutting; the other feminine, consisting in biting. The latter type made use of a penis hidden within the feminine genitalia as its executive organ.[22] Behind the idea that the mother had robbed the father of his penis, which remained menacingly within her, like a shining jewel or a hidden sword, there lay the earlier one that the vagina was a hollow penis tucked in like a glove-finger. The return of the repressed from beneath repression showed that the purpose behind this supposition was to obliterate all traces of the possibility of castration which had been demonstrated *ad oculos* by the woman's lack of penis; the hollow penis eventually became a secreted penis which had been stolen from the father, and in this way what was originally meant for a denial of castration became a very dangerous castration instrument.

For a time the patient's impotence took the form of a premature recession of erection after it had set in promptly. He had the impression that his penis "withdrew inside him," became a hollow penis. His impotence thus represented his transformation into a woman. The change of the penis into a hollow penis—indeed the whole idea of a hollow penis—was a prophylactic measure against castration. *Transformation into a woman with an imagined hollow penis was, therefore, a means of avoiding castration.* Thus the form which the impotence took led to the discovery of the mechanism with which the patient sought to protect himself from the menace to his virility, i.e. a secondary mother-identification.

His early sexual observations had left him with a prohibition which influenced all his later sexual activities and was especially directed against his excessive sadistic impulses, which had only been strengthened by regression. Frequent parental quarrels furnished an objective foundation for his rooted sadistic conception of the sexual act. In his fantasies and dreams he repeatedly saw symbols of the maternal and feminine genitals covered with blood. This aggression that was to be inhibited was, however, undoubtedly directed to a far greater degree against his own sex and originally against his father. There was a condensation here of inimical and sadistic impulses. Not only did he occasionally feel, to his extreme horror, murderous impulses against his father, but by mistake he had brought about two shooting accidents in which he had nearly killed his father in reality.

This compensating reactive inhibition dominated the patient's character. He was quiet and reserved, avoiding every kind of action that had in any way the appearance of aggression. Owing to his impotence he shunned all sexual aggressiveness, and had been potent only in the affair in which the woman took the active part. Otherwise he was afraid of his sadistic impulses because he expected castration by the woman as a revenge. He never protected himself against wrong, and allowed himself to be taken advantage of constantly. Even as a child he had always been "good" and quiet, and had never been able to refuse anyone a request. His slow progress in school and later on in his profession was because, it appeared, he might otherwise have outstripped his contemporaries and thus injured them. His masochism had therefore in typical fashion originated at first in the turning of his sadism against himself, in the transformation of activity into passivity. In this connection his tendency to self-destruction was by no means slight; the shooting accidents in which his father was nearly killed led, after a turning against himself, to his exposing himself recklessly in the direct line of enemy fire during the war; he was utterly unconscious of his own intention in so doing.

This transformation of sadism into masochism coincided with the reversion to the feminine attitude already mentioned. One had the impression that the compulsory inhibition of aggression due to the castration anxiety had been, so to speak, turned to advantage by the feminine attitude, with the view of extracting the maximum of pleasure from a situation of enforced deprivation. This outlet would not have been possible had a previous object love for the father not pointed the way to it. And of course the masochistic "depression" could also occasionally be used for the sadistic tormenting of other persons.

Analysis of the various repetitions in the transference of this all-important turning against the self showed that the *moral masochism,* the ceaseless self-punishments and self-restrictions, owed their origin to the same regressive transformation as the scanty feminine masochistic impulses. A single episode may be given as an example of many others similar to it:

While traveling to meet a woman friend he took part in a game of chance with some unknown men on the train and lost a sum of money which for a man in his circumstances was very large. As a result of this loss he could not pay the analyst his current fee, nor take the intended excursion with his friend. He was surprised that the analyst neither scolded nor punished him on this account; immediately on reaching the end of his journey he had said to his friend penitently that she ought to beat him. It occurred to him further that during the journey he had felt an urgent need to defecate, but had not paid any attention to this in the excitement of the game; it was not until later that he satisfied this need and soiled his fingers in doing so.

There are several points in this material that we are able to observe very clearly: (a) The strata-like structure of the feminine and infantile attitudes in masochism. (b) The eroticizing of the need for punishment. The repetition of the passive, feminine attitude evoked by the analysis leads to self-punishment in the form of loss of money. This loss, however, is at the same time a "crime due to a sense of guilt," as well as a sadistic injury of the father (analyst) and the mother (friend), and a repetition of the offense that needed punishment—a passive homosexual act. The punishment which he seeks for this, the request to be beaten, is again a satisfaction of a purely passive sexual trend. (c) The coincidence of regression to the feminine stage with regression to the anal. (d) The progressive building up in layers of feminine and moral masochism. *The regression from morality to the oedipus complex* is clearly evidenced in the need, following on self-punishment (itself also a crime), to be thrashed in punishment by his father or his mistress. The penalizing superego in this case is the surrogate of the actual father, from whom the patient seeks punishment as a form of regressive instinctual satisfaction. This falls into line with the fact that the patient grew more and more insistent in his requests to the analyst for *punishment* or—*hypnosis*. He had heard that Professor Forster was not particularly mild in his treatment of pathological patients, and he wished to go to him to be cured of his impotence. "He would make a thorough examination of my penis, and then give me a good scolding."

He also displayed unmistakably another unpleasant concomitant of moral masochism: the negative therapeutic reaction. As a result of the interpretation of his self-punishments his self-reproaches became gradually more conscious, and his "depressions" approximated more and more to pure melancholia.

The determining mother-identification was established in the ego totally unknown to the patient, who was constantly engaged in the endeavor to imitate his father. In vivid contrast to his supposed ideal, his conduct in life was like his mother's. His exhibitionistic and other instinctual characteristics could be traced to the behavior of his mother, while his father's abrupt temperament furnished him with the material and occasion for his fantasies.

This mother-identification was rendered possible by:

(a) *An early object-relation to the father,* which was continued in the adoption of the father into his superego; this had a further existence in the borrowed sense of guilt which will be discussed later on.

(b) *An anal eroticism of extraordinary strength,* which accompanied the sado-masochistic fantasies and was again regressively cathected at the same time as the genital inhibition of aggression took place. The copious anal symptoms of the patient showed clear traces of the mother-identification. Even his dread of castration was here regressively transferred to the anal zone. He had the impression that there was something behind in his body that was cut in two. He even realized an anal castration in his childhood by breaking a chamber pot under him and injuring himself on the seat, and later when he was grown up by undergoing an intestinal operation, of which he formed a similar conception.

(c) *Early visual sexual observations of his parents,* which activated the bisexual attitude, and found its issue in the sight of the maternal genitalia that had such important results. A whole series of screen memories and dreams suggested that an observation of this kind should be presumed. His skepticism, too, could be traced to the doubt whether he had seen correctly, whether there could really be anyone without a penis. In this way he often gave expression to the most grotesque doubts regarding psychoanalysis. In a *déjà vu* kind of reminiscence he recognized that during puberty he had cherished a similar doubt regarding the possibility of sexual intercourse between his parents. Occasionally even at the date of the analysis he expressed manifest scoptophilic desires.

A dream that brought into the transference the traumatic scoptophilic experience and its consequences is given in brief. It consists of two parts, and runs as follows:

(a) *He has to go to the elementary school and start from the very beginning.* (b) *A little girl is about to undergo an operation on the abdominal cavity or on the mouth. He asks a nurse: "Is the operation over? Ah! Has it already begun?" She says: "It is just over" or perhaps something else; she expresses herself very obscurely.*

The day's residues: A short time previously the patient's potency had been restored by the treatment; he took advantage of this by indulging to excess in sexual intercourse with his mistress. The day before it had been said that he might be right in suspecting that this was the cause of his feeling so worn out and "depressed." He therefore made up his mind not to have intercourse again; but, as a matter of fact, that same evening, in defiance of the supposed prohibition, he had intercourse again.

Associations: *For the first part:* When he was at school he always had to hurry in order not to be late. Anyone who was late in arriving at school was punished. When he was afraid he would not be on time his father used to give him roses out of their garden to take with him as a present to the teacher, and in that way he escaped being punished. That, however, should not have been allowed. When he was sixteen years old there had been on one occasion a scandal in the school. A youth had done something, he did not know what, to a little girl, and had been soundly thrashed for it. *"To start over again from the very beginning":* If he could begin the analysis over again from the start, he would be "nicer," would give better associations: i.e., he would bring roses with him for the analyst, so as not to be punished for the coitus of the previous evening.

For the second part: A woman friend of his had an operation for carcinoma in the tongue. The girl in the dream is her daughter. Something in her mouth was cut open, something that had been closed was opened: i.e., a vagina was formed, she was castrated. He now adds that in the dream he was perhaps to have been operated on himself. His intention in being there was to observe the operation. As an adult—it was shortly after the amputation of his finger—he had overheard a coitus through the thin walls of an hotel bedroom. At the operation in the dream everything was very obscure—the instruments and the apparatus were mysteriously large. Then he recalled that when he was about fourteen he had set a little girl of two on a chamber pot, and in so doing he had observed her genitals. Thus he had committed the same transgression as the youth at school—i.e., he replaced his recent misdemeanor in the matter of the coitus by the offense of scoptophilia; in the memory of the thrashing the youth had received as punishment, and in the repeated assertion that bringing the roses was a wrong action, he was therefore asking to be thrashed; he identified himself with a girl, and was castrated. Recently, when he had asked how long it would be before the analysis was finished, he had received just as "obscure" an answer as he had to the analogous question in the dream.

The coitus which preceded the dream had mobilized his sense of guilt in such a way that he desired the penalizing castration and forthwith sexualized it in a passive feminine attitude (identification with the woman). In doing so, however, he betrayed the fact that he considered his inspection of the feminine genitals to be the all-important guilty act.

In connection with his memories of sexual curiosity, it came to his mind that he had the idea he must infect himself with pathogenic bacteria in order to be ill and be made much of: i.e., a disguised idea of self-destruction, which represented self-punishment for the offense of scoptophilia. This was, however, again sexualized in the passive feminine sense; the infecting bacteria represented impregnating spermatozoa.

Once more then we will summarize the development of the mother-identification: The patient, warned as to the reality of castration by his observation of the mother's lack of a penis, first regressed from the genital to the sadistic-anal stage of organization. The reinforced sadism then gave way under castration anxiety into the reaction formation of inhibited aggression, and turned into masochism; this united with the newly cathected anal eroticism and wakened his former love for his father in such a way that a transition from father-identification to mother-identification was the result.

In order to gain a complete understanding of the moral masochism we must now continue to follow the vicissitudes of the older father-identification. Its libido flowed only in part back again to the old object relation. Part of the father-identification was retained in the superego; in the recognition that the self-punishments were made use of for satisfying homosexual trends there was implied an admission that the penalizing authority was a surrogate of the father. What further significance, however, was due to the father-identification only became manifest when it came to light with surprising clarity that the sense of guilt was *borrowed* from the father and that this borrowing—quite in the way Freud has described in the passage mentioned before—represented the residue of an old object love toward him.

A little episode, which occurred after repeated discussion of the conditions that have been already described here, may be mentioned. Heaping bitter reproaches on himself—as he now did frequently—the patient declared that he lived too extravagantly; he must discipline himself; he ought, for example, to sell his scarfpin. He informed me a week later in reference to this that his mother was complaining in her letters about his father's irresponsibility; for instance, the week before she had told him in a letter that his father had bought himself an expensive scarfpin.

By his proposal to sell his own scarfpin the patient was saying to his mother in the sense of the oedipus complex: "Just take me, I am better than Father." But he told her this in a peculiar fashion. The reference to his father's offense had mobilized his own sense of guilt; he had to atone for his father's sins.

Many details of the patient's behavior now became intelligible. For instance, he was ashamed when another person got into trouble. He felt that he himself was responsible when acts were censured of a kind for which he was really not at all to blame. The self-reproaches that were now becoming acute in his depression had the same significance as the latent reproaches against the analyst; "the likeness to melancholia" was "unmistakable."

The following facts have to be noticed: The patient had an extraordinary respect for his father, had set up for himself an ideal image of him, though the accounts he occasionally gave of his father's actual behavior did not at all fit in with this ideal. He was thereupon ashamed of his father, but made light of his feelings, and was patently engaged in endeavoring to close his eyes to the contradictions between the ideal father and the real.

But they continued, nevertheless, to exert their influence—to such an extent, indeed, that *it seemed as if he had committed his father's offenses himself, and was being called to account for it by the ideal father.*

For instance, it was remarkable that the patient's sense of guilt—first unconsciously, then consciously—should be aimed so particularly at his sexual life, as if he were a horrible debauchee. He quite groundlessly reproached himself with infidelity to his mistress and was oppressed after every occasion on which he had been in her company. The suspicion was now put to him that possibly his father had committed the offense of the (imagined) dissipation and infidelity, but it was indignantly thrust aside, although since he had been grown up he had already heard of two girls to whom his father had made sexual approaches. On his return, however, from a short visit to his parents, he related with amazement that he had only then noticed how his father would cast lascivious looks at any woman and frequently made offensive remarks about them; this had no doubt always been so, only he had never noticed it before. We could only express entire agreement with this supposition. Evidently as a child he had felt that similar behavior on his father's part was an *infidelity toward his mother,* but had refused to accept the knowledge implied in this observation, and by adopting ("borrowing") the guilt he turned the reproaches concerning excess and infidelity against himself. The father's infidelity gave him indeed access to his mother, made it possible for him to woo her—as we saw in the case of the scarfpin—and the oedipus guilt could also hide itself behind the borrowed sense of guilt that related to the "infidelity." This now furnished an explanation of what at first seemed so interesting and paradoxical—i.e., that the sense of guilt which the patient felt in connection with every other sexual action was lacking precisely in connection with that mother-figure with whom he had had happy relations: the sense of guilt borrowed from his father in relation to his *infidelity* of necessity made itself more noticeable in the case of persons unlike his mother than in that of persons like her.

The analysis was also able to discover the prototype—perhaps the original one—for the infidelity of his father; a sister of his father's had stayed with them for some time and frequent quarrels occurred, the aunt and the father taking sides against the mother. The child had a fantasy that the father had taken the aunt for his wife and forsaken the mother. This grievous accusation he then diverted from the ideal father-imago and turned against himself. Precisely the same took place here as in a case of moral masochism described by Lampl, where the guilt-borrowing took its origin in the father's adultery (in this case actual).[23]

The borrowing of guilt can only be explained by an original impulse to commit the same sin as the father. As a matter of fact, as a child the patient had tried to make a sexual attack on this aunt but had been repelled. This wish to imitate the father was frustrated by castration anxiety. He may not do all that the father does, but he has to take on himself the penalties his father merited. "Thus the shadow of the object fell on the ego." [24] The paternal superego demands punishment, not only for all the actions of the ego disapproved by it, but also for those of the real father. [25] The adoption of the father into the ego had of course miscarried, but had nevertheless in some degree been effected, though certainly not in a manner approved by the ego. It was a compromise between the struggles of the id (to enjoy the father's sexual freedom) and of the superego (not to do the same as the father), and the ego had to suffer from it.

The father-ideal had thus become independent of the actual father. It had to be kept intact at all costs. In this way, however, there accrued very great libidinal gains in the direction of passive homosexuality, which became predominant after the regression: he could now overrate the beloved father without restraint, and the self-punishment which took the place of the original genital wish (to imitate the father) was enjoyed in a regressive fashion as a *passive feminine gratification through the father.*

When we recall that Freud has recently described [26] as a powerful motive, urging towards homosexual object choice, regard for the father or fear of him (the mechanism, namely, of "withdrawing from rivalry with him"), we can see now that "guilt-borrowing" is also such a form of withdrawal. By its means everything is permitted to the actual father; he is placed beyond criticism; while the ego with its inhibitions of aggression not only desists from all aggressiveness against the father but is even punished for his misdeeds. We know how great an increase of (unconscious) homosexuality in our case went hand in hand with this withdrawal. The idea that is so fundamental in religion and ethics of *suffering for the guilt of others* may have its roots in a similar mechanism.

There was abundant material in the transference to confirm our hypothesis. This material consisted of an alternation between occasional attempts of the hitherto inhibited aggression to break out, and exacerbations of the depressions, which became more and more like pure melancholia. He cast the same reproaches alternately at the analyst and at himself. On the one hand he developed a quite extraordinary attentiveness to the "little sins" of the analyst, and on the other he declared that the analyst could do all that he himself could not do. While he lived a licentious life, the analyst certainly never had intercourse with women. He said this after he had seen a lady leaving the consulting-room and had spun fantasies about a relation between the analyst and her. He thus repeated directly his behavior in relation to his infantile sexual observations of his father. He does not wish to have seen anything, and feels that he is guilty himself. More and more memories gradually emerged of scenes in which his father had not conducted himself in accordance with his ideal of him. He had forgotten that he had once seen his father's penis, but had reproached himself on account of his exhibitionistic inclinations. Gradually the material of a normal oedipus complex came through, and the cure of his impotence ensued entirely in the form of a liberation of the aggression and a struggle against his homosexuality. He was potent for the first time, when in a sudden uprush of defiance, he kept his mistress with him all night against the expressed prohibition of his landlord. Later on erection took place after a castration ceremonial, the thought suddenly springing up in him like a revelation, "I am really alone with her!" It appeared that up till then he had always felt himself threatened from behind by a gigantic ghost on every occasion of the sexual act.

We know now the fate of the identifications with both parents which had begun in the primal scene: the identification with the father had partly undergone a regressive change into (repressed) homosexual object love, and partly had been idealized and established in the superego; there it raged against the ego, driving it to perpetual self-injuries, and affording by the sexualization of these self-injuries a homosexual gratification to the id. The identification with the mother had been effected chiefly in the ego; it dominated the actual character of the patient and was completely unconscious. He would prefer to be like his father and was—without knowing it—like his mother. The opposition between the two parental identifications was similar to the one which Reich has described as a type of masculine "mistaken sex-identity."[27] We might say that the perpetual self-punishments signified an intrapsychic continuation of the abuse he had as a child heard his father giving his mother.

We reach the same result as so many other psychoanalytic writers do at the conclusion of their investigations. We find that a great part of what we have discovered has long ago been uttered in Freud's writings. The "adoption of guilt" turns out to be a new way of regarding a process which was described in *Group Psychology and the Analysis of the Ego* and even in *The Interpretation of Dreams* as "hysterical identification on the basis of the same etiological claim."[28] If all the girls in a class at school imitate the attacks of another girl, instead of, as they really wish, having a similar love affair to hers,[29] then in their case, too, the identification has been effected only in the negative form. In "A Child Is Being Beaten," too, Freud has, in the first place, depicted the danger for the masculine character of a regressive homosexual fantasy of being beaten by the father, leading to perpetual self-injury being inflicted throughout life, and has further pointed out that the outcome of a feminine attitude without (manifest) homosexual object choice is "specially remarkable" in the development of the passive fantasy of being beaten.[30] Our patient had had the fantasy of being beaten by a woman only very seldom and with very slight affect. We believe we have shown why *moral* masochism with its strong ingredient of the death instinct was the particular form which the patient's masochism took. But that also made a "feminine attitude without a homosexual object choice" possible for him. His homosexuality, through his introjection of his father and his unconscious rage against himself, became a drama that was enacted within his personality, and hence required no real object.

IV

We have little more to add. We hope we have succeeded in reproducing the impression received in the treatment of patients of this class. That impression may be regarded as an immediate clinical confirmation of the Freudian doctrine of the instincts, and the view that the sense of guilt is a unique, primitive, ruthless thing, which would not shrink from the destruction of the patient's own ego, and is not synonymous with passive sexual libido. It is the clinical representative of the mute death instincts. We have seen that in the neurotic clinical picture it appears always in instinctual fusion with the more noisy sexual impulses, that the proportion of both components in the fusion can be very different, and that this combination is extremely important for prognosis. We have further got to know a series of possible connections between the instinctual demands of the id and the demands of the superego for punishment. In the first case we see, particularly in the symptoms, the various condensations of deed and punishment, the quality of punishment attaching to deeds and that of wish fulfillment to punishments; the combination of "criminality from a sense of guilt," punishment as a license for further sins, and the part played by external projection of the superego in paranoid neurotics and probably also in criminals. In the second case we saw the genesis and constitution of moral masochism; the excessive sexualizing in it of all penalizing actions; the turning of the sadistic trends against the patient's self, and the change of the normal oedipus complex into the inverted form as a preliminary; further, the mechanism of guilt-borrowing as its most advantageous expression. Unfortunately, in regard to the therapeutic aspect, we cannot say anything more hopeful than Freud has already said in his footnote on the subject of the borrowed sense of guilt.

NOTES

1. S. Freud, "Some Character-Types Met with in Psycho-Analytic Work," II, III, *Coll. Pap.*, Vol. IV, London, Hogarth, 1948.
2. S. Freud, "The Economic Problem of Masochism," *Coll. Pap.*, Vol. II, London, Hogarth, 1948, p. 263.
3. S. Freud, *The Ego and the Id*, London, Hogarth, 1947, p. 72 footnote.
4. In his lectures at the Berlin Psychoanalytic Institute in 1924, S. Rado suggested original ambivalence and instinctual defusion arising at a very early stage and there, to all appearances, irreversible, as constituting the limits of susceptibility to analytical treatment. In the face of destructive instinctual components which cannot be erotically bound our therapeutic efforts are as yet powerless.
5. Cf. the competent researches of T. Reik, *Gestaendniszwang und Strafbeduerfnis*, Vienna, Int. Psa. Verlag, 1925; F. Alexander, "A Metapsychological Description of the Process of Cure," *Int. J. Psa.*, Vol. 6, 1925; and W. Reich, *Der triebhafte Charakter*, Vienna, Int. Psa. Verlag, 1925.
6. S. Freud, "Certain Neurotic Mechanisms in Jealousy, Paranoia and Homosexuality," *Coll. Pap.*, Vol. II, p. 242.
7. T. Reik, *op. cit.*, p. 213.
8. Cf. G. Groddeck, "Wunscherfuellungen der irdischen und goettlichen Strafen," *Int. Z. Psa.*, Vol. 6, 1920.
9. T. Reik, *op. cit.*, pp. 208–209.
10. S. Hollós, "Die Psychoneurose eines Fruehgeborenen," *Int. Z. Psa.*, Vol. 10, 1924.
11. The clear insight the patient had into his pyschic mechanisms will not astonish us, having regard to the nature of his symptoms.
12. T. Reik, *op. cit.*, p. 94.
13. F. Boehm, "Beitraege zur Psychologie der Homosexualitaet, III. Homosexualitaet und Oedipuskomplex," *Int. Z. Psa.*, Vol. 12, 1926.
14. S. Freud, "On Narcissism: An Introduction," *Coll. Pap.*, Vol. IV.
15. S. Freud, *Beyond the Pleasure Principle*, London, Hogarth, 1948, p. 33.
16. S. Freud, "Certain Neurotic Mechanisms in Jealousy, Paranoia and Homosexuality," *Coll. Pap.*, Vol. II.
17. S. Freud, "On Narcissism: An Introduction," *Coll. Pap.*, Vol. IV, p. 53.
18. S. Freud, "Psycho-Analytic Notes upon an Autobiographical Account of a Case of Paranoia (Dementia Paranoides)," *Coll. Pap.*, Vol. III, London, Hogarth, 1948.
19. W. Reich, *op. cit.*, p. 108.
20. S. Freud, "A Child Is Being Beaten," *Coll. Pap.*, Vol. II, p. 193.

21. S. Freud, "The Passing of the Oedipus-Complex," *Coll. Pap.*, Vol. II.
22. F. Boehm, "Beitraege zur Psychologie der Homosexualitaet, II. Ein Traum eines Homosexuellen," *Int. Z. Psa.*, Vol. 8, 1922.
23. H. Lampl, "Contributions to Case History. A Case of Borrowed Sense of Guilt," *Int. J. Psa.*, Vol. 8, 1927.
24. S. Freud, "Mourning and Melancholia," *Coll. Pap.*, Vol. IV, p. 159.
25. Many traits of the borrowed sense of guilt could be explained by the idea, "What I do to myself my father should do to himself," and reminded us in this way of the "magic gestures" which Liebermann has described in his "Monosymptomatischen Neurosen" (lecture at the Salzburg Congress, 1924). We mentioned that the *anal* symptoms of our patient were based on the mother-identification. Now he had to defecate immediately after taking any food. That meant that the mother was not to become pregnant again. He also refused to eat fish, mushrooms, or asparagus. His mother, he said, was very fastidious about what she ate.
26. S. Freud, "Certain Neurotic Mechanisms in Jealousy, Paranoia and Homosexuality," *Coll. Pap.*, Vol. II, p. 241.
27. W. Reich, "Mutteridentifizierung auf analer Basis," *Der triebhafte Charakter*, pp. 48 ff.
28. S. Freud, "The Interpretation of Dreams," *The Basic Writings*, New York, Modern Library, 1938, p. 228.
29. S. Freud, *Group Psychology and the Analysis of the Ego*, London, Hogarth, 1948, pp. 64–65.
30. S. Freud, "A Child Is Being Beaten," *Coll. Pap.*, Vol. II, p. 196.

16. The Characteristics of Masochism (An Excerpt)

Theodor Reik

Are there any characteristic elements possessed in common and invariably found in the different forms of masochism? The sexological and psychological literature surely offers sufficient observational material—often one might believe too much—but even today the assertion may be ventured that the phenomenology of masochism has not yet been adequately investigated. That is to say there is still lacking a description of the peculiar features of masochism in its usual forms.

It will be worth while to cite some illustrative material. In the selecting of examples the primary consideration will be that there can be no doubt of their masochistic character. The differences as to sex will be as little considered as the question of whether it concerns a masochistic phantasy or an actual scene of perversion. The three following examples may from this standpoint claim to be representative of the essentials.

A young girl had the following phantasy which showed in the course of many years but trivial variations: it is late evening, she goes through the streets to the butcher-shop which has already closed its shutters. She knocks, when the butcher opens the shutters she says: "Please, I would like to be butchered." He grants her request and lets her in. She undresses at the back of the store and lies down naked on the meatblock. She has to lie there a long time waiting. The butcher is busy cutting up some calves. Once in a while one of his fellow workmen comes by and grasps her body and tests the flesh like an expert testing an animal to be slaughtered. Finally the butcher himself comes and he also tests with his fingers various portions of her body, hauling her about for this purpose as if she were a dead calf. He grabs the butcher

Reprinted by permission of Johns Hopkins University Press, from *American Imago* 1 (1940):26–59.

knife but before he makes a cut puts his finger in her vagina. At this moment she has an orgasm.

The unquestionably masochistic phantasy of this woman can be compared with its counterpart from a man: a 37-year-old father of three children is sexually potent only with the aid of an especially widespread and varied set of phantasies. From among them I will select one at random: To a barbaric idol somewhat like the Phoenician Moloch there is to be sacrificed over a lengthy period a great number of young athletes. They will be undressed and laid on the altar one by one. There is heard the rumble of drums to which are joined the songs of the temple choir. The highpriest followed by other priests approaches. He tests with a critical eye each of the young men. They must satisfy certain requirements as to beauty of form and athletic appearance. The highpriest takes the genital of each victim in his hand and tests its weight and form. Many of the young men will be rejected as distasteful to the god or unworthy of being sacrificed, if the genitals are not pleasing to the priest. The highpriest gives the order for the execution and the ceremony continues. With a sharp cut the genitals and surrounding parts are cut away. The patient who belongs to the visualizing type is able to picture to himself very plastically the progress of the scene. He is himself not a participant, only an onlooker.

Here the question might be raised whether such a phantasy is masochistic or sadistic. During the phantasy, which was used at first in masturbation and only later was called into aid in intercourse with his wife, the ejaculation occurred at the moment when the highpriest showed the knife. The decision as to whether a phantasy is primarily masochistic or is more sadistic in character must be based on information as to whom the person identifies with. In our case it was certain that the day-dreamer identified with one of the victims, usually not the one who was being castrated but with the next who was obliged to look on at the execution of his companions. The patient shared every strong affect of these victims, felt their terror and anxiety with all its signs since he imagined that he himself would experience the same fate in a few moments.

Rather than take the third example from the field of phantasy we will select an actual instance of masochistic perversion. A middle aged man goes from time to time to a prostitute and carries out the following scene: on entering he asks her if she gives Russian lectures. The word is used for masochistic practices in announcements in certain newspapers of his country. In the mind of the patient the expression connotes the terrors of pogroms and scenes in Russian prisons which he has read about. If the girl says yes, he tells her what she has to do. She must scold him as if he were a little boy who has been naughty or has committed some misdeed. She must say to him that he deserves a severe beating with a club and so on. He exposes himself obediently and receives a blow on the buttocks. In many instances the blow is unnecessary since the ejaculation has already occurred. In coitus the patient was impotent.

It is not to be doubted that these three examples are representative of masochism as a perversion. It is perhaps accidental that in none of them does the sensation of pain or the perception of it play any kind of role or receive any significance. Even in the phantasy of the execution of the young men there can be no question of pleasure in picturing that, rather is the pleasure in the idea of the anxiety and terror. What was pleasurable in the ideas, we should remember, was the fright the next victim must feel at the moment of castration of his predecessor. The castration itself appeared in the phantasies merely as a surgical operation. No stress was laid on the sensation of pain.

If we have excluded then, the pleasure in pain as an inevitable element what remains as a common factor? Surely everything else that hitherto was considered as characteristic of masochism: the passive nature, the feeling of impotence and the submission to another person, the terrible, degrading and shameful treatment by this person and the sexual excitement which appears in consequence of this treatment. There is nothing new in all this. Yet we intend to produce something new, something not previously disclosed as characteristic or at least something which has been insufficiently valued. These characteristics must appear as those which necessarily and inevitably constitute the essence of masochism. Naturally they do not always appear in the same form nor with the same intensities, yet they are always present. Where they are lacking we cannot speak of masochism. In what follows I wish to describe three such constituent elements, which can be demonstrated in masochism as a perversion as well as in its desexualized forms. They are: the *peculiar significance of phantasy*, the necessity of a distinctive course of excitement or the *suspense factor*, and the *demonstrative character* of the phenomena. It will also appear that these three factors are intimately associated, that they are only different modes of expression of a more deeply hidden essential.

THE SIGNIFICANCE OF PHANTASY FOR MASOCHISM

If we review the examples cited above feature by feature, then the significance of the phantasy as a preparation for and means of producing sexual tension cannot be doubted. The young girl in the butchershop scene must wait, until the butcher has finished his other business. When he turns to her, first must come the testing of the meat, then the feeling of and hauling about of the body. The prisoner in the phantasy of the young men must participate in all the religious ceremonials, experience the slow approach of the priests, the preparations for the execution and the castration of his comrades. He must listen to the cries of anguish of the other victims, must share in their moanings and writhings. The prelude to the scene which the masochist plays with the prostitute is more important than the blow on the buttocks. The entrance, the speech, question and answer, the scolding, the forced and yet desired exposure of the person, the waiting for punishment were the features designated by the patient himself as those most important and essential for producing pleasure.

This peculiar significance of phantasy for the masochistic excitement is demonstrable not only in the later forms. It can be observed already in the original scenes which gave rise to the perversion. For example, take the basic scene in the case of the young Dutch girl. As a child she had lived in the neighborhood of a slaughterhouse. Because of his trade the parents would not associate with the butcher although he was an uncle. This circumstance may have contributed to the fact that the activities of this uncle had a mysterious significance for the child and her somewhat older brother. The two had many opportunities to watch the activities of the butcher-uncle and his fellow workmen. The children watched closely when their uncle cut up animals and then played, in the garden attached to the house, a game of "slagertje" (Dutch for butcher). The little girl laid on the bench in the garden and the brother carried on like a butcher. First he was busy elsewhere, came at last to where his sister lay and played at cutting her up as he had seen his uncle do. With light flat strokes of the extended open hand he cut the body—still clothed—into pieces. The preliminaries to the procedure were themselves already in some dim way pleasure-toned for the girl. The light blows on the body produced sensations in the clitoris. The example shows that already in the situation where the masochism originated phantasy is significant for sexual stimulation, or speaking more exactly, is so in one of the situations decisive for its genesis. To wait to be slaughtered, an anticipation of being handled, stirred up, even at that time, a sexual tension in the little girl.

Another requirement is satisfied by the masochistic phantasy when, as in my patient's Moloch scene, it anticipates terrible future possibilities. The material for this phantasy was again easily recognizable as a working over of childhood ideas. The religious clothing came from later years and showed the traces of the effects of a varied reading. When the patient was a small boy his some years older brother was operated on for a phimosis and later showed the little one his wound. The later phantasies of the boy sprang from his impressions then, and were directed at his good but stern father before whom he felt very helpless and afraid. He must have assumed at that time, that he also later like the brother would have his penis operated on by his father or by a doctor. In this idea appear homosexual stirrings which had mixed with those springing from the need for punishment and became arrested as a reaction to masturbation. In the Moloch phantasy there is to be recognized in the young men before the altar a series of brothers among whom he has his place. It is a noteworthy characteristic that he identifies with the one who watches the operation and experiences the anxiety of him who is next.

Nevertheless, is the significance of phantasy for sexual stimulation actually so surpassing just in masochism? Its role in normal sexual life is certainly also not denied a degree of importance. Does masochism show a departure here from other perversions in which the preliminaries of a desired situation are demonstrably so prevalent in phantasy? It is indeed the essence of perversion that the phantasies linger on the preparatory activities instead of progressing to genital satisfaction. We may compare, then, the significance which phantasy has in the sexual stimulation in sadism and in peeping. Naturally also in the sadist and the voyeur the situation desired comes about in phantasy and through such ideas produces a sexual tension. It would seem then that the difference reduces to a plus and minus of the excitability. However, this is not the case. The difference is rather, that the masochist cannot miss the phantasy, that it represents a preliminary which is indispensable, a condition *sine qua non*. The sadist or the voyeur is also capable of satisfaction without such preparation. If a voyeur out walking, let us say, in the woods has opportunity to see a woman exposed, no preliminary phantasy is necessary to produce in him strong sexual excitement. Compare with this the situation about as it would be in a masochist. Let us assume that his specific condition for excitement is to receive a box on the ear from a corpulent woman and to be cursed at. Let us assume further, that this situation eventuates without preparation, that is, without the usual preliminary phantasies. The man in question, let us say, goes peaceably out on the street, a huge woman comes up to him, showers him with words of abuse and gives him a mighty box on the ear. To give the scene some verisimilitude it is only necessary to assume that the poor man is the victim of a mistaken identity. The woman so prone to strike believes she has recognized in him a man who had wronged her.

Will the masochist be sexually stimulated by the sudden attack? That is almost impossible. Of course it is quite possible, that the scene will subsequently be used in phantasy to produce sexual stimulation, but its momentary effect will not be of this sort even though it exactly reproduces a desired situation. This assumed situation is designed to make clear the significance of phantasy for the masochistic gratification. Here the assertion is not, that phantasy is not essential as a preparation in the other perversions, but that for masochism it is absolutely indispensable.

Yet there are two objections to such an opinion. The first would bring up that phantasy is of especial importance as a preliminary in exhibitionism. Experience shows that this is really the case. We are thus compelled to make a correction and are obliged to say: in the perversions with a passive instinctual goal there is a particular necessity for a preliminary phantasy in order that sexual excitement may be attained. Psychologically this is quite intelligible, for these perversions depend not alone on the will of the person in question but as much or even more on the will of the particular object. It is left to this partner, how one shall react. If his reaction is not the desired one, then no or only a slight sexual effect is produced. This reaction is more important for the masochist and the exhibitionist than for the sadist and the voyeur, who are less dependent on the behavior of their partner. It has been reported that once in some woods near Paris an exhibitionist suddenly appeared to an English woman and—it was at a lonely spot on a winter evening—exposed his genitals. The woman with great presence of mind went up to him and said: "My good man, won't you catch cold?" One may venture to assume that this thoughtfulness had a very moderating effect. For all that it is not quite the case that phantasy is as important for the exhibitionist as for the masochist. A group of young girls who have just come along the path can instantly bring it about that the exhibitionist decides to expose himself.

Another objection has it that in certain cases the sudden appearance of a detail can suffice to generate a masochistic excitement. Thus a colleague referred me to a case treated by him in which the beating of a dog became the central point of a masochistic phantasy. Later the mere sight of a dog whip was sufficient to produce sexual excitement in the patient. It thus appears that in such a case a frank preliminary phantasy is needless. But this is only the appearance, for in actuality the preparation is very extensive and of ancient date. The material has been gone over so often, that everything is prepared. The glimpse of the dog-whip is simply the factor that stirs into activity this already prepared psychic material. Such a glimpse reminds us of something that can come forward at any moment because it is always ready. It is exactly as when we hear faintly touched on the piano the first notes of an old familiar melody. As a counter-part I would refer to the patient with the Moloch phantasy cited above. A low degree of sexual excitement could be detected by him when he saw strong young men in certain postures, indeed sometimes, even when he merely looked at their photograph. These postures had to be of the sort that reminded him of the posture of the victim in the Moloch phantasy. Thus the form of a young man lying on a couch brought back to him, with the corresponding sexual excitement, the image of the sacrificial victim on the altar of the terrible idol. The objection then is not so strong as it would seem. There is in these cases not a less but a greater degree of phantasy preparation. The fetishistic mechanism which is effective in such cases is the well known displacement on to a detail, whereby the detail becomes a substitute for and representative of the whole. In this there is nothing peculiar to the excitability of any perversion. The sexual erotogenic effects of such surrogate details can be shown also in the field of normal sexuality. A trifling sketch in a recent newspaper pictured a young woman stopping on a street corner to fix her garter. For this purpose, of course, she had to raise her skirt a bit. One of two men happening to pass by remarks to the other: "It's not much, but it gives you a kick."

The objections we have considered were not adequate to make us revise our opinion. It still stands then that the preliminary phantasy has an especial importance for masochism. The phantasy is the primary thing. Masochistic practices are only an acting out of preceding phantasies. Every thorough analysis shows that the masochistic perversion is a realization in practice of imagined situations with which the person has long concerned himself. The actual scene corresponds thus to the staging of a drama and is related to the phantasy as is the performance to the dramatist's conception. It is exposed to the same accidents and necessary adaptations to the means at hand and is just as dependent on the mood and concurrence of the actors. Only rarely does the performance surpass the ideas of the author. More often, even as with the masochistic scene, it falls short of the conception. It is in accordance with the theatrical element in masochism that it seldom becomes a matter of "deadly earnest" as with the sadistic perversion.

Some unconnected remarks about the peculiarities of masochistic phantasy are here in order. A particular feature is the tendency to synchronization, an admirable expression I obtained from the patient with the Moloch phantasies. A phenomenon he had observed in himself was that the sexual excitement ran a temporal course corresponding completely to the course of events in the phantasy which, incidentally, proceeded at a pace in such consonance with his feelings that it was clear he identified masochistically with the victim. Thus the ejaculation always occurred in the Moloch phantasy at approximately the same place, when the highpriest produced the knife.

Striking and certainly in keeping with the essence of masochism is the conservativism or tenacity of the phantasy. Masochistic situations are frequently maintained for years with little or no change and are found in the phantasies to remain exciting. Such alterations as do occur are usually restricted to trifling displacements and substitutions of persons, times and places while the main theme, if it may be called such, is adhered to. After long intervals, however, great and very extensive alterations are introduced bringing about a complete change of theme, a process comparable perhaps to the reform in an old institution produced by the introduction of efficiency. The masochistic situation appears to be wholly altered. The new content in turn will be maintained for a long time and with little variation. At intervals the old "worn out" phantasies obtrude again into the picture. It is thus possible to distinguish long periods during which the psychic processes are dominated by this or that sharply circumscribed phantasy content. The patient referred to above spoke of these phantasy groups as "cycles." So he could speak of the period of the Aztec cycle during which he was sexually excited by the idea of the sacrifice of prisoners in the Aztec kingdom, or of the queen cycle, a phantasy group in which a terrible empress subjected her lovers to horrible torments and so on. One gets the impression that after a long while the masochistic phantasy loses its exciting quality and is superseded. It was only after considerable analytic experience that I became convinced that this tenacity of phantasy is characteristic of masochism.

It is noteworthy that masochistic phantasy and action are not restricted to the visual field. According to my impressions speech also plays a great part. There are verbal masochists who become sexually excited when they are insultingly abused or humiliated. These situations are frequently anticipated and enjoyed in their phantasies. If the scene should then become actual, the masochist will expect and hope to hear just those insulting and abusive words of which a certain choice, succession or emphasis appears important for great sexual stimulation.

The material in masochistic phantasies is more frequently capable of extension and circumscription than in other perversions. It can assume the form of a story and bring many people on its phantasy stage to act and suffer. It frequently finds support in the patient's reading, the influence of which can be clearly detected in its conformation. In one case observed by me the phantasies of a school boy took as a point of departure for many situations that of Marsyas who was flayed by Apollo. This nucleus proved to be so strong and persistent that twenty years later in altered form it still exercised its exciting effect when the man saw in the Brussels Museum the picture by David of the flaying of the judge Marsyas.

Related to a characteristic to be discussed shortly, the factor of suspense, is the fact that masochistic phantasies cling to, select or test out details. The fact is, however, that the different pictures or scenes undergo a selection according to their capacity for producing sexual excitation and if they do not prove adequate are discarded, as in a kaleidoscope different individual pictures appear and persist for a longer or shorter period. Naturally it occurs that some aspects of the phantasy are effective for long periods and are later rejected depending on a diminution of the sexually stimulating value. To the conservatism of the masochistic phantasy then, there is opposed a need for variation which represents only an expression of the psychic alterations in the phantasying person. Whether a phantasy "succeeds" or not depends on various factors. A successful phantasy is, of course, one giving or accompanied by a satisfactory orgasm. With other phantasies there is none or, at most, a flat orgasm.

It is not always clear beforehand with whom the phantasying person identifies. Surely with the victim, the passive person in the phantasy, but also with the active terrible figure, frequently also with a nonparticipating onlooker, though one to whom is known the feelings of the active and of the suffering figures. The often quoted stanza of the masochistically inclined Charles Baudelaire:

"Je suis la plaie et le couteau!
Je suis le soufflet et la joue!
Je suis les membres et la roue,
Et la victime et le bourreau!"
L'Héautontimorouménos. *Les Fleurs du Mal.* Edition critique. Paris, 1917.

is in this sense incomplete. The masochist is in his phantasies the spectator at the execution and experiences the pleasure of watching which clearly seems to be an attenuated or displaced sadistic gratification.

The property of evoking sexual excitation is certainly not the only factor involved in the selection of the images referred to above. Other factors such as conformity with the reality situation are influential. Frequently the imagination dwells on the details until they shall seem to conform to reality, arranges and alters the situation until it shall show no gross contradiction with other details. It is the more striking then, that at other times the phantasying person is completely indifferent to such considerations. In the Moloch phantasy, for instance, the patient many times dwelt for long on the idea of a red-hot grill, on which the victims were to be laid, striving to make this detail technically correct in all particulars. On the contrary he gave no thought to the great anachronisms introduced into his phantasy; impossibilities with respect to time and place were, of course, not hidden to his observation but they didn't concern him. This attitude could be compared to the behavior of a poet who sometimes brings his story into conformity with some particulars of an historic event only to permit himself great poetic license at other points. This patient, for instance, had had a long and extensive interest in Mexico and Peru, knew not only the general works dealing with these lands but also special investigations on their sacrificial rites and had even himself searched the remains of these dead cultures for altars, temples and so on. Of course, he was well aware that the ritual sacrifice with the Aztecs was not a castration, nevertheless in his phantasies he insisted on the notion of castration which excited him. As an example of such a phantasy: an English officer has fallen into the hands of the ancient Aztecs, who periodically make ceremonial sacrifice of prisoners to the god by castrating them. Up to the moment of execution the prisoner dwells in the house of the man who captured him and who also will officiate at the sacrifice. On one occasion he takes the officer who in general is treated in a very friendly manner, into a room in which are displayed as trophies the genitalia of earlier victims. At this point there enters into the phantasy a characteristic hesitation or deliberation: just how are the genitals displayed? In the beginning the patient imagined that they were deposited in a chest. This idea was rejected in the course of the phantasy because the flesh would become decayed and shrunken. Also the possibility of their being stuffed like a dead bird was discarded. The phantasier finally decided they should be preserved in bottles of alcohol. Here is the covert intrusion of a childhood experience, the bit of reality from which the whole started. As mentioned above the older brother of the patient, who was four years old at the time, was operated on because of a phimosis. The youngster must in his imagination have connected the operation with a cutting off of the penis. Later on he could persuade himself by looking that the penis of the brother although wounded was still present, but this impression was presumably less strong than the earlier one which had the character of reality for his phantasies. Some years later the old impression must have been reanimated when the same brother underwent an operation for appendicitis. This time the patient was shown the amputated appendix preserved in alcohol. Here then is that feature out of the reality which has crept back into the phantasies incognito by way of a detour. Some of the material out of which the phantasy was constructed is clearly recognizable. The doubt relating to the detail about the means of preservation represents surely the one then arising in the child, and probably others still preserved in the Unconscious of the adult: if father castrates his son, will I also be castrated? The patient's attitude to his phantasies was ambiguous, on the one hand he devoted to their elaboration a great deal of energy and cleverness, on the other he found them ridiculous and was ashamed of them and did not understand why such grotesque stuff could so intensively occupy his mind and excite him. . . .

A Peculiarity of the Masochistic Achievement
of Pleasure

The other characteristic feature of masochism is an especial form of getting sexual gratification which, hitherto, has received at most inadequate or superficial consideration. The tension is the clearest indication of the phenomenon. Two features show up here and are demonstrably different from anything in normal sexuality: the preponderance of the anxiety factor and the tendency to prolongation of the act. The sexual tension in masochistic experience shows more strongly than in the normal a vacillation between the pleasurable and the anxious and a tendency to being maintained as long as possible, in opposition to the natural impulse towards discharge. Apparently there is an intrinsic relation between these two features. First of all one is tempted to assume that the vacillation between anxiety and pleasure brings to expression an uncertainty which is designed to avoid a decision. However, a deeper insight into the psychic facts corrects this guess. While in normal sexual life the tension shows no note of anxiety or, at least, none worth speaking about, this is a regular feature in the experience of the masochist. This bit of anxiety always receives support either in the phantasy or in the scene itself. There is a difference between the normal and the masochistic tension-curve which in English can be made clear in a word. For the curve of normal sexual excitement the word "tension" (Spannung) is completely adequate, for the other the best designation is "suspense." These two words may be contrasted. Tension denotes a simple state of excitation in which there is a tendency to reach a climax which, it is self-evident, will be subsequently discharged. Suspense on the contrary connotes the element of the uncertain, the hesitating, the being poised and at the same time the idea that there is no definite duration or termination to this state. One can speak of an "agony of suspense" thus designating the painful, even unbearable element in it. But the words can also designate the expectations of children as they sit watching the closed door on Christmas eve awaiting the appearance of Saint Nicholas with his presents. The public that awaits the verdict of the jury is in "suspense" just as is the reader of a detective story. The German language knows no corresponding expression. At best perhaps the "Hangen und Bangen" of Goethe approximates like "suspense" to something of the quality of pleasurable anxiety of a state of excitation. It is certainly no accident that being hung on some kind of contraption is one of the masochistic practices. It is described by perverse devotees as affording an especial pleasure. Presumably it gives a functional objectivity to the suspense sensation.

The second characteristic of the tension-curve in masochism is a tendency to prolongation of the state while the opposite intention of resolving the tension is subordinated. We will put it cautiously: it seems as if such an intention existed in masochism. From a superficial point of view it is possible to believe that the masochist strives to prolong the pleasure and consequently drags out the tension in the sense of all pleasure: "For joys all want— eternity."[1] But this is only the appearance; a more critical investigation shows that his striving is to prolong the forepleasure, or what is more important, to avoid the end-pleasure. Here masochism can be distinguished from all of those other perversions which cling to the stage of the fore-pleasure. In masochism the end-pleasure is avoided *because it involves anxiety.*

The postponement and ultimate renunciation of the end-pleasure can easily be explained by an analogy: we all know children who leave a bit of food of which they are especially fond until the last. If this tendency to reserve the best of the food for the end continues such a habit could appear to a teacher as a valuable asset for life. In the meantime he should not overlook the danger which results from the hypertrophy of this practice: that the child finally renounces entirely that particular bit of food. The reservation has become a renunciation, from the training in self-control an ascetic characteristic. I know of a case in which a youngster put a Swiss pastry of which he was very fond into a box to preserve it and kept up a continual struggle against his desire to eat it. When finally he did decide to do so and after several days opened the box he found the chocolate cake quite spoiled.

The corresponding sexual behavior is not uncommonly observed at puberty: a typical form of masturbation consists in avoiding discharge by interrupting the manual activity and diverting the thoughts. After a while the masturbation is resumed and the excitement again cut off just before ejaculation. The youth given to this sort of masturbation frequently does this for the sake of maintaining the sexual pleasure as long as possible but the result is usually that ejaculation occurs prematurely and without satisfaction or is entirely omitted: thus there is renunciation of the end-pleasure of orgasm. . . .

Up to this point we have considered the suspense factor only as developing its effectiveness in sexual intercourse in the absence of masochistic practices. When the individual has not experienced punishment, abuse or pain before sexual gratification the intervention of the suspense factor will inhibit the attainment of end-pleasure. There is thus an alternative: preliminary punishment, humiliation or pain—orgasm; or, no preliminary pain—suspense and no orgasm, eventually end-discontent. Expressed in another way: if the masochist has experienced directly physical pain or psychic discomfort he is quite capable of having the orgasm and of feeling intense pleasure. The climax of excitation is normal. If no serious discomfort has preceded, there appears in place of the excitation climax a suspense, which later leads to disturbance of potency and finally to impotence. This picture of the alternative is correct beyond a doubt. It can be demonstrated in any case of masochistic attitude. . . .

We have said that masochistic practices were offshoots of phantasies; they show that the masochist is seeking the way of return to reality. To avoid anxiety he assumes beforehand the burden of suffering, displeasure or punishment which threatens him, in order to be able to enjoy a sexual pleasure. In this sense he represents a pendant to the ascetic or saint who has visitations of sexuality. The masochist atones in advance. He scourges himself or has himself scourged that he may then without punishment have the orgasm. The ascetic punishes himself because of the emerging sexual excitement. With the masochist the discontent is wiped out by the sexual gratification, with the ascetic or saint the sexual excitement by the discontent or by the self-punishment. By association and contrast the two types become clearer if one opposes concrete examples of each. There are countless typical cases in which a corporal chastisement, which the masochist inflicts on himself flows over into sexual excitement and orgasm. It seems that a definite degree of pain or displeasure must be reached so that the transition to a heightened sexual excitement may occur. Thus, perhaps one must be beaten for such and such a length of time, say until he bleeds from many wounds, before the orgasm can occur.

THE DEMONSTRATIVE FEATURE

I promised to describe the characteristic features which cannot be missed in any case of masochism. The surpassing importance of phantasy seems to me the primary feature, the factor of suspense taking second place. The third striking feature will for the moment be called the demonstrative, a designation which will be justified later. By it, I mean that in no case of masochism can the fact be overlooked that the suffering, the discontent, humiliation or abuse is shown, brought to notice so to speak, put in a show case. In many instances this feature shows up so clearly that one may wonder why it has been so long under-estimated. Many observers, as for example, *J. Lampl, K. Menninger,* have referred to it in passing since they have commented on the narcissistic character of masochism. I will later show that not only this designation seems misleading but also—what's in a name—that it represents a wrong conception.

In the practices of the masochist the exposure and display of the person with all their psychic concomitant phenomena play so great a role that a constant relation between masochism and exhibitionism could be spoken of. If I prefer to designate this feature rather as demonstrative then it is for two reasons. In the first place to avoid a certain misunderstanding by which the idea of exhibitionism is associated only with the display of what is believed to be beautiful or that which is stimulating. And secondly under the term 'demonstrative' reference is intended to be made also to a hidden meaning of such display, which I shall hope to make clear in what follows. Here it will suffice to remark that in an example such as that of Rousseau, who was impelled despite all shame to show to any lady passing by his naked buttocks, not only does the exhibitionistic nature of masochism become clear but also that important closely related feature which I shall designate as the *provocative*. The showing off or desire to let the other see would indeed be furthered by the sexually gratifying punishment.

Occasionally the demonstration in phantasy—or less frequently in reality—suffices to touch off the masochistic satisfaction. I would remind you here of the girl with the phantasy of the butcher. The lying-there-naked which she felt as most degrading and humiliating, was one of the most pleasurable moments, especially when she imagined that none of the butchers paid any particular attention to her. In the third example referred to above of the man who went to the prostitute and had himself beaten because he was "bad," the undressing and exposure of the backside was almost as important as the blow which followed. Here is to be noticed what distinguishes such demonstration or exhibition from narcissism. At first glance it seems immaterial whether what is to be seen by the other or others is imagined to be beautiful or ugly. While in some cases the body will be felt by the exhibitionist to be striking and stimulating it appears in other cases to be felt as terrifying or disgusting. Closer consideration shows, of course, a more complicated situation. In the cases with conscious pride in their own bodies or who take especial pleasure in it, the punishment or the pain which follows is perceived as more severe or the disgrace as deeper. Where the body seems hateful to the person, the presentation or depictation of it being felt to be disgusting, this feeling itself will become a feature of the masochistic pleasure and effectively contributes to the sexual excitement. We will recall the example of the extensive sacrificial phantasies of the man who took his sexual satisfaction in imagining that young men were being offered up to Moloch or to an Aztec god. For this terrible death in the fire only the most beautiful youths of the tribe were chosen. They were shown to the whole of the people. Here, of course, a narcissistic pride could be spoken of in relation to the idea that these youths—all "doubles" of the daydreamer—stood before the idol "with nothing on but a smile." Their beautiful bodies stirred the admiration of all. They themselves, however, considered it as a distinction that they should be called to suffer the terrible death in the flames. The severe chastisement in this phantasy may be contrasted with the deep feeling of impotent humiliation and degradation in the phantasies of a young girl of being watched while urinating or defecating which, nevertheless, brought her a clearly masochistic pleasure. In place of bodily hurt or pain these people often put on a shameful or degrading exhibitionistic display of bodily or psychic awkwardness which in their imagination has a stimulating effect. The "embarrassing situation" is enjoyed with the same anxious-pleasant feeling which accompanies bodily punishment.

With this we are already at the threshold leading to the desexualized forms of masochism. With these there can be no question of perversion in the grosser meanings of the word, but where the masochism becomes a dominating attitude to life, this demonstrative feature is clearly recognizable. When *Wilhelm Reich* in his book finds a close relation between masochism and inhibited exhibitionism he has allowed himself to be duped by the external aspects of the phenomena. A conscious suppression of exhibition does not, of course, contradict a hidden and yet victorious tendency in the opposite direction. The resultant of such conflicting forces is at most a demonstrative concealment or an exhibition with reversed indications. A young woman, who as a girl had elaborate masochistic phantasies gave no indication of these but she neglected no opportunity of any sort however unfitted to emphasize that she could do nothing, had no distinct character, was inferior to other women in charm and desirability. It was as if she would show to the whole world her complete insignificance. But just in this was the striking feature, she always referred to her lack of attractiveness at the moment when she could have taken pride in it. The onlooker or listener is here also a *conditio sine qua non.* Such display or glorification of one's own defects does not accord well with an inhibition of exhibitionism. It is not to be understood why these "inferior" people do not practice a reticence or discretion as might be expected of them. The self-abasement and self-depreciation which *Reich* feels is so striking, exists indeed but the essential thing in it is that it is so *strikingly present.* The young woman for instance, of whom I have just spoken, was once asked if she could typewrite. "Not very good, really not at all," she answered. Next day she mentioned as if she had just happened to think of it, that she possessed a diploma in typewriting. So there is often a divided or ambiguous attitude. One might say, "Pride cometh after the fall." The demonstrative factor in those who are on the quest for suffering is so general that it can be found also where opposing psychic tendencies have forced displacements, hybrid forms and reaction formations. Generally the result, as already mentioned, is a compromise formation of showing and hiding. That sounds as paradoxical as it is. But just such remarkable blends are to be met with in life. Take a commonplace example: a man enters a room in which a woman sits very free and easy with crossed legs. She will certainly immediately alter her position, and pull down the edge of her skirt. Now there are cases in which this so happens that the pudicity is stressed or demonstrated. The movements which she makes can betray a mixture of such wishes to display and to hide. There is to be encountered in masochism such blends from the most refined to the grossest forms. The following instance made quite an impression on me: a patient had to go to a gala concert of a famous orchestra. She wished to wear her new evening dress and the pearls she had recently been given. But, she resisted this with the thought that in the small city so magnificent a toilette would attract attention. After long hesitation she decided—*pour épater les bourgeois*—to go in her usual clothes. The result, naturally was that she was the only woman there not in evening dress and was critically inspected by all. Now she had really attracted attention which was just what she had sought to avoid. She felt humiliated and yet superior. In this public display, the realization of which might be called almost cunning, a *coincidentia oppositorum* was reached. The goal was still—to be noticed; the result was—she was looked at. The original wish struggling with its counter-impulse, had led to a masochistic compromise expression, to a sort of negative demonstration or an exhibitionism with reversed signs. . . .

To return to the individual psychic life we have to add that the same characteristic cannot be missed in the transformation from perverse to desexualized masochism. In self-depreciation and self-derision before others this feature reappears. Many of these people even when alone behave unlike the queen in the fairy tale: "Mirror, mirror on the wall, who is stupidest and ugliest in all the land?" The attention of others must be drawn to the ego through clumsiness and bad conduct, indeed even by criminal acts. In one case I could study such a transition in detail. A man in middle life who had for years only a masochistic sexual gratification, during the analysis dropped his perversion and attained a normal sexual life. His character had, however, slowly undergone a noticeable development. He went much into society and greatly amused his friends and associates by relating many experiences in which he appeared as the boob or poor fish. He produced a constant stream of witticisms—killing ones moreover more often than not—which made unmerciful fun of his own stupidity, tactlessness or egotism. Generally he simply played the clown whose job it is to make others laugh at himself. Out of the sexual perversion had arisen, so to speak, a social one. His masochism had persisted in assuming the role of a Schlemihl, a self-deriding wit. The self-depreciation had become a social mask. In displaying his own worthlessness, in cynicism directed at his own ego, he brought in again the self-demonstration. Where earlier he had exposed his buttocks in the whipping scene, he now presented himself in his psychic nudity. I would not like at this point to neglect stressing, that consideration of the result of such psychic development leads to valuable psychological insight into the personality of wits—particularly of that type which turns the shafts against itself—as well as into the genesis of the intentionally comic. Thus the production of laughter by a self-recognition before the world of defects is a kind of masochistic demonstration. Certainly it is no contradiction, that such intentional demonstration of weakness and stupidity occasionally discloses, as in the comical figures of Falstaff and Don Quixote, the masochistic character of suffering. So we find in the clown often enough the peculiar mingling of disclosure and concealment. "Laugh, Pagliacco, make foolish faces . . ." sings Leoncavallo's hero. But that laugh should not merely conceal suffering, it should also betray it. Making people laugh, is only the special form of masochistic gratification in the comical individual.

An objection easily disposed of, is based on the fact that the definitely perverse can develop out of solitary practices. Self-flagellation before a mirror is not an infrequent practice with some young people. In one case the patient who brought on an orgasm in this manner, had to see in the mirror the bloody weals he had produced on his buttocks by beating. The solitude is, to be sure real, but not psychologically actual. The person concerned phantasies a spectator, is himself that spectator many times. This imagined witness has to look on at the exposure and beating and share the pleasure. He cannot be left out for he is the carrier of the pleasure bringing action. As in self-pity where unconsciously another person (mother, father) is phantasied as present and sympathizing as they once actually did when they saw us in trouble so here in the practices of masochism in solitude an active onlooker is essential. For the rest it can easily be guessed how such mirror-beating scenes come about. They are attempts primarily pictured only in phantasy to put into execution a situation in which the one person has taken over the role of the second. Such attempts signify a step away from phantasy and towards the realization in practice of a masochistic scene with a partner who will later actually be sought for. At this point we are reminded of what was said earlier as to the significant and primary role of phantasy in masochism.

Perhaps it would be well at this point to offer some justification for the designation "demonstrative" as applied to the just described characteristic, and at the same time, to differentiate it from analogous designations. It has been said already that the word "exhibitionistic" is not adequate because it presupposes that the show-off is proud of what he displays as if it were beautiful or magnificent. This, on the contrary, is not the case with either perverse or moral masochists. Much rather do they consciously feel their exposure or degradation to be shameful and unworthy. In the best case one could speak only of an exhibitionism with reversed signs as with the Gueux, that Dutch nobility who seized on a designation once abusive ('gueux' means 'beggar') to make it afterwards a term of honor and wore small silver or copper begging bowls on their hats and belts to show they belonged to the order. Even if one could—with these restrictions—designate the typical feature as exhibitionistic, it would still be wrong to coordinate it with narcissism as many observers have done *(Lampl, Menninger)*. I have described how the tendency of the masochist passes on to an actual exposing of himself for the sake of attracting attention. We will for the moment abstain from deciding whether this is to receive punishment or evidence of love from the other. It is quite puzzling to me, how one can call such behavior narcissistic. We understand by this term an attitude of being in love with the self. As its most certain index or most visible expression appears the characteristic of self-satisfaction. The beautiful youth of the Greek myth who fell in love with his mirror image had certainly no need to draw the attention of others to himself. He was immersed in his own looks and cared nothing about the rest of the world. How different an impression the masochist produces on us. His self display and showing off have indeed every characteristic of the aspiration to make himself noticeable. His conduct is directly the opposite of a narcissistic demeanor. It would be much more correct to say, it is evident the narcissism of these masochistic persons is deranged in the deepest levels since such great exertions are made to draw the attention of others to themselves. The typical attitude of the masochist, which has been described above, could be called narcissistic with as great justification as comparing a gourmet who gives himself up in solitude to the enjoyment of reading about foods to the man who, with his inflammatory placards, parades in front of a hunger demonstration. The onesidedness and lack of discrimination so frequently to be met with in analytic literature, the to me often terrifying misuse of analytic terminology is shown in such giving of names and misleading characterizations.

The designation "demonstrative" for the pathognomonic feature was selected because of all possible choices it can give best an idea of the typical behavior just described. It seems to me furthermore the most neutral term, since it says nothing as to the aim striven for by the masochistic showing off. For this reason also I would renounce the unambiguous term "exhibitionism." So when I wish to specify the goal which the demonstrative feature tries to attain I would speak neither of the exhibitionistic nor of the narcissistic nature of masochism. A long continued and ever renewed critical observation of the manifold phenomena of masochism shows that the first and most essential goal of the demonstration is universally the same. It can also be conceived as a primary one and be named. The demonstrative feature has the unconscious intention, many times also capable of becoming conscious, of liberating definite reactions in the surroundings: or better of evoking them. I would call this feature "provocative." The demonstration is thus on the psychological side a provocation. What it would provoke, how it attains its goal, and what concealed meanings it has, will be considered later. If I do not on this occasion pursue this theme any further it is because we have here to do only with the universal and typical features of masochism. The provocatory character of the masochistic attitude, however, shows already its intimate relationship to sadistic strivings.

—Translated by G. WILBUR

NOTES

1. F. Nietzsche, *Thus Spake Zarathustra*, p. 321, Modern Library Edition.

17. The Role of Object Relations in Moral Masochism

Bernhard Berliner

I

'Moral masochism' is used in this paper as a general term for those forms in which masochism appears as a 'norm of behavior' *(6)* in contradistinction to masochistic sexual perversion or 'sexual masochism'. Freud defined moral masochism as the form that has 'loosened its connection with what we recognize to be sexuality', in which 'it is the suffering itself that matters'. However, the motivation is found in an unconscious feeling of guilt or need for punishment by some parental authority. Freud concludes that the œdipus complex is regressively reactivated and morality is resexualized. Libido is after all the driving force in moral masochism as well as in sexual perversion.

However, there are forms of nonsexual masochistic behavior in which a need for punishment in terms of the œdipus complex does not appear to be the primary motivating force and in which 'morality' is not manifestly involved. Other terms have therefore been proposed, such as 'social masochism' (Theodor Reik) or 'neurotic masochism' (Otto Sperling) or 'psychic masochism' (Edmund Bergler). In searching for more elementary psychodynamic mechanisms I find it impossible to draw a line of demarcation with regard to forces of morality. As the term 'moral masochism' has long been in general use and has outgrown the original narrower definition I see no reason not to apply it to all 'nonsexual' masochistic phenomena.

In psychoanalytic practice, however, the concept of masochism itself has become somewhat clouded because the term is often used for any form of self-inflicted neurotic suffering. The most frequent confusion is between

Based on a paper presented at the midwinter meeting of the American Psychoanalytic Association, December 3, 1955.
Reprinted by permission of the author's estate and *The Psychoanalytic Quarterly* 27 (1958):38–56.

moral masochism and obsessional neurosis. What, then, are the criteria essential for masochism?

Two main theories have been proposed. Freud's later concept was based upon the hypothesis of a death instinct. In the present state of our knowledge the assumption of a death instinct is a profound and stirring speculation, but it cannot be used for understanding the individual or in therapeutic work. If there is such a silent force within all living substance directed toward return to the inanimate, we do not have today the knowledge to comprehend in what ways and by what means it may produce a will to suffer or may be turned outward as a force of destruction.

Most analysts are inclined to follow Freud's earlier theory, which considers masochism a turning of the person's sadism upon the self, whereby the active aim is changed into a passive one and some person is sought as an object who takes over the original sadistic role of the subject. However, the turning of sadism upon the self is not yet masochism. Freud *(7)* has made an important statement on this point which apparently is often overlooked. He writes that in obsessional neurosis 'we have the turning upon the subject's self without the attitude of passivity toward another. . . . Self-torment and self-punishment have arisen from the desire to torture, but not masochism.' This means that masochism is not simply self-torment and self-punishment. A prerequisite for it is a relation to *another person*. This is the point of departure for my presentation. My thesis is that the other person does not enter into the picture only after the passive aim is established. The other person is a reality from the very beginning and is instrumental in bringing about the whole masochistic process.

The term masochism was introduced by Krafft-Ebing for the masochistic sexual perversion. Phenomenologically, the sexual masochist is in love or sensually infatuated with a person who gives him ill-treatment. The partner is always a sadist,—for example, a phallic woman with a whip,—or at least a person who does the masochist the favor of acting the role of sadist. The sado-masochistic performances depict in genital patterns scenes between a love-hungry child and a parent who is cruel and punishing but also sexually complying. By that, as Rudolph Loewenstein *(14)* has pointed out, the parent figure undoes the castration threat and gratifies the incestuous genital desire.

What justifies the use of the term masochism for the nonsexual or moral form? First, there is no sexual masochist who is not also a severe moral masochist.[1] The perversion is a superstructure over a character formation which the pervert and the moral masochist have in common. This is evident in all descriptions of masochistic perverts, including the biography of Sacher-Masoch himself and the characters in his novels (2). But the analogy goes deeper.

In previous presentations (1, 3) I have proposed the view that masochism is neither a peculiar instinctual phenomenon (death instinct), nor the expression of a component sexual drive; nor is it the subject's own sadism turned around upon his self; it is, I suggested, in the sexual as well as in the moral form a disturbance of object relations, a pathologic way of loving. Masochism means loving a person who gives hate and ill-treatment. This is manifest in sexual perversion, and analysis makes it evident in moral masochism too, where the superego and transference manifestations take the place of an original sadistic love object. Masochism is the search for love or, in sexual perversion, for sexual pleasure, through the troubled medium of displeasure which originally was forced upon the subject and thereafter bends the search for gratification of erotic needs in the specifically masochistic direction.

Masochism (I shall speak henceforth only of the moral form) is the neurotic solution of an infantile conflict between the need for being loved on the level of oral and skin erotism and the actual experience of nonlove coming from the person whose love is needed. It is also a defensive structure against this need for love and experience of nonlove. Nonlove is to be understood in the widest sense of the word. There are cases in which a parent has been outrageously cruel to the child. In other cases milder forms of rejection have occurred, including traumatic events in weaning or toilet training, discipline against masturbation, absence of the mother (studied by Spitz), appearance of a sibling, demanding or overauthoritarian attitudes or œdipal defenses on the part of a parent, and many other forms of deprivation which may leave in the child a serious feeling of frustration and a lasting distortion of the relationship of parent and child. The constitutional intensity of the child's erotic needs is, of course, another important variable, and so is a re-enforcement of these needs by pampering preceding the frustration. I do not want to be misunderstood. I do not emphasize the environmental factors in order to deny the libido theory, as does the school of Karen Horney. I adhere strictly to the dual instinct theory. Both sides are important: the libidinal drive in the subject and its relations with the environment. In masochism, however, the decisive forces in the environment are the aggressive ones.[2]

The conflict between the infantile need for being loved and the experience of suffering at the hands of the love object is the basic and most clearly causal pattern in all the cases I have seen. The masochistic attitude is the bid for the affection of a hating love object. Childhood experiences of this kind result in a character structure that keeps the original situation alive through transferences to any person or set of circumstances. Masochistic suffering represents in the unconscious the original personal love object that once gave suffering. *Masochism is the sadism of the love object fused with the libido of the subject.* Freud's concept which bases masochism upon an unconscious sense of guilt or need for punishment should be supplemented in two directions: 1, regarding the motivations of the sense of guilt or the need for punishment, and 2, its place in the ego and its relation to outside objects. To explain the sense of guilt from the œdipus complex alone is not sufficient. Our cases regularly show that the œdipus complex itself is under the influence of masochistic mechanisms of earlier origin. The same holds true for the castration complex.

It should be remembered that in the Œdipus legend the father's attempt to kill his infant son, the crippling injury he does to the child's feet, and his tearing the child away from the mother, precede the son's deed. It is the technique of the Greek tragedy, and apparently of myth formation in general, to illustrate with external events the motivations operating within a person. George Devereux, in his paper Why Œdipus Killed Laius *(4)*, has dealt with the Œdipus legend in great detail. He calls attention to the widespread failure to recognize the parents' participation in the œdipus situation and to the adult's deep-seated need to place all responsibility for the œdipus complex upon the child.

Freud assumed a phylogenetically inherited foundation of the sense of guilt. In Moses and Monotheism *(8)*, he says that 'men have always known that once upon a time they had a primeval father and killed him'. If this statement is correct, it may be equally correct to say that men have always known that once upon a time, — and still in historic times, — it was customary and legally permitted to kill unwanted children. Freud was not far from making this assumption, for he attributed a phylogenetic inheritance to the castration complex as well as to the œdipus complex. Parental cruelty is a frequent theme in fairy tales. In legend both Œdipus and Moses, who meant so much in Freud's thinking, were unwanted children who were exposed to die but were rescued and raised by foster parents. Neither became a masochist but rather the opposite; they became parricidal rebels. And when we read in Freud's book on Moses the references to Christ we cannot fail to remember that in the infancy of Christ too there is the threat of death coming from a father figure and the rescue from it while a multitude of other infants were slain. Otto Rank *(15)* has shown that the theme of the unwanted or feared child who is exposed to die but is saved and later becomes the hero who takes revenge on the cruel father occurs in numerous sagas of various peoples.

Freud says in Totem and Taboo *(9),* 'I have supposed that the sense of guilt for an action has persisted for many thousands of years and has remained operative in generations which can have had no knowledge of that action. I have supposed that an emotional process, such as might have developed in generations of sons who were ill-treated by their father, has extended to new generations which were exempt from such treatment for the very reason that their father had been eliminated. It must be admitted that these are grave difficulties; and any explanation that could avoid presumptions of such a kind would seem to be preferable.' With this passage Freud himself opens the door wide for a new approach to the problem of guilt and of masochism. We can avoid Freud's 'grave difficulty' if we examine what we hear daily not only of the childhood of our patients but also of the hostilities toward their children revealed by men and women in their analyses. From this we learn that the ill-treating parent does not belong to the dim prehistoric past, that he has not been done away with once for all by the parricidal gang of brothers; this parent is, rather, still very much alive. If there is an inborn knowledge of ill-treatment by parents, it can perhaps help to explain certain childhood fantasies and the disproportionate sensitivity of some children to minor degrees of traumatization. At any rate, I do not favor explaining such sensitivity solely on the basis of projection of instinctual aggression and of sadistic fantasies on the part of the child, as Rank did with regard to the myths he had collected. Such an assumption would ignore a vast amount of empirical facts regarding primary impulses of cruelty in adults to which the child reacts.

Whatever importance we may attribute to hereditary patterns, they are of no help in our clinical work. As far as the sense of guilt and the need for punishment are concerned, I contend that they mean the need for the love of a person who punishes and makes one feel guilty. This love, or the imagination of it, can be attained through submission and suffering. Masochism I do not consider an instinctual phenomenon like sadism or aggression. Masochism is a defensive reaction, motivated by libidinal needs, to the sadism of *another person.* Without this reference to an individual, a need for punishment as the moral form of an instinctual 'lust for pain' does not seem to exist. Sense of guilt and need for punishment are secondary to object dependency and part of the defensive structure against the original conflict.

The defense mechanisms involved are primarily denial and libidinization of suffering. The experience of hate and ill-treatment is repressed. The child, in its imperative need for love, accepts this hate and ill-treatment as if they were love and is not conscious of the difference. Suffering thus libidinized is introjected. Essentially the same process underlies depression. Moral masochism can also be defined as the manifestation, with regard to object relations, of a depressive character. When the introjection occurs, the pain-giving love object and the suffering caused by it become constituents of the superego. The libidinization makes the trauma egosyntonic and protects from a too deleterious degree of suffering, but it does not heal the narcissistic wound. The superego throughout life forces the subject to relive and to re-enact the original trauma which the analysis detects in the unpleasurable situations that the masochist not only must experience but must actively bring about. The masochistic phenomena represent a regression to an early libidinal phase plus its traumatic disturbance. Like the melancholic, the masochist hangs on, so to speak, to a breast which is not there and which he has to repudiate when it could be there, symbolically. The goal of the masochistic defense (denial and libidinization) is not suffering but the avoidance of suffering. However, like every neurotic defense, it is unsuccessful and even helps the return of the repressed. Suffering, repressed in its original form, reappears as the price to be paid for obtaining a little bit of love or the imagination of it.

II

There are few individuals, mainly depressed children, in whom masochism appears in the asthenic form of search for love through libidinized suffering only. The majority of our patients show aggressive attitudes as an essential part of their masochism.

The aggressiveness of the masochist is only to a small extent conscious to him. We meet in our work with very unpleasant types. They are often greatly astonished and resistive when attention is called to their nastiness. The motivation for this repression is simple. Hostility would cause loss of the love object. With the repression of hostility and the acceptance of suffering instead, this ever-present danger is denied. But this defense is also unsuccessful. Hostility manifests itself all the more in character traits.

To understand the aggressive behavior of the masochist is the most difficult problem we have so far encountered with this condition. Freud expressed a pessimistic view even in his last work, An Outline of Psychoanalysis *(10)*, with regard to severe cases of masochism: 'It must be confessed that these are cases which we have not yet succeeded in explaining completely'. They present a 'form of resistance, our means of combating which are especially inadequate'.

Aggression appears in several ways and with different motivations which for better understanding should be studied separately.

1. Hostility can be a remnant of a justified and normal hatred against a hating love object. The struggle for self-preservation is not entirely left to denial and libidinization. This hate may be repressed from consciousness because the need for love serves as a repressing force; in itself it would not be masochistic. Masochism does not simply mean to defend against hate, it means to attempt to save love through suffering.

2. More important, therefore, is the aggression exercised in the service of the masochistic need for love. It is an intensified bid for affection. The masochist inflicts himself upon his love object with possessiveness and reproachfulness. He tries to extort love. Being loved means in his mind also being given the license to be naughty. His provocative attitude gives the impression that he needs and asks for punishment, but such an interpretation, if it is given, remains unintelligible to him. He knows only that he is unhappy and needs love, and he acts as if it were the partner's duty to love him. Of course, that is the duty of a parent.

Hostility does not supersede the masochistic search for love. The latter remains the operational basis and the purpose of the aggression. When the masochist not only accepts but even seeks suffering and exhibits it in the way of martyrdom, it is not because he wants to suffer and to punish himself; it is because suffering gives him a feeling of increased love-worthiness, a narcissistic gratification. Feeling sorry for himself does him good and he also feels that he has a claim not only to being loved but also to prestige and domination, which means the privilege of exercising aggression. He is a grievance collector who collects and retains causes for resentment. Having a cause against the object is more important for him than having the object. His object relations have started 'against' instead of 'with'. Masochism is an unsuccessful attempt to substitute the 'with' for the 'against'. The masochist welcomes being hurt, not because it hurts, but because it makes him right over others. He would rather be right than happy. Being right also emphasizes his love-worthiness, and so do his megalomania and exhibitionism These attitudes serve the continuation of the denial of rejection. However, the motivation of this righteousness does not lie in any primary aggressive need. It is one of the means to put pressure on his love objects,—those of childhood, of course,—that they may change their minds and give more love. He feels and acts as if he could force his past to change—an irrational magic gesture.

3. The ambivalent blending of the plea for affection with aggression appears particularly in the attitude expressing the idea, 'You will be sorry'. The love object which cannot be given up is punished through self-destructive attitudes destined to make the other person guilty, but simultaneously concerned for the subject. The vindictiveness is kept in repression by this libidinization and by suffering. I am not referring here to a defense against feeling of guilt by denial and projection. Projection of hostility is of course frequent; it is one of the ways in which the masochist arranges for trouble. This is not the principle I have in mind here. I refer rather to the insistence upon being loved by the hating object. There is more projection of love into the hating partner than projection of hostility. A sense of guilt may have the meaning of an unconscious sense of the guilt of the parent,—the not infrequent phenomenon of 'borrowed guilt'. The need for love results in a need to exonerate the parent, as if saying: 'I am the bad one, not you'. This may be the same process that we find, in higher degrees, in the self-accusations of the melancholic which, as Freud (11) has shown, do not fit the patient but relate to another person who is a frustrating love object. Making sorry results from the need to get back at, to get even with, the frustrating love object; in other words, to punish the object that formerly did the punishing (again a magic revival of the past) but that nevertheless must be preserved as a needed love object. Forms of self-sabotage such as being 'wrecked by success' or the negative therapeutic reaction or the so-called fate neurosis may be caused by a sense of guilt as described by Freud; if so, we are dealing with the pathology of obsessional neurosis, not of masochism. The masochistic form of these processes derives from the *drive to punish* the love object with the help of failure and unhappiness which simultaneously emphasize loveworthiness and the bid for affection.

The aggressive attitudes of the masochist, which I need not further describe, look very much like sadism, sometimes more oral, sometimes more anal, but if the diagnosis masochism is right they are secondary to his bid for the affection of a hating object in a transference situation. The quarrels and troubles in which he involves himself are an acting out of the repressed original situation between the child and a rejecting or ill-treating parent. The primary defense against suffering at the hands of a love object, denial and libidinization, leads into a painful state of neurotic depression (in serious cases it may even be psychotic). Against this condition a secondary defense is established in the form of aggression, that is, turning passivity into activity. However this defense, too, fails because it embodies all the elements of the conflict against which it is directed. I have previously proposed to call this aggressive defense a 'countermasochistic attitude' in analogy to the counterphobic attitude described by Fenichel.

I see no objection to explaining also as adaptational phenomena what I have described as defenses. There is only a difference in the point of view. 'Defense' refers to mechanisms and motivations, 'adaptation' to the result.

III

In the drive to punish, the original traumatic situation is reenacted by *identification* in the masochist with the frustrating love object. I have come to recognize that the analysis of this part of the masochistic character structure is the most important part of our work.

The defense mechanism involved here is that described by Anna Freud *(5)* as identification with the aggressor. In the case of the masochist the aggressor is the original parental person who gave the child hate or rejection, all that I have referred to previously as nonlove.

This identification is the most powerful mechanism in the masochist and in his neurotic defense against guilt and suffering. I presented my ideas about it ten years ago. My work since then has increasingly convinced me that they are correct. Therefore, I may be permitted to quote from my previous paper *(3)*.

The drive to punish is associated with a feeling of righteousness. However, it is not the feeling that punishing the rejecting parent would be a just revenge. That would not be masochistic at all. It is a feeling . . . that arises from the superego. Analysis regularly reveals that the person feels he is doing the right thing according to the sadistic object whose love he craves, and that he will gain the love and approval of the object when he expresses aggressive trends which copy those of the object. These aggressive trends, originally experienced in the love object, appear in two ways: they are directed against the ego, causing self-inflicted suffering or what appears to be self-punishment; or they are directed against the external world in the way the original love object has treated or would treat external objects.

The permanent wish to please the once rejecting, introjected [love] object causes the person to lose his identity. To accommodate [and to appease] a hating parent [figure] he may make himself as unlovable as he feels the parent wants him to be. He may deny his good qualities or his intelligence, often to the degree of pseudodebility; he fails to exploit his opportunities or to seek legitimate enjoyments, confusing an irrational asceticism with virtue that earns love; he [pleads guilty and] 'lives down' to the views of those who resent him in order to be accepted by them. He feels that he has to make efforts and sacrifices to reconcile the world with his existence, and he does so by suffering as well as by being hostile or mischievous, which lowers his value as a love object and releases the hater from having to love him. He is stigmatized with unwantedness and displays his stigma as his bid for affection.

On the other hand, with submission to the parental power the masochist borrows the authority for his drive to punish. . . . The aggressiveness of the masochist is not the manifestation of his primary sadism; the latter only furnishes part of the energy with which the identification with the hater is set into action. It is this imitation, out of his search for love, which makes the masochist feel that by being aggressive he is the way he is *supposed* to be. This accounts for the fact that these persons are often so astonishingly unaware of their provocative behavior. The superego shields the ego and furnishes the motives for aggression. . . .

The identification with the hating and punishing love object is the motivation for what Freud, in his earlier theory, considered the essential mechanism in masochism, namely, the turning of sadism against the self. However, what is turned against the self is not the person's own sadism, but the sadism of a love object incorporated, through the oral need for the object's love, in the subject's superego. The blending of the subject's libido with the sadism of the other person makes the original aggressor unrecognizable except through analysis.

The need for punishment which Freud considered the central motive of moral masochism is the acceptance, in form and content, of the drive to punish which operates in the love object, resulting in punishing oneself and in punishing others, thus developing one's own drive to punish and passing it on to the next generation. The identification with the parental drive to punish seems to be the strongest foundation of our moral standards. . . . It accounts for the universality of moral masochism in our culture. No death instinct needs to be postulated to explain masochism.

It may be mentioned parenthetically that this mechanism tends to raise large problems of countertransference in therapeutic work.

The statement that the subject's own sadism furnishes part of the energy with which the identification with the hater is set into action may need some amplification. The introjected and libidinized sadism of the object and the subject's own sadism are operative in various proportions for constitutional reasons. In some cases the subject's own sadism seems to be only the instinctual potentiality for identification with the aggressor, while the libidinal component prevails as the motivating force. In other cases with a stronger sadistic endowment it may be more accurate to say that the sadism of the object steers the sadism of the subject against the self and against the outside. These are the cases nearer to the pathology of obsessional neurosis with motivations derived from masochistic mechanisms. There is a wide variety in the degree to which masochistic suffering serves both instincts, the need for love and the gratification, with the help of justification, of aggression. In any case I do not think that the diagnosis masochism should be made if the introjection of another person's sadism is not the essential pattern.[3]

IV

It has been my purpose to outline the psychodynamic factors specific for masochism. This outline provides a guide for therapeutic procedure and it also helps to detect and treat accordingly those masochistic features that are admixtures in the structure of almost any other neurotic illness. On the other hand, in the analysis of a predominantly masochistic person we have to deal with hysterical, obsessional, or paranoid features too, in which, however, masochistic motivations play their part.

The analysis of moral masochists is generally considered difficult. Transference resistances can be very strong, negative therapeutic reactions, and resistances against final success are frequent. However, it seems that the main technical intricacies have arisen from erroneous theoretical premises, namely: 1, that the masochist 'wants' to suffer because pain and humiliation are for him substitutes for sexual pleasure; 2, that the masochist has to satisfy his need for punishment because of his guilt for either incestuous or aggressive impulses (this holds true for obsessional neurosis, not for masochism); 3, that his self-damaging attitudes are the expression of his own sadism turned upon his self, (also belonging to the pathology of obsessional neurosis), or perhaps even of his death instinct.

Some analysts believe that with a moral masochist they must be very stern and cool, even openly unfriendly, in order to bring the sadistic trends of the patient into the open. It has also been stated that such an attitude corresponds to the rule of abstinence which requires that we establish an impediment against the sticky love-seeking attitude of the masochistic patient. I have found this to be a mistake. A rejecting attitude in the analyst, or any reference to the theoretical premises mentioned above, makes the patient feel criticized and confronted with his own nastiness and guilt in the same way as he once was criticized or reproved or punished by a parent. A transference is established in which the analyst comes too close to being a new edition of this parent, and the analyst may have exercised a countertransference of the same order and lent himself to the acting out of the patient's masochistic tendencies. To dissolve this transference situation analytically can be very difficult.

As to the rule of abstinence, I find it better to afford the patient an emotional atmosphere in which he finds abstinence from his habitual search for libidinized suffering and in which, perhaps for the first time in his life, he has the experience of a human being who gives him a friendly understanding instead of the criticism and punishment to which he has been accustomed. Such an attitude conforms also with the principle that in the transference situation the analyst should be as different as possible from the original role that is being transferred upon him.[4]

I follow the theory that masochism is a libidinal reaction to traumatic influences from outside, originating in infancy and being re-enacted throughout life. Freud *(12)* has stated: 'There can be no doubt that, when the etiology of the neurosis is traumatic, analysis has a far better chance. Only when the traumatic factor predominates can we look for . . . such a re-enforcement of the ego that a correct adjustment takes the place of that infantile solution of the patient's early conflicts which proved so inadequate.'

The analysis of masochism offers the opportunity to take advantage of this view. We must not forget, of course, that besides the traumatic experience, the form and strength of the libidinal needs are also determinants.

The masochistic patient appears in a double light: he is the *victim* of a traumatic childhood, and he is a *troublemaker* who entangles himself in actual conflicts by which he continuously makes himself the victim again. He is sinned against and sinning, to paraphrase Shakespeare. We give the analysis of the victim priority over the analysis of the troublemaker.

I have found it helpful to do what I can to slow down the development of an intense emotional transference to the person of the analyst. This is accomplished by examining with the patient the transferences he forms to his external world at large before analyzing his transference to the analyst's person.

The patient talks about his unhappy reality situation; he complains and accuses. The analyst makes no criticism, expresses no doubt; but he notes, and in due time shows to the patient, that the persons the patient accuses are always in some sense love objects, either in actuality or in transference representations. The picture of suffering at the hands of a love object is thus established in the analysis. The patient becomes aware of his passivity and dependence and how he acts out the unhappy experiences of his childhood and invites others to treat him with the same rejection as that he encountered from his earliest love objects. I have seen analysis penetrate in this way to very early oral traumata, which could be reliably reconstructed. The patient is helped to arrive at a more mature evaluation of those beloved but unloving persons who started his neurotic suffering. He will find that he is not guilty and needs no punishment, but that he has been the recipient of a parental drive to punish. The sense of guilt is analyzed by breaking it down into elements that are not guilt, namely, the need for affection and the experience of the punishing parent, and thus the sense of guilt is deprived of its moralistic aspect. 'Sense of guilt', it seems to me, is sometimes a wrong name for what more accurately should be called 'sense of defeat'. It is the defeat by a rejecting parent or parent substitute in transference; and it is this defeat rather than guilt that is introjected and forms a character pattern for acting out. Although it sounds almost trivial to say that a prerequisite for a need for punishment is the existence of a punishing parent, the function of this parent has so far been much less recognized than the instinctual processes in the child.

In this way we try to conduct the analysis with a minimum of acting out in the analytic situation itself. When it occurs it is easier to analyze. The analyst can point out not only that the patient sees in him a new edition of an original of his childhood, but also that the analyst shares this role with numerous other figures in the patient's life.

The first preliminary goal is to make the patient realize that it is his need for the love of rejecting love objects that makes him accept suffering as if it were love. The recognition of this 'plus quality', as a patient has called it, is a great help against the ever-present resistance caused by the expectation and invitation of criticism. The second goal, after this, is to make the patient better acquainted with his sadistic tendencies and with the fact that his drive to punish the love object is responsible for the maintenance of his suffering. In the transference situation achieved by the first part of the work this can now be done without arousing the feeling of being criticized or accused.

The identification with the aggressor constitutes the phase of working through. All the features of the illness are recapitulated in the analysis of the identification. This work often greatly stimulates the interest and coöperation of the patient. The recognition of the feeling of 'being supposed to' is a very effective revelation. The superego relaxes. The patient learns to differentiate between love and hate and to adjust his life accordingly.

Lest this picture of the therapeutic process appear too optimistic, a word of caution may be in place here regarding the nature of the masochistic acting out. We have to deal mainly with preœdipal factors, and there is an important difference in the operation of defenses according to whether they are directed against œdipal or against preœdipal conflicts. It is comparatively easy to bring the incestuous love of the œdipal situation into consciousness and to free actual relations from the re-enactment of those old bondages. Preœdipal conflicts are much farther removed from consciousness and more deeply engraved in the unconscious. In particular, the earliest traumatic experiences in the oral phase cannot be remembered at all; the analysis has to rely here on reconstruction alone. These unrecallable early conflicts leave in the personality a permanent tendency to acting out in which the person returns into an early symbiosis, a symbiosis lived with no possibility of conscious ego participation, which therefore left an identification not only with persons but also with situations and with special traits in these persons, such as their punitiveness. What is being acted out is neither the libidinal need in itself nor the defense against it. It is always the total conflict, the libidinal striving plus the outer and inner forces that oppose it. The person needs love but can never find it. What he finds is only frustrated, unhappy love, a re-enactment of the original situation with which he is identified. When it seems that the longing for love can find a fulfilment, the counterforces, stemming from deep unconscious sources, may be simultaneously stimulated and intensified to such a degree that the individual must perish from this fulfilment. While the danger of suicide is usually not too great so long as the transference is well in hand, there is always the danger that the patient will get himself into very unfortunate life situations, and there is particular danger of psychosomatic complications. The recognition, late in his life, that there are hostilities in people near him of which he had not been aware because of his defenses may result in temporary depressive and paranoid reactions. There are types reminding one of the Flying Dutchman. Although the legend calls it redemption, what happens is death. That the Dutchman for his salvation needs the love of an absolutely faithful woman, such as only an ideal mother can be, makes the legend a symbolization of a very early traumatic situation with its only solution annihilation. Persons with self-destructive tendencies must be watched for their acting out of a preœdipal libidinal need that has deep and intense association with frustration. This association precludes any self-healing of the masochistic character. The analysis of these cases belongs to our most laborious but also most rewarding tasks.

NOTES

1. The manifest character of a pervert does not always show this. There are some active and seemingly masculine types among them. However, this seems to be a compensatory reaction-formation analogous to the 'ulcer personality'.
2. In reporting these observations at the midwinter meeting of the American Psychoanalytic Association in 1955, Dr. Martin H. Stein (16) remarked, 'This would imply that we should be able to find a truly cruel parent in the history of masochists'. The overstatement is not mine. What is meant by 'truly cruel'? Cases of severe and overt cruelty occur, but they are not the rule and may not be the most pathogenic ones for masochism; perhaps they are more likely to lead to rebellion or delinquency. In my cases I have seen the 'untruly' cruel parent, one whose ambivalence tends more toward the hostile side and enjoins ill-treatment or guilt upon the child under the guise of love.
3. On some differential points between masochism and obsessional neurosis, see Ref. 3, p. 470.
4. This recommendation is not an innovation by the Chicago Institute for Psychoanalysis, as a recent publication from that Institute (13) makes it appear. This principle is as old as psychoanalytic technique.

   Dr. Martin H. Stein, in his report cited above (16), finds that I recommend 'that the analyst play the directive role of the "improved" or ideal parent, in order to accomplish the purpose of avoiding interpretation which might be regarded by the patient as accusatory or insulting'. It is difficult to see how such avoidance, which is indeed my principle, can be called 'playing a directive role'. I should reserve such a term for exactly opposite behavior. Dr. Stein is here in error; there is nothing of role-playing or manipulation of the transference in the technique outlined here. It is entirely nondirective, taking its direction only from what the patient says and not from any educational function of the analyst.

REFERENCES

1. Berliner, Bernhard: *Libido and Reality in Masochism. Psychoanal. Quart.*, IX, 1940, pp. 322–333.
2. ———: *The Concept of Masochism.* Psa. Rev., XXIX, 1942, pp. 386–400.
3. ———: *On Some Psychodynamics of Masochism. Psychoanal. Quart.*, XVI, 1947, pp. 459–471.
4. Devereux, George: *Why Œdipus Killed Laius.* Int. J. Psa., XXXIV, 1953, pp. 132–141.
5. Freud, Anna: *The Ego and the Mechanisms of Defense.* New York: International Universities Press, Inc., 1946.
6. Freud: *The Economic Problem in Masochism.* Coll. Papers, II.
7. ———: *Instincts and Their Vicissitudes.* Coll. Papers, IV, p. 71.
8. ———: *Moses and Monotheism.* New York: Alfred A. Knopf, 1939, p. 159.
9. ———: *Totem and Taboo.* In: *The Standard Edition of the Complete Psychological Works of Sigmund Freud, Vol. XIII.* London: The Hogarth Press, 1953, pp. 157ff.
10. ———: *An Outline of Psychoanalysis.* Int. J. Psa., XXI, 1940, pp. 58ff.
11. ———: *Mourning and Melancholia.* Coll. Papers, IV, p. 158.
12. ———: *Analysis Terminable and Interminable.* Int. J. Psa., XVIII, 1937, p. 377.
13. Johnson, Adelaide M.: Psychoanalytic Therapy. In: *Twenty Years of Psychoanalysis.* Edited by Franz Alexander and Helen Ross. New York: W. W. Norton & Co., Inc., 1953.

14. Loewenstein, Rudolph M.: *A Contribution to the Psychoanalytic Theory of Masochism* J. Amer. Psa. Assn., V, 1957, pp. 197–234.
15. Rank, Otto: *The Myth of the Birth of the Hero.* New York: Nervous & Mental Disease Monograph Series, No. 18, 1914.
16. Stein, Martin H.: Report on the Panel Discussion: *The Problem of Masochism in the Theory and Technique of Psychoanalysis.* J. Amer. Psa. Assn., IV, 1956.

18. The Masochistic Character: Genesis and Treatment

Charles Brenner

Masochism is a subject which is of interest to psychoanalysts from both a theoretical and a clinical aspect. This was first noted by Freud (17, 18) who from the clinical side emphasized the unfavorable prognostic significance of a strong unconscious need for punishment and from the theoretical side pointed out the paradoxical position which masochistic phenomena occupy in human mental life and behavior: whereas we ordinarily think of man as avoiding pain for the sake of pleasure, in masochism man seems to seek pain as a source of pleasure.

The present paper will consist of three parts. The first part will be a summary of Freud's views on the subject plus a summary of the views of subsequent authors in so far as they add to or diverge from those of Freud. The second part will contain some formulations concerning the genesis of masochistic character traits and of their place in psychic functioning. The third part will be a discussion of some problems involved in the treatment of patients with masochistic character traits.

I

The essence of masochism appears to consist in an intimate relationship between pleasure and pain, or more generally between pleasure and unpleasure. It may perhaps best be defined as the seeking of unpleasure, by which is meant physical or mental pain, discomfort or wretchedness, for the sake of sexual pleasure, with the qualification that either the seeking or the pleasure or both may often be unconscious rather than conscious.

Freud raised the question: How can we explain the phenomena of masoch-

Reprinted by permission of the author and International Universities Press, Inc., from *JAPA* 7 (1959):197–226.

ism when at the same time we maintain the existence and importance of the pleasure principle in mental functioning? His first answer to this question is contained in "Instincts and Their Vicissitudes" (13). He there explained masochism as a secondary phenomenon: it was sadism which had been turned back on the self. That is to say, in the first instance the masochistic individual had had sadistic impulses or wishes toward an outside object, but for one reason or another the outside object had been replaced by the self, resulting in self-directed sadism, or masochism. The commonest or best known mechanism by which this result might occur, Freud said, was the mechanism of identification with a lost object which had been both loved and hated, as described in "Mourning and Melancholia" (14). At the same time Freud believed that an alternative or auxiliary factor was at work in the production of masochism, a factor which was more nearly independent of environmental factors than such an instinctual vicissitude as turning against the self. This was the capacity of the organism to experience any intense stimulation, even painful stimulation, as sexually exciting (12). Freud suggested that this human capacity, which might well be greater in one individual than in another, could account for the fact that masochistic perverts experienced sexual excitement and even orgasm in situations in which bodily pain was inflicted upon them, in some cases by themselves, more often by a partner. Subsequent experience in analyzing patients with masochistic behavior or fantasies convinced Freud that the relationship between pain and sexual excitement in masochists is not quite so simple (15) and that it might perhaps be more accurate to say that for masochists pain is a *condition* for sexual pleasure rather than to say that it gives rise to it directly. Freud (18) therefore amended his view that painful stimuli, or other excessive tension, normally produce sexual excitement in infancy and continue to do so throughout life in masochists. In 1924 he stated that even though the capacity of pain to produce sexual excitement in infancy "dried up" or disappeared in later life, it was "the physiological substrate which is then covered by a psychic superstructure to form erogenic masochism," the type of masochism which he considered to be its basic form.

It will be appreciated that this first explanation of Freud's, based on the two factors just outlined, was one which permitted the phenomena of masochism to be subsumed under the pleasure principle. At least it was an explanation which did not expressly contradict the view that the pleasure principle was the guiding principle of the functioning of the psychic apparatus, an assumption which Freud had made as early as 1900, in Chapter VII of *The Interpretation of Dreams*. However, Freud later suggested a different explanation which was intended to contribute to the understanding not only of masochism but of the wide range of other phenomena as well which attest the importance of destructive tendencies in the human mind.

In *Beyond the Pleasure Principle* (16) Freud advanced the hypothesis of a death instinct. According to this new hypothesis a self-directed, destructive impulse was assumed to be present in the mind from birth and to operate independently of the pleasure principle and even in contradiction to it. Masochism, or rather its infantile prototype, was thus considered to be the primary phenomenon in human psychology and sadism the secondary one which was due to deflection of the destructive instinctual drive from its primary object, the self, outward onto other objects. To be sure, the sadism which arose in this way could again be turned back upon the self by such means as identification with the hated object, in which case secondary masochism would appear.

Whether or not the death instinct is a valid hypothesis is probably a matter for biologists rather than for psychoanalysts to decide, as Fenichel (10) and others have pointed out. However, the concept of a destructive instinctual drive as an innate component of human mental life has become an integral part of psychoanalytic theory and analysts in general seem to be content to leave unanswered the question whether this drive is originally self-directed or not. Whatever may be the answer to this particular question, it is generally accepted that there is an important connection between the destructive or aggressive drive and the phenomena which we call masochism.

As far as one can judge from his writings Freud's chief interest in masochism lay in the problems it posed with respect to the theory of drives and of the regulatory principles of the mind: the pleasure principle and the repetition compulsion. However, his occupation with these matters of psychoanalytic theory did not preclude his making the first, fundamentally important *clinical* contribution to the subject which is contained in the paper "A Child Is Being Beaten" (15). He there advanced the idea that a perversion, like a neurosis, is a consequence of infantile sexual conflicts, in particular, of oedipal conflicts. In the case of beating fantasies the perverse wishes or practices are masochistic ones. Thus masochistic fantasies of phenomena were shown to be a part of the "legacy of the oedipus complex," as Freud so aptly put it. It might be added that the wish to be beaten was considered by Freud to be a regressive representative of oedipal strivings and to stem originally from the anal-sadistic phase of libidinal organization (18).

In addition to relating masochism to the oedipus complex, Freud (18) proposed to distinguish clinically three forms of masochism. The first of these he called erogenic masochism, by which he meant essentially perverse masochism in which pain or humiliation are associated with conscious sexual excitement and gratification. He considered this form to be the basic one which was fundamental to the development of either of the other two: feminine masochism, in which suffering was the consequence of an unconscious fantasy of being a woman in either sexual intercourse or childbirth, and moral masochism or masochistic character formation.

We see, therefore, that Freud attempted to explain the phenomena of masochism in the following ways.

(i) He assumed its physiological basis, what one might call its developmental *sine qua non,* to be the tendency of the infant to respond to any increase in psychic tension with sexual excitement; he believed that even painful stimuli produced sexual responses in infancy, that an exceptionally great tendency to respond sexually to painful stimuli in infancy would provide a constitutional basis for later masochism, and that although this tendency "dried up" or disappeared in later life (18), it was the "physiological substrate which is then covered by a psychic superstructure to form erogenic masochism," the basic form of masochism.

(ii) He assumed its instinctual basis to be the death drive, which was originally self-directed, giving rise to primary masochism. He assumed (16) that some of the death drive remained self-directed, while the rest was deflected from the self toward objects in the outer world during the course of infantile development. This outwardly deflected part of the death drive might be again self-directed as a vicissitude of later life and would then reinforce that part of the death drive which had remained self-directed from the beginning, a development which might be spoken of as secondary masochism. It might be added that in Freud's view there would have to be some degree of fusion of self-directed destructiveness and self-directed libido to account for *pleasure* from pain as distinct from a mere tendency to self-injury or self-destructiveness, since he considered the discharge of destructive energies alone to be unaccompanied by the subjective quality of pleasure.

(iii) He concluded that some and perhaps all of the masochistic fantasies and behavior met with in clinical practice are consequences of the psychic conflicts of the oedipal period. This would presumably be an example of the phenomenon just referred to as secondary masochism.

(iv) In addition, and obviously in close connection with (iii), Freud (18) pointed to the intimate relationship between masochistic phenomena and the superego, a concept then new to psychoanalytic theory (17).

(v) Finally, Freud proposed to distinguish three forms of masochism: erogenic, feminine, and moral, of which he considered the first to be basic to the other two.

Subsequent authors have dealt with masochism within the framework of Freud's ideas, although their conclusions have sometimes differed from his either in content or in emphasis. The contributions of recent years may be summarized briefly as follows. The emphasis will be on additions to Freud's views and modifications of them. For a more detailed review of pertinent literature the reader is referred to Loewenstein (21).

II

We may proceed now to some formulations concerning the genesis of masochistic character traits and their place in psychic functioning.

The first of these formulations is one which was mentioned by Reik (25) but which otherwise has received little direct attention in the literature on the subject. It is the proposition that masochistic phenomena play a part in the lives of all of us, the normal as well as the neurotic.

The clearest and usually the most extensive evidence of this in the course of normal psychic development is afforded by the genesis and functioning of the superego. As Reik (25) remarked, following Freud's (18) views on the relation between moral masochism and an unconscious need for punishment, a *need* or *wish* for punishment, as opposed to a *fear* of punishment, is in itself a masochistic phenomenon. We may add that a need for punishment, whether it be a conscious or an unconscious one, is invariably a part of normal superego functioning. It follows therefore that some degree of masochism is ubiquitous.

To clarify this point let us consider, for example, what happens in the mind of a boy in the oedipal phase who fears that his father will castrate him as a punishment for his desire to castrate and kill his father and to take father's place with mother. The expected result of the boy's fear will be the development of a whole series of defensive measures, measures which will differ from one another in a variety of ways but which will have in common the purpose of avoiding the fantasied danger, castration. Now among these defensive measures we normally expect to find a tendency on the boy's part to win his father's sympathy and love by hurting or punishing himself or by making his remorse or suffering apparent to his father. Indeed, we shall not be surprised to find these tendencies linked with the boy's passive, feminine, oedipal strivings with the result that the wish to be a woman and to be loved by father in mother's place comes to serve the defensive purpose of averting the fantasied danger of being castrated by father as a vengeful rival for mother to which we referred above. These oedipal conflicts and wishes and the fantasies and fears connected with them normally become unconscious as the boy grows older, but they leave their mark in that aspect of superego function to which we refer as remorse and as a need for punishment; as a wish for penance and expiation, whether the wish be conscious or not.[1]

If this view is correct, it follows that masochism is a normal component of character formation. The question then arises whether the difference between what might be called normal and pathological masochism is one of degree or one of kind.

Such a question can be answered only on the basis of clinical experience. Perhaps future observation will reveal differences in kind, that is, qualitative differences between normal and neurotic manifestations of masochism, but so far as experience goes at present it would appear that the differences are only quantitative ones. It is true that such quantitative differences may be very great ones and of the utmost practical importance. Nevertheless, the best available evidence at the present time suggests that no sharp line can be drawn between what is called a normal character and what is called a masochistic one.

This view has important clinical implications. For one thing it makes intelligible the fact that the syndrome which is called masochistic character or moral masochism is so difficult to separate diagnostically from a variety of other pathological conditions. According to the view advanced here, masochistic phenomena or tendencies are a part of every individual's mental life. They can and often do exist together with many sorts of neurotic symptoms and with a variety of other character disturbances. In other words, the diagnostic category of masochistic character, though nosologically useful, is by no means an exclusive one.

Bak (1) has drawn attention to the masochistic aspects of paranoia and Fenichel (10) has done the same with respect to obsessional neurosis, while many analysts have commented on the fact that it is frequently difficult to decide whether a particular case is to be diagnosed as masochistic character or as depression. However, it is equally true, though less frequently commented upon, that masochism plays a large role in the mental lives of many other patients as well. For example, one need only think of the patients with conversion hysteria whom one sees in any large general hospital to realize how unmistakably large is the role played by masochistic trends in the unconscious mental lives of the great majority of such patients. *"La belle indifférence"* is a characteristic of conversion hysteria which is hallowed by long usage and enshrined in the literature, but conscious suffering and the unconscious pursuit and enjoyment of suffering are in fact far more frequently found in patients with serious conversion symptoms than is indifference. One may also find masochistic tendencies playing a large role in patients with phobias, in addicts, in patients with impulsive character disorders, in many criminals, and so on.

Two brief clinical examples may be to the point here. A thirty-five-year-old man came to analysis because of recurrent bouts of alcoholism. The importance of his masochistic problems may be indicated by the fact that his conscious masturbation fantasies from the age of eight years until well into puberty were of a naked boy being beaten in public. This patient's alcoholic bouts were regularly precipitated by the prospect of success, a prospect which had for him unconsciously the commonplace oedipal significance of competing with and supplanting his father. The drinking had a variety of unconscious meanings, as might be supposed, but the one which is apropos here is that it was self-destructive, self-castrative, and very nearly suicidal. In fact each bout of drinking was an expression of an unconscious wish to be the prodigal son who, after riotous, profligate living returned in rags and despair to be rescued by his loving father. This patient's alcoholism thus had a specifically masochistic character: a bout of drinking was a way of producing suffering, misery, and helplessness which would lead to being loved and gratified by father.

The other example is a twenty-two-year-old man whose chief complaints were that he was generally anxious and that after dark he feared and avoided empty or ill-lighted streets. It was soon apparent that his fears were a consequence of unconscious sadomasochistic fantasies in which he was the beaten and tortured partner. In adolescence he had been an overt masochistic pervert for a time, deriving sexual gratification with orgasm from being bound naked and whipped by a girl. At the time he came for treatment he was consciously bisexual without apparent conflict, but he was increasingly terrified by his unconscious wish to be beaten, tormented, and castrated by a man, a wish which had given rise to the phobias and to the anxiety state which brought him to treatment.

These clinical notes will serve to illustrate the point that masochistic trends are of importance in patients from a variety of diagnostic categories, e.g., alcoholism and phobias. It may be added that for the purpose of emphasis the two cases chosen were rather extreme ones. There are many patients in whom masochistic trends are of great importance who yet give no history of conscious beating fantasies or of masochistic perversion, as did the patients just cited.

The view that as regards masochism what is pathological differs from what is normal in degree rather than in kind has the further effect of inclining one to think of infantile factors as increasing or diminishing the individual's tendency toward masochistic character formation or behavior rather than to try to discover or establish a "cause" in infancy for the development of masochistic phenomena in later life. Most of all, this view will make impossible the idea that masochistic phenomena are per se pathological.

It may be of interest to consider for a moment the question why masochism should be universal if indeed it is so. One answer to this question might be based on the dual instinct theory (16): the psychic state of the neonate is assumed to be one in which both the destructive and the erotic drives are self-directed. This state Freud (16) called primary masochism. In view of the universal tendency toward repetition of earlier states during later life it might be expected that the instinctual position of the neonate would tend to be reinstated, at least partially, resulting in later or secondary masochism.

Another answer, related more closely to observable clinical data, would be that the adaptive efforts of the child during the stormy instinctual conflicts of childhood inevitably result in some degree of masochism in the child's psychic functioning. In other words, given the psychic equipment of the child, its instinctual drives and its ego capacities, on the one hand, and the child's environment on the other, including its available gratifications and inescapable frustrations, it would appear to be unavoidable that there be at least some degree of masochism in the patterns of psychic functioning that develop in the child's mind as it lives through this period of its life.

It should be noted, by the way, that the two answers just suggested neither contradict nor exclude one another.

There is another clinically important point about the masochistic character that derives directly from clinical experience, though it is probably related to the topic just under discussion, i.e., to the ubiquity of masochism. This is the fact that sadistic and masochistic tendencies are always seen together, never separately. For the problem of masochism this has the consequence that one expects a patient's behavior or fantasies to have a sadistic or hostile meaning as well as a masochistic or passive one. It is then no surprise to be told by one author that the unconscious fantasy behind a masochistic patient's behavior is one of mollifying his parent and winning his live by submission to him and to learn from another author that such behavior represents an unconscious fantasy of humiliating and triumphing over one's parent. On the contrary, one expects that there will be *both* a sadistic and a masochistic, both a submissive and an aggressive, meaning to every patient's masochism.

Moreover, the relationship between the two opposing tendencies of sadism and masochism is not simply one of polarity or competition. Each has a defensive function as well as being a means of instinctual gratification, for example. In fact the complex phenomena of masochism can be best understood and most nearly unraveled only by viewing them in the framework of the structural hypothesis, that is, in reference to the interrelated functions of ego, superego, and id. It will be remembered that Brenman (6) was the author who most strongly emphasized the multiple function of a masochistic character formation, and rightly so. But in fact, masochistic character formation is in no way unique in this respect. On the contrary, as Waelder (27) pointed out, *every* psychic act may be viewed as a compromise among the various parts of the psychic apparatus.

The concept of intrapsychic compromise is an old one in psychoanalysis. It was introduced sixty years ago by Freud (11) in connection with the formation of psychoneurotic symptoms and has been a basic part of the psychoanalytic theory of symptom formation ever since. What is apparently not always so clearly kept in mind, though it certainly should be since Waelder called attention to it so explicitly in 1936, is that the concept of compromise formation or multiple function is applicable to many psychic acts and products other than neurotic symptoms. For example, and this is what is important for our present purpose, it is equally applicable to the formation of character traits, whether masochistic or otherwise, to the extent that such character traits resemble symptoms in arising on the basis of intrapsychic conflict.

If one uses the concept of multiple function as his frame of reference in viewing the clinical phenomena of the masochistic character, it is possible to observe in one's own patients that many of the apparently unrelated explanations that have appeared in the literature as constituting the unconscious motivation of masochistic behavior are indeed coexistent in the same patient and are mutually cooperative, if the word is permissible in such a context. A single set of masochistic fantasies and behavior will serve a great variety of functions in an individual, as the following clinical excerpt may show.

The patient was a single woman who began analysis at the age of thirty-two because of anxiety and depression. Despite these symptoms, which continued during several years of analysis, at times with considerable exacerbation, she was able to carry on her work without interruption and to function in a superior way in positions of responsibility. Actually the principal effect of her symptoms was to make her chronically unhappy and uncomfortable and to deprive her of many of the pleasures and satisfactions of life which otherwise would have been accessible to her on the basis of her real abilities and achievements.

Several factors appear to have been significant in the genesis of the masochistic character traits which were prominent in the patient's symptomatology. (i) The patient grew up in a semi-rural community in which there was a downtown gambling and red-light district in which her father spent every Saturday night. There was much talk among the children of fights, prostitutes, and killings, which was both exciting and frightening. Moreover, the patient's mother was constantly fearful that her husband would be killed or seriously hurt in his drunken revels, something which in fact never happened. As might be expected, the fantasy of being herself a prostitute figured prominently among the patient's childhood fantasies as far as could be ascertained by their revival in the transference. In these fantasies coitus was represented sadomasochistically as a violent fight between man and woman. In fact the patient's parents did quarrel often and violently, though the violence was limited to verbal exchanges. The intensity of the patient's emotional involvement in these scenes may be judged from the fact that on one occasion during a quarrel between her parents at the table when she was nine years old, she threatened to stab her father with a fork. (ii) The mother's generally expressed attitude was one of suffering and martyrdom. Though this attitude was often belied by the fact that the mother gave as good as she took in her battles with the patient's father, identification with her mother had for the patient the consequence of seeing herself as an abused and mistreated individual whose lot in life was to suffer at men's hands while at the same time she strove to revenge herself on them. (iii) Both her father and brother died suddenly and bloodily. The former event was the more traumatic and the more significant for her masochistic character formation. It occurred when the patient was seventeen years old as the terminal event of a year's illness which was understood by the patient to be the consequence of many years of dissipation. Her father arose one morning, had a massive hematemesis, and exsanguinated before the patient's eyes. Her brother killed himself some years later. The first of these two events contributed considerably to her unconscious guilt and to her fear that her murderous wishes could really kill, attitudes which were still further reinforced by her brother's death. As a consequence of this guilt and fear it was characteristic of her in adult life that self-punishment appeared instead of anger and revenge when a man failed to love her as she would have wished.

As might be expected, this patient's transference resistance took the form of masochistic suffering: she had a strong tendency toward a negative therapeutic reaction, getting worse or at best failing to improve with each interpretation, and in addition she was miserable, complaining, reproachful, and often silent for long periods of time. By these means she unconsciously expiated her guilt for her unconscious sadistic wishes toward me at the same time that she gratified them, still unconsciously, by triumphing over me and depriving me of what she regarded as my most precious possession: my therapeutic potency. In addition, her sulkiness and suffering duplicated her mother's behavior toward her father, so that it appeared that her masochistic transference reaction was a way of unconsciously acting out the fantasy that she and I were married and living together as mother and father had done. Again, from the point of view of her conflict with her superego, it was abundantly clear that her suffering behavior served not only as a submissive expiation but also as a defense against her guilt feelings, since by her suffering she demonstrated that it was I who was the cruel and guilty one and not she, who was on the contrary quite obviously the meek and gentle victim.

It must be understood that these many unconscious meanings did not emerge all at once nor with equal ease. They became accessible only gradually and over a long period of analysis, but each of them proved to be of importance in motivating the patient's masochistic behavior. It must also be understood that in other masochistic characters the significant unconscious motives for and functions of masochism may be at least partly different. It seems unlikely, to be sure, that in any case of masochistic character an adequate analysis would fail to find convincing evidence of an unconscious need for punishment and atonement. However, other factors may vary greatly in importance from case to case. For example, separation anxiety appeared to play a relatively minor role in the genesis of the masochistic character traits in the case just outlined, while in other cases it may play a very large role indeed.

It would seem therefore that it is probable that the various authors who have emphasized one or another particular genetic factor in masochistic character formation or one or another particular motive or function in its operation have each been correct in what they have said and have erred only in what they have omitted to say. The importance of this in clinical practice is that the analyst must expect that the proper analysis of the masochistic character traits in any patient in whom they bulk large will uncover a number of unconscious motives and functions for these traits rather than one or two, and that he will find, moreover, that these motives and functions vary somewhat from case to case.

This is particularly important to bear in mind in view of a tendency in the literature during the last several years to discuss the genesis and function of masochism solely in terms of object relations. This has been done explicitly by such authors as Berliner (2, 3, 4) and Menaker (22), and has been either implied or suggested by such others as Bernstein (5), Brenman (6), and Bromberg (7).

There can be no doubt that in many patients masochistic fantasies and behavior function, among other things, as a defense against fears of losing an object or the love of an object or both. However, it is equally true that these are not the only fears against which masochism serves as a defense. It may be recalled that Freud (19) outlined a typical sequence of infantile and childhood fears which he believed corresponded to successive stages in psychic development: fear of object loss, fear of loss of love, castration fear, and superego fear, or guilt. In a given patient, whatever his symptoms may be, one or another of these fears will play the major role, though it is rare for any of them to be really unimportant or absent. Moreover, they are often interrelated. A familiar example of this is furnished by the boy to whom his father's love is important as a guarantee against castration. In such a case the fear of loss of love and the fear of castration are hardly to be distinguished. An equally familiar example is that of the girl who equates possession of a penis with being her parents' favorite and in whom the fear of loss of love contributes in a major way to her painful mortification at being without a penis.

Such considerations concerning the origin and content of the typical fears of childhood are of general importance to the understanding of any neurotic symptoms in adult life, and masochistic fantasies and behavior are no exception. It is likely that each of the fears mentioned plays an important role in every case of masochistic character formation, with the major emphasis being on castration fear or its feminine analogues in some cases and on fear of loss of an object or of the object's love in others.

III

We may turn now to problems involved in the treatment of individuals in whom masochistic character traits play a considerable role. The particular technical problem which complicates the analyses of such patients is that which arises when masochistic behavior dominates the transference. This corresponds essentially to what Freud (17, 18) called the negative therapeutic reaction, that is, a paradoxical exacerbation of symptoms due to an unconscious need to suffer or be punished.

The most extensive discussions in the literature of the problems involved in treating masochistic patients are those by Eidelberg and Berliner. Of these Eidelberg was concerned with problems in the treatment of patients with masochistic sexual practices as well as of those with masochistic character traits, while Berliner was concerned only with the latter group of patients. It should be added, however, that the two groups frequently overlap to an appreciable degree.

According to Eidelberg (9, 26), "the problem of the recognition and final elimination of the infantile omnipotence is of decisive importance." Thus one must focus on the manifestations of the patient's fantasy of omnipotence, that is, on his using his ability to produce failure and to provoke punishment as proofs of magical control of the environment, especially as these manifestations appear in the transference; having done this one must then convince the patient that to stop being masochistic does not mean that he will become the helpless slave of the environment. In addition, or rather, as a preliminary, one must demonstrate to the patient that his suffering is not in spite of himself, but that on the contrary it is self-induced.

Berliner (4, 26) made three quite different points: (i) the analyst must be warm and friendly to avoid seeming like the patient's real parents; (ii) the analyst must take the patient's side against those whom the patient feels to be hostile to him; and (iii) the analyst must show the patient that his hostility is not his own, but is derived from his parents' real hostility toward him in childhood.

There are not many recommendations or observations elsewhere in the literature concerning the technical problems which arise in the psychoanalysis of patients with masochistic character formations. Menaker (22) offered recommendations which were very similar to those of Berliner. It will be recalled that the ideas of the two authors concerning the genesis of masochism were also very similar. Freud (15, 17, 18, 20) remarked on the negative therapeutic reaction exhibited by patients with masochistic character formation in whom the characteristically strong, unconscious need for punishment regularly resulted in a worsening of the patient's symptoms following a correct interpretation instead of in a symptomatic alleviation, as one would expect. Freud expressed pessimism concerning the possibilities for success in analyzing such patients, though he noted that he had occasionally been successful when the origin of the patient's masochism was in fact an identification with a masochistic parent: an incorporated rather than a genuine masochism, so to speak. Freud's pessimism has found an echo in the minds of many since the time he first voiced it and one frequently hears the opinion that masochistic character disturbances have a poor or hopeless prognosis.

Such pessimism and such considerable deviation from usual analytic technique as that recommended by Berliner and Menaker do not seem justified at our present stage of technical development. No one can claim that analytic technique has progressed to the point at which all patients are analyzable, but masochistic character traits are not unanalyzable as such. They may be present and even prominent in a patient who is unanalyzable for any one of many reasons. The mere fact of their presence, however, does not preclude analytic success, and in many cases conventional analytic technique will lead to a successful result.

By the same token a masochistic transference reaction, though doubtless a serious obstacle to the progress of analysis, is not necessarily an insuperable one per se. The approach to it should be to analyze it, in the same way in which one would analyze any other transference resistance in a patient with a character disorder; to direct the patient's attention to it as an object of analysis, to view it objectively oneself, to attempt to discover as much evidence as possible about its present role in the patient's unconscious mental life as a defense, as a means of gratification, as an expiation or punishment, etc., as well as evidence concerning its genesis, and finally to communicate to the patient one's conjectures as to its genesis and its present role in a suitable way and at an appropriate time. It is not always an easy matter to maintain an analytic attitude toward a patient whose continual, daily complaints are of being victimized by an analyst whose efforts to cure him only succeed in making him worse, but it is just as necessary to do so as to maintain an analytic attitude toward any transference reaction which functions as a resistance. One must remember that all patients to a greater or less extent use "reality" to relive infantile desires and conflicts, and sadomasochistic patients are no exception to this rule.

The following clinical excerpts are intended to illustrate both that a considerable degree of masochism does not necessarily preclude good therapeutic progress in analysis and that the degree of therapeutic success, or the rate of progress, achieved in the analysis of a masochistic patient is not simply a function of the severity of his masochism. At the same time an attempt will be made to illustrate certain of the general principles just mentioned which should guide the analyst in dealing with a masochistic transference reaction. It will be noted that in the examples to be given success was not achieved in a crucial analytic hour or by a single, crucially important piece of analytic understanding suitably interpreted to the patient. Such dramatically impressive events may occur in the analysis of a patient with masochistic character traits, as they may in the analyses of patients with any other type of psychological disturbances. The individual circumstances of the particular case determine whether or not this will be so. However, in the majority of masochistic patients what seems at least to be of vital importance for a satisfactory therapeutic result is the steady day-to-day work, always with as clear a view as possible of the conflicting forces at work within the patient's mind.

A. and B. were both single male patients in their early thirties with serious masochistic character disturbances. A. came to analysis complaining of a general feeling of unhappiness, worse at some times than at others, and of an inability to fall in love and marry. B's chief complaints were of occasional impulsive episodes of homosexual behavior in which his partners performed fellatio upon him and of acute attacks of anxiety during the preceding two and a half years which seriously interfered with his work. Despite the lack of similarity suggested by the differences between their chief complaints, further acquaintance with the patients revealed that they were very much alike. Thus A. had strong unconscious homosexual tendencies and had all his life worried that he would be considered a sissy or a homosexual. Indeed in boyhood he had felt himself to be effeminate and had deliberately striven against appearing to be so. Moreover both patients had made up their minds before ever seeing me that they weren't going to have any personal feelings toward their analysts, A. because that would be "sissyish" and B. because it would mean he "really was" a homosexual, a thought that terrified him. Thus despite the absence of overt homosexual behavior A. resembled B. very closely in this respect. It also turned out that B., llke A., had never felt happy during his life, or at least never since very early childhood. In both cases it developed during the course of treatment that loneliness had been an important part of the chronic unhappiness which each had felt, though neither had been aware of feeling lonely prior to treatment.

A wish to be beaten played a considerable role in the lives of both patients. A. remembered a childhood game in which a male friend of his parents would pretend to spank him whenever he visited A's home, a game in which A. took great delight. He also recalled a childhood belief that the man who lived next door beat his wife and several daughters with a whip. When his own father occasionally spanked him in boyhood he recalled feeling sexually excited as well as frightened and fearing that his penis would fall off. In adult life he masturbated occasionally with intense excitement at times when he felt acutely helpless, unhappy or lost, with a vague conscious idea that something unpleasant or painful was being done to him. In B's case there had been conscious fantasies of beating or rape which had accompanied masturbation ever since adolescence, fantasies in which he identified with the maltreated woman. Both patients had a considerable degree of anal fixation or regression which had been evident in various ways during their lives. In particular, both arranged their lives unconsciously so that they were taken advantage of financially. Both had many affairs with women in adult life with normal potency but inadequate pleasure. Neither was habitually overtly sadistic or masochistic during the sexual act itself, though there were natu-rally many sadomasochistic features in the relationship of each with women.

The tendency to be taken advantage of by others was more pronounced in B. than in A., or at any rate it had led to more serious consequences. Thus B. continued to be exploited by his parents and employers to an incredible degree right up to the time of his entry into analysis, so much so, indeed, that it nearly wrecked his career. A. on the other hand had been able to break away from home in late adolescence rather than remaining to be exploited by his parents who would have been glad to employ him in his father's business all his life for a pittance, as they had done with one of his brothers.

A few words should be said about the outstanding events and influences of early childhood which seemed to be directly connected with the two patients' psychological difficulties in later life. A's mother was separated from him and from the rest of the family when he was three by a chronic physical illness from which she subsequently died, so that he was left dependent on a succession of nurses for mothering. His father was a very passive, fearful man who was quite obviously jealous of his sons, and the patient greatly envied a baby sister who was clearly the family favorite. Some idea of his intense longing for love and of his feminine identification in childhood may be indicated by the fact that at the age of nine or ten he begged so hard for a tonsillectomy that he finally gained his wish. The operation was performed under local anesthesia and was followed by a severe otitis media. In B's early childhood the most important single event was a circumcision at the age of five. Until that time he had been a habitual bed wetter and he recalled being told that the operation was to help him stop his enuresis. In that respect it was completely successful. He was never enuretic thereafter. Indeed he was a model child, though an unhappy one, who ever after, until the day he started analysis, turned over all his earnings to his parents without ever asking or receiving an accounting for the money. Throughout boyhood he served his mother as a maid of all work about the house and in adolescence was a menial in various of his father's enterprises, while the latter traveled about "on business." It was only by making great sacrifices and by continuing to work as a laborer for his father that he was able to attend college and eventually to equip himself for a professional career.

It is hoped that this brief comparison has served to establish, first, that the two cases are comparable symptomatically, and second, that the manifestations of masochistic tendencies in patient B. were at least as severe as those of patient A., if not somewhat more so. Thus B. had more overtly masochistic sexual disturbances with frightening, conscious beating and rape fantasies often accompanying masturbation; B's unconscious need to find someone to exploit and to mistreat him in ordinary social relationships was greater than was the case with A. and had led to the virtual destruction of his career by the time he started analysis; and finally, the fact that B. was submissive to his parents and willing to be exploited by them well into adult life seems likewise to argue that he was more masochistic than A., who broke away from home at a much earlier age.

If the severity of the masochistic disorder is the factor which is decisive in limiting therapeutic success in such patients one would expect A's analysis to be the more successful of the two, yet in fact the reverse was the case. A's analysis dragged on for years, was characterized by a stubborn, masochistic transference resistance with all the classical features of a negative therapeutic reaction that erupted on the occasion of the first discussion of his then unconscious homosexual wishes and that repeatedly brought the patient close to fleeing from treatment. B. on the other hand made relatively rapid progress toward being able to face his homosexual and sadomasochistic wishes and the conflicts underlying them, as well as toward remembering many of the significant pathogenic events of his childhood. In addition, the rate of symptomatic improvement was much greater for B. than for A., and under this heading are included improvement in feelings and behavior toward women with whom he had sexual relationships, improvement in other social relationships, improvement in career, improvement in ability to handle money, and changes in feelings of self-esteem and in his ability to enjoy life. Finally the manifestations of resistance which appeared in the transference in B's case were analyzable, despite the sadomasochistic nature of the fantasies involved and they did not lead to any serious negative therapeutic reaction.

These data would appear to suffice to demonstrate both that a considerable degree of masochism does not necessarily preclude good therapeutic progress in analysis and that the rate of progress achieved in the analysis of a masochistic patient is not simply a function of the severity of his masochism. It is more difficult to perform the final task that has been set for this section, namely, to indicate how one deals in practice with a difficult masochistic transference reaction, but perhaps the following will serve to accomplish it in some measure. It concerns an episode in A's analysis.

The pertinent facts were as follows. For some weeks A. had been trying to get a favor from me, a favor disguised as a concession on my part with regard to our long-established arrangement about fee. A. presented his desire for this concession as something quite impersonal, a matter that had nothing to do with more than a purely business matter between us, and something that it was reasonable and justifiable for him to desire on purely external grounds. However, his dreams and associations indicated more and more openly as time went on that his wish for this concession was a repetition in the transference of his childhood wish to be the favorite child. It will be recalled that he had been very envious of a baby sister in early childhood.

As long as he was hopeful of gaining what he wished, A. behaved in an exemplary fashion in treatment. He worked hard during each hour at facing his passivity and its origins, and at recognizing his envy and the material wishes as well as the rage connected with them, emotions which both frightened him and made him guilty, and which he attempted as always to deal with by masochistic fantasies and behavior. Nevertheless there was no evidence of insuperable resistance or of a negative therapeutic reaction as yet. However, the most important aspect of all that was going on was not at first contained in the increased insights and understanding being gained through analysis. It was that the patient was endeavoring by his behavior to win a material token of love from me by his exemplary behavior. Eventually it was possible for him to verbalize even this and to talk humorously of wanting to kill me if I didn't grant his wish.

When he understood that his wish would not be granted, however, the entire analytic picture changed. A. felt angry, mistreated and desperately unhappy, but without recognizing the connection between these feelings and the frustration of his wish for something from me. On the contrary, he attributed all of these feelings to the fear that his current girl friend no longer loved him and he tried very hard to provoke her into unloving behavior, unsuccessfully as it happened. When the motives of his provocative behavior with her were made clear to him and the spurious idea that it was her coldness that desolated him became untenable, which took only a few days, A. came in, lay down on the couch, and announced that he was leaving analysis as of that day: analysis was too slow, too expensive, and he could see no good results from it. In fact he only felt worse than he had when he had started years before.

This decision was announced with complete soberness, deliberation, and finality, yet within a few minutes its unconscious motivations were clearly indicated by A's behavior: after announcing his decision he fell silent and, as he admitted, wanted me to say something. He vehemently denied wanting me to persuade or encourage him to stay in analysis, but he could admit wishing that I would say something that would indicate sympathy and interest on my part, and after some little time he was able to confess that the closer he had come that day to my office the more aware he had been of feeling that he would miss me when he left analysis. In fact this very feeling of "dependence" on me made it seem to him the more necessary to break away from me once and for all.

It was possible to interpret to A. the connection between my refusal to grant him the favor he wanted from me and his subsequent rage, loneliness, misery, exacerbation of symptoms, and decision to leave, and in fact he remained in treatment. It took weeks, however, before his stubborn masochistic transference resistance could be overcome and his decision to leave treatment was repeated more than once during that time, so that there were considerable periods during which he was in treatment from day to day. It will be understood that during the course of analyzing this episode it was possible to relate it to similar disappointments and reactions in A's childhood and that much more was learned and interpreted concerning A's unconscious responses to my refusal than has been specifically mentioned.

When such a masochistic transference resistance and negative therapeutic reaction are presented as this one has been with a list of the precipitating factors and of the appropriate and efficacious interpretations, it may not seem that any very difficult therapeutic problem is involved. It is not quite so simple when it happens, however. Then is when one must extract from all the many facts of the situation the particular ones that are decisive; that is, the analyst must understand what is really going on in his patient's analysis, and this is often no easy matter.

It would seem that an analyst is most likely to be successful in understanding correctly a patient's masochistic transference reaction if certain conditions are met. First, that the analyst is not himself unconsciously tempted to participate with the patient in some sort of sadomasochistic behavior: to become angry at the patient, to feel hopeless and defeated by him, or to demonstrate either affection or aversion in whatever way. Second, that the analyst bear in mind the various meanings which masochistic behavior may have and the purposes it may serve in a patient's mental life so that he is ready to perceive those meanings and purposes, however well disguised and rationalized they may be. If these conditions are met, the analyst is able to demonstrate to the patient as well as may be done the true significance of the patient's masochistic reaction in the transference: that it is at once defensive, expiatory, unconsciously gratifying, and above all a repetition of the patient's way of reacting to the instinctual conflicts of early life.

A model of behavior for the analyst to follow in dealing with such situations which is somewhat homely but perhaps useful is that of an understanding adult who has the task of dealing reasonably with a sulky, stubborn, provocative child. If the adult is wise and not unduly involved emotionally with the child, he is not upset or disturbed by such a child's behavior but remains calmly observant and understanding whatever may be the child's attempts to seduce and provoke him into a sadomasochistic episode. Nearly everyone will agree that this is easier said than done, but it must be added that difficult though it be, it is not impossible, and that in any case it is essential to the optimal analytic treatment of the masochistic patient.

SUMMARY

1. The views of Freud and those of later authors relative to masochism have been briefly reviewed.

2. It is suggested that it is useful to view the problem in the following way. (a) Masochism is a normal component or characteristic of the human personality, as witness the part it plays in superego formation and functioning. (b) The difference between the normal and the masochistic character is one of degree rather than of kind. (c) Masochistic character traits and masochistic tendencies may be associated with many sorts of neurotic symptoms and a variety of other character disturbances. (d) In practice masochistic fantasies and character traits are always associated with sadistic ones; the label "sadomasochistic" would really be more appropriate than the label "masochistic." (e) Masochistic character traits and fantasies exhibit a multiple function and are multiply determined; this multiple function is most conveniently expressed in terms of coexisting tendencies of the ego, superego, and id. (f) Though there are similarities in the functions and genesis of masochistic traits and fantasies from case to case, there are also differences; not all cases are identical. (g) Masochistic character traits and fantasies are a legacy of infantile sexual conflicts, principally of oedipal conflicts in most cases. (h) As such they are related to the principal danger situations of early childhood, which are typically the dangers of object loss, of loss of love, and of castration, but the importance of each of these dangers as a motive for defense will vary from one masochistic patient to another. (i) The analysis of a patient with masochistic character traits is no different in principle from any other character analysis. The special difficulties presented by such analyses lie in the handling of the sadomasochistic transference relationship and of the related negative therapeutic reaction. (j) Like any other transference relationship which serves the function of resistance, a sadomasochistic transference may or may not be analyzable. If a suitably objective attitude is maintained and if the analyst persists in analyzing the patient's reactions rather than himself reacting to them in any other way, a successful result is attainable more often than would appear to be generally recognized.

NOTES

1. It should be noted that this is only one aspect of superego genesis and functioning, an aspect which is emphasized here because of its importance in the theory of masochism and not because it is conceived of as the prime factor in superego formation. The importance of the fear of punishment (castration or analogous genital injury) in the formation and functioning of the superego is presumed to be of principal significance in most cases in accordance with the abundant literature on the subject since Freud (17).

BIBLIOGRAPHY

1. Bak, R. Masochism in paranoia. *Psychoanal. Quart.*, *15*:285–301, 1946.
2. Berliner, B. Libido and reality in masochism. *Psychoanal. Quart.*, *9*:322–333, 1940.
3. Berliner, B. On some psychodynamics of masochism. *Psychoanal. Quart.*, *16*:459–471, 1947.
4. Berliner, B. The role of object relations in moral masochism. *Psychoanal. Quart.*, *27*:38–56, 1958.
5. Bernstein, L. The role of narcissism in moral masochism. *Psychoanal. Quart.*, *26*:358–377, 1957.
6. Brenman, M. On being teased; and the problem of "moral masochism." *The Psychoanalytic Study of the Child*, *7*:264–285. New York: International Universities Press, 1952.
7. Bromberg, N. Maternal influences in the development of moral masochism. *Am. J. Orthopsychiat.*, *25*:802–809, 1955.
8. Eidelberg, L. A contribution to the study of masochism (1934). *Studies in Psychoanalysis.* New York: International Universities Press, 1952, pp. 31–40.
9. Eidelberg, L. Technical problems in the analysis of masochists. *J. Hillside Hosp.*, *7*:98–109, 1958.
10. Fenichel, O. *The Psychoanalytic Theory of Neurosis.* New York: W. W. Norton, 1946.
11. Freud, S. Further remarks on the defence neuropsychoses (1896). *Collected Papers, 1*:155–182. London: Hogarth Press, 1924.
12. Freud, S. Three essays on sexuality (1905). *Standard Edition, 7*:125–243. London: Hogarth Press, 1953.
13. Freud, S. Instincts and their vicissitudes (1915). *Standard Edition, 14*:109–140. London: Hogarth Press, 1957.
14. Freud, S. Mourning and melancholia (1917). *Standard Edition, 14*:237–258. London: Hogarth Press, 1957.
15. Freud, S. "A child is being beaten" (1919). *Standard Edition, 17*:175–204. London: Hogarth Press, 1955.
16. Freud, S. Beyond the pleasure principle (1920). *Standard Edition, 18*:3–64. London: Hogarth Press, 1955.
17. Freud, S. *The Ego and the Id* (1923). London: Hogarth Press, 1927.
18. Freud, S. The economic problem of masochism (1924). *Collected Papers, 2*:255–268. London: Hogarth Press, 1924.
19. Freud, S. *The Problem of Anxiety* (1926). New York: W. W. Norton, 1936.
20. Freud, S. Constructions in analysis (1938). *Collected Papers, 5*:358–371. London: Hogarth Press, 1950.

21. Loewenstein, R. M. A contribution to the psychoanalytic theory of masochism. *JAPA*, 5:197–234, 1957.

22. Menaker, E. Masochism—a defense reaction of the ego. *Psychoanal. Quart.*, 22:205–220, 1953.

23. Monchy, R. Masochism as a pathological and as a normal phenomenon in the human mind. *Int. J. Psychoanal.*, 31:95–97, 1950.

24. Reik, T. The characteristics of masochism. *Am. Imago*, 1:26–59, 1939.

25. Reik, T. *Masochism in Modern Man*. New York: Farrar & Rinehart, 1941.

26. Stein, M. H. Report of panel on the problem of masochism in the theory and technique of psychoanalysis. *JAPA*, 4:526–538, 1956.

27. Waelder, R. The principle of multiple function: observations on overdetermination. *Psychoanal. Quart.*, 5:45–62, 1936.

19. The Excitement of Sadomasochism

Stanley J. Coen

. . . .

The psychoanalytic literature, by and large, regards the etiologic differences between masochistic character disorder and masochistic perversion as
unknown. The interrelations between masochistic character disorder and
masochistic sexual excitement are complex. It is not sufficiently appreciated
that sadomasochistic enactments, both sexual and not explicitly sexual, are
exciting, often intensely so. We will focus on this excitement, sexual and
nonsexual, in sadomasochistic object relationships. This focus will help us to
explore patients' difficulty with relinquishing sadomasochistic relationships.

Stoller (1976) proposed that sexual and nonsexual excitement involves
rapid oscillation among fantasied danger, repetition of prior trauma, and
fantasied triumph and revenge. He especially emphasized sexual excitement
as defense against anxiety. Shapiro (1981) suggested that what is exciting for
the sexual sadomasochist is playing at giving in to fantasies of dominance
and submission. This dynamic, however, in no way distinguishes the moral
masochist from the masochistic pervert. This formulation leaves us wonder-
ing why all moral masochists are not perverts inasmuch as they all share
conflicts about dominance and submission.

It will be helpful to bear in mind Freud's (1905) early proposal that sadism
and masochism are erotic expressions of aggression. That is, a focus on the
erotic in sadomasochism will keep us close to the excitement. Sadomasochistic object relations are a way of loving (and hating) others and oneself and
are especially concerned with intense ways of engaging another so as to
mitigate dangers of separateness, loss, loneliness, hurt, destruction, and
guilt. Aggression and sexuality are adapted to this end of intense connected-

Reprinted from S. Coen, from *The Misuse of Persons: Analyzing Pathological Dependency,*
190–208, by permission of the publisher. Copyright © 1992 by The Analytic Press.

ness with another person. Multiple defensive and adaptive functions are subserved. Sadomasochistic object relations can be viewed schematically as a complex defensive system against destruction and loss, within which relationships are continually pushed to the brink, with the reassurance that the relationship (at least some imaginary parent-child relationship) will never end. To the degree that separateness is too frightening to be tolerated, the patient will fear and be unable to relinquish such sadomasochistic bonding. Despite the threats, fights, provocations, and excitement, sadomasochistic object relations tend to be stable, enduring, and highly resistant to change.

Here is a brief sample from Sacher-Masoch's (1870) *Venus in Furs* to illustrate the need to manage both separateness and destructiveness in sadomasochism:

Severin: "I want your power over me to become law; then my life will rest in your hands and I shall have no protection against you. Ah, what delight to depend entirely on your whims, to be constantly at your beck and call! And then—what bliss!—when the goddess shows clemency, the slave will have permission to kiss the lips on which his life and death depend" [p. 163].

Wanda to Severin: "You are no longer my lover, and therefore, I am relieved of all duties and obligations towards you; you must regard my favors as pure benevolence. You can no longer lay claim to any rights, and there are no limits to my power over you. Consider that you are little better now than a dog or an object; you are my thing, the toy that I can break if it gives me a moment of pleasure. You are nothing, I am everything; do you understand?" [p. 164].

The contract between them: "Mrs. von Dunajew may not only chastise her slave for the slightest negligence or misdemeanor as and when she wishes but she will also have the right to maltreat him according to her humor or even simply to amuse herself; she is also entitled to kill him if she so wishes; in short, he becomes her absolute property" [fragment, p. 184].

Usually, layers of anxiety, defense, and guilt cover the excitement of sadomasochism. In my experience, patients with sadomasochistic character disorder have sadomasochistically distorted sexuality (not, however, structured perversions). Like the excitement more generally, this distortion is not readily apparent; it is uncovered only by analysis.

Certain similarities in defense and adaptation should be noted between sadomasochistic object relations and sadomasochistic perversion. The content of the excitement and the dynamic uses made of it are similar in both. Sadomasochistic excitement involves entering into what is ordinarily dangerous and forbidden: incestuous, exploitative, inappropriate, hurtful, infantile, regressive. Excited, intense feelings and experiences substitute for genuine love and caring and defend against negative feelings in oneself and in the other. When one feels unloved and unloving, illusions of intense, excited involvement with another are substituted. The couple has difficulty being separate and feeling valuable, so that they must be with each other and at each other. This dilemma is then idealized as if it were wonderful love. "You can't stand to be without me; you can't resist me; I'm the most important person in the world to you!"—such grandiose, exciting, seeming adoration fills in the gap of one's feeling unloved. When the promise of such adoration is frustrated, then rage, hurt, and rejection are evoked. These feelings threaten disruption of the bond and lead to more provocation and attack so as to reconnect, even more intensely, with the partner. Such patients become addicted to the exciting illusion of special (grandiose) adoration. This becomes the background for erotized repetition. Genetic and dynamic links, especially in relation to defense against hostile aggression, are described among sexual seductiveness, sexualization, and sadomasochism. Similarities are noted in the object relations (perverse misuse of others) of certain patients with sadomasochistic character disorder and sadomasochistic perverts. Patients with masochistic character disorder are relatively able to express conflict in fantasy, to handle it within their own mind. Masochistic perverts differ in being impelled to enact unconscious fantasies into concrete reality so as to render them valid and credible. They cannot accomplish this process intrapsychically; their ability to symbolize and to resolve conflict in fantasy is impaired.

EROTIZED REPETITION

Contemporary psychoanalysts have tended to overly desexualize masochism. (See Maleson, 1984, and Grossman, 1986, for discussions of this). These writings have helped to differentiate moral masochism from masochistic perversion and to trace Freud's views of sadism and masochism as component instincts. Further, a multiple-function approach to masochism must certainly emphasize the variety of nonsexual meanings encompassed in clinical descriptions. Nevertheless, this tack has tended to minimize the motivational pressure, the driven excitement, in sadomasochism. Defensively sexualized repetition remains a useful perspective from which to view clinical samples of sadomasochism. Sexualization of hostile aggression is an important contributor to sadomasochism. Sexualization as defense is usually considered in relation to painful affects, hostile aggression, and narcissistic needs. To be sure, not all samples of sadomasochistic behavior can be demonstrated to involve defensively sexualized repetition. But I am impressed with the confluence of moral masochism with defensively sexualized repetition. Similar genetic and dynamic issues tend to occur where sexualization is used as a predominant form of defense and in sadomasochistic character pathology. Separateness, loss, helplessness, and destruction are central dangers to be defended against by sexualization and by moral masochism. Sexualization and sadomasochism are both especially useful ways to manage intensely frightening destructiveness.

It is exciting to feel able to induce intense affective responses in another person, to overcome the other's barriers, to feel in control and dominant, able to make the other feel bad, guilty, weak, inferior, defective. It is exciting to hold another person in the palm of one's hand, to push another to the point of losing control, attacking, and leaving, and then to be reassured that this loss will not occur. Others can be simultaneously gotten rid of and held onto. When one is terrified of separateness and destructiveness, it is very reassuring, indeed, to feel able to combine getting rid of and holding on. It is not my intention here to attempt a comprehensive review of the literature on masochism. What I am after, instead, is focusing on why masochistic object relations are held onto so tenaciously. Parkin's (1980) view of masochistic enthrallment is relevant as the attempt to share in and borrow the mother's power and fury. I prefer, however, to emphasize the masochist's willingness to surrender to the hostile (critical) parental view of him in order to feel the illusion of magical protection, caring, and specialness under the domination of the powerful (destructive) parent. Surrender protects both child and parent from the dangers of the hatred and destructiveness in both of them and makes possible some relationship between them. The child (patient) accepts his role as the worthless, defective, shitty one in submission to the hostile, rejecting parent as the good, idealized one. This becomes a kind of "seduction of the aggressor" (Loewenstein, 1957). It is seductive, indeed, to offer the other the grandiose prospect of doing whatever he pleases with you. The child (patient) can then extract some caring from the parent, protect the parent from his guilt at hating/rejecting the child, and enhance his own worthiness through his suffering. He plays at the illusion that since he is the bad one, when he finally becomes good, the parent will love him. To face the fact of the parent's inability or deficiency in loving and the parent's hatred and destructiveness is too barren a prospect for the child. To face one's own rage and destructiveness is too frightening. The masochist seeks mastery and control and associated narcissistic enhancement through the provocation and exaggeration of suffering. The willingness to continue to view oneself through the hateful and distorted eyes of a rejecting parent, because of all of these defensive and compensatory gains, can be strong, indeed. The wish to surrender, to hate oneself, to feel depressed, shitty, worthless, incapable, crippled is in these terms, an appeal to a parent for love, caring, and protection, especially from the rage and destructiveness in the patient and in the parent.

Underneath the layer of game playing in sadomasochistic object relations is a more serious destructiveness—destroying another's integrity, self-respect, autonomy, and free choice. This point is where it becomes frightening to face the parent's destructiveness in wanting to cripple oneself as well as one's own destructive hatred of the parent. If one feels terrified of separateness and of one's destructiveness and continues to crave parental loving, it becomes impossible to integrate one's hatred and destructiveness and to let go of the pathological relationship with the destructive parent. Sadomasochism's combined destroying/getting rid of and holding onto avoids this more mature integration. Instead of facing what has been wrong, the patient becomes excited in repeating what a parent (mother) did with one. Indeed, the excited, erotized repetition serves to ward off the horrors of destructiveness, mother's and one's own. Erotization tames destructiveness; one can pretend that it is a kind of loving relatedness, an exciting game sought by both participants. Playing this game is very different from acknowledging that one person hates, envies, and begrudges another his own life and his own separateness and autonomy and wants to destroy them. Dangers of fusion through passive masochistic surrender are defended against by the illusion of sadistic omnipotent control, the ability to render another helpless. That is, the masochist is hardly just a passive victim. Under that pose are his hungry destructiveness, his wish to control, dominate, rob, and despoil the other. Submission to a stronger object serves to protect the masochist from fears of his own destructive wishes and affects.

THE GENETIC BACKGROUND OF EROTIZED SADOMASOCHISM

One common genetic background for both sexualization (when extensively used) and sadomasochism is a relationship with a relatively unavailable, depressed mother who is sometimes inappropriately and overly seductive but much of the time is unresponsive and unempathic. Extractiveness in the service of mother's pressing needs combines with her sexualized defense against her own destructiveness and rejection of the child. These motivations are commonly expressed in a sadomasochistic relationship between mother and child. Terrors of loss and destruction are countered by the illusion that mother and child will remain tightly bound together forever. Such mothers resent the burdens of child care. They wish to be the one who is cared for. They envy the child his new chance in life, his autonomy, capacities, strength, youth, attractiveness, phallus (i.e., whatever they feel they lack). Out of envy and hatred, the mother unconsciously wishes to destroy these attributes of the child. She cripples the child and bonds the child forever to her, with a reversal of roles. Idealization of pretended loving (reaction formation) and seductive overstimulation emphasize that the mother-child relationship is good and loving rather than exploitative and destructive. The child identifies with mother's predominant defensive positions and relates to her in a complementary way. This encourages both sexualization and sadomasochism as defensive and adaptive phenomena to contain and soothe intolerable affects.

Sadomasochistic provocation of a child can lead to overstimulation of sexuality and aggression, overwhelming the child with affects of arousal, rage, hurt, and humiliation. Being the object of such intense attention from a parent, in sexually seductive or sadomasochistic ways, stirs feelings of specialness and exception. These alternate with feelings of neglect and loneliness, guilt at one's transgressions (sexual or sadomasochistic), overstimulation, rage, and helplessness at one's exploitation and neglect. Defensive identification and erotic or sadomasochistic repetition aim to master the overwhelming affects, as well as to repeat the idealized pleasures. Being the child of sadomasochistic parents can be a chronic strain trauma. That is, the child is frequently and chronically flooded with anger and sexual arousal, without adequate parental protection for modulating these affects. As with Q, whom I shall describe shortly, there may be a lack of clear boundaries between family members. Autonomy is not to be respected, but to be destroyed in the service of intense neediness. Family members are not to be separate and different, each responsible for tolerating and resolving his own difficulties. The destruction of autonomy encourages and perpetuates interactive defensive modes, pathological forms of object relating, and defensive analization. Mixing and merging of self and other, of good and bad confuses boundaries, identity, and psychic contents. One blames the other and tries to make the other responsible and guilty for what is wrong within oneself. This mode of relating must interfere with separateness and increasing tolerance and responsibility for one's own affects and wishes. The more uncomfortable a person feels with his own psychic contents, the more he must turn to another for protection. Once this tendency has become automatic, change, even within a psychoanalysis, can become very difficult indeed. Bear in mind that masochism need not have this particular genetic background; there need not have been sadomasochistic parents. What is emphasized here are the consequences of having had sadomasochistic parents.

Here is a brief example, reported to me by the horrified father, my patient. Q, a toddler, was watching her parents in another intense, sadomasochistic fight. Mother was screaming obscenities at father and trying to claw at him; she seemed to be out of control. Father, angry and helpless, grabbed his wife's hands and yelled at her to stop fighting in front of Q, who became excited, overstimulated, overwhelmed. She, too, began to scream, "Shut up, you fuckin' bitch!" and grabbed at her mother. Father was appalled, thinking that Q looked just like his wife—she was becoming a toddler sadomasochist!

Q had been overindulged, the parents making conscious attempts to keep her from feeling frustrated. Q had been allowed unlimited access to the parental bed and to the mother's body; the mother had overidentified and confused herself with the frustrated child. Q had not been provided with reasonable limits to her need satisfaction and reasonable experiences of frustration. These would have been necessary for her to develop tolerance and patience while learning to soothe and comfort herself. She was encouraged to identify with both parents' urgent demandingness and wish that there be no frustration or (reasonable) separateness. Parents and child repeatedly re-created an exciting and entitled primal scene from which none of them was to be excluded. Q, too, could go after whatever bodily gratifications she desired. In these fighting scenes, this young child had to deal with her parents' being out of control, enraged, and destructive. There was a temporary loss of a protective parent to help modulate her affects.

PSYCHODYNAMICS OF EROTIZED
SADOMASOCHISM

The child attempts to get and maintain some mothering in an otherwise very difficult situation. Rage, hurt, humiliation, exploitation, neglect, and betrayal require powerful regressive defenses. Both sexualization and sadomasochism are especially useful for the illusion that destructiveness is caring. Excited, intense feelings and experiences are idealized and defensively focused on. Here are important dynamic similarities among sadomasochistic character, sexualization, and perversion. The excitement, from mixing together intense hostile aggression and sexuality, allows such patients, like perverts, temporarily to master rage and other negative affects. During imaginary, as well as enacted, seductive and provocative encounters, there occurs a temporary defensive transformation of negatively toned, aggressively infiltrated images of self and other(s) into positive, pleasurably regarded ones. Sexual arousal, masturbation, and enactment of seductive fantasy all help temporarily to disown negative aspects of the self and to appropriate dangerous aspects of the object. Sexual responsiveness, in fantasy or in actual enactments, reassures against fears of loss or destruction of the object or oneself.

An extreme example of a sexualized defense occurred in Ms. W, a psychotically delusional patient whose analyst spoke to her about hospitalization because the patient and the treatment relationship had become unmanageable. For the entire session, she smiled, stared seductively into the analyst's eyes and insisted she would never leave him and he could never leave her. Words did not count, nor did they have anything to do with what was real—an intense, exciting, passionate bond that could never be broken. The more she feared loss or destruction of the relationship with the analyst, the more Ms. W needed to tempt, seduce, and provoke the analyst into excited interaction with her. She had long overtly and implicitly offered to be the analyst's most adoring one, so that she and he would share the grandiose splendor of being god and goddess of the world. This union was now to be consummated. Ms. W would never be apart from him, a merger that she attempted to enact! She covered over her destructive wishes to devour and drain the analyst with seductiveness, adoration, and loving words; however, her hungry destructiveness (and primitive guilt about it) and terror of separation broke through the "loving" cover to spoil it. Ms. W refused to leave the analyst's office, followed him home, phoned him repeatedly during the night, and tried to enter his home. She dealt with her guilt about her hostile aggression by insisting that the analyst was now the cause of the problem. If only he would leave his family, live with her, and love her, everything would now be fine!

In less extreme form, in neurotic sadomasochism, the illusion of loving conceals destructiveness and the wish to misuse the other. We could also discuss "aggressivization" of object relations in sadomasochism; abundantly available aggressive drive derivatives infiltrate libidinal object relations in the service of intense attachment, relatedness, and domination.

In the sexual seductiveness of sadomasochistic object relations, the object cannot be left alone, outside of one's own orbit. The pair can neither be comfortably together nor be apart. Hatred drives the couple apart; fear of separateness and loneliness forces them together. Control, domination, submission, and arousal of intense affects by omnipotent manipulation keep the couple engaged. Denial and projective identification aim to put into the other what cannot be tolerated within oneself. The other is made the "bad one," who must then seek absolution and loving forgiveness from oneself. Badness is then repeatedly made not to count. It is magically turned into goodness. Fixed, clear moral standards have little force. What matters is to be accepted by the other, however this acceptance is accomplished. During phases of sexualized reunion, each partner feels accepted, forgiven, and no longer bad. The badness in each has been magically repudiated. Both partners are now good; it is others who are bad.

CLINICAL VIGNETTES

Ms. O complained of feeling depressed and hopeless that she would ever have a satisfactory love relationship. She had again broken up with Xa, although this relationship was, she thought, the best she had yet had. Xa had told her repeatedly that he would not tolerate her provocative fighting. They had just resumed their relationship after another "ending." On Christmas Day, Ms. O gave Xa a number of gifts. The previous day she had complained on the phone that Xa had not gotten her any gifts. He arrived with a lovely bouquet of flowers. As Xa unwrapped the gifts Ms. O had gotten him, she became more and more incensed that he had not gotten her anything besides the flowers. She tried to ignore her feelings but, instead, found herself boiling up, wanting to go at Xa. Finally, she could not resist. She attacked Xa for his lack of generosity and worked herself and him into a frenzy. He tried to calm her down and briefly got her interested in sex, but there was no stopping Ms. O. Xa left, again announcing that the relationship was over. The patient called his home repeatedly, then took a long cab ride to his home. She left him a note and multiple messages on his answering machine and apologized, saying that she wanted to see him again. This provocation was a repetitive pattern. When she felt ignored, neglected, or abandoned,

Ms. O would attack the other person; she would try to provoke him into fighting with her and make him feel guilty and responsible for her. She was now well aware how exciting provocative fighting was and how difficult it was for her to resist the temptation to engage others in such scuffles.

With the analyst also, especially before separations, she would be provocative, attacking, guilt provoking, trying to worry him and make him responsible for what would happen to her in his absence. She sought to elicit some intense reaction from the analyst that would reassure her that she, in effect, would be emotionally inside him during the separation. If the analyst felt worried about her, guilty or angry with her, she could imagine that she was with him during the separation. The patient would repeatedly become more demanding and difficult with the analyst up to the point where he was expected to lose control, get angry, and threaten to get rid of her. When she feared this result might happen, she would quickly change and behave herself to undo the danger of being gotten rid of. In this enactment of a beating wish, she also wanted the analyst to restrain and contain her hatred and destructiveness. The analyst was to spank her and thus show her that he both loved her and was strong enough to protect both of them from her intense destructiveness. She could not at all take for granted the analyst's concern and ability to help her to contain her destructiveness.

The reader will need some background to appreciate why Mr. P felt so anxious and uncomfortable on an initial date with V, an attractive, capable woman. Mr. P was a very rigid, consciously paranoid and schizoid, single corporate executive who was afraid of his own feelings, of intimate contact with others, and of others' controlling and dominating him. With me, Mr. P was controlled and guarded, fearful of really becoming emotionally involved, of any spontaneity. He was referred to me with low back pain syndrome. His hesitation to resume his life fully, while some leg pain persisted, conveyed the feeling that, if he actively made a move on his own behalf, he would be punished. That expectation is, indeed, what he had felt as a child with his tyrannical, sadistic, alcoholic mother as well as in relation to a serious gastrointestinal disease. Mother was prone to rage attacks and torturing of the family, especially of the father, who was repeatedly humiliated (as not being a man) in front of the children. Mr. P's passive father seemed to surrender at home to mother's sadistic attacks, and he seemed uninvolved with the patient. Mother would competitively exhibit her intelligence to Mr. P, so that he felt stupid and worthless by comparison. His childhood gastrointestinal disease, not diagnosed until he was six, also contributed to his intense self-restraint and sense of detectiveness. Unpredictable vomiting, diarrhea, failure to gain weight, hospitalization, and violent reaction to foods were all part of his early years. Life became easier for him once this disease was diagnosed; he could then have more control over his body by avoiding certain foods.

Mr. P had good reason to be guarded and mistrustful, to expect nothing good from other people. His best feelings as a child involved helping mother to admire herself, usually at his own expense. Intense feelings of disappointment, neglect, deprivation, hunger, rage, and sadism were warded off by Mr. P's sadomasochistic, paranoid system, in which all emotion was carefully regulated. He maintained object ties through his negatively experienced contact with "tormentors" at work. Mr. P was very frightened of closeness with others; he had not had any satisfying intimate relationships. Especially when he seemed to want to feel closer to others, he would experience them as wanting to force him into "being friendly," behavior that he would resent and resist fiercely. His need not to give in to others or to himself was striking.

It was touching to observe this very schizoid man begin to cry for himself about his deprivation and abuse and begin to want something more for himself. He began to feel the right, less colored by shame, to want the analyst to be there for him, really to help him. So much of the time he had tried to go through the motions of just talking for the sake of talking and wanted nothing from the analyst. He began to allow himself to feel angry at the analyst's absences, to want caring and intimacy with the analyst. I was moved when he was able to complain that I seemed less involved in a particular session, that he wanted to feel my concern. He was surprised to discover that he could turn to me for help during a particularly difficult period; not only would I not turn him away, but I welcomed his allowing himself to need me. He sobbed as he allowed himself to thank me; he contrasted my emotional availability with his childhood neglect and rebuff. Increasingly, he began to tolerate and integrate his considerable rage from underneath his masochistic submissiveness, self-hatred, and self-restraint.

Now let us return to his date with V. That V had been "all over him" physically that night had especially made him anxious. He thought there was an inconsistency between her apparent strength and her so quickly coming on to him. Mr. P's anxiety was related, in part, to his own wishes to have sexual control over V. He was very uncomfortable with his wishes that V would become so aroused sexually that he could do anything he wanted with her. She would go helplessly out of her mind with desire, so that Mr. P could, in effect, lead her around by her genitals. He relished V's feeling humiliated and debased as she abjectly desired that he satisfy her. He would be cool, indifferent, powerful, strong. Then Mr. P would not have to fear that V could humiliate or hurt him.

To the wish sexually to dominate V, Mr. P associated an adolescent memory he had recently recalled. When he was 16, mother had had one of her usual drunken fights with the entire family and had especially taunted father for not being a man, for being a fairy. Removing her blouse and bra, mother had stood, bare-breasted, in front of their home and defied father and patient to stop her, inviting sexual attack from "anyone man enough to handle her." Mr. P recalled, and now could allow himself to feel with hatred, lust, and tears, how much he wanted to go at his mother. He wanted to teach her a lesson, to make her behave herself; she should act like a normal mother, who would not humiliate and attack his father and himself. He also wanted to possess this wild sexual animal that was his mother. Mr. P could now connect his masturbatory fantasies of strangling women by squeezing their necks with his hands with wanting to shut his mother up. By attacking his mother, he would stop her from saying all those horrible things. He wanted to destroy mother (women) while also enjoying her body as he pleased. In this necrophilic fantasy, the woman was safe only if totally dominated (dead). The intensity of his sexual sadism frightened him. He quickly resumed his defensive posture and felt anxious, insecure, vulnerable; his aggression was again projected onto others.

If Mr. P did not control and dominate the woman, he feared becoming trapped forever. It was difficult for him to tolerate his own wishes for passive masochistic surrender. He was eventually able to describe wishes to get fully inside the body of the woman, where he would feel safe from her critical attacks, neglect, or abandonment. If he became part of the woman, she would not attack herself, so she would not hurt him. The only way he felt he had connected with his mother was by entering into her world. He had seductively offered to give himself up for her greater glory: "My mother couldn't resist that I would give up everything for her. That was too seductive!" It remained very hard for him to believe that anyone would want him otherwise, for himself.

Eventually, Mr. P came to acknowledge that underneath the image of the dangerous mother was his view of how fragile and vulnerable she seemed. He had been so afraid of his mother's emotional collapse in the face of his criticism or anger that he had felt constrained to be protective with her. Much of his terror of his sadism and destructiveness was connected with this exaggerated danger of his power. When he became freer to criticize me angrily, he would quickly feel the need partially to undo attack and would acknowledge how I was helping him. He was able to feel his fearfulness that I could not withstand his angry attacks.

ON THE WAY TO PERVERSE ENACTMENT

In both sexual seductiveness and sadomasochistic object relations, intensity of arousal and connectedness substitutes for genuine love and caring. The more that negative feelings in oneself and in the other must be denied, the more need there is for repetitive arousal of the other and of oneself. Erotized repetition seeks to recapture and cling to aspects of infantile love because one does not feel securely loved and safe. Simultaneously, erotized repetition attempts to master hostility, fears of loss, narcissistic injury, and even specifically sexual conflicts, such as about homosexuality (Blum, 1973).

Both sexual seductiveness and sadomasochism between parent and child lead to attempts to idealize the intensely exciting encounters. What becomes special and emphasized for the parent-child couple is their intense, exciting bond. They do what others dare not. Each will give himself totally to the other, will do whatever the other wants. That this enmeshment is mutual using and extracting, not love and respect for a separate other, is denied and covered over by passion. The psychology of the exception not only is used as protection against guilt about such transgression and misuse but also is elaborated more generally to protect against hatred and destructiveness. Superego corruption is fostered between parent and child by denial of complicity in such seductive and sadomasochistic transgressions (Blum, 1973). Specialness, entitlement, and the ability to seduce and arouse others are all used to defend against superego criticism for one's destructiveness. Such patients have, by and large, not completed the task of superego integration; they remain with harsh, personified, poorly integrated superego forerunners. During childhood, the ordinary rules and expectations did not apply. At times, a parent could do as he wanted, regardless of the consequences for the child. Reality was not reasonably assessed and clarified for the child by the parent. Reality could be what such a needy parent deemed it to be. Such children had to struggle between times of great indulgence and attention, with sexual and sadomasochistic arousal, and times of feeling ignored, neglected, and abandoned by the parent, who could not remain appropriately emotionally involved with the child. Of course, such children will seek to reengage the parent in whatever ways work (sexual seductiveness or sadomasochistic provocation). They will have little reason to assess themselves according to ordinary reality. They will seek to share in the parent's narcissistic specialness as expressed in special indulgence, stimulation, excitement, and even special shared guilt. Here they can again feel grandiose rather than worthless. Erotized or sadomasochistic repetition seeks to recapture such specialness.

One aspect of what is exciting is the sense of what is ordinarily forbidden, what should not be, which is transgressed: incestuous, exploitative, inappropriate, hurtful, infantile, regressive. The excitement itself and excited repetition serve to ward off guilt at awareness of what one should not do. Immersion in the excitement and idealization of the forbidden and wrongful behavior are focused upon to distract from more realistic, guilty self-assessment. Sade prescribes sexualized excitement clearly: any horrible feeling can be avoided if only one gets sufficiently excited. Sadomasochistic excitement, like sexual seductiveness, involves similarly entering into dangerous and forbidden territory. It always has the meaning of special adoration, which feels magnetic, irresistible. The masochistic patient gives in to regressive wishes to escape from autonomy by becoming embroiled with another in hostile aggressive and erotic contact. This interaction stirs up and mixes up who is who, in an exciting and consuming surrender. Remember that this merger need not be psychotic. At neurotic levels, such defensive analization of object relations (reversibly) plays at merging and mixing. This protects against separateness, destruction, responsibility (and guilt) for what is within oneself and whatever is dangerous about the other (by pretending that it is one's own, a kind of introjective denial in fantasy). The knowledge that this behavior is wrong, destructive to oneself and to the other, and infantile and regressive adds to the excitement (and guilt). The patient disclaims responsibility for his behavior. He plays the sadomasochistic game with the analyst, who is to try to stop him—or become so frustrated, angry, hopeless, and defeated that he is unable to help the patient. But in his angry frustration, the analyst is never to let the patient go, thereby proving his love and reassuring that separation will never occur. What is dissociated here is the patient's difficulty with autonomy and self-regulation and acknowledgment of the serious destructiveness embedded within such sadomasochistic game playing. The excitement of the game denies the seriousness of the intended destructiveness.

Sexual seductiveness and sadomasochism tend to come together in nonperverse masochistic patients once defenses against such awareness have been interpreted. It becomes exciting for such patients to make another person vulnerable or to become vulnerable oneself to being controlled, dominated, exploited, and humiliated through sexual arousal. With interpretation of defense, nonperverse masochistic patients, to a degree, tend toward playing at perverse sexual misuse of others. This does not become structured perversion but perverse sexual desires, which are partly enacted and partly contained in pleasurable fantasy. That is, the patient does not become a sadomasochistic pervert, although his desires to torture and be tortured may become sexually exciting. In analyzing masochistic, pathologically dependent patients who are not perverts, the analyst should expect such perverse trends to emerge often. That the patient regards perverse sexual misuse of others as "play" conceals his more destructive intent. To arouse and control another through his own intense sexual arousal makes the patient feel powerful, an irresistible seducer, and it gives him the illusion that he is loved. Negative qualities in the object and in oneself are warded off by emphasis on one's own magical ability to bring the other to life sexually. For the moment it is as if nothing else matters. The need to seduce others, too, may repeat childhood patterns of seductiveness in a sadomasochistic relationship with a parent. Exploitation, misuse, and humiliation of the vulnerable one, with associated rage, hurt, and betrayal, are defended against by excited sexualized repetition. Even though there is a reversal from passive to active in the initiation of such scenes, the patient inwardly clings to the regressive and destructive parent-child relationship. Excited repetition puts off until another day the need to relinquish the parent-child relationship and to take responsibility for one's own affects and wishes.

Sadomasochism, in this sense, is a complex regressive defense against varied dangers of autonomy. It is a kind of running home to what is safe and familiar. One person is to beat and punish another repetitively to contain and atone for what is "bad" within himself. The patient runs away from what frightens him within himself and runs toward his craving for protection against such dangers. To the degree that autonomy (and responsibility for one's own wishes and affects) is frightening, regressive defensive solutions will be sought.

We have not discussed sexuality other than as an excited, sadomasochistic capturing or surrender to another; however, we are still not in the area of perversion. Patients may, indeed, feel driven to arouse, seduce, and conquer in the service of sadomasochistic exploitation, bondage, and domination.

Unless this behavior is obligatory for adult sexual functioning, unless there is no other way, this is not structured perversion. The need to enact seductive fantasy with another, who is made to fit one's own fantasies, does move toward perversion.

SADOMASOCHISTIC PERVERSION

The sadomasochistic pervert, in contrast to the neurotic, tends to have a sexual fantasy life that is rigid and impoverished. He has only one way to become sexually aroused. Unlike the neurotic, the pervert is relatively unable to resolve conflict solely within fantasy. Hence, the patient's obligatory fantasy must be repetitively enacted so as to validate his needed illusions. I find it useful to make a schematic division of perverts into higher and lower level types and to think of higher and lower level functions within these types. The higher level sadomasochistic pervert uses perverse behavior primarily to permit sexual functioning and orgasm as a defense against castration anxiety and oedipal guilt. He attempts by his act to validate his unconscious fantasy (of the phallic woman: signifying that castration does not occur) in order to defend against intense castration anxiety, so as to be able to function sexually. The lower level sadomasochistic pervert uses sexualization in the service of narcissism, closeness, need satisfaction, defense, repair, adaptation, and the preservation of psychic equilibrium and structure. Of course, the lower level pervert is also enabled to function sexually through his perversion, although that function is not his primary goal. Rather, he needs to use sex to accomplish other, more pressing tasks.

The object relations of the higher level sadomasochistic pervert can resemble those of neurotics, except for the focal sector of the concretely perverse defense against castration anxiety and oedipal guilt. The object relations of the lower level pervert are grossly impaired. Typically, there is incomplete self-object differentiation, with extensive use of projective identification. The external object is used primarily to satisfy the lower level pervert's needs, with little acknowledgment of the other as a separate person entitled to the satisfaction of his own needs.

Sadomasochistic perversion involves some humiliation or suffering, usually not intense physical pain. For example, the man may be insulted or humiliated by the woman, tied or blindfolded, urinated on, or symbolically dominated. At the highest level, the humiliation or suffering represents a punishment, symbolic of castration but precluding castration, for incestuous wishes and actual sexual functioning. By participating with him, the woman reassures him against castration and is a willing accomplice to his incestuous wishes. By participating with him and administering a token "punishment" under the patient's absolute control and staging of the performance, she undoes the danger that she will actually castrate him. Seduction of the castrator, a variant of Loewenstein's (1957) term, seduction of the aggressor, is an apt way to describe this attempt to change the woman's image from aggressive and threatening into accepting and participating. The woman usually is dressed in "phallic" clothing to counter castration anxiety further. Dangerous qualities in another and in oneself can be changed, easily and magically, by change of clothing, gesture, or appearance. This sexual magic is theater.

The patient's control and staging of the performance must be respected by his actress. If the woman steps out of her assigned role, the game is spoiled; for example, if she hits too hard, enjoys her role too much, or functions too autonomously.

The masochistic pervert, more than the neurotic masochist, exploits and clings to erotization and action. For the pervert, action has a magical defensive quality (action "makes it so"), involving repetitive reenactment of childhood seductive experiences. The magical quality of action for the pervert may be partly determined by the fact of childhood seduction or seductionlike experiences. Childhood seduction contributes to the illusion that, magically, the child's wishes have been actualized. "Magical happenings" may then be used to deal with frustration and painful affects. Sexual magic is not only used to achieve sexual arousal; the magic of action becomes an important defensive illusion, which is sought to eliminate whatever cannot be tolerated. The exciting sexual event (for example, "She lets me do anything I want with her") disavows absence, hurt, and rage with someone, like the analyst, who cannot be so fully controlled. Other nonperverse patients also tend to go into action so as to avoid painful feelings ("action tendencies"). Here the emphasis is on the exploitation of excitement and specialness in the service of varied defensive needs. Confusion between reality and fantasy protects against negative affects and frightening perceptions associated with childhood sexual overstimulation (Shengold, 1963, 1967, 1971, 1974; Blum, 1973). Denial and/or destruction of reality assumes a prominent role in defense. Masturbation and seduction of others become vehicles for demonstrating one's magical powers to affect oneself and others. Illusions of magical ability protect against felt helplessness and inadequacy. Even in nonperverse sadomasochistic object relations, action tends to be regarded as magical. Especially where there has been childhood parent-child sadomasochistic overstimulation, does this mode of relationship bear similarities to perversion: the magic of action and the specialness of what has transpired between parent and child become central to the psychopathology. This concept of the magic of action complements the view that repetition of seductive gratifications is both desired and attempts to master and repair the associated traumatic affects of overstimulation, rage, and helplessness.

THE PERVERSITY OF OBJECT RELATIONS
IN SADOMASOCHISM

Note the similarity in the object relations of lower level perverts with patients overtly involved in sadomasochistic object relations. The other person is, to a degree, to be used for the patient's imperative needs. A partial denial of his separate identity allows for his illusory transformation into a needed fantasy object. Dehumanization, degradation to the status of part-object, projective identification, omnipotent manipulation, and exploitation occur in both. The other person is to be controlled within one's own subjective world and denied his separateness and autonomy. Of course, masochism is seen at every level of psychic integration and object relations. Patients for whom sadomasochistic excitement becomes irresistible tend to resemble perverts in what they need from their partners, in the illusory games they play, and in their relatively perverse misuse of others. Sexual, sadomasochistic, and perverse excitement is similar in the promise of what will occur with one's partner. The patient is beckoned by something forbidden, something that should not happen, something dangerous, appealing, leading backward. He returns to the exciting, special games of yesterday. Once again he is embroiled in a dangerous, destructive relationship with an enticing, exploitative parent. If he can keep repeating the excitement that beckons him, then he need not face the horrors to which he has made himself a party. Excited, endless repetition avoids the truth of abuse, neglect, misuse, and exploitation—destructiveness in the parent and destructiveness and complicity in oneself.

Repetitive exploitation is, indeed, perverse misuse of others. The child/ patient felt used by the parent, who tended to destroy the child's (and the parent's own) perception of objective reality and the validity of the child's separate needs in favor of the parent's own neediness. Hence, the patient now feels entitled to enact a reversal of misusing others. We cannot, however, claim that every such patient was actually exploited by a parent. Feelings of hatred and deprivation, without sufficient ability to contain and balance these feelings against some sense of feeling loved and cared for, can similarly evoke a pathological relationship involving misuse. The patient feels entitled to extract what he desires from the other, who exists predominantly to gratify him. The patient's rage, demandingness, and destructiveness in such misuse of others tend to be dissociated and justified. In embroiling himself in repetitive excitement with the other, he makes the other responsible for him and uses the other to manage what the patient feels he himself cannot. This mode of relating is a form of pathological dependency in which one invites, entices, insists that the other must take care of him. The other is to provide the illusion of caring and love, of which the patient feels so deprived. The other is to reassure the patient against his terrors of separation, loss, destruction, castration, and guilt, by his responsiveness, continual availability, and punishment or forgiveness. The other becomes the repository for whatever the patient cannot tolerate in himself: aspects of id, ego attitudes, and superego judgments. The relationship with the other is to take the place of, and deny/undo, whatever is wrong within the patient, which no longer counts. This becomes extractive, destructive misuse of another person for one's own needs; the separateness and needs of the other are then denied and ignored. The excited illusion that the couple is involved in the most special kind of loving hides the ruthless exploitation and destructiveness. To the degree that the patient can extract the illusion of being loved, he can temper and disown his rage and destructiveness. The addiction to feeling loved is needed to calm one's destructive anger.

REFERENCES

Blum, H. 1973. The concept of erotized transference. *J. Amer. Psychoanal. Assn.* 21:61–76.

Freud, S. 1905. Three essays on the theory of sexuality. *S.E.* 7:123–243.

Grossman, W. 1986. Note on masochism: A discussion of the history and development of a psychoanalytic concept. *Psychoanal. Quarterly.* 55:379–413.

Loewenstein, R. 1957. A contribution to the psychoanalytic theory of masochism. *J. Amer. Psychoanal. Assn.* 5:197–234.

Maleson, F. 1984. The multiple meanings of masochism in psychoanalytic discourse. *J. Amer. Psychoanal. Assn.* 32:325–56.

Parkin, A. 1980. On masochistic enthralment: A contribution to the study of moral masochism. *Int. J. Psycho-Anal.* 61:307–14.

Sacher-Masoch, L. von 1870. *Sacher-Masoch, an Interpretation by Gilles Deleuze, together with the entire text of "Venus in Furs."* Trans. J. M. McNeil, London, Faber and Faber, 1971.

Shapiro, D. 1981. *Autonomy and Rigid Character*. New York: Basic Books.

Shengold, L. 1963. The parent as sphinx. *J. Amer. Psychoanal. Assn.* 11:725–41.

———. 1967. The effects of overstimulation: rat people. *Int. J. Psycho-Anal.* 48:403–15.

———. 1971. More about rats and rat people. *Int. J. Psycho-Anal.* 52:277–88.

———. 1974. The metaphor of the mirror. *J. Amer. Psychoanal. Assn.* 22:97–115.

Stoller, R. 1976. Sexual excitement. *Arch. Gen. Psychiat.* 33:899–909.

PART V

MASOCHISM AND FEMALE PSYCHOLOGY

Introduction

There is a controversial aspect to the papers in this section on masochism and female psychology. We can ask first if a separate section on masochism and female psychology should be included. Almost everything that has been written on masochism applies to both sexes. Yet, the male cases by Smirnoff (1969; chapter 3 in this volume), Fenichel (1925; chapter 15 in this volume), or Bak (1946; chapter 9 in this volume) differ from the female cases by A. Freud (1922; chapter 14 in this volume), Reich (1940; chapter 21 in this volume), Chasseguet-Smirgel (1993; chapter 23 in this volume). The structure of the Oedipus, both negative and positive, is different; the receptive sexual aim, to be penetrated, in the positive Oedipal phase is unique for girls. The sadomasochism in the anaclitic bond is different for the little girl who identifies with the femininity of the mother in that bond, than for the boy who identifies with the masculinity of the father while being bonded to the mother. The complexity of identifications in both sexes (Benjamin 1987) does not mean that there is symmetry for the genders.

While Freud finally eschewed an identity between passivity and femininity (1931), he had forged an even closer link between masochism and femininity through his idea that penis envy involved a humiliation necessary to feminine sexuality (1925). The Freudian vision of normal feminine masochism as needing the acceptance of "castration" as a condition for feminine sexual pleasure (Kristeva 1981), was always held in significant doubt (Horney 1933; Blum 1976; Fliegel 1986).

The theory of masochism in normal female sexuality has not received anything like the clinical validation that other aspects of the theory of masochism have had. Much would depend on having access to the unconscious fantasies of normal little girls, which is not easy to do (Galenson and Roiphe 1976). As an aspect of male perversion, "feminine masochism" (Freud 1924a; chapter 13 in this volume) delineates unconscious fantasy identifications of the male with the mother in pain (Fenichel 1925; Bak 1946). As an aspect of normal female sexuality, feminine masochism has no clear manifestation. Loewenstein (1957; chapter 2 in this volume) first noted that it was inconsistent to denote normal female sexuality as "masochistic" in a pathological sense (Blum 1976).

Some contemporary papers on feminine masochism and fantasy (André 1991; Lax 1992) have returned to the beating fantasy in the female Oedipus complex to explore gender specificity in masochism. Few would now assert that women are "more" masochistic than men, except as child-rearing, socialization, maternal ego-ideals, and male power lead them toward the "seduction of the aggressor" (Loewenstein 1957; Benjamin 1987; Meyers 1988). Nonetheless, women's fiction, from Charlotte Brontë to Alice Munro, shows a strong fascination with the female psyche in its particular sexual submissions and humiliations, and employs literary techniques set to bring to light denials of sadomasochism (Hanly 1992; Fitzpatrick 1984; Fitzpatrick-Hanly 1993). The possibility of a feminine masochism, with gender specificity for women, has not quite been laid to rest (Benjamin 1987; André 1991).

Loewenstein (1957) explored the normal passivity of infantile sexual life—longings to be held, caressed, and fed—as these blurred into the "protomasochism" of skin erotism, and then, into the "seduction of the aggressor" associated with infant play. The passive infantile longings, which are filled with mild or intense excitations and anxiety, have a universal place in human sexuality, providing a bedrock of universal masochistic tendencies (Kernberg 1991). Loewenstein attributes no gender specificity to infantile passivity and protomasochism.

In "The Economic Problem of Masochism" (1924a), Freud noted that feminine masochism in men involved the wish to be treated "like a small helpless child, but, particularly like a naughty child." He went on to note that in extreme cases the subject was placed, in fantasy, in a charateristically female situation, "that is, being castrated, or copulated with, or giving birth to a baby." Freud writes that he has called this form of male pathology "feminine" masochism, "although so many of its features point to infantile life." The specific nature of infantile sexual fantasies (largely unconscious) including primal scene fantasies and theories of where babies come from and how they come out, affects the degree of sadomasochism in the adult sexuality for both genders (Chasseguet-Smirgel 1993).

Helene Deutsch's paper on the function of masochism in female sexuality (1930; chapter 20 in this volume) had a key role in deepening Freud's conviction about castration and masochism in women, despite his having little clinical evidence (Fliegel 1986). Horney's criticism of Helene Deutsch's

(1930) position was strong: "She contends that what woman ultimately wants in intercourse is to be raped and violated; what she wants in mental life is to be humiliated; menstruation is significant to the woman because it feeds masochistic fantasies; childbirth represents the climax of masochistic satisfaction" (1939, 110). While Horney seems to leave aside the unconscious nature of these masochistic fantasies, she focused the problems in Freud's theory. Horney agreed with Freud's contention that woman's basic fear is that of losing love, which makes her vulnerable to masochistic submissiveness (see also Benjamin 1987). In conclusion Horney quotes Freud (1933): "But we must take care not to underestimate the influence of social conventions, which force women into passive situations. . . . The repression of their aggressiveness, which is imposed on women by their constitutions and by society, favors the development of strong masochistic impulses, which have the effect of binding erotically the destructive tendencies which have been turned inwards" (p. 118).

In the dialectic of the argument on masochism and female sexuality, Annie Reich (1940) presented an implicit corrective to the Freudian position. Without entering the controversy, Reich indicates how submissiveness and humiliation comprise a pathological, not a normal, masochism in her women patients. Reich illuminates narcissistic problems in her female patients which stem from disturbances in the passive dependent relationship with the pre-phallic mother, and which result in the overvaluation of the penis and the sense of ineffable bliss in orgasm, and utter despair in neglect or disappointment. She gives examples of the wish to destroy which underlies a sham warmth, thus delineating the full sadomasochistic dynamic in the submissive woman: "The relentless, destroying attitude, which the prostitute lives out in her love life, the submissive woman attempts to master by repression (p. 429 in this volume)." Boundaries are indicated beyond which submissiveness is not "normal" in women; pre-Oedipal and narcissitic issues are well thought through.

Despite many reasons to abandon the idea of a gender specific masochism for women, Bonaparte (1952) opened up the issue of female masochism from the point of view of early genital anxiety, which accompanies the fantasy of sexual pleasure in being penetrated, and which sets up an anlage for the experience of pleasure in pain in a particular way in women. In "Some Biopsychical Aspects of Sado-Masochism" (1952; chapter 22 in this volume), Bonaparte, quoting extensively from Freud and from de Sade, harks back to Krafft-Ebing and Freud in their intuition that masochism was a sort of "pathological overgrowth of psychical feminine factors" (that is, passive sexual longings). She looks at the human experience of being penetrated, by food for nutrition, and if a female, by the male sperm for reproduction, and, then, by traumatic penetration, infraction, and wounding, causing suffering and death. She posits a psychical confusion in the little girl's unconscious between the erotic and wounding penetration. Bonaparte, then, in terms of the biopsychical—of the unconscious fantasies rooted in physical nature— asks when the female child apprehends that she is destined to perpetuate herself through internal impregnation? While Bonaparte's sense that a female's biology creates a unique tendency to masochism is deplored by many contemporary thinkers, her theory is also a forerunner of contemporary theories of primary gender identity and female genital anxieties (Mayer 1985; Bernstein 1990; Renik 1990).

There are other perplexing issues concerning masochism and female psychology. The explicit sadomasochism in the lesbian counterculture requires the revision of older ideas about the gender specificity of certain "male" perversions. In "Feminine Guilt and the Oedipus Complex," Chasseguet-Smirgel (1970) explored a special feminine guilt which resulted from a split off, or repressed, aggression toward the father and his penis, a split that was possible through the idealization of the father in Oedipal love, and a regressive attachment of hostility to the phallic mother. The delineation of a particular feminine guilt represents an important theoretical contribution to masochism and gender specificity.

In "Auto-Sadism, Eating Disorders, and Femininity," Chasseguet-Smirgel (1993) examines the relationship of auto-erotic activities and fantasies in eating disorders, to the adolescent's desperate need to control the body. She sees the bondage of daughter to mother as made up of the early ambivalent identifications. The growing body threatens to become a maternal dominance from the inside of the developing girl. The sadism felt toward the mother gets bent back onto the body as it becomes more like that of the mother.

The unconscious fantasies of particular female aggressions and split-off guilt, which have contributed to the masochistic functioning of many women, are being more and more uncovered and understood. What this implies about "female masochism" is not yet clear. Gender specificity in masochism has meaning at the level of particular symptoms and unconscious fantasies in pathology. Whether, the unique sexual functions of women create a gender specific vulnerability to masochism is not settled in the literature.

BIBLIOGRAPHY

André, J. 1991. La sexualité féminine: Retour aux sources. In *Psychanalyste à l'Université*. Paris: Presses Universitaires de France.

Bak, R. 1946. Masochism in Paranoia. *Psychanal. Quarterly* 15:285–301. (Chapter 9 in this volume.)

Benjamin, J. 1987. The Alienation of Desire: Women's Masochism and Ideal Love. In *Psychoanalysis and Women: Contemporary Reappraisals*, ed. J. Alpert. Hillsdale, N.J.: The Analytic Press, pp. 113–39.

Bernstein, D. 1990. Female Genital Anxieties, Conflicts and Typical Mastery Modes. *Int. J. Psycho-Anal.* 71:151–65.

Blum, H. 1976. Masochism, the Ego Ideal and the Psychology of Women. *J. Amer. Psychoanal. Assn.* 24,5 (Suppl.): 157–92.

Bonaparte, M. 1935. Passivity, Masochism and Femininity. *Int. J. Psycho-Anal.* 16:325–33.

———. 1952. Some Biopsychical Aspects of Sado-Masochism. *Int. J. Psycho-Anal.* 33:373–84. (Chapter 22 in this volume.)

Brierly, M. 1936. Some Problems of Integration in Women. *Int. J. Psycho-Anal.* 17:163–80.

Chasseguet-Smirgel, J. 1970. Feminine Guilt and the Oedipus Complex. In *Female Sexuality*, ed. J. Chasseguet-Smirgel. Ann Arbor: University of Michigan Press, pp. 94–134.

———. 1976. Freud and Female Sexuality. *Int. J. Psycho-Anal.* 57:275–86.

———. 1993. Auto-Sadism, Eating Disorders, and Femininity. In French, in the *Canadian Journal of Psychoanalysis* 1, no. 1:101–22. (In English, chapter 23 in this volume.)

Deutsch, H. 1930. The Significance of Masochism in the Mental Life of Women. *Int. J. Psycho-Anal.* 11:48–60. (Chapter 20 in this volume.)

Fenichel, O. 1925. The Clinical Aspect of the Need for Punishment. In *The Collected Papers of Otto Fenichel: First Series*. New York: Norton, 1953, pp. 71–96. (Chapter 15 in this volume.)

Fitzpatrick, M. 1984. Projection in Alice Munro's *Something I've Been Meaning to Tell You*. In *The Art of Alice Munro: Saying the Unsayable*. Waterloo, Ont.: University of Waterloo Press. pp. 14–20.

Fitzpatrick-Hanly, M. 1993. Sadomasochism in Charlotte Brontë's *Jane Eyre*. *Int. J. Psycho-Anal.* 74:1049–61.

Fliegel, Z. 1986. Women's Development in Analytic Theory: Six Decades of Controversy. In *Psychoanalysis and Women*, ed. J. Alpert. Hillsdale, N.J.: The Analytic Press, pp. 3–31.

Freud, A. 1922. Beating Fantasies and Daydreams. *Int. J. Psycho-Anal.* 4:89–102. (Chapter 14 in this volume.)

Freud, S. 1905. Three Essays on the Theory of Sexuality. In *S.E.* 7:135–243. (In excerpt form, chapter 4 in this volume.)

———. 1923. The Infantile Genital Organization of Libido. In *S.E.* 19:141–53.

———. 1924a. The Economic Problem of Masochism. In *S.E.* 19:159–72. (Chapter 13 in this volume.)

———. 1924b. The Dissolution of the Oedipal Complex. In *S.E.* 19:173–82.

———. 1925. Some Psychical Consequences of the Anatomical Distinction between the Sexes. In *S.E.* 19:248–58.

———. 1931. Female Sexuality. In *S.E.* 21:225–43.

———. 1933. Femininity. In *S.E.* 22:112–35.

Galenson, E., and Roiphe, M. 1976. Some Suggested Revisions Concerning Early Female Development. *J. Amer. Psychoanal. Assn.* 24 (Suppl.):29–57.

Greenacre, P. 1950. Special Problems of Early Female Development. *Psychoanal. Study Child.* 5:112–38.

Grossman, W. I. and Stewart, W. 1976. Penis Envy: From Childhood Wish to Developmental Metaphor. *J. Amer. Psychoanal. Assn.* 24, 5 (Suppl.):193–212.

Hanly, C. 1992. Autobiography and Creativity: A Case Study. In *The Problem of Truth in Applied Psychoanalysis:* New York: The Guilford Press.

Horney, K. 1933. Contribution to the Problem of Femininity. *Psychoanal. Quarterly* 2:489–518.

———. 1939. Feminine Psychology. In *New Ways in Psychoanalysis.* New York: Norton.

Kernberg, O. 1991. Sadomasochism, Sexual Excitement, and Perversion. *J. Amer. Psychoanal. Assn.* 39:333–62.

Kristeva, J. 1981. Women's Time. In *Essential Papers on the Psychology of Women.* New York: New York University Press, 1990.

Lax, R. 1992. A Variation on Freud's Theme in "A Child Is Being Beaten"—Mother's Role: Some Implications for Super-Ego Development in Women. *J. Amer. Psychoanal. Assn.* 40:455–73.

Loewenstein, R. 1957. A Contribution to the Psychoanalytic Theory of Masochism. *J. Amer. Psychoanal. Assn.* 5:197–234. (Chapter 2 in this volume.)

Mayer, E. L. 1985. Every Body Must Be Just Like Me: Observations on Female Castration Anxiety. *Int. J. Psycho-Anal.* 66:331–48.

Menaker, E. 1953. Masochism—A Defense Reaction of the Ego. *Psychoanal. Quarterly.* 22:205–21.

Meyers, H. 1988. A Consideration of Treatment Techniques in Relation to the Functions of Masochism. In *Masochism: Current Psychoanalytic Perspectives.* Hillsdale, N.J.: The Analytic Press, pp. 175–88.

Person, E. 1974. Some New Observations on the Origins of Femininity. In *Women and Analysis,* ed. J. Strouse. New York: Grossman, pp. 250–61.

Reich, A. 1940. A Contribution to the Psychoanalysis of Extreme Submissiveness in Women. *Psychoanal. Quarterly* 9:470–80. (Chapter 21 in this volume.)

Renik, O. 1990. Analysis of a Woman's Homosexual Strivings by a Male Analyst. *Psychoanalytic Quarterly* 59:41–53.

Schafer, R. 1974. Problems in Freud's Psychology of Women. *J. Amer. Psychoanal. Assn.* 22:459–89.

Smirnoff, V. 1969. The Masochistic Contract. *Int. J. Psycho-Anal.* 50:665–71. (Chapter 3 in this volume.)

Stoller, R. J. 1968. The Sense of Femaleness. *Psychoanal. Quarterly* 37:42–55.

20. The Significance of Masochism in the Mental Life of Women

Helene Deutsch

PART I
'FEMININE' MASOCHISM AND ITS RELATION
TO FRIGIDITY[1]

In the analysis of women we became familiar with the masculinity-complex before we learnt much about the 'femininity' which emerges from the conflicts accompanying development. The reasons for this later recognition were various. First of all, analysis comes to know the human mind in its discords rather than in its harmonies, and, when we turn the microscope of observation upon the woman, we see with special distinctness that the main source of her conflicts is the masculinity which she is destined to subdue. It followed that we were able to recognize the 'masculine' element in women earlier and more clearly than what we may term the nucleus of their 'femininity'. Paradoxical as it may sound, we approached the feminine element with greater interest when it formed part of a pathological structure and, as a foreign body, attracted a closer attention. When we encountered in men that instinctual disposition which we designate feminine and passive-masochistic, we recognized its origin and the weighty consequences it entailed. In the case of women we discovered that, even in the most feminine manifestations of their life—menstruation, conception, pregnancy and parturition—they had a constant struggle with the never wholly effaced evidences of the bisexuality of their nature. Hence, in my earlier writings[2] I shewed with what elemental force the masculinity-complex flares up in the female reproductive functions, to be once more subdued.

My aim in this paper is different. I want to examine the genesis of

Reprinted by permission of the author's estate and the *International Journal of Psycho-Analysis* 11 (1930):48–60. Copyright © Institute of Psycho-Analysis.

'femininity', by which I mean the feminine, passive-masochistic disposition in the mental life of women. In particular I shall try to elucidate the relation of the function of feminine instinct to the function of reproduction, in order that we may first of all clarify our ideas about sexual inhibition in women, that is to say, about frigidity. The discussion will concern itself with theoretical premises rather than with the clinical significance of frigidity.

But first let us return to the masculinity-complex.

No one who has experience of analysis can doubt that female children pass through a phase in their libidinal evolution, in which they, just like boys, having abandoned the passive oral and anal cathexes, develop an erotogenicity which is actively directed to the clitoris as in boys to the penis. The determining factor in the situation is that, in a certain phase, sensations in the organs, which impel the subject to masturbate, tend strongly towards the genital and effect cathexis of that zone which in both sexes we have called the 'phallic'.

Penis-envy would never acquire its great significance were it not that sensations in the organs, with all their elemental power, direct the child's interest to these regions of the body. It is this which first produces the narcissistic reactions of envy in little girls. It seems that they arrive only very gradually and slowly at the final conclusion of their investigations: the recognition of the anatomical difference between themselves and boys. So long as onanism affords female children an equivalent pleasure they deny that they lack the penis, or console themselves with hopes that in the future the deficiency will be made good. A little girl, whom I had the opportunity of observing, reacted to the exhibitionistic aggression of an elder brother with the obstinate and often repeated assertion: 'Susie *has* got one', pointing gaily to her clitoris and labia, at which she tugged with intense enjoyment. The gradual acceptance of the anatomical difference between the sexes is accompanied by conflicts waged round the constellation which we term penis-envy and masculinity-complex.

We know that, when the little girl ceases to deny her lack of the penis and abandons the hope of possessing one in the future, she employs a considerable amount of her mental energy in trying to account for the disadvantage under which she labours. We learn from our analyses what a large part the sense of guilt connected with masturbation commonly plays in these attempts at explanation. The origin of these feelings of guilt is not quite clear, for they already exist in the phase in which the Œdipus complex of the little girl does not seem as yet to have laid the burden of guilt upon her.[3]

Direct observation of children shows beyond question that these first onanistic activities are informed with impulses of a primary sadistic nature against the outside world.[4] Possibly a sense of guilt is associated with these obscure aggressive impulses. It is probable that the little girl's illusion that she once had a penis and has lost it is connected with these first, sadistic, active tendencies to clitoral masturbation. Owing to the memory-traces of this active function of the clitoris, it is subsequently deemed to have had in the past the actual value of an organ equivalent to the penis. The erroneous conclusion is then drawn: 'I once did possess a penis'.

Another way in which the girl regularly tries to account for the loss is by ascribing the blame for it to her mother. It is interesting to note that, when the father is blamed for the little girl's lack of a penis, castration by him has already acquired the libidinal significance attaching to this idea in the form of the rape-phantasy. Rejection of the wish that the father should have been the aggressor generally betokens, even at this early stage, that rejection of the infantile feminine attitude to which I shall recur.

In his paper 'Some Consequences of the Anatomical Difference between the Sexes', Freud sees in the turning of the little girl to her father as a sexual object a direct consequence of this anatomical difference. In Freud's view, development from the castration to the Œdipus complex consists in the passing from the narcissistic wound of organ-inferiority to the compensation offered: that is to say, there arises the desire for a child. This is the source of the Œdipus complex in girls.

In this paper I shall follow up the line of thought thus mapped out by Freud. After the phallic phase, where the boy renounces the Œdipus complex and phallic masturbation, there is intercalated in the girl's development a phase which we may call 'post-phallic'; in this the seal is set upon her destiny of womanhood. Vaginal cathexis, however, is as yet lacking.

In spite of my utmost endeavours, I am unable to confirm the communications that have been made with reference to vaginal pleasure-sensations in childhood. I do not doubt the accuracy of these observations, but isolated exceptions in this case prove little. In my own observations I have had striking evidence in two instances of the existence of vaginal excitations and vaginal masturbation before puberty. In both, seduction with defloration had occurred very early in life.[5] If there were in childhood a vaginal phase, with all its biological significance, it surely could not fail to appear as regularly in our analytical material as do all the other infantile phases of development. I think that the most difficult factor in the 'anatomical destiny' of the woman is the fact that at a time when the libido is still unstable, immature and incapable of sublimation, it seems condemned to abandon a pleasure-zone (the clitoris as a phallic organ) without discovering the possibility of a new cathexis. The narcissistic estimation of the non-existent organ passes smoothly (to use a phrase of Freud's) 'along the symbolic equation: penis— child, which is mapped out for it'. But what becomes of the dynamic energy of the libido which is directed towards the object and yearns for possibilities of gratification and for erotogenic cathexes?

We must also reflect that the wish-phantasy of receiving a child from the father—a phantasy of the greatest significance for the future of a woman— is, nevertheless, in comparison with the reality of the penis, for which it is supposed to be exchanged, a very unreal and uncertain substitute. I heard of the little daughter of an analyst mother who, at the time when she was experiencing penis-envy, was consoled with the prospect of having a child. Every morning she woke up to ask in a fury: 'Hasn't the child come *yet*'? and no more accepted the consolation of the future than we are consoled by the promise of Paradise.

What, then, does happen to the actively directed cathexis of the clitoris in the phase when that organ ceases to be valued as the penis? In order to answer this question we may fall back on a familiar and typical process. We already know that, when a given activity is denied by the outside world or inhibited from within, it regularly suffers a certain fate—it turns back or is deflected. This seems to be so in the instance before us: the hitherto active-sadistic libido attached to the clitoris rebounds from the barricade of the subject's inner recognition of her lack of the penis and, on the one hand, regressively cathects points in the pregenital development which it had already abandoned, while, on the other hand, and most frequently of all, it is deflected in a regressive direction towards masochism. In place of the active urge of the phallic tendencies, there arises the masochistic phantasy: 'I want to be castrated', and this forms the erotogenic masochistic basis of the feminine libido. Analytic experience leaves no room for doubt that the little girl's first libidinal relation to her father is masochistic, and the masochistic wish in its earliest distinctively feminine phase is: 'I want to be castrated by my *father*'.[6]

In my view this turning in the direction of masochism is part of the woman's 'anatomical destiny', marked out for her by biological and constitutional factors, and lays the first foundation of the ultimate development of femininity, independent as yet of masochistic reactions to the sense of guilt.

The original significance of the clitoris as an organ of activity, the masculine-narcissistic protest: 'I won't be castrated' are converted into the desire: 'I want to be castrated'. This desire assumes the form of a libidinal, instinctual trend whose object is the father. The woman's whole passive-feminine disposition, the entire genital desire familiar to us as the rape-phantasy, is finally explained if we accept the proposition that it originates in the castration-complex. *My view is that the Œdipus complex in girls is inaugurated by the castration-complex.* The factor of pleasure resides in the idea of a sadistic assault by the love-object and the narcissistic loss is compensated by the desire for a child, which is to be fulfilled through this assault. When we designate this masochistic experience by the name of the wish for castration, we are not thinking merely of the biological meaning—the surrender of an organ of pleasure (the clitoris)—but we are also taking into account the fact that the whole of this deflection of the libido still centres on that organ. The onanism belonging to this phase and the masochistic phantasy of being castrated (raped) employ the same organ as the former active tendencies. The astonishing persistency of the feminine castration-complex (including all the organic vicissitudes with which is associated a flow of blood) as we encounter it in the analyses of our female patients is thus explained by the fact that this complex contains in itself not only the masculinity-complex, but also the whole infantile set towards femininity.

At that period there is a close connection between the masochistic phantasies and the wish for a child, so that the whole subsequent attitude of the woman towards her child (or towards the reproductive function) is permeated by pleasure-tendencies of a masochistic nature.

We have an illustration of this in the dream of a patient whose subsequent analysis unequivocally confirmed what had been hinted in the manifest content of her dream; this occurred in the first phase of her analysis before much insight had been gained.

'Professor X. and you (the analyst) were sitting together. I wanted him to notice me. He went past my chair and I looked up at him and he smiled at me. He began to ask me about my health, as a doctor asks his patient; I answered with reluctance. All of a sudden he had on a doctor's white coat and a pair of obstetrical forceps in his hand. He said to me: "Now we'll just have a look at the little angel". I clearly saw that they were obstetrical forceps, but I had the feeling that the instrument was to be used to force my legs apart and display the clitoris. I was very much frightened and struggled. A number of people, amongst them you and a trained nurse, were standing by and were indignant at my struggling. They thought that Professor X. had specially chosen *me* for a kind of experiment, and that I ought to submit to it. As everyone was against me, I cried out in impotent fury: "No, I will not be operated on, you shall not operate on me".'

Without examining the dream more closely here, we can see in its manifest content that castration is identified with rape and parturition, and the dream-wish which excites anxiety is as follows: 'I want to be castrated (raped) by my father and to have a child'—a three-fold wish of a plainly *masochistic character.*

The first, infantile identification with the mother is always, independently of the complicated processes and reactions belonging to the sense of guilt, *masochistic,* and all the active birth-phantasies, whose roots lie in this identification, are of a bloody, painful character, which they retain throughout the subject's life.[7]

In order to make my views on frigidity intelligible I had to preface them with these theoretical considerations.

I will now pass on to discuss those forms of frigidity which bear the stamp of the masculinity-complex or penis-envy. In these cases the woman persists in the original demand for possession of a penis and refuses to abandon the phallic organization. Conversion to the feminine-passive attitude, the necessary condition of vaginal sensation, does not take place.

Let me mention briefly the danger of the strong attachment of all sexual phantasies to clitoris-masturbation. I think I have made it clear that the clitoris has come to be the executive organ, not only of active but of passive masochistic phantasies. By virtue of its past phase of masculine activity, a kind of organ-memory constitutes it the great enemy of any transference of pleasure-excitation to the vagina. Moreover, the fact that the whole body receives an increased cathexis of libido (since it has failed to find its focus) brings it about that, in spite of an often very vehement manifestation of the sexual instinct, the libido never attains to its centralized form of gratification.

In far the largest number of cases, feminine sexual inhibition arises out of the vicissitudes of that infantile-masochistic libidinal development which I have postulated. These vicissitudes are manifold, and every form they assume may lead to frigidity. For instance, as a result of the repression of the masochistic tendencies a strong narcissistic cathexis of the feminine ego may be observed. The ego feels that it is threatened by these tendencies, and takes up a narcissistic position of defence. I believe that, together with penis-envy, this is an important source of so-called feminine narcissism.

Akin to this reaction of repression is another reaction-formation which Karen Horney calls 'the flight from femininity,' and of which she has given a very illuminating description. This flight from the incest-wish is, in my view, a shunning not only of the incestuous object (Horney), but most of all of the masochistic dangers threatening the ego which are associated with the relation to this object. Escape into identification with the father is at the same time a flight from the masochistically determined identification with the mother. Thus there arises the masculinity-complex, which I think will be strong and disturbing in proportion as penis-envy has been intense and the primary phallic active tendencies vigorous.

Repression of the masochistic instinctual tendencies may have another result in determining a particular type of object-choice later in life. The object stands in antithesis to the masochistic instinctual demands and corresponds to the requirements of the ego. In accordance with these the woman chooses a partner whose social standing is high or whose intellectual gifts are above the average, often a man whose disposition is rather of an affectionate and passive type. The marriage then appears to be peaceful and happy, but the woman remains frigid, suffering from an unsatisfied longing—the type of the 'misunderstood wife'. Her sexual sensibility is bound up with conditions whose fulfilment is highly offensive to her ego. How often do such women become the wretched victims of a passion for men who ill-treat them, thus fulfilling the women's unconscious desires for castration or rape.

I have also observed how frequently—indeed, almost invariably— women whose whole life is modelled on the lines of masculine sublimation-tendencies are markedly masochistic in their sexual experiences. They belong to that reactive masculine type which yet has failed to repress its original masochistic instinctual attitude. My experience is that the prospect of cure in these cases of relative frigidity, in which sexual sensation depends on the fulfilment of masochistic conditions, is very uncertain. It is peculiarly difficult to detach these patients from the said conditions and, when analysis has given them the necessary insight, they have consciously to choose between finding bliss in suffering or peace in renunciation.

The analyst's most important task is, of course, the abolition of the sexual inhibition in his patients, and the attainment of instinctual gratification. But sometimes, when the patient's instincts are so unfortunately fixed and yet there are good capacities for sublimation, the analyst must have the courage to smooth the path in the so-called 'masculine' direction and thus make it easier for the patient to renounce sexual gratification.

There are women who have strong sexual inhibition and intense feelings of inferiority, the origin of which lies in penis-envy. In such cases it is evidently the task of analysis to free these patients from the difficulties of the masculinity-complex and to convert penis-envy into the desire for a child, i.e. to induce them to adopt their feminine rôle. We can observe that during this process the 'masculine aims' become depreciated and are given up. Nevertheless we often find that, if we can succeed in making it easier for such women to sublimate their instincts in the direction of 'masculine tendencies' and so to counter the sense of inferiority, the capacity for feminine sexual sensibility develops automatically in a striking manner. The theoretical explanation of this empirically determined fact is self-evident.

It is but rarely in analytic practice that we meet with such cases of conditioned frigidity as I have described or indeed with any cases of frigidity unaccompanied by pathological symptoms, i.e. of sexual inhibition without symptoms of suffering. When such a patient comes to us, it is generally at the desire of the husband, whose narcissism is wounded, and who feels uncertain of his masculinity. The woman, actuated by her masochistic tendencies, has renounced the experience of gratification for herself, and, as a rule, her desire to be cured is so feeble that the treatment is quite unsuccessful.

As we know, hysteria which expresses itself in symptom-formation is extraordinarily capricious and varied as regards the nature of the sexual inhibition displayed. One type of hysterical patient is driven by an everlasting hunger for love-objects, which she changes without inhibition: her erotic life appears free, but she is incapable of genital gratification. Another type is monogamous and remains tenderly attached to the love-object, but without sexual sensibility; she exhibits other neurotic reactions which testify to her morbid state. Such women often dissipate the sexual excitation in the fore-pleasure, either owing to the strong original cathexis of the pregenital zones or because by a secondary and regressive reaction they are endeavouring to withhold the libido from the genital organ which prohibitions and their own anxiety have barricaded off. Here one often receives the impression that all the sense-organs, and indeed the whole female body, are more accessible to sexual excitation than is the vagina, the organ apparently destined for it. But conversion-symptoms turn out to be the seat of false sexual cathexes. Behind the hysterical, pleasure-inhibiting, genital anxiety we discover the masochistic triad: castration, rape and parturition. The fixation of these wish-phantasies to the infantile object here becomes, as we know, the motive factor in the neuroses. If this attachment is resolved by analysis, sexual sensibility as a rule develops.

In touching briefly on the question of frigidity accompanying phobias and obsessions, mention must be made of the remarkable fact that in these cases the sexual disturbance is emphatically not in direct ratio to the severity of the neurosis. There are patients who remain frigid long after they have overcome their anxiety, and even after they have got rid of the most severe obsessional symptoms, and the converse is also true. The uncertainty of obsessional neurosis—in so far as the genital capacity of female patients is concerned—is most plainly manifested in certain cases (several of which have come under my observation) in which the most violent orgasm may result from hostile masculine identifications. The vagina behaves like an active organ, and the particularly brisk secretion is designed to imitate ejaculation.

At the beginning of this paper I endeavoured to show that the masochistic triad constantly encountered in the analyses of women corresponds to a definite phase of feminine libidinal development and represents, so to speak, the last act in the drama of the vicissitudes of the 'feminine castration-complex'. In neurotic diseases, however, we meet above all with the reactions of the sense of guilt, and hence we find this primary-libidinal feminine masochism already so closely interwoven and interlocked with the moral masochism, originating under pressure of the sense of guilt, that we miss the significance of that which is in origin libidinal. Thus many obscure points in connection with the feminine castration-complex become clearer if we recognize that, behind the castration-anxiety, there is further the repressed masochistic wish characteristic of a definite infantile phase of development in the normal feminine libido.

The task of psycho-analysis is to resolve the conflicts of the individual existence. The instinctual life of the individual, which is the object of analytical scrutiny, strives towards the ultimate goal, amidst conflicts and strange vicissitudes, of *attainment of pleasure*. The preservation of the race lies outside these aims, and, if there be a deeper significance in the fact that the same means are employed to achieve the racial aim as to subserve the pleasure-tendency of man's instincts, that significance is outside the scope of our individualistic task.

Here I think we have a fundamental and essential difference between 'feminine' and 'masculine'. In the woman's mental life there is *something* which has nothing at all to do with the mere fact of whether she has or has not actually given birth to a child. I refer to the psychic representatives of motherhood which are here long before the necessary physiological and anatomical conditions have developed in the girl. For the tendency of which I am speaking the attaining of the child is the main goal of existence, and in woman the exchange of the racial aim for the individual one of gratification may take place largely at the expense of the latter. No analytical observer can deny that in the relation of mother to child—begun in pregnancy and continued in parturition and lactation—libidinal forces come into play which are very closely allied to those in the relation between man and woman.

In the deepest experience of the relation of mother to child it is masochism in its strongest form which finds gratification in the bliss of motherhood.

Long before she is a mother, long after the possibility of becoming one has ended, the woman has ready within her the maternal principle, which bids her take to herself and guard the real child or some substitute for it.

In coitus and parturition the masochistic pleasure of the sexual instinct is very closely bound up with the mental experience of conception and giving birth; just so does the little girl see in the father, and the loving woman in her beloved—a child. For years I have traced out in analyses this most intimate blending of the sexual instinct with that of the reproductive function in women, and always the question has hovered before my mind: When does the female child begin to be a woman and when a mother? Analytic experience has yielded the answer: *Simultaneously,* in that phase when she turns towards masochism, as I described at the beginning of this paper. Then, at the same time as she conceives the desire to be castrated and raped, she conceives also the phantasy of receiving a child from her father. From that time on, the phantasy of parturition becomes a member of the masochistic triad and the gulf between instinctual and the reproductive tendencies is bridged by masochism. The interruption of the little girl's infantile sexual development by the frustration of her desire for the child gives to the sublimation-tendencies of the woman a very definite stamp of masochistic maternity. If it is true that men derive the principal forces which make for sublimation from their sadistic tendencies, then it is equally true that women draw on the masochistic tendencies with their imprint of maternity. In spite of this symbiosis, the two opposite poles, the sexual instinct and the reproductive function, may enter into conflict with one another. When this occurs, the danger is the greater in proportion as the two groups of tendencies are in close proximity.

Thus, a woman may commandeer the whole of her masochistic instinctual energy for the purpose of direct gratification and abandon sublimation in the function of reproduction. In the relation of the prostitute to the *souteneur* we have such an unadulterated product of the feminine masochistic instinctual attitude.

At the opposite end of the pole, yet drawing upon the same source, we have the *mater dolorosa,* the whole of whose masochism has come to reside in the relation of mother to child.

From this point I return to my original theme. There is a group of women who constitute the main body figuring in the statistics which give the large percentage of frigidity. The women in question are psychically healthy, and their relation to the world and to their libidinal object is positive and friendly. If questioned about the nature of their experience in coitus, they give answers which show that the conception of orgasm as something to be experienced by themselves is really and truly foreign to them. During intercourse what they feel is a happy and tender sense that they are giving keen pleasure and, if they do not come of a social environment where they have acquired full sexual enlightenment, they are convinced that coitus as a sexual act is of importance only for the man. In it, as in other relations, the woman finds happiness in tender, maternal giving.

This type of woman is dying out and the modern woman seems to be neurotic if she is frigid. Her sublimations are further removed from instinct and therefore, while on the one hand they constitute a lesser menace to its direct aims, they are, on the other, less well adapted for the indirect gratification of its demands. I think that this psychological change is in accordance with social developments and that it is accompanied by an increasing tendency of women towards masculinity. Perhaps the women of the next generation will no longer submit to defloration in the normal way and will give birth to children only on condition of freedom from pain.

And then in after-generations they may resort to infibulation and to refinements in the way of pain—ceremonials in connection with parturition. It is this masochism—the most elementary force in feminine mental life—that I have been endeavouring to analyse.

Possibly I have succeeded in throwing light on its origin and, above all, on its importance and its application in the function of reproduction. This employing of masochistic instinctual forces for the purpose of race-preservation I regard as representing in the mental economy an act of sublimation on the part of the woman. In certain circumstances it results in the withdrawal from the direct gratification of instinct of the energy involved and in the woman's sexual life becoming characterized by frigidity without entailing any such consequences as would upset her mental balance and give rise to neurosis.

Let me now at the close of my paper give its main purport: *Women would never have suffered themselves throughout the epochs of history to have been withheld by social ordinances on the one hand from possibilities of sublimation, and on the other from sexual gratifications, were it not that in the function of reproduction they have found magnificent satisfaction for both urges.*

NOTES

1. Read at the Eleventh International Psycho-Analytical Congress, Oxford, July 27, 1929.
2. Helene Deutsch: *Psychoanalyse der weiblichen Sexualfunktionen.* Neue Arbeiten zur ärztlichen Psychoanalyse, Nr. V.
3. Freud: 'Some Psychological Consequences of the Anatomical Difference between the Sexes' (*International Journal of Psycho-Analysis,* Vol. VIII, 1927). The argument in this paper of Freud's is that the Œdipus complex does not develop in girls until after the phase of phallic onanism. Cf. also Deutsch: *Op. cit.*
4. In his paper on 'The Economic Problem in Masochism' (*Collected Papers,* Vol. II), Freud points out that the important task of the libido is to conduct into the outside world the instinct of destruction primarily inherent in living beings, transforming it into the 'instinct of mastery'. This is effected by means of the organ of motility, the muscular system. It appears to me that part of these destructive tendencies remains attached to the subject's own person in the earliest form of masturbation, which has as yet no libidinal object, and that it is thus intercalated between organic pleasure and motor discharge into the outside world. At any rate I have been able with some degree of certainty to establish the fact that children who are specially aggressive and active have a particularly strong urge to masturbation. (I am speaking here of the earliest masturbation, which is as yet autoerotic). We see too that in little children frustration may provoke an outburst of rage and at the same time attempts at masturbation.
5. Even if further observations should prove the occurrence of vaginal sensations in childhood, the subsequent cathexis of the vagina as a sex-organ would still seem to be scarcely affected by the question of whether it had transitorily been a zone of excitation, very soon repressed so as to leave scarcely a trace, or whether it were only in later years of development that it assumed for the first time the rôle of the genital apparatus. The same difficulties arise in either case.
6. That 'feminine' masochism has its origin in this regressive deflection of the libido is clear evidence of the identity of 'erotogenic' and 'feminine' masochism.
7. In the second section of this paper I will revert to the part that the sense of guilt plays in feminine masochistic phantasies. In the present argument I am indicating the purely libidinal origin of feminine masochism, as determined by the course of evolution.

21. A Contribution to the Psychoanalysis of Extreme Submissiveness in Women

Annie Reich

The aim of this contribution is to further our understanding of a morbid development in the character of the woman who is extremely submissive to men and to explain a certain neurotic aspect of her love life. An investigation of this type of disturbance of the relationship to objects may also throw some light on certain properties of immature object relationships in general.

In the German language there exists the special expression *Hörigkeit* for which there seems to be no precise English equivalent; the term 'extreme submissiveness' will serve. By this term we understand a special dependency of one adult upon another: the impossibility of living without the partner, the willingness to comply with all the partner's wishes thereby sacrificing all interests of one's own, all independence and self-reliance. I think that such extreme submissiveness is a clear-cut clinical picture which may best be regarded as a perversion. It is found in men as well as in women but since my clinical material happens to comprise only female cases I will restrict myself to discussing the mechanisms at work in women. It is possible that the mechanisms in men are similar.

Susan, twenty-nine years of age, had been living in such a submissive relationship with a very brilliant but very narcissistic man for nine years. This man was very disturbed sexually and had deep objections to intercourse. It took six years before he finally gave in to Susan's importunate sexual needs, but even after that he was willing to have intercourse only on very infrequent occasions. Life with this man was a perpetual courtship on Susan's part. Notwithstanding the fact that her life had become a long chain of

Read before the annual meeting of the American Psychoanalytic Association at Chicago, May, 1939.
Reprinted by permission of the author's estate and *The Psychoanalytic Quarterly* 9 (1940):470–80.

disappointments and rejections, she lived for this man only. Before him Susan had had several intimate friends, but somehow he was the 'right' one. She wanted only to be near him, to share his life. She followed him everywhere to the neglect of her vocation, her family, all her former interests.

For all this Susan felt recompensed by the overwhelming happiness which she experienced whenever she succeeded in sleeping with her lover; then she was utterly happy and had the feeling of being completely fused with him. 'We become one person', she said. 'He is I and I am he.'

The overvaluation of sexual intercourse seen in Susan is typical of all similar cases. Another example of this was Mary, thirty-one years old, married to a narcissistic man who maltreated her and went around with other women. Like Susan, Mary was deeply bound to her husband in an extremely submissive way. She endured all his insults and brutalities only to feel the bliss of having intercourse with him. Describing her feelings during intercourse, she said: 'The walls between him and me do not exist any more. I feel what he feels; I even think what he thinks. We are one person, and the only wish I have is to die that very minute.'

Intercourse is an experience of extraordinary intensity in these cases of extreme submissiveness in women. Since the feeling of bliss in this *unio mystica* cannot be explained by the orgastic sensation alone, let us try to probe the matter a little deeper.

In the submissive woman the special ecstasy of intercourse must be viewed against the background of anxiety, despair and helplessness which are experienced when she is separated from the object of her love or when her lover turns away from her. Mary described this in the following way: 'I am quite disturbed, as if I were poisoned. It is as if I were in an empty, cold and dark world all by myself. It is absolute solitude.' The description given by Susan was somewhat similar: 'I feel as though I were in a dark hole, all alone. All other men are dead. I am unable to do anything.'

It is worthy of note that the self-esteem of the submissive woman falls to a strikingly low level when she is away from her lover. The man, on the other hand, is overrated; he is considered to be very important, a genius. He is the only man worthy of love.

The submissive woman seems completely to have renounced her own narcissism. It is as if she had projected her narcissism onto the man; she develops a sort of megalomania in regard to him. In the magic of the *unio mystica* she finally regains through identification the narcissism which she had renounced.

Susan's history shows this clearly. She was a very ambitious girl with a wild urge towards perfection. She was characteristically compulsive in her work: for instance, she felt that she could never find a composition book of the 'right' size in which to copy the most complicated matters of science in the 'right' order. If after innumerable struggles she once managed to do so, she would then fall into a state of narcissistic enthusiasm. She began to study philosophy but finally gave it up as too difficult. A short time afterward she became acquainted with the man who later became her husband. He was a philosopher, and she fell helplessly in love with him. She was quite conscious of the fantasy that she would come to understand philosophy through her love for this man. In her analysis it became quite clear that the perfection which Susan could not achieve through her own efforts but only through having a man in intercourse was the penis.

Mary, our other submissive patient, had also fought for masculinity desperately and unsuccessfully. She too found vicarious satisfaction in her husband's greatness. Speaking of her handsome husband, she said: 'He is tall, slender, sinewy and muscular. His body is like a large penis!'

As children both women had imagined that during intercourse the woman would get the penis from the man and keep it. But the presence of this fantasy alone does not clarify the problem of submissiveness. The process of achieving the desired penis in a magic way through intercourse seems frequently to be the solution of the masculine conflicts of normal girls. The normal girl too has to renounce her masculine desires of puberty and is also partially recompensed by the love of a man. Hence we have to look for factors more specifically determining the development of extremely submissive conduct. The question as to what distinguishes the normal woman from the submissive one is the more important in as much as under certain social conditions, for example those prevailing in the nineteenth century, the obedient wife who was submissively dependent upon her husband represented the ideal of society.

A factor more specifically bearing upon the question of submissiveness in certain women is their tendency to fall in love with men who abuse and humiliate them. If we suppose that these humiliations are an inseparable part of their love life, we must look for further signs of masochistic tendencies. These signs are indeed to be found. For one thing, these women consider intercourse an act of violence, or in a more sublime way the act may be experienced as a mystic dissolution of the person which has its climax in death during orgasm. Likewise, the humiliations to which the submissive woman is subjected are obviously a part of the love play: the deeper the despair resulting from abuse or separation from the lover, the greater the happiness of the reunion. There seem to be two parts to the process: that which is destroyed in the first part is restored in the second. The masochistic nature of yielding to the great can also be seen clearly in the masturbation fantasies of childhood. Little Mary dreamed: 'A father operates on the penis of a little boy. Then he loves the boy very much.' Intercourse in later life is a living out of this fantasy: the woman has first to be castrated and destroyed by the man in order to be loved afterwards. In that ecstatic experience we find a unification of contradictory trends and emotions. The ecstasies represent at the same time castration and the restitution of the penis as well as death and resurrection.

Before we can fully understand this strange process we must examine another aspect of the behavior of submissive women: their extreme passivity. The submissive woman is helpless if she has to accomplish something un-aided and alone. This is not because she lacks ability—all the submissive women I have analyzed were intelligent, distinguished and highly devel-oped—but because the impulse towards activity was missing. The submis-sive woman wants to remain passive far beyond the realm of sexuality. The man has always to take the first step; she wants only to be his executive organ. If the man inspires or orders something she can do it, but independent action has no such pleasure attached to it.

The main symptom for which Susan came to analysis was her incapacity to do anything by herself. During the analysis she came to understand that every action undertaken by herself was initiated against great resistance because it showed that she was all alone and without her friend. Mary too was full of complaints about her lack of initiative and her unproductiveness. Only if someone else gave orders was she capable of doing anything. In conversation she always had to agree with her partner because, as she put it, she did not have brains enough to make independent evaluations. In fact she found pleasure in this type of intellectual subordination and she built up in each conversation a kind of submissiveness in miniature.

The inclination to be passive reveals a very intense sexualization of the whole life. Women showing this type of submissiveness continually want attention and love from their men. The necessity of independent action already represents for them loneliness and lack of love. They only partly learn to renounce continuous gain of pleasure and to adjust themselves to the requirements of reality. Their very childish attitude is clearly crystallized in the fantasy: 'I have no penis; I cannot do anything alone; you must continually give me something; you must always do something for me'.

Further analysis of the submissive woman characteristically reveals that her problems arise earlier than the phallic phase. They are rooted in a childish fixation to the mother. From her the child expects protection, tenderness, food—in short, all kinds of attention. This was most clearly seen in the analysis of another submissive woman. Frances, thirty years old, had lost her mother when she was four, after which she was sent from one foster home to another for a year until her father finally provided a new mother by marrying again. The child clung to her new mother desperately and wanted all the time to be cleaned, fed, loved and cared for. In her later life the same continual demand for attention of all kinds was seen. In masochistically yielding to a very brilliant man she tried to find fulfilment of these desires through the bliss of an ecstatic union.

In Mary's childhood this special dependency on the mother played a large rôle. She did not want to do anything without the help of her mother. She had a daydream of a mighty being who knew exactly what she needed and who fulfilled her every need without her asking. What in later childhood she hoped to get from her mother was the penis. Originally her desires had been anal and oral ones. Those tendencies remained unchanged, crossing each other, overlapping, and both extending into her submissive relationship to her husband. Desires that were originally meant for the mother reappear in an ecstatic love relationship to a man.

In describing this ecstatic state we emphasize repeatedly that individuality is dissolved in complete union with the man. We might also understand this union with the great and mighty as a magic fusion with the mother. It is like relapsing to a time in which the ego is about to be formed and when the boundaries between the ego and the outer world were still blurred and only painfully experienced in moments of frustration and tension. Helene Deutsch[1] believes that the sensation of ecstasy is based upon the restitution of some larger unit in the ego when she describes the ecstatic orgastic experience in terms of the fusion of the ego instincts and superego and at the same time with an otherwise hostile, denying outer world.

That the ecstatic experience of orgasm meant a fusion with the mother was substantiated in Mary's analysis. Whenever she was separated from her mother in childhood, Mary feared that her mother had died. She suffered terribly when her mother was dissatisfied or angry with her. On seeing her mother again after an absence or at reconciliation, she felt the same intense happiness she later experienced in her union with a man. She recalled having fallen asleep in her mother's bed with an indescribable feeling of bliss, cuddled up to the warm back of the mother. She used later to fall asleep in the same position after intercourse.

The fear which hung over Mary's childhood that the mother might die we recognize of course to be an expression of the repressed hostility directed against that at times callous fountainhead of all fulfilment. This hostility was later diverted from the mother and directed towards the husband, but it remained repressed. Thus the extreme infantile ambivalence was not overcome by the later change of object but merely directed into other forms. The most important transformation was into masochism. The hostility which had been repressed was explosively discharged upon herself during intercourse through identification with the brutal, sadistic man. At these times she would feel intense lust but would experience a sort of split of her personality. At the same time that she was feeling sexual pleasure as a woman she would also feel like a bystander watching the conquest of a woman. She frequently had the fantasy of being a man and doing the same thing to a young girl. Likewise some of her masturbation fantasies revealed this coëxistence of active and passive attitudes: first, a boy is castrated by his father; then the grandfather performs the same operation upon the father.

The anxiety and despair which Mary experienced when separated from her husband were secondarily erotized to increase the intensity of the later sexual gratification. During analysis she realized that in such a state of despair she really felt hatred and envy towards the man who denied her his greatness, his penis. In such a state she once bit savagely into her husband's shaving brush, and her subsequent dreams showed clearly that she wanted to bite off his penis. But such an undisguised outburst of rage could occur only when her marriage was about to end in failure. This expression of rage signified a breakdown of the whole mechanism of submissiveness. So long as the marriage was working, her basic hostility was sufficiently neutralized by its secondary erotization; she was able to endure the torture of being alone in order to increase the bliss of the ensuing reconciliation. When the marriage started to go on the rocks, repression failed.

Although a certain overvaluation of the object is characteristic of a normal love relationship, the submissive woman tends to endow her object with a special greatness. Only with such an object is the *unio mystica* possible, the ecstatic intercourse in which all secret wishes are fulfilled, all aggression, all anxiety and all guilt neutralized.

What happens if this type of woman is thrown into a relationship with an 'average' man? Here, in contrast to her behavior with an admired man, her aggression breaks through. This can be illustrated in the case of Frances, cited earlier, whose fixation was determined by her mother's death when she was four. Frances had been bound submissively to an 'important' man for ten years. This liaison came to a sudden end when her lover's child died. A little later Frances began a new sexual relationship but of a very different kind. Her new lover, many years younger than she, was a nice, plain fellow who felt great love and admiration for her. From him she demanded and got economic security. But in this relationship there was nothing of her former devoted yielding. Here she dominated, but she had to struggle with intense feelings of guilt. 'I don't love this man', she would muse. 'I abuse his young body, his tenderness, his money. If I don't want him I put him in the icebox, so to speak, to have him ready when I need him again.' She used the man like a tool. To her he was not a human being but only a penis conveniently at her disposal. She dreamed of satisfying herself with a detached penis.

Susan likewise felt egotistic and guilty when she had a sexual relationship with a man who was not the 'right' one. 'I do not love him', she felt; 'I just abuse him'.

In this form of sexual relationship the object is not intact; the man does not figure as a human being but only as a means of gratifying an instinct.

This lack of consideration for the object is characteristic of the prostitute. She may be submissive and masochistic in the hands of a bully while she abuses, exploits and destroys numerous other men. Here there is no identification with the object, no sentiment, no interest in individuality.

The relentless, destroying attitude which the prostitute lives out in her love life, the submissive woman attempts to master by repression. She tries hard to preserve her faith in the greatness and singularity of her man because this overvaluation alone enables her to maintain the underlying hatred in repression. A blind, unqualified glorification of the object insures a lasting relationship to it.

This strained repression, however, is frequently difficult to maintain. Mary, for instance, was always furtively and anxiously evaluating her admired husband to see whether he was really as great, as brilliant and as beautiful as she had made him out to be. She had continual anxiety that she might discover in him something that was stupid, ugly, ridiculous. To stifle this dread she naturally had to pump hard in order to maintain her object in a perpetual state of inflation. Were this bubble to break there would emerge the primitive, aggressive, coprophagic and cannibalistic impulses which in early childhood were predominant in relation to the mother.

The struggle to maintain this balance is characteristic of all object relationships in submissive women. There is towards all things a tendency to sham kindliness, sham warmth, sham attachment.

This inclination to destroy, present as a chronic tendency, is not in this form characteristic of the early infantile attitude from which it is in fact derived. This impulse dominates the emotional state of the infant only if its feeling of well being is interrupted by pain and frustration. Then the denying object is wanted intensely but only then is it at the same time hated and destroyed.

This alternation between unlimited love and the wish to destroy, depending on whether or not immediate wishes were gratified, was observed clearly in the analysis of a schizophrenic patient. At one moment the world was wonderful, its beauty entering his body like a stream of warm milk; in the next instant everything was gray, colorless, hateful. The development of a minor internal tension was sufficient to produce this change: for instance, if he became thirsty and the desired drink did not come to him magically without the necessity of his getting up and getting it. Or if his girl kept him waiting two minutes his love vanished; there was nothing left but hatred and the wish to destroy.

This patient behaved like a baby in its first month of life. At this stage there is a complete intolerance of tension and frustration. The object is beloved only so long as it fulfils every need. Life is a succession of discrete moments; there is no recollection of any kind. The fact that the object was kind until now is emotionally meaningless. The infant cannot remember nor can it wait or understand that there may be a later gratification. All it can do is rage.

Conformity to the reality principle, emotional continuity and the minimization of mood swings is achieved in a variety of ways in the course of normal development. In submissive women this is attempted by the narcissistic elevation of the object, by the pleasure gratification of the ecstatic love experience, and finally by the transformation of aggression into masochistic behavior. Instead of the loose, unstable relationships of the early stage there is developed a single, unchangeable, exaggerated fixation to the object.

This solution of an infantile conflict is not the most successful one which could be achieved. The 'phallic girl' described by Fenichel,[2] for instance, has worked out a somewhat similar but more stable arrangement. This woman identifies herself with the desired organ of the object by magic incorporation. She is now a part of the man—his penis. The 'phallic girl' is not driven to masochism and is not so much threatened by an unstable ambivalence towards the object as is the submissive woman. By incorporating the desired organ of the object she is enabled to live always in a state of satisfied narcissism.

SUMMARY

A healthy relationship to objects is one where the love of an object can be maintained even if the object be the agent of temporary disappointments or frustrations. This is possible by the development of an ego that is capable of mastering reality. Where there is interference with this development a perpetuation of early infantile conflicts results. Masochistic submissiveness in women is one way of attempting to solve these conflicts.

NOTES

1. Deutsch, Helene: *Zufriedenheit, Glück, Ekstase.* Int. Ztschr. f. Psa., XIII, 1927.
2. Fenichel, Otto: *Die symbolische Gleichung: Mädchen-Phallus.* Int. Ztschr. f. Psa., XXII, 1936, pp. 299–314.

22. Some Biopsychical Aspects
of Sado-Masochism

Marie Bonaparte

We all know Freud's two theories of sadomasochism. The first, originally presented in *Three Essays on the Theory of Sexuality* (1905) reads thus: 'The most common and the most significant of all perversions—the desire to inflict pain upon the sexual object, and its reverse—received from Krafft-Ebing the names of 'sadism' and 'masochism' for its active and passive forms respectively. Other writers have preferred the narrower term 'algolagnia'. This emphasizes the pleasure in *pain,* the cruelty; whereas the names chosen by Krafft-Ebing bring into prominence the pleasure in any form of humiliation or subjection.

'As regards active algolagnia, sadism, the roots are easy to detect in the normal. The sexuality of most male human beings contains an element of *aggressiveness*—and a desire to subjugate; the biological significance of it seems to lie in the need for overcoming the resistance of the sexual object by means other than the process of wooing. Thus sadism would correspond to an aggressive component of the sexual instinct which has become independent and exaggerated and, by displacement, has usurped the leading position.

'In ordinary speech the connotation of sadism oscillates between, on the one hand, cases merely characterized by an active or violent attitude to the sexual object, and, on the other hand, cases in which satisfaction is entirely conditional on the humiliation and maltreatment of the object. Strictly speaking, it is only this last extreme instance which deserves to be described as a perversion.

'Similarly, the term masochism comprises any passive attitude towards sexual life and the sexual object, the extreme instance of which appears to be

Paper read at the 17th International Psycho-Analytical Congress, Amsterdam, 1951. Translated by John Rodker.
Reprinted by permission of the author's estate and the *International Journal of Psycho-Analysis* 33 (1952): 373-84. Copyright © Institute of Psycho-Analysis.

that in which satisfaction is conditional upon suffering physical or mental pain at the hands of the sexual object. Masochism, in the form of a perversion, seems to be further removed from the normal sexual aim than its counterpart; it may be doubted at first sight whether it can ever occur as a primary phenomenon or whether, on the contrary, it may not invariably arise from a transformation of sadism. It can often be shown that masochism is nothing more than an extension of sadism turned round upon the subject's own self, which thus, to begin with, takes the place of the sexual object. Clinical analysis of extreme cases of masochistic perversion shows that a great number of factors (such as castration complex and the sense of guilt) have combined to exaggerate and fixate the original passive sexual attitude.

'The history of human civilization shows beyond any doubt that there is an intimate connection between cruelty and the sexual instinct: but nothing has been done towards explaining the connection, apart from laying emphasis upon the aggressive factor in the libido. According to some authorities this aggressive element of the sexual instinct is in reality a relic of cannibalistic desires—that is, it is a contribution derived from the apparatus for obtaining mastery, which is concerned with the satisfaction of the other and, ontogenetically, the older of the great instinctual needs. It has also been maintained that every pain contains in itself the possibility of a feeling of pleasure. All that need be said is that no satisfactory explanation of this perversion has been put forward and that it seems possible that a number of mental impulses are combined in it to produce a single resultant.

'But the most remarkable feature of this perversion is that its active and passive forms are habitually found to occur together in the same individual. A person who feels pleasure in producing pain in someone else during a sexual connection, is also capable of enjoying as pleasure any pain which he may himself derive from sexual relations. A sadist is always at the same time a masochist, although the active or the passive aspect of the perversion may be more strongly developed in him and may represent his predominant sexual activity.

'We find, then, that certain among the impulses to perversion occur regularly as pairs of opposites; and this, taken in conjunction with material which will be brought forward later, has a high theoretical significance. It is, moreover, a suggestive fact that the existence of the pair of opposites formed by sadism and masochism cannot be attributed merely to the element of aggressiveness. We should rather be inclined to connect the simultaneous presence of these opposites with the opposing masculinity and femininity

which are combined in bisexuality—a contrast which often has to be replaced in psycho-analysis by that between activity and passivity.'

In a later work, *Instincts and their Vicissitudes* (1915), Freud, still maintaining his first theory of instincts, wrote: Whether there is, besides this, a
more direct masochistic satisfaction is highly doubtful. A primary masochism
not derived in the manner I have described from sadism, does not appear to
be met with.

'The conception of sadism is made more complicated by the circumstance
that this instinct, side by side with its general aim (or perhaps rather, within
it), seems to press towards a quite special aim: —the infliction of pain, in
addition to subjection and mastery of the object. Now psycho-analysis would
seem to show that the infliction of pain plays no part in the original aims
sought by the instinct: the sadistic child takes no notice of whether or not it
inflicts pain, nor is it part of its purpose to do so. But when once the
transformation into masochism has taken place, the experience of pain is
very well adapted to serve as a passive masochistic aim, for we have every
reason to believe that sensations of pain, like other unpleasant sensations,
extend into sexual excitation and produce a condition which is pleasurable,
for the sake of which the subject will even willingly experience the unpleas-
antness of pain. Where once the suffering of pain has been experienced as a
masochistic aim, it can be carried back into the sadistic situation and result
in a sadistic aim of *inflicting pain,* which will then be masochistically
enjoyed by the subject while inflicting pain upon others, through this identification of himself with the suffering object. Of course, in either case it is not
the pain itself which is enjoyed, but the accompanying sexual excitement,
and this is especially easy for the sadist. The enjoyment of pain would thus
be a primary masochistic aim, which, however, can then also become the
aim of the originally sadistic instinct.

If we compare these two extracts we grasp the difficulty which Freud
confronted in presenting his first concept of sado-masochism. Whatever he
may first have thought, sadism could never be primary, for how could
pleasure be felt in inflicting pain if one had not already experienced both
these antagonistic and mysteriously linked sensations?

Passivity, generally, precedes activity. Freud thus comes to deny that any
real primary sadism exists, since he denies the child any pleasure in its
cruelty, widespread though that is, which hardly seems to conform to the
facts.

With his second theory of instincts, however, Freud was to go much further along the path leading to the acceptance of masochism as the forerunner of true sadism, and even so far as to deny the existence of this primary phase of primitive infantile sadism which cannot yet be qualified as true sadism, and which is precisely our own point of view.

In *Beyond the Pleasure Principle* (1920), Freud abandons the dualism of ego and sexual instincts in his first theory of instincts, and establishes his second theory restoring this dualism to the death and life instincts, the latter taking to themselves the libidinal object drives and primary ego instincts which become the narcissistic libido.

As to the death instincts, there described for the first time, their tendency would be to return all living substance to its original inorganic condition. Nevertheless, the aggression which animates all creatures still remained unexplained, and it was not until *The Economic Problem of Masochism* (1924) was published that Freud's views on the subject became clear, and precisely on this subject of sado-masochism.

We have a right to describe the existence of the masochistic trend in the life of the human instincts as from the economic point of view mysterious. For if mental processes are governed by the pleasure-principle, so that avoidance of 'pain' and obtaining pleasure is their first aim, masochism is incomprehensible. If physical pain and feelings of distress can cease to be signals of danger and be ends in themselves, the pleasure-principle is paralysed, the watchman of our mental life is to all intents and purposes himself drugged and asleep.

In this light, masochism appears to us as a great danger, which is in no way true of sadism, its counterpart. We feel tempted to call the pleasure-principle the watchman of our lives, instead of only the watchman of our mental life. But then the question of the relation of the pleasure-principle to the two varieties of instincts that we have distinguished, the *death-instincts* and the *erotic (libidinal) life instincts* [1] demands investigation . . .

Freud then posits three types of masochism; erotogenic, feminine, and moral, and, after describing the feminine masochism observed by him in various male patients who delighted in being, or imagining themselves, 'pinioned, bound, beaten painfully, whipped, in some way mishandled, forced to obey unconditionally, defiled, degraded', he concludes that 'the feminine type of masochism . . . is based entirely on the primary erotogenic type, on the 'lust of pain' which cannot be explained without going very far back.'

Now follows the backward glance which Freud invites us to take:

'In my *Drei Abhandlungen zur Sexualtheorie,* in the section on the sources of infantile sexuality, I put forward the proposition that sexual excitation arises as an accessory effect of a large series of internal processes *as soon as the intensity of these pleasures has exceeded certain quantitative limits;*[1] indeed, that perhaps nothing very important takes place within the organism without contributing a component to the excitation of the sexual instinct. According to this, an excitation of physical pain and feelings of distress would surely also have this effect. This *libidinal sympathetic excitation*[1] accompanying the tension of physical pain and feelings of distress would be an infantile physiological mechanism which ceases to operate later on. It would reach a varying degree of development in different sexual constitutions: in any case it would provide the physiological foundation on which the structure of erotogenic masochism is subsequently erected in the mind.

The inadequacy of this explanation is seen, however, in that it throws no light on the regular and close connection of masochism with *sadism,*[1] its counterpart in the life of the instincts. If we go a step further back to our hypothesis of the two varieties of instincts which we believe to be active in animate beings, we come to another conclusion which, however, does not contradict the one just mentioned. In the multicellular living organism the libido meets the death or destruction instinct which holds sway there, and which tries to disintegrate this cellular being and bring each elemental primary organism into a condition of inorganic stability (though this again may be but relative). To the libido falls the task of making this destructive instinct harmless, and it manages to dispose of it by directing it to a great extent and early in life—with the help of a special organic system, the musculature—towards the objects of the outer world. It is then called the instinct of destruction, of mastery, the will to power. A section of this instinct is placed directly in the service of the sexual function, where it has an important part to play: this is true *sadism.*[1] Another part is not included in this displacement outwards; it remains within the organism and is "bound" there libidinally with the help of the accompanying sexual excitation mentioned above: this we must recognise as the original *erotogenic masochism.*[1]

'We are entirely without any understanding of the physiological ways and means by which this subjugation of the death-instinct by the libido can be achieved. In the psycho-analytical world of ideas we can only assume that a very extensive coalescence and fusion, varying according to conditions, of the two instincts takes place, so that we never have to deal with pure life-instincts and death-instincts at all, but only with combinations of them in different degrees. Corresponding with the fusion of instincts there may under certain influences occur a "defusion" of them. How large a part of the death-instincts may refuse to be subjugated in this way by becoming attached to libidinal quantities it is at present not possible to ascertain.

'If one is willing to disregard a certain amount of inexactitude, it might be said that the death-instinct active in the organism—the primal sadism—is identical with masochism. After the chief part of it has been directed out-wards towards objects, there remains as a residuum within the organism the true erotogenic masochism, which on the one hand becomes a component of the libido and on the other still has the subject itself for an object. So that this masochism would be a witness and a survival of that phase of development in which the amalgamation, so important for life afterwards, of death-instinct and Eros took place. We should not be astonished to hear that under certain conditions the sadism or destruction instinct which has been directed out-wards can be introjected, turned inward again, regressing in this way to its earlier condition. It then provides that *secondary masochism*[1] which supplements the original one.

The erotogenic type of masochism passes through all the developmental stages of the libido, and from them it takes the changing shapes it wears in the life of the mind. The fear of being devoured by the totem-animal (father) is derived from the primitive oral stage of libido-organization; the desire to be beaten by the father from the next-following sadistic-anal stage; castration, although it is subsequently denied, enters into the content of masochistic phantasies as a residue from the phallic stage; and from the final genital stage are derived of course the situations characteristic of womanhood, namely, the passive part in coitus and the act of giving birth. The part played by the nates in masochism is also easily intelligible, apart from its obvious founda-tion in reality. The nates are the special erotogenic bodily regions which have preference in the sadistic-anal stage, as the nipple in the oral stage and the penis in the genital stage.

Freud then goes at length into the question of moral masochism, which plays so great a part in so many lives as the need for punishment and the tendency to frustration. Highly desexualized though it may seem, this form of masochism also arises on the biological foundation of erotogenic masochism. We shall not, however, continue to follow Freud here, since our main enquiry is into the biopsychical origins of erotogenic sado-masochism.

But first another voice merits attention: that of the man from whom sadism takes its name.

In that verbose romance, *Histoire de Juliette: Les Prospérités du Vice,* the notorious Marquis de Sade intersperses his countless scenes of exquisite and cruel lust with metaphysical or philosophical discussions. I shall quote from among those where he seeks to justify what today we term sado-masochism.

Some noblemen, voluptuaries, admiringly described as 'ferocious', have gathered, one evening, round a festive board which is lit by candles so stuck as to roast the private parts of a number of little girls. Our noblemen, however, complacently continue their philosophizing.

'Noirceuil,' said Saint-Fond, 'while our little novices roast, explain, I beg, with your usual metaphysics, how one may manage to obtain pleasure from watching the sufferings of others or from suffering oneself?' 'Listen then,' said Noirceuil, 'and I will prove it to you.'

'*Pain,* logically speaking, *is nothing but a feeling of aversion inspired in the soul by certain responses, opposed to its structure, in the body it animates.* So says Nicole, who distinguished an aerial substance in man which he termed soul, as opposed to the material substance we call body. Personally, since I do not at all accept that frivolous idea and see man only as a kind of purely concrete vegetation, I would merely say that pain is a consequence of the disharmony between foreign bodies and the organic molecules of which we are constituted, with the result that the atoms emanated by these foreign bodies, instead of attaching themselves to our nervous fluid, as they do in the shock of pleasure, only make an angular, prickly, repellent approach, so that they never link up together. Yet, though their effects are repellent they are nevertheless always effects and, whether it be pleasure or pain we are offered, they will always provoke a shock to the nervous fluid. Now, what is to prevent this shock of pain, infinitely keener and more vigorous than the other, from exciting in this fluid that same widespread conflagration which arises through attachment of the atoms emanated by objects of pleasure? If we must have sensations, what is to prevent one getting used, through habit, to being made just as happy through the repellent atoms as through those which attach? Satiated with the effects of those which produce only simple sensations, why should I not get equally used to receiving pleasure from those which give *poignant* sensations? They both strike in the same place, the only difference being that while one is keen, the other is mild and, to the satiated, is not the former infinitely preferable to the latter? Do we not, every day, see folk who have accustomed their palates to an irritation they like, and others who could not endure that irritation for a moment? And is it not nowadays true (once you grant my hypothesis) that, in their pleasures, men always try to rouse the objects that serve their enjoyment in the same way that they themselves are roused, and that this practice, in the metaphysics of enjoyment, is considered as resulting from "delicacy"? What is there strange, then, in a man, endowed with the organs we describe, by the same practices as his adversary and acting on the same principles of delicacy, imagining he will stir the object that serves his enjoyment by means that affect him himself? He has done no worse than the other, he has only done what the other did. The consequences differ, I agree, but the original motives are the same: the former was no crueller than the latter, and neither of the two has done wrong: both, on the object of their enjoyment, have used the identical means they employ to get pleasure.

'But, the creature at the mercy of a brutal lust will reply: *That does not please me;* in which case I must see whether I can compel you to like it or not. If I cannot, go away and let me be; if, on the other hand, my money, credit or position give me some mastery over you or some earnest that I can abolish your objections, then silently suffer whatever I may please to impose, because enjoyment I must have, and I can only enjoy by tormenting you and seeing your tears flow. In any case, do not be surprised, or blame me at all, because I obey the motions with which nature endowed me, or follow the path she makes me take; in a word, by subjecting you to my harsh and brutal lusts, those alone which succeed in bringing me to the acme of pleasure, I act from those same principles of delicacy as the effeminate lover who only knows the roses of a feeling which I can but see as thorns. For, in tormenting and rending you, I do the only thing by which I am stirred, just as he, drearily raking his mistress, does the only thing that stirs him agreeably. Let us leave effeminate delicacy to him, however, because it could never stir such powerfully made organs as mine. Yes, friends,' continued Noirceuil, 'you may be sure that no being, truly passionate for the joys of lust, could ever indeed mix delicacy with it, that delicacy which merely poisons these pleasures and implies a sharing that is impossible to whoever seeks real pleasure: any power shared is weakened thereby. It is a commonplace that, if you try to give enjoyment to the object that serves your pleasure, you will soon see it is at your own expense. There is no passion more egotistic than that of sensuality; not one that demands to be served more sternly. One must absolutely never think about anyone but oneself, when in erection, and never consider the object that serves us except as a kind of victim offered to the rage of that passion. Do not all passions demand victims? Well, the passive object, in the lust act, is that of our lustful rage; the less it is spared, the better the aim is fulfilled; the keener that object's pangs, the more utterly is it degraded and humbled and the more complete is our enjoyment. It is not pleasure we should make that object taste, but sensations that we should produce in it and, since that of pain is infinitely keener than that of pleasure, it is indubitable that it is better for the shock this outer sight produces on our nerves to happen through pain, rather than pleasure. There you have the explanation of the mania of those numerous libertines who, like ourselves, never manage to achieve erections and seminal emissions except by committing acts of atrocious cruelty, or by gorging themselves on their victim's blood.[2] Some would not even experience the slightest erection, despite the worst extremities of pain in their object, but for the thought that they themselves were the prime cause of those pangs in the sorry thing sold to their lustful rage. You desire to subject your nerves to a violent shock, you feel that that of pain will be stronger than that of pleasure, you use those means and find yourself well contented. But beauty, some idiot objects, softens and moves; it urges to kindness, pardon. How resist a pretty girl's tears when, with clasped hands, she implores her torturer? Well, indeed! that's just what one wants; it is the very prerequisite from which the libertine in question derives all his delightful enjoyment; he would indeed deserve to be pitied were he acting on an inert, unfeeling creature, and this objection is as ridiculous as would be a man's who declared one should never eat mutton because the sheep is an inoffensive creature.'

Comparing these extracts with Freud's hypothesis of the origins of sado-masochism, we see that de Sade, evidently at first hand, seems to subscribe in advance to the first Freudian concept of masochism, forerunner of true sadism, as expressed in *Instincts and their Vicissitudes.* 'Where once the suffering of pain has been experienced as a masochistic aim, it can be carried back into the sadistic situation and result in a sadistic aim of *inflicting pain,* which will then be masochistically enjoyed by the subject while inflicting pain upon others, through his identification of himself with the suffering object.'

In other pages, however, and best in the words he lends Pope Braschi, de

Sade even seems to go so far as to accept the Freudian concept of the death-instincts, every whit as eternal and dominant as the life-instincts, as in this dithyramb by his mitred philosopher.

'In all beings, the principle of life is no other than that of death: we receive and foster them in us, both at the same time. In that instant we call *death,* everything seems to disintegrate: we believe so, owing to the extreme change then found in this portion of matter which no longer seems animate. This death, however, is but imaginary; it is merely figurative and without reality. Matter, bereft of that subtle portion of matter which communicated motion to it, is not thereby destroyed; it merely changes its form, it corrupts, and already you see a proof of the activity it retains in it; it gives sap to the earth, fertilizes it, and serves to regenerate other kingdoms, besides its own. In fine, there is no essential difference between the first life we receive and this second which is that we call death. For the first comes about through the matter formed and organized in the female womb and the second, likewise, from the matter renewed and reorganized in the bowels of the earth. Thus, in its new womb, this extinguished matter again becomes the germ of particles of etherealized matter which, but for it, would have remained apparently inert. There you have all the wisdom of the laws governing these three kingdoms, laws they received on their first irruptions, laws which confine nature's urges to gush forth in new ways; these are the only ways in which the laws inherent to these kingdoms operate. The first generation, which we call life, provides us with a sort of example. These laws only succeed in reaching the first generation through exhaustion; they do not reach the other save by destruction. For the former a sort of corrupt matter is needed; for the second, putrified matter. That is the sole cause of these huge successive creations; in one and all there are but these prime principles of exhaustion or annihilation, which thus makes clear that death is as necessary as life, that there is no death and that all the scourges we have mentioned . . . (those wars and famines with which she (nature) overwhelms us, those pestilences which, from time to time, she visits on the globe in order to destroy us, those scoundrels she multiplies, those Alexanders, Tamerlanes, Genghis Khans, all those heroes who ravage the earth) . . . the tyrants' cruelty, the villain's crimes, are as necessary to the laws of these three kingdoms as are the deeds which rebrought them to life; that, when nature visits them on the earth, meaning to annihilate these kingdoms which deprive it of the capacity to produce new upsurges, it merely performs an impotent act, since the first laws received by these kingdoms when they first gushed forth, stamped this productive capacity upon them for ever and ever; this, nature could never abolish except by totally destroying herself, which is not in her power, since she herself is subject to laws from whose sway it is impossible for her to escape, and which will endure eternally. Thus the villain, by his murders, not only assists nature's intentions towards ends she will never be able to fulfil, but even assists the laws which the kingdoms received at their first upsurge. I say first upsurge, to ease comprehension of my system, for since there never was an act of creation and since nature is eternal, the gushes are perpetual while creatures exist; they would cease to be, if no more occurred, and would then encourage secondary gushes, which are those that nature desires but to which she cannot attain except by total destruction, the intended aim of crime. Whence it results that the criminal who could overwhelm all three kingdoms at once by annihilating them and their productive capacities would be he who had served nature best.'

Thus, the anthropomorphized sadism of nature, which Goethe personified in Mephisto as 'the spirit that always denies', would prevail, and the ultimate trend of the death-instincts postulated by Freud would have overshot their mark: that of the return of organic matter to the inorganic state.

I do not, of course, imagine that the death-instincts, as conceived by de Sade, are identical with those philosophically postulated by Freud. I merely wish to draw attention to some rough, though interesting, points of agreement.

Nevertheless, despite de Sade, and even Freud, the cardinal problem of sado-masochism in which Pleasure and Pain, Libido and Destruction, are so enigmatically, so paradoxically intertwined, does not seem entirely solved.

I say Destruction and not Death, for, to me, the destructive and aggressive instincts are not identical in essence, as regards that silent fading into the inorganic of all things living as they move towards death. This seems to me, as to other analysts, an entropy as it were, a running down of the life-force, which must be 'unlived', faster or slower, in each species, through life. Does not Freud himself allude to this, in *Beyond the Pleasure Principle,* in regard to the transient rejuvenation of living substance by conjugation of the reproductive cells?

Nor is it very clear how a simple entropy, a negative concept such as the dissipation of energy, can turn outwards and assume the active, positive form of living aggression. Aggression seems much more wholly to derive from life and its cravings. In any case, aggression is not a hypothesis but an observable fact.

And the just as obvious fact of sado-masochism, in which, whether active or passive, destruction mingles inextricably with Libido, continues to challenge all our sagacity.

Where greater men than ourselves have tried, dare we venture to cast some light into such darkness?

It is clinically, in the pervert that masochism as an entity is met. It has already been described; the need to be bound, beaten, humiliated, or suffer in different ways in order to achieve sexual enjoyment.

It is clinically, too, in the sadist, that sadism is met, with its manifold cruelty and the frightful lust-murders committed by these rare criminal perverts who, from time to time, terrify yet enthral the public.

What roots are we to postulate for such extremes of sadism, as of masochism? There seem to be several, some biological, others psychological.

The living cell is a speck of protoplasm bounded by a more or less protective membrane. The cell is not, however, hermetically sealed: it not only receives impressions, but can be entered in three ways.

For nutrition, it must draw such substances from its environment as are needed to keep it alive; to assimilate and reject.

For reproduction, if a female cell, it must undergo penetration by another living cell; be impregnated by the male cell. Both these penetrations are beneficent and serve life. They differ from each other in that the nutritive process works on organic though dead substances, substances which have lost their living identity and can only at that price become part of the cell that ingests them, whereas impregnation is unique in that one live cell is penetrated by another and does not undergo destruction and death but, on the contrary, creates life.

The third sort of cellular penetration is traumatic: infraction and wounding causing suffering and death.

If we now apply all this to multicellular organisms, we also find these three possible kinds of penetration which, as regards the penetrated organism, imply three different kinds of response:

Appetite for substances able to serve nutrition;

Erotic attraction towards the sexual partner;

Terror of infraction and wounding that may cause suffering and death.

.   .   .

In the animal world, however, at a certain point in the scale, internal fecundation is established. Not only the sex-cell, the ovum, must be penetrated, but the very body of the female, by the penis. It is so with all mammals.

As a result a psychical confusion may arise in the female between the erotic and the wounding penetration, whence results the flight from the male of many mammalian females and, in our own species, so many cases of feminine frigidity.

Erotism, however, tends to bind this terror of infraction and often succeeds, either by largely masochizing the confusion between wounding and erotogenic penetration, or by establishing such penetration as preeminently erotogenic. Nevertheless, some homœopathic dose of masochism remains needful for acceptance of even the most erotogenic feminine penetration.

Even to Krafft-Ebing, years ago, masochism seemed, in fact, 'a sort of pathological overgrowth of psychical feminine factors; a sort of morbid intensification of certain psychic characteristics of women.'

Freud too, as we saw in his *Three Essays,* wrote that 'we should rather be inclined to connect the simultaneous presence of these opposites' (sado-masochism) 'with the opposing masculinity and femininity which are combined in bisexuality—a contrast which often has to be replaced in psychoanalysis by that between activity and passivity.'

I do not know whether some unimaginable, basic masochism exists in the cell, or what forms masochism may assume in the course of evolution, but, to me, it seems that the erotogenic masochism of the totality of a multicellular organism could only truly appear when internal fecundation had been established.

Thereupon the same confusion between erotogenic and wounding penetration which, so often, makes the mammalian female flee from the male, may operate in the contrary manner. We then find ourselves faced, in that crown of nature which is man, by those final forms of erotogenic masochism whose clinical shapes we know. Only the vital biological instinct of self-preservation can then halt the erotically wished-for aggression at the point where danger to life would begin.

These then, would be the phylogenetic roots of human masochism which plunge into man's remotest evolutionary past. Thus, through countless ages, erotism would be linked with every infraction, every disturbance of living tissue, including unpleasure and pain.

.   .   .

We may also, however, seek the biological roots of masochism ontogenetically. When does the human child apprehend, following the laws which govern its species, that it is destined to perpetuate itself through internal impregnation? Something, in the depths of its tissue, may well sense it. Yet, from this angle, a primordial happening in childhood must instruct it as to its future destiny as man or woman; that primal scene which so many children have witnessed, while the adults imagine them too young to notice. Observation of the coupling of animals, in any case, is never absent from an infantile anamnesis and provides a substitute from which the child will imagine what happens between the parents.

Psycho-analytic observation enables us to establish that coitus is always interpreted, by the childish observer, as a brutal, aggressive act, committed by the male on the female; that is the sadistic concept of coitus. Then, depending upon the amount of masculinity or femininity it includes, the child will thenceforth identify itself predominantly with either the man or the woman, but, always, given its original bisexuality, in some degree with both.

If the child is a girl, fear of male aggression may result, depending on the degree of masculinity she harbours, and lead to a recathecting of her defensive masculine positions. Unless, that is, a truly feminine masochism is constituted. If the child, however, is male, his masochism, also, may become strengthened, depending on the degree of innate femininity present, though sadism should predominate in some acceptable form. As though the little male already felt that penetration would be spared him; that, like the spermatozoon which would later shoot from his body, he too, luckier than the female, would not be penetrated but penetrate.

Thus, from the memory of the primal scene, lost in the mists of infantile amnesis, and from the traces which it leaves in each unconscious, the resulting sadistic concept of coitus may make the female draw back from accepting the penetrative phallus, imaginarily likened to some piercing weapon. But it may also, at times, in the sadistically predisposed male, create the very counterpart to this sadistic concept of coitus in which the erotogenic concept of wounding, of a piercing weapon, is phallicized and eroticized. In that case the phallic symbolism of the knife is taken literally by the mind.

It is this erotogenic concept of the wound that the great sadists like Kürten or Vacher expressed concretely, and that Baudelaire sang, in such sublimated form, in his poem *A celle qui est trop gaie.*[3] No more poetic or clearer expression could be given to this confusion between penetration in its wounding and erotic aspects. It is not only the phallic symbolism of the knife that shows through here, but the poison symbolism of semen which so many neurotic symptoms reveal. So classical, so transparent, are the sadistic symbols of the poem, that the judges immediately sensed them when this poem in *Les Fleurs du Mal* was condemned as obscene. Yet these are universal sexual symbols which only the unique span of the human imagination could contrive. We must now turn to its other achievements.

There are forces other than biological, however, which help to make human beings masochistic or sadistic; psychological forces which bring into play the psychical mechanisms of associated ideas and imaginative identification with others.

The universe is full of hostile forces which deny the child and individual the satisfaction which their instincts desire. From birth, from the cradle, it is at the mercy of hunger and cold, for the mother or breast do not always turn up in time to soothe it when needed. Later, privations, accidents, punishments cannot always be avoided. Nevertheless, the pleasure-principle reigns deep in the young creature and tends to over-cathect even painful emotions and feelings as, for instance, the whippings of ill-inspired upbringers. Doubtless that is why, as Freud says: 'It may well be that nothing of considerable importance can occur in the organism without contributing some component to the excitation of the sexual instinct'[4] which would therefore, *par excellence*, be the hedonistic instinct. Thus 'an excitation of physical pain and feelings of distress would surely also have this effect.'[5]

The mechanism governing the association of ideas being thus actuated, with pleasure arising at the same time as pain, certain kinds of pain soon seem to be sought for themselves, thus often establishing paradoxical hedonistic responses for life.

Since all beings are basically bisexual, however, every masochist is more or less a sadist, the male factor which he includes taking to itself the pleasure-pain in order to project them centrifugally outwards in accordance with the objectives of convex masculine eroticism. Many women, also, may be sadistic, owing to the male element they include, but it is mainly among males that sadism assumes its most striking forms. Since the male, like the spermatozoon, is not penetrated but penetrates another organism in the generative act, sadism is essentially male, as well as being vitally important.

Thus, when the pain-pleasure pair have taken a centrifugal path and turned outwards, the vital instinct of self-preservation ceases to be threatened and no longer raises barriers against it. On the contrary, it combines with the sadism, which then, in possessive, destructive fashion strives to annex the maximum amount of living-space round it, and to master and rule in supremely egotistic fashion. And the sadist will allow himself orgies of blood that the masochist must deny. Here enters the second and prime psychological condition needful to sadism, namely, human imagination, which allows that identification of aggressor with aggressed from which arise those intense, safe, and boundless masochistic pleasures because imagined, which, when combined with the egocentric intoxication of power, find satisfaction in the cruellest lust.

Thus the sadist, in the integrity of his ego, in the security of his own body, delights in the pain he inflicts, as it were by proxy, much in the way we safely enjoy the dramatic mishaps of our tragedy heroes. But, a more powerful relish, the play is real and the triumph his own.

Again, the essential ambivalence of Eros finds satisfaction in sadism. Born of the lover's eternal but unattainable desire to unite with his beloved, this ambivalence craves the destruction of that object in order that the vain, and thus painful, striving may end. Yet, though the great criminal sadist will at times partially devour his victim, true union with her is still withheld, as to all lovers. Then only the destruction of that ephemeral plaything of his passion will establish a more or less enduring truce which, for a time, assuages the sadist's torturing, unappeasable desires.

Such seem to be some of the biological and psychological roots which help to give rise to the great masochists and sadists.

Fortunately, however, masochistic like sadistic drives do not culminate in such extremes of perseveration. And though we all retain some masochistic or sadistic infantile residues in the unconscious, it is mostly in *inhibited* or *transformed* shapes.

What inhibits masochism, as we have shown, is the limitations placed upon it by the vital instinct of self-preservation. What inhibits sadism is precisely that on which, in other cases, it rests; the psychical mechanism of identification.

Depending on whether the sadist, innately, is more or less masochistic, i.e. ready to cathect the experienced pain with pleasure, he will likewise enjoy inflicted pain by imaginatively placing himself in the position of the victim and will, in some degree, be sadistic. But if the barrier of the vital instinct of self-preservation in himself strongly opposes the masochism in him, the same barrier will function in the potential sadist against the infliction of pain on others, through identification with them. This mechanism which inhibits sadism through *reaction-formation* we call pity. That is to say that the less innately masochistic one is, the less sadistic one will be, which is hardly surprising.

Sado-masochism may also be liable to vicissitudes other than those of *perseveration* or *inhibition* through *reaction-formation*. It may also undergo a transformation destined to great achievements, that of *moralization*.

Human morality could never have arisen, through the ages, save by the strong repressing the weak, to which the weak, resentfully, submitted. Nevertheless, to endure this constraint they had, perforce, to eroticize such painful moral and, at times, physical pressure. This is still true today, even in enlightened homes. Analysis, however, has enabled us to see that the prohibitions instituted by the child's upbringers are introjected by degrees and, combined with the individual's internalized aggression, later constitute its super-ego or moral conscience. The masochism in the ego then maintains the child's masochistic attitude to the super-ego which, modelled on those who brought it up, will be harsh and even sadistic. By this employment of our universal sadomasochism, man's moral conscience has arisen.

In this *moralization* of sado-masochism, are we encountering a *sublimation* of these aweinspiring drives? It may be so, since sublimation implies deflecting a drive to another than its original objective. Yet virtue is often so ferocious, both to oneself and others, that we may doubt whether such moralization of sadomasochism can be called a true sublimation. All the more in that we find precisely these same self-torturing mechanisms at work at the roots of the psycho-neuroses, which clearly reveals the basic ferocity of sado-masochism, even when transformed into moralistic shapes.

Moral masochism, though least spectacular, is the most widespread of all. To it many unfortunates owe their failure in life, and the more readily in that the blows they account to fate are often inflicted by those petty moral sadists who, like themselves, swarm everywhere. These petty moral sadists may be frankly malevolent or virtuous people, since virtue is often sadistic. In any case, moral masochists seem to invite the blows of their sadistically moral counterparts, which thus helps to turn their lives into an ever-thorny path.

· · ·

Of the three noble entities praised by the Philosophers: the Good, the Beautiful, the True: goodness, therefore, does not seem properly able to sublimate sado-masochism successfully.

Do the Beautiful and the True succeed any better?

It would seem so, for sadism feeds both the enquiring and the scientific spirit, though it is that sublimated sadism which, through the intellect, strives to penetrate the universal body. Only the surgeon reveals a certain regression, in this spirit, as actual penetrator of human flesh, though with permitted and beneficent intents.

The maximum sublimation of sado-masochism, however, is achieved by art; and that in its most direct though least concrete form, thanks to the incomparable power of human imagination. The great works of art are cruel, whether one thinks of Shakespeare's or Sophocles' tragedies, to mention but these. Nowadays the cinema, that mass substitute for antique tragedy, delights in murderous plots.

This salutary catharsis of the most dangerous human instincts may be experienced by the spectator without peril, as without remorse, for, peacefully seated in his place, he well knows that after the bloodiest death, the screen- or play-hero will have gone home to bed.

As for the creative artist, his achievements, issuing from instinctual depths, have no doubt often saved him from sadistic deeds by allowing him to act his sadism. What would a Poe or a Baudelaire have become, but for the safety-valve of their sovereign art? Even a de Sade who, as a rarely gifted writer, could imaginatively indulge his monstrous sadism, was doubtless thus saved from committing worse crimes than savagely flogging a Rose Keller, or distributing sweets containing cantharides at an orgy.

Yet, from the example of the 'divine Marquis', we can see how much more intensely sadism, i.e. imaginative masochism combined with a triumphant masculine egocentricity, fascinates man than its humbler brother, primary masochism. For though the works of a Sacher-Masoch still keep their documentary value for the psychiatrist or psychologist, they cannot claim the enduring lustre of the work of a de Sade. And that, even ignoring their unequal talents. The content here lends lustre to the form, since sadism, compared with simple masochism, triumphs by linking the vital and male with the pleasure of inflicting pain.

Thus sado-masochism, whose roots plunge into the matrix of the first living tissue, penetrated now by life and again by death, beholds its rule confirmed in that internally impregnated mammal, man, due to the original confusion communicated to the total human body through the long chain of evolution. This is the biological, the phylogenetic determinant of sadomasochism.

This awareness that internal impregnation takes place finds additional confirmation in each generation by what the child experiences in witnessing the primal scene; from this arises the sadistic concept of coitus. In this concept the child, depending on the degree to which it is innately female or male, identifies itself more or less with the female or male adult. The foundations thereupon begin to be laid for a more or less sadistic or masochistic nature which will manifest itself later; this is the biological and ontogenetic determinant of sado-masochism.

The following determinants are more specifically psychological. Masochism, under the primacy of the pleasure-principle and the inevitable suffering which life brings all creatures, becomes intensified by erotization, throughout childhood, which associated ideas should lead us to meet misfortune bravely.

If the child, however, declares itself more male than female, its original sadism will dominate; this will serve to project the masochism outward through identification of aggressor with aggressed and thus enable the child to enjoy its masochistic pleasures in security, since they are mirror-images, while remaining a conqueror itself. This triumph it owes to the illimitable imagination of man. In that respect the animal creation can never equal man, Taine's 'fierce, lustful gorilla!' And the essential ambivalence of Eros, which blossoms in our species, finds gratification in the destruction of the sexual partner.

In that super-cerebral creature man, however, many different vicissitudes await his sadomasochism. His extreme *perseverations* which culminate in the great perversions are, happily, not the rule. As for the masochism, that is shackled by *inhibitions* and the vital instinct of self-preservation, whereas his sadism is inhibited by *pity,* which is also determined by identification, though no longer masochistic, with the possible victim. Another vicissitude to which sado-masochism is subject is that of *moralization,* accompanied by moral torturings of oneself and others. Finally, *sublimation,* its transmutation into Science and Art, is the most highly developed form which man can give to sado-masochism, for he then employs it to serve civilization.

Even in the highest cultures, however, human sado-masochism remains active, demanding and insatiate. The occasional perverts which it here and there produces; the spectacular recital of crimes in the press; the occasional executions that thrill the public; the moral masochism to which, more or less, every civilized being is subjected and the sublimations of science and art; often do not suffice man any longer. It is as though, in a nostalgia for its origins, it once more desired the penetration of flesh. So the sportsman kills for pleasure and the soldier for the fatherland or an ideal. Truly, though with grim irony, it has been said that the art of war is to convey as much metal as possible into the most human flesh, not to mention the vast ancillary destruction. True, aggression here seems stripped of eroticism. And yet, some echo of our primitive sado-masochistic reactions stirs deep in the hearts of the fighters, as of those in the rear who read, or hear, victorious communiqués announcing that twenty thousand tons of bombs, more or less, have been dropped on troop concentrations or populous towns.

It seems, indeed, that physical aggression, stripped of hedonistic appeal, that is, of all sadism, is impossible to that animal with imagination, man. And the vast blood-bath of war enables sado-masochism to rediscover its original path on an immensely magnified scale, desexualized though it appear; that of the triumphant, death-dealing penetration of the living body.

Herein lies an obstacle to any true conversion of the peoples' hearts to pacifism, despite the increasing horror of modern wars.

NOTES

1. Author's italics.
2. As did Kürten, the vampire of Düsseldorf.
3. Mad woman who maddens me,
   I hate thee as much as I love thee!

   Thus, I would like, some night,
   When the hour of lust strikes,
   To crawl, I, a craven, in silence,
   Towards the treasures that are thine.

   In order to chastise thy joyous flesh,
   To bruise thy pardoned breast
   And to inflict on thy surprised flank
   A deep and hollow wound.

   And, giddy with the sweetness of it,
   Through these new lips of thine
   More beautiful and more radiant,
   Infuse in thee my venom, O sister of mine!

   (Trans. M. B.)

4. *Three Essays on the Theory of Sexuality.*
5. *The Economic Problem of Masochism.*

BIBLIOGRAPHY

Alexander, Franz. 'The Need for Punishment and the Death-Instinct', *Int. J. Psycho-Anal.*, **10**, 1929.

Berg, Karl. 'Der Sadist', *Deutsche Z. f. d. ges. gerichtliche Med.*, **17**, 1931.

Bonaparte, Marie. 'Passivity, Masochism and Femininity', *Int. J. Psycho-Anal.*, **16**, 1935.

——'Some Palæobiological and Biopsychical Reflections', *Int. J. Psycho-Anal.*, **19**, 1938.

——'De la Sexualité de la Femme', *Revue Française de Psychanalyse*, **13**, 1949.

Deutsch, Helene, 'The Significance of Masochism in the Mental Life of Women', *Int. J. Psycho-Anal.*, **11**, 1930.

Ellis, Havelock. 'Studies in the Psychology of Sex', *Society of Psychological Research*, 1904.

Federn, Paul. 'Beiträge zur Analyse des Sadismus und Masochismus', *Int. Z. Psychoanalyse*, **1** and **2**, 1913–1914.

Freud, Sigmund. *Three Essays on the Theory of Sexuality.* 'Instincts and their Vicissitudes', *Collected Papers*, **4**; 'A Child is being beaten', *Collected Papers*, **2**; *Beyond the Pleasure Principle*, 'The Economic Problem of Masochism', *Collected Papers*, **2**.

Horney, Karen. 'Das Problem des weiblichen Masochismus', *Int. Z. Psychoanalyse*, **12**, 1926.

Krafft-Ebing, Richard v. *Psychopathia Sexualis.* (Stuttgart, 1886.)

Laforgue, René. 'De l'Angoisse à L'Orgasme', *Revue Française de Psychanalyse*, **4**, 1930–31.

Meisenheimer, Johannes. *Geschlecht und Geschlechter.* (Jena, 1921.)

Nacht S., and Loewenstein, R. 'Le Masochisme', *Revue Française de Psychanalyse*, **10**, 1938.

Reich, Wilhelm. 'Der masochistische Charakter', *Int. Z. Psychoanalyse*, **18**, 1932.

Reik, Theodor. *Geständniszwang und Strafbedürfnis.* (Wien, 1925.)

Sacher-Masoch (Leopold von). *Die Damen im Pelz*, 1881.

Sade, Donatien Alphonse Francois, Marquis De. *Justine: Les malheurs de la Vertu*, 1791.

——*Histoire de Juliette: Les Prospérités du Vice*, 1792.

——*Les 120 Journées de Sodome*, 1800.

Sadger, Isidor. 'Ein Beitrag zum Verständnis des Sado-Masochismus', *Int. Z. f. Psychoanalyse*, **12**, 1926.

Weiss, Edoardo. 'Todestrieb und Masochismus', *Int. Z. Psychoanalyse*, **12**, 1935.

23. Auto-Sadism, Eating Disorders, and Femininity: Reflections Based on Case Studies of Adult Women Who Experienced Eating Disorders as Adolescents

Janine Chasseguet-Smirgel

These reflections arise from the observation that seven out of ten of the female patients currently undergoing psychoanalysis or psychotherapy with me, aged between 20 and 56, experienced eating disorders when they were teenagers. Knowing that some patients have experienced these disorders in the past, the therapist will be more watchful and will also realize how surprisingly common they are.

I can add to my own material that of several other analyses conducted by young colleagues under my supervision. Most of these women generally overcame their symptoms—usually spontaneously—long before beginning their therapy. Nevertheless, their personalities still bear the imprint of what caused their "adolescent breakdown" (Laufer & Laufer, 1984), and the reasons which caused them to look for help go way back to the very roots of their bulimia and/or anorexia.

I am well aware that these disorders are in vogue nowadays and, it seems, more widespread than they used to be. But I think at least two factors can be added to the social factors that are sometimes put forward:

(i) Eating disorders are spotted today better than they were when only their dramatic, life-threatening aspects received any real attention, so that some of my patients' eating disorders went unnoticed by their families,

This article appears by permission of the author and The Canadian Psychoanalytic Society. It was originally published in French in The *Canadian Journal of Psychoanalysis* v.1, no. 1 (1993: 101–22.

or, if they were noticed, it was not thought necessary to ask for professional help in connection with them.

(ii) Tuberculosis, an illness that even up till the 1950s struck and killed
millions of western adolescents, has virtually disappeared. The role it
played in the psychic economy of young people is possibly played
nowadays, to some extent, by eating disorders.[1]

In this study I should like to put forward the hypothesis that during female
development and particularly at puberty, there is a more or less violent wish
to escape from the biological order manifested essentially through eating
disorders. This revolt is repeated during the menopause though it no longer
expresses itself in the same way.

I believe it was Mara Selvini-Palazzoli (1963) who first emphasized that
the anorexic patient is not as much afraid of food as of her own *body*.
This author considers that interpretations of anorexia as a "defence against
cannibalistic impulses" or "the fear of being poisoned" are secondary and
even inappropriate (to this may be added the fear/envy of incorporating the
penis, becoming pregnant, etc.). She resolutely asserts that the anorexic
patient "is afraid of her body and *she experiences food intake as an increase
of the latter at the expense of her ego*" (p. 87).

By thus displacing the emphasis from food to the *body* in eating disorders
(for I think that her assertion is also true—paradoxically—of bulimia on one
level), Selvini-Palazzoli has opened the way to the comprehension of the
correlation between these disorders and femininity.

She also says: "To the anorexic, *being a body* is tantamount to being a
thing" (p. 87); and again " . . . *the body has become a threatening force that
must be held in check*". To my mind, bulimia is the self-same endeavour to
control the body, the same hopeless attempt to dominate it. (I shall be
coming back to this point.) I should like to emphasize from the outset that,
contrary to certain classical hypotheses and to the apparent meaning of eating
disorders, they are not hysterical and genital in nature, or, for that matter,
simply oral.

Moses & Egle Laufer (1984) focused their study of adolescence on the
developmental breakdown which occurs at this moment in life, by highlighting its essential bodily changes (note, however, that these authors are
not specifically concerned with eating disorders and are referring here to boys
as well as girls; this paper nevertheless owes a great deal to them):

We define developmental breakdown in adolescence as the unconscious rejection of the sexual body and an accompanying feeling of being passive in the face of demands coming from one's own body (. . .). It is a breakdown in the process of integrating the physically mature body image into the representation of oneself (p. 22).

Unlike the child or the adult patient, the adolescent patient experiences his body as the constant representative of that which will overwhelm him with painful or frightening fantasies and emotions.
[He often projects] the hatred of his own body on to the mother, with the feeling that he has now surrendered to her (p. 23).

Adolescents struggle within themselves around the question of "ownership of the body". They often feel their bodies as belonging to their mothers and view them as an enemy or as separate from themselves (p. 39). Susan, one of the case studies, speaks of her body as "that filthy ugly horrible mass which is fastened to me".

One of my patients, who is now 43 and suffered from bulimia as a teenager, made the following slip of the tongue when speaking of her body: "I found it repugnant. I don't understand how women like you (sic) can feel comfortable inside their 'pigs'." She explained that this was an involuntary condensation of "body" (corps) and "skin" (peau), which led to "porc" (pig). Let it be noted, incidentally, that although she has not been bulimic for over twenty years now, nevertheless she still almost consciously regards her body as a pig.

According to R. Stoller's ideas concerning proto-femininity (e.g., Stoller & Herdt, 1982), it is boys who are confronted with the difficult task of freeing themselves from the mother's femininity in the first years of their lives. In my view, a no less difficult task faces girls at puberty and during adolescence, when, more than at any other time, they must struggle to separate their own bodies from those of their mothers in a specific way, and eating disorders are a major pathological expression of this struggle.

Tota mulier in utero. This misogynous adage, shown by clinical experience to be motivated by male envy and the correlative fear of maternal creativity, corresponds, however, to the intimate representation that certain adolescent girls have of themselves and against which they rebel. It is commonplace to observe that the boy's body, at puberty, undergoes changes that are less spectacular and less dramatic than those undergone by the girl. Moreover, for the boy, puberty coincides with the acquisition of secondary sexual characteristics which differentiate his body from that of his mother once and for all. Conversely, *at puberty the girl's body becomes similar to that of her mother*. In eating disorders, the patient's body *is* simultaneously, in a persecutory mode, the mother's. It is an alien body which is, so to speak, imposed from outside, forcibly, by the biological order represented by the mother.

In a way, the teenage girl has to begin all over again the effort of integrating the body ego and the psychic ego, just as had to be done at life's start. Tausk (1919), in his classic study, "The Influencing Machine", writes this sentence which fits my subject extraordinarily well:

Man in his struggle for existence is constantly compelled to find and recognize himself anew (p. 544).

And also:

. . . self-discovery and self-choice repeat themselves with every new acquisition of the ego, to this effect, that, under the guidance of conscience and judgement, each new acquisition is either rejected, or cathected with libido and attributed to the ego (p. 547).

The girl's pubescent body is *par excellence* a new acquisition which will be "either rejected or cathected with libido and attributed to the ego".

My clinical experience shows me that all the cases who experienced eating disorders as teenagers have also experienced disorders in the sphere of infantile auto-erotism, which are often still there but in a displaced form.

At this point I must issue a "warning to the reader". What I am about to offer is likely to be less than idyllic. The cases to be discussed involve or have involved some unappetizing forms of auto-erotic behaviour in which the secretions and/or excretions of the patients' own bodies take pride of place and give rise to secret practices which cannot be confessed to. In most cases, they are only eventually revealed with enormous difficulty. Admittedly, all of us to some degree or other indulge in hidden auto-erotic activities, but those of my female patients are characterized by great *violence* directed against themselves. Again, those who practise these activities directly associate them on the unconscious level with their eating disorders. Note, too, that adults also find it embarrassing to confess to such disorders even if they have been over and done with for thirty years. For instance, an approximately thirty-year-old patient in psychotherapy, a dietician by profession, admitted her past eating disorders to me as follows: "When will I ever manage to separate myself from mother? I feel as if I were stuck to her. I had a disgusting dream. My face and body were covered all over with pustules. A yellow pus like custard was oozing out of them. I never told you this, but I used to be bulimic; I used to make myself be sick. My sister is anorexic. She bites her nails until her fingers bleed. She goes for her pimples mercilessly."

This fragment of a session thus presents us with a chain of associations: a mother-as-secretions seen as equivalent to food, bulimia with vomiting, and violent auto-erotic activities.

A little later, the same patient dreamt of seeing a group of patients suffering from dermatosis at the hospital where she worked. Their faces were full of excrescences which she called *"madeleines"*, which she associated with some disgust with the cakes of that name and with an aunt Madeleine who used to look after her during the holidays (her parents would go away on long trips every year without her).

I contend that what is specific to eating disorders is their *autarkic* aim. The anorexic tries to preserve the illusion that the body can live indefinitely without any contribution from outside. It is a victory of the mind over the body. In bulimia, the *autarkic illusion* is maintained by the fantasy that everything ingested is a production of the subject's own body, and that he is feeding on his own secretions and excretions—in other words, he is *autopha-gous*. Something must be added to my earlier statement that eating disorders are not hysterical in nature (or are only seemingly so): they in fact belong to the category of narcissistic pathologies.

Another patient, Ana, of whom I shall speak at length (she suffered from bulimia and anorexia), would pluck out her hair, so much so that she had a bald patch on the top of her head. Likewise, Bessy, also bulimic and anorexic, would bang her head against the bars of her cot, to the extent that her parents had to have her wear a thick woollen bonnet. Today, she makes her beauty spots and fleshy excrescences bleed. Bona, who after six months' therapy overcame her bulimia, still scratches her thumbs with her forefingers, so much so that the distal phalanges are twisted and her thumbs bleed. She also scratches the inside of her ears. Bettina, a former bulimic, eats her nasal secretions. Another former bulimic would talk of "mucking up her ugly mug" by scratching herself with a pin and working unceasingly at her pimples. A former anorexic spoke of her compulsive masturbation, in the course of which she would make herself bleed.

In the context of merycism, Michel Fain (1974) put forward a number of hypotheses as to the deviations of infantile auto-erotism. He presents a case study of a little girl whose mother had tied her arms to stop her from sucking her thumb (something that would have been a normal form of auto-erotic satisfaction). The author compares merycism—which comprises the regurgitation of food, some of which is kept in the mouth and never-endingly chewed—to the "game with the reel" described by Freud (1920). In the latter there is an identification with the mother and the constitution of an ego ideal, opening up the prospect of development; whereas merycism, with its manipulation of the alimentary bolus, is a "caricature of a refusal of dependence" and forebodes a particularly sombre future.

Michel Fain emphasizes that "auto-erotic stimuli are developed to compensate for the lack of narcissistic elements the mother should normally provide" (p. 121).

Philippe Jeammet (1990) distinguishes two types of auto-erotism which seem to fit in with Michel Fain's developments. In one case, the infant internalizes a good relationship with its mother and its auto-erotism bears the trace of the relationship it experienced with its object. The child gradually becomes autonomous thanks to the relatively stable introjection of the mother. On the other hand, in the second case, the mother's excessive stimulation or lack of stimulation induces another type of auto-erotism developed not from a link to the object but "instead of such a link or even against it" (p. 56).

This conception of positive and negative auto-erotism (developed by Michel Fain and then by Philippe Jeammet) can be associated with that of Frances Tustin, who writes (1986):

It is suggested that in aberrant development, auto-erotism and auto-sadism have developed precociously, which means that erotism and sadism are not directed towards external objects in an appropriate way. This has happened in psychogenic autism (p. 60).

She refers to Winnicott (1958), who

has shown finding the thumb leads to exploration of the world outside the child's own body. Sucking the thumb or the fingers becomes associated with rich fantasies and ideas which enables the child to wait until more appropriate and authentic satisfaction comes (p. 110).

On the contrary, this is a healthy kind of auto-erotism, which forms a part of normal development.

Ferenczi (1913) showed that the care the child is given—the soothing rocking, the dimly lit room, the warmth of its cot—can be interpreted as a post-natal substitute for the womb the environment provides the new-born child with. The environment-as-mother clothes the infant with a narcissistic envelope. If it were faultless, the fusion of subject and object would perpetuate itself. The introduction of gradual discontinuity into this narcissistic envelope enables the ego to separate itself from the object and to develop in a reasonably harmonious way. The infant's sexuality is simultaneously going to become detached from its vital needs and auto-erotism will appear. It may be presumed that the pleasure afforded by sucking is partly linked with the necessity of calming the pain caused by the tearing away from the object, already present in the more or less permanent sensation of hunger. We can suppose that sexuality inevitably contains a certain dose of aggression that can be integrated thanks to the satisfaction afforded by the object. In a way, "healthy" auto-erotism—i.e., an auto-erotism not accompanied by excessive auto-sadism (although it inevitably contains some auto-sadism owing to the frustration of vital needs which gives rise to it)—can only develop if the vital needs are deemed to include the narcissistic needs for envelopment, rocking and love. If, however, de-fusion takes place abruptly, the maternal narcissistic envelope right from the start being very deficient or even non-existent, the ego will form too precociously and in a fragmented way. The child's sexuality will awaken in a context of hatred and destruction. The absence of any soothing, satisfying experiences afforded by the object will stamp the child's auto-erotism with violence and sadism, the infant's own body being too soon and too poorly differentiated from that of the object. The auto-erotic activity will aim primarily to subdue the object, to triumph over it, to gain the illusion of being able to do without it, in order to soothe the raw narcissistic wound resulting from the tearing away of the maternal envelope or its absence.[2] Auto-erotism will then lose its soothing function in favour of a frantic quest for excitation, or will mix the quest for rhythmic satisfaction with violent excitation, as in the tales where the devil is a violinist who makes the dancers dance till they die of exhaustion.[3] These dancers are ill-treated like the kind of horses that ought to be put out of their misery, and they are easy to identify: in anorexia as in the bulimia, the object is not food itself but the subject's own body, which is not distinguished from that of the mother. The aim of anorexia is to triumph over the body-as-mother. It is well known that anorexia often goes with intense motor activity. One of my patients, a former anorexic, told me that as a teenage student she would go for walks of at least 12 miles a day. She added: "It was like a rider tiring out his horse." She dreamt of a horse called, like her mother, Joséphine. She later joined the army.

I once had a 20-year old patient telling me she had been anorexic when she was 15 and that at the same time she had decided to sleep on the floor in an unheated room, her body having to endure it all. "So you set out to be its tamer?" I asked. This prompted her to ask: "Why did you use the word *tamer?* Because of *mater?*"[4] This showed that by curbing her body she was in fact trying to curb her mother.

Despite first appearances, I cannot see any fundamental difference with bulimia. The patient's body is used in a way that has nothing to do with satisfying vital needs, yet in a way which is not merely sexual either. What is involved is first and foremost an act of mastery, by forcing the body-as-mother to distend itself and making it gulp down any old thing in any old order, suffocating it, stuffing it, showing it up in all its monstrosity, ridiculing it, deforming it and making it spew.

The anal meaning of such behaviour is often obvious. A patient with bulimic tendencies would look at herself in the mirror and sing Marguerite's aria from Gounod's *Faust:* "Ah! Je ris de me voir *poubelle* en ce miroir".[5]

The clinical examples I am now going to examine will highlight, among other things, the relation between anality and bulimia. This is nothing new, Wulf's pioneering paper (1932) having outstandingly brought it to the fore. Marion Oliner (1988) has recently reviewed the question. But what I intend to do is to show how the bulimic's excremental world is linked up with the negative nature of the patient's early infantile auto-erotism.

However, beforehand, I should like to include a brief reference to Mike Leigh's film *Life is Sweet* (1991), which to my mind describes in an exemplary way the relationship between anality and bulimia as well as many other aspects of the problems teenagers have with their bodies. For lack of time I cannot describe the characters of the parents which have been remarkably portrayed by this director and I have to leave aside the social aspect stressed by the author. The heroines are two teenage sisters. One of them eats nothing at all at mealtimes and shows her disgust at her mother's scabrous sexual conversations. The other daughter is a plumber and relates how a woman customer once took her for a young man. One night, the former, apparently an anorexic, opens a suitcase lying under her bed, throws herself bestially on the food, and then makes herself vomit into a paper bag. Her sister (the plumber) in the adjacent room listens all the while. The bulimic girl also has a facial twitch, perpetually rubs her sternum and pulls at her hair. She has a boyfriend she treats haughtily because she doesn't want to buckle under. But in fact, she has herself tied up, has chocolate cream poured all over her breasts and makes her boyfriend lick her. He would like to have "normal" sexual intercourse without this preliminary ritual, but she refuses and he jilts her.

In the middle of the film, there is a long episode in which an obese youth, a friend of the family, opens up a so-called French restaurant. All the dishes on the menu are composed of offal—e.g., kidneys "à la rhubarb", ox tongue with apple, etc.,—apart from one dish that we actually see being prepared. It's a redcurrant jelly tart with a huge shrimp in the middle of it, surrounded by yoghurt.

The restaurant is decorated with the most disparate objects, including the stuffed head of a cat. Someone objects that it will smell. There is also a gas mask.

At the end, the two sisters are talking to each other and the plumber—the one who seems to be reasonable and who has found a sort of peace in her male identity—tells her sister, so as to reassure her, that she too has done some disgusting things: at work she dips her hands in shit.

I cannot give a detailed interpretation of the various elements of the film, which I have very imperfectly summed up. However, I would like to insist on the fact that the suitcase, placed *under* the bed, the dirty, smelly caravan bought in one episode by the father to make hamburgers and sausages in, and the restaurant with its gas mask, can be understood as representations of the rectum, and the food there—the offal, the awful mixture of foods that normally are only to be found together in the digestive tract—represents excrement.

But the key to the story seems to me to lie in the plumber's final admission: dipping her hands in shit.

The early negative auto-erotism of my patients who had eating disorders probably manifested itself—either in reality or in fantasy—in anal masturbation. Its displacement is particularly visible in such activities as scratching the inside of one's ears to get the wax out, sticking one's finger up one's nose, furiously pressing one's spots or scratching off one's fleshy excrescences. D. Meltzer's famous paper (1966) on anal masturbation highlights the fact that it is inspired by hatred.

One of the consequences of this act and of the related fantasy is the identification with the internal mother. The other consequence is to see the rectum "as a source of food".

Although to the best of my knowledge the author has not applied his views to eating disorders, it seems to me that they are relevant to bulimia and to the *autarkic* fantasy referred to above in which the subject eats his own faeces; the suitcase under the bed, the cupboard, the larder, the refrigerator, the cellar containing food that the patient generally eats in secret, are all extensions of the subject's own body—inexhaustible rectums. The fact that certain bulimics force themselves to throw up confirms the autarkic fantasy, for unconsciously it comes down to eating what has been vomited in a sort of endless cycle. Paul Denis (oral communication) told me of a case (non-psychotic) in which the vomited food really was swallowed again. Monique Cournut (oral communication) told me about a bulimic patient who even ingested her menstrual blood. The same fantasy is at work in my bulimic patient's habit of eating her nasal secretions, or in the dream of another patient who had once been hospitalized for anorexia but had also suffered from bulimia: "I am in hospital. They have found a way of turning the patients' poohs back into food". There is no need to underline the rejection of the analyst that such a self-sufficient dream implies.

The triumph of the mind over the body-as-mother is assured by the utter contempt in which "this bag of guts" (Céline) is held, by its degradation into absolute filth, by the identification of ingesta with excreta. The latter are surely the ideal embodiment of *matter,* as denoted by classical medical usage—"the matter of vomit, the matter of perspiration, purulent matter" (Littré's Dictionary, 1873), and the use of the plural noun "excreta". Language, it seems, reveals a universal Gnostic tendency which ultimately views matter as equivalent to dejecta. If *matter* and *mater* have a common etymology, language may surely be said to provide us with the unconscious association which we make between the bodily, the material and the ma-ternal.

I have noticed a number of common features among former bulimic and/or anorexic female patients:

(1) *The autarkic illusion and pseudo-independence:* This is the basic char-acteristic of eating disorders, as described above, and is summed up almost concretely in the way Bessy, in her daydreams as a young child living in France during the war, but knowing that the French suffered

from food rationing, spent hours imagining how she would procure food for herself to live on even when there was none available in the shops. In her second preliminary interview with me, she told me a dream she had just had: she threw all the drugs in her medicine cabinet out of the window (she was on antidepressants and anxiolytics at the time), and then tried to suck her own breast, which she was biting. Suddenly she felt sad and it occurred to her to jump out of the window. I do not wish to interpret this dream in detail, but would point out that it immediately reveals her autarkic wish (to feed from her own breast), a wish that is frustrated in the dream itself. It was only much later that I learnt of the trauma her mother had inflicted on her, which I shall discuss later.

(2) *Kleptomania:* Stealing is an activity which implies the avoidance of any object-relation, a way of indirectly obtaining what one wants from the object, backhandedly so to speak. Moreover, according to Meltzer, anal masturbation implies robbing the mother of faeces-as-food.

(3) *The equivalence of food and faeces:* This leads to the confusion of representations concerning kitchen and toilets, eating and defecating, ingesting food and taking in excrement.

For example, an anorexic patient of mine with bulimic episodes explained to me that she couldn't eat in front of people, because "eating is like going to the toilet". The dream of another patient is typical of the dreams bulimics have. The dream occurred after we had talked about her bulimia as an adolescent (when she had weighed 80 kg, or 176 lbs) and the fact that she found it difficult to accept my interpretations. "I'm with a woman who is a kind of nurse. We are in a big building. She is showing me the way, and then she disappears. I find myself in a huge kitchen where all sorts of strange dishes are being prepared. In the middle of the room there are two enormous white toilets." (She abandons me to relapse into an autarkic style of feeding behaviour in which rectum, food and breasts are all muddled up.)

In bulimia the food eaten is swallowed up in any old order; sometimes it is raw, at other times it is even picked out of the dustbin. It is often—but not always, of course—chocolate.

The link with faeces is obvious. Anal masturbation is the image clearly evoked by this patient, who was always gobbling up Chocolate Fingers.

(4) *Sexual behaviour:* When compulsive sexual conduct exists, it is often a quest for coloured, preferably *black,* partners.[6]

(5) *Sexual relations:* The patient's sexual behaviour is characterized by activity, which stems from fear of the mother's intrusion, the sexual partner being insufficiently differentiated from the mother. Thus the patient who picks at her thumbs says that when she is on the verge of orgasm she sometimes holds it back "so as not to owe it to anyone". Similarly, she has a way of constantly dominating me by skipping sessions, changing the times, pestering me with questions, etc. She would always poke into her mother's weak points in order to make her cry.

The patient who eats her nasal secretions can only reach orgasm if she mounts her partner. Orgasm can be terrifying, experienced as a disintegration, a fragmentation, an atomization which, owing to the loss of control that is linked to the orgasmic experience, allows the dangerous mother to seize hold of the subject. However, such active behaviour (cf. Laufer, forthcoming) hides passive desires that are unavowed since they are experienced as shameful and dangerous.

(6) *Homosexuality:* This is important and sometimes manifest. In the best of cases, it can help the girl or woman to shake off the mother's femininity by projecting her ego ideal on to another woman—a teacher or aunt, for example—experienced as unconventional, or the analyst in the transference. Sometimes splitting proves impossible. In this case the patient's homosexuality is violently rejected, thus increasing the risk of psychosis.

(7) *Penis envy:* This is characterized here more than elsewhere by the wish to acquire the organ the mother is without in order to differentiate from her, to dominate her or satisfy her by being the desired boy who will at last be loved.

(8) *The father:* He is often physically violent and sometimes almost incestuous. He has usurped the maternal function. In short, he fails to play his role as a father, being insufficiently differentiated from the maternal imago. This renders oedipal triangulation very fragile and encourages pregenital regression.

(9) Sometimes, without there being any stable perverse organization, *perverse behaviour* appears. In thinking about the constitution of auto-erotism, insofar as this depends upon the mother's attitude, it can be said that eating disorders related to early maternal deficiencies are to

femininity what perversion is to masculinity. The mother of the pervert-to-be overcathects her son narcissistically and erotically, putting him in the place of the father.

In the far rarer case where the boy, like the girl, suffers from a lack of narcissistic cathexis, his perverse behaviour will not be organized but will be manifested in perverse "flashes".

(10) In parallel with her struggle for independence and autonomy, the girl does not give up her *dream of fusion* with the primary object, the fusion being seen as repairing the discontinuity the child experienced at a very early age. In analysis and in object-relationships, this gives rise to intense intolerance of any separation and the fantasy of emptying the mother's body of its contents (the father, the penis, her babies) in order to smooth it out entirely so that the subject can return to its former place inside it (the apocalypse fantasy: Chasseguet-Smirgel, 1984).

The following case histories will help me to throw more light on some of these points.

Ana, who first came to me when she was 34, had been bulimic when she was 13, then anorexic at 15 when her parents went abroad. Since the age of 16½, she has eaten normally. At 19 she complained to her mother that she could hear clocks ticking away inside the walls of the house. So her parents sent her along for an analysis with a woman to whom she never stopped lying from the day she learned that one of her sisters (Ana is the youngest of four girls) had also been in analysis with this therapist, who had never mentioned the fact to her. She did all she could to make the analyst think she was cured. The therapist had allegedly diagnosed Ana as "schizophrenic".

When she was 13, Ana would implore the maid to go and fetch her forty chocolates (she would gobble them up one after the other) from the grocer's where her mother had an open account (in this way she would steal her mother's faeces by entering her mother's grocery-store-rectum-body without her mother knowing it). She would also steal money from her mother's purse. She grew so fat that one day her father, seeing her from a distance with a little friend, asked: "Who is the monster that has come to play with Ana?" *She* was. When she was anorexic, she felt on top of the world. She had always lied to her mother. It was, so she said, the only way of escaping from her constant intrusions. At the same time this mother never touched her daughters, never cuddled them, leaving them with maids, and never the same ones at that. The mother had become pregnant with Ana against doctor's orders. She had wanted to have a boy, at long last. Ana's father was an authoritarian, violent man.

The first dream that Ana brought me was about a sort of rubber bra on which a pair of breasts was drawn. Ana associated with the fact that her mother had not been able to breastfeed her daughters since her nipples had been inverted. This representation seemed to symbolize Ana's relationship with her mother.

A long and difficult analysis in which I felt that I would never be able to get through to her in fact showed that Ana had transformed *herself* into an elusive breast. She had made herself smooth so as to be able to carry on with those secret activities from which I was excluded. It was she as a little girl who would pull out her hair, an auto-erotic and sadistic practice of which the eating disorders and stealing were specific aspects. The hallucinatory episode of the clocks—perhaps a nascent influencing machine—enables us to see the possible serious consequences of a rejection of the body expressed through eating disorders.

I would like to take up one point in the analytical material of Bettina, aged 29, who eats her nasal secretions. This point concerns the type of sexuality she had as a teenager when she was bulimic. She herself qualifies it as self-destructive. She had a large number of sexual partners, mainly Arabs and blacks. "Without any tenderness. It was simply having sex with blokes, like blokes with me. And underlying all that, a huge sense of emptiness, immense loneliness." Here we can distinguish the struggle against passivity (male identification), and at the same time the auto-erotic nature of the compulsive sexual intercourse with blacks, which combines anal masturbation with bulimia. (She would wolf chocolate cakes from a pantry where her mother would leave all sorts of provisions.)

Bessy was over 53 when she came to see me. She is depressed, anxious, suffers from suicidal tendencies. She has spent six months in a clinic. As stated earlier, a psychiatrist gave her drugs which were necessary because of her condition. "But I need to understand. It's vital," she says. This remarkably intelligent patient was afraid that her depression had a genetic origin, as her mother had gone through a manic type of episode on her husband's death and had been labelled as "manic-depressive" by a psychiatrist. Before long, this fear, which was often formulated during therapy, appeared as being based on persecutory fantasies of her mother's taking over her body to the very cells. Even during the preliminary session, Bessy told me that her mother had had no milk and had fed her on vegetable stock. She associated this immediately with the little woollen bonnet they had put on her head to prevent her from hurting herself as she banged her head rhythmically against the bars of her cot. Her mother had subsequently had six more children, all boys. She had breastfed them.

Bessy wrote several novels, which she tore up after they were turned down by the one and only publisher to whom she had submitted them. But actually, the first novel hadn't really been turned down. The reader has suggested one or two changes. Bessy had not been able to bear that.[7] At the time, she was about 20 years old. In this novel, she described a cave full of rubbish to which a young girl is taken by a group of boys who have sexual intercourse with her on a semenstained mattress. The story reveals Bessy's central masturbatory fantasy, whose anal character—the rubbish-filled cave—is obvious. She has always been fascinated by tramps. Actually, Bessy often talks about the films she has seen. Her favourites always include the element of refuse. One of them, *Turkish Delight,* whose plot she has already related with great fascination two or three times, features a very beautiful woman suffering from brain cancer. Chemotherapy causes her to go bald. Her lover gives her a blond wig and when she is in hospital he brings her a box of Turkish delights that she gobbles up greedily. In the end she dies and her beautiful blond wig is thrown into a refuse skip.

As a teenager, Bessy would either put on make-up and dress provocatively or go out at midnight disguised as a boy, having drawn a moustache on her upper lip and flattened her breasts.

For a long time the material she brings to the analysis revolves around her repulsive, old-woman's breasts that she feels compelled to hide; she also brings me suicidal dreams.

When she was about 15, Bessy had become bulimic. She also went through a phase of kleptomania. She would swallow up disgusting things such as leftovers from the fridge embedded in solidified fat. She also went through periods in which she would eat only raw carrots so as to save money to buy an umbrella *(sic)* that could only be procured in Venice. In a second period she ate only tomatoes. Finally there was a third episode in which, when she was on holiday in a mining town, she would pick up dog-ends that she smoked instead of eating. Bessy's mother was always beautiful and smart, with breasts that my patient describes as like artillery shells. When Bessy was eight, her mother locked them both inside the bathroom, bared her breasts and asked her daughter to suck them because they hurt (she had just had another child). She asked Bessy to keep quiet about it. Bessy's father, a strict Roman Catholic, beat his sons and tried to breathe his strength into his daughter by hugging her tight. When Bessy divorced, he wanted to adopt his grandchildren—i.e., to become the father of his daughter's children. As a very small child, Bessy would take refuge in a tent that she had built. She also took refuge in poetry. When she was two, she was invited to the court of the prince of the country in which her parents lived so as to recite the poems she had composed.

This precocious intellectual maturity can be understood both as an attempt to create a positive form of auto-erotism (poetry as a way of rocking oneself), offsetting auto-sadism (banging her head against the bars of her cot), and as a first attempt to bring others to accept her fantasy world.

Bessy's present depression, her anxiety, her suicidal ideas (a compulsive attempt to swallow barbiturates occurred during a long stay she was obliged to make abroad), her self-destructive fantasies (a recurring dream, for example, was that from one point in her body her flesh comes undone as though it were a ribbon of putty)—all these elements prove to be connected mainly with her menopause, experienced as yet another attempt on the part of her mother to control the daughter's body. An example of this fantasy is the feeling of despair that fills Bessy on buying a new kitchen: "As if, once and for all, I were entering the realm of women, as though I were imprisoned." She told me in the following session that when she was an adolescent somebody had told her she looked like her mother (an extremely beautiful woman). She had retorted: "If someone says that to me again, I'll kill myself." On reaching the menopause, Bessy experiences her mother as destroying her daughter's capacity for engendering, as spoiling her breasts and her sexually attractive body in retaliation for the daughter's hostile feelings towards those pregnancies, the breastfeeding her brothers enjoyed and her feminine seduction, traumatically inflicted on the daughter herself.

Bessy told me of an exhibition of Fang art she had visited on emerging from a depression that had lasted for three years. She had admired powerful wooden statues with eyes inlaid with human teeth. She told me that before her analysis and at the beginning of it still, she had had recurrent dreams in which either her eyes would fall out of their sockets or a tooth would fall from her gums: the holes thus formed would grow and grow until they ate up her whole body. This material resembles F. Tustin's observations of autistic patients (1986). Some of the patients I describe may well have autistic traits.

It is indeed paradoxical to find the same conflicts at the menopause as at puberty, as the physiological changes are the other way round. Yet at both of these stages the young girl and the adult woman are obliged, by a body they cannot master, to comply with the biological order—i.e., to submit to the dictates of the mother.

CONCLUSION

These hypotheses certainly do not apply to all women. On the contrary, the constitution of a positive auto-erotism makes it possible to avoid the dramas which eating disorders show up, allowing the bodily ego to be integrated with the psychic ego at the different stages in a woman's life. Anorexia probably represents a victory over bulimia, which fulfils in a quasi-conscious and concrete manner the Gnostic conception of the body as waste and excrement. It no longer seeks to deny the body by rising towards anorexic purity and immateriality, but pushes debasement of the subject's own body (confused with that of the mother) to its extreme limit.

Eating disorders reveal the daughter's rebellion against womanhood. They manifest the wish to escape from the grip of a mother who has forever incarcerated her daughter within her own body.

—Translated by PHILIP SLOTKIN
London

NOTES

1. A study cited by Hilde Bruch (1973), conducted in the days before the introduction of antibiotic treatments for tuberculosis in Europe, shows that anorexia used to be virtually non-existent in adolescents suffering from TB.

2. Ferenczi noted (1913) that post-natal care tends to reproduce physiological rhythms transmitted in the womb from mother to infant (her heartbeat, breathing, the rhythm of her footsteps). After birth the infant's environment impresses rhythmic movements upon it, present in particular during rocking and in lullabies, and these the infant reproduces when suckling and in auto-erotic finger sucking. A continuity exists between the *rhythmicity* of suckling and sucking and that of masturbation and, later on, coitus. But if sadistic auto-erotism prevails over rhythmic soothing activities, this denotes a weakness of primary object narcissistic conduct in favour of the baby and an accompanying inability to introject this.

3. In my very first paper (1958)—a commentary on a study of the psychoses by S. Nacht & P. C. Racamier—I correlated precocious primary de-fusion with the phenomena of depersonalization.

4. In French *to tame* is *mater*.

5. The actual wording is "Ah! Je ris de me voir *si belle* en ce miroir" [Ah! I laugh to see myself *so beautiful* in this mirror], so that the patient, instead of rejoicing in the reflection of her loveliness (si belle), was seeing herself as a dustbin (poubelle).

6. In this case the manifest anti-racism conceals an unconscious contempt for this penis equated with the black fingers of masturbation.

7. I cannot speak here of the various conceivable hypotheses regarding the meaning of writing for my patient, her intolerance of any criticism and her self-destructive behaviour, as long and complicated explanations would be necessary. However, it can be supposed that the criticism of her first novel containing her central masturbatory fantasy was felt as a denunciation of its being a shameful and guilty activity.

REFERENCES

Bruch, H. 1973. *Les yeux et le ventre*. Paris: Payot.

Chasseguet-Smirgel, J. 1958. Intervention sur le rapport de S. Nacht et P. C. Racamier, *La théorie psychanalytique du délire* (XXième Congrès de Psychanalystes Romanes, 1958). *Rev. Franc. Psychanal*. 22:536–37.

————. 1984. The Archaic Matrix of the Oedipus Complex. In *Sexuality and the Mind*. New York: New York University Press, 1986.

Chasseguet-Smirgel, J.; Luquet, P.; Parat, C.; Grunberger, B.; McDougall, J.; Torok, M.; and David, C. 1964. *Female Sexuality*. London: Karnac Books, 1992.

Fain, M. 1974. In *L'enfant et son corps*, ed. L. Kreisler, M. Fain, and M. Soule. Paris: Payot.

Ferenczi, S. 1913. Stages in the Development of the Sense of Reality. In *First Contributions to Psycho-Analysis*, trans. E. Jones. New York: Brunner/Mazel, 1952.

Freud, S. 1920. Beyond the Pleasure Principle. In *S.E.* 18:7–64.

Geist, E. 1989. Self-Psychological Reflections on the Origin of Eating Disorders. In *Psychoanalysis and Eating Disorders*, ed. J. Bemporad and D. Herzog. New York: Guilford Press, pp. 5–27.

Jeammet, P. 1990. Le destin de l'auto-érotisme à l'adolescence. In *Actes du Deuxième Congrès National sur la Post-Analyse*. Paris: Presses Universitaires de France, pp. 53–79.

Kestemberg, E.; Kestemberg, J.; and Decobert, S. 1972. *La faim et le corps*. Paris, Presses Universitaires de France.

Laufer, E. forthcoming. The Female Oedipus Complex and the Fear of Passivity.

Laufer, M., and Laufer, E. 1984. *Adolescence and Developmental Breakdown*. New Haven: Yale University Press.

Meltzer, D. 1966. The Relation of Analmasturbation to Projective Identification. *Int. J. Psycho-Anal*. 47:335–42.

Oliner, M. 1988. Anal Components in Overeating. In *Bulimia: Psychoanalytic Treatment and Theory*, ed. H. J. Schwartz. Madison: International Universities Press.

Pasche, F. 1959. Le génie de Freud. In *À partir de Freud* Paris, Payot, 1969, pp. 61–77.

Selvini-Palazzoli, M. 1963. *Self-Starvation*. Haywards Heath: Human Context Books.

Stoller, R., and Herdt, G. 1982. The Development of Masculinity: A Cross-Cultural Contribution. *J. Amer. Psychoanal. Assn*. 30:29–59.

Tausk, V. 1919. The Origin of the "Influencing Machine" in Schizophrenia. *Psychoanal. Quarterly* 2:519–56.

Tustin, F. 1986. *Autistic Barriers in Neurotic Patients*. London: Karnac Books.

Winnicott, D. 1958. *Collected Papers: Through Paediatrics to Psychoanalysis*. New York: Basic Books.

Wulf, M. 1932. (On an Interesting Oral Symptomatic Complex and Its Relation to Addiction.) Sur un intéressant complexe symptomatique oral et sa relation à l'addiction. In *La boulimie*. Tr. A. Grandon et M. Cl. Rose. Paris: PUF, 1991, pp. 47–62.

PART VI

MASOCHISM AND THE NEGATIVE THERAPEUTIC REACTION

Introduction

In the "Wolf Man" case, Freud (1918) observed that, shortly after a symptom had been cleared up there was a brief recurrence. He likened this to the way children do something one more time after a prohibition has been imposed, to try to show through a last defiance that they are stopping of their own accord. This hint of an intimate relationship between the negative therapeutic reaction and the child's capacity to say "no" has been part of the theoretical discussion from Joan Riviere's essay (1936; chapter 24 in this volume) to that of Pontalis (1988).

In *The Ego and the Id* (1923) Freud elaborated his thoughts concerning those who become engaged in the negative therapuetic reaction: "There is no doubt that there is something in these people that sets itself against recovery and dreads its approach as though it were a danger." Freud notes that after we subtract the primary and secondary gains from the illness, and the defiant attitude to the analyst, the greater part of the reaction still remains. And so he came to see the syndrome as related to "a sense of guilt which is finding atonement in the illness and is refusing to give up the penalty of suffering."

Some of the discussion since Freud's formulation has centered around the nature of the unconscious guilt and the inability to give up suffering. Is this guilt an Oedipal, superego guilt, (Freud 1923; Fenichel 1925, chapter 15 in this volume; Schafer 1988) or is it more related to a regressed sadomasochistic attachment to a depressive pre-Oedipal mother (Riviere 1936)? Should we speak of superego precursors as well as superego where the negative therapeutic reaction is concerned (Modell 1965)? Some have answered that the negative therapeutic reaction like the sadomasochism with which it is linked, has multiple determinants, differing in different patients (Brenner 1959; chapter 18 in this volume). Others have seen the reaction, in its most full-blown manifestations—reactive, negative, massively resisting the analyst and the analytic progress—as predominantly pre-Oedipal, tied to the developmental stage of appropriate negativity, the "no" stage, in which the child experiences the peculiar vulnerability of the anaclitic bond with the powerful, invasive mother (Riviere 1936; Olinick 1964, chapter 25 in this volume; Pontalis 1988).

What is the relationship of the negative therapeutic reaction to the drives, to the sadomasochism which is acted out in the transference, or, to the primary masochism of the death drive? Those analysts who are comfortable with the dual instinct theory formulated in terms of sexual and aggressive drives see the negative therapeutic reaction as related to vicissitudes of libido and aggression, along with adaptive strivings (Brenman 1952; Brenner 1959; Olinick 1964). The transference is overtly hostile, but it is the pressure of the drives and affects in the positive transference that reactivates the massive resistance, the self-punishment through a worsening of symptoms and, simultaneously, through what Joseph (1982; chapter 26 in this volume) calls "the doing down" of the analyst and analytic work. How much the explicit sexual component is present in the sadomasochism of the transference varies. In a patient suffering from a severe version of the reaction, the analyst can be experienced as having taken over the drives so that the patient has no right to her own desire (Pontalis 1988) or, no right to his own life (Modell 1965). The fixation of sadomasochism, the unconscious guilt and the attachment to suffering (Valenstein 1973) are as multidetermined as the case histories presented throughout this volume.

In "Analysis Terminable and Interminable" Freud goes beyond the negative therapeutic reaction as a deep-seated resistance which comes from certain relations between ego and superego, and he speaks of

a force which is defending itself by every possible means against recovery and which is absolutely resolved to hold on to illness and suffering. . . . If we take into consideration the total picture made up of the phenomena of masochism immanent in so many people, the negative therapeutic reaction and the sense of guilt found in so many neurotics, we shall no longer be able to adhere to the belief that mental events are exclusively governed by the desire for pleasure. (1937, 242–43)

The Pandora's box of masochism, and the death instinct opens up. How necessary is the idea of the death instinct to an understanding of the reaction and to the interpretive strategies which emerge from this understanding? The intractable nature of the masochism, of the attachment to the analysis as self-punishment has lead some analytic writers to posit the working of a primary self-destructive instinct. But many writers who use the notion of the death instinct give us what is almost an alternative formulation when they describe the deeply disturbed early object relations, in the light of which they sometimes find effective interpretations (Loewald 1972). Those analysts who write on the negative therapeutic reaction using the idea of the death instinct, often present cases from the more severely disturbed portion of the patient population, and some have, as Freud did, a realistic caution concerning the limitations of analysis, where the death drive is unbound by the superego (Brenner 1959; Panel 1970; Loewald 1972).

The possibility that the patient, still bound to a depressed or hating pre-Oedipal mother imago, must say "no" to the analyst in order to resist a repetition of a takeover of his soul is elaborated by Joan Riviere (1936) and by Pontalis (1988). The study of the libinal, aggressive, and narcissistic factors in the negative therapeutic reaction extends into the consideration of internal object relations. When the patient must save his loved (and hated) objects, before he thinks of himself, our offer of analysis can be experienced as a direct seduction, a betrayal. In the early stage when the "no" is a link with the loved mother (Levy 1982; Renik 1991), in the anaclitic bond, an overly controlling mother can produce a superego so filled with ambivalent introjects, so much guarding against id wishes, that there results a sort of "boycott" on life (Olinick 1964). The positive transference will arouse the defensive reaction again. Valenstein's (1973) work on the attachment to painful feelings emphasizes the patient's need to deny the sadistic parent (Berliner 1958; chapter 17 in this volume) and to play out the trauma once again with the analyst.

All types of negative therapeutic reaction place special pressures on the analyst. One of the clearest indications of the reaction is that the analyst will experience the pain of helplessness, the anxiety of having no curative power, the loss of balance from having good work cause an exacerbation of symptoms, the fatigue that emerges from ceaseless attacks. The reaction becomes a fruitful place for the examination of the response of the analyst. If the analyst is not open enough to feel a certain anxiety, pain, and/or anger in response to these patients, he may deny the existence of the negative therapeutic reaction (Riviere 1936) or simply fail in the analytic task (Olinick 1964). The very attitude needed for receptivity to the analyst's preconscious or unconscious responses, which indicate what will be an effective interpretation, comes perilously close to a vulnerability which can lead to countertransference enactments. These minor countertransference enactments can indicate the nature of the betrayal or loss the patient feels the analytic work will entail for him (Renik 1991).

The psychoanalysis of the therapeutic reaction began with Freud's (1923) understanding of the unconscious "need for punishment," that is, with his exploration of the workings of moral masochism. The spiral has come round so that the transference and countertransference issues in the negative therapeutic reaction have been showing us more about the object relations, the anxieties, the fantasies, involved in the "need for punishment."

BIBLIOGRAPHY

Berliner, B. 1958. The Role of Object Relations in Moral Masochism. *Psychoanal. Quarterly* 27:38–56. (Chapter 17 in this volume.)

Brenman, . 1952. On Teasing and Being Teased: And the Problem of Moral Masochism. *Psychoanal. Study Child* 7:264–85.

Brenner, C. 1959. The Masochistic Character: Genesis and Treatment. *J. Amer. Psychoanal. Assn.* 7: 197–226. (Chapter 18 in this volume.)

Fenichel, O. 1925. The Clinical Aspect of the Need for Punishment. In *The Collected Papers of Otto Fenichel: First Series.* New York: Norton, 1953, pp. 71–96. (Chapter 15 in this volume.)

Freud, S. 1918. From the History of an Infantile Neurosis. In *S.E.* 17:3–123.

————. 1923. The Ego and the Id. In *S.E.* 19:1–66.

————. 1937. Analysis Terminable and Interminable. In *S.E.*23:209–53.

Horney, Karen. 1936. "The Problem of Negative Therapeutic Reaction. *Psychoanalytic Quarterly.* 5:29–44.

Joseph, Betty. 1982 Addiction to Near-Death. *Int. J. Psycho-Anal.* 63: 449–56. (Chapter 26 in this volume.)

Levy, Joshua. 1982. A Particular Kind of Negative Therapeutic Reaction Based on Freud's "Borrowed Guilt." *Int. J. Psycho-Anal.* 63:361–68.

Limentani, Adam. 1981. On Some Positive Aspects of the Negative Therapeutic Reaction. *Int. J. Psycho-Anal.* 62:379–90.

Loewald, Hans. 1972. Freud's Conception of the Negative Therapeutic Reaction, With Comments on Instinct Theory. *J. Amer. Psychoanal. Assn.* 20:235–45.

Meyers, H. 1988. A Consideration of Treatment Techniques in Relation to the Functions of Masochism. In *Masochism: Current Psychoanalytic Perspectives.* Hillsdale, N.J.: The Analytic Press, pp. 175–88.

Modell, Arnold. 1965. On Having the Right to Life: An Aspect of the Super-ego's Development. *Int. J. Psycho-Anal.* 46:323–31.

Olinick, Stanley. 1964. The Negative Therapeutic Reaction *Int. J. Psycho-Anal.* 45:540–48. (Chapter 25 in this volume.)

Panel. 1970. Negative Therapeutic Reaction. *J. Amer. Psychoanal. Assn.* 18:655–72.

Pontalis, J.-B. 1988. Non, deux fois non. In *Perdre de vue.* Paris: Gallimard, pp. 73–101.

Renik, Owen. 1991. One Kind of Negative Therapeutic Reaction. *J. Amer. Psychoanal. Assn.* 39:87–105.

Riviere, Joan. 1936. A Contribution to the Analysis of the Negative Therapeutic Reaction. *Int. J. Psycho-Anal.* 17:304–20. (Chapter 24 in this volume.)

Schafer, R. 1988. Those Wrecked by Success. In *Masochism: Current Psychoanalytic Perspectives,* ed. R. Glick and D. Meyers. Hillsdale, N.J.: The Analytic Press, pp. 81–91.

Valenstein, A. F. 1973. On Attachment to Painful Feelings and the Negative Therapeutic Reaction. *Psychoanal. Study Child* 28:365–94.

24. A Contribution to the Analysis of the Negative Therapeutic Reaction[1]

Joan Riviere

In this contribution my aim is to draw attention to the important bearing recent theoretical conclusions have on the practical side of the problem of the negative therapeutic reaction. I mean the latest work of Melanie Klein and in particular her Lucerne Congress paper on the depressive position.[2]

To start with, it is necessary to define what is meant by the negative therapeutic reaction. Freud gave this title to something that he regarded as a specific manifestation among the variety of our case-material, though he says that in a lesser measure this factor has to be reckoned with in very many cases. When I referred to Freud's remarks on this point, I was interested to find that actually they are not exactly what they are generally remembered and represented as being. The negative therapeutic reaction, I should say, is generally understood as a condition which ultimately precludes analysis and makes it impossible; the phrase is constantly used as meaning unanalysable. Freud's remarks on the point are almost all in *The Ego and the Id*, the last eighteen pages of which deal with the problem of the unconscious sense of guilt. He says, 'Certain people cannot endure any praise or appreciation of progress in the treatment. Every partial solution that ought to result, and with others does result, in an improvement or temporary suspension of symptoms produces in them for the time being an exacerbation; they get worse instead of better'. This last sentence might imply that they are unanalysable; but he does not actually say so, and has just said the exacerbation is for *the time being*. He says the obstacle is 'extremely difficult to overcome'; 'often there is no counteracting force of similar intensity'; and that 'it must be honestly confessed that here is another limitation to the efficacy of analysis'—but he

Reprinted by permission of the Melanie Klein Trust and the *International Journal of Psycho-Analysis* 17 (1936):304–20. Copyright © The Melanie Klein Trust and the Institute of Psycho-Analysis.

does not say a preventive. Clearly the point is merely one of degree, and he might concur in the general attitude taken up. He is not, however, actually as pessimistic about it as people incline to suppose; and this interested me, because it is not intelligible why one reaction should be thought more unanalysable than another. The eighteen pages in *The Ego and the Id* are in fact part of his contribution towards analysing it; and our understanding of it has now been very greatly advanced by Melanie Klein.

Freud's title for this reaction, however, is not actually very specific; a negative therapeutic reaction would just as well describe the case of any patient who does not benefit by a treatment; and it would describe those psychotic or 'narcissistic' patients whom Freud still regards as inaccessible to psycho-analysis. It seems to me that this specific reaction against a cure described by him may not differ so very greatly in character from those more general cases of therapeutic failures I mentioned, and that the difficulty may be due to some extent to the analyst's failure to understand the material and to interpret it fully enough to the patient. The common assumption is that even when the analyst has fully understood and interpreted the material, the super-ego of certain patients is strong enough to defeat the effects of analysis. I shall try to show that other factors are at work in this severity of the super-ego that until recently have not been fully understood and therefore cannot have been sufficiently or fully interpreted to our patients.

It will be clear now that what I propose to talk about is in fact the analysis of specially refractory cases. I do not think I can go much further in defining the type of case to which my remarks refer, partly because any one analyst's experience is necessarily limited, even of refractory cases; moreover, my expectation is that similar unconscious material may probably exist in other difficult cases of a kind I have not personally met with. I would say this, however, that the cases in which I have made the most use and had greatest advantage from the new understanding have been what we call difficult character-cases. The super-ego of the transference neurotic, it must be remembered, has always been placated by his sufferings from his sense of guilt, and by his symptoms, which are a real cause of inferiority and humiliation to him whatever epinosic gain he has from them; the character-case has never placated his super-ego in these ways; he has always maintained the projection that 'circumstances' have been against him. After some analysis he may guess that he has punished others all his life and feel that what he now deserves is not 'cure', but illness or punishment himself; and he unconsciously fears that that is what analysis may bring him if he submits to it. Of course we find these motives for or against co-operation in all cases; I merely suggest that in character-cases they may have peculiar strength.

With reference to this matter of character-resistances I shall recall to your minds a paper of Abraham[3] in which he described and commented on a certain type of difficulty in analysis, that he virtually names the *narcissistic type* of character-resistance. He tells us that such analyses are very lengthy and that in no such case did he obtain complete cure of the neurosis, and we can see that the degree of negative therapeutic reaction in this type is what led him to distinguish it. The narcissistic features of this type are, shortly: that they show a chronic, not merely occasional, inability to associate freely, in that they keep up a steady flow of carefully selected and arranged material, calculated to deceive the analyst as to its 'free' quality; they volunteer nothing but good of themselves; are highly sensitive and easily mortified; accept nothing new, nothing that they have not already said themselves; turn analysis into a pleasurable situation, develop no true positive transference, and oust the analyst from his position and claim to do his work better themselves. Under a mask of polite friendliness and rationalization they are very mean, self-satisfied and defiant. Abraham shows the relation of all these features to anal omnipotence, and he especially emphasizes the *mask of compliance*, which distinguishes this type of resistance from an open negative transference and renders it more difficult to handle than the latter. And 'These patients', he says, '*shut their eyes to the fact that the object of the treatment is to cure their neurosis.*'. Incidentally, I do not suppose that Abraham was guilty of it, but I feel that analysts themselves are not always incapable of shutting their eyes to a fact too, namely, that when a patient does not do what he ought, the onus still remains with the analyst: to discover the cause of his reaction. In my opinion the patient was entirely in the right who said, 'Yes, doctor, when you have removed my inhibitions against telling you what is in my mind, I will then tell you what is in my mind', and the situation is similar in regard to getting well.

This paper of Abraham's suggests what I take to be a generally valid proposition, that in specially long and difficult analyses the core of the problem lies in the patient's narcissistic resistances. One surmises, further, that this narcissism may not be unconnected with the inaccessibility to treatment of the 'narcissistic neuroses', as Freud has called certain psychoses. There is nothing very new, or immediately helpful, in the idea that narcissism is the root of the problem—for what is narcissism? I will mention only two general points in this connection. One—the old one—is that any marked degree of narcissism presupposes a withdrawal of libido from external objects into the ego, and secondly, the newer point, that ego-libido can now be recognized, especially in the light of Melanie Klein's more recent work, to be an extremely complex thing. Freud speaks of the secondary narcissism derived from the ego's 'identifications', which most of us here now regard as including the ego's *internal objects*. And Melitta Schmideberg[4] suggests that love for the introjected objects is a part of narcissism. And now the significance of the ego's relations to its internalized objects shows clearly that this great field of object-relations within the ego, within the realm of narcissism itself, needs much further understanding; and it is my belief that more light in this direction will do much to explain such hitherto inexplicable analytic resistances as the narcissistic ones of Abraham and the super-ego one of Freud.

The concept of *objects* within the ego, as distinct from identifications, is hardly discussed in Freud's work; but it will be remembered that one important contribution of his to the psychology of insanity is built up almost entirely on this conception—I mean of course his essay on 'Mourning and Melancholia', dealing with the problems of *depressive* states. His discussion in *The Ego and the Id* of the unconscious sense of guilt, too, is closely interwoven with aspects of the melancholic condition. This brings me to my second point. Observations have led me to conclude that where narcissistic resistances are very pronounced, resulting in the characteristic lack of insight and absence of therapeutic results under discussion, these resistances are in fact part of a highly organized system of defence against a more or less unconscious depressive condition in the patient and are operating as a mask and disguise to conceal the latter.

My contribution to the understanding of especially refractory cases of a narcissistic type will therefore consist in the two proposals *(a)* that we should pay more attention to the analysis of the patient's inner world of object-relations, which is an integral part of his narcissism, and *(b)* that we should not be deceived by the positive aspects of his narcissism but should look deeper, for the depression that will be found to underlie it. That these two recommendations are not unconnected might be guessed from Freud's paper, which links the two, and from Melanie Klein's view that the internal object-situation in this position is of supreme importance. The depressive position might be described as a miscarriage of introjection, she says; and *this* is the unconscious anxiety-situation that our narcissistic patients are defending themselves against and that should be the true objective of analysis in such cases.

Now this particular anxiety-situation, the depressive, has its own special defence-mechanism, the manic reaction, of which Melanie Klein also gives a general outline. The essential feature of the manic attitude is omnipotence and the *omnipotent denial of psychical reality,* which of course leads to a distorted and defective sense of external reality. (Helene Deutsch[5] has pointed out the inappropriate, impracticable and fantastic character of the manic relation to external reality.) The *denial* relates especially to the ego's object-relations and its *dependence on its objects,* as a result of which *contempt* and depreciation of the value of its objects is a marked feature, together with attempts at inordinate and tyrannical *control and mastery of its objects.* Much could be written about the manic defence, and I hope will be, for in my opinion the future of psycho-analytic research, and therefore of all psychology, now depends on our belated appreciation of the immense importance of this factor in mental life. It is true that we have known of many of its manifestations and even had a name which would have represented it, if we had known how to apply it—the word omnipotence—but our knowledge and understanding of the factor of omnipotence has never yet been organized, formulated and correlated into a really useful theoretical unit. Omnipotence has been a vague concept, loosely and confusedly bandied about, hazily interchanged with narcissism or with phantasy-life, its meaning and especially its functions not clearly established and placed. We ought now to study this omnipotence and particularly its special development and application in the manic defence against depressive anxieties.

It will not be difficult to see how characteristic the most conspicuous feature of the manic attitude, omnipotent denial and control by the ego over all objects in all situations, is of our refractory patients with their narcissistic resistances. Their inaccessibility is one form of their *denial;* implicitly they deny the value of everything we say. They literally do not allow us to do anything with them, and in the sense of co-operation they do nothing with us. *They* control the analysis, whether or not they do it openly. If we are not quick enough to be aware of it, too, such patients often manage to exert quite a large measure of real control over the analyst—and can even do this when we are quite aware of it. So far, it seems to me, we have not known, or not known enough, exactly where to place this tendency or how to relate it to the rest of the analytic context and so—we have not been able to analyse it. We have tended to see it as a negative transference and as an expression of aggressive attitudes towards the analyst. We have understood these as defences against anxiety, but we have not realized that a *special* fear lay beneath this special way of attaining security. I think Abraham's whole description, with every detail of the 'narcissistic' resistances he describes, in fact presents an unmistakable picture of various expressions of the manic defence—the omnipotent control of the analyst and analytic situation by the patient—which yet, as he points out, is often enough extremely cleverly masked. The conscious or unconscious refusal of such patients to produce true 'free associations', their selection and arrangement of what they say, their implicit or explicit denials of anything discreditable to themselves, their refusal to accept any alternative point of view or any interpretation (except with lip-service), their defiance and obstinacy, and their claim to supersede the analyst and improve on his work all show their determination to keep the upper hand and their anxiety of getting into the power of the analyst. Free association would expose them to the analyst's 'tender mercies'; love for the analyst, a positive transference, would do the same; and so would any admission of failings in themselves. Along with their self-satisfaction and megalomanic claims, their egotism is shown in pronounced meanness, and often in an absence of the most everyday acknowledgements or generosity. Certain patients of this type especially withhold from us all 'evidence' of an indisputable character in support of our interpretations. They leave us with dreams, symbols, voice, manner, gesture; no statements, no admissions from themselves. So we can say what we like, nothing is proved—yet of course they accept the help they get, but refuse us all help and all acknowledgements. Abraham interprets this trait as anal omnipotence. Beside this connection, it signifies especially their need to reserve and preserve everything of any value, all good things, to themselves, for various reasons, and especially for fear that others (the analyst) will gain in power by means of them. Above all, however, the trait of *deceptiveness,* the mask, which conceals this subtle reservation of all control under intellectual rationalizations, or under feigned compliance and superficial politeness, is characteristic of the manic defence. This mask owes its origin undoubtedly to the specialized dissimulation of the paranoiac; but it is exploited in the manic position not as a defence in itself but as a cover for the defence of securing exclusive control. To this description of this type of patient I would here add an important further detail: they shew a quite special sensitiveness on the point of consciously feeling any anxiety; it is quite apparent that they have to keep control so as not to be taken unawares by, and not to be exposed to, a moment's anxiety. Abraham comments on their lack of affect, and this in my view is to be taken first as a dread of *anxiety*-affect. But their complete incapacity for any feeling of guilt is equally astonishing and is of course one of their most psychotic traits in its lack of the sense of reality: they deal with guilt-situations entirely by projection, denial and rationalization.

Now it might be objected here that no analyst worth his salt has failed to interpret these manifestations in precisely this way time and again in his practice and this of course is true; but in my view there is all the difference in the world between what may be called single isolated interpretations, however correct and however frequent they may be, and the understanding and interpretation of such detailed instances as part of a general *organized system of defence* and resistance, with all its links and ramifications spreading far and wide in the symptom-picture, in the formation of character and in the behaviour-patterns of the patient. Analysis has to concern itself with daily details because only the immediate detail of the moment has affect and significance for the patient, but the analyst has to be careful not to become too affectively interested in working out detailed interpretations: he has to be careful not to lose sight of the wood for the trees. He must aim, not merely at understanding each detail in itself but at knowing where to place it in the general scheme of the patient's mental make-up and in the continuous context of the analytic work. Of course, what have been called 'spot-analyses' or snapshot interpretations have long been condemned, and Ella Sharpe, for instance, once led a crusade against meaningless *ad hoc* symbol-interpretations which do not form part of a whole picture. What I am urging now is only a further application of this principle. I suggest that the common tendency we often see in patients to control the analysis and the analyst is even more widespread than we suppose, because it is largely masked and disguised by superficial compliance, and that it forms part of an extremely important general defensive attitude—the manic defence—which has to be understood as such.

Now what is the specific relation between this special line of defence and the negative therapeutic reaction; why does the need to control everything express itself so particularly in not getting well? There are certain obvious answers to this, all of which would show that not getting well is an unavoidable indirect result of these resistances. For instance, I have just suggested that hitherto these tendencies in patients to usurp all control have been regarded as expressions of a negative transference and hostility to the analyst.

This interpretation, so far as it goes, is certainly correct; the patient is extremely hostile; but that is not all. Things are not so simple. The very great importance of analysing aggressive tendencies has perhaps carried some analysts off their feet, and in some quarters is defeating its own ends and becoming in itself a resistance to further analytic understanding. Nothing will lead more surely to a negative therapeutic reaction in the patient than failure to recognize anything but the aggression in his material.

The question why the defence by omnipotent control leads so characteristically to the negative therapeutic reaction cannot be answered fully until we consider the anxiety-situation underlying this defence; but I think there is one direct connection between the two which may be stated here. There actually is a kind of wish in the patient not to get well and this wish is itself partly in the nature of a defence. It comes from the desire to preserve a *status quo,* a condition of things which is proving bearable. It is built upon many compromises; the patient does not finish the analysis, but neither does he break it off. He has found a certain equilibrium and does not intend it to be disturbed. To my mind, this is an important general explanation of the phenomenon Freud comments on. He says[6] 'A few words of praise or hope or even an interpretation bring about an unmistakable aggravation of their condition'. If the patient is changing, or is being changed, he is losing control; the equilibrium he has established in his present relation with the analyst will be upset; so he has to reinstate his former condition, and regain his control of things. Actually, this anxiety-reaction to the idea of making progress often disappears on being itself interpreted; and of course not interpreted only in this general way, but the detailed connection of the immediate resistance to the immediate anxiety made clear. Incidentally, there are many ways in which this aspect of the defence by control (namely, that of prolonging and maintaining the *status quo*) verges on and merges into the obsessional technique of prolonging in time and preserving in space certain distances, always maintaining a relative, never an absolute or a final relation. But the connection between the manic and the obsessional forms of defence is not part of my subject here.

If the patient desires to preserve things as they are and even sacrifices his cure for that reason, it is not really because he does not wish to get well. The reason why he does not get well and tries to prevent any change is because, however he might wish for it, he has no faith in getting well. What he really expects unconsciously is not a change for the better but a change for the worse, and what is more, one that will not affect himself only, but the analyst as well. It is partly to save the analyst from the consequences of this that he refuses to move in any direction. Melitta Schmideberg said something of the same kind in the paper quoted already: 'Inaccessibility in patients is due to a fear of something "even worse" happening'. Now what is the still worse situation which the patient is averting by maintaining the *status quo*, by keeping control, by his omnipotent defences? It is the danger of the *depressive position* that he is guarding himself and us against; what he dreads is that that situation and those anxieties may prove to be a reality, that that psychical reality in his mind may become real to him through the analysis. The psychic truth behind his omnipotent denials is that the worst disasters have actually taken place; it is this truth that he will not allow the analysis to make real, will not allow to be 'realized' by him or us. He does not intend to get any 'better', to change, or to end the analysis, because he does not believe it possible that any change or any lessening of control on his part can bring about anything but the realization of disaster for all concerned. I may say at once that what this type of patient ultimately fears most of all—the kernel, so to speak, of all his other fears—is his own suicide or madness, the inevitable outcome, as he feels it unconsciously, if his depressive anxieties come to life. He is keeping them still, if not dead, as it were, by his immobility. Patients I have analysed have felt this dread of losing the manic defence quite consciously during the analysis of it, have both threatened and implored me to leave it alone and not 'take it away', and have foreseen that its removal would mean chaos, ruin to himself and me, impulses of murder and suicide: in other words, the depression that to some extent supervenes as the defence weakens. But I need hardly say the analyst has not this despair, for as the capacity to tolerate the depression and its anxieties gradually increases, very notable compensations accompany it and the capacity for love begins to be released as the manic stranglehold on the emotions relaxes.

The content of the depressive position (as Melanie Klein has shewn) is the situation in which all one's loved ones *within* are dead and destroyed, all goodness is dispersed, lost, in fragments, wasted and scattered to the winds; nothing is left *within* but utter desolation. Love brings sorrow, and sorrow brings guilt; the intolerable tension mounts, there is no escape, one is utterly alone, there is no one to share or help. Love must die because love is dead. Besides, there would be no one to feed one, and no one whom one could feed, and no food in the world. And more, there would still be magic power in the undying persecutors who can never be exterminated—the ghosts. Death would instantaneously ensue—and one would choose to die by one's own hand before such a position could be realized.

As analysis proceeds and the persecutory projection defences, which are always interwoven with the omnipotent control position, weaken along with the latter, the analyst begins to see the phantasies approximating to this nightmare of desolation assuming shape. But the shape they assume is that of the patient, so to speak; the scene of the desolation is himself. External reality goes on its ordinary round: it is *within himself* that these horrors dwell. Nothing gives one such a clear picture of that inner world, in which every past or present relation either in thought or deed with any loved or hated person still exists and is still being carried on, as the state of a person in depression. His mind is completely and utterly preoccupied and turned inward; except in so far as he can project something of this horror and desolation, he has no concern with anything outside him. To save his own life and avert the death of despair that confronts him, such energy as he has is all bent on averting the last fatalities within, and on restoring and reviving where and what he can, of any life and life-giving objects that remain. It is these efforts, the frantic or feeble struggles to revive the others within him and *so* to survive, that are manifested; the despair and hopelessness is never, of course, quite complete. The objects are never actually felt to be dead, for that would mean death to the ego; the anxiety is so great because life hangs by a hair and at any moment the situation of full horror may be realized.

But struggle as he may and does under his unconscious guilt and anxiety to repair and restore, the patient has only a slenderest belief unconsciously in achieving anything of the kind; the slightest failure in reality, the faintest breath of criticism and his belief sinks to zero again—death or madness, his own and others', is ever before the eyes of his unconscious mind. He cannot possibly regenerate and recreate all the losses and destruction he has caused and if he cannot pay this price his own death is the only alternative.

I think the patient's fear of being forced to death himself by the analysis is one of the major underlying factors in this type of case and that is why I put it first. Unless it is appreciated many interpretations will miss their mark. All his efforts to put things right never succeed *enough;* he can only pacify his internal persecutors for a time, fob them off, feed them with sops, 'keep them going'; and so he 'keeps things going', the *status quo,* keeps some belief that 'one day' he will have done it all, and *postpones* the crash, the day of reckoning and judgement. One patient had woven this into a lifelong defensive pattern: his death would be exacted, yes, but he would see to it that this was postponed until his normal span had elapsed. He had reached a position of success and recognition in his own department of the world's work, so in old age his obituary notices would eventually serve him still as last and final denials and defences against his terrible anxieties and his own fundamental disbelief in any real capacity for good within himself.

I said before that understanding of these refractory cases lay on the one hand in our recognizing that the narcissistic and omnipotent resistances were masking a depressive position in these patients. This has been my own experience, but I might substantiate this theoretically in a simple way. The patient does not get well. The analysis has no effect on him (or not enough), because he resists it and its effect. Why? Now analysis means unmasking and bringing to light what is in the depths of his mind; and this is true in the sense both of external conscious reality and of internal psychic reality. What he is resisting, then, is precisely this: becoming aware consciously of what is in the depths of his mind. But this is a truism; all of us and all patients do this, you will say. Of course that is true; only these patients do it *more* than the others, for the simple reason that in them the underlying unconscious reality is more unbearable and more horrible than in other cases. Not that their phantasies are more sadistic; Glover has often reminded us that the same phantasies are found in everybody. The difference is that the *depressive position* is relatively stronger in them; the sense of failure, of inability to remedy matters is so great, the belief in better things is so weak: despair is so near. And analysis means unmasking, that is, to the patient, displaying in all its reality, making real, 'realizing', this despair, disbelief and *sense of failure,* which then in its turn simply means death to the patient. It becomes quite comprehensible why he will have none of it. Yet, with what grains of hope he has, he knows that no one but an analyst ventures to approach even to the fringes of these problems of his; and so he clings to analysis, as a forlorn hope, in which at the same time he really has no faith.

The patient's inaccessible attitude is the expression, then, of his denials of all that the analyst shows him of the unconscious contents of his mind. His megalomania, lack of adaptation to real life and to the analysis are only superficially denials of external reality. What he is in truth concerned to deny is his own *internal reality.* Here we come to my second point: the internal object-relations which are an integral part of his narcissism.

When we come to close quarters with the importance of the internalized objects in this connection, one general aspect of the situation will at once become clear in view of what has already been said about the depressive position. The patient's conscious aim in coming for analysis is to get well himself: unconsciously this point is relatively secondary, for other needs come first. Unconsciously his aim is: (1) on the paranoid basis, underlying his depressive position, his task is something far more urgent than getting well; it is simply to avert the impending death and disintegration which is constantly menacing him. But more even than this (for the paranoid aspect of things is not the most unbearable), unconsciously his chief aim must be (2) to cure and make well and happy all his loved and hated objects (all those he has ever loved and hated) before he thinks of himself. And these objects now to him are within himself. All the injuries he ever did them in thought or deed arose from his 'selfishness', from being too greedy, and too envious of them, not generous and willing enough to allow them what they had, whether of oral, anal or genital pleasure—from not loving *them* enough, in fact. In his mind every one of these acts and thoughts of selfishness and injury to others has to be reversed, to be made good, by sacrifices on his own part, before he can even be sure that his own life is secure—much less begin to think about being well and happy himself. Our offer of analysis to make him well and happy is unconsciously a direct seduction, as it were, a betrayal; it means to him an offer to help him to abandon his task of curing the others first, to conspire with him to put himself first again, to treat his loved objects as enemies, and neglect them, or even defeat and destroy them instead of helping them. On his paranoid level, this is all very well, and he wants nothing better; but there is always something more than the paranoid position; there is the only good thing he has, his buried core of love and his need to think of others before himself at last, to make things better for them and so to make himself better. And the analyst's offer to help him seems to him unconsciously a betrayal of them—of all those others who deserve help so much more than he. In addition, he does not for a moment believe that any good person really would be willing to help him before all the others who need it so greatly; so his suspicions of the analyst, and of his powers and intentions; are roused. One might suppose one could perhaps allay these suspicions by emphasizing how others will benefit by his cure; but on this point of technique I must here make an important digression. It will have struck you how incongruous and contradictory this picture of the patient's unconscious aim—one of them—(to make all his objects well and happy) is compared with his manifest egoistic behaviour. But its incongruity is of course no accident; the terrific contrast of extreme conscious egotism as against extreme unconscious altruism is one of the major features of the defence by denial. In order to disprove one underlying piece of reality, he parades its opposite extreme. So I have to remind you that his unconscious aims are really *unconscious* and that we cannot use them directly as a lever to help on the analysis. We cannot say 'What you really want is to cure and help other people, those you love, and not yourself', because that thought is precisely the most terrible thought in all the world to him; it brings up at once all his despair and sense of failure—all his greatest anxieties. Any such imputation, if at all plainly and directly expressed, has the immediate effect of producing a paranoid resistance as a defence; because, when we see through his denials, the manic defence has failed him. We have to be as guarded about directly imputing any altruistic motives to such patients as about imputing sadism or aggression to a hysteric. Nevertheless, when we know the unconscious situation, we know how to watch our steps; and even if we cannot use this lever ourselves for a very long time at least, we know it is there and can bring into play any indications of it there are, in subtle, indirect and gradual ways which do not rouse instant and unmanageable resistances.

This difficulty—that the patient unconsciously feels himself utterly unworthy of analytic help and, moreover, feels he is betraying the only good side of himself in accepting analysis, the side which would devote his life to making his loved ones happy—can only be got over in one way, namely, through the possibility that analysis, by making him better, will in the end make him at last capable of achieving his task for others—his loved ones. His *true* aim is the other way round—to make *them* better first and so to become well and good himself; but that is indeed impossible, both externally and internally, for his sadism is still unmanageable. The nearest hope is this reversal, again on the lines of a contradiction, or this compromise—to be cured himself in order then to cure others. It is only on this understanding, so to speak, unconsciously, and by placing all responsibility on the analyst, that such patients accept analysis at all; and I think this hope, and this only, is the ultimate source of the endless time, suffering and expense that such patients will bring to continue analysis. We have to recognize that they do this much, even if they do not get well. Why they do it has not hitherto been fully understood. This single unconscious motive then, that he is to be cured in order at last to be capable of fulfilling his task to others, and not for his own ends, is the one slender positive thread on which the analysis hangs. But we can see at once how impotent this motive can remain, how it is weakened, obstructed and undermined by innumerable counteracting forces. For one thing the patient does not for a moment believe in it; his fear of his own id and its uncontrollable desires and aggression is such that he feels no sort of security that he would eventually use any benefits obtained through analysis for the good of his objects; he knows very well, one might say, he will merely repeat his crimes and now use up the analyst for his own gratification and add him to the list of those he has despoiled and ruined. One of his greatest unconscious anxieties is that the analyst will be deceived on this very point and will allow himself to be so misused. He warns us in a disguised way continually of his own dangerousness.

Further, over and above this anxiety of accepting analysis on false pretences and deceiving and betraying his good objects again by it, there is an even greater fear, one which concerns the ego's fear for itself again, and links up with the fear of death unconsciously so strong in his mind. This is the dread that if he were cured by analysis, faithfully and truly, and made at last able to compass the reparation needed by all those he loved and injured, that the magnitude of the task would then absorb his whole self with every atom of all its resources, his whole physical and mental powers as long as he lives, every breath, every heartbeat, drop of blood, every thought, every moment of time, every possession, all money, every vestige of any capacity he has—an extremity of slavery and self-immolation which passes conscious imagination. This is what cure means to him from his unconscious depressive standpoint, and his uncured *status quo* in an unending analysis is clearly preferable to such a conception of cure—however grandiose and magnificent in one sense its appeal may be.

I hope that while I have spoken of the patient's unconscious aim of making others well and happy before himself, you will have borne in mind that the others I refer to always are the loved ones *in his inner world;* and these loved ones are also at the same moment the objects of all his hatred, vindictiveness and murderous impulses! His egoistic self-seeking attitude corresponds accurately enough to one side of things in his unconscious mind—to the hatred, cruelty and callousness there; and it represents his fears for his own ego if the love for his objects became too strong. We all fear the dependence of love to some extent.

I have spoken, too, of the contrast and incongruity of his love and need to save with his egoism, his tyranny, his lack of feeling for others. This egoism *is* his lack of a sense of reality. For his object-relations are not to real people, his object-relations are all within himself; his inner world is *all* the world to him. Whatever he does for his objects he does for himself as well; if only he could do it! he thinks; and in *mania* he thinks he *can*. So it is the overwhelming importance of the inner world of his emotional relations that makes him in real life so egocentric, asocial, self-seeking—so fantastic!

The unconscious attitude of love and anxiety for others in the patient is not identical with Freud's unconscious sense of guilt, though the feeling that the patient deserves no help till his loved ones have received full measure corresponds to it. This unworthiness finds atonement, as Freud says, in the illness, but only some atonement; the illness or the long analysis are compromises. To my mind it is *the love for his internal objects,* which lies behind and produces the unbearable guilt and pain, the need to sacrifice his life for theirs, and so the prospect of death, that makes this resistance so stubborn. And we can counter this resistance only by unearthing this love and so the guilt with it. To these patients if not to all, the analyst represents an internal object. So it is the positive transference in the patient that we must bring to realization; and this is what they resist beyond all, although they know well how to parade a substitute 'friendliness', which they declare to be normal and appropriate and claim ought to satisfy us as 'not neurotic'. They claim that their transference is resolved before it has been broached. We shall be deluded if we accept that. What is underneath is a *love* (a craving for absolute bliss in complete union with a perfect object for ever and ever), and this love is bound up with an uncontrollable and insupportable fury of disappointment, together with anxiety for other love-relations as well.

In Freud's remarks on the difficulties of the negative therapeutic reaction he has a footnote which in this connection is extremely interesting. He says that this unconscious sense of guilt is sometimes a 'borrowed' one, adopted from some other person who had been a love-object and is now one of the ego's identifications. And, 'if one can unmask this former object-relation behind the unconscious sense of guilt, success is often brilliant'. This is the view I have just stated; the love for the internal object must be found behind the guilt (only Freud regards the love as past and over). He adds a link, too, with the positive transference. 'Success may depend, too', he says, 'on whether the personality of the analyst admits of his being put in the place of the ego-ideal'. But Freud's suggestion that the guilt is 'adopted' from a now internal object shows us that the brilliant success rests on a *projection* (or localization) *of the guilt on to an object, though an internal one;* and this is an extremely common feature of the manic defence (which may of course have been built up on some facts in experience). And his suggestion that the personality of the analyst determines whether or not he plays the part of ego-ideal indicates that consciousness and external circumstances are being allowed to blur the issue—exactly as the manic patient employs them to do if he can. The analyst *is* unconsciously the ego-ideal, or prototype of it, already to these patients; if they can rationalize their overmastering love and idealize it, then they can to some extent realize it without analysis; and this is in part a reparation, of course. The true aggressive character of their love, and their unconscious guilt of that, is still denied. Freud admits that this is a 'trick method' which the analyst cannot use. But the patient tries his utmost to trick us in this way. A great deal of our therapeutic success in former years in my opinion actually rested, and still may do, on this mechanism, without our having understood it. The patient exploits us in his own way instead of being fully analysed; and his improvement is based on a manic defensive system. Nowadays I regard this possibility as a danger, even if it was not so formerly; for the analysis of primitive aggression now rouses severe anxieties, while recognition and encouragement by the analyst of the patient's attempts at reparation (in real life) allay them merely by the omnipotent method of glossing over and denying the internal depressive reality—his feeling of failure. The result is that the patient may develop a manic defensive system—a denial of his illness and anxieties—instead of a cure, because the depressive situation of failure has never been opened up. In my experience the true analysis of the love and guilt of the depressive anxiety-situation, because they are so deeply buried, is far the hardest task we meet with; and the instances of success Freud quotes seem to be last-minute evasions of it by the patients' chosen methods of projection and denial.

The most important feature to be emphasized in these cases is the degree of unconscious falseness and deceit in them. It is what Abraham comments on; he, however, did not connect it with an unconscious sense of guilt. To us analysts both the full true positive and true negative transference are difficult to tolerate, but the *false* transference, when the patient's feelings for us are all insincere and are no feelings at all, when ego and id are allied in deceit against us, seems to be something the analyst can see through only with difficulty. A false and treacherous transference in our patients is such a blow to our narcissism, and so poisons and paralyses our instrument for good (our understanding of the patient's unconscious mind), that it tends to rouse strong depressive anxieties in ourselves. So the patient's falseness often enough meets with denial by us and remains unseen and unanalysed by us too.

NOTES

1. Read before the British Psycho-Analytical Society, October 1, 1935.
2. Klein, 'A Contribution to the Psychogenesis of Manic-Depressive States', *International Journal of Psycho-Analysis,* Vol. XVI, Pt. 2.
3. Abraham, 'A Particular Form of Neurotic Resistance Against the Psycho-Analytic Method' (1919), *Selected Papers on Psycho-Analysis,* p. 303.
4. 'Persecutory Ideas and Delusions', *International Journal of Psycho-Analysis,* Vol. XII, 1931.
5. 'Don Quichote und Donquichotismus', *Imago,* Bd. XX, 1934.
6. *New Introductory Lectures.*

25. The Negative Therapeutic Reaction

Stanley L. Olinick

The accumulated man-years of psycho-analytic practice since Freud's (1923) formulation of the negative therapeutic reaction have produced only a few attempted contradictions or additions. Most psycho-analytic writers now deal with the syndrome as a component of masochism; appropriate technique in treatment has involved attention primarily to the masochism and other prevailing pathology. But there is an aspect of the syndrome that has been de-emphasized since Freud's description and discussion of it in *The Ego and the Id* (1923), and which had been prominent in his earlier, less well-known description (Freud, 1918). This is the negativism that is a *sine qua non* of the reaction. In the patient's own idiom of expression and communication, the presenting fact of the negative therapeutic reaction is negativism—a fact that is still compatible with the usual considerations of sense of guilt, need for punishment, and moral masochism.

I propose here to re-examine the ego psychology of the negative therapeutic reaction as a special case of negativism. This point of view facilitates the understanding and therefore the management of the syndrome, by permitting us to view from a new vantage point certain technical and theoretical problems concerning the concomitance of negativism, sadomasochism, and depression.

The syndrome itself represents the nucleus of the patient's defences; and its appearance is analogous to the recapitulation of the neurosis that is evinced in the terminal phase of analysis. These defences are highly cathected, narcissistic devices, originally evoked in the face of dire necessity during infancy and childhood, and now re-evoked in the genetic and dynamic regression of transference. In their negativistic rejections of the psychic and external realities of their situations, the patients may repudiate success and

Reprinted by permission of the author and the *International Journal of Psycho-Analysis* 45 (1964):540–48. Copyright © the Institute of Psycho-Analysis.

fulfilment, sometimes endangering their lives with exacerbated symptoms and actions. It is my view that the negative therapeutic reaction is often unrecognized as such, or otherwise becomes unmanageable, when the analyst has become infected with the patient's negativistic rejection. He identifies with the negativism, mistrusting his own valid interpretation, and failing to give due attention and credence to the sequence of events in the patient's life leading up to the reaction. However, even in the absence of such undue involvement, these patients present complicated problems in treatment.

HISTORICAL DEVELOPMENT

In 1918, Freud wrote of the patient who has since become known as the Rat Man:

> . . . In fact he never gave way to fresh ideas without making one last attempt at clinging to what had lost its value for him. . . . He still behaved in just the same way during the analytic treatment, for he showed a habit of producing transitory 'negative reactions'; every time something had been conclusively cleared up, he attempted to contradict the effect for a short while by an aggravation of the symptom which had been cleared up. It is quite the rule, as we know, for children to treat prohibitions in the same kind of way. When they have been rebuked for something . . . they repeat it once more after the prohibition before stopping it. In this way they gain the point of apparently stopping of their own accord and of disobeying the prohibition (Freud, 1918).

The syndrome so described was given further definition and refinement in *The Ego and the Id,* and assigned the aptly paradoxical designation of 'negative therapeutic reaction'. Significant changes were made in the formulation:

> Every partial solution that ought to result, and in other people does result, in an improvement or a temporary suspension of symptoms produces in them for the time being an exacerbation of their illness . . .
> There is no doubt that there is something in these people that sets itself against their recovery and dreads its approach as though it were a danger. We are accustomed to say that the need for illness has got the upper hand in them over the desire for health. If we analyse this resistance in the usual way—then, even after we have subtracted from it the defiant attitude towards the physician and the fixation on the various kinds of advantage which the patient derives from the illness, the greater part of it is still left over; and this reveals itself as the most powerful of all obstacles to recovery, more powerful even than such familiar ones as narcissistic inacessibility, the assumption of a negative attitude towards the physician or a clinging to the advantages of the illness.

In the end we come to see that we are dealing with what may be called a 'moral' factor, a sense of guilt, which is finding atonement in the illness and is refusing to give up the penalty of suffering (Freud, 1923).

The formulation of 'superego resistance' in 1925 (Freud, 1926) further clarified the dimensions of guilt and need for punishment. Since then, negative therapeutic reactions have come to be subsumed under this heading, or even identified with it (Glover, 1955).

Abraham (1918) gave an account of 'A Particular Form of Resistance Against the Psycho-Analytic Method'. He described markedly narcissistic patients who while overtly compliant with the methods of psycho-analysis resisted genuine free associations and produced only ego-syntonic material. They were 'particularly sensitive to anything which injures their self-love. They are inclined to feel "humiliated" by every fact that is established . . . and they are continually on their guard against suffering such humiliations.' He characterized them as anal-sadistic-omnipotent. Towards the analyst their attitudes were antagonistic, begrudging, negativistic, demanding, and exacting. Abraham did not explicitly refer to 'negative therapeutic reaction', but there is no doubt that he was referring to the same type of patient.

In 1935, Joan Riviere presented before the British Psycho-Analytical Society 'A Contribution to the Analysis of the Negative Therapeutic Reaction' (Riviere, 1936), a paper which drew upon Melanie Klein's theoretical views. She stressed the crucial roles of hypomanic denial and infantile omnipotence as defences against depression. Horney (1936) analysed various forms of the negative therapeutic reaction in terms of conflicts of rivalry and affection, and the fear of success. Gero (1936), with later confirmation by Lewin (1950, 1961), noted that negative therapeutic reactions characterized the analyses of patients with depression. Eidelberg (1948) referred the reaction to the masochist's intolerance of success: the patient's megalomania requires that defeats be self-imposed. Sullivan (1953) drew attention to the 'malevolent transformation of personality', referring to the sadomasochistically developed person who, under the stress of severe and chronic anxiety when needing tenderness, acts in a defensively malevolent way, thereby bringing his malevolence back on to himself. Fenichel (1941, 1945) and W. Reich (1933) have also written on the subject, and will be referred to below.

Glover (1955) maintained that superego resistance, 'sometimes called the "negative therapeutic reaction" ', is operative throughout therapy; that on the one hand it prevents a full expansion of transference, and on the other hinders a resolution of transference; and that these resistances cannot be effectively uncovered apart from the transference.

Melanie Klein saw the negative therapeutic reaction as formed in part by the splitting off of envy and hate from 'The original wish to please the mother, the longing to be loved, as well as the urgent need to be protected from the consequences of their own destructive impulses . . .' (1957).

MISCONCEPTIONS

Notwithstanding the work already done, there continue to be misconceptions as to the nature of the reaction, failure to recognize its presence, and lack of clarity as to its significance for ego psychology and therapeutic technique. These misconceptions may be grouped as follows:

(1) The concept is outmoded, as being descriptive only of symptoms. It is said to stem from a period in the history of psycho-analysis when symptom-interpretation was the sole method of treatment, as compared with what later came to be known as resistance-analysis or character-analysis. It is evident from the quotations cited that Freud, far from dealing only with symptoms, sought and elicited the meta-psychology of the reaction and discussed it as character-defence. He did, however, leave the negativism on a relatively descriptive and meagrely developmental level of understanding.

(2) It would be more accurate and useful to consider the reaction as a therapeutic impasse, resulting from some mismanagement by the physician of the analyst-patient relationship. This view, that the reaction is no more than a consequence of an incompetently managed negative transference, was first expressed by Wilhelm Reich (1933). He claimed, on the basis of the experience of the Vienna Seminar for Psychoanalytic Therapy between 1923 and 1930, that the negative therapeutic reaction did not occur if one followed two rules: first, to make conscious the 'secret negative attitude' of the patient, while liberating and securing discharge for all aggression, and treating any masochistic tendency as a 'masked aggression' outwards; second, to leave positive manifestations of love alone until they either 'turn into hatred' ('disappointment reactions'), or concentrate in ideas of genital incest.

It must be emphasized that even if adherence to Reich's two rules were followed with successful results, it does not prove that they were successful because, as Reich (1933) claimed, negative therapeutic reactions are results of 'inadequate technique for dealing with the latent negative transference'.

Also, there is evidence that the reaction is prone to occur in the presence of latent *positive* transference. Clinical experience disposes of the proposition that the phenomenon is solely an artifact of poor technique, while acknowledging that it may in fact be exacerbated by poor technique.

(3) One occasionally still hears the term employed as a designation for any and all worsenings of the patient's condition during treatment. This gratuitously nullifies the meticulous clinical observations of previous writers.

(4) Fenichel (1945) held that not all negative therapeutic reactions resulted from moral masochism, and referred to those exacerbations that occur when an interpretation is given from the id side, before complete analysis of the defence. This I should prefer to call a counterfeit negative therapeutic reaction: it is limited to this one occasion; its origin can readily be traced; and it does not have the immediately self-damaging, character-rooted quality of the true reaction. That is, it is likely, assuming the analyst does not make the same mistake again, that it will neither endure for long, nor again recur, as the masochistically rooted reactions tend to do. Fenichel referred also to the adverse reaction of some patients to a change for the better in their neurotic equilibrium. This also, as he pointed out, is not necessarily due to masochism, but to an investment in the neurotic state as the lesser of two evils (1945).

REFORMULATION AS SPECIAL CASE
OF NEGATIVISM

To a valid and properly timed interpretation of defence that contains the tacit promise of understanding and eventual autonomy, or to any situation holding forth the hope or possibility of emancipation from the old, crippling form of living, certain persons react not with clinical improvement, but with worsening of their condition. This exacerbation occurs in the affective context of an often resoundingly dramatized 'No!', utilizing a combination of defences of which denial by action or acting out, negation, and negativism are prominent. I stress *dramatized* in order both to emphasize the power of their behaviour to stir the emotions of the other person, and to indicate that the negativism may be totally or partly non-verbal. The behaviour need not be theatrical or melodramatic. 'Acting out' in the classical sense (Freud, 1914) is frequently an important part of the reaction.

This dramatic enactment of the negative, with its effect on the other person, is a reformulation that extends the concept of symptom- and illness-exacerbation to include also patterns of living—i.e. the fluctuations of character-defences. The people who are prone to negative therapeutic reactions are in fact special instances of the 'neuroses of destiny' (Fenichel, 1945).

(1) For examples, we turn first to one of Freud's instances of 'Those Wrecked by Success' (1916):[1] the spirited young woman who ran away from home in search of adventure. After many changes of fortune she came to live with an artist who appreciated her finer qualities, and to whom she became a faithful companion. There followed years of rehabilitation, during which he reconciled his family to her, and prepared to make her his legal wife. From that time, she began to neglect the house, imagined herself persecuted by the lover's family, hindered her lover in his work and social life, and finally succumbed to an incurable mental illness. The paradoxical behaviour of this woman resulted from the imminent fulfilment of wishes that were felt to be dangerous (Freud, 1916, 1936), and it is to be seen as a negativistic rejection of that which was wished for but forbidden.

(2) Another illustration of this paradoxical, negativistic quality: an obsessional patient boasts that he has not had his habitual headache for weeks; soon he proceeds to suffer from one (1925).

(3) A young man entered treatment with principal complaints of sexual impotence, an angry attitude towards friends and colleagues, and generally over-compensated reactions to passivity, submission, and dependency. His voice was loud and booming, his gestures emphatic, and his opinions categorical and unyielding. He reviewed his history with reproachful indignation that life had not dealt more kindly with him.

Questioning by the analyst, intended to clarify or inform, led to angry rejections, although in subsequent sessions the patient might bring up these matters himself. In minor ways, the patient picked up various of the analyst's traits of speech. Concurrent with these signs of a covert identification, and reflecting a conflicted father-transference, he complained bitterly that the psycho-analytic work was not producing the desired effects of improvement in his work and marriage, and in his general well-being. Business contacts which were vital to his career he also dealt with ambivalently at best, and often destructively. His behaviour during analytic sessions gradually produced in the analyst feelings of dissatisfaction and doubts about his own ability to continue to work with a patient who was so completely negativistic to all that was said to him.

One could discern, behind his vigorous and bombastic complaints and his imperious commands that he be treated as he saw fit, a frightened little boy pleading for father's affection and assistance, and for mother's nurturing; but the reaction formations to dependent needs were violent in the extreme, and the positive transference remained latent.

Enuretic as a child, he had been subjected to painful and repeated urethral dilatations. He and his younger sister had received enemas from the compulsive, depressive mother. Always sickly, the sister had early succumbed to a chronic illness, and now became moribund and died of carcinoma of the bowel while he was still early in treatment.

This patient's defences were so heavily invested with the drive derivatives against which he was defended; he was in such turmoil of manifest contradictions; and the transference was so quickly developed in terms of impossible demands and expected disappointment and humiliation, that only the most tentative and tactfully expressed interventions could be attempted. Even these were rejected, usually with eruptions of negativistic, reproachful attacks on the analyst. The sister's marriage, final illness, and death, during his first year of treatment also increased his anxieties. His grief was masked by an increase of sadomasochistic behaviour, which led to the termination of this analysis. His analyst was at the time inexperienced in the management of negative therapeutic reactions, and fell prey to the sadomasochistic provocations. A longer period of work with a second analyst also ended in failure.

(4) A muted version of the same theme presented itself in another young man. To him the interpretation was offered that his feelings and behaviour were comprehensible as a duplication of his father's depression and work disability. The characteristic sequence developed of quick denial, evasions of the subject, and, in the following hour, bitterness and reproaches towards the analyst with worsened symptoms. Over a period of time, the interpretation came to be accepted.

It is the greater tribute to the dissembling ability of these people, that it is so often accepted at face value that they are dogged by ill-fortune. This effect on the observer is unconsciously intended. No one must suspect the presence of forbidden wishes; consequently, the wish is repressed and the prohibiting agency attributed to the fates. Success or, for that matter, sympathy over failure will induce shame, guilt, depression, and resentment, for both threaten his narcissistic sense of perfection, and seductively confront him with his forbidden id derivatives. Therefore, he must suffer the strictures of his superego, or again reconstitute his defences. The projection on to the fates having failed, it is once more projected, but perhaps this time on to a 'persecuting' sympathizer.

Supposing now that these events occurred in the course of treatment, as they do following confrontation or interpretation, wherein is this a negative therapeutic reaction, rather than the effect of an economically and structurally wrong interpretation?

(a) The reaction is paradoxically negativistic, in that it refuses, repudiates, and renounces inappropriately to the external situation. The negativism is directed not so much at the issue raised by the confrontation or interpretation as at the person of the confronter or interpreter in an intensification of transference.

(b) This transference is overtly negative and hostile, but it is latently or unconsciously positive. It is the pressure of the drives and affects encompassed by the positive transference that arouses the sequence of defensive rejection, self-punishment by symptom-exacerbation, and alloplastic attack upon the therapist.

(c) The general orientation is sadomasochistic, and resistance arises from the superego.

(d) Out of this matrix there develops the dramatic, alloplastic intent. It is not only that the patient projects on to the analyst, but he also vigorously attempts to mould the analyst into the very prototype of the hated yet beloved introject. The transferred impulses and affects are ambivalent, pregenital, and intense.

(e) There is, finally, an uncanniness about these reactions (Kris, 1951), which I believe to be related to the resonant affects and impulses in the analyst induced by the patient's profound narcissistic conviction that his very existence depends on his ability to transform reality in accord with his infantile omnipotence.

CHARACTER-DEVELOPMENT

Negativism

What René Spitz (1957) calls 'the ideational concept of the negative' he finds to be first expressed between the fifteenth and eighteenth months in the head-shaking gesture of 'No'. He demonstrates that, normally, 'the phylogenetically preformed pattern of . . . rooting behaviour becomes the matrix of the semantic gesture of negative head-shaking'. Negativism was stressed by

Freud as essential in the subsequent development of critical judgment and discrimination (1925), and Spitz sees it as also essential in the replacement of action by communication, and in the eventual humanization of the individual.

Interruptions of the child's activity, as for instance with prohibitions, invite or enforce a return to passivity, a regressive step towards the narcissistic organization of the ego. Impelled, as Spitz says, by the biological urge to progress from passivity to activity, and further motivated by the aggressive cathexis provoked by the frustration experience, the child 'at the end of the first year of life and throughout the second year' conspicuously employs 'in practically every situation requiring mastery or defense' the adaptive mechanism of identification, and in particular identification with the aggressor or frustrator. In this, 'The "No" (gesture or word) is the identificatory link with the libidinal object . . . [and] the suitable vehicle to express aggression . . .' (Spitz, 1957).

As with other of the ego's synthetic functions and defences, the line between the adaptational and the regressively pathological is thin and fluctuating. Consider for instance a possible development of a child's 'No', first as the aggressive warding off of excessive stimulation. At this point, the anxiety-signal leading to the 'No' might be conceptualized as 'Too much to be safe'—that is, too much excitation to be assimilated. Later, when additional external forces are introjected as part of the superego system, ordinarily gratifying experiences will evoke negativistic responses, as being 'Too good to be true' or, as one patient quoted her envious mother, 'More than the law allows'. Moreover, as Anna Freud and others have shown (A. Freud, 1952; Bychowski, 1958; Sterba, 1957), the now self-abnegating negativism, although inappropriate to many of the processes of living, may come to be defensively employed in the face of the subjective feeling of threatened emotional surrender or enslavement in a regressed, submissive, helpless, dependent position. The automatic obedience and 'waxy flexibility' of some catatonics, for example, represents a degree of regressive compliance that ambiguously says both Yes and No.

Many years ago, Rank (1929) commented that the first manifestation of what he called 'Will', or 'dynamic organization of the impulse life', was to be found in the very young child's negativism. Observation of any two-year-old in this phase of development confirms that there is indeed self-affirmation and assertiveness in this behaviour. Frequently this expresses an urge to master lest one be mastered. Albert Camus (1951) stated it boldly as, 'I rebel, therefore I am'. The small child struggles thus in the necessary distinguishing of self from non-self, and such a struggle for autonomous identity is pursued through all of life (Erikson, 1956).

NEGATIVE THERAPEUTIC REACTION

From reconstructions, it is my impression that those people who display the negative therapeutic reaction were endowed from birth with greater than average funds of aggressive orality and anality. This in turn made the mothering relationship stressful (as it may later the analytic), by investing it with realistic anxieties about filling an assigned role with these masterful infants and children. One is reminded of the earlier observations of Riviere (1936) and of Horney (1936), who separately pointed out the prevalence of defences entailing tyrannical control of self and of others. Inevitably the mother's resentful helplessness and overcompensating, possessive demands, and the infant's or child's impotent aggressiveness will reinforce each other, with the result that the child grows up to be a welter of contradictions: demanding, but so fearful of disappointment as to be spuriously independent and rejecting; apprehensive of intrusion, yet fearful of isolation; wanting love, but able only to command or buy its counterfeit, dependence on and from the partner.

At the same time, the father has become unavailable, either psychologically, or through divorce, death, or desertion. Whether his abdication is the result primarily of his own renunciation of the paternal role, or whether he is pushed aside by the joint efforts of mother and child, or both, I am not prepared to say. In any case, mother and child form an alliance wherein are intermeshed their defences against dependency and fear of abandonment. Needless to say, no true oedipal triumph has ensued. The child's superego consists of pre-oedipal, ambivalent introjects, and he is therefore constantly guarded against the fulfilment of his id wishes. From the superego, a generally negative attitude is erected against temptation and wish. Phobic, obsessional, and counterphobic defences are seen. Should all fail, there is released a sadomasochistic rage and/or depression.

Frequently, the history of these patients contains references to the severe illness or death of a sibling or friend. Gastrointestinal disturbances are prominent in their own medical histories. These findings are relevant to the importance of passive-active and oral-anal conflicts (Olinick, 1959).

Freud (1923) observed that the patients we are considering do not feel guilty but ill, although harried by a punitive superego. Their discomfort is largely that of 'social anxiety', with hypersensitivity to neglect and the possibility of aloneness, and the expectation of humiliation and mortification. Consequently, they resort to an irritable guardedness. That is, their character defences take the form of a rude querulousness, of the kind sometimes seen in the over-indulged child who has also been subjected to importuning and nagging by an insecure and possessive parent. Their early passive experiences of frustrated, guilt-imbued needs have led to the development of defences that, as one patient put it, are intended to 'boycott' life. The usual 'If you can't lick them, join them' (identification with the aggressor) evolves into 'If you can't lick them or join them, destroy them'.

This failure of the defence of identification follows a disturbance in the delicate internal balance of activity-passivity, increases the imbalance, and results in the threat of guilt and annihilation. The patient, in other words, in his impotent efforts towards self-aggrandizement, rages destructively at his introjects. Meanwhile he rejects those external temptations that conspire to fulfil his fantasies, and thus precipitate his crisis. Alternatively, he may project his guilt, and find a scapegoat who will accept the guilty role.

DEPRESSION, SADOMASOCHISM, AND NEGATIVISM

Riviere stated that it is an underlying depression against which these patients direct their complicated defences. The depression is dreaded as death or destruction: the world will be empty, and they will be abandoned, drained, and alone (1936). To this should be added the proposition that the dread is of *regression,* and specifically regression to what Anna Freud has referred to as 'primary identification with the love object', a forerunner of object-love proper (1952). This is feared as a loss of intactness, or annihilation of self, and is defended against by negativism. I would further propose that this dreaded helplessness and emotional surrender is inherent in the *ambivalent identification with a depressed, pre-oedipal maternal* love object.

Lest this dread circumstance develop and endure, the patient offers himself as a reciprocating partner in the dialectic of sadomasochism, as though preferring a relationship in which some control remains to one in which he is helplessly engulfed (Eidelberg, 1948). In the sadomasochistic relationship, the patient experiences his partner variously as the introjected or projected bad object—the depressed, devouring, but positively needed maternal imago. Lewin's concept of the oral triad is useful here in comprehending the vacillations between hypomanic denial and depression (Lewin, 1950).

The frequently observed, overdetermined coincidence of depression and masochism may be due in part to the masochism—itself a negative attitude towards the processes of living—functioning as a defence against depression. That is, on the basis of the regular effect of the masochistic behaviour on the other person—the dramatic quality of the negative therapeutic reaction—it would be legitimate to refer to the mechanism of this defence as the projection of depression, and its induction by provocation, in the other person. For, in raging against himself, the masochist dramatically and effectively evokes the experience of helplessness, guilt, and rage in the other person: not he is depressed, but the other one. (The more usual forms of this response in the analyst may include the defences of boredom, irritability, and dozing (Olinick, 1959).) Stated differently, in the course of the life or death struggles with his hated and hating introject, his sadomasochistic techniques of relatedness may result in his finding an actual partner who is himself prone to dependency, depression, and sadomasochism, and to whom he is at the same time acceptable as an introject. In such a relationship, it is now necessary to defend by negativism against that which was induced in and projected into the partner. The No-saying, then, is defensive against that same dependent depression and masochism, as it is now perceived in the other person. Sadomasochism 'projects' depression, and negativism 'rejects' depression.

When the negativism is thus admixed with sadomasochistic components, with rage and destructiveness from and against the introjects, and not least, also admixed with a flair for the dramatic or alloplastic in behaviour, we then have the negative therapeutic reaction. I may now denote this reaction as a depressive, sadomasochistic rage, which is projected and induced in the other person, in a desperate effort at defence against the expectation of inner loss and helpless regression. Negativism is the linkage between the various parts of the picture, the common denominator among the varied elements.

THERAPEUTIC MANAGEMENT

The technical problem of the negative therapeutic reaction is the management in the patient of an acute, recurrent, negativistic emotional crisis in a sadomasochistic person who is prone to depression. The reaction occurs during a latent positive transference, and it is the press of the forbidden positive feelings and impulses that triggers the automatic 'No'. The matrix in which the reaction develops is one that requires the presence of others with whom the patient can attempt to enact his intrapsychic conflicts of omnipotence versus dependent gratification. At the same time, he is likely to deny their importance, except as intrusive agents of frustration and pain.

The conditions of the psycho-analytic situation, inviting and enforcing the dynamic and genetic regression of transference, establish once again in a susceptible patient the requirements of reinforcing the infantile, defensive 'No'.[2] The dominant-submissive axis of the therapeutic relationship is enhanced (Olinick, 1959), the patient experiencing as dangerous the requirement of voluntary receptivity and submission to the subjective experiences of the couch and to the interventions of the analyst. The physician is encountered as a frustrating and untrustworthy figure who must be resisted lest utter passivity and helplessness be exacted. The crisis is precipitated when he is perceived as tempting opposition to the patient's superego mandates and restrictions. The resulting negativistic rejection may be in the form of a 'simple' repudiation of success on the one hand, or a violent sadomasochistic storm at the opposite extreme. The more regressed the patient, the more violent will be this superego crisis.

It is only when the patient has recognized the importance of the other person as a vehicle for his own projections and provocations that the sadomasochism, having become ego-dystonic, can begin to yield to psychoanalysis. Until then, one has been able only to point out systematically and consistently, and with infinite patience and tact, that the patient's negativism is obstructing further understanding. Until then, also, the patient uses the analyst as he uses his other partners, as an adversary who may divest him of his magic cloak of secret megalomanic wishes, evoke superego reproaches, and so expose him to defeat and helplessness. In the face of these expected dangers, it is not surprising that the patient 'chooses' the lesser threat of maintaining the *status quo,* by frustrating his own wishes for recovery.

It is usual in the literature on the subject (e.g. Brenner, 1959; Eidelberg, 1948) to emphasize that the principles of treatment of these patients are not different from those in other character analyses. With this I am in full agreement. However, the often repeated statement that the analyst must and can remain calm, observant, and understanding in the face of the patient's skilful provocations and discouraging negative therapeutic reactions says too much in too few words. To the neophyte analyst, these words are heard as an exhortation, perhaps to emulate his idealized seniors; to the more experienced but not yet fully seasoned analyst they may not evoke the guilt of failing to measure up to the ideal, but instead a puzzled *pro forma* acquiescence that may inadvertently touch off his own defences and dissociate him from the patient.

Needless to say, by reason of the conditions of his work the analyst is in a peculiarly vulnerable position. His 'freely hovering attention', empathic identification, and the usual motivations that enter into his choice of profession tend to open his ego boundaries to the operations of the patient. This is necessary and useful, but, under certain regressive conditions, it may overcarry. The dominant-submissive axis of the therapeutic relationship is then reversed, with the patient dominant, although only in the temporary sense of a child in a tantrum.

For example, in the course of one negative therapeutic reaction, the patient worked himself into a cold, articulate attack upon the analyst as incompetent and malicious. In so doing, he was guarding himself from feeling guilty and helpless. Yet such was the intensity of effort, the subtlety of the twisted logic, and the distortion of facts, as to produce in the analyst the apprehension that perhaps the patient was right. Momentarily, the analyst felt guilty and helpless. Recognizing that he had introjected 'something bad', he could extricate himself from the role he was being forced into, and await his opportunity to interpret the defence.

In such instances, distinction must be made between humane consideration for the patient's anguished defence, and undesirable acquiescence in the dramatically alloplastic transference. In fact, the analyst's angry assertiveness against such manipulation is at times indicated, if it is tactfully motivated and timed, and clearly intended as the setting of limits. Not so, however, in the instance cited above. Here it was indicated to wait out the period of time until the patient could hear it said that his repudiation was one of a long chain of automatic No-saying. With much working through, it was then possible to take up the second part of the defence, having to do with the attack on the analyst. This was the more difficult, as it dealt with a projection, and considerable time elapsed before the occasion was right, and more time for working through. The sadomasochistic induction and projection of guilt and helplessness was a measure employed to protect from depression, and therefore it was particularly important that the defence be not reinforced nor the depression abruptly precipitated.

The analytic *pas de deux* must always be conducted with special, tactful attention to the patient's pace, rhythm, and capacity of expression, and here is one of those many areas in psycho-analytic practice where science and art have to be delicately combined. The analyst must sustain himself against the patient's ambivalent need to destroy, always recognizing the presence of the other side of the ambivalence, but interpreting only when the patient is, as one perceptive woman put it, 'almost not saying "No" '. By not yielding to the projections of guilt and depression, the analyst becomes available as a guilt-free introject, and this strengthens the patient's non-malevolent and accepting potentialities.

In order to be utilized as a good object, the analyst must know that the uncanny threat of destruction that he feels from the patient during the negative therapeutic reaction is only secondarily if at all the result of disappointment of therapeutic zeal. Primarily, this threat is felt to be aimed at his own sense of psychological integrity and identity, and is the counterpart of the patient's fear of annihilation. In fact, the patient's continuing negativism and projections must sooner or later impinge upon the most wholesomely developed analyst, however lightly and temporarily, or it is a sign that the instrument of empathic identification has given way to defences.

For work with these patients, it is essential that the analyst has a capacity for empathic identification in a context of having worked through his own projective distortions and sadomasochistic defences, and has developed his own realistic sense of the relativity of values. There is now a realistic appraisal and appreciation of the irony of a critical situation when confronted with these people. The approach is throughout intended to establish within the patient a new set of introjects that are less hateful and hated than those already present. With less stringent superego and ego ideal demands, the freed psycho-analytic process may be expected to work through the mourning and depressive constellations. The final therapeutic task is the analysis of the 'primary identification' with the depressed, pre-oedipal mother. None of this should imply, however, that the analytic course is one of successive removal of layer upon layer of defence. The intricate network of defence and impulse is a formidable challenge to the fortitude and perceptivity of both analyst and patient.

SUMMARY

(1) Misconceptions about the syndrome of the negative therapeutic reaction are reviewed and discussed. A selective review of the historical development of the concept of the reaction is presented.

(2) The ego psychology of the negative therapeutic reaction is reviewed

and discussed as a special case of negativism—that is, as an acute, recurrent, negativistic emotional crisis in a sadomasochistic person who is prone to depression. The syndrome represents a category of superego resistance.

(3) The recurrent pattern of living of those prone to the negative therapeutic reaction is of intolerance of gratification. At its height, the depressive, sadomasochistic rage is projected and often induced in the other person. Defences are directed against expected inner loss and helpless regression to the primary identification with the depressed mother. Schematically, sadomasochism 'projects' depression, and negativism 'rejects' depression.

(4) The therapeutic management is presented with particular emphasis on the frequent transference-countertransference tensions. Schematically, interpretation proceeds from the side of negativism through the alloplastic, projective defences, to the task of analysis of depression.

NOTES

1. It is a curious and noteworthy fact that a culling of the literature, while it produces an abundance of references to the negative therapeutic reaction, elicits only a handful of clinical descriptions; e.g. Freud (1916) and Lewin (1950).
2. The analyst, although he stands as the advocate of individual integrity, inviolability, and spontaneity, is at the same time the initiator and agent of a process that for painfully long periods of time must be traced through a maze of submissiveness and intrusiveness. The necessity to assist the patient to the point of his ego's freedom to choose along a route of dependence, via the psychoanalytic processes of dynamic and genetic regression, constitutes a paradox, upon the solution of which depends the outcome of the therapy. There is no lessening of its stress from the fact that this paradox confronts every parent and indeed every authority figure in a society where the privileges and obligations of the individual are traditionally honored' (Olinick, 1959).

REFERENCES

Abraham, K. (1918). 'A Particular Form of Neurotic Resistance Against the Psycho-Analytic Method.' In: *Selected Papers*. (London: Hogarth, 1948.)
Brenner, C. (1959). 'The Masochistic Character.' *J. Amer. Psychoanal. Assoc.*, **7.**
Bychowski, G. (1958). 'The Struggle Against the Introjects.' *Int. J. Psycho-Anal.*, **39.**
Camus, Albert (1951). *The Rebel*. (New York: Knopf, 1954.)
Eidelberg, L. (1948). 'A Contribution to the Study of Masochism.' In: *Studies in Psychoanalysis*. (New York: Int. Univ. Press.)
Erikson, E. (1956). 'The Problem of Ego Identity.' *J. Amer. Psychoanal. Assoc.*, **4.**
Fenichel, O. (1941). *Problems of Psychoanalytic Technique*. (New York: Psychoanalytic Quarterly, Inc.)
——(1945). *The Psychoanalytic Theory of Neurosis*. (New York: Norton.)

Freud, Anna (1952). 'A Connection Between the States of Negativism and of Emotional Surrender.' Author's Abstract in *Int. J. Psycho-Anal.*, **33.**

Freud, S. (1914). 'Remembering, Repeating, and Working-Through (Further Recommendations on the Technique of Psycho-Analysis II).' *S.E.*, **12.**

———(1916). 'Some Character-Types Met With in Psycho-Analytic Work.' *S.E.*, **14.**

———(1918). 'From the History of an Infantile Neurosis.' *S.E.*, **17.**

———(1923). *The Ego and the Id. S.E.*, **19.**

———(1925). 'Negation.' *S.E.*, **19.**

Freud, S. (1926). *Inhibitions, Symptoms, and Anxiety. S.E.*, **20.**

———(1936). 'A Disturbance of Memory on the Acropolis.' *S.E.*, **22.**

Gero, G. (1936). 'The Construction of Depression.' *Int. J. Psycho-Anal.*, **17.**

Glover, E. (1955). *The Technique of Psycho-Analysis.* (New York: Int. Univ. Press; London: Baillière.)

Horney, K. (1936). 'The Problem of the Negative Therapeutic Reaction.' *Psychoanal. Quart.*, **5.**

Klein, M. (1957). *Envy and Gratitude.* (New York: Basic Books; London: Tavistock.)

Kris, E. (1951). 'The Development of Ego Psychology.' *Samiksa*, **5.**

Lewin, B. (1950). *Psychoanalysis of Elation.* (New York: Norton.)

———(1961). 'Reflections on Depression.' *Psychoanal. Study Child*, **16.**

Olinick, Stanley L. (1959). 'The Analytic Paradox.' *Psychiatry*, **22.**

Rank, Otto (1929). *Will Therapy and Truth and Reality.* (New York: Knopf, 1945.)

Reich, Wilhelm (1933). *Character Analysis.* (New York: Orgone Inst. Press, 1945.)

Riviere, J. (1936). 'A Contribution to the Analysis of the Negative Therapeutic Reaction.' *Int. J. Psycho-Anal.*, **17.**

Spitz, R. (1957). *No and Yes.* (New York: Int. Univ. Press.) Sterba, R. (1957). 'Oral Invasion and Self-Defence.' *Int. J. Psycho-Anal.*, **38.**

Sterba, R. (1957). 'Oral invasion and Self-Defence.' *Int. J. Psycho-Anal.*, **38.**

Sullivan, H. S. (1953). *The Interpersonal Theory of Psychiatry.* (New York: Norton.)

26. Addiction to Near-Death

Betty Joseph

There is a very malignant type of self-destructiveness, which we see in a small group of our patients, and which is, I think, in the nature of an addiction—an addiction to near-death. It dominates these patients' lives; for long periods it dominates the way they bring material to the analysis and the type of relationship they establish with the analyst; it dominates their internal relationships, their so-called thinking, and the way they communicate with themselves. It is not a drive towards a Nirvana type of peace or relief from problems, and it has to be sharply differentiated from this.

The picture that these patients present is, I am sure, a familiar one—in their external lives these patients get more and more absorbed into hopelessness and involved in activities that seem destined to destroy them physically as well as mentally, for example, considerable over-working, almost no sleep, avoiding eating properly or secretly over-eating if the need is to lose weight, drinking more and more and perhaps cutting off from relationships. In other patients this type of addiction is probably less striking in their actual living but equally important in their relationship with the analyst and the analysis. Indeed, in all these patients the place where the pull towards near-death is most obvious is in the transference. As I want to illustrate in this paper, these patients bring material to analysis in a very particular way, for example, they may speak in a way which seems calculated to communicate or create despair and a sense of hopelessness in themselves and in the analyst, although apparently wanting understanding. It is not just that they make progress, forget it, lose it or take no responsibility for it. They do show a strong though frequently silent negative therapeutic reaction, but this negative therapeutic reaction is only one part of a much broader and more

Presented to the scientific meeting of the British Psycho-Analytic Society, 20 May 1981.
Reprinted by permission of the author and the *International Journal of Psycho-Analysis* 63 (1982):449–56. Copyright © the Institute of Psycho-Analysis.

insidious picture. The pull towards despair and death in such patients is not, as I have said, a longing for peace and freedom from effort; indeed, as I sorted out with one such patient, just to die, although attractive, would be no good. There is a felt need to know and to have the satisfaction of seeing oneself being destroyed.

So I am stressing here that a powerful masochism is at work and these patients will try to create despair in the analyst and then get him to collude with the despair or become actively involved by being harsh, critical or in some way or another verbally sadistic to the patient. If they succeed in getting themselves hurt or in creating despair, they triumph, since the analyst has lost his analytic balance or his capacity to understand and help and then both patient and analyst go down into failure. At the same time the analyst will sense that there is real misery and anxiety around and this will have to be sorted out and differentiated from the masochistic use and exploitation of misery.

The other area that I am going to discuss as part of this whole constellation is that of the patient's internal relationships and a particular type of communication with himself—because I believe that in all such patients one will find a type of mental activity consisting of a going over and over again about happenings or anticipations of an accusatory or self-accusatory type in which the patient becomes completely absorbed.

I have described in this introduction the pull of the death instincts, the pull towards near-death, a kind of mental or physical brinkmanship in which the seeing of the self in this dilemma, unable to be helped, is an essential aspect. It is, however, important also to consider where the pull towards life and sanity is. I believe that this part of the patient is located in the analyst, which in part, accounts for the patient's apparent extreme passivity and indifference to progress. This I shall return to later.

It will be seen that much that I have outlined in this introduction has already been described in the analytic literature. For example, Freud (1924) discusses the working of the death instinct in masochism and distinguishes the nature of the inner conflict in a negative therapeutic reaction from that seen in moral masochism. He adds at the end of the paper 'even the subject's destruction of himself cannot take place without libidinal satisfaction'. In the patients that I am describing it seems to me that the near destruction of the self takes place with considerable libidinal satisfaction, however much the concomitant pain. The main additional aspects, however, that I want to discuss are: the way in which these problems make themselves felt in the transference, and in the patient's internal relationships and his thinking; and the deeply addictive nature of this type of masochistic constellation and the fascination and hold on them that it has. Later I want to add a note on some possible aspects of the infantile history of these patients. I shall start by getting into the middle of the problem by bringing a dream.

This dream comes from a patient who is typical of this group. He started analysis many years ago, and was then cold, rather cruel, loveless, highly competent, intelligent, articulate and successful in his work—but basically very unhappy. During the treatment he had become much warmer, was struggling to build real relationships and had become deeply but ambivalently emotionally involved with a gifted but probably disturbed young woman. This was a very important experience for him. He was also now deeply attached to the analysis although he did not speak of it, did not acknowledge it, was often late and seemed not to notice or be aware of almost anything about me as a human being. He often had sudden feelings of great hatred towards me. I am going to bring a dream from a Wednesday. On the Monday he had consolidated the work we had been doing on a particular type of provocation and cruelty silently achieved. By the end of the session he had seemed relieved and in good contact. But on the Tuesday he 'phoned just at the time of the end of his session and said that he had only just woken up. He sounded very distressed, but said that he had hardly slept in the night and would be here the following day. When he arrived on Wednesday he spoke about the Monday, how surprised he was that following the better feeling in the session he had felt so terrible and tense physically, in his stomach and in every way on the Monday night. He had felt much warmer towards K, the girl friend, and really wanted to see her, but she was out for the evening. She said she would 'phone him when she got back, but she didn't, so he must have been lying awake getting into a bad state. He also knew that he very much wanted to get to analysis and he expressed a strong positive feeling that he felt was emerging since the last session. He had found the work we had done during the Monday session very convincing and a real culmination of the work of the last period of analysis. He altogether sounded unusually appreciative and absolutely puzzled about the complete sense of breakdown, sleeplessness and the missing of the Tuesday session.

When he was describing the pain and misery of the Monday night, he said that he was reminded of the feeling that he had expressed at the beginning of the Monday session, the feeling that perhaps he was too far into this awful state ever to be helped out by me or to get out himself. At the same time during and immediately after the session there had been feelings of insight and more hope.

He then told a dream: *he was in a long kind of cave, almost a cavern. It was dark and smoky and it was as if he and other people had been taken captive by brigands. There was a feeling of confusion, as if they had been drinking. They, the captives, were lined up along a wall and he was sitting next to a young man. This man was subsequently described as looking gentle, in the mid-twenties, with a small moustache. The man suddenly turned towards him, grabbed at him and at his genitals, as if he were homosexual, and was about to knife my patient, who was completely terrified. He knew that if he tried to resist the man would knife him and there was tremendous pain.*

After telling the dream, he went on to describe some of the happenings of the last two days. He particularly spoke first about K. He then spoke about a meeting he had been to, in which a business acquaintance had said that a colleague told him that he, the colleague, was so frightened of my patient, A, that he positively trembled when on the 'phone to him. My patient was amazed, but linked this with something that I had shown him on the Monday, when I had commented on a very cold, cruel way in which he dealt with me when I queried a point about another dream. This association was connected with the idea of the man in the dream looking so gentle but acting in this violent way, and so he felt that the man must somehow be connected with himself, but what about the moustache? Then suddenly he had the notion of D. H. Lawrence—he had been reading a new biography of Lawrence and remembered that he was enormously attracted to him in his adolescence and felt identified with him. Lawrence was a bit homosexual and clearly a strange and violent man.

I worked out with him that it seemed therefore that this long, dark cavern stood for the place where he had felt he was too far in to be pulled out by himself or by me; as if it was his mind, but perhaps also part of his body. But the too-far-in seems to be linked with the notion that he was completely captured and captivated, possibly, by the brigands. But the brigands are manifestly associated with himself, the little man linked with Lawrence, who is experienced as part of himself. We can also see that the giving-in to this brigand is absolutely terrifying, it is a complete nightmare, and yet sexually exciting. The man grabs his genitals.

Here I need to interpose—I had been impressed for some time about the pull of despair and self-destructiveness in this man and one or two other patients with similar difficulties, and was driven to conclude that the actual despair, or the describing of it in the session, contained real masochistic excitement, concretely experienced. We can see it in the way these patients go over and over their unhappinesses, failures, things they feel they ought to feel guilty about. They talk as if they are attempting unconsciously to pull the analyst into concurring with the misery or with the descriptions or they unconsciously try to make the analyst give critical or disturbing interpretations. This becomes a very important pattern in the way that they speak. It is familiar to us and has been well described in the literature (Meltzer, 1973; Rosenfeld, 1971; Steiner, 1982) that such patients feel in thrall to a part of the self that dominates and imprisons them and will not let them escape, even though they see life beckoning outside, as expressed in my patient's dream, outside the cavern. The point I want to add here is that the patient's experience of sexual gratification in being in such pain, in being dominated, is one of the major reasons for the grip that the drive towards death has on him. These patients are literally 'enthralled' by it. In this patient A, for example, no ordinary pleasure, genital, sexual or other, offered such delight as this type of terrible and exciting self-annihilation which annihilates also the object and is basic to his important relationships to a greater or less extent.

So, I think the dream is clearly a response, not just to the girl friend K being out on the Monday night and A lying in bed getting more and more disturbed about it, of which he was conscious, but to the fact that he had felt better, knew he had and could not allow himself to get out of his misery and self-destruction—the long cavern—or allow me to help him out. He was forced back by a part of himself, essentially sado-masochistic, which operated also as a negative therapeutic reaction, and which used the distress about the girl friend as fuel. I also stressed here, and shall return to, his triumph over me when our work and the hope of the last weeks is knocked down and he and I go under.

I am discussing here, therefore, that it is not only that he is dominated by an aggressive part of himself, which attempts to control and destroy my work, but that this part is actively sadistic towards another part of the self which is masochistically caught up in this process, and that this has become an addiction. This process has always, I believe, an internal counterpart and in patients really dedicated to self-destructiveness, this internal situation has a very strong hold over their thinking and their quiet moments, their capacity for mulling things over or the lack of it. The kind of thing that one sees is this. These patients pick up very readily something that has been going on in their minds or in an external relationship and start to use it over and over again in some circular type of mental activity, in which they get completely caught up, so that they go over and over with very little variation the same actual or anticipated issue. This mental activity, which I think is best described by the word 'chuntering', is very important. The Oxford Dictionary describes chuntering as 'mutter, murmur, grumble, find fault, complain'. To give an example, A, in the period when I was trying to explore in him this dedication to masochism, described one day how he had been upset the previous evening because K had been going out with somebody else. He realized that on the previous evening he had, in his mind, been rehearsing what he might say to K about this. For example, he would talk about how he could not go on like this with her, while she was going around with another man; how he would have to give up the whole relationship; he could not go on like this, and so on. As he went on speaking about what he was planning to say to K, I got the feeling, not only from the ideas, but from his whole tone, that he was not just thinking what he might say to K, but was caught up in some kind of active cruel dialogue with her. Slowly then he clarified the ideas that he had had, and how he had been going over things in his mind. On this occasion and indeed on others, he realized that he would be saying something cruel, for example, and that K in the fantasy would reply or cry or plead or cling, she would become provocative, he would get cruel back, etc. In other words, what he then called 'thinking about what he would say' is actually actively being caught up in his mind in a provocative sado-masochistic fantasy, in which he both hurts and is hurt, verbally repeats and is humiliated, until the fantasy activity has such a grip on him that it almost has a life of its own and the content becomes secondary. In such cases unless I could begin to be aware of the problem of their being caught up in these fantasies and start to draw my patients' attention to them these fantasies would not come into the analysis, although in some way or another they are conscious. Patients who get so caught up in these activities, chuntering, tend to believe that they are thinking at such times, but of course they are living out experiences which becomes the complete antithesis of thought.

Another patient, when we had finally managed to open up very clearly the enormous importance and sadistic grip that such going over and over in his mind had on him, told me that he felt that he probably spent two thirds of his free time absorbed in such activities; then in the period when he was trying to give them up he felt that he had almost too much free time on his hands, and had a vague feeling of let-down or disillusionment as he began to do without them; the sense of let-down coming from the relinquishing of the exciting pain of this internal dialogue.

My point about the circular mental activities being the antithesis of thought is, of course, important in the analytic situation. I am stressing that the internal dialogue, the chuntering, is lived out in the analytic dialogue as well as in these patients' lives. Such patients use a great deal of analytic time apparently bringing material to be analysed and understood, but actually unconsciously for other purposes. We are all familiar with the kind of patient who talks in such a way as, they hope unconsciously, to provoke the analyst to be disturbed, repetitive, reproachful or actually critical. This can then be used by the silently watchful masochistic part of the patient to beat himself with, and an external 'difficulty' can be established in the analysis and perpetuated internally, during the session, with the patient silent and apparently hurt; or outside in an internal dialogue. We can then see that it is not 'understanding' that the patient wants, though the words are presented as if it were so. These self-destructive patients appear very often to be passive in their lives, as on one level did A, and a very important step is taken when they can see how active they are, by projective identification, for example through the kind of provocation that I am describing or in their thinking and fantasy. But there are other ways of expressing this type of self-destructiveness in the analysis. For example, some patients present 'real' situations, but in such a way as silently and extremely convincingly to make the analyst feel quite hopeless and despairing. The patient appears to feel the same. I think we have here a type of projective identification in which despair is so effectively loaded into the analyst that he seems crushed by it and can see no way out. The analyst is then internalized in this form by the patient, who becomes caught up in this internal crushing and crushed situation, and paralysis and deep gratification ensue.

Two issues arise from all this. First, that this type of patient usually finds it very difficult to see and to acknowledge the awful pleasure that is achieved in this way; and, second, I believe it is technically extremely important to be clear as to whether the patient is telling us about and communicating to us real despair, depression or fear and persecution, which he wants us to understand and to help him with, or whether he is communicating it in such a way as primarily to create a masochistic situation in which he can become caught up. If this distinction is not clearly made in the analysis from moment to moment, one cannot analyse adequately the underlying deep anxieties because of the whole masochistic overlay and the use that is being made of this. Further, I think that one needs to distinguish very clearly between the masochistic use of anxieties that I am discussing and dramatization. I am here describing something much more malignant and much more desperate to the personality than dramatization.

I want now to bring an example to illustrate further this connexion between actual anxieties and the exploitation of anxieties for masochistic purposes: and the connexion between genuinely persecuted feelings and the building up of a kind of pseudo-paranoia for masochistic purposes. I shall bring material from the patient A in a period when he was in great distress. It had been indicated to him that he would be likely to be promoted to a very senior position in the firm where he worked, but he got into a bad relationship with a principal man—himself probably a difficult and tormenting person. For a period of about two years things quietly deteriorated until there was a major reorganization in which he was to be demoted. He was deeply disturbed and decided he would almost certainly have to leave rather than be put in an inferior position. It should, however, be remembered that in his position there would be no likelihood of his having difficulty in finding other high-grade and financially rewarding work.

I bring a session from a Monday at this time. The patient came in most distressed, then remembered he had not brought his cheque, but would bring it the following day; then described the happenings of the weekend and his talk with his principal on Friday and how worried he felt about his job. K, his girl friend, had been helpful and kind, but he felt sexually dead and as if she was wanting sex from him, which became rather horrifying. Then he queried, 'was he trying to be cruel to her?'—already that question has something a bit suspect about it, as if I was supposed to agree that he was trying to be cruel to her and get caught up in some kind of reproaching of him, so that the question became in itself masochistic rather than thoughtful. He then brought a dream. In the dream, *he was in an old-fashioned shop at a counter, but he was small, about the height of the counter. There was someone behind it, a shop assistant. She was by a ledger but was holding his hand. He was asking her, 'was she a witch?' as if wanting a reply, persistently asking, almost as if he wanted to hear from her that she was a witch. He felt she was getting fed up with him and would withdraw her hand. There were rows of people somewhere in the dream and a vague feeling of being blamed for something he had done. In the shop a horse was being shod but with a piece of white plastic-looking material, about the shape and the size of the material one would put on the heel of a man's shoe.*

In his associations he spoke about his anxiety about his relationship with K at the moment and his sexuality. He was the height of a child in the dream. He had tremendous feelings of panic and anxiety at night. What would he do? Would he really run out of money, and what would happen to his whole position? We spoke about the realities of this a bit more.

He had seen a lot of horses being shod as a child and well remembered the smell of the iron going into the horse's hoof. He spoke about his guilt about the situation that he felt he had helped to create at work and realized that he must actually have acted very arrogantly with his principal and that this had probably really helped to bring the ceiling down on him.

I linked the ledger with the forgotten cheque and his anxiety about finances. He is worried about his lack of sexual interest at the moment, but seems to want me to be nasty about the cheque, and K about his lack of libido. In the dream he wanted the woman to say that she was a witch and this attitude appears to be an old story, since he is the height of a child. The guilt, I believe, is not just about his faulty handling of his work situation, his arrogance and harsh attitude, which has really led to serious work problems, but this is used both in his mind and actively in the transference in an attempt to draw me into agreement with his despair, to criticize his arrogance in his relationship with K and shatter him and create utter despair and a sense of uselessness in both of us. This is the masochistic use of anxiety in his mind and in the session. We can then see something about the sexualized excitement, of a very cruel kind, that he gets in this attitude by looking at the associations to the shoeing of the horse. There is the picture of a burning iron being put into the horse's foot and the fascination and horror of this as a child, feeling that it is bound to hurt, though in fact one subsequently knows it doesn't. So, I could then show him the indulgence in a tremendously masochistic attitude that was going on visibly in the dream, currently in the session, as misery, despair and pseudo-paranoia were being built up. There is almost a fragment of insight in this dream, as when he demands that the woman tells him if she is a witch and vaguely he knows that he hopes that she will agree that she is. As we went over this he began to see it again very clearly and his whole attitude became more thoughtful and quiet, as opposed to desperate and hopeless. He slowly added that, of course, there is the problem that this kind of sexual excitement and horror seems so great that nothing else can be so important and exciting to him. Now, when he said this, at first there was clearly a sense of insight and truth about, but then there began to be a different feeling in the session as if he really meant there was nothing one could do about it. Even the insight began to contain a different message. So I showed him that there was not only insight, not only anxiety and despair about being so much caught up in this kind of masturbatory excitement, but now there was also a triumph and a kind of sadistic jab at me, as if he were digging a burning iron into my heart to make me feel that nothing we were achieving was really worth anything and nothing could be done. Once again he could see this and so it was possible to link the desperate sexualized masochistic excitement with the triumphant doing down of his object, external and internal.

I have tried to show in this example how this masochistic excitement was covering up at that time deep anxieties stirred up by his work situation, connected with feelings of rejection, being unwanted, failure and guilt. But it is only possible to get through to them if the masochistic use, exploitation, is first dealt with. If one does not do this then one gets a situation which is so common with these patients that interpretations may appear to be listened to, but some part of the patient's personality will treat the analyst with contempt, with sneering and with mockery, though the mockery and and contempt will be silent.

But we are still left with a major problem as to why this type of masochistic self-destruction is so self-perpetuating; why it has such a grip on this type of patient. One reason which I have discussed in this paper—the sheer unequalled sexual delight of the grim masochism—is undeniable, yet it is usually very difficult for a long time for such patients to see that they are suffering from an addiction, that they are 'hooked' to this kind of self-destruction. With A, by the time we reached the dream about the sexual assault in the cavern, we had worked through a lot of this, and he felt consciously that he was in the grip of an addiction from which he believed he would like to be free. But he felt that the part of him that would like to be freed was nothing like as powerful nor were the possible results as attractive as was the pull of his addiction. And this he could not understand.

This problem needs considering from the angle of these patients' passivity that I mentioned at the beginning of the paper when I described how the pull towards life and sanity seems to be split off and projected into the analyst. One can see this in the transference, in severe cases going on sometimes over years, roughly like this. The patient comes, talks, dreams, etc. but one gets the impression of very little real active interest in changing, improving, remembering, getting anywhere with the treatment. Slowly the picture builds up. The analyst seems to be the only person in the room who is actively concerned about change, about progress, about development, as if all the active parts of the patient have been projected into the analyst. If the analyst is not aware of this and therefore does not concentrate his interpretations round this process, a collusion can arise in which the analyst carefully, maybe tactfully, pushes, tries to get the patient's interest or to alert him. The patient briefly responds only quietly to withdraw again and leave the next move to the analyst, and a major piece of psychopathology is acted out in the transference. The patient constantly is pulling back towards the silent kind of deadly paralysis and near complete passivity. When these lively parts of the patient remain so constantly split off it means that his whole capacity for wanting and appreciating, missing, feeling disturbed at losing, etc., the very stuff that makes for real whole object relating is projected and the patient remains with his addiction and without the psychological means of combatting this. To me, therefore, the understanding of the nature of this apparent passivity is technically of primary importance with these patients. Moreover, it means that with such splitting-off of the life instincts and of loving, ambivalence and guilt is largely evaded. As these patients improve and begin to become more integrated and relationships become more real, they begin to feel acute pain sometimes experienced as almost physical—undifferentiated but extremely intense.

I think it is often at these periods of analysis, when concern and pain near to guilt begin to be experienced, that one can see a quick regression to earlier masochistic methods of avoiding pain linked essentially with infantile and childhood behaviour. To give a very brief example—A, following a good analytic experience had a dream in which *his mother, dead or near dead, was lying on a slab or couch, and he, to his horror, was pulling off bits of sunburnt skin from one side of her face and eating them.* I think that instead of becoming aware of, and guilty about, the spoiling of the good experience, he is showing here how he again becomes identified with his damaged object by eating it up, and it is also important to see the link between the painful exciting physical horror and his earlier nail-biting and skin-tearing, familiar to us.

Freud, of course, describes this process of identification in 'Mourning and melancholia' (1917) and he also adds 'the self tormenting in melancholia . . . is without doubt enjoyable . . .' Despite certain important similarities the patients that I am describing are not 'melancholic'—their guilt and self-reproach being so much evaded or swallowed up by their masochism.

My impression is that these patients as infants, because of their pathology, have not just turned away from frustrations or jealousies or envies into a withdrawn state, nor have they been able to rage and yell at their objects. I think they have withdrawn into a secret world of violence, where part of the self has been turned against another part, parts of the body being identified with parts of the offending object, and that this violence has been highly sexualized, masturbatory in nature, and often physically expressed. One sees it, for example, in head-banging, digging nails into fists, pulling at one's own hair and twisting and splitting it until it hurts, and this is what we are still seeing in the verbal chuntering that goes on and on. As one gets into this area and these patients are able to recognize, usually at first with great difficulty and resentment, the excitement and pleasure they get from these apparent self-attacks, they can usually show us their own particular personal predilection. One of my young male patients of this group was still pulling at and splitting his hair when he was well into his analysis. Another, an older man, who spoke of the amount of time used up by his chuntering, used, in times of great disturbance, to lie on the floor drinking and putting on his radio as loud as possible, as if caught up in a wild orgy of rhythmical bodily experience. It seems to me that instead of moving forward and using real relationships, contact with people or bodies as infants, they retreated apparently into themselves and lived out their relationships in this sexualized way, in fantasy or fantasy expressed in violent bodily activity. This deeply masochistic state, then, has a hold on the patient, that is much stronger than the pull towards human relationships. Sometimes this is to be seen as an aspect of an actual perversion, in others it is part of a character perversion.

It will be seen that in this paper I have not attempted to discuss the defensive value of the addiction, but there is one aspect of this problem that I would like to mention before ending. It has something to do with torture and survival. None of the patients whom I have in mind as particularly belonging to this addictive group, have really very seriously bad childhood histories, though psychologically in a sense they almost certainly have—as, for example, a lack of warm contact and real understanding, and sometimes a very violent parent. Yet in the transference one gets the feeling of being driven up to the edge of things, as I indicated, and both patient and analyst feel tortured. I get the impression from the difficulty these patients experience in waiting and being aware of gaps and aware of even the simplest type of guilt that such potentially depressive experiences have been felt by them in infancy, as terrible pain that goes over into torment, and that they have tried to obviate this by taking over the torment, the inflicting of mental pain on to themselves and building it into a world of perverse excitement, and this necessarily militates against any real progress towards the depressive position.

It is very hard for our patients to find it possible to abandon such terrible delights for the uncertain pleasures of real relationships.

SUMMARY

This paper describes a very malignant type of self-destructiveness seen in a small group of patients. It is active in the way that they run their lives and it emerges in a deadly way in the transference. This type of self-destructiveness is, I suggest, in the nature of an addiction of a particular sado-masochistic type, which these patients feel unable to resist. It seems to be like a constant pull towards despair and near-death, so that the patient is fascinated and unconsciously excited by the whole process. Examples are given to show how such addictions dominate the way in which the patient communicates with the analyst and internally, with himself, and thus how they affect his thinking processes. It is clearly extremely difficult for such patients to move towards more real and object-related enjoyments, which would mean giving up the all-consuming addictive gratifications.

REFERENCES

Freud, S. (1917). Mourning and melancholia. *S.E.* 14.
———(1924). The economic problem of masochism. *S.E.* 19.
Meltzer, D. (1973). *Sexual States of Mind*. Perthshire: Clunie Press.
Oxford English Dictionary, (1979). *Compact Edition*. London: Oxford Univ. Press.
Rosenfeld, H. (1971). A clinical approach to the psychoanalytic theory of the life and death instincts: An investigation into the aggressive aspects of narcissism. *Int. J. Psychoanal.*, 52:169–178.
Steiner, J. (1982). Perverse relationships between parts of the self: A clinical illustration. *Int. J. Psychoanal.*, 63:241–252.

Name Index

Abelin, E.C., 256–257
Abraham, K., 225, 229, 479, 482, 496
Adler, A., 23
Alexander, F., 29
Amiel, H. F., 196
Andre, J., 406

Bak, R., 4, 52, 78, 156, 157, 182–195, 247, 267, 268, 365, 405
Balint, M., 243
Ballet, G., 22
Benjamin, J., 405, 406
Bergler, E., 8, 54, 200, 201
Bergman, M., 258
Berliner, B., 5, 54, 80, 196, 200, 201, 269, 270, 270–271, 344–359, 371, 372, 475
Bernfield, R., 298
Bernstein, D., 408
Bernstein, L., 371
Bettelheim, B., 55
Bieber, I., 237
Binet, A., 22
Blos, P., Jr., 3, 242
Blum, H., 2, 82, 134, 139, 258, 271, 395, 399, 405–406
Boehm, F., 307
Bonaparte, M., 7, 50, 407, 432–452
Bouvet, M., 212
Brenman, M., 52, 54, 55, 141, 269, 271, 368, 474
Brenner, C., 5–6, 79, 134, 141, 153, 155, 156, 268, 269, 360–382, 473, 474, 475, 506
Brinich, P. M., 242, 246
Bromberg, N., 371
Brunswick, R. M., 50, 192
Bychowski, G., 502

Cain, J., 250
Cameron, N., 183

Chasseguet-Smirgel, J., 3–4, 7, 8, 268, 405, 406, 453–470
Codet, H., 29
Coen, S., 2, 6, 155, 156, 157, 267, 270, 383–401
Cooper, A., 8, 272

Darcourt, G., 62
De M'Uzan, M., 155–156
Deutsch, H., 6–7, 50, 406, 411–422, 427, 481
Diatkine, G., 209
Dickes, R., 223
Dooley, L., 141

Eidelberg, L., 1, 8, 43, 197, 372, 496, 504, 506
Ellis, H., 22, 145
Erikson, E., 503
Escalona, S. K., 245
Eulenberg, A., 22

Fain, M., 457–458
Federn, P., 23
Feldman, S. S., 200
Fenichel, O., 3, 43, 80, 153, 156, 237, 268, 300–323, 362, 365, 405, 430, 473, 496, 498, 499
Ferber, L., 237
Ferenczi, S., 143, 182, 458–459
Ferre, C. 22
Fish-Murray, C. C., et al., 128
Fitzpatrick, M. A., 406
Fitzpatrick-Hanly, M. A., 406
Fliegel, Z., 79, 405, 406
Fliess, W., 220, 223, 226, 228, 229
Fraiberg, S., 131–132
Freud, A., 5, 136, 249, 267, 269, 286–299, 353, 405, 502–504
Freud, S., 1, 3, 4, 5, 22–24, 26–27, 28–32, 41, 43, 44, 44–45, 49, 50, 52, 55, 62, 67,

Freud (*Continued*)
77, 78, 81, 84–89, 90–103, 104–122,
125, 126, 127, 133, 138, 139, 141, 142,
153, 154, 156, 159–181, 182, 183,
184,192, 194, 197, 200, 201, 209, 215,
220, 221, 222, 227, 228, 229, 237, 237–
238, 258, 262, 267, 268, 270, 274–
285, 286, 295, 300, 307, 308, 311, 319,
321, 322, 345, 347, 348, 350, 351,
360, 361, 362, 363, 364, 367, 368, 371,
372, 373, 383, 405, 406, 407, 432–
438, 473, 477–478, 480, 491–492, 494,
495–496, 498, 499, 502, 503, 512, 521
Furman, E., 246, 252, 257
Furman, R., 257

Galenson, E., 129, 133–134, 405
Gauthier, M., 81
Gedo, G., 496
Gianino, A., 241
Glenn, J., 129, 136, 243
Glick, R., 2
Glover, E., 496
Gorski, P. A., 131
Green, A., 77, 78
Grossman, W. I., 3, 79, 81–82, 125–150,
261
Grunberger, B., 4, 153, 157, 196–214, 268,
269, 269–70, 272

Hanly, C., 406
Hartmann, F. R., 258
Hartmann, H., 52, 55, 56
Herzog, J. M., 129, 130, 131, 137, 143–144
Hesnard, A., 29
Hoffer, W., 226
Horney, K., 16, 201, 405, 406–407, 417,
496, 503

Isaacs, S., 132

Jacobson, E., 80, 81
Jeammet, P., 458
Jones, E., 25
Joseph, B., 8, 474

Keiser, S., 202, 229
Kernberg, O., 2, 8, 125, 126, 142, 153, 155,
271, 272, 406

Khan, M.M.R., 65
Klein, M., 184, 209, 227, 427, 480, 485–
486, 497
Krafft-Ebing, R. F., 21–22, 23, 64
Kretschmer, E., 183
Kris, E., 52, 55, 56, 501
Kucera, O., 22, 80, 156, 225, 228

Lagache, D., 62, 63
LaForgue, R., 16, 29
Lamb, M. E., 256
Lampl-de Groot, J., 8, 50, 197, 318
Laplanche, J., 3, 15, 77, 79, 80, 104–124,
156
Laufer, E., 453, 454–455
Laufer, M., 453, 454–455
Lax, R., 79, 132
Lebovici, S., 209
Lewin, B. D., 227, 496, 504
Lewinsky, H., 198
Litman, R. E., 237
Loewald, H., 474, 475
Lorenz, K., 218, 219
Low, B., 275
Lowenstein, R., 2, 15–16, 55, 79, 81,
133–134, 135, 145, 155, 156, 200, 237,
238, 242, 345, 386, 389, 405–406

Mahler, M. S., 226
Maleson, F. G., 126, 237, 250, 261
Mayer, E. L., 408
Mayer-Gross, W., 183
McDevitt, J. B., 138
Meltzer, D., 461
Menaker, E., 201, 269, 270, 371, 372–373
Meyers, D., 2, 405
Meyers, H., 406
Modell, A., 271, 473, 474

Nacht, S., 2, 15, 18–33, 52, 62, 79, 156,
196, 197, 199, 200, 201, 209, 267, 268,
269
Niederland, W. G., 252
Novick, K., and Novick, J., 4, 79, 126, 136,
155, 237–264, 270, 271
Nunberg, H., 29, 184

Odier, C., 197
Oliner, M., 460

Olinick, S. L., 8, 244, 473, 474, 475
Orgel, S., 242, 246

Parkin, A., 386
Pontalis, J. B., 473, 474, 475

Rank, O., 348, 502
Rado, S., 200
Reich, A., 7, 78, 271, 405, 407, 423–431
Reich, W., 16, 32, 54, 62, 201–309, 320, 496, 497
Reik, T., 5, 19, 23, 29, 62, 81, 156, 157, 196, 198, 200, 201, 204, 267, 268, 272, 306, 324, 343, 364
Renik, O., 408, 475
Richards, A., 7
Riviere, J., 8, 473, 475, 477–493, 496, 503, 504
Roheim, G., 184
Roiphe, H., 136, 405
Rosenberg, B., 15, 81, 82
Rosenblatt, B., 256
Rosenfeld, H., 8
Rubinfine, P. L., 246, 254

Sacher-Masoch, 1, 16, 17, 21, 63–71, 384, 449
Sandler, J., 256
Sadger, J., 23
Schafer, R., 8, 127, 473
Schrenck-Notzing, A. von, 22

Schulter, H., 182
Selvini-Palazzoli, M., 454
Shapiro, D., 156, 383
Shapiro, T., 2
Shengold, L., 2, 4, 77, 80, 144, 145, 156, 215–236, 270, 399
Shuren, I., 221, 223
Simmel, E., 227
Smirnoff, V., 2, 62–73, 153, 155, 156, 157
Solomon, R. L., 126, 138
Spitz, R. A., 501–502
Starcke, A., 183
Steckel, W., 23
Sterba, R., 502
Stern, D. W., 245
Stoller, R. J., 145, 383, 455
Stolorow, R. D., 271
Sullivan, H. S., 496

Tausk, V., 456
Tronick, E., 241

Valenstein, A., 8, 243, 261, 474
van Ophuijsen, J.H.W., 183

Waelder, R., 16, 47, 52, 368
Weiss, E., 29
Winnicott, D. W., 70, 242
Wulf, M., 460

Zanardi, C., 2
Zinnser, H., 217, 218

Subject Index

Aggression: identification with aggressor, 352–354; inhibition of, 312–313; morality and, 41; murderous, 218; need for love and, 349–352; oral, 226; pain and, 137–142; pain, fantasy, and, 128–129; sadomasochism and, 104–124; sexualized self-directed, 136

Ambivalence, 94, 100–101

Anaclisis (or propping), 105–109

Anality: anal phase and masochism, 251–252; bulimia and, 461–465; castration of father and, 190; erotism and, 3, 38, 217, 219, 224; in masochism, 314; passive anal cravings, 233

Anorexia, 459–460

Anxiety: 16, 37, 47; formation of masochism and, 371–372; masochistic fantasy and, 293; masochistic use of anxieties, 517–518; negative therapeutic reaction and, 484–485; pleasure in masochism and, 198–199, 335–336; recoil from pleasure and, 198

Auto-eroticism, 95; eating disorders and, 458–460

Beating fantasy: 3–4, 24, 41–41, 159–181, 286–299; beater as a condensed object, 204; disturbance of normal omnipotence and, 242; father's love and, 193; feminine position and, 175; male paranoia and, 186; men and, 174–179; narcissistic goals and, 248; paradigmatic masochistic fantasy as, 117–122; as substitute for super-ego, 258; unconscious and, 168–169

Bisexuality, 44

Cannibalism, 215–222

Castration, 19, 43, 72; cannibalism and, 20, 224–225; father and, 204–206; self-castration, 43; wishes, 252

Castration anxiety, 36, 39, 228; inhibition

and, 311–312; masochism and, 199–200; penalizing and, 316

Castration complex, 20; rape fantasy in women and, 415

Clinical technique: masochism and, 258–261; negative therapeutic reaction and, 490–492, 505–508

Co-excitation, 48, 79–81, 110–111; foundation for erotogenic masochism, 277, 361; "libidinal sympathetic excitation," 115

Component instincts, 162–163

Counter-transference: sadomasochistic patients and, 140–141

Daydreams, 287–299

Death instinct, 18, 19–20, 29, 45, 81–82, 274–276, 278–280, 362, 363

Defense: mechanisms of, 47; masochism as defense against destructive wishes, 248

Depression, 318, 319; manic defense and, 480–483

Destruction, 218; behavior, trauma, and, 129–130; castration and, 221; death instinct and, 81–82, 278–279; destructive parents, 387; penetration as, 233

Drive: aim inhibited, 296; sadomasochism as sexual, 105–107

Erotic: complicity, 46; satisfaction, 18, 38

Excitation, 80, 93; looking and, 85; touching and, 85

Excitement, 292, 297; as defense against guilt, 396; sadomasochism and, 389–390

Exhibitionism, 85, 91, 93–94; negative and, 340

Fantasy, 5–6; masochism and, 40, 117, 327–334; impoverishment of fantasy in perversion, 398–400; masturbation and, 40, 117; pain, aggression, and, 128–129; provocative sadomasochistic, 516; revenge and,

Fantasy (*Continued*)
224–225; sacrifice and, 68; significance of fantasy for masochism, 327–334; slave fantasy, 41–42; unconscious fantasy, 20
Female masochism, 6–7, 22, 24, 50, 53; ambivalence to mother and, 427–428; as "anatomical destiny," 414–415; beating fantasy and, 254–255; frigidity and, 412, 416–418; girl's love for father as masochistic, 414; masculinity complex and, 170, 412, 425; reproduction and, 412
Femininity, 44; maternal instinct and, 420; penis envy and, 412–415, 417–418; as masochistic, 419–421
Fetishism, 38, 67, 70

Genital satisfaction, 18, 56; masochistic perversion and, 213; masochism and weak genital organization, 172
Gratification, 48
Guilt, 5–6, 20, 24, 37, 45, 49, 288; beating fantasy and, 117; borrowing of, 318–319, 351, 491–492; incestuous fantasy and, 167–168; insufficient reason for masochism, 347–348; masochism and relief of, 208–210; moral masochism and unconscious, 279–281; penalizing castration and, 316

Hate, 96–101; erotic character of, 101
Helplessness, 36, 292
Homosexuality, 171; paranoia and, 182–194
Humiliation, 1, 16, 37; in female masochism, 424–426; as punishment, 292; sadism and, 86; sexual excitement and, 126
Hysteria, 286

Incest: love and, 295; reunion, mother, and, 42; wish fantasy and, 296
Incestuous gratification, 39
Inhibition, 1; masochists and, 197–198
Isolation, 215, 221–222; "double-think" and, 222–223

Libidinization: beating and, 190; as distinct from fusion and binding, 246
Love, 96–101; fantasy and, 296

Masochism: as addictive, 515–523; as defense against paternal castration wishes, 204–208; delusion and, 70; as demonstrative, 337–343; depression and, 349–350; erotogenic, 30–31, 53, 126, 138, 278–279; feminine, 31, 44, 276–279; "idealized evil woman" and, 70–71; infantile rage, 430; melancholia and, 317–318; moral masochism, 18, 31–32, 55–56; multiple functions of, 368–369; narcissistic need and, 350–351; negative exhibitionism, 340; negative therapeutic reaction and, 512–523; normal masochism and, 364–365; object relations and, 344–357; oedipus complex and, 279–283, 362; oral passive masochism, 217, 220–221, 226; overstimulation and, 221, 227, 232; in paranoia, 182–194; passive, 111–112; perverse fantasy and, 341–342; primary, 19, 81–82, 107, 115, 274–276; as provocative, 338; reflexive, 111–112; secondary, 279; submission and, 219; in transference, 314, 315, 519–520
Masochistic: ceremony, 68; character, 18, 54, 55; contract, 16–17, 64–66, 72; "depression," 315; expectancy, 67; feminine ideals, 69; girl's love for father as, 414; ordeal, 67; position, 65, 66; proto-, 46–47; proto-masochistic defenses, 15; scenario, 16, 330–331
Masturbation; perversion and, 174–175; beating fantasy and, 165, 168–169, 255–256

Narcissism, 8–9, 96–97; beating fantasy and, 119–121, 242; delusion of omnipotence, 253, 254; as distinct from masochism, 338–339, 342; hate and, 100; masochism as passive, 172; narcissistic function of masochism, 271–272; narcissistic goals and beating fantasy, 248; narcissistic masochistic position, 63; narcissistic specialness and overstimulation, 396; omnipotence, 481–483; paternal phallus and, 211; primary, 97; as reason for aggression, 350–351; secondary, 26; in submissive women, 424–426
Negative Oedipus complex, 32
Negative therapeutic reaction, 7–8, 140, 370,

373; anxiety and, 484–485; "borrowed guilt" and, 491–492; despair and, 511–523; Klein's theory of depressive states and, 477–493; libidinal satisfaction and, 512–515; love and guilt in, 491; masochism and, 511–523; negativism and, 498–503; review of, 473–476, 494–497; sadomasochism and, 504–505; super-ego resistance and, 496–497
Nirvana principle, 274–275

Object: incestuous, 16; primary sexual, 72
Object relations, 5, 6, 16; as defining aspect of masochism, 271; excitement and sadomasochistic, 383–385; masochism and, 116–117; negative therapeutic reaction and internal, 487–489; perverse object relations in sadomasochism, 400–401; sadomasochism and, 52; in submissive women, 430
Oedipus Complex, 24, 26–28, 44, 53; beating fantasy and, 237–238, 240, 252–254; females and, 413; masochism and, 170–173, 287–288, 296; moral masochism, 279–283, 362
Omnipotence: in the negative therapeutic reaction, 481–483
Oral: oral fantasy as defense, 212; sadistic libido, 217, 225–229
Orgasm: anxiety and, 40; masochistic fantasy and, 325, 326, 332, 336–337
Overstimulation, 221, 227; altered states of consciousness, 232

Pain, 33, 35, 48, 62, 65, 66; aggression, fantasy, and, 128–129; as indirect source of sexual excitement, 110–111; mastery of pain through fantasy, 142–145; neo-natal pain syndrome, 130; pain seeking, 251
Paranoia: masochism and, 173, 182–195
Passivity, 15–16, 23–24, 36, 44, 92–97: as distinct from receptivity, 250; in female masochism, 426–427; male negative oedipus and, 310–311; passive masochism and search for object, 111–112; role and, 294
Persecution, 219
Perversion: beating fantasy and, 124, 159–181; as distinct from sadomasochistic character, 383–385; "feminine" masochism in

male perversion, 276–279; Freud on, 86–87, 91–96; Loewenstein on, 37–39; masochistic, 21, 35–42, 51–52, 53–54, 153–157, 383–385; masturbation and, 174–175; oedipus complex and, 170–171; Reik on, 324–343; Sacher-Masoch and the scenario, 63–66, 69–72; sadomasochistic, 398–400
Phallic: power, cannibalism and, 220; mother as, 229; woman, 16, 36, 72
Pleasure principle, 30–31, 35, 98, 274–276
Primal scene: identifications in, 320; sadistic intercourse theory and, 252; sadomasochism and, 389
Prohibition, 46: in masochists, 197–198, 312
Projection, 228; of aggressive sadistic component, 209–210; of cannibalistic aggression, 229–230; excitation and, 307–308
Propping. See Anaclisis
Punishment, 24, 25, 37, 39, 42, 287; beating as, 160–161; fear of separation and, 250–251; need for punishment, 20, 31–32, 280–283, 352–353, 371; provocation of, 49; punishment scene, 294; self-punishment, 49, 295; undoing of, 49

Regression: ego, 221–224; healthy fantasy and, 168–169; from sublimated homosexuality to masochism, 168, 169
Repetition, 43, 385–387
Repression, 25, 28, 162; beating fantasy and, 168–169
Revenge, 1, 232

Sacrifice, 66–67, 68
Sadism, 23, 68–69, 72, 92; anal, 215, 220; anal organization and, 100, 215; father and, 232; oral, 215, 220; Marquis de Sade, 442–448
Sadomasochism, 126; negative therapeutic reaction and, 504–505; in object relations, 383–87; pain and, 129–133; strong, weak characters and, 297
Sadomasochistic object relations: as defense against destruction and loss, 383–387
Scopophilia, 85, 91, 93–94
Screen memory, 39, 40, 67
Seduction, 38, 47; of aggressor, 40, 46–47, 57, 386; childhood, 234

Self-destruction, 18–19; addiction to, 511–522

Sexual excitement, 287, 330; fantasy in passive perversion and, 329; in the masochistic transference, 519–520; negative therapeutic reaction and, 515–517; rage and, 231; sexual tension in masochistic fantasy, 328

Sexual instinct, 84, 90

Sexuality, 2–3, 15, 23, 35, 56; aberrations, 84; gratification and, 295; sexual aims, 84–87; sexual pleasures emerging from non-sexual activities, 106–108

Sexualization: of masochism, 252–254; of morality, 42, 282–283

Slave: "mentality of," 55

Stimulation, 47

Submissiveness: rage and, 428–429; search for, 63; in women, 423–431

Suffering, 18, 19, 38; as purifying, 208–209; for sexual pleasure, 336–337

Super-ego, 25, 26–28, 49; fixed beating fantasy and, 258; moral masochism and, 280–283; mystified by masochism, 207–208, 211; penalizing, 313–314; turning of aggression on self and, 135

Torture, 215–217, 294

Trauma, 38, 41, 67, 348–351; mastery of trauma through fantasy, 142–145; parental pathology, suicide, and, 252; sexual fantasy and, 131

About the Editor

Margaret Ann Fitzpatrick Hanly is a psychoanalyst in private practice in Toronto, Canada, a member of the faculty of the Toronto Psychoanalytic Institute, and an adjunct professor in the Department of Psychiatry, University of Toronto. She received her Ph.D. in English Literature from the University of Toronto where she taught for several years. She trained as a psychoanalyst in the French Canadian "Société Psychanalytique de Montréal." Dr. Fitzpatrick Hanly has published works on Keats's oral imagination, on projection in Alice Munro's short stories, and on sadomasochism in Charlotte Brontë's *Jane Eyre*.